More Praise for This Book

"Keep this book by your bedside, on your desk, or in your backpack. In an era where our greatest asset is our ability to learn, Elaine has convened the brightest minds in the field to help us and our organizations to learn, grow, and develop. If you are leading talent development today or aspiring to do so tomorrow, this handbook will become your go-to resource."
—André Martin, Ed Tech Advisor; Former CLO, Google, Target, Nike, Mars

"*ATD's Handbook for Training and Talent Development* has long been a must-have resource for managers, L&D practitioners, coaches, and students. This newest handbook, masterfully edited by Elaine Biech, responds to the urgency needed to learn, navigate, and lead with optimism and clarity through the turbulence of a shifting workforce landscape. Every chapter is informed by the latest research while offering practical insights and actionable advice to optimize organizational performance."
—Portia R. Mount, VP Marketing, Commercial HVAC Americas Region, Trane Technologies

"The demand for new skills and fresh, nimble thinking in the post-pandemic world is enormous, which is why there's never been a more exciting and important time to work in training and talent development. This book provides an exquisite map of where the field is heading—and what professionals can do right now to ensure that they and their colleagues thrive."
—Vice Adm. John R. Ryan, USN (ret.), Former President and CEO, Center for Creative Leadership

"*ATD's Handbook for Training and Talent Development* is a brilliant coupling of notable experts with proven industry leaders offering unique and authentic insight into the future of work. The impressive roster of trainers and corporate professionals recognizes the importance of an interprofessional approach. This handbook, with dynamic web tools, is revolutionary."
—Kimberly R. Cline, President, Long Island University

"The ATD handbook continues to be a staple for the future of training and development! Filled with expert advice and relevant practices, *ATD's Handbook for Training and Talent Development* provides insights for the changing world of HR. An excellent must-read!"
—Marshall Goldsmith, *Thinkers50* #1 Executive Coach; *New York Times* bestselling author, *Triggers, Mojo,* and *What Got You Here Won't Get You There*

"This compendium of authors, topics, and experiences should help anyone inside an organization, whether they're a talent development leader or not, understand what makes training, HR, or leadership development an integral part of a growing company. I'll put Elaine up against any person called the Greatest of All Time (GOAT) whether in this domain or sports. Move over Tom Brady and Simone Biles!"
—Rear Adm. Gib Godwin, USN (ret.), President and CEO, Mercy Medical Angels

"It is a rare thing in any field to consistently overachieve. However, Elaine Biech has once again managed to assemble the best insights from some of the best minds available in a concise, readable compendium that should be on everyone's shelf! This third edition of the handbook is not to be missed—its tools and diverse inputs will open new ways of thinking about training and talent development."
—Capt. Will Brown, USN (ret.), Former Talent Manager, Office of Naval Research

"Imagine having more than 100 talent development luminaries and thought leaders on speed dial. If you have questions about learning science, growing your TD career, strategic partnering with core business leaders, the future of TD, or a host of other topics, pick up *ATD's Handbook for Training and Talent Development*. If you're looking for insight, inspiration, or innovation for our field, voila, here it is!"
—Dana Alan Koch, Learning Scientist; Co-Host, *Learning Geeks Podcast*; Team Lead, Accenture's Institute for Applied Learning Sciences

"Written by professionals for professionals, *ATD's Handbook for Training and Talent Development* is your go-to guide to ensure your TD staff are using the most up-to-date content available. The accompanying website also includes tons of tools, checklists, and planning templates to make your job easier."
—William A. Gentry, Interim VP, Student Life, High Point University; Author, *Be the Boss Everyone Wants to Work For*

THIRD EDITION

ATD's Handbook for **Training and Talent Development**

ELAINE BIECH
EDITOR

Alexandria, VA

© 2022 ASTD DBA the Association for Talent Development (ATD)

All rights reserved. Printed in the United States of America.

25 24 23 22   1 2 3 4 5

No part of this publication may be reproduced, distributed, or transmitted in any form or by any means, including photocopying, recording, information storage and retrieval systems, or other electronic or mechanical methods, without the prior written permission of the publisher, except in the case of brief quotations embodied in critical reviews and certain other noncommercial uses permitted by copyright law. For permission requests, please go to copyright.com, or contact Copyright Clearance Center (CCC), 222 Rosewood Drive, Danvers, MA 01923 (telephone: 978.750.8400; fax: 978.646.8600).

Portions of chapter 2 were adapted with permission from Pluth, B. 2016. *Creative Training: A Train the Trainer Field Guide*. Minneapolis: Creative Training Productions.

Chapter 45 is adapted from *Learning Leadership: The Five Fundamentals of Becoming an Exemplary Leader*, by James M. Kouzes and Barry Z. Posner. San Francisco: The Leadership Challenge, A Wiley Brand. Copyright © 2016 James M. Kouzes and Barry Z. Posner. All rights reserved.

Chapter 40 is adapted from *Building Your Independent Practice: From Startup to Market Leadership*, by Andrew Sobel, 2014. andrewsobel.com/wp-content/uploads/2014/03/Building-Your-Independent-Practice-From-Startup-To-Market-Leadership.pdf.

ATD Press is an internationally renowned source of insightful and practical information on talent development, training, and professional development.

ATD Press
1640 King Street
Alexandria, VA 22314 USA

Ordering information: Books published by ATD Press can be purchased by visiting ATD's website at td.org/books or by calling 800.628.2783 or 703.683.8100.

Library of Congress Control Number: 2021952596

ISBN-10: 1-953946-34-8
ISBN-13: 978-1-953946-34-8
e-ISBN: 978-1-953946-35-5

ATD Press Editorial Staff
Director: Sarah Halgas
Manager: Melissa Jones
Content Manager, L&D: Eliza Blanchard
Developmental Editor: Kathryn Stafford
Production Editor: Hannah Sternberg
Text Design: Shirley Raybuck
Cover Design: Rose Richey
Text Layout: PerfecType, Nashville, TN

Printed by Data Reproductions Corporation, Auburn Hills, MI

Contents

Foreword ix

Acknowledgments xi

Introduction xiii

Section I. Learning and Development Basics 1

    Luminary Perspective: Our Job Is to Deliver Breakthrough Moments 3
    Tacy Byham

    1. **The Evolution of Talent Development** 13
       Lorrie Lykins

    2. **Critical Adult Learning Basics in Action** 35
       Becky Pike Pluth

    3. **A Learning Science Strategy: Deepening the Impact of Talent Development** 51
       Jonathan Halls

    4. **The Business Case for Learning** 65
       Preethi Anand

Section II. Planning a Career in Talent Development 77

    Luminary Perspective: Talent Development Mindsets 79
    Beverly Kaye

    5. **The Talent Development Capability Model** 83
       Morgean Hirt

6. Give Your Career a Boost With Certification 95
   Rich Douglas

7. Thriving in Your Career: Powerful Plans for Lifelong Learning 107
   Catherine Lombardozzi

8. The Irreplaceable Growth Mindset 119
   Ryan Gottfredson

9. An Oath of Ethics for Learning and Development Professionals 131
   Travis Waugh

10. What's EQ Got to Do With a TD Career? 143
    Jean Greaves

Section III. Training and Development Basics 159

Luminary Perspective: Train to Add Value and Make a Difference 161
Bob Pike

11. ADDIE: The Origin of Modern-Day ISD 167
    Angel Green

12. Using Evidence to Assess Performance Gaps 187
    Ingrid Guerra-López

13. Design Thinking for TD Professionals 199
    Sharon Boller

14. Innovative Design: Uncovering the Art of the Possible 211
    Brian Washburn

15. We Need It Personalized, Accurate, and NOW! 223
    Lisa MD Owens and Crystal Kadakia

16. Delivering as if Learning Depended Upon It! 239
    Hadiya Nuriddin

17. 21st-Century Media Skills: Put Learning Where the Work Is 257
    Mhairi Campbell

18. Using Story Structure to Influence 271
    Nancy Duarte and Jeff Davenport

19. Implementing the Four Levels of Evaluation 285
    Jim Kirkpatrick and Wendy Kayser Kirkpatrick

20. Impact and ROI: Results Executives Love 299
    Jack J. Phillips and Patricia Pulliam Phillips

Section IV. Enhancing and Supporting Talent Development 311

Luminary Perspective: Talent Development Changes in a Changing Time! 313
Elliott Masie

21. The Journey to Learning Experience Design 319
    George Hall

22. **Keys to Designing and Delivering Blended Learning** 327
    Jennifer Hofmann

23. **The Many Aspects of Accessibility** 341
    Maureen Orey

24. **Learning Transfer: The Missing Link** 351
    Emma Weber

25. **Critical Tools to Support the Fundamentals of E-Learning** 363
    Diane Elkins

26. **Designing and Delivering Virtual Training** 385
    Cynthia Clay and Cindy Huggett

Section V. Required Forward-Focused Proficiencies and Attitudes 401

Luminary Perspective: Slowing Down to Go Fast 403
Rita Bailey

27. **Essential Skills for TD Professionals** 411
    Wendy Gates Corbett

28. **Initiating a Talent Development Effort** 423
    David Macon

29. **Working Effectively With SMEs** 439
    Greg Owen-Boger and Dale Ludwig

30. **Perfecting Your Facilitation Skills: The Facilitative Trainer** 455
    Michael Wilkinson

31. **Communicating With Executive Leadership to Gain Buy-In** 469
    Dianna Booher

32. **Integrating DEI Principles Into TD Initiatives** 479
    Maria Morukian

33. **Digital-Age Requirements for Talent Development Professionals** 497
    Alex Adamopoulos

Section VI. Expanded Roles of Talent Development 509

**Luminary Perspective: Make Your Future Happen:
Plan Beyond Your Current TD Role** 511
Kimo Kippen

34. **Building Your Organization's Learning Technology Ecosystem** 515
    JD Dillon

35. **Equip Your Managers to Become Masters of Development** 533
    Wendy Axelrod

36. **Talent Development's Role in Strategic Workforce Planning** 547
    Barbara Goretsky

37. **From Ward to Steward: Enhancing Employee Ownership of Career Development**... 561
   Halelly Azulay

38. **Implement a Mentoring Program That Works**.. 577
   Jenn Labin and Laura Francis

39. **Consulting on the Inside: Roles, Competencies, and Challenges** 587
   B. Kim Barnes and Beverly Scott

40. **Becoming a Successful Consultant: From Startup to Market Leadership**... 603
   Andrew Sobel

41. **Building Teams and Understanding Virtual Teamwork**.. 617
   Tammy Bjelland

42. **The Trifecta: Project Management, L&D, and Talent Development**................ 631
   Lou Russell

Section VII. Aligning the Learning Function to the Organization 643

Luminary Perspective: Be the Leader People Want and Organizations Need... 645
Ken Blanchard

43. **Learning and Development's Role in Achieving Corporate Vision**................... 651
   Jack Zenger and Joe Folkman

44. **Structuring TD to Meet the Dynamic Needs of the Organization** 663
   William J. Rothwell, Angela Stopper, and Aileen G. Zaballero

45. **The Five Fundamentals of Learning Leadership**.. 675
   Jim Kouzes and Barry Posner

46. **Building Your Business Acumen** 689
   Kevin Cope

47. **Supporting Your Organization's Onboarding Efforts** 697
   Norma Dávila and Wanda Piña-Ramírez

48. **Determining Talent Development's Organizational Impact**............................... 715
   David Vance

49. **Best Practices for a Talent Development Department of One**........................... 725
   Emily Wood

Section VIII. Talent Development's Role for Future Success 739

Luminary Perspective: The Future Is Closer Than You Think 741
John Coné

50. **6 Essentials for a Thriving Learning Culture** 749
   Holly Burkett

51. **Sustaining Diversity, Equity, and Inclusion** 773
    Tonya Wilson

52. **How L&D Can Partner With Executives** 791
    Andy Trainor

53. **Organizational Design Practices That Can Make or Break
    Your Organization** 799
    David C. Forman

54. **Agility for the Future Workforce** 813
    Christie Ward

55. **Developing a Change-Ready Organization** 825
    Jennifer Stanford

56. **Emerging Technology and the Future of Learning** 835
    Karl Kapp and Jessica Briskin

57. **Talent Development's Role in Aligning People Analytics
    With Strategy** 847
    Larry Wolff

Appendix A: Glossary 859

Appendix B: List of Tools 901

Index 909

About the Editor 931

About ATD 933

Foreword

The talent development field has undergone monumental changes in recent years. Massive upskilling and reskilling of the workforce, shortages in available labor, changes in technology, and the COVID-19 pandemic have demanded that TD professionals juggle the development priorities of learners, clients, organizations, and themselves; it has been an incredible feat.

Elaine Biech notes in the introduction that "the timing couldn't be better" for this new edition of the *ATD Handbook*. She's right. More than 100 authors—deep subject matter experts in the profession with many decades of experience—offer their practical insights to help all of us understand industry trends, how to focus on our own development, the best ways to move teams forward, and opportunities to contribute to the success of individuals and organizations.

This handbook is an ideal resource for your own growth and development—one to add to your professional library to refer to again and again. Whether you're faced with a new challenge or confirming your own knowledge, you will find it in a chapter here—there are 57 in all—that will have the answer you're seeking.

Karl Kapp, a contributing author of this handbook, champions the need to focus on our own growth. In an ATD blog post reflecting on the events of the previous years and considering 2022 trends, he writes that "it's more important than ever to spend some time focusing on our own personal growth and development. It's time to reflect on what is important, strengthen the areas that need improvement, and get out of our comfort zone and move forward. We aren't going to be able to accomplish this without some effort."

This handbook also features ATD's Talent Development Capability Model, which provides the foundation for the knowledge and skills needed for success in our field. Chapter 5 provides deep background about how the Capability Model sets standards for the field, helping to prepare talent development professionals for the future of work by broadening the scope of knowledge and skills that will make them effective. If you're not familiar with this model, I encourage you to invest time to learn how it can help you develop a lifelong learning mindset and help your organizations navigate the future of learning.

ATD's Handbook for Training and Talent Development came to life because of Elaine's countless hours of hard work during many months. ATD is grateful for the energy and dedication she brought to this edition and those that have come before it.

ATD is honored to bring the work of so many talented authors and experts to you in this powerful resource. I know your work will benefit from the time you invest with the content and expertise included here.

Thank you for partnering with ATD to create a world that works better.

Tony Bingham
President and CEO
ATD

Acknowledgments

It is an honor to edit *ATD's Handbook for Training and Talent Development* for the third time. It's impossible for anyone to complete a task like this alone. Providing you with the absolute best resources takes a team—but not just any team. It must be a team of dedicated, talented professionals who are not afraid to work long hours and meet insanely short timelines with incredibly high-quality standards. And that's the team that delivered this handbook to exceed your expectations.

So, who are these wise, committed, and talented team members? I am thankful for the thousands of hours contributed by these dedicated people:

- First and most important, thanks to the 101 authors who responded to our call for content. We appreciate your expertise. I am especially grateful for your willingness to accept the topic we defined, conduct your research, and create a chapter that enhanced the flow of the handbook and met the needs of our readers. Lead authors are listed in the table of contents, but you will also find sidebar authors and contributing authors within several of the chapters.
- Thank you to the eight luminary guest authors who shared their wisdom in each section's introduction: Tacy Byham, Bev Kaye, Bob Pike, Elliott Masie, Rita Bailey, Kimo Kippen, Ken Blanchard, and John Coné. I know your time is limited and I appreciate that you dedicated some of it to this project. A double thanks to each of you.
- Thank you to the ATD staff who recommended timely topics and awesome authors. Your ability to extend our reach to seasoned and new authors was a bonus, as proven in the table of contents. I am grateful to Holly Batts, Justin Brusino, Kristen Fyfe-Mills,

- Patty Gaul, MJ Hall, Jack Harlow, Jennifer Homer, Melissa Jones, Paula Ketter, Kathryn Stafford, and Courtney Vital.
- Thank you to the fabulous people beyond the ATD staff who helped me connect with exceptional authors, including Howard Farfel, Cheryl Flink, Jonathan Halls, Michael Hansen, and Walt McFarland.
- Thank you to everyone who helped to ensure that this handbook represented a diverse audience.
- Writing the content is the first big task, but honing it into clear, concise, coherent, consistent, and grammatically correct language is the second task—almost as big as the first. I, and all the authors, value the various editing tasks that it takes to make a superb book: developmental editing, copyediting, content editing, structural editing, and proofreading. We appreciate Caroline Coppel, Melissa Jones, and Kathryn Stafford for your editing prowess. You make all of us look good!
- Thanks to everyone who helped me wrap up the details, including Renee Broadwell, Fred George-Hiatt, Jeanenne Ray, and Melissa Smith. You went above and beyond.
- A special and delayed thank you to Capt. (ret.) Joe Ruppert. Without his trust in me, most of this would never have happened.
- Last—but probably should be first—an interminable thanks to Dan Greene, who supports and encourages me to assume these enormous projects. Thank you for your devotion and trust.

And of course, thank you to ATD, Tony, Justin, Jennifer, and Courtney, for continuing to offer me projects that allow me to grow, develop, and be a lifelong ATD volunteer.

Introduction

Much has changed since March 2020. With organizations moving quickly to adjust operations and a large portion of the workforce working remotely because of COVID-19, talent development (TD) departments have scrambled to determine how best to develop employees. Some of this change has been difficult, but many of the results are positive.

TD departments had to rethink how to deliver their services in a matter of days, without a needs assessment or a plan to guide them. Many were completely unprepared for such an upheaval in terms of tools and competencies. Still, they rose to the challenge. Talent development practitioners switched to virtual instructor-led training, they chunked learning into specific lessons, they made it interesting for those distracted by working from home, and they got creative when new technology wasn't in the budget. And they did it all in days instead of months.

The timing couldn't be better for this handbook. Many of its chapters relate practitioners' experiences and offer tools that you can use as you face the challenges ahead.

Why This Handbook?

It is an honor to edit *ATD's Handbook for Training and Talent Development* for the third time. Through each edition, the topics have changed to reflect the times and the needs of the profession. You'll find different sections and different chapters. In fact, it's all new. The topics have changed, and the emphasis has too.

But one thing that hasn't changed is the thousands of hours that we've invested in bringing you a resource that you will turn to again and again. This book delivers the content you need, written by experts you respect, to help you comprehend what's important in your changing role. While it addresses what you need to know today and into the future, it also affords you an opportunity to delve into the historic roots of our profession.

This handbook brings together 101 thought leaders in talent development to provide a multitude of cutting-edge topics—the author list reads like a who's who in talent development. The wisdom of the best minds in the profession has been woven together to help you create your professional persona. Each section, chapter, and topic has been selected based on what you need to know at this time and in the future. You would need to purchase dozens of books to garner the same critical content that is condensed between these two covers.

Yes, our roles have expanded due to the pandemic, but they were already changing—COVID-19 simply made them transform more rapidly. This handbook provides a definition of the changes, an understanding of why change was required, and some predictions for what you can expect in talent development in the future. All of these changes require a voice of reason, and the handbook answers that call. In its pages you'll find the rationale to help you sort what's important and what's not, what's new and what's the past rehashed.

Many practitioners, whether new to the profession or highly experienced, do not have a clear understanding of the history of talent development. There is always a fire to put out, an immediate question that must be addressed, or a development opportunity to create, thus leaving little time to research our history. Why do we do the things we do? It's highly unlikely that you will readily find information about the history of training and the theories and practices that support it in most of your current resources. However, it is important to know that there is scientific evidence behind what we do and that some options work better than others. A fundamental purpose of this handbook is to provide you with a description of how talent development has evolved and the gurus who led the early efforts.

What's in This Handbook?

ATD's Handbook for Training and Talent Development is divided into eight sections, representing key areas of the TD profession. You will find that the sections are less ADDIE-dependent and more focused on the expanding role that you are experiencing in the profession.

Although the design does not match the Talent Development Capability Model, care has been taken to ensure that the content in the handbook aligns with ATD's Talent Development Body of Knowledge (TD BoK). For example, the glossary has new and different words with their own meanings, but if the word also appears in the TD BoK glossary, you will find the same definition. Consistency is critical, especially for those who are preparing for certification.

Each of the eight sections is introduced by a luminary—a unique individual who has reached legendary stature in the TD profession and has had an active role in developing and leading the topic addressed in that section. Let's look closer at each section:

1. **The Foundations of Learning and Development.** As you might expect, the handbook starts with a strong foundation and builds on that. I am so excited to share our leadoff luminary, Tacy Byham's, perspective on what it takes to have a strong foundation. She challenges us with 10 simple words: "Match the demands of the business with ready-now talent." This section prepares you to create the business case for learning in your organization by creating your own strong foundation as you review critical adult learning basics and the science of learning.

2. **Planning a Career in Talent Development.** There's no one better to initiate a section for developing a TD career than Bev Kaye, the indisputable authority on career development. You'll love her perspective on the eight talent development mindsets. The rest of this section introduces you to the Talent Development Capability Model and certification, the importance of lifelong learning, and the relationship of EQ and mindset to your professional success. You'll also gain Jean Greaves' advice about how EQ is important for you as well as the clients you develop.

3. **Training and Development Basics.** Bob Pike, the trainer's trainer, kicks off section III, sharing some of his favorite models and his Learning Preference Continuum. The rest of the section offers 10 chapters that focus on the various elements of ADDIE, plus new ways to think about ADDIE. Check out the chapter by Nancy Duarte, the Storyteller of the Valley, and Jeff Davenport; they advise us to use story structure to influence others—because "stories stick." Another must-read chapter is written by Mhairi Campbell, award-winning media producer and executive at the BBC, who addresses 21st-century media skills. Don't miss the excellent chapters in this section that take you beyond the basics.

4. **Enhancing and Supporting Talent Development.** Who better to introduce a section that requires us to modify our thinking than the provocative and entertaining Elliott Masie? This section addresses many of the questions we have about the future of talent development. These topics include blended learning, accessibility, learning transfer, critical tools that support e-learning, and advice for those designing and delivering virtual training. We are fortunate to have authors whose names you'll recognize share their best with you. Who? Have you heard the names Hofmann, Orey, Elkins, Clay, or Huggett? Yes, I thought so.

5. **Required Forward-Focused Proficiencies and Attitudes.** One of the most forward-thinking people I know, Rita Bailey, sets the standard in this section. She asks you to consider the knowledge, skills, and attitudes you require to be successful as you experience "change on steroids." She offers a checklist for assessing your readiness for the future and even relates her skydiving experience to what our profession is currently experiencing. This section also offers a list of the essential skills required of TD professionals, suggestions to work with SMEs, tips to perfect your facilitation skills, advice to improve your communication with executives, and ways to integrate DEI into talent development.

6. **Expanded Roles of Talent Development.** The ever-positive Kimo Kippen, a native Hawaiian, opens this section by encouraging us to upskill and reskill ourselves and our colleagues to ensure success for our organizations. You've probably experienced some of the new roles that TD professionals are being asked to play—coaching managers to develop their people, supporting workforce planning, or implementing a mentoring program. Perhaps you've been tasked with encouraging employees to take ownership of their careers or transforming a dysfunctional team into a productive team. You may have even been asked to play the role of an internal consultant. Each of these new roles helps define the ways the TD profession is expanding. Read more about each topic in this section.

7. **Aligning the Learning Function to the Organization.** The highly respected and influential Ken Blanchard starts our discussion about how we can help ensure our organization's success. It requires that we become leaders, and Ken shares the three steps you can take to "become the kind of leader people want and organizations need." This section continues with Kouzes and Posner's take on the five leadership fundamentals, then Zenger and Folkman share L&D's role in achieving a corporate vision. To align the learning function to the organization, you'll also learn how to structure talent development, build your business acumen, support onboarding efforts, and measure your impact. Be sure to review the steps Dean Griess shares for working successfully with their leaders. Finally, there's a chapter just for the TD department of one.

8. **Talent Development's Role for Future Success.** The distinguished futurist and thought leader John Coné challenges us to let go of yesterday's approaches, look beyond the concerns of today, and prepare to build the future of tomorrow. I encourage everyone to read his perspective on what's possible in the future. This section also challenges you to determine how to sustain DEI and create a thriving learning culture. You can explore emerging technology, people analytics, workforce agility, and organizational design practices. Be sure to check out a special contributor, Andy Trainor, VP of Walmart US Learning, as he shares secrets to partnering with executives.

That's a lot of content to compile in one book, and even more for you to digest within its 900+ pages. Yet I can't think of one topic I'd remove. Our profession has become more complex, and this handbook can help you make sense of it all. If I sound excited about this content, it's because I am! I can't wait for you to read it and share your perspectives as well.

What Should You Watch For?

While you are reading, you may want to look for themes throughout. You may also want to compare authors' perspectives. They aren't all the same, but they are all thoughtful. I've read most of the books and articles that our authors have published, and knew they had the necessary expertise.

We asked more of them than just to write 3,000 words. We asked each author to ensure that their submission was practical and implementable by you, the readers. We asked them to address diversity in their chapters when appropriate and to recommend additional resources so you could go more in depth on topics that intrigued you. We also asked them to provide tools that you could download from the website to make it easier for you to implement their ideas. Finally, we asked for a list of glossary terms and definitions that they thought were critical to their submissions.

I believe that there is something in the handbook for everyone in the TD profession:

- You will find the basics of L&D. It couldn't be called a handbook without covering the basics, and they are all here.
- We incorporated the Talent Development Capability Model. While we certainly didn't want to repeat what's in the TD BoK, we did expand on several topics. The TD BoK addresses what and why; the handbook goes beyond to address how.
- The handbook is relevant to what we've experienced throughout the pandemic. COVID-19 and its variants have thrown entire businesses into disarray. Every one of the 101 authors lived through that experience and you will find mention of it throughout. (However, we did remove some references because you don't need to be reminded of the pandemic more than necessary.)
- You should find a focus on diversity in three ways: First there are whole chapters devoted to DEI and accessibility, and both are mentioned in many other chapters as well. Second, my goal was to include diversity in contributions including country and culture, race and ethnicity, age and generation, gender, sexual orientation, religious and spiritual beliefs, disability, and socioeconomic status and background. Where appropriate you will see the diversity peek through. For example, we maintained spellings that are culturally unique. And finally, you'll see diversity of thought as I sought contributors who are not only in the TD profession, but from education, IT, and corporate areas.

Finally, you will see several themes running through the handbook. These themes should be a wake-up call to all of us in the profession:
- Be prepared for the future.
- Gain new skills for new responsibilities.
- Promote DEI.
- Stay abreast of the warp speed of change.
- Ensure your organization is successful.

Watch for these themes throughout the handbook. Then ask yourself these questions:
- How prepared am I for the future?
- What skills do I need to traverse the changes in my organization?
- Who could mentor me to build the competency and the confidence to do more?
- How can I be a better lifelong learner?

How Can You Get the Most Out of Your Handbook?

If you need some motivation, I suggest you start with John Coné's luminary introduction to section VIII, Talent Development's Role for Future Success. John has a wonderful ability to inspire others, and in this case, his rousing projection of the future is stimulating and thought provoking.

If you are new to the profession, get a serious dose of learning and development philosophy in section I. Then move on to section III, Training and Development Basics, to explore the skills you'll need from assessment to evaluation and everything in between.

Are you looking for that illusive seat at the table? Have we got resources for you! Turn to section VII, Aligning the Learning Function to the Organization, where Ken Blanchard discusses being the leader your organization needs. Next check out chapter 43 by Jack Zenger and Joe Folkman, and chapter 45 by Jim Kouzes and Barry Posner to discover the five fundamentals of learning leadership.

If you are still wondering about the changes from training to talent development, check out section VI, Expanded Roles of Talent Development. Explore your role in workforce planning, helping your managers coach their employees, implementing a mentoring effort, building teams, and consulting. Yes, our role is changing, and we need to accept the responsibility to change with it. Get a pep talk from luminary Kimo Kippen then slip on over to Halelly Azulay's chapter 37 to learn how to take ownership of your own career development.

Finally, remember the tools on the website (ATDHandbook3.org). Choose your favorite chapter and download the tools that will help you implement the content.

How can you get the most out of this handbook? To quote Jim Kouzes and Barry Posner, "You have to make learning a daily habit." Use this book to enhance your knowledge. Turn to any page or any chapter to learn something every day. The handbook makes it easy.

Final Thoughts

Much has changed since March 2020. We live in a dynamic world. Thankfully we are also part of a vibrant, prepared profession. The training and talent development landscape has been changed forever. However, we have proven that we can quickly rise above to successfully address the challenges our organizations face. Talent development is made up of professionals who will find a way to support and lead—no matter the challenge. I am delighted to share this handbook to help guide you into your professional future.

Elaine Biech, CPTD Fellow
Norfolk, VA
May 2022

SECTION I
LEARNING AND DEVELOPMENT BASICS

LUMINARY PERSPECTIVE

Our Job Is to Deliver Breakthrough Moments

Tacy Byham

Breakdown or Breakthrough?

Tanya worked in supply chain management for an aeronautics manufacturer. She excelled in her job as an individual contributor and had a real knack for anticipating things that might become problems later. So, when she was promoted to her first leadership role—and was relocated to Florida, an added perk!—she felt both proud and ready. It was her time.

When she met with her team, a group of more seasoned contributors, on her first day, Tanya talked about how excited and privileged she felt to lead them, and acknowledged their unique role in the organization. So far, so good. "They were smiling, nodding, and asking great questions," she recalls.

Then it was her turn to listen.

The team took turns reporting on projects, accomplishments, and bottlenecks: One talked about the new vendor exploration, while another shared progress on the inventory management system. Then an associate passed out the team's monthly dashboard, a common report that had been distributed to the operations team earlier that day. When Tanya saw the report, she panicked.

And in a single moment, Tanya damaged everything she'd worked for until that point.

"*WHAT?!?!?*" Her shriek jolted the team out of their collective happy place and into a defensive crouch. "*This report just went to MY boss? Who else on our team read this over?*" she remembers exploding. "I complained about the grammar, the graphs, the formatting, and the data. Everything." She publicly yelled at the associate for letting the document out the door.

When Tanya shared this story in a leadership training session—between deep gulps and face palms—the pain of her mistake was still fresh, even though it was eight years later. "I was labeled as a hothead and a perfectionist by everyone on the team," she says, noting that even worse things were probably said that she wasn't aware of.

> It takes 20 "atta boys" to overcome that one "oh @##$%!" moment. And sometimes that doesn't even help.

All it took was one moment—one breakdown—to destroy her reputation. And it took her years to recover it.

We all have moments when our surprise and emotions get the better of us. But that's exactly where training kicks in. With the right training, we can rewire ourselves to do better.

As learning and development professionals, this is our gift to give. We help people, especially leaders like Tanya, develop the foundational skills that serve them in every moment of their jobs. We help them deal with those big, scary, stressful moments, when they don't know where to turn for help and they need help fast. We are their lifeline and their coach so their pathway to success is easier the next time around.

And when we do this well? We turn breakdowns into breakthrough moments. Instead of spending years overcoming a bad moment, we give them the tools to make the best of each experience.

The Crack in the Foundation

Our challenge in 10 simple words is to "match the demands of the business with ready-now talent." We've devoted our careers to pursuit of this straightforward ideal. We build visions of robust talent pipelines, with multiple qualified people ready to step up to any given challenge.

Can it happen? Absolutely. According to DDI's *Global Leadership Forecast 2021*, about one in 10 organizations (11 percent) says it has a "strong" or "very strong" bench. But most of us aren't doing that well. In fact, bench strength is at its lowest level in the last 10 years.

Where are the other 89 percent of us going wrong?

As you dig into this "Learning and Development Basics" section, you'll find three clear differences in the practices and programs that result in a robust leadership pipeline, based on success rates of more than 1,700 organizations (Neal, Boatman, and Watt 2021):

1. Shorten transitions to help leaders become successful in new roles quickly. Ninety days or less is ideal.
2. Give leaders self-insight via a high-quality assessment as a catalyst for development.
3. Deliver personalized, relevant leadership development experiences that support people in key moments.

Each of these topics deserves its own chapter, if not a full book or semester of university study. And yet, I urge you to pause for a moment of reflection. If you were to assign a letter grade to your company's adoption of these principles, would you be an A student or a C student (or worse)? And what impact does that have on the speed and quality with which you fulfill your mission of "matching the demands of the business with ready-now talent?"

Let's build a case for the cumulative power of these three practices.

The Urgency of Successful Transitions

As we learned from Tanya's story, you can make a mistake on your first day in a new role. And it can haunt you for years. Yet companies rarely apply a sense of urgency to support leaders in their transitions. That's why our first pillar of foundational training is around support in transitions. For example, here are a few things some of our research has revealed about leadership transitions:

- On average, it takes four years for a first-time leader to get training, leaving them to sink or swim (DDI 2019).
- The longer it takes for leaders to get up to speed, the more stressful it is. More than a third of leaders at every level describe their transition as overwhelming or extremely stressful. Five percent frequently dream of quitting (DDI 2021).
- The stress isn't temporary. Regardless of how long ago it was, leaders who report long and stressful transitions are significantly less engaged in their roles. They're more than three

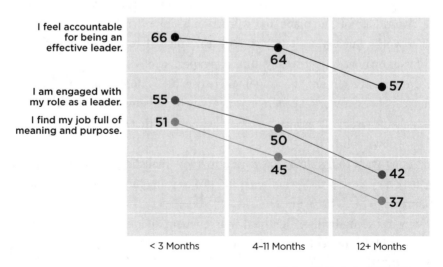

The Cost of Long Transitions

© Development Dimensions International, Inc. 2021. All rights reserved.

times as likely to report burnout compared with their peers with low-stress transitions. Worse, they feel less accountable for being a good leader for their team and find their work to have less meaning and purpose (DDI 2021).

Are you likely to hear about any of this? Probably not. For many people, especially leaders, it feels too risky to admit they're struggling. What if their boss holds it against them? What if their team loses confidence in them? What if they don't get a raise or promotion because of it?

So they put a smile on and stay silent. They assume there's something uniquely wrong with them, because everyone else seems to be fine (even though they're experiencing the same thing). And eventually they leave, opening up yet another gap in your pipeline.

And don't expect the leader to be the only one who leaves. The risk stretches into their teams as well. A single disengaged leader has a compounding effect on the organization, and their poor skills can drive talented people out the door long before they throw in the towel themselves.

As learning and talent professionals, this is where we have the power to change things. If you wait to deliver training until someone asks for it, it's probably too late.

> If you wait to deliver training until someone asks for it, it's probably too late.

Our job is to anticipate what's ahead for these roles and create development experiences that prevent leaders from falling into deep pitfalls. We need to give them the foundation they need before they know they need it.

"Know Thyself"

Stepping into a new role is like being asked to fly a plane, despite never having done it before. You might have ridden on the plane and worked in a support role, and you might understand how the plane works. But as you sit in the pilot's seat, you realize you're suddenly responsible for hundreds of lives on board. It's a totally different experience.

There's very real risk in not knowing if you're capable of doing something. Simply "faking it until you make it" doesn't work. Leaders may not only be missing some key skills—their previous instincts may also be wrong. They may have to unlearn things that were strengths in a previous role because they're now liabilities.

Leaders don't want to fly blind. They want to know that they can handle the responsibility. And if they have a weakness, they want to fix it. The last thing they want to do is fail, especially in front of their team.

That's why our second pillar, high-quality assessment and feedback, is so important. In fact, assessment is one of the top requests leaders would like more of from their employers (Neal, Boatman, and Watt 2021).

But not all assessments are the same. What leaders are telling us, loudly and clearly, is that they want objective feedback on their skills. In our experience, high-quality assessments should:
- Be competency based.
- Offer an objective view of strengths and development areas.
- Pinpoint the exact behavior that a leader needs to focus on within a competency.
- Give insights about readiness for future roles.
- Support development after the assessment.

When done well, insight from assessment data drives the success of your development program. Leaders know why they need development, and how it's going to drive relevance on the job. They can accelerate their success by understanding where they need to pull back, where they need to focus, and where they need to add something new to their leadership repertoire.

The results are undeniable. On average, combining high-quality assessment with any development program boosts bench strength by 30 percent. Furthermore, HR leaders with strong formal assessment programs say they can fill 56 percent of critical leadership roles immediately, compared with 43 percent at other organizations (DDI 2021).

In short, assessment helps you answer the fundamental question: Does our development strategy help us match the demands of the business with ready-now talent? If you've done the assessment, you can answer that question easily, proving the value of the investment in learning and leadership development.

Create Experiences for the Moments

Earlier, we mentioned that the third pillar of creating a robust leadership pipeline depends on delivering personalized, relevant development experiences that support people in key moments. When we talk to most L&D clients about this, their mind first goes to the type of technology they might use.

Technology is certainly an important part of the equation, but it doesn't get to the heart of the problem. People aren't asking for what technology will make learning personal and relevant. Rather, they are wondering what they can learn that is personal and relevant to their *problem right in this moment*.

It might sound a bit basic, but it's one of the most common fundamentals of learning that I see companies overlook. So often, we get caught up in the details and tactics of the huge array of learning options that we overlook our real goal, which is the impact we have on people's lives and the moments within them.

In what ways are they struggling? How can we design learning experiences that go beyond conveying information to changing their behavior in those moments? And how do you measure the impact of those moments?

For leaders, these moments might be big changes that happen over time, like taking on a new role or driving a transformation. Or they might be small and quick, like resolving a team conflict. Or they might be large but urgent, like reacting to a crisis.

The mistake we often see companies make is trying to deliver the same type of learning for every moment. For example, they might offer only live group courses, which are great for learning proactive skills during big moments of change but are rarely timely enough to solve on-demand problems. Or they might swing the other way completely, offering only on-demand courses or microlearning. While these approaches can be helpful for giving quick advice, they are ineffective at building major skills.

In short, you can think of it like a pendulum, with each extreme living on either end. In addition, companies may offer multiple types of training content, but they come from different sources. For example, they might develop a few courses in-house for proactive moments and supplement them with an online learning library. The problem? If the content is inconsistent, leaders are likely to get mixed messages.

The Pendulum of Digital vs. Classroom Learning

All Classroom
- Proactive
- Cohort-based
- Episodic

All Digital
- Reactive
- Individual
- On demand

Instead of swinging wildly across the pendulum, L&D professionals should be looking to find balance by focusing on key moments, then designing consistent content that meets those needs but offers flexibility in timing and modality.

Let's take a look at a couple examples.

Moment 1: Stepping Into a Leadership Role for the First Time

Becoming a leader for the first time is a big moment of transformation that changes a person's career. And they need a lot of support to develop in these moments.

Here are a few considerations for meeting new leaders in the moment:
- **Group or individual?** Ideally, this is a moment when leaders really benefit from learning together. It helps to share challenges and build a network with other new leaders who can support one another over time. However, it may be a challenge to build cohorts that help leaders as quickly as they need it. So you may have to consider providing individual learning first, and following up later with group experiences.
- **How fast?** As we learned from Tanya, speed is critical. If you have identified someone in advance as a high-potential leader, you can start building skills before they get into the role. If the promotion is a surprise or fast decision, start developing them as soon as possible.
- **How complex are the new skills they need?** Leadership requires learning significant new skills, and leaders will need to put in significant time to master them. Learning theory won't be enough. They will need the opportunity to practice.
- **How personalized should it be?** It's crucial for first-time leaders to build a core set of skills and have an approach that's consistent with the organization's leadership culture. However, as they are building their own leadership brand, personal insight is critical. Each leader might also want to explore some specific topics where they are personally struggling.

A lot of companies we've worked with try to meet these needs by building great onboarding experiences. Ideally, they kick off with an assessment to personalize the experience, then bring leaders together to learn and practice new skills over a few days or a few months.

While these onboarding programs are excellent, I caution L&D professionals to make sure they move fast enough. Many hold onboarding only once a year, or they wait until there are enough people for a cohort. But that can leave leaders waiting for a long time. In many cases, it would be best to provide some on-demand learning to get them started quickly, even if they go through a larger program down the road.

When leaders are met in this moment, it can change the entire course of their career at the company. But the big mistake is that many companies stop with basic training.

Moment 2: Resolving a Team Conflict Right Away

While proactive learning is extremely helpful, new problems pop up all the time. For example, a leader might have a conflict on their team, and they need some guidance to resolve it.

These spur-of-the-moment issues create the "Google problem" for L&D professionals. Basically, every employee's first instinct is to type their question into their browser and click on whatever comes up first. The problem? They could find literally anything. It could be bad advice. Or outdated advice. Or simply an approach that doesn't fit within your company culture.

These moments are common, and they are worth our attention. We need to be better than Google. We need to provide resources on demand that people can trust to help them in these critical moments. Consider how new leaders would answer these questions about their development:

- **Group or individual?** For the moment, individual is fine, although they may need or want to practice their skills with a group later.
- **How fast?** Now!
- **How complex are the new skills they need?** At this point, they should be building on their foundational skills. As long as what they are learning is consistent with what they learned in those core skill-building programs, they should easily be able to expand their skills.
- **How personalized should it be?** It doesn't necessarily need to be personalized, but leaders may benefit from tools that help them quickly assess themselves and their situation. For example, if they need to resolve a conflict, they might benefit from a tool that helps them quickly assess their natural approach to the topic.

So, consider this the moment where you pull out all your digital tools! How can you leverage 10-to-15-minute microcourses to quickly build skills? Employ digital tools that can help employees understand their approach and, ideally, help them quickly practice their newfound skills.

Above all, make sure that what you put together is proven, so leaders can trust what they're learning in the moment. Otherwise, they'll be off to find their own approach!

Making Development a Way of Work

These are just two examples of the many moments leaders experience. But they illustrate a few key things:

- Think of the moment of need first and how to solve that problem.
- Build your content and approach on the same foundational set of principles. Otherwise, leaders will get mixed messages.
- Fit and flex the modality for the moment, rather than dictate how people learn. Going all-or-nothing on any side of the pendulum leaves huge gaps in development. Rather, you can flex the modality to meet people with the speed and type of learning they need right now.

When you do this well, you can achieve a big goal: Making development a way of work. When you meet people in their moment of need—big or small—you teach them how to truly integrate learning into their job, and not as something extra.

Our Calling Is to Deliver Breakthrough Moments

In the rest of this section, you'll learn a lot about the fundamentals of learning, including the science, the history, and the strategy behind it. But as you dive in, I hope to impress upon you the importance of the human moments in all that we do.

As learning and development professionals, we aren't here to just convey information. We work to create breakthrough moments of learning that change how people view themselves, their jobs, and their relationships (at work and often outside it). We can ease their stress in tough moments and prepare them to achieve great things.

When we do that well, we've done so much more than effectively build a skill. We've changed lives. We can spark a hunger for learning and constant improvement. And when we do this not only in individuals, but throughout organizations as well, we can alter the trajectory for success in our entire companies.

And that's why we have one of the best—and one of the hardest—jobs in the world.

About the Author

Tacy Byham is passionate about empowering leaders to declare their true worth and ignite their impact in the workplace, from the start of their careers all the way to the C-suite. She is CEO of Development Dimensions International (DDI), a global award-winning leadership consultancy that helps the world's most successful companies transform the way they select, develop, and accelerate leaders. An internationally recognized presenter on leadership, Tacy co-wrote the global bestseller *Your First Leadership Job*, and her featured articles have appeared in *Forbes*, *Fast Company*, and *Inc.*, as well as numerous blog postings on LinkedIn via the Forbes Coaches Council. Tacy also launched the #LeadLikeAGirl movement, which provides women with practical strategies and real-world wisdom to ignite their careers. Learn more about Tacy and DDI at ddiworld.com.

References

DDI. 2019. *The Frontline Leader Project*. Pittsburgh, PA: DDI.
DDI. 2021. *Leadership Transitions Report*. Pittsburgh, PA: DDI.
Neal, S., J. Boatman, and B. Watt. 2021. *Global Leadership Forecast 2021*. Pittsburgh, PA: DDI.

Recommended Resources

Byham, T.M., and R.S. Wellins. 2015. *Your First Leadership Job: How Catalyst Leaders Bring Out the Best in Others*. Hoboken, NJ: John Wiley & Sons.

Paese, M.J., A.B. Smith, and W.C. Byham. 2016. *Leaders Ready Now: Accelerating Growth in a Faster World*. Pittsburgh, PA: DDI Press.

CHAPTER 1

The Evolution of Talent Development

Lorrie Lykins

The continuously evolving theories and practices of learning, training, and talent development are integral to the story of human history, with accounts of formal training frameworks and approaches dating back to ancient Greece, Egypt, and Rome. Storytelling (which encompasses, among other things, today's case studies, TED Talks, interviews, classroom learning, and on-the-job training with a mentor) is the foundation on which the acquisition and passing down of knowledge and skill was built.

Over time, the training profession has seen its initial focus on skills training progress from an emphasis on individual development, to systems theory and organization development, to learning, to, most recently, performance and the development of talent.

> **IN THIS CHAPTER:**
> - Explore the historic roots of training, learning, and talent development theories and practices
> - Discover how the profession of talent development has evolved

Today's organizational learning and development function is reflective of the breathtaking speed of continuous change that has taken place over the past several years. It has transformed from functioning as a fixed locus of learning content creation and delivery for the organization into a dynamic hub of talent development with trainers acting as facilitators, coaches, advisors, and curators—increasingly of user-generated content that is produced across the enterprise.

As learning becomes more easily accessible and personalized to each individual's abilities, aptitudes, and potential, the organizational culture is also transforming. For example, talent acquisition professionals look at talent in new ways—eschewing the outmoded approach of screening out candidates driven by rigid requirements of knowledge and skills to *screening in* for learning agility.

As CEOs and senior leadership teams recognize the bottom-line business impact that training, learning, and development delivers, the identity and role of L&D to include reporting lines, titles, remit, and so forth continue to change and vary worldwide; training departments and the professionals therein can be known as:

- Learning and development
- Learning and talent development
- Learning and performance management
- Learning and workforce experience
- Talent and employee experience
- Talent and organizational effectiveness
- Talent management and organization development
- Talent, learning, and culture
- Talent and inclusion

While this is not an exhaustive list, it illustrates the evolution of the profession and its expanding role, specifically, as a key pillar of talent management—which takes a holistic view of developing individuals throughout the employee life cycle as well as building and sustaining the capacity of the organization's entire workforce.

What follows is an overview of the history and evolution of training and development. Use this knowledge to help frame your thinking about where we have been, where we are today, and what might be ahead.

Early Learning Models and Practices

The earliest documented form of training was on-the-job training (OJT), with records dating back to ancient Egypt, Greece, and Rome. Sometimes referenced as an "earn while you learn" or "sit by me" scenario, on-the-job training takes place when an individual learns by observing an experienced worker performing a job in the work setting. This remains a popular approach for some industries, in part because of the simplicity (Shay 2019).

Apprenticeships

Apprenticeships are the gold standard of on-the-job training—nine out of 10 apprentices are employed after completing their apprenticeship, with an average starting wage of more than $50,000. Apprenticeships are a reliable source of highly skilled and loyal workers for employers, and an apprentice worker's lifetime compensation can be more than $300,000 compared with that of their peers (i4cp and Aspen Institute 2016a).

The concept of the apprenticeship—passing down mastery of a trade, craft, art, or profession from master to novice—remains largely unchanged from its earliest documented origins. Evidence of this more formal arrangement of on-the-job training survives in contracts written on papyrus during the 600-year Roman occupation of ancient Egypt: Heraclides was apprenticed as a nail smith in 18 BC; Panechotes had a two-year apprenticeship to learn shorthand with his master in 155 AD (Lewis 1983; Westermann 1915).

Apprenticeships took firm root during the Middle Ages, with the types of these arrangements varying widely, and distinctions were made between teaching contracts and apprenticeship contracts, which sometimes included indenture (Morgan 2001). The latter was more likely to include the master providing room, board, and even clothing, because the work of the apprentice immediately benefited the master's business (Westermann 1915). Although apprenticeships are generally thought of as applying only to artisanal crafts, they were not restricted to such jobs and could apply to medicine, law, and education (Steinmetz 1976).

In some strata of society, apprenticeships were highly sought after because they were often how people could ensure both a livelihood and position in society, which sometimes came with such opportunities. For example, the Inns of Court provided legal education to young men in Britain beginning in the 1300s. Men learned the practice of law by living at the Inns, reading and discussing law books, and attending court daily. The Inns also became centers of intellectual and social activity in Renaissance England. While many of the men who attended them became practicing lawyers, others used the Inns to make connections with members of high society and better their future prospects (Friedman 1985).

Apprenticeships were an integral part of the colonial period in the United States; as colonial society developed and commercial activity increased, so too did the need for competent legal counsel. Law apprentices combined self-directed reading of law books (sometimes loaned by tavern owners) with guidance from lawyers before being examined for admission to the bar (Friedman 1985).

Today, apprentices in the US are safeguarded by the US Department of Labor (USDOL), which ensures equality of access to apprenticeship programs and provides employment and training information to sponsors and the employment and training community. Apprenticeships are rebounding in popularity—the USDOL reported that the number of registered apprenticeships increased by 64 percent between 2010 and 2020 (Cooper 2021).

Apprenticeships also remain the preferred method of vocational worker training in many countries and, according to a 2013 World Bank survey, they're increasing in use worldwide. Today's apprentices are paid employees who are engaged in the process of mastering the work skills of a particular trade or occupation (Cantor 2015). In Germany, they are an important part of the successful dual education system, which combines apprenticeships with vocational education.

Guilds

Also developed in the Middle Ages in England, the guild system was made up of "associations of people [guilds] whose interests or pursuits were the same or similar. The basic purpose was mutual protection, assistance, and advantage" (Steinmetz 1976). The guild system controlled the quality of products by establishing standards and regulating the people who were authorized to produce them. This also meant that apprenticeships came under the authority of the guild, which determined when a worker had reached a certain level of proficiency. Guilds also strictly regulated worker hours, tools, prices, and wages, and required that all workers have the same privileges and pursue the same methods.

Vocational and Manual Schools

The onset of industrialism sparked the rapid and continuous evolution in business we see today, as well as changes in training and learning practices. It was during this time that vocational and manual schools were created.

Vocational education or vocational education and training (VET)—also known as career and technical education (CTE) or "trade school"—is traditionally nonacademic and prepares learners for jobs in specific occupations. The one-to-two-year learning period submerses the learner in a trade or vocation, such as welding, plumbing, nursing, firefighting, the culinary arts, court reporting, or mechanics. One of the earliest vocational schools was established by the Masonic Grand Lodge of New York in 1809; in 1824, Rensselaer Polytechnic Institute in Troy, New York, became the first technical college; and in 1828, the Ohio Mechanics Institute opened in Cincinnati, Ohio (Miller 2008; Steinmetz 1976).

Vocational schools have fluctuated in popularity in the US—in 1999, 9.6 million students were enrolled in a trade school, but by 2014, this number had increased to 16 million, according to the National Center for Education Statistics (2021). Trade schools are an important force in training, especially in Europe, which included vocational training in the draft Constitutional Treaty establishing the European Community.

Agriculture and Mechanical Education

Postsecondary teaching of agricultural and mechanical (A&M) arts via land-grant colleges began in the US in the 1840s and is credited to Jonathan Baldwin Turner (1805–1899), a classical scholar, botanist, and political activist. Turner's idea and advocacy resulted in the 1862 passage of the Morrill Land Grant Act during the Civil War, in which federal lands were given to the states to sell and use the proceeds to establish A&M colleges (Turner 1961). In signing this act into law, Abraham Lincoln provided a way for average people to get an education, which had previously been restricted to the wealthy.

A second Morrill Act, passed in 1890, required each state to demonstrate that race was not an admissions criterion, or required each state to designate a separate land-grant institution for people of color (LII n.d.). Many of today's historically Black colleges and universities (HBCUs) can trace their beginnings to this act.

However, the legacy of the land-grant acts is not without criticism and ongoing controversy, as much of the land used for the program was seized from Native Americans (Lee and Ahtone 2020).

Factory Schools and Vestibule Training

The New York City printing press manufacturer R. Hoe & Company is credited with providing the first on-site classroom learning to employees in the 1870s. It was described as "evening school for the firm's apprentices, six months in the year … with suitable books and appliances competent teachers are employed. They are instructed in the various branches of a common English education according to their needs and capabilities, and those who are sufficiently advanced are also taught mathematics and mechanical drawing" (Tucker 1973).

Near the turn of the 20th century, an innovation came about that addressed some of the challenges of classroom training: vestibule training, in which new employees learn the job in a setting that approximates the actual working environment as closely as possible. Using simulated cockpits to train airline pilots is an example of this type of training. Vestibule training is generally used when the actual equipment would be too risky for untrained employees to use or when the actual work setting would be unconducive to learning (Law 2009).

The 20th Century: World Wars and Systematic Training

US historians assert that training and development in the 20th century took form during World War II, when a surge in demand for products came at the same time that scores of experienced workers were enlisting in the armed forces. The expanding wartime economy, technological innovations, and a dramatic increase in the demand for trained workers all combined to drive rapid maturation of the training and learning profession and growth of employee training and development, as well as the rise of the US labor movement (Torraco 2016).

When men were drafted for the war, large numbers of untrained women and men over the age of 40 surged into the workforce to replace them. When the supply of vocational school instructors could not meet the demand, the Training Within Industry Service of the War Manpower Commission developed the Job Instructor Training (JIT) program. The JIT's purpose was to teach first- and second-line supervisors how to teach their skills to others (Shaw 1994; Steinmetz 1976). These train-the-trainer programs became known as J programs and expanded to include topics such as human relations, job methods, safety, and program development. Influences on these topics included Abraham Maslow's *A Theory of Human Motivation* (1943) and Kurt Lewin's first experiments with group dynamics (1948).

In concert with systematic training came a systematic approach to instructional design. During World War II, the military applied a systems approach to learning design, which became the forerunner for today's instructional systems design (ISD). The research and theories of B.F. Skinner on operant conditioning affected the design of these training programs, which focused on observable behaviors. Training designers created learning goals by breaking tasks into subtasks, and training was designed to reward correct behaviors and remediate incorrect behaviors.

B.F. SKINNER (1904-1990)

B.F. Skinner was a renowned behavioral psychologist and a major proponent of behaviorism, an influential school of psychological thought that was popular between World War I and World War II.

Skinner believed that the best way to learn about human nature was to explore how an organism responds to stimuli, both from the external environment and from internal biological processes, in a controlled, scientific study. Skinner's scholarly interests were influenced by psychologists such as Ivan Petrovich Pavlov, Bertrand Russell, and the founder of behaviorism, John B. Watson. Skinner's major works include *The Behavior of Organisms* (1938), *Walden Two* (1948), and *Science and Human Behavior* (1953).

His research found that in most disciplines, learning is most effectively accomplished when it is taught through incremental steps with instantaneous reinforcement, also known as reward, given to the learner for acceptable performance. Programmed learning should be implemented using teaching machines, which present the user with a question, allow the user to answer, and then immediately provide the user with the correct answer. Programmed learning as an educational technique has two major types: linear programming and branching. Linear programming rewards student responses that lead toward the learning goal; other responses go unrewarded. A correct response also moves the learner along through the program.

In addition, the industry came to recognize how important it was to train supervisors. As Steinmetz (1976) puts it, "Management found that without training skill, supervisors were unable to adequately produce for the defense or war effort. With it, new production methods were being established by the aged, the handicapped, and industrially inexperienced women." The need for leadership in training had become obvious, and so the title of *training director* became increasingly common in management hierarchies. In 1942, during a meeting of the American Petroleum Institute in New Orleans, Louisiana, the American Society of Training Directors (ASTD) was formed.

In addition to developing leadership in the training function, organizations realized the need for development in leadership more generally. This led to the emergence of the first management development programs, which were sponsored and guided by universities and colleges that offered college-level courses in management and technology (Steinmetz 1976).

The 1950s—The Influence of Educational and Behavioral Psychology

Following World War II, the industry's newfound efficiencies to accommodate the demands of war production were channeled into peacetime reconstruction. However, some of the methods that had been used to achieve those efficiencies—specifically, scientific management—were beginning to prove demotivating to employees. As a result, human relations training grew increasingly popular, and many supervisors were trained in psychology (Shaw 1994).

Individualized instruction was later automated using teaching machines in the 1960s and also formed the basis for early computer-based training. It had the advantages of enabling learners to learn at their own pace, giving them privacy to correct mistakes, and reducing training time and error rates when back on the job. However, individualized instruction could be expensive to produce, included only what the designer put into it, and required the learner to transfer knowledge back to the workplace. Another development in ISD that occurred during the 1950s was the introduction of Benjamin Bloom's taxonomy of educational objectives. Bloom published his classification of learning objectives, which describes cognitive, psychomotor, and affective outcomes, in 1956. The six levels of behavior are knowledge, comprehension, application, analysis, synthesis, and evaluation.

Cognitive outcomes, or knowledge, refer to the development of intellectual skills. Psychomotor outcomes, or skills, refer to the physical movement, coordination, and use of motor skills to accomplish a task. Affective outcomes, or attitudes, refer to how people deal with things emotionally. These categories are often referred to as KSAs (knowledge, skills, attitudes) and relate to the way that learning objectives are written to specify the types of learning to be accomplished. For example, a knowledge objective might be to describe how the increased production needs of World War II dramatically affected the field of training and learning.

At the end of the decade, ASTD published Donald Kirkpatrick's articles about the four levels of evaluation in *Journal of the American Society of Training Directors* (later *T+D* and then *TD*), which introduced a new theme into the field: measurement.

> **BENJAMIN BLOOM (1913-1999)**
>
> Benjamin Bloom was an educational psychologist whose contributions to education involved his model of talent development and his Taxonomy of Educational Objectives in the cognitive domain.
>
> The focus of Bloom's research was the study of educational objectives. He proposed that any given task favors one of three psychological domains—cognitive, affective, or psychomotor:
> - The cognitive domain deals with the ability to process and use (as a measure) information in a meaningful way.
> - The affective domain is concerned with the attitudes and feelings that result from the learning process.
> - The psychomotor domain involves manipulative or physical skills.
>
> Bloom is credited with being instrumental in shifting instructional emphasis from teaching facts to teaching students how to apply the knowledge they learn.

The 1960s

The introduction of measurement into the field of training was closely linked to another theme that started to emerge in the 1960s: the need to understand the business. During the 1950s, more publications appeared noting the importance of involving top management in training, and in 1960 Gordon M. Bliss, then executive director of ASTD, urged members to seek "wider responsibilities" and to understand "the vernacular which is used to report profits" (Shaw 1994). To reflect this broader focus, in 1964 ASTD changed its name to include the word *development*.

Another sign that the training profession was broadening its horizons was the adoption of organization development (OD). According to the Organization Development Network, a professional organization for OD practitioners, "Organization development is a values-based approach to systems change in organizations and communities; it strives to build the capacity to achieve and sustain a new desired state that benefits the organization or community and the world around them." Its roots lie in the behavioral sciences, using theories about organization change, systems, teams, and individuals based on the work of Kurt Lewin, Douglas McGregor, Rensis Likert, Richard Beckhard, Wilfred Bion, Ed Schein, Warren Bennis, and Chris Argyris (Haneberg 2005).

The wider focus on business results was also related to the emerging field of human performance improvement (HPI) or human performance technology (HPT). Performance improvement is a systematic, systemic, results-based approach to helping organizations meet their goals through the work of people. The work of Thomas Gilbert, Geary Rummler, Donald Tosti, and Dale Brethower moved the field of workplace learning from a singular focus on training to a wide variety of activities that improve business results.

More popular during this period was the psychology of influence, motivation, and attitude change. Topics related to the emerging US civil rights movement, such as workplace diversity, were also becoming more common.

In the areas of learning theory and design, the 1960s saw Jean Piaget, a Swiss developmental psychologist, create a model of cognitive development with four stages:
- The sensorimotor stage (birth to two years)
- The preoperational stage (ages two to seven)
- The concrete operational stage (ages seven to 11)
- The formal operational stage (ages 11 and up)

His theories form the foundation for the development of constructivism, which began to appear in the 1970s and 1980s.

Robert F. Mager proposed his model for instructional objectives in his 1962 book, *Preparing Objectives for Programmed Instruction*. This model indicates that objectives should have three components: behavior, condition, and standard. That is, the objective should describe the specific, observable behavior that the training should accomplish; indicate the conditions under which the behavior should be completed; and state the desirable level of performance. This type of objective is alternatively known as behavioral, performance, or criterion-referenced objectives.

Mager's theory of objectives was originally developed for use in programmed instruction. In the 1960s, programmed instruction became increasingly automated through the briefly popular use of teaching machines, which were electromechanical devices for delivering programmed instruction. Another development in technology in the mid-1960s was the increasingly wide availability of minicomputers.

ROBERT F. MAGER (1923-2020)

The criterion referenced instruction (CRI) framework developed by Robert F. Mager is a comprehensive set of methods for the design and delivery of training programs.

Some of the critical aspects include:
- Goal/task analysis—to identify what needs to be learned
- Performance objectives—exact specification of the outcomes to be accomplished and how they are to be evaluated (the criterion)
- Criterion-referenced testing—evaluation of learning in terms of the knowledge and skills specified in the objectives
- Development of learning modules tied to specific objectives

Training programs developed using the CRI format tend to be self-paced courses involving a variety of different media (such as workbooks, videotapes, small group discussions, and computer-based instruction). Students learn at their own pace and take tests to determine if they have mastered a module. A course manager administers the program and helps students with problems.

In 1965, Robert Gagné published *Conditions of Learning*, which describes eight types of learning and nine corresponding approaches of instruction. His theory is that there are different types or levels of learning and a need for types of instruction that complement them. He asserted that learning tasks for intellectual skills can be organized in a hierarchy according to complexity: stimulus recognition, response generation, procedure following, use of terminology, discriminations, concept formation, rule application, and problem solving. The primary significance of the hierarchy is to identify prerequisites that should be completed to facilitate learning at each level. Prerequisites are identified by doing a task analysis of a learning or training task; learning hierarchies provide a basis for the sequencing of instruction (Gagné 1985).

ROBERT MILLS GAGNÉ (1916-2002)

Conditions of learning theory:
- Gaining attention (reception)
- Informing learners of the objective (expectancy)
- Stimulating recall of prior learning (retrieval)
- Presenting the stimulus (selective perception)
- Providing learning guidance (semantic encoding)
- Eliciting performance (responding)
- Providing feedback (reinforcement)
- Assessing performance (retrieval)
- Enhancing retention and transfer (generalization)

The 1960s also heralded the era of corporate universities, which began with the founding of Hamburger University by the McDonald's Corporation in 1961. Hamburger University was designed exclusively to instruct personnel employed by McDonald's Corporation or by McDonald's independent franchisees in the various aspects of the business and operations. By the end of the 20th century, Hamburger University had branches in England, Japan, Germany, and Australia. Other corporations soon followed McDonald's lead (Schugurensky 2009).

The 1970s

Sociotechnical-systems theory, which indicates that the interaction of social and technical factors supports or hinders the successful functioning of an organization, became widespread in the 1970s (Shaw 1994; Pasmore 1988). Trainers began to understand that to achieve peak performance, both the technical and the social aspects of organizations had to be considered and optimized together. This aligned with the broader focus for the field that OD and HPI started establishing in the 1960s.

Social issues such as racism, discrimination against women and members of other underrepresented groups, and political and environmental concerns were at the forefront of popular culture in the 1970s; these issues also began to influence changes in how training took place in organizations.

Another emerging focus during the 1970s was sensitivity training—also known as the laboratory method—which was a form of human relations training that took place in groups and was designed to raise self-awareness and understanding of group dynamics, enabling attendees to modify their own behavior appropriately. The method had vocal detractors who did not think it was appropriate for workplace training to help "managers achieve authenticity and develop self-esteem," but Chris Argyris of the National Training Laboratories was its principal defender (Shaw 1994).

Chief among other new forms of training developed during the 1970s was the case method, which had been used in business schools but not in training programs. The case method involves the use of a case study to explore a topic. Storytelling trainers also began to teach management by objective, introducing expectancy theory as a way to predict employee behavior (Shaw 1994).

Learning theory also saw several developments; Malcolm Knowles's book *The Adult Learner: A Neglected Species* introduced adult learning theory in 1973. Although he wasn't the first to suggest that adults learn differently from children (Eduard C. Lindeman challenged the notion that pedagogy was appropriate for adults in *The Meaning of Adult Education* in 1926), Knowles coined the term *andragogy* and presented key principles that affect the way adults learn (see the sidebar for more).

At about the same time, Robert M. Gagné and Leslie J. Briggs presented the nine events of instruction in their 1974 book, *Principles of Instructional Design*. The nine events represented a new theory in learning called cognitivism. While behaviorism focuses on outward behaviors, cognitivism focuses on how information is processed, stored, and retrieved in the mind.

Another emerging learning theory in the 1970s was constructivism. With roots in Piaget's theories about cognitive development, constructivism posits that learning is a process of constructing new knowledge. Jerome Bruner, an important theorist related to constructivism, saw learning as "a social process, whereby students construct new concepts based on current knowledge. The student selects information, constructs hypotheses, and makes decisions, with the aim of integrating new experiences into his existing mental constructs" (Thanasoulas 2002). With the constructivist learning theory, the impetus in learning design is to create learning experiences that enable learners to discover and construct learning for themselves.

> **MALCOLM KNOWLES (1913-1997)**
>
> Regarded as the father of adult learning, Knowles made numerous contributions to the theory and practice of human resource development, but is best known for popularizing the term *andragogy*, which is the art and science of teaching adults. Andragogy recognizes that adults learn differently than children and as a result need to be treated differently in the classroom. In 1973, Knowles defined four assumptions about adult learning in his book *The Adult Learner: A Neglected Species*. These were expanded to six assumptions in a subsequent edition (1984):
> - Adults need to know why it is important to learn something before they learn it.
> - Adults have a concept of self and do not like others imposing their will on them.
> - Adults have a wealth of knowledge and experience and want that knowledge to be recognized.
> - Adults become ready to learn when they know that the learning will help them with real problems.
> - Adults want to know how the learning will help them in their personal lives.
> - Adults respond to external motivations, such as the prospect of a promotion or an increase in salary.

The 1980s

Productivity in the US slowed in the 1980s, and many organizations underwent large downsizings while global economic competition simultaneously became their biggest business challenge (Shaw 1994). This led organizations to look more closely at their training budgets, compelling training and development leaders to focus more on the bottom line and prove the value training brings to organizations. For this reason and others, cost-benefit analysis and the concept of return on investment (ROI) became increasingly hot topics.

In addition, women were entering the T&D field at an unprecedented rate in the 1980s; by 1989, women made up 47 percent of ASTD's members. Assertiveness training flourished, as did training topics such as behavior modeling, teamwork, empowerment, diversity, adventure learning, feedback, corporate culture, and trainer competencies (Shaw 1994).

Trainer competencies were the topic of two competency models published in the 1980s, which positioned the field of training and development as part of the broader field of human resources work. The first modern attempt to define *training and development* was the 1983 report *Models for Excellence: The Conclusions and Recommendations of the ASTD Training and Development Study*, which captured this expansion of the role of training (McLagan 1983). By 1989, career development and organization development had been added to the repertoire of training and development work, as noted in *Models for HRD Practice* (McLagan 1989). That report used Leonard Nadler's term for the field, *human resource development (HRD)*, defining it as "the integrated use of training and development, organization development, and career development to improve individual, group, and organizational effectiveness."

In technology, the first electronic workstations came on the market in 1981. As laser discs began to be used with training, providing immediate access to video segments, the training community became more enamored of multimedia as a way to engage the learner. Laptop computers soon emerged, followed by smaller disc formats for interactivity and storing media (IBM's Ultimedia and CD-i by Philips, both of which eventually gave way to the CD-ROM). The rise of these technologies revolutionized much of how learning was designed, delivered, and managed in organizations.

The 1990s

The summer of 1991 heralded an inflection point in technological and human progress when Tim Berners-Lee published the code for what would become known as the World Wide Web (Berners-Lee 2000). The internet introduced the era of limitless access to information. Proponents of e-learning, computer-based training, and online learning proclaimed that classroom learning was over. Early e-learning followed the same behaviorist model that had informed the programmed instruction of the 1950s and the learning machines of the 1960s, in which learners went through a sequence of steps, after which they responded correctly (or incorrectly) and then continued to the next learning element or doubled back as required.

The benefits were also similar: Learners could learn at their own pace, make mistakes, and get feedback without being embarrassed, while also repeating sections until they mastered them. E-learning had the additional benefit of more branching capabilities than the earlier programmed instruction and learning machines, which allowed learners to automatically bypass sections they already knew and focus more on problem areas. Multimedia capabilities also made e-learning more effective by stimulating more of the senses and appealing to different types of learners. And finally, it allowed greater accessibility to training by minimizing costs associated with travel to training, time off work to attend, and facilities fees.

However, the early days of e-learning had some challenges, such as low learner engagement due to rudimentary e-learning programs. And while systems-based training took off in the format, e-learning did not work quite as well for training interpersonal skills. Controlling costs and keeping programs current were also concerns.

In response, more organizations adopted a blended learning strategy by combining e-learning with live classroom elements. Learners could use e-learning elements to complete any prerequisite training so that once a classroom session started, everyone was at the same point. This helped minimize time spent to get everyone up to speed and maximize time on the new skills and knowledge to be learned. Additionally, while asynchronous training became the early norm for e-learning, technology-based synchronous training gained in popularity, allowing students to mimic the classroom environment online, no matter where they were physically.

Another development in HRD was the concept of the learning enterprise. Peter Senge's 1990 book, *The Fifth Discipline*, presented this concept: A learning organization commits itself to disciplines that will allow it to develop its learning capacity to create its future. Ideas underlying the learning organization are systems thinking, mental models, personal mastery, and shared vision and dialogue.

The last two topics—performance support and learning organizations—were popular training topics in the 1990s. Other popular topics included reengineering, reorganization and transformation of work, customer focus, global organizations, "visioning," and balancing work and family (Shaw 1994).

The 21st Century

In learning theory, behaviorism continues to have strong influence on learning design; cognitive and constructivist learning theories use Gagné's nine events of learning and discovery learning. Knowles's theory of adult learning informs most training by emphasizing making learning relevant, using learners' experience as a platform for learning, and giving learners some say in how or what they learn.

While the basic ISD model has evolved, the industry has also developed new models of instructional design that are applicable to varying situations and have different emphases, such as rapid prototyping and learning modules. But the legacy theories of the 1950s and 1960s—Bloom's taxonomy, and Mager's model for learning objectives—continue to influence how learning objectives are written by specifying first the type of learning (knowledge, skill, or attitude) and then the behavior, condition, and degree.

Measurement also remains a key concern in the field of training and development. Kirkpatrick's classic four levels of evaluation—reaction, learning, behavior, and results—and the work of Jack and Patti Phillips in ROI continue to dominate how learning content is measured and reported.

In 2010, a group of industry thought leaders and preeminent practitioners coalesced to create standards for learning and development to provide the learning profession with templates to operate more like a business. The result was the Talent Development Reporting principles (TDRp). The nonprofit Center for Talent Reporting (CTR) was created in 2012 to be the permanent home for TDRp. Since then, hundreds of organizations around the world have adopted TDRp, and CTR has further refined the principles, measures, and reports based on feedback from the early adopters (Vance and Parskey 2016). This guidance includes a simple yet comprehensive framework for planning, collecting, defining, and reporting the critical outcome, effectiveness, and efficiency measures needed to deliver results and contribute to the success of the organization.

Other significant developments in the learning community included the widespread use of social and informal learning throughout the enterprise and increased leveraging of user-generated content. In an ode to the oft-cited 70-20-10 model, based on studies by the Center for Creative Leadership, training departments have slowly evolved from being the sole provider and deliverer of content in their companies to a role that fosters sharing knowledge in the organization and becoming a connector of people. In a study by i4cp and ASTD, informal learning was shown to play an acknowledged role to varying degrees in the organizations of 97 percent of participants; 27 percent reported that informal learning represented more than half of the total learning taking place in their companies (ATD and i4cp 2013).

Technology has taken center stage in learning; easy-to-use content generation tools have enabled the workforce to share knowledge and expertise in an environment centered on performance support. Furthering the concept of performance support, the ubiquity of mobile devices and internet connectivity has hastened the adoption of mobile learning and instant access to information, which the newest generation of workers has grown up with and expects. A big piece of this, of course, is the capacity to deliver learning in simple, quick, mobile ways that mirror the instant connections and transactions we're all accustomed to making daily. Microlearning, highly customized learning, and apps that provide learners with assistive chatbots and daily nudges appeal to a wide range of workers across all generations.

The continuous evolution of and advancement in technology demands upskilling and reskilling that is also continuous. The rapid increase in the adoption of advanced work automation including AI, machine learning, and robotics has already fueled a significant capability gap in knowledge and skills, according to research conducted by i4cp, which found that only 16 percent of the organizations surveyed reported having focused upskilling or reskilling programs to close this capability gap (Stone 2019).

The Emergence of Talent Management

In 1997, McKinsey & Company published a seminal article, "The War for Talent"; the overarching theme was that organizations must compete for talent (Chambers et al. 1997). This competition was cooled by the slumping economy in the dot-com bust and recession of the early 2000s, but the concept of talent management was born and has expanded exponentially since.

In *The Executive Guide to Integrated Talent Management,* co-authors Kevin Oakes and Pat Galagan (2011) made the case that learning professionals often act as partners, collaborating with others or working with function owners to support talent management integration, or to serve as facilitators who provide guidance and support for integration efforts. This shift in thinking presents an opportunity for learning professionals to play leading roles in developing and managing talent across an organization.

Human resources in most organizations has historically functioned in siloed departments, meaning that each area rarely shared data with others or worked collaboratively to have a more holistic view of talent. For example, some of the strategic areas that commonly exist under HR but function separately include:

- Talent acquisition (recruitment, selection, assessment)
- Total rewards (compensation, benefits)
- Diversity, equity, and inclusion
- Engagement (employee experience)
- Leadership development
- Learning and training
- Performance management
- Succession planning

Organizations have moved swiftly in recent years to integrate these functions to create a unified view of their current talent and for strategic workforce planning, which asks these questions:

- What is the inventory of skills, capabilities (including languages spoken, backgrounds, subject matter expertise), and relevant experiences among the workforce?
- What are the gaps between current technical and professional capacity and the capacity required in the next one to three years?
- How will the jobs at your firm today be augmented or perhaps replaced by automation in the next three to five years? (Martin 2020)

Social and Collaborative Learning

A study by i4cp and ATD defined *social learning* as information and experience sharing, collaboration, and co-creation between and among networks (both employees and outsiders) using interactive discussions and conversations, social media, internal networking platforms, and other technology-based methods that facilitate social interactions and communication (such as blogs, forums, internal or external social networks, and video sharing). The study found that while most organizations encourage and support content sharing, few track user-generated content or reward workers who regularly share content (ATD and i4cp 2016b).

Organizations are more focused on how to implement continuous learning across the entire enterprise. This is accomplished by producing more curated, user-generated content (created by learners for other learners, which may include text, video, or images) and facilitating collaboration that allows employees to connect (in person or virtually) with internal subject matter experts for quick tutorial or mentoring check-ins. Part of this shift can mean focusing more on user experience and less on tracking and reporting on ROI for some organizations, recognizing that social learning happens continuously and much of it is not trackable.

The most common current approach to measuring social learning is tracking activity rather than learning quality or effectiveness. But the ability to track and measure where social learning happens and where it's working well so organizations can adjust or redesign their approaches remains largely aspirational. This will likely change as social learning is viewed less as a self-directed learning option and more as a strategy linked to enhancing collaboration, innovation, and improved talent development performance. Beyond tracking access to specific learning assets, the other most common measures of social learning are activity in online learning communities, use of specific social media tools, popularity of shared content, type of content shared, and the number of users who share content. But more organization are likely to start measuring what high-performance organizations are more likely to measure: tracking activity in online learning communities, tracking the type of content employees shared on social media, and measuring the results produced when social learning was linked to workers' individual performance objectives (ATD and i4cp 2016a).

What's ahead? More emphasis on designing learning for delivery through social media, tying social learning to organizational business goals, and accurately measuring learning that takes place via social media. It's likely that we will see wider adoption of connecting social learning to specific business objectives and measuring the related key performance indicators. And the inclusion of social media capabilities in competency models will likely become more common as a tool to encourage employees to contribute to social learning content, share knowledge and information, and collaborate on projects.

Upskilling and Reskilling

Workforce capabilities are the lifeblood of enterprises, directly affecting such vital considerations as competitive market ability, strategic execution, critical role and leadership pipelines, and organizational agility. As a result, ongoing changes in markets, customer preferences, technologies, and other potentially disruptive events are turning upskilling and reskilling programs into critical talent strategies for many companies.

In his 2015 State of the Union address, President Barack Obama called on US employers to adopt or expand additional measures to help frontline workers gain the training and credentials needed to advance into better paying jobs—including paying for college education, offering on-the-job training for career progression, and increasing access to technology-enabled learning tools. The following day, the UpSkill America initiative was launched.

In support of Upskill America's work, the Institute for Corporate Productivity and the Aspen Institute partnered to study worker development and found a high correlation with bottom-line business impact when frontline workers took advantage of development opportunities. Yet, a large gap exists at most organizations between what is being done and what should be done to ensure the development of this critical worker segment, which often provides the most direct link between an organization and its customers but receives the least amount of development (i4cp and Aspen Institute 2016a).

A form of upskilling that is receiving renewed attention is rotation programs, in which employees move through different jobs or assignments to gain new experience or skills. These programs have a long history in developing new leaders but can also be a valuable learning experience for frontline workers in a time when skills are rapidly changing or becoming obsolete. Through internal talent marketplaces driven by AI technology, employers are able to track and analyze the skills of employees and offer rotations in other parts of the organization (i4cp and Aspen Institute 2016b).

Workforce Readiness

Among the many lessons learned from the COVID-19 pandemic was a reinforcement of the importance of organizational agility. Indeed, the ability to anticipate, adapt, and act on change is no longer a nice-to-have. An essential component of agility is establishing and fostering a culture of continuous learning, and this need for ongoing learning will continue to accelerate.

Consider these two findings from the World Economic Forum's 2020 report, *The Future of Jobs*, which asserts that by 2025:
- 44 percent of the skills that employees need to perform their roles effectively will change.
- Companies hope to internally redeploy nearly 50 percent of workers displaced by technological automation and augmentation.

Talent shortages are a growing challenge for employers, who also recognize they cannot hire their way to the skills they need now and in the future. The need for upskilling and reskilling is real, accelerating, and requisite for organizational sustainability and worker relevance. Ideally, organizations will redirect the resources currently applied to tracking learning activity to focus on tracking and enabling workforce readiness—the real driver toward sustainable organizational success.

Final Thoughts

The most effective and resilient organizations are those that have created cultures in which continuous learning is a foundational element of their mission and guiding principles. The critical role of talent development in promoting a strong organizational learning culture cannot be overemphasized. A workplace in which learning is a valued way of life, knowledge is readily shared, and performance steadily improves—at both the individual and organizational levels—is the vision that drives companies to establish, invest in, and expand cultures of learning. Organizations are more competitive, agile, and engaged when knowledge is constantly and freely shared and celebrated.

From ancient papyrus to classroom, social, mobile, virtual, and performance-based learning, the uninterrupted thread in each evolution of learning has been the drive to acquire new knowledge and skills.

As we navigate the post-pandemic era, organizations will look for new ways to make training and development more accessible, flexible, individualized, and integral to overall employee experience. High-performance organizations will continue to invest in and expand on such offerings and learning opportunities, which in turn will provide a competitive advantage in attracting and retaining the talent they need.

Now more than ever, employers recognize the importance of training to the overall expansion and growth of the business as well as the strengthening of organizational culture—in turn, learning and talent development professionals will continue to rise in importance to the enterprise. New history is created constantly by this profession, and the easiest prediction to be made for the future is that it will continue to change and evolve in areas we can't imagine. You are more capable than most of not only imagining that future, but also bravely leading into it, inspiring others to accomplish what may have seemed unachievable not that long ago.

About the Author

Lorrie Lykins is vice president of research at the Institute for Corporate Productivity (i4cp), a research firm focused on helping organizations better anticipate, adapt, and act in a constantly changing business environment. Prior to joining i4cp, she was a research analyst at the Human Resource Institute, and a correspondent and columnist with the *Tampa Bay Times*. She is a contributing author to *ATD's Foundations of Talent Development: Launching, Leveraging, and Leading Your Organization's TD Effort* (2018) and *The ASTD Leadership Handbook* (2010). She has served as an adjunct professor in the adult education program at Eckerd College in St. Petersburg, Florida, since 2003. Lorrie is based in New York City. You can reach her at Lorrie.Lykins@i4cp.com and learn more about her work at lorrielykins.contently.com.

References

ATD and i4cp. 2013. *Informal Learning: The Social Evolution.* Alexandria, VA: ATD Press.
ATD and i4cp. 2016a. *Building a Culture of Learning.* Alexandria, VA: ATD Press.
ATD and i4cp. 2016b. *Social Learning Developing Talent Through Connection, Contribution, and Collaboration.* Alexandria, VA: ATD Press.
Berners-Lee, T. 2000. *Weaving the Web: The Original Design and Ultimate Destiny of the World Wide Web.* New York: Harper Business.

Bloom, B. 1956. *Taxonomy of Educational Objectives, Handbook 1: Cognitive Domain*, 2nd ed. Boston: Addison-Wesley Longman.

Cantor, J. 2015. *21st-Century Apprenticeship*. Westport, CT: Praeger.

Chambers, E.G., M. Foulon, H. Handfield-Jones, S.M. Hankin, and E.G. Michaels III. 1997. "The War for Talent." *The McKinsey Quarterly* 3.

Cooper, P. 2021. "Apprenticeships Have Risen by 64% Since 2020. How Should Policymakers Support Them?" *Forbes*, May 7. forbes.com/sites/prestoncooper2/2021/05/07/apprenticeships-have-risen-64-since-2010-how-should-policymakers-support-them/?sh=36fb4dc638e0.

Friedman, L. 1985. *A History of American Law*. New York: Simon & Schuster.

Gagné, R. 1985. *The Conditions of Learning*, 4th ed. New York: Holt, Rinehart & Winston.

Gagné, R.M., and L.J. Briggs. 1974. *Principles of Instructional Design*. New York: Holt, Rinehart, and Winston.

Haneberg, L. 2005. *Organization Development Basics*. Alexandria, VA: ASTD Press.

i4cp. 2021. *Accelerating Total Workforce Readiness*. Seattle, WA: i4cp.

i4cp and the Aspen Institute. 2016a. *Developing America's Frontline Workers*. Seattle, WA: i4cp.

i4cp and the Aspen Institute. 2016b. *Rotation Programs as Upskilling Strategies*. Seattle, WA: i4cp.

Knowles, M.S. 1973. *The Adult Learner: A Neglected Species*. Houston, TX: Gulf Publishing.

Knowles, M.S. 1984. *The Adult Learner: A Neglected Species*, 3rd ed. Houston, TX: Gulf Publishing.

Law, J. 2009. *A Dictionary of Business and Management,* 5th ed. New York: Oxford University Press.

Lee, R., and T. Ahtone. 2020. "Land Grab Universities." High Country News, March 30. hcn.org/issues/52.4/indigenous-affairs-education-land-grab-universities.

Lewin, K. 1948. *Resolving Social Conflicts; Selected Papers on Group Dynamics*. New York: Harper & Row.

Lewis, N. 1983. *Life in Egypt Under Roman Rule*. New York: Oxford University Press.

LII (Legal Information Institute). n.d. *7 U.S. Code § 323. Racial Discrimination by Colleges Restricted*. law.cornell.edu/uscode/text/7/323.

Lindeman, E.C. 1926. *The Meaning of Adult Education*. New York: New Republic.

Mager, R.F. 1962. "The Evolution of the Training Profession." Chapter 1 in *Preparing Objectives for Programmed Instruction*. Belmont, CA: Fearon Publishers.

Mager, R. 1975. *Preparing Instructional Objectives,* 2nd ed. Belmont, CA: Lake Publishing Co.

Martin, K. 2020. "Workforce Readiness: The Learning Metric That Leads to Real ROI." Institute for Corporate Productivity.

Maslow, A.H. 1943. "A Theory of Human Motivation." *Psychological Review* 50(4): 370–396.

McLagan, P.A. 1983. *Models for Excellence: The Conclusions and Recommendations of the ASTD Training and Development Study*. Alexandria, VA: ASTD Press.

McLagan, P.A. 1989. *Models for HRD Practice*. Alexandria, VA: ASTD Press.

Miller, V.A. 2008. "Training and ASTD: An Historical Review." In *The 2008 Pfeiffer Annual Training*, edited by E. Biech. San Francisco: Pfeiffer.

Morgan, K. 2001. "The Early Middle Ages." In *The Oxford History of Britain*. Oxford: Oxford University Press.

National Center of Education Statistics. 2021. "Postsecondary Education: Undergrad Enrollment." nces.ed.gov/programs/coe/indicator/cha.

Northern Illinois University Center for Innovative Teaching and Learning. 2020. "Gagné's Nine Events of Instruction." *Instructional Guide for University Faculty and Teaching Assistants*. niu.edu/citl/resources/guides/instructional-guide/gagnes-nine-events-of-instruction.shtml.

Oakes, K., and P. Galagan. 2011. *The Executive Guide to Integrated Talent Management*. Alexandria, VA: ASTD Press.

Pasmore, W.A. 1988. *Designing Effective Organizations*. New York: John Wiley & Sons.

Schrager, A. 2018. "The Modern Education System Was Designed to Teach Future Factory Workers to Be "Punctual, Docile, and Sober." *Quartz*, June 29. qz.com/1314814/universal-education-was-first-promoted-by-industrialists-who-wanted-docile-factory-workers.

Schugurensky, D. 2009. "1961: McDonald's Starts First Corporate University." History of Education: Selected Moments of the 20th Century. schugurensky.faculty.asu.edu/moments/1961mcdonalds.html.

Senge, P. 1990. *The Fifth Discipline*. New York: Doubleday.

Shaw, H.W. 1994. "The Coming of Age of Workplace Learning: A Time Line." *Training & Development* 48(5): S4–S12.

Shay, C. 2019. "The History of On-the-Job Training." OJT.com, May 15. ojt.com/history-ojt.

Shrestha, P. 2017. "Ebbinghaus Forgetting Curve." Psychestudy, November 17. psychestudy.com/cognitive/memory/ebbinghaus-forgetting-curve.

Skinner, B.F. 1953. *Science and Human Behavior*. New York: Macmillan.

Steinmetz, C.S. 1976. "The Evolution of Training." In *Training and Development Handbook*, edited by R.L. Craig and L.R. Bittel. New York: McGraw-Hill.

Stone, T. 2019. "Work Automation and AI: Mind the Three Gaps." Seattle, WA: i4cp.

Thanasoulas, D. 2002. "Constructivist Learning." Teaching Learning. seasite.niu.edu/tagalog/teachers_page/language_learning_articles/constructivist_learning.htm.

Torraco, R.J. 2016. "Early History of the Fields of Practice of Training and Development and Organization Development." *Faculty Publications in Educational Administration* 15. digital commons.unl.edu/cehsedadfacpub/15.

Tucker, S.D. 1973. *History of R. Hoe & Company, 1834-1885*. Worcester, MA: American Antiquarian Society.

Turner, M.C. 1961. *The Life of Jonathan Baldwin Turner*. Urbana: University of Illinois Press.

Vance, D., and P. Parskey. 2016. "Introduction to Talent Development Reporting principles (TDRp)." Center for Talent Reporting, November 9. roiinstitute.net/wp-content/uploads/2019/01/Click-5-intro-to-TDRp-052118-1.pdf.

Westermann, W.L. 1915. "Apprentice Contracts and the Apprentice System in Roman Egypt." *Classical Philology* 9(3): 295–315. jstor.org/stable/261714.

World Economic Forum. 2020. *The Future of Jobs Report 2020*. WEF, October 20. weforum.org/reports/the-future-of-jobs-report-2020.

CHAPTER 2

Critical Adult Learning Basics in Action

Becky Pike Pluth

The basics. It sounds like a chapter you could skip reading because you have slogged through years of hard work in learning and development. However, is it possible to have years of experience that just equate to a single year of experience that is simply on a rinse-and-repeat cycle? Sometimes going back to the basics is a great place to reignite your passion for training, as well as for those who are new to the industry. It's a great place to lay a foundation for excellence and kick-start your career.

IN THIS CHAPTER:

- ♦ Explore instructor-led participant-centered (ILPC) learning and how to put it into action
- ♦ Discover the CORE elements of interactive content and select from 36 ideas to use immediately
- ♦ Examine the six different hats that trainers wear

When I was a student at Bethel University, I started as pre-med. I was also a teacher's assistant, campus tour guide, and member of the track team. The busier I was, the more I used my "free" time to ensure I did well in all my classes. One night, midway through my junior year, I had an epiphany: I was studying with peers and noticed that while the concepts seemed to come very easily to them, for me it was painstaking effort to attain an equivalent grade (or lower!). At that moment I asked myself, *Who would you want to be your doctor in this group?* The answer was definitive—it was not me. I wanted a doctor who chose to work hard, practiced even harder, got top scores, and was passionate about what they were doing.

Despite my effort, others were far more naturally talented and passionate about learning medicine. That night, with teary eyes, I called my mom and told her that I was going to change my major to K–12 teaching. Her response was somewhere along the lines of, "I wondered when you would realize that teaching was your calling."

As you read and percolate on each concept in this chapter, you may have your own aha moment. Are you in the right space, teaching content you are passionate about? Are you willing to put in more effort than required to strive for excellence? Have you finished resting on your laurels and decided it's time to jump back in, rejuvenate, and get better and better? These concepts are for you but with a focus on your participants.

Cognitive Neuroscience Versus Cognitive Neuropsychology

Is there a difference between neuroscience of the brain and neuropsychology, and does one matter more when it comes to teaching and learning? In simple terms, cognitive neuroscience is all about the brain and how it is structured. Functional magnetic resonance imaging (or functional MRI or fMRI) measures brain activity by detecting changes associated with blood flow. Different parts of the brain light up during various activities, and scientists use that information to understand how the brain works. Cognitive neuropsychology, on the other hand, focuses on the mind and behavior (Thomas, Ansari, and Knowland 2019). For example, someone will have a bigger boost in knowledge retention when learning is spaced out over time and using a variety of methods. It includes the social component of learning by yourself and with others.

An easy way to improve both the brain and behavior is in creating a positive atmosphere in the classroom. Have a welcome sign on the door, play upbeat music in the background as people arrive, create slides that allow participants to get to know you and create connection. Or incorporate puzzles or pictures to create curiosity and start engaging the brain right away. For example, you could place a printed word search or puzzle of some kind at each chair so those who prefer to work alone have something to work on while waiting. Both neuroscience and neuropsychology play an important role in education, but after 24 years of teaching and training, I can definitely say

I use psychology more often when I am presenting. However, having a foundational understanding of neuroscience is what allows me to design a session that will be recalled and used back on the job.

Two Radio Stations

Every session you lead has two radio stations: WII-FM (What's in It for Me?) and MMFG-AM (Make Me Feel Good About Me). WII-FM starts long before the session begins. It doesn't matter whom you are training or even what type of presentation you are doing—from a keynote to a workshop. When learners sign up for a class they don't always read the description, so it is important to help them get on the WII-FM wavelength immediately. One way to help them discover the program's value is by having a handout and giving them a minute to flip through the pages to see what's ahead and note areas of top interest. They are likely to do this anyway while you are trying to talk, so why not make a point of it and have them share a page or two with a partner?

These ideas help tune people in to WII-FM:
- Use a schedule-at-a-glance to ensure you get to the WII-FM and set participants up for success early in your opening.
- Have an agenda, without times but in order, to allow people to see what's ahead. It meets the needs of both a specific and a general learner and gives each one a small sense of control.
- If there are a couple of sections of content that will take longer than others, share that at the beginning of the session so learners don't begin to panic when they feel behind.
- It is motivating for learners when they are engaged and actually get what you are teaching. Try to present concepts as single ideas so they don't get lost in the content.
- Make sure you have plenty of variety in how concepts are taught. Mix up segments with storytelling, panel discussions, gamification, practical application time, partner work... the list goes on.
- Use language that is common to the audience.
- Use case studies that are specific to the learners' areas of expertise and applicable to their roles.

There is also a social and emotional side of training, and that's where the sister radio station, MMFG-AM, comes into play. Start by using participants' first names. Honor their experience by allowing them to share examples or what they are taking away from the training session. MMFG-AM taps into the hippocampus of the brain, which plays a major role in learning and memory (Anand and Dhikav 2012). It is also the gateway to the prefrontal cortex (PFC), which is the part of the brain responsible for cognition, critical thinking, problem solving, and focus. In Patrick Sweeney's interview of Mo Milad at Harvard's neuroscience lab, Milad explained, "Rather than erasing old fearful memories, when we create courage and face our fears we actually write new, more powerful memories, with more positive outcomes in the PFC" (Sweeney 2020). When the brain is experiencing fear, anxiety, stress, uneasiness, uncertainty, or tension, the hippocampus protects the prefrontal cortex by putting up a wall that limits access to it. As presenters, our job is more than just teaching a theory or helping people discover and use information; our job is also to help reduce tension in the classroom to increase retention.

Here are some ideas to tune people in to MMFG-AM:
- Use music for background noise as people enter, exit, or have discussions.
- Use examples from the audience.
- Watch your audience for their excitement or boredom levels and move through content at their pace.
- Explain the why and how behind the content so learners are in the know.
- Ask questions that start with facts before feelings.
- Randomly select team leaders in advance of an activity so learners know the expectation.
- Follow the safety scale for working together. Start by having learners work in pairs, then the next most comfortable in groups of three, followed by small groups, and last would be in front of a large group.
- Give directions for activities in one or two steps at a time.
- Take baby steps with new or difficult content to allow mastery little by little.
- Create stretch goals *with* the participant rather than *for* the participant.
- Add in time for practice during the session so learners are not doing something for the first time outside the classroom.

Instructor-Led Participant-Centered Methodology

Part of what has made me who I am today as a speaker, trainer, and consultant is having just enough ego to get onstage in front of 1,000 people and having enough humility to know it is not about me. Great sessions are always about the audience and those they will turn around and teach. The goal is for each learner to teach at least one other learner. And triple transfer—when the person a trainer teaches is able to then teach that information to another learner—is the ultimate goal. Over the past 40 years, the Bob Pike Group has used instructor-led participant-centered (ILPC) methods to achieve triple transfer.

My dad, Bob Pike, believes that "there is no such thing as dry, boring content, only dry, boring presentations." In other words, as trainers we need to make sure that the technical content is relevant and add interactivity and engagement throughout so learners see a personal payoff in their learning. The brain doing the talking is the brain doing the learning, so it is imperative that trainers be a guide on the side and let the participants do the heavy lifting. It takes practice to design classes that are structured with the learner being the center of the learning and actively engaged throughout, but it reaps rewards.

There are many components within ILPC learning, but for now we will keep it super simple and stick to three that can be implemented immediately and have a big impact.

- **Doing = Learning. Action Planning = Retention.** The concept here is to provide time during training for focused practice. Research on the world's top athletes, musicians, and chess players finds they require a minimum of 10 years of practice to reach their peak performance (Ericcson 2006). Once a participant leaves the room there is no guarantee that the information will be applied and used, so provide opportunities for practice that include peer-to-peer or instructor feedback. Feedback from an instructor is valuable if it is positive, specific, and constructive. Self-reflection through journaling and action planning is another alternative—all the better if participants share their work with at least one other person. Providing lots of options and choices also helps to increase their level of engagement.
- **People don't argue with their own data.** This component of ILPC learning has you tap into your participants' prior experience and expertise to promote faster buy-in to your content. Having participants share allows them to critically think about past coaching, learning, and methods. It has them analyze for themselves and listen to one another. To dig deeper into this, use lots of questions to get participants to the aha moment for themselves. Ask questions that start with "how" to tap into cognitive processing versus just absorbing and listening to a lecture. This also honors their experience and what they bring to the table. Each person will identify with learning in ways that are comfortable for them.
- **People have different learning preferences.** Note the subtlety between preferences and styles in Figure 2-1. There are thousands of learning theories, styles, approaches, and intelligences. How do we cut through the noise and find what really works? George Ojemann has studied more than 100 brains using electrical stimulation mapping, and to no surprise they've all mapped differently—uniquely. Because no two brains are the same, there is no single best method of instructing, which brings me to the concept of preferences. As you design and present, think about variety on both ends of the spectrum. Whether it is informative or practical, specific or general, reflective or participative, having a variety of interactions helps you toss the widest net and meet a wide array of learning types. You can find 55 ways to add variety to your training by turning to the tools on the handbook website, ATDHandbook3.org.

Figure 2-1. Learning Preferences Continuum

LEARNING PREFERENCES CONTINUUM
Name of participant: _____

Informative Learner ◀――――――――――▶	**Practical Learner**
Give informative learners a lot of additional "nice to know" information, such as extra examples or more reading material.	Give practical learners just the "need to know" information that will help them learn the specific content you are teaching.

Specific Learner ◀――――――――――▶	**General Learner**
Create a lot of structure for specific learners. Let them know your agenda and objectives, give them specific timeframes for the class, and give them a sense of the flow of information and exercises.	Give general learners a global overview of what you will be covering, but allow them the opportunity to structure the information in such a way that works for them.

Reflective Learner ◀――――――――――▶	**Participative Learner**
Allow reflective learners time to study and learn on their own when appropriate. Let them read and reflect on the material, and then you can answer questions they might have.	With participative learners, have a lot of discussions and activities to keep them engaged.

Used with permission from Pluth (2016)

Getting to the CORE of Training

I love to attend a session where I can walk away with tips to apply immediately. Not just theory. If you are like me, then you will like these activities to get started with ILPC implementation.

CORE is an acronym for the four components of interactivity you want in every session. Not activity for the sake of interaction, but intentional, essential CORE components that are proven to increase retention and pull through. You can allocate more or less time for each component by selecting the best activities to align with the timeframe of your session. Just don't fool yourself into thinking there isn't enough time.

Closers

What does an effective closer look like?

There are three key components to closing out a session well, and they conveniently create the acronym TIE:
- Tie things together.
- Include everyone.
- Examine next steps.

A single effective closing activity should embody these three components—it should direct participants to consider how they will apply their new knowledge; it should celebrate their hard work during the session; and it should allow participants to mentally connect the new information with their prior knowledge, tying up any loose ends of the new content into a nice, neat bow.

A deadly sin of trainers is closing with, "In closing, let me summarize…." I cringe at the thought. In that situation, the person doing the talking is doing the learning. An ILPC trainer would close by saying something like, "Take four minutes to work as a team at your table and brainstorm five ways you plan to implement skills or ideas you learned today." *That* is facilitating action planning—it's setting up your participants to plan how they will act on the information they've learned.

The role of instructor is to set the activity up; the participants decide on their takeaways. This reflection and planning time helps them focus on what they will do differently because of what they learned. Through this brief planning, they are participating with the content (promoting retention), communicating with one another, gaining a greater awareness of their next steps, and building a better attitude toward applying the content—all before they walk out of the session.

In general, I find that trainers are less likely to do a solid closer and more likely do an effective opener, so here are some tips and several quick closer examples:

- **Action idea list.** This is a blank page in the participant workbook where learners can record important ideas to use in the future. It is helpful to make this page a unique color so it's easy to find.
- **Get one, give one.** Participants take their action idea list, meet up with another participant, share their best idea of the class so far, and get their partner's best idea. They then move on to another partner and share their second-best idea. They continue the process for a prescribed time limit.
- **High-five review or toe touch.** Participants partner up and, when the instructor asks a question, they answer between themselves. Once they have a sufficient answer, they give a high five (or tap toes if social-distancing protocols are in place).
- **Journaling.** Allow participants time to write concepts and ideas in their own words. Offer guidance to ensure participants can effectively "close" around the topics being taught.
- **Key concepts.** Working with a group of people, share the key concepts, ideas, or takeaways from the learning session.

- **One word whip.** Each participant shares one word that describes how the training session has gone for them, what they learned, or how they are feeling about the day.
- **Polls.** Using physical space, written cards, or virtual tools, ask directed questions or statements to find out which action ideas are most important to participants and what concepts they are going to use first.
- **Pop-ups.** One person stands up, briefly shares an idea, and then sits back down. The next person will do the same and so on.
- **Sit-stand.** Participants begin by standing. The instructor shares a fact or piece of information. If it is true for the participant, they sit down and stand back up.

Openers

What exactly is an opener? The goal of a strong opening is to move participants into a place of learning as quickly as possible. If you typically open your session with a test or by presenting your agenda, *stop*! While the course objectives and agenda are important, the priority should be breaking the preoccupation of those in the room to capture their interest in the training and create buy-in. In some circumstances, trainers are required to present safety procedures as a first order of business. If this applies to you, then the opener should come immediately after completing the safety precautions.

An opener is a purposeful activity that is relevant to the content. There are three questions we can ask about an activity to help decide if it is a good opener or not. We refer to this as raising the BAR. Does the activity:

- Break preoccupation.
- Allow for networking.
- Stay relevant to content.

If you can answer "yes" to these, the activity qualifies as an opener and not just an icebreaker.

Open with your most important message and provide opportunities for learners to feel good about themselves. For example, use their first names, honor their years of experience, share bits and pieces of personal information (as appropriate), and say "thank you" when they've shared a good idea. In class, once we've had partners work together, I may ask them to give their partner a high five or fist or elbow bump or to just say "thank you" as a way to show appreciation and build their confidence.

If you want to gain the attention of your participants, you need to "hook" them in right away. Your audience will decide in the first few seconds of your presentation how interested they are in what you have to say. In a spoken presentation, your hook must capture your participants' attention in the first few sentences and make them want to listen attentively.

Here are a few quick openers that will grab the attention of your audience:
- Outline an incident.
- Ask for a show of hands.
- Ask a rhetorical question.
- Ask a discussion question.
- Make a promise.
- Make an outstanding statement.
- Use an unusual statistic.
- Use a visual or prop.
- Use a metaphor or an analogy.
- Share a compelling story.

In general, you should avoid these when beginning your presentation:
- Apologizing
- Beginning with a joke
- Admitting you are unprepared
- Asking how much time you have

The scientific principle of primacy shows that people are most influenced by and remember best whatever they hear first. A strong opening is critical to the success of any presentation. Start strong!

Revisiters

Revisiting is when the learners do the work. They take the time to connect the dots and to put a content frame around what they just learned. It is their chance to understand the meaning of what was said. Revisiting requires analysis and synthesis, which also builds critical thinking skills. There is a time and place for both revisiting and reviewing, but in ILPC training we primarily focus on the revisiting to keep the learner actively engaged in the process.

This is a great way to help space the learning and reinforce key messages, which also helps to move information from short-term memory into long-term memory. When learners don't have a chance to use their newfound knowledge, it is very easily forgotten (Litman and Davachi 2008).

For this to be effective, revisiting activities need to be well designed and executed. When you're creating your revisiters, remember the acronym DO IT:
- Don't announce it, just do it.
- Oriented to action.
- Includes everyone.
- Think reinforcement.

What is designed into the program usually happens, so make sure to include revisiters in your schedule. It takes repeated effort for information to move into long-term memory. Of course, reviewing the information over time is most effective, but revisiting during class is important too.

Just as participants typically dread inactive learning, they also typically dislike mundane types of review, like pop quizzes or making flashcards. Make the revisit fun and interesting. Bring it to life by revisiting the content solo, with partners, or in small groups. When using a game, ensure that everyone is able to buzz in and engage. Watching others revisit content is just review! You want to build and facilitate revisiters that engage all participants.

Energizers

Energizers are fun activities that get people up from their chairs and moving around before getting back to work. If you ever met me, you could easily guess that energizers are one of my favorite things. I just love to see participants go from tired to pumped for what is next. I am full of energy, and I love to share it with others—people often ask if I can bottle my energy and sell it to them. Unfortunately, energizers are as close as it gets.

A great energizer stimulates the mind and body all at once. They can be used during a transition time, to break up a long section of content, or after a quiz. Energizers should be used whenever the energy in the classroom seems low. Oftentimes this is late in the morning or late in the afternoon, once participants' candy bars or meals are processed and they begin to crash.

Energizers do not have to relate to the content, but they can. Sometimes I ask people to stand up and use their thumbs and pointer fingers to massage their ear lobes for 30 seconds. Besides feeling good, this actually triggers a stress relieving, mind-focusing effect on the body. If you choose an energizer that does not relate to the content, make sure it is quick.

If your energizer links to the content you have been teaching, it also becomes a physical revisiter. Here are some quick ideas that can be used either way:

- **Action idea list.** Learners record important ideas on a blank page in their participant workbook that they want to use in the future. It is helpful to make this page a unique color so that it is easy to find.
- **Field trips.** A technique where learners explore concepts and learning outside the classroom setting.
- **Four corners.** Label each corner of the room with A, B, C, or D. Ask questions and tell participants to go to the corner that best represents their answer.
- **Gallery walk.** Hang posters of content up on the walls and have learners move around the room, recalling information and adding new insights to learning that has already taken place.

- **Human lineup.** Have participants line up on an imaginary continuum. For example, more experienced to the right, less experienced to the left. Participants will have to talk to one another to figure out who goes where. This is an example of a visual survey.
- **Human scramble.** After giving participants criteria on information to share, have them meet up with one (or more) people, share the information, and then move on to meet as many new people as possible in the time allowed.
- **Matching.** In this process, one idea is connected to another as the participants choose an option from a list of possibilities.
- **Mirror race.** Ask participants to pair up, with one being the follower and one being the leader. Tell the leader to move around while the follower tries to match their movements. Have participants switch roles and try again. Feel free to tie this exercise into content!
- **Mnemonics.** This is a memory tool like a rhyme, a visual, or an acronym.
- **Sit-stand.** Participants begin by standing. The instructor shares a piece of information. If it is true for the participant, they sit down and stand back up.
- **Top 10 list.** Have participants generate a top 10 list of ideas or concepts related to the topic at hand working in groups or individually. This activity helps home in on the most important concepts.
- **Touch three walls.** To increase the energy in the room, tell participants to "touch three walls, give two high fives, and return to your seats as fast as you can. Go!!!"
- **Wall chart list.** This is any activity that gets learners up and standing by a wall where they can write on a chart or whiteboard.

When used correctly, revisiters and energizers will get participants back into a learning mode with a refreshed body and refocused mind. Most participants will make the connection between the activity and the purpose for which it was intended—to help the learning process. You can find a checklist for how to facilitate each activity by turning to the tools on the website for this handbook at ATDHandbook3.org.

Consider the Social Component of Learning

You may remember a time you attended a course and at the end of it thought, "I have no idea who was in class with me, but I did learn the content. Now I wish I had someone to follow up and connect with to bounce ideas off of." Connection and community are important, and if you have not included them you are missing an important piece of learning. In fact, one study found that starting the day with a simple relationship-building activity—such as welcoming participants at the door—can increase academic engagement by 20 percentage points while reducing difficult behavior by nine (Cook, Fiat, and Larson 2018). Connection also forms relationships.

At the Bob Pike Group we developed the CIO model: control, included, and openness. A sense of belonging can be achieved by giving learners control through choices. The choices do not have to be life shattering. As you think about choices, pick ones that fit your personality and consider whom you are training. Here are some easy examples to start you off:

- Work alone or with a partner.
- Write your ideas on a whiteboard or in your workbook.
- Select a team leader.
- Write down your own goals.
- Stand and stretch or sit and stretch when you are finished with the exercise.
- Answer the poll questions using clickers or your smart device.
- Collect points during class.
- Listen to a podcast and report back.
- Take a test on your own or with a partner.
- Choose your own seat.
- Create a name tag and put down your two favorite pastimes and one idea you want to use from yesterday.

Providing these choices for participants to make creates a safe environment in which learning can occur and long-lasting relationships can be built. Purposefully create times of connection so that participants can get to know one another. If you provide time for writing down goals and then let learners share them, they may discover a commonality that fosters a relationship. The social component of learning helps reduce tension and give learners control, which makes them more open to learning. In addition, remind participants to create action plans and share them with one another to create accountability. From those plans people can break into smaller groups that share similar ideas for additional networking. People like people like themselves, and this is one way to build bonds that will last beyond the four walls of the classroom.

Oh, the Many Hats a Trainer Wears

When I first began training, I had no idea that the term *facilitator* was different from *presenter* or *speaker*. Here are the main distinctions:

- **Speaker.** This term is often synonymous with keynoting. This could be a formal lecture or more edutaining or motivational. One of my favorite speakers is a woman named Jeanne Robertson. She is a true humorist and a storyteller! I want to be her when I grow up. A speaker can get across a message in a lot of ways, but it is typically a one-way communication style in which ideas are shared by a thought leader.
- **Trainer.** These people show how things are done. Most of this chapter was dedicated to this role. Learning happens through watching the presenter role-model, through the content itself, and through learning from peers throughout the session.

- **Facilitator.** When working with clients, I often have to ask what they mean when they say, "Facilitate a session." The word *facilitation* comes from the Latin word *facilis*, which means "to make something easier." This term is often associated and commingled with a presentation, a speaking gig, or a training session. However, it is different. Facilitation occurs when you are not the content owner and instead are responsible for asking questions and leading a group through a process to come to an end result. It is important to keep in mind that a facilitator is not sharing opinions or a bias, and is not the interesting one but the interested one.
- **Coach.** Take a moment and pause to think about the best coach you know. This would be someone you learned from, but in an indirect manner. When you put on this hat you provide guidance to learners to help them reach their goals and potential by asking good questions and helping them figure it out for themselves.
- **Mentor.** You may think of a mentor as having a one-on-one relationship, but a mentor can also be an inspiration to many. For example, *The Creative Training Techniques* podcast is my way of being a mentor to many. If you find that you are looking to grow in your role as either a virtual or face-to-face trainer and speaker, I encourage you to sign up for this free weekly podcast, where you can find ideas, tips, and tactics that are practical and immediately usable in the L&D world.
- **Author.** As a presenter, authorship may be a little more niche; you may not think about this role if you are an employee, but it can be a differentiator for you. I recommend starting small by creating a blog or publishing shorter articles. The internet has made it easy for us to post articles and provide a place for content curation in the written form. For example, on LinkedIn you can create content and share it quickly as a post, or you could take a little more time and make it into an article. There is a lot of "noise" to cut through on social media, but the idea is to get started using baby steps to help build confidence. Once you have established yourself, find ways to get published in an industry magazine or ezine writing about your area of expertise. This can help you become an authority on your topic. This book is a perfect example of how you can get published without writing an entire book on a single topic. It may take a lot of work to get noticed, but it's worth it once you do.

Final Thoughts

Yes, you may be an experienced TD professional. Still, I hope that you've gained a few ideas as you reach the end of this chapter about the basics. I've always believed that it's good to return to the basics to get grounded and reignite your passion. It's important for you and your learners because nothing beats a good foundation on which to build an action-packed, experiential learning session.

About the Author

Becky Pike Pluth, MEd, CSP, is not your typical speaker. With more than 24 years of experience in training delivery and design and business operations, Becky has been the owner of the Bob Pike Group for the past eight years. She has designed and delivered more than 5,000 interactive webinars, face-to-face training, and keynotes on a variety of topics including sales, customer service, train-the-trainer, performance consulting, and virtual presentation skills. A Certified Speaking Professional for the National Speakers Association, Becky's in-person sessions at conferences hosted by *Training* magazine and the Association for Talent Development have drawn standing-room-only audiences for the last 15 years. She also is the author of *Creative Training: A Train-the-Trainer Field Guide* and nine other influential books and resources. Her *Creative Training Techniques* podcast has more than 375 free lessons to learn from. Learn more at bobpikegroup.com.

References

Anand, K.S., and V. Dhikav. 2012. "Hippocampus in Health and Disease: An Overview." *Annals of Indian Academy of Neurology* 15(4): 239–246. doi.org/10.4103/0972-2327.104323.

Anderson, M., and S. Della Sala. 2013. *Neuroscience in Education: The Good, the Bad, the Ugly*. New York: Oxford University Press.

Cook, C.R., A. Fiat, and M. Larson. 2018. "Positive Greetings At the Door: Evaluation of a Low Cost, High-Yield Proactive Classroom Management Strategy." *Journal of Positive Behavior Interventions* 20(3). journals.sagepub.com/doi/abs/10.1177/1098300717753831.

Ericcson, K.A. 2006. "The Influence of Experience and Deliberate Practice on the Development of Superior Expert Performance." In *The Cambridge Handbook of Expertise and Expert Performance*. New York: Cambridge University Press.

Kostyrka-Allchorne, K., A. Holland, N.R. Cooper, W. Ahamed, R.K. Marrow, and A. Simpson. 2019. "What Helps Children Learn Difficult Tasks: A Teacher's Presence May Be Worth More Than a Screen." *Trends in Neuroscience and Education* 17 (December). doi.org/10.1016/j.tine.2019.100114.

Litman, L., and L. Davachi. 2008. "Distributed Learning Enhances Relational Memory Consolidation." *Learning Memory* 15(9): 711–716.

Pluth, B. 2016. *Creative Training: A Train the Trainer Field Guide*. Minneapolis: Creative Training Productions.

Riley, H., and Y. Terada. 2019. "Bringing the Science of Learning Into Classrooms." Edutopia, January 14. edutopia.org/article/bringing-science-learning-classrooms.

Sweeney II, P.J. 2020. *Fear Is Fuel: The Surprising Power to Help You Find Purpose, Passion and Performance*. London: Rowman & Littlefield.

Thomas, M.S.C., D. Ansari, and V.C.P. Knowland. 2019. "Annual Research Review: Educational Neuroscience: Progress and Prospects." *J Child Psychol Psychiatry* 60:477–492. doi.org/10.1111/jcpp.12973.

Recommended Resources

Pluth, B. *Creative Training Techniques*. Podcast, The Bob Pike Group.

Pluth, B. 2018. *Training Difficult People*. Minneapolis: Creative Training Productions.

Pluth, B. 2021. *Webinars With WOW Factor,* 2nd ed. Minneapolis: Creative Training Productions.

Pluth, B., and R. Meiss. 2014. *SCORE! for Webinar Training*, vol 5. Minneapolis: Creative Training Productions.

Pluth, B., and R. Meiss. 2017. *CORE Activities and Games for Face-to-Face Training*, vol 3. Minneapolis: Creative Training Productions.

CHAPTER 3

A Learning Science Strategy: Deepening the Impact of Talent Development

Jonathan Halls

If your doctor suggests a course of medication, they might discuss why you need it, how it helps, and its possible side effects. The reason most people trust their doctor's prescriptions is because the doctor is a professional. Your doctor, meanwhile, is confident about their diagnosis because they have likely based it on science. So, here's the question. Are you as confident offering learning solutions to your clients and stakeholders as your doctor is prescribing you medicine? And by confident, we mean are you assured they'll work?

> **IN THIS CHAPTER:**
> ♦ Explore what learning science is and why we need it to deepen talent development
> ♦ Discuss how learning happens, drawing on a cognitive framework
> ♦ Determine how a learning science mindset can affect our approach to workplace learning and talent development

In this chapter, we look at what the emerging field of learning science is and how it can provide talent professionals with the confidence to offer learning solutions that help move the needle of performance. Given the size of this field, we'll focus on an area within learning science to explore how learning happens, then consider some mindset changes that may deepen the impact of talent development in our organizations. While many conversations about learning science focus on the instructional event itself, such as how to make content easier to understand and remember, the field offers as many insights for executives and organizational stakeholders as it does for trainers and instructional designers. So, what is learning science, anyway?

Learning science is an interdisciplinary research-based field that works to further the understanding of learning, learning innovation, and instructional methodologies (ATD 2020). Drawing on neuroscience, cognitive science, instructional design, data analytics, anthropology, linguistics, computer science, psychology, and education, learning science explores things like genetics, environment, brain chemistry, and other influences that can foster or inhibit learning (Applied Learning Sciences Team 2017; Science of Learning Institute n.d.). Because it's an interdisciplinary field, scientists are able to explore learning from multiple perspectives, which leads to a richer understanding of learning.

Science

The word *science* comes from the Latin word *scientia*, which literally means "knowledge." *Science* is often used to describe bodies of knowledge, such as environmental science or biology. But it also describes the processes researchers follow to acquire that knowledge, which is represented by theories that provide a reasoned explanation of an observable phenomenon. A key aspect of scientific theories is that they are supported by overwhelming evidence (Olson 2004).

Strong evidence is important. Consider a new trainer who's tasked with teaching a class. Over the years, he has found that he works best while listening to classical music. So, he decides to play Bach's "Brandenburg" Concertos during class while learners complete their exercises. On the surface, it sounds like a nice idea. Creative, in fact. But how can he be sure it really helps learners do their best work? After all, he is drawing on his personal subjective experience. Does he know whether using classical music has worked for anyone else? Scientific theories require objective observation and measurement of ideas. And the ideas must be tested on enough people to be sure they apply to the broad population, and then be tested multiple times to ensure the findings can be replicated.

Learning science provides insight into how learning works, putting us in a better position to explain to learners and other stakeholders what we are doing and why. While learning science is a relatively new field, the notion of evidence-based learning in the world of training is not. An evidence-based approach has been championed by authors and learning authorities such as Ruth

Colvin Clark, Patty Shank, Clark Quinn, and Elaine Biech, to name a few. However, our field has often been drawn to theories that lack rigorous inquiry, such as learning styles, left- and right-brain theory, and multitasking.

That said, not all science is foolproof. We need to be discerning with how we use it. Theories evolve as new evidence and new ways of measuring that evidence are found. And like any endeavor involving humans, it's vulnerable to bias, fraud, and misunderstanding. Thirty years ago, scientists believed saturated fats caused heart disease, whereas today they believe sugar does (Cleveland Clinic 2017). Theories evolve. And as for bias, therapies like acupuncture, which successfully treated pain for thousands of years in China, were considered quack medicine by Western doctors until the 1990s because they hadn't been studied empirically (Lu and Lu 2013). Fraud and sloppy research are also serious problems, with an alarming number of studies failing to pass replicability tests (Harvey 2020; Samarrai 2015). But overall, research gives us confidence that a theory or technique has been tested and is likely to work.

Learning

Philosophers and researchers have attempted to define learning since the days of Plato and Aristotle, led by the context in which learning takes place, its purpose, and their own philosophical frames of reference. Our frame of reference is adult learning in the workplace. Malcolm Knowles—who is probably the most influential thinker in adult learning—described learning as the process of gaining knowledge or expertise (Knowles, Holton, and Swanson 1972). But it doesn't happen by accident. Theorist Robert Gagné (1970) believed that learning was an intentional process stretching beyond mere growth, involving the development of a skill that is retained over a period of time. So, we can classify learning as the intentional process of building workplace skills and consider learning science to be the collection of research-based theories and techniques from multiple disciplines that describes how learners can intentionally build workplace skills.

One discipline that has guided adult learning since the 1950s is cognitive science, which was developed when researchers started exploring attentional and decisional processes with advanced mathematical modeling (Malmberg, Raaijmakers, and Shiffrin 2019). At a high level, cognitive science deals with memory and cognition.

One of the most influential models for memory research is the Multi-Store Model of Memory, developed by Richard Atkinson and Richard Shiffrin in 1968 (Malmberg, Raaijmakers, and Shiffrin 2019). The model divides memory into three structural components: sensory register, short-term store, and long-term store (Table v). Many theorists use this framework to describe memory functions, although most in education refer to the short-term store as the working memory, based on subsequent work by Alan Baddeley and Graham Hitch in 1972.

Table 3-1. Multi-Store Model of Memory

Sensory register	Acts as the gatekeeper for information entering the brain.
Working memory*	Acts as the thinking space where new information is connected with existing memories to build understanding. It has very limited capacity.
Long-term memory	Acts as the file cabinet where memories are structured and stored as schema. There is no known limit on how much it can store.

Originally the short-term memory, this is now mostly referred to as the working memory.

The *sensory register* acts like a gatekeeper for information entering the brain. Sensory information can be anything we see, hear, taste, smell, or feel, although most educational research focuses on visual and auditory information. The *working memory* acts like the RAM on your computer and processes this information to make sense of the world and perform day-to-day tasks. It has an extremely limited capacity, holding only three to five new chunks of information at any one time (Cowan 2010). The *long-term memory* acts like a filing cabinet for all the memories we need to keep. It is said to have an indefinite capacity, and no actual limit to its capacity has been found (Ericsson and Pool 2016).

Memory isn't important just in cognitive science. Malcolm Knowles's andragogy prioritizes adults' experiences, while John Dewey (1938), in *Experience and Education* sees memories as crucial building blocks of knowledge. An influential cognitive theory suggests that memories are mental representations called *schemata*. Think of schemata (or schema in the singular) as schematic diagrams we hold in our mind of events, ways of performing a task, or details about a concept. First suggested by German philosopher Immanuel Kant, schema theory was proposed by Cambridge psychologist Frederick Bartlett in 1934, popularized by Swiss psychologist Jean Piaget, and more recently researched by educational psychologist David Rumelhart. Schemata are also referred to as mental models.

Schema theory suggests that as a matter of survival, our brains organize and categorize our memories so they are easy to access when we need them. Rumelhart (1980), who called memories the building blocks of cognition, described them as "data structures representing generic concepts stored in memory." They are like computer programs our brain uses to think and perform tasks. On one level, it's easy to think that learning professionals are in the business of delivering learning content. But from a cognitive perspective, we're really in the business of helping learners build schemata that they can then use to perform their jobs.

Making Sense of Learning

To make sense of how these things work together, let's break learning into three separate steps:
- **Understanding** how to perform a task

- **Remembering** how to perform a task
- **Mastering** a task so it is performed on the job efficiently, creatively, and with few mistakes

Understanding a Task: Connection

In most cases, you need to understand a task before you can perform it. At first blush, it may seem like a one-way process. Learners listen to a presentation or watch a demonstration and voilà—they understand. However, what they're doing is cognitively connecting new information, such as what they hear in a presentation, with something they already know, which, as we've seen, is a schema held in the long-term memory. As such, classroom presentations are not the only ways for learners to understand a skill or task. Experimentation, field trips, critical reflection, and conversations are among many ways people make sense of new ideas and tasks. The important thing is connecting new information from new experiences to existing memories and then manipulating it to create a new memory.

If you attend a class about workplace tension that focuses on how the lack of role clarity can increase stress, you might recall a personal experience you had where role clarity made your work life very stressful. As the trainer talks about it, you will use your own experiences to analyze and make sense of what the trainer is saying (Figure 3-1).

Figure 3-1. Building Understanding

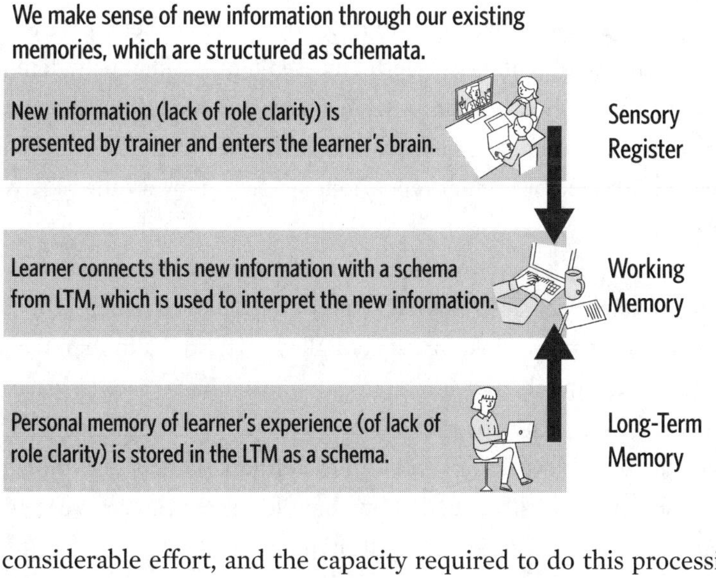

We make sense of new information through our existing memories, which are structured as schemata.

New information (lack of role clarity) is presented by trainer and enters the learner's brain.	Sensory Register
Learner connects this new information with a schema from LTM, which is used to interpret the new information.	Working Memory
Personal memory of learner's experience (of lack of role clarity) is stored in the LTM as a schema.	Long-Term Memory

This takes considerable effort, and the capacity required to do this processing in the working memory is called cognitive load (Lovell 2020). When learning a new task for which we have little prior knowledge or experience, the cognitive load is considerably higher, which can cause learners to be overwhelmed and confused. This is the crux of cognitive load theory (CLT), which was developed in the 1970s by educational psychologist John Sweller. Hugely popular in K–12 education, this theory is backed by a plethora of studies and offers a detailed understanding of how to make it easier for learners to build their understanding.

There are two principal types of cognitive load in CLT. Intrinsic load refers to how complex the topic is itself. The actual level of complexity is affected by the learner's prior knowledge or experience. Extraneous load refers to how information is conveyed by the trainer, as well as the instructional materials and other factors like distractions in the learning environment. We can make the process of understanding new information easier by reducing extraneous load and optimizing intrinsic load (Lovell 2020).

CLT offers research-based techniques to actively reduce extraneous load, including managing redundancy, split attention, transient information, and dual coding. Strategies that optimize intrinsic load include sequencing and matching instructional techniques to appropriate skill levels. Matching skill level to the instruction is based on a theory called the expertise reversal effect, which confirms the suspicion many trainers have that mixing different levels of experience in the same class is not always productive (Kalyuga 2003).

Remembering a Task: Practice

To perform a new task back on the job, a learner needs to not just understand it but remember how to perform it. Intentionally building memory happens through *practice*.

Humans aren't good at remembering stuff; it doesn't matter whether it's the name of someone you just met or a telephone number. Hermann Ebbinghaus famously demonstrated this in a series of experiments published in 1885 in which he introduced the concept of the forgetting curve. Recently replicated, Ebbinghaus's experiments showed that despite our tendency to forget, memory decays can be arrested by regular repetitions spaced out over time (Murre and Dros 2015; Ebbinghaus 1885).

The more times we bring a memory from long-term memory into our working memory, the stronger it becomes (Figure 3-2). This is what practice is all about, which probably isn't surprising, especially if you've ever performed in a school play or learned a foreign language. You likely learned your lines by practicing them over and over, and used flash cards to learn a new language. But mindlessly repeating something over and over a process called massed practice, doesn't lead to longer-term memory. It may work for short-term retention, such as cramming for an exam, but those memories are shown to quickly decay. Ebbinghaus found that creating a space between practices is more effective and leads to greater long-term retention.

Figure 3-2. Building Memory

We build memory by drawing schemata from the long-term memory into the working memory through rehearsal or practice. The more we do this following intentional practices, the stronger the memory.

We build long-term memory by drawing memories in and out of WM and LTM.

Working Memory

Long-Term Memory

We can use techniques such as spaced practice to help learners remember a task. *Spaced practice* involves practicing a task or skill multiple times with space—perhaps a day or two or even a few hours—between each practice. *Interleaving*, which during instruction can feel messy, could also be called "mixing it up." For example, let's say you're learning three tasks. Rather than practicing task A for an hour, then task B for an hour, and then task C for an hour, you'd practice all three tasks in that three-hour window, switching back and forth between each. *Retrieval practice* involves pulling a schema from long-term memory into working memory and processing it.

How many corporate training experiences involve practice time? A lot of energy is put into crafting presentations, but how much time do we put into activities for learners to reflect and refine their performance? The science tells us that just presenting or sharing information is not enough. We need to plan time for practice.

> Facilitator tip: Give learners lots of time and space to practice what they learn. Without the practice, they will likely forget much of the information that has been presented.

Mastering a Task

Understanding how to perform a task requires us to connect new information to a schema and manipulate it. Remembering that task requires us to practice it. But what is necessary for doing it well? *Intentional practice.*

The science of expertise and expert performance offers insight into what it takes to be really good at something. One of the leading proponents of expertise, Anders Ericsson, suggested that top performers are superb at what they do because of the amount of time they put into practice and the very specific way they do it. He calls this *deliberate practice*. Thousands of hours of practice—sometimes 15,000 to 25,000 hours—are necessary to be good enough at a skill to be considered an expert (Ericsson, Prietula, and Cokely 2007). Deliberate practice goes beyond interleaving or retrieval practice because it zeroes in on weaker areas of performance, using goals to stretch learners out of their comfort zone and expert feedback that is direct and often harsh to keep them on track. The bottom line—becoming an expert at anything is generally hard work and time consuming.

If talent development is about equipping people to be not just performers but high performers, there's no escaping the fact that they need to invest lots of time. It doesn't matter if that's in or out of the classroom. And while achieving high performance may not quite require the number of hours needed to become an expert, a two-day learning event, which accounts for 10 to 14 hours, will likely fail to provide the necessary time. Unfortunately, this is not what many supervisors want to hear—many like to send staff to a training program to gain skills like people send a car through the car wash to clean it up.

Deepening the Impact of Talent Development

What does all this mean? While we've explored only a tiny area within the broader field of learning science, we can still glean insights that may help us deepen the impact of talent development. Many involve evolving our mindset about training. Here are some initial thoughts.

A Learner-Centered Mindset

Many people approach training and talent development with the mindset that it is about delivering content. That's why so much energy is focused on what the trainer does, which then leads to low retention rates and a lack of opportunity for learners to improve their performance. Learning is about connecting new information with existing schemata, practicing it, and then going deeper with deliberate practice. This doesn't diminish our training role, which still includes sharing information in presentations; however, we will have a greater impact if we help learners navigate this process rather than simply presenting it to them. The notion of shifting from "sage on the stage" to "guide on the side" is a helpful metaphor, as is seeing the trainer not as a mini keynote speaker, but as a professional whose work more mirrors a physiotherapist's (Halls 2019).

A Research Mindset

Many trainers are not given the resources they need to develop an evidence-based practice, so they end up using techniques they've seen others use or have heard about at conferences. We need to take time to reflect on the instructional techniques we use through the lens of research—not just through cognitive science but the other disciplines within learning science as well. For example, it's amazing how many trainers still use learning styles, which have been conclusively proven to have no impact on learning (Colvin Clark 2015). This means purging practices that we cannot reliably argue are supported by research and adopting new approaches that lead with evidence, such as those proposed in cognitive load theory. We also need to look at every aspect of talent development from a research perspective because it can inform the strategy as much as the tactics.

A Talent Continuum Mindset

Training is often seen as what might be described as a retail experience. A supervisor looks at a catalog, sends one of their direct reports to a class, and expects them to return to the job with new skills. Sure, they may return with some basic proficiency, but it won't be enough to be a high performer. Rather than approaching learning as an instructional event—a one-day class or one-hour online module—we need to see learning as a continuum that lasts months, years, or even a whole career. Trainers don't have to be an intricate part of every moment within that continuum, but they should be key influencers. It's a daunting thought; while it's easy to plan and feel in control of a two-day instructional event, a learning continuum mindset includes many unpredictable dynamics. As a profession, we need to explore how to make this work in the spirit of a learning organization, with the understanding that research shows the learner needs lots of time and intentional methodologies that stretch beyond those two days to develop high performance.

A Learning Ecosystem Mindset

Another common mindset in today's profession is that learning happens in a classroom or an online module. However, the truth is that learning happens anywhere or with anything that causes learners to connect, practice, and refine their skills. We don't need a classroom, workshop, or laboratory for every learning situation. In fact, the workplace itself offers more productive resources that support learning. Maybe it's time to adopt a learning ecosystem mindset in which we see the whole organization as the classroom, the people in it as the teachers, and the equipment as the instructional resources (Theodotou 2020). How can we tap into this? How can we use Peter Senge's learning organization approach to support this?

A Professional Learner Mindset

As we discussed earlier, science is never settled. New data and methods of reading that data constantly expand our perspectives. The same goes for learning; even the most seasoned learning professionals will say they can't possibly know all there is to know about learning. Therefore, it's incumbent on learning professionals to also be professional learners seeking to find out more about how to help other people be better at what they do. Scientists are never satisfied with a theory and will constantly evaluate it and seek to either disprove or affirm it. We too should approach learning and talent in such a way.

Nothing New Under the Sun

To be fair, these aren't all new suggestions. Adult learning theory has always talked about emphasizing active learner participation, drawing on experiences and problem solving over a formal presentational approach. And while the idea of a learning ecosystem has been discussed extensively over the past decade, notions of the learning organization have been with us for 30 years. Learning science, however, gives us greater clarity, more insights, and a framework to deepen our practice. In tension with a learning philosophy, it offers incredible opportunities for us to reimagine our practice.

Challenges for Talent Professionals

Learning science doesn't speak just to people who craft individual learning experiences, but to anyone involved in an organization who is interested in improving performance—from the learning and talent executives to the people doing the learning. And it speaks to strategy as much as it does to tactics. Here are some questions for different people in the talent world to consider about their roles.

Learning and Talent Executives

Learning executives can usually influence substantive change, and as such bear much of the responsibility in evangelizing a learning science approach. They should ask:
- How can I help trainers and instructional designers review their practice based on research?
- Should I offer them further training or time to stay up to date or learn new techniques?
- How can I help trainers and designers, especially subject matter experts, get comfortable with presenting information and shift from a keynote to physiotherapist mindset?
- How can I educate key stakeholders across the broader organization to see learning as a talent continuum that they also have significant influence over?
- How can I equip people throughout the learning ecosystem with skills that ensure their influence is constructive?
- Can I redefine the role of trainer or instructional designer to clearly encompass the talent continuum and learning ecosystem?
- How can I model a learning science approach in my decisions and the practical support and feedback I give to my teams?

Trainers and Instructional Designers

In some organizations, trainers and designers are different roles; in others, they are integrated into the same role. These are the people who have direct influence over the development of workplace performance. Questions they should ask include:
- How can I increase my knowledge of current research around learning? Not just in the cognitive field but in the broader fields, such as biology, anthropology, or mathematics?
- How can I consistently manage cognitive load in the classroom through planning, preparing content such as learning aids, and my facilitation techniques?
- How can I shift from being a content deliverer to a performance improver by crafting experiences that help learners access their memories to practice and refine performance?
- How can I extend constructive learning beyond the classroom?
- How can I better network across the organization to ensure all resources are being tapped as part of talent development?

Organizations

Many innovations start with enthusiasm and die at the feet of organizational disinterest. What should we think about organizationally to take talent development from being a catalog of classes to a strategy that improves performance with a long-term view? Organizations should ask:
- Do we need to change policies around appraisals and independent development plans? Does that involve changing the way they are done or equipping incumbents to better facilitate them?
- Do we need a leadership-driven cultural change initiative that emphasizes the importance of learners taking control of their learning?
- Should we review the reward structures associated with performance development?
- What policies, resources, infrastructure, or other aspects of an organization that might prevent growth in this new direction need to be changed or challenged?

There are two self-assessments on the handbook's website at ATDHandbook3.org. One is for trainers and instructional designers and the other is for talent executives.

Final Thoughts

So where does this leave us with learning science? Can it deepen the impact of talent development for you? Many organizations throughout the world have a good record on talent development; others are struggling. Some already implement solutions they are confident will move the needle of performance because they know their methods are based on research; some have already seen great results. Learning science is more than just a bunch of theories to write in your notes at a conference or plug into the trainer's toolkit. It's a mindset that gives us greater confidence that our work will have long-lasting impact. And it increases our credibility because we'll be able to better explain what we do, and clients and stakeholders will see real results. Just as we feel confident taking prescriptions from our doctors.

About the Author

Jonathan Halls helps learning and talent leaders reinvigorate their training and talent departments with a focus on boosting credibility with stakeholders. He specializes in supporting learning science and digital media content. A former BBC learning executive, Halls has worked with clients in 25 countries over 30 years and was a member of the advisory panel for ATD's new Talent Development Capability Model. He has both a master's and bachelor's in adult education and is an adjunct professor at George Washington University. He runs professional development workshops for learning and talent professionals and has written a number of books, including *Confessions of a Corporate Trainer*. Learn more about his work at JonathanHalls.com.

References

Applied Learning Sciences Team. 2017. "What Is Learning Science?" McGraw Hill, February 28. medium.com/inspired-ideas-prek-12/what-is-learning-science-a1dc07ec4ce.

ATD (Association for Talent Development). 2020. "Talent Development Body of Knowledge." Alexandria, VA: ATD Press.

Atkinson, R.C., and R.M. Shiffrin. 1968. "Human Memory: A Proposed System and Its Control Processes." In *The Psychology of Learning and Motivation,* vol. 2, edited by K.W. Spence and J.T. Spence. New York: Academic Press, 89–195.

Baddeley, A.D., and G. Hitch. 1974. "Working Memory." *Psychology of Learning and Motivation* 8:47–89. doi.org/10.1016/S0079-7421(08)60452-1.

Cleveland Clinic. 2017. "Why a Sweet Tooth Spells Trouble for Your Heart." Cleveland Clinic, Health Essentials, April 6. health.clevelandclinic.org/sweet-tooth-spells-trouble-heart.

Colvin Clark, R. 2015. *Evidence-Based Training Methods*. Alexandria, VA: ATD Press.

Cowan, N. 2010. "The Magical Mystery Four: How Is Working Memory Capacity Limited, and Why?" *Current Directions in Psychological Science* 19(1): 51–57.

Dewey, J. 1938. *Experience and Education,* 1997 reprint. New York: Free Press.

Ebbinghaus, H. 1885. *Memory: A Contribution to Experimental Psychology*. Translated ed. 1913. Teachers College, Columbia University.

Ericsson, K.A., M.J. Prietula, and T.T. Cokely. 2007. "The Making of an Expert." *Harvard Business Review*, July-August.

Erricsson, K.A., and R. Pool. 2016. *Peak: Secrets From the New Science of Expertise*. New York: Mariner Books.

Gagné, R. 1970. *The Conditions of Learning*, 2nd ed. New York: Holt, Rinehart & Winston.

Halls, J. 2019. "Trainers Aren't Keynote Speakers." ATD blog, May 1. td.org/insights/trainers-arent-keynote-speakers.

Harvey, L. 2020 "Research Fraud: A Long-Term Problem Exacerbated By the Clamour for Research Grants." *Quality in Higher Education* 26(3): 243-261. DOI: 10.1080/13538322.2020.1820126.

Kalyuga, S. 2003. "The Expertise Reversal Effect." *Educational Psychologist* 38(1): 23–31.

Knowles, M.S., E.F. Holton, and R.A. Swanson. 2005. *The Adult Learner: The Definitive Classic in Adult Education and Human Resource Development*. New York: Elsevier.

Lovell, O. 2020. *Sweller's Cognitive Load Theory in Action*. Woodbridge, AU: John Catt Educational.

Lu, D., and G.P. Lu. 2013. "An Historical Review and Perspective on the Impact of Acupuncture on U.S. Medicine and Society." *Medical Acupuncture* 25(5): 311–316.

Malmberg, K.J., J.G.W. Raaijmakers, and R.M. Shiffrin. 2019. "50 Years of Research Sparked by Atkinson and Shiffrin (1968)." *Mem Cogn* 47:561–574. doi.org/10.3758/s13421-019-00896-7.

Murre, J.M., and J. Dros. 2015. "Replication and Analysis of Ebbinghaus' Forgetting Curve." *PLoS One* 10(7): e0120644. doi: 10.1371/journal.pone.0120644.

Olson, S. 2004. "Science Produces Explanations That Can Be Tested Using Empirical Evidence." In *Evolution in Hawaii: A Supplement to Teaching about Evolution and the Nature of Science*. Washington, DC: National Academies Press.

Rumelhart, D. 1980. "Schemata: The Building Blocks of Cognition." Chap. 2 in *Theoretical Issues in Reading Comprehension*, edited by R.J. Spiro, B.C. Bruce, and W.F. Brewer. New York: Routledge.

Samarrai, F. 2015. "Massive Study Reports Challenges in Reproducing Published Psychology Findings." UVA Today, August 27. news.virginia.edu/content/massive-study-reports-challenges-reproducing-published-psychology-findings.

Science of Learning Institute. n.d. "About Us." John Hopkins University. scienceoflearning.jhu.edu/about-us.

Senge, P. 1990. *The Fifth Discipline: The Art & Practice of the Learning Organization*. New York: Doubleday.

Theodotou, M. 2020. "Learning Ecosystem: Why You Need One, How to Build It." ATD Blog, December 14. td.org/insights/learning-ecosystem-why-you-need-one-now-and-how-to-build-it.

Recommended Resources

Biech, E. 2016. *The Art and Science of Training*. Alexandria, VA: ATD Press.

Erricsson, K.A., and R. Pool. 2016. *Peak: Secrets From the New Science of Expertise*. New York: Mariner Books.

Kirschner, P.A., and C. Hendrick. 2020. *How Learning Happens: Seminal Works in Psychology and What they Mean in Practice*. New York: Routledge.

Quinn, C. 2018. *Millennials, Goldfish & Other Training Misconceptions: Debunking Learning Myths and Superstitions*. Alexandria, VA: ATD Press.

CHAPTER 4

The Business Case for Learning

Preethi Anand

In the early 2000s, when most learning leaders realized the potential of their function in driving business strategies to execution, it was hard to convince CEOs and business leaders of their value proposition. It is absolutely refreshing to see that today there is a growing interest—curiosity even—among business leaders about how learning and talent development can add value to their business strategy.

> **IN THIS CHAPTER:**
> - Recognize the key trends in the world of business and how they are affecting the way organizations are run
> - Explore what CEOs look for in the learning and development function and how that knowledge helps us become their strategic partners
> - Distinguish the critical success factors for a forward-looking learning and development strategy

Today there is a very real opportunity to make learning and development a critical part of business success. Excitement aside, expectations from the function are also very high. But by incorporating a practical understanding of the current business landscape with foresight around the future of work, we can make a compelling business case for learning. So, what has changed? Why are we in the spotlight? Where do we begin? And how do we make the most of it? This chapter will answer these questions by describing the fundamental changes in the world of business, how it has set the stage to create a powerful business case for learning, and how we can play an active role in helping businesses flourish and stay competitive.

The World of Business: What Changed?

Imagine being CEO of a business in the 1920s. There were very few industries, significantly less competition, more available labor than jobs, rarely changing regulations, and business models that had been relevant for decades. Fast-forward to 2020—we can agree that a CEO's life today is dramatically different.

I've heard people say that it was much easier to be a CEO then versus now, because these are unprecedented times with disruptive changes. But if we look back to the 1920s, we can see that it was the beginning of an era in which the industrial revolution was on full speed, mass production was changing consumer trends, and scientific management principles were emerging—it was a much bigger disruption regarding work or creating a livelihood. Consider even the 1980s and 1990s; when computers entered the workplace, they caused a huge disruption and were definitely unprecedented. So, we have survived disruption in business before.

The next argument is typically that there was much less competition in the 1920s, and hence a CEO could sleep peacefully, worrying less about becoming obsolete. But on the other hand, there were also fewer opportunities to become a CEO in the 1920s, which made it an unfulfilled fantasy for many back then.

I strongly believe that understanding the nuances that define the context in which a 2020 CEO operates will be extremely valuable in appreciating and empathizing with their cause; this understanding can help us offer a promising value proposition for the learning function. Here are several key factors that define today's business context and the associated challenges and opportunities:

- **Growing possibilities with technology.** We live in a world in which technology has pervaded practically all aspects of work and life. Name a task and there's an app for it! This gives businesses immense opportunity to transform operations, rethink value propositions, innovate new products and services, and even create new business models. It also means that today's CEOs are constantly aware of the fact that their competitors, by leveraging the latest in technology, can make their entire business obsolete. Technology is growing at a much faster rate than we can attain, so fast that, to a CEO, a wild imagination might give them a bigger advantage than prosaically understanding how technology works.

- **Fewer barriers to start a business.** In the 1980s, when my father entered the workforce and considered settling down in a city in India, he literally had to choose between two companies to work for. Today there are three companies operating on my street! (One of them is operating from a garage, so I better make friends with them before they become a technology giant.) Many reasons make starting a business easy today: better access to funds, governmental support in the form of tax breaks and subsidies, and (the rarely acknowledged) better access to information. Reduction of entry barriers is an important factor for CEOs of organizations big and small, because it translates to more competition in an already crowded marketplace. It also reminds us of the fact that emerging companies are more nimble, with a faster reaction time to change. So pace becomes very important to business leaders.

- **Deconstruction of value chains.** The first time I heard this phrase, it sounded like something Tom Cruise would say in the movie *Minority Report*. But this is becoming a wildly important factor influencing business strategy. Let's examine how we managed finances back then compared with now. Just 15 years ago, all our financial management started and ended with banks: We used checks, demand drafts, and wire transfers for payments. We bought bonds, got mortgages, and opened accounts to deposit our earnings. Today, if we look closely at the payments space, there are so many players in the market, and banks no longer hold a monopoly. These players, which include many technology firms, took one link in the bank's value chain and transformed it to offer an easier, faster, and better experience to customers. This completely redefined the competitor landscape. For example, Google's autonomous cars could potentially affect Toyota's market share in the same way Google Pay has eaten into the banking business's pie. So, this makes constant innovation not a luxury, but a necessity for survival.

- **Increased stakeholder influence on business.** Stakeholders have always played a vital role in how businesses operate. But a few decades ago, when CEOs spoke of their stakeholders, they often alluded to customers or shareholders, the simple reason being these were the stakeholders who could affect business performance. Today, we are talking about the dawn of a new age where the stakeholders' footprint is much larger in the business landscape. Klaus Schwab, in his brilliant book *Stakeholder Capitalism*, talks about how companies are moving away from just delivering value to shareholders to also trying to create long-term value for all stakeholders (Schwab 2021). In simple terms, the expectations of a business from employees, clients, partners, governments, and other stakeholders is not just around profits anymore, but also about their plans to affect people and the planet. This has brought in a renewed focus on diversity, equity, and inclusion (DEI) initiatives and sustainability programs, among other things. Such programs are moving away from being ad hoc charity programs to becoming more closely tied to business strategy. HSBC, for example, has set an ambitious net zero carbon emissions target across its entire customer base by 2050 at the latest and is providing between $750 billion and $1 trillion in financing to help clients make the transition.

The New Learning Paradigm: What the CEO Wants You to Know

As challenging as it sounds, many CEOs have made their businesses thrive in this new normal. Large-scale transformations in marketing, operations, and research and development have played a major role in making this happen. Now, CEOs are also turning to the function that can influence transformations to bring the best out of their biggest assets, people. But the ask of the learning and talent development function is entirely different from what it was a few years ago. In fact, in a 2021 survey of Fortune CEOs, 71 percent of leaders said that the focus of their transformation efforts was around workforce and talent development (Deloitte 2021). Let's explore what CEOs want us to know when we design the learning and development function's business case.

On the Larger Focus of Our Business Case

If I were to use a metaphor for how CEOs are leading their businesses, I would probably compare it to walking on a treadmill on high speed (and yes, I have forgotten all about walking outside, thanks to the COVID-19 pandemic). When you walk on a treadmill, each step you take is a product of how you planned it five seconds ago. And when you take a step, your mind is already focusing on the next step, and the cycle continues; it's always all eyes ahead. With the complexities that exist in the business landscape, CEOs are investing more resources on preparing for the future than solving the problems of the present. Books like *The Signals Are Talking*, by quantitative futurist Amy Webb, which explores a systemic way of evaluating emerging ideas in technology to better understand the future, are growing in popularity among business leaders. Hence, a learning function's strategy should have a future-focused approach.

CEOs will appreciate a learning and talent development strategy that not only supports the business in providing learning solutions for performance challenges of today, but also has a vision for the future that mirrors that of the business. There are several ways in which learning leaders are approaching this: by investing in the identification and development of future skills, by exploring artificial intelligence and machine-learning-powered technology to amplify learning impact, by working toward creating a sustainable learning culture, and by designing transformation programs to reimagine the learning function for the future. I don't recommend simply replicating all these best practices. The idea is to understand and synthesize your specific business's strategy and craft a targeted learning strategy that aims to accelerate the organization's plans for the future. In business terms, CEOs are seeing learning and development initiatives less as a *cost* of doing business and more as an *investment* in the future. We will discuss the financial angle to this shortly, but this perspective will help us rethink our initiatives. Traditionally, most of our initiatives are focused on improving performance and saving costs. But increasingly, business leaders expect us to seek solutions for and invest in initiatives that may give us returns in the long run, like future skills initiatives. If we want a seat at the table, we need to rethink our value proposition and re-engineer our function as one poised to prepare the business for the future.

On Financial Impact

Let's be honest, learning leaders don't often have coffee-table conversations about finances, but we all know that financial acumen plays a critical role in positioning our function as a strategic arm of the business. And the idea is not just to know about the key terms used in our financial statements, but to be able to read and interpret them. Financial statements give a raw picture of the entire business, and many experts decode how businesses are run by just looking at them. While this level of expertise would definitely play to our advantage, having an understanding of the financials in an organization would also help us in looking through the CEO's lens.

Let's discuss this with an example: Kamala is the head of learning and talent development in a multinational corporation. Her organization has consistently generated significantly higher revenue year over year, despite operating in a highly competitive market. However, its operating cost has also increased, reducing the profit margin. This prompted the CEO to focus on creating cost efficiencies across the organization. Kamala, equipped with this information, worked with her peers to study the factors responsible for the high operating costs. They realized that two different manufacturing units were hiring in huge numbers during the holidays and in the spring, respectively, owing to a surge in demand. Kamala and her peers proposed cross-training a significant portion of the workforce in both units to create a fungible pool of workers and avoid hiring costs. The solution was well received by all the stakeholders, and Kamala was tapped to lead a task force with HR, learning and development, and operations for the pilot program. In the first year of implementation, the project reduced costs associated with hiring and induction by 75 percent and increased engagement among employees in both business units. Kamala's CEO now wants them to come up with a large-scale cross-skilling strategy for the business. This solution was possible only because Kamala understood the critical factors involved and how an optimal solution could influence the operating costs. Kamala is now a strategic partner to the CEO.

As L&D professionals, our mission in appreciating business finance does not stop with delivering value; we must also show it in quantitative terms. Today every business arm has to report on the financial impact of its initiatives to justify its requests for more funding. As learning leaders, we should also be able to make a powerful business case, supported by hard-hitting numbers. The Phillips ROI Methodology, for instance, provides a great framework to get started in this journey. When we think of measuring training impact, we often take the approach of doing a cost-benefit analysis. Business leaders use different methods to measure impact. It is important that we understand the financial measures commonly used in our organizational context so as to accurately portray the financial impact of our projects. Understanding measures like the internal rate of return, net present value, and payback period and applying them to specific learning initiatives will help business leaders immediately relate to the impact we showcase. Thus, learning leaders may want to design meaningful dashboards to represent the quantitative impact of the function.

On the Business Need for Skills and Skilling

One of the reasons I love being a learning professional in this age is the new level of excitement around skills, reskilling, upskilling, and cross-skilling. Skilling might be new to a business leader's dictionary, but it has been in ours for decades. So why the sudden interest? In this age of massive competition and evolving technology, we know that an organization's agility is its biggest competitive advantage. For many years, building an agile organization often meant having agile processes, agile strategies, or increased technology. In recent years, however, one idea around agility has been gaining in popularity: the idea of having a fungible workforce, one that adapts faster to changes and transforms with the evolving organization. And it didn't take long for organizations to realize that using a skills-based approach could bring order to this potentially chaotic exercise.

Skills are objective; they can be tagged and classified to form an ontology that can be managed at scale. Josh Bersin (2021) explains on his blog that "SkillsTech" (tools that help in managing, assessing, analyzing, and developing skills in organizations) has a massive market because "every time the CEO wants to go in a new direction, skills and capabilities are fundamental to execution." Many CEOs are excited about this idea because, for the very first time, they can see what their workforce is capable of and how it is evolving.

Skills ontologies are gaining in significance for two main reasons. First, technology has evolved so much that we are questioning the fundamental value add of many existing job roles, if not professions. Because automation and machine learning have made human intervention redundant for many job roles, organizations are supporting reskilling plans to prepare these employees for emerging roles. There are several success stories of such initiatives across the globe, like how a consortium of public and private partnerships in Sweden enabled reskilling airline-cabin staff to become assistant nurses to support hospitals burdened by the pandemic (AP 2020). Second, and more commonly, jobs are constantly evolving with agile ways of working, changes in organizational processes, and increased influence of technology. This makes the traditional idea of having job descriptions with skills and competencies that are reviewed every two years a thing of the past. We need to be able to systematically understand the changes in skills that are required to be successful in different roles and be empowered to take action real time. Several HR and learning platforms have already started moving toward becoming future focused and have integrated skills-powered engines, which provide intelligent insights for decision making.

Critical Ingredients for a Successful Learning Strategy

Armed with an understanding of the current business landscape and the key expectations of L&D from the CEO, let's explore some of the critical factors that we will need to incorporate in our learning strategy for its successful execution.

Solve for the Present and Future Business Needs

There are great initiatives around learning and talent development led by experts and leaders in the field. Some of them are path breaking, while others are simple yet genius solutions to business challenges. Reading about them might tempt us to replicate them in our organizations. But every business leader will tell you that the simple "cut-copy-paste" approach will never really work for business strategies; it is more nuanced than that. I believe that it is very important to follow trends, not only in our field, but also in technology, psychology, and business strategy, and among our competitors. These trends, however, need to serve more as inspirations than blueprints for our initiatives. Our learning and talent development strategies will work only if what we create is a specialized solution for our organization. Our strategy needs to also mirror our business's strategy, calling out the ways in which we will specifically be adding value to the organization today and how we will prepare the organization for the future.

Design Thinking Is a Way of Learning and Leading

Some of the world's most forward-looking organizations have embraced human-centered design and design thinking to empathize with and design for the customer in mind. The brilliance of the framework is its ability to help people fixate on the "why" of a product or service and push designers to continually reinvent the "how."

Let's look at Company Z's L&D planning off-site. Its business is going through a massive digital transformation. All of its processes, procedures, and ways of working are changing, as are nearly 60 percent of its job roles. Business leaders have asked the L&D team to present a paper on how the function will support the transformation. Unfortunately, the team has just invested in a proof of concept for an LMS and purchased three massive content libraries to support skill building for roles that will soon become redundant. The team comprises 10 trainers, three learning business partners, two instructional designers, and, of course, the head of the function. After a long (and heated) debate, the team members finally agree on an approach; they simply list all the digital assets and resources that they have on one side of a whiteboard; on the other side they list every bullet point from the business strategy document. They then go on to "match the following."

I am sure some of you are cringing reading this example, but I'd also bet that you've been part of a similar scenario in the past. Clearly, this cannot be the right approach. Design thinking can be the beacon that guides us toward accomplishing our business goals by making the most of our available opportunities. Similar to the way it has helped businesses suddenly turn around revenues from products and services, design thinking can also help us take the much-needed turn if we embrace it with open arms and open minds.

Skills and Capabilities of the Learning Team

The previous example also brings up an extremely crucial aspect of the learning strategy—the learning team's skills and capabilities. We are vocal advocates for massive reskilling and upskilling initiatives for the business, yet we often forget to focus on reskilling our own functions. We know digital is a massive disruptor, yet very few on our teams truly understand how to work within the digital environment. While many organizations are working on reskilling their L&D teams, there are some that simply do not have the funding for it. It is time we acknowledge the significance of reskilling the torchbearers of (ironically) the organization's reskilling plans. This needs to be baked into our function's strategy and must be a nonnegotiable expenditure, because several studies support its massive impact on the business. In IBM's *2019 HR 3.0* study, companies with world-class HR skills were found to be five and a half times more likely to be "significantly more profitable than peers" and six times "significantly more innovative" than others (Wright et al. 2020). If we can help business leaders understand that the primary intent is to support business strategy and showcase the potential impact and financial benefits of a reskilling program, we will be able to make this happen.

From Custodians to Catalysts for Learning

The half-life of a skill is probably the most intriguing concept I have heard about in the last five years. It refers to how long a job skill is relevant before declining in importance. Typewriting skills, for example, must have been relevant for at least 20 years. Today the half-life of a job skill is an average of five years, which means that in five years a learned skill will be only half as valuable. It is quite evident that as a function, we cannot produce learning content and programs at the pace at which skills change. So, the best way we can enable learning in this context is by moving away from a "command and control" model of learning to designing and promoting a culture of learning. Many of us have already embraced social learning, employee-to-employee learning programs, and self-directed learning experience platforms, moving away from the traditional learning management system (LMS). For the same reason, there is also an increasing focus on building learning agility among employees.

Possibilities With Technology

There was a time when we explored technology as a means to execute our strategy. Even CEOs and business leaders are now learning the nuts and bolts of technology because the tables have turned. Today's technology offers more possibilities than we can realize, possibilities that can help us put our best foot forward and gain a competitive edge. We need to explore the potential of learning systems and technologies as an integral part of our learning strategy. Be it artificial intelligence and machine learning, block chain, or natural language processing, technology can help us amplify our value proposition to the business.

Partnerships and Stakeholders

When I started my career, there was a very clear line separating the business support functions like HR, marketing, learning, and operations. Today I struggle to see those lines; instead, several learning projects are executed in partnership with one or more support functions. And then there are those projects that cut across even organizational boundaries. We truly are in an era of hyper-collaboration, which is probably the primary reason we were able to accomplish so much so fast (Kolk et al. 2018). Hence, identifying and creating a plan to manage our key stakeholders is one of the most important factors for reaching our function's goals. In fact, several learning organizations have partnered with public initiatives, not-for-profits, organizations in their supply chain, and even peers and competitors to enable learning for organizational success.

Final Thoughts

In 1966, Robert Kennedy said, "Like it or not, we live in interesting times. They are times of danger and uncertainty; but they are also the most creative of any time in the history of mankind." Here we are in 2022, and this feels like it could be the tagline for the last two years. The COVID-19 pandemic gave us a shockingly sudden change in our context. As individuals, it helped us sort through our priorities in life, and despite all the darkness, we saw humanity at its best. As organizations, it was a litmus test on the resilience of our strategic plans, with technology playing a huge role in sustaining the business. We were already on a path toward a massive transformation as a function a few years ago, and the last two years may have accelerated these efforts. None of us can be certain what the future holds. But I believe that the next few years will be a time of paradoxes as we try to better understand our new normal and get comfortable with our new context. For example, while we are exploring all the possibilities of data and technology, we are also realizing the ethics and moral implications of those possibilities, and we might put an end to them before they are realized.

This will truly be interesting times for us, as I believe that we could be tasked with finding answers for questions we were never asked before. (Some organizations have already started asking us these questions.) Like, how can you build and sustain a learning organization? What are the ethical implications of your skilling initiatives? What is the plan of action for removing biases and making our learning systems inclusive? Can you make a forecast for emerging skills for our business plans? How can a human learn to work with an intelligent machine? How do you plan to train robotic processes? Can you make a proposal for building emotional intelligence among customer-facing robots? How do you build subject matter expertise when most of the job is automated? Can you show me a real-time heat map of key behavioral skills enabling and deterring team performance in teams? How can the learning function support global sustainable development goals? Can you look at organizational capabilities and propose how to reimagine the business model?

Our possibilities are endless.

About the Author

Preethi Anand is AVP of the Operations Technical Training Academy at HSBC. She is a learning and development professional with more than 12 years of experience in learning strategy and solutions design. With work experience at AIG, Polaris, and Intellect (a FinTech startup), Preethi has managed several portfolios ranging from competency mapping and development to branding for the learning function. She holds a bachelor's degree in English literature and a master's in social work, and recently completed an executive management program with Cornell University. She is also a PMI Agile Certified Practitioner. A frequent contributor to *TD* magazine and *Training Journal* (UK), she won the Bronze Award in the category Global L&D Professional of the Year, conferred by *Training Journal* in 2017. She was also named a 40 under 40 in HR by CNBC and Jombay in 2019.

References

AP (Associated Press). 2020. "Coronavirus: SAS Airline Employees Train to Assist in Health Care." *USA Today*, April 2. usatoday.com/story/travel/airline-news/2020/04/02/coronavirus-sas-airline-employees-train-assist-nursing-homes-hospitals/5110477002.

Bersin, J. 2021. "Understanding SkillsTech, One of the Biggest Markets in Business." Business Trends, April 18. joshbersin.com/2021/04/understanding-skillstech.

Deloitte. 2021. "2021 Fortune/Deloitte CEO Survey." Deloitte, Fall. deloitte.com/us/en/pages/chief-executive-officer/articles/ceo-survey.html.

Kennedy, R.F. 1966. "Day of Affirmation Address." University of Capetown, Capetown, South Africa, June 6. jfklibrary.org/learn/about-jfk/the-kennedy-family/robert-f-kennedy/robert-f-kennedy-speeches/day-of-affirmation-address-university-of-capetown-capetown-south-africa-june-6-1966.

Kolk, M., R. Eagar, C. Boulton, and C. Mira. 2018. "How Hyper-Collaboration Accelerates Ecosystem Innovation." *Strategy and Leadership* 46(1): 23–29. researchgate.net/publication/323131982_How_hypercollaboration_accelerates_ecosystem_innovation.

Schwab, K. 2021. "What Is Stakeholder Capitalism?" World Economic Forum, January 22. weforum.org/agenda/2021/01/klaus-schwab-on-what-is-stakeholder-capitalism-history-relevance.

Wright, A., J. Mertens, D. Gherson, and J. Bersin. 2020. "Accelerating the Journey to HR 3.0: Ten Ways to Transform in a Time of Upheaval." IBM Institute for Business Value and Josh Bersin Academy. ibm.com/thought-leadership/institute-business-value/report/hr-3.

Recommended Resources

Anand, P. 2017. "Executive Dashboards to Win Over the C-Suite." *TD at Work*. Alexandria, VA: ATD Press.

Horowitz, B. 2014. *The Hard Thing About Hard Things: Building a Business When There Are No Easy Answers*. New York: Harper Business.

Iansiti, M., and K.R. Lakhani. 2020. *Competing in the Age of AI: Strategy and Leadership When Algorithms and Networks Run the World*. Boston: Harvard Business Review Press.

Roose, K. 2021. *Futureproof: 9 Rules for Humans in the Age of Automation*. New York: Random House.

SECTION II
PLANNING A CAREER IN TALENT DEVELOPMENT

LUMINARY PERSPECTIVE

Talent Development Mindsets

Beverly Kaye

If you're thinking about a career in talent development, it would be natural to assume it's all about education and skill sets. After all, you can earn a degree in instructional design, leadership development, organizational psychology, or adult learning. You can invest in L&D certifications to help you upskill and stay current on the profession's various roles and responsibilities. And of course, you can access ATD's Talent Development Capability Model for a list of the personal, professional, and organizational skills you will need to develop yourself and others within organizations. These include hard skills like business insight, technology application, and learning sciences; soft skills like servant mentality, persuasion, flexibility, and creativity; and what I call "Velcro skills," which link the two types together, like lifelong learning, cultural awareness, and inclusivity.

So, while it's undeniable that degrees, certificates, and skills are critical components of a TD career, what you bring to the profession is so much more than just your CV and skill set.

Aptitude and Attitude

You can earn a coaching certificate and make it part of your resume, but if you lack enthusiasm and positivity, if you don't believe behavior can change, or if you lack the patience to provide personal mentorship to your team or others who ask, you should probably avoid a coaching path. Likewise, while your education can provide the methodology to identify a business problem and your experience might tell you what has worked and what hasn't, if you don't bring sufficient curiosity, vision, and commitment to the problem you probably won't be a very successful business partner. Success in the talent development profession is about more than your aptitude. It's also about your attitude.

Attitude is defined as a mindset or settled way of thinking or feeling about something, typically one that is reflected in a person's behavior. I believe certain mindsets are especially important for those in talent development and can make the difference between their ability to simply perform and the attitude necessary to excel and thrive. I've identified eight for you to consider. If you want to give yourself an action-producing exercise, rate yourself on each or ask others for their opinion.

The Inquirer

Inquirers are unusually curious, willing to ask questions, and able to evaluate the validity of the answers. If you are an inquirer, you:

- Are curious about your future, that of the business you represent, and the individuals you work with
- Don't allow important questions to go unasked at strategic planning meetings and in other critical decision-making venues
- Believe there is always more to learn
- Quickly and willingly access your inner observer and from there gain useful information about what you are capable of, passionate about, and most satisfied by
- Want to know how you are perceived by others, are open to feedback, and are willing and able to examine the truth of it
- Pay attention to gaps between your self-image and the feedback you receive
- Will question the alignment between the intent of your behavior and its impact on others

The Envisioner

Envisioners can imagine things that don't currently exist. If you are an envisioner, you:

- Don't allow yourself to see only with your eyes and won't be boxed into limited vistas
- Can visualize the changes you want for yourself and your organization
- Are able to picture yourself at work in the future talent development world
- Can imagine yourself in that future and picture how success looks, feels, sounds, and tastes
- Consider multiple possibilities before making a decision
- Delight in the challenge of seeing yourself in expanded, comprehensive frames, and are willing to stretch beyond what is currently comfortable to fit into them
- Can anticipate the inspiration, trust, and respect that will exist between yourself and your colleagues, which fuels your future ambitions

The Ambiguity Appreciator

Ambiguity appreciators can sit in uncertainty without trying to escape immediately. If you are an ambiguity appreciator, you:

- Have a higher tolerance for uncertainty than others and may even relish it because you know uncertainty is a close relative of change

- Are able to take a first step without knowing exactly where the next one lies
- Can see that the greater the distance between past and future scenarios, the more time you have to devise the best plan

The Pulse Checker

Pulse checkers are vigilant and alert to vital signs, trends, and threats. If you are a pulse checker, you:
- Feel your creative juices bubbling and flowing in concert with the beat of the business
- Are on the lookout for aha moments, and as they emerge, seize them with gusto and gratitude, and investigate them further
- Borrow perspectives from every Zoom call and article and check to see if it changes your "reading" of ideas or situations
- Check your own pulse for how engaged you still are

The Conscious Connector

Conscious connectors naturally identify and see alignment between seemingly disparate concepts and ideas. If you are a conscious connector, you:
- See potential relationships that others don't
- Are always connecting with those who can provide feedback on your performance or open a new door for you
- Give your personal connections enough time to share their wisdom with you, and you always offer your own knowledge
- Sniff out talent trends and look for ways to turn them into an organizational advantage

The Bottom Liner

Bottom liners approach problems, decisions, and projects with a business case mentality. If you are a bottom liner, you:
- Calculate the ROI—return on investment—on an initiative or an innovation and apply this information to the decisions you make and the changes you propose
- Use business strategy and goals as a measure of success in your own role
- Operate as if you are an owner of the business, not just its employee

The Change Chaser

Change chasers both react to and instigate change. If you are a change chaser, you:
- Can see shifts in the business conditions driving your work and respond appropriately
- Pursue change when necessary to achieve business goals
- Understand that your reputation is not static, and you will pursue changes in your attitude and behavior to help maintain positive aspects of how others see you

The Network Finder and Minder

Network finders and minders identify and maintain relationships with those critical to their success and that of the organization. If you are a network finder and minder, you:
- Seek and nurture contacts that will facilitate involvement and innovation, as well as extend or influence your own point of view
- Invite colleagues to challenge your thinking
- Practice "quid pro quo" for all who help you
- Notice and make connections between:
    - Plans and the skills needed to implement them
    - Individual and team skills gaps and the best available learning content, methodology, and venues
    - Talent resource problems and the opportunities for addressing them

Final Thoughts

Success is not a skill. You might spend your talent development career attracting and retaining employees, identifying development gaps, creating strategies for closing them, or designing and implementing performance management, leadership development, or employee assessment programs. Whatever you choose, you can be confident that your degrees, certifications, and skills will enable you to demonstrate your aptitude, but without attitudes like those outlined here, your success cannot be ensured. If opportunity is an accident meeting a prepared mind, then talent development career success is a close collaboration between aptitude and attitude.

About the Author

Beverly Kaye is recognized internationally as one of the most knowledgeable and practical professionals in the areas of career development, employee engagement, and retention. Her contribution to the field includes the *Wall Street Journal* bestseller, *Love 'Em or Lose 'Em: Getting Good People to Stay,* now in its sixth edition. Her recent books include *Up Is Not the Only Way* and *Help Them Grow or Watch Them Go,* which helps managers blend career conversations into their everyday routine. In 2018, ATD honored Beverly with a Lifetime Achievement Award recognizing her contributions to the profession. The Association of Learning Professionals honored her with their 2018 Thought Leadership Award. In 2019, Beverly was recognized with a Lifetime Achievement Award from the Institute for Management Studies.

CHAPTER 5

The Talent Development Capability Model

Morgean Hirt

The Talent Development Capability Model is a research-based framework for what talent development professionals need to know and do to be successful. Developed with input from more than 3,000 professionals around the world in a wide range of roles and working in a diverse set of organizations, the Capability Model elevates the talent development function to the level of a key contributor to an organization's success.

> **IN THIS CHAPTER:**
> ♦ Review the Talent Development Capability Model
> ♦ Describe the value of the Talent Development Capability Model
> ♦ Apply the Talent Development Capability Model to your own career, your team, and your organization to elevate your talent development practice

The Talent Development Capability Model offers a new standard for the field, helping prepare talent development professionals for their future of work by broadening the scope of knowledge and skills that will make them effective. There is no professional model better positioned to help organizations navigate the changes that are coming, and talent development professionals themselves need to be ready to meet that change.

ATD has been developing competency models since 1978. Each model has focused on the specific technical skills required of those in talent development, which in turn helped build a solid foundation of skills for TD professionals. However, when developing its new framework in 2019, ATD decided to move in a slightly different direction—away from competencies and toward capabilities. *Competence* has become a somewhat outdated and passive term, as it refers to a person's current state and their having the knowledge and skills necessary to perform a job. *Capability*, on the other hand, is about integrating knowledge and skills and adapting and flexing to meet future needs. By shifting from a competency model to a capability model, ATD is helping talent development professionals put their knowledge and skills to work to create, innovate, lead, manage change, and demonstrate impact.

How the Model Was Developed: The Latest Study

The research for the 2019 capability model began with capturing the major shifts in society and the larger business landscape that had occurred since the previous model was published. Major changes were identified through a comprehensive literature review, expert practitioner interviews, and advisory group discussions. These trends spanned a variety of areas in business, technology, learning, science, and the profession itself, and were directly incorporated into the research to determine their impact on future skills requirements for practitioners.

The results of the trends research overwhelmingly indicated that the role of the TD professional has moved beyond the traditional realm of training design and delivery. Effective talent development requires a proactive, business-partner approach to anticipate and respond to changing needs and to leverage personal capabilities to support organizational strategy and generate competitive advantage. The research data collected formed the basis for ATD to craft competency statements. Because this was the first study done under the banner of talent development, defining the full scope of what encompasses the field was a key goal.

The competency statements were then included in an occupational survey, which ended up being the largest ever done by ATD. That study determined which competency statements would be included in the final framework. The range of data obtained in the study enabled ATD to reflect on the global nature of the work TD professionals are doing and showed little difference between what those in varying parts of the world, different size organizations, or disparate industries need to know and be able to do in order to succeed. Having information from such a wide range of levels of practitioners, rather than just those who are midlevel career, helps ensure all TD professionals can build their skill set and create a more mobile workforce, establishing an international standard for TD practice.

The Model and Its Structure

ATD's recent competency research shows that the future of work will require talent development professionals to leverage interpersonal skills, along with their professional expertise, to work as a true business partner to help achieve organizational goals.

Overwhelmingly, respondents rated the importance of tasks related to business partnering and those that affect organizational strategy and success equally to, and in some cases higher than, those traditionally viewed as necessary in the learning and development field, such as instructional design and training and facilitation. Similarly, the high ratings of knowledge and skill areas that were once considered "foundational" or "enabling"—such as communication, business acumen, and having a global mindset—showed the increased importance of these interpersonal abilities to success.

The resulting Talent Development Capability Model has three equal domains of practice, centered on three key areas: personal skills, professional expertise, and contributing to organizational success. Among these, there is no hierarchy of importance of the knowledge and skills to be developed. Talent development professionals will need to leverage topics across these domains for the greatest level of success and effectiveness.

Under each of the three domains are 23 capabilities, which detail the specific knowledge and skills that can be harnessed for maximum impact (Figure 5-1).

Figure 5-1. The Talent Development Capability Model

Building Personal Capabilities

This domain of practice embodies the foundational or enabling abilities all working professionals should possess to be effective in the business world. These largely interpersonal skills, often called soft skills, are needed to build an effective organizational or team culture, trust, and engagement. The Building Personal Capabilities domain includes the following capabilities:

- **Communication.** As talent development professionals become critical business partners, they will need to articulate the appropriate messages for a particular audience.
- **Emotional intelligence and decision making.** Emotional intelligence and the ability to make good decisions are paramount to professional success. Regulating your own emotions and correctly interpreting the verbal and nonverbal behaviors of others are key strengths in building rapport and trust with others.
- **Collaboration and leadership.** Leadership is about influence and vision, which also helps to facilitate collaboration. Being good at collaboration requires the ability to foster environments that encourage teamwork and respectful relationships, especially cross-functionally. Effective leaders inspire trust and engagement with their employees and teams.
- **Cultural awareness and inclusion.** Cultural awareness and the ability to foster an inclusive work environment are requirements in today's global business climate. Being effective at both means conveying respect for different perspectives, backgrounds, customs, abilities, and behavior norms, as well as ensuring all employees are respected and involved by leveraging their capabilities, insights, and ideas.
- **Project management.** Effective project management requires being able to plan, organize, direct, and control resources for a finite period to complete specific goals and objectives.
- **Compliance and ethical behavior.** Compliance and ethical behavior refer to the expectation that a talent development professional acts with integrity and operates within the laws that govern where they work and live.
- **Lifelong learning.** Lifelong learning is sometimes called continuous learning, agile learning, or learning drive. It is marked by traits such as self-motivation, insatiable curiosity, and intelligent risk taking. Talent development professionals should model the value of lifelong learning by pursuing knowledge for personal and professional reasons.

These areas are of particular value to talent development professionals who need to be able to persuasively communicate solutions and guide individuals and teams to improved performance, and to do so in an inclusive way. The need to focus on and elevate these knowledge and skill areas is echoed by research being done by others. A recent IBM report on the future of work states that "skilled humans fuel the global economy. Digital skills remain vital; however, executives tell us soft skills have surpassed them in importance" (La Prade et al. 2019).

Developing Professional Capabilities

This domain of practice encompasses the knowledge and skills talent development professionals should possess to be effective in their roles of creating the processes, systems, and frameworks that foster learning, maximize individual performance, and develop the capacity and potential of employees. The core professional skills that have been the mainstay of the field, such as instructional design, evaluating impact, and training delivery, are all found in this domain of the new model as key elements, alongside new and expanded skill sets such as learning sciences and technology application.

The Developing Professional Capabilities domain includes the following capabilities:

- **Learning sciences.** Organizations with highly effective learning programs incorporate key principles from the learning sciences, which is an interdisciplinary research-based field that works to further the understanding of learning, learning innovation, and instructional methodologies.
- **Instructional design.** Instructional design is an essential element of an effective learning effort. The creation of learning experiences and materials is what results in the acquisition and application of knowledge and skills.
- **Training delivery and facilitation.** Training delivery and facilitation are means by which talent development professionals help individuals improve performance at work by learning new skills and knowledge. The practitioner serves as a catalyst for learning.
- **Technology application.** Disruption via technology will continue to be a reality for organizations and talent development functions. Talent development professionals must have the ability to identify, select, and implement the right learning and talent technologies that serve the best interests of the organization and its people.
- **Knowledge management.** Knowledge management is the explicit and systematic management of intellectual capital and organizational knowledge. In a knowledge economy, lost institutional knowledge can be costly for organizations in the form of turnover, recruitment, and training expenses.
- **Career and leadership development.** Creating a culture of career development in an organization can be a competitive advantage. Being effective at career and leadership development requires the ability to create planned processes of interaction between the organization and the individual.

- **Coaching.** Coaching is a discipline and practice that is an essential capability for any talent development professional, and it has the power to catalyze breakthroughs to enhance individual, team, and organizational performance.
- **Evaluating impact.** Evaluating the impact of talent development programs is correlated with learning and business effectiveness. Talent development professionals should be able to implement a multilevel, systematic method for assessing the effectiveness and effort of learning programs.

These specialized skills are necessary for identifying, developing, and delivering effective learning solutions. Practitioners not directly involved in development and delivery will be better business partners and advocates if they understand these key elements of talent development.

Impacting Organizational Capability

This third domain of practice includes the knowledge, skills, and abilities needed by professionals to ensure talent development is a primary mechanism driving organizational performance, productivity, and operational results. Talent development professionals are in the unique position of having insight into an organization's workforce, coupled with the ability to link that human capital to the skills most needed to attain business-critical missions and goals. If all TD professionals had the knowledge and skills to serve as business partners, regardless of their role, organizations could achieve their goals more quickly and effectively.

The Impacting Organizational Capability domain includes the following capabilities:
- **Business insight.** Business insight is the understanding of key factors affecting a business, such as its current situation, influences from its industry or market, and factors influencing growth. Having business insight is essential to strategic involvement with top management and ensuring talent development strategies align with the overall business strategy.
- **Consulting and business partnering.** Being seen as a valued business partner should be a goal for talent development professionals. Consulting and business partnering use expertise, influence, and personal skill to build a two-way relationship that facilitates change or improvement in the business.
- **Organization development and culture.** To remain relevant, organizations must continually develop capability and capacity. Organization development (OD) is an effort that focuses on improving an organization's capability through the alignment of strategy, structure, management processes, people, rewards, and metrics.
- **Talent strategy and management.** Talent strategy and management are the practices used to build an organization's culture, engagement, capability, and capacity through the implementation and integration of talent acquisition, employee development, retention, and deployment processes, ensuring these processes are aligned to organizational goals.

- **Performance improvement.** Organizational competitiveness is fueled by improvement in human performance. Performance improvement is a holistic and systematic approach to meeting organizational goals by identifying and closing human performance gaps.
- **Change management.** Talent development professionals are well positioned to facilitate change because they connect people, process, and work. Change management is the capability for enabling change within an organization by using structured approaches to shift individuals, teams, and organizations from a current state to a future state.
- **Data and analytics.** Data and analytics are key drivers for organizational performance and should also be drivers for talent development. This is about the ability to collect, analyze, and use large data sets in real time to influence learning, performance, and business.
- **Future readiness.** The increasing pace of change requires constant upskilling and reskilling of the workforce. Future readiness requires intellectual curiosity and constant scanning of the environment to stay abreast of forces shaping the business world, employees and their expectations, and the talent development profession.

This domain comprises the knowledge, skills, and abilities (KSAs) that enable TD professionals to be key business partners who can present data to the C-suite in a way they understand, showing that L&D functions are not disposable but essential drivers toward competitive advantage and business success. All talent development professionals, regardless of role or experience, should strive to understand how interconnected their work is to the success of an organization and how they can influence that success.

While the Talent Development Capability Model has a new framework and set of labels for what talent development professionals need to know and be able to do, many of these concepts could be found in previous models. However, they had not been surfaced in a way that led professionals to focus on developing them. The Capability Model demonstrates the need for TD professionals to blend their knowledge and skills across the three domains and each of the capabilities to be most effective. Even entry-level professionals can begin to see the necessity of collaborating with key business units, uncovering the true needs of the business, and effectively presenting ideas and solutions that are tied to organizational goals. If TD professionals develop themselves and their teams in line with this new standard for talent development, they can best position themselves to drive a learning agenda that will help organizations navigate the future.

Using the Talent Development Capability Model

In addition to introducing a new visual framework for talent development capabilities, ATD also developed tools and an interactive website that are available to anyone at no cost. The site is designed to assist professionals in exploring the Capability Model, assessing themselves against the new standard to identify skills gaps and areas for development, and connecting with resources to assist them in their own professional growth and development. You can find these tools and job aids at the handbook's website, ATDHandbook3.org.

The Talent Development Capability Model defines the standard of excellence and helps lead the profession by empowering professionals to elevate their skills and enabling organizations to strategically align learning and talent development opportunities to business outcomes. However, the real utility of a capability model is in its application. Practitioners and organizations must invest in skill-building opportunities, quantify the importance and impact of talent development, and boost their credibility within the organizational landscape.

Individuals may use the model to explore skills that will lead to role or career expansion or to help prepare for professional certification. Academic institutions, professional groups, and others involved in educating those who will perform talent development functions may use the model to benchmark and align their curriculums. And talent development managers and leaders may use the model to establish which roles they need to fill and which skill sets are required of their staff. Each stakeholder group will have different needs in relation to how they use the model.

The Talent Development Capability Model provides a common language and consistent way to communicate about the profession. It conveys the scope of the profession to those exploring career or professional development. It can also help demonstrate the value of talent development to organizational leaders and the workforce at large.

For Individuals

The interactive website allows individuals to explore the model and identify how knowledge and skills blended across the model can enhance their practice. The domains and capabilities complement each other but also provide a deeper dive into the various areas of practice, from instructional design, to organization development, to technology application. A built-in self-assessment encourages professionals to benchmark their current knowledge and skill proficiency against this new standard. The assessment can identify knowledge and skills gaps and then be saved to a user's ATD profile.

Users can prioritize identified gaps for development and access direct links to ATD resources that can help close those gaps. Various learning paths can help users achieve their goals and were designed to develop knowledge and skills specific to those goals. Users can choose among paths that are role based, can help deepen their practice throughout their career, are designed for developing readiness to pursue a professional certification, are customizable, and allow them to create their own learning path. At any time, a user can come back to the self-assessment to reassess against the standard and update learning goals.

The self-assessment can also help uncover how a professional's career might evolve over time, what jobs they might want to pursue in the future, and which skills are necessary for those roles. Professionals with more tenure in the field can use the model to hone knowledge and skills in areas they may not have encountered over the course of their career or develop new skills as a result of changes in the field or society.

The new model also serves as the foundation for the two credentials currently offered by the ATD Certification Institute. The Associate Professional in Talent Development (APTD) is designed for individual contributors who are still early in their career or for whom talent development is only part of their role. The Certified Professional in Talent Development (CPTD, formerly the Certified Professional in Learning and Performance) is for more experienced practitioners and those who wish to play a more strategic role in their organization. The appropriate subset of knowledge and skills for each designation is included on the respective credentialing exams.

STACKABLE CREDENTIALS

By identifying specific gaps through self-assessment, professionals can target their skill development through programming designed to focus on specific knowledge or skills. This can be done through a range of resources and activities, such as reading books, participating in conferences or webinars, and reading articles. Targeted courses focused on these skills can then be built on or combined to complete larger certificates in a specific capability or area of practice. Those seeking a deep dive or who want a capstone project to demonstrate their proficiency level can participate in an assessment-based certificate program, such as the ATD Master series, that includes those elements. Skill development can culminate in demonstration of the ability to apply knowledge and skills on the job by achieving an APTD or CPTD professional certification from the ATD Certification Institute.

For Managers and Teams

Managers can also use the new model to design job roles and structure teams, departments, and the talent development function. The model can provide insight into what talent development capabilities are needed by line managers, subject matter experts, and other nonpractitioners who are responsible for developing or educating others. The flexibility of the model allows practitioners to personalize the areas in which they place their focus.

Managers can use the interactive model to have members of their teams complete self-assessments to identify common gaps and develop team learning plans. ATD resources—from

TD magazine articles and job aids, to downloadable books or webcasts, to education courses—are linked directly to the knowledge and skill areas that need to be developed, making it easy to identify personalized or group learning solutions.

The model can also serve as a template to show talent development managers and leaders what success looks like now and in the future. It can be leveraged to set performance expectations and incentivize staff to expand and enhance their skills to align to those expectations, thereby enhancing the image and credibility of the profession with business leaders. The integration of personal, professional, and organizational impact capabilities in the Capability Model makes it especially well suited to communicating the talent development function's strategic value.

For Organizations and Their Leaders

The Capability Model is a useful framework for leaders at multiple levels—from a manager of a talent development team, to a senior talent leader, to a C-suite executive—because it provides insight into the range of functions talent development performs in the organization. It also articulates how professionals serving in these roles can add significant value to the organization through their work in fostering learning, improving performance, and supporting the organization through change. Leaders can use the model to support discussions about the value of upskilling the TD team by demonstrating the link between talent development and organizational performance.

Once an organization determines which functions its talent development team will perform, the Capability Model can be used to create a road map of the knowledge and skills team members need to support those functions. Job descriptions can be scoped to match those skills, which in turn can be used to upskill current team members or recruit new members with complementary skill sets.

Because the model is designed to be a blended, flexible set of knowledge and skills, it can also be used to identify skill sets for ancillary team members—such as subject matter experts, technology team members, and those in analytics or human resources—whose roles intersect with the talent development function. This can help create a common language and understanding of expectations that will enhance overall performance across the learning and development function.

Final Thoughts

The ATD Capability Model defines the standard of excellence and helps lead the profession by empowering professionals to elevate their skills and enabling organizations to strategically align learning and talent development opportunities to business outcomes. The interactive model can serve an informational role in capturing what is most needed among TD professionals now and in the future, but its value stems from its potential application through assessment, personalized learning plans, and direct links to learning solutions. It has been designed for individuals and organizations to place themselves in its center and apply or customize it to their needs. Practitioners and organizations must invest in skill-building opportunities, quantify the importance of talent development, and boost their credibility within the organizational landscape. The ATD Capability Model provides talent development professionals with a common language and standard against which knowledge and skills can be developed to leverage expertise for maximum impact on an organization's success.

About the Author

Morgean Hirt is director of credentialing at ATD and responsible for the overall management and leadership of the ATD Certification Institute. She was instrumental in the development of the Talent Development Capability Model. Morgean has devoted her career to advancing professions through the establishment of industry standards, providing strategic leadership and technical expertise in developing and implementing competency and credentialing programs. Morgean has led several organizations through establishing industry standards, including clinical research, K–12 ed tech leaders, and healthcare information systems. Prior to joining ATD, Morgean was CEO of Certified Fund Raising Executives International and was responsible for establishing international support across six continents for a unified standard of fundraising practice. Morgean lives in Alexandria, Virginia, and is active with the Institute for Credentialing Excellence (ICE).

References

La Prade, A., J. Mertens, T. Moore, and A. Wright. 2019. *The Enterprise Guide to Closing the Skills Gap*. IBM Institute for Business Value. ibm.com/thought-leadership/institute-business-value/report/closing-skills-gap.

Vital, C., M. Hirt, and P. Galagan. 2019. *Capabilities for Talent Development: Shaping the Future of the Profession* Alexandria, VA: ATD Press.

Recommended Resources

"Talent Development Body of Knowledge." Association for Talent Development. td.org/tdbok.

CHAPTER 6

Give Your Career a Boost With Certification

Rich Douglas

Harvard University president Derek Bok once said, "If you think education is expensive, try ignorance." Ask yourself, "Who is looking out for your professional development?" Talent development professionals focus on their clients, customers, and employees. But what about their own growth and development? Who develops the developer? You do.

> **IN THIS CHAPTER:**
> - Define the requirements that make talent development a profession
> - Name useful distinctions between growth and development
> - Describe three types of professional credentials
> - Select credentials most relevant to your professional development
> - Discuss the potential impact of earning a professional degree

Your education can make a huge difference as you perform your jobs and roles. But often that's not enough. It helps if other stakeholders in your career—your employers, clients, and training subjects—know what you've learned as well. You can go just about anywhere to learn something, but you need a credential to prove to others that you've completed the course or workshop.

Let's look at your options to earn career-related credentials to boost your career and your position in the talent development profession. We'll discuss what identifies a profession, the differences between your growth and development, and three categories of credentials, as well as an in-depth argument for one of them. Along the way we'll hear from practitioners who have earned talent development certifications and how those pursuits influenced their careers. Finally, we'll wrap with some questions (and answers) about earning credentials.

Talent Development—Occupation or Profession?

Are you a professional at what you do as a talent developer? Is talent development even a profession, or is it an occupation instead? This section answers these questions, makes the argument for why you should be a talent development professional, and offers ways to become one.

> When my manager introduced me to the Association for Talent Development, I got a lot of reference material and realized that this profession has multiple dimensions. —Patricia Torres, APTD

An occupation is a job family that is distinct from other job families, such as tollbooth operator, postal carrier, or pool cleaner. A profession, on the other hand, is distinctly different and includes three requirements: a body of knowledge, entry requirements and certifications, and a professional organization.

- **Body of knowledge.** Does your occupation have a distinct body of knowledge? The skills, abilities, and values practitioners agree are necessary to practice effectively? Talent development does. The Association for Talent Development (ATD) recently published its first body of knowledge, which is designed around ATD's Talent Development Capability Model and the knowledge that TD professionals require. The Talent Development Body of Knowledge (TD BoK) describes the personal, professional, and organizational capabilities talent development professionals need to master to practice at the top of their profession. Personal capabilities, for example, include emotional intelligence, communication skills, and lifelong learning. Professional capabilities include skills such as learning sciences, instructional design, and training delivery. Organizational capabilities include knowledge such as business insight, consulting, and change management. Together, these sets of skills describe a talent development professional's required capabilities.

- **Entry requirements.** Typically, a profession has a set of entry requirements. Some, like medicine and law, are controlled by the government, while others, like talent development, HR, and coaching, are prescribed and controlled by members of the profession. Because it is not controlled by law, anyone can call themselves a "talent development professional." Talent development, as a profession, sets its entry requirements through certification and organizational membership.
- **Certification.** An important indicator that you are part of a profession instead of an occupation is the presence of a certification process. Are practitioners in your field being recognized by the field for what they know, what they can do, and what they value? The field of talent development has two—the Associate Professional in Talent Development (APTD) and the more advanced Certified Professional in Talent Development (CPTD)—which are offered by the Association for Talent Development Certification Institute. Both credentials are earned by meeting the criteria and successfully passing a certification examination. Here are brief descriptions of each:
  - *APTD*. The capabilities covered in the APTD exam are the basics of talent development that professionals can use every day, no matter the level within an organization or company.
  - *CPTD*. The Certified Professional in Talent Development (CPTD) is a professional certification for TD professionals with at least five years of experience. It is broad and measures a professional's knowledge and skill application across the breadth of talent development capabilities.
- **Professional organization.** The Association for Talent Development was established in 1943 to advance the practice of trainers and developers around the world. The world's largest organization of its kind, ATD has more than 30,000 members from more than 120 countries, with more than 100 local chapters. As the leading professional organization in our field, ATD sets forth the profession's standards of practice and certification requirements, and advances the practice of talent development throughout the world.

> The CPTD exam was just the first step of my journey into the learning and development field. —Madeline Mbeh, CPTD

Clearly, talent development qualifies as a profession. So, are you a talent development professional? There is no one right answer to the question—it's a sliding scale—but there are many things you can do to establish yourself in the talent development profession:

- **Join ATD and your local chapter.** Get involved in activities and take advantage of the resources available to members.

- **Earn a higher degree in a segment of the talent development field,** like training and development, coaching, or organization development.
- **Earn a credential.** Whether it's the APTD or CPTD, a certificate, or another degree, get recognized for the abilities you have as a talent developer.
- **Advance the profession (and your career)** by being the best talent developer you can be!

A solid rationale exists for choosing talent development as a profession. Knowing a path exists to give your career a boost is helpful. So, how can you focus on your own growth and development?

Growth and Development

The terms *growth* and *development* are frequently lumped together, but they are two distinct concepts. When considering the pursuit of a career-enhancing credential, it is vital to know which one you are pursuing.

- **Growth** is horizontal, focused on the present. Think about taking a new position. Sure, there are a lot of things you are already good at—they hired you, right? However, typically, you'll have to learn a lot of other things to become proficient at your new job: things you need to know and be able to do, and values you will need to adopt. Only by consolidating (becoming completely capable) at this level can you be ready to develop to the next.
- **Development** is vertical, focused on the future. In career terms, horizontal growth is focused on consolidating what is required in your current situation or position. Vertical development leads to building greater capacity and toward larger responsibilities and opportunities.

Think of yourself as a bucket that can be filled with capabilities. Vertical development is about increasing your capabilities—building a bigger bucket. By paying attention to growth (filling the bucket with more capabilities) and development (making the bucket bigger by increasing capacity), you can progress in your career as a talent development professional. Earning a credential can help you accomplish either one—or both.

> While I am an effective career coach and trainer, I soon realized that I wasn't always speaking the same language as those who do talent development full time, highlighting my lack of industry expertise. —Craig Engstrom, CPTD

Credentials

Credentials document an individual's mastery of a body of knowledge—and performance-related accomplishments—and are issued by external bodies. They act as proxies—that is, they speak about your abilities when you're not there. When put on a resume, website, business card, book jacket, or LinkedIn page, they say something about you, your abilities, and your experience. The type of credential issued, who issued it, and what you did to earn it can go a long way in defining your place in the talent development profession.

Credentials matter to professionals. The three most common credentials are certificates, certifications, and degrees, and we'll look at each in more detail here. Use the Credential Consideration Tool to identify the factors to consider when selecting which credential to pursue. You will find it on the handbook website at ATDHandbook3.org.

> Like many others in the talent development field, I'm what we call an "accidental trainer." One day I was an architect and the next I was in learning and development. I started considering a certification soon after my promotion but always hesitated and doubted my readiness. Then I heard about the APTD pilot. The thrill of the unknown as well as the idea of contributing to something bigger got me. —Aya Medhat, CPTD

Certificates

Not to be confused with certification, certificates document the completion of a learning program. These programs can be as short as one day or as long as several months. There are no controls on who issues a certificate or for what. It's up to each person—both the recipient and others who see it—to decide how much to make of a certificate. While you might not want to put a certificate issued by your employer for completing a workplace safety seminar on your resume or LinkedIn page, be sure to highlight that three-month executive development program you took over the summer at an Ivy League school!

Certifications

Certifications differ from certificates in many substantial ways. First, certifications are issued by either governmental agencies (these are often called licenses) or professional associations. Second, where a certificate might cover a subject related to your profession, a certification represents mastery of the knowledge, skills, and values of the entire profession. Finally, certification typically requires passing an examination, demonstrating extensive experience in the profession, and adhering to a code of ethics. Certifications also differ from certificates in that they must be maintained—through additional education and/or experience—and renewed periodically. If your profession has a certification—and talent development does—being a member of that profession means you should be certified by it.

> With no degree and limited experience, doors didn't open easily for me. When I was able to find training roles, it was usually for junior positions because companies couldn't see the value I could bring to them. At the time, the CPLP seemed a bit too lofty and didn't feel like the right fit for me. When the APTD pilot was announced, I jumped at the chance and studied hard. I saw the APTD as an opportunity to quantify my years of experience. —Rob Hoitt, CPTD

Earlier, I mentioned the two certifications issued by the ATD Certification Institute—the APTD and the CPTD. But they are by no means the only professional certifications relevant to talent development professionals. Here are a few others to consider:

- **SHRM-CP/SCP.** The Society for Human Resource Management (SHRM) issues two credentials, which are targeted toward either less-experienced practitioners (the Certified professional; SHRM-CP) or more experienced (the Senior Certified Professional; SHRM-SCP).
- **PHR and SPHR.** Some HR professionals hold credentials from the HR Certification Institute—the PHR (Professional in Human Resources) and SPHR (Senior Professional in HR).
- **PMP.** The Project Management Institute issues the Project Management Professional (PMP) designation. Talent developers are often faced with creating a learning project that requires scheduling, staffing, communication, risk management, and so on. Having a solid background in project management—a sure thing once you've obtained the PMP certification—can contribute to every talent development engagement's success.
- **ICF.** The International Coaching Federation is the most prominent professional association in the burgeoning field of coaching, offering three levels of certified coaches (associate, professional, and master). Coaching can contribute mightily to talent development because you'll be working with clients far beyond the classroom (or online) curriculum and can help alleviate the challenge of transferring learning into performance.

Degrees

Another form of professional credentialing is the degree. Unlike certificates (which can be issued by just about anyone) and certifications (which are managed by professional associations), degrees are awarded only by colleges and universities. They require one to several years of full- or part-time study. Earning a degree, especially one related to your profession, can be extremely valuable. While they come in many forms, there are three basic types to consider:

- **Bachelor's.** Awarded for four years of study (or the equivalent), this degree covers a batch of knowledge, both in the area of specialty (major) and across a wide array of general educational topics. Earning a bachelor's degree demonstrates you have learned the basics of your profession. (This assumes your degree is related to your profession. It may not be.)
- **Master's.** Typically requiring one or more years of study beyond the bachelor's degree, master's program graduates have mastered the skills and knowledge in their fields. Unlike the bachelor's degree, the entire curriculum of a master's degree is focused on the major field of study.
- **Doctorate.** With two or more years of study beyond the master's degree, people who complete a doctorate go beyond their field's established body of knowledge, creating new knowledge or practice to advance the entire profession.

Credentials and the Talent Development Professional

When talent development professionals pursue higher credentials—certificates, certifications, or degrees—there are many benefits. Here are a few:

- **Increased relevance of talent development.** Our field has been fighting for decades to get the respect and attention it deserves in the organizational culture. Increasing the credentialing—and the professionalism—of its practitioners contributes to that effort.
- **Improved organizational results.** If we accept as an axiom that talent development leads to better performance, then so will improving the capabilities of practitioners.
- **Competition.** As a talent development professional, you compete everywhere you go. You compete for recognition and respect—and thus opportunities for impact—from your senior leaders. You compete for budgets and other resources. And you compete for future opportunities. Relevant credentials, along with the knowledge gain and recognition that come with them, can make you more competitive wherever you practice.

> I am a dentist with a scientific background and a vocation for education and sharing knowledge. I had the drive; I shape it through the certification. At some point I thought about recertifying to return to clinical practice, but now I am elated with the turn my profession has taken. I am not only a dentist, but also an Associate Professional in Talent Development who can provide knowledge about the clinical application of dental products in a way that is in sync with adult education principles. —Patricia Torres, APTD

But it's not just talent development professionals who benefit from earning credentials. Hiring managers can make better distinctions among job applicants. Employers get better results from more talented and capable staff—both the talent developers and the employees they develop. Finally, all the employees you work to develop will gain from your increased knowledge and capabilities as well.

> Whoever controls the tone of training and narrative of education has the most impact in organizations. —Shermaine Perry-Knights, CPTD

The Special Case for the Professional Doctorate

There are two types of academic doctorates: scholarly and professional. (A third type, the first-professional doctorate, is for specific fields like medicine and law and beyond our scope.)

Scholarly doctorates typically result in the award of a doctor of philosophy (PhD). These degrees are primarily (but not exclusively) designed to make original contributions to an academic discipline and prepare one for entering academia. However, many people earn a PhD and enter the workforce, and many who are already in the workforce opt for pursuing a PhD.

The *professional doctorate* is similar to the scholarly doctorate, with three big differences:
- The degree is designed for working professionals to continue in their careers.
- The research usually contributes to practice instead of scholarship or theory.
- PhD is not the degree designation—it is instead profession-specific, like doctor of education (EdD), doctor of business administration (DBA), or doctor of social science (DSocSci).

A person can also hold scholarly and professional degrees; for example, I have both a PhD and a DSocSci.

So, why would a talent development professional or other working professional consider pursuing a professional doctorate? Let's look at a few reasons:
- **Become a thought leader.** If you're so inclined, completing a doctorate can lead to other means and situations where you can share insights regarding your field. You can actually shape its future by mastering your field, connecting not only with the most forward-thinking people in your profession but also with the underlying scholarly theory and thinking that makes your field go.
- **Contribute to your field.** Not only will you master the knowledge of your particular field, you'll contribute to it. In a professional doctorate, you will develop methods and thinking that other practitioners can use to advance the profession.
- **Develop yourself.** You will also learn a lot as you're pursuing your doctorate. Not just from the curriculum, but also from the research you'll do for class assignments and your

dissertation. It will light a fire under you to push the boundaries of your profession and learn what lies beyond.
- **Advance in your career.** Earning a doctorate can be a career enhancer. Some employers will be intrigued by what you studied and what you learned—thinking that those are the people to work with.
- **Go into private practice.** Whether due to retirement, a need to get out of the rat race, or a desire to define and conduct your own practice your own way, there often comes a time when it makes sense to stop working for someone else and begin working for yourself. Earning a doctorate can help define who and what you will be in the future, a key aspect to understanding how you will practice. Plus, the credential can add credibility when engaging your clients.

Is pursuing a professional doctorate right for you? If you want to learn more about the complete field of study, as well as contribute to advancing it, then starting a professional doctorate in a field related to talent development might be an option for you.

Practitioners' Stories

Talent development professionals have a variety of credentialing experiences. Here is a sample:
- "On a day-to-day basis we fill a role, but we don't have a real understanding of an organization. I have 10 years of experience working in the industry and four of them with a more open-minded and contextual vision that my APTD certification gave me. Today, I realize how important it is for every employee to understand their contribution to the business objectives. An organization with employees who are clear about the vision and mission of the company will always be high performing. Change and transformation in a society and in organizations are possible thanks to the commitment of its members. My APTD helped me better understand what the business is about, and how each employee contributes to the organization's success and social evolution." —Patricia Torres, APTD
- "After earning the APTD and landing in my current role, I went back to college to complete a BA in education studies from the University of Arizona Global Campus. Last year, I also took advantage of the CPTD pilot and am now proud to hold that credential. To me, the biggest value of earning both credentials is that I now have the confidence to present myself to my current and future employers as a valuable asset to the teams I will be asked to support in the future." —Rob Hoitt, CPTD
- "The APTD and CPTD credentials gave me far more than four letters. They gave me guidance, direction, and a seat at the table. I may still be unsure of where I want to be, but I know where I stand now. Preparation made me aware of my strengths and development

areas, which made setting my next learning goal easier. After all I went through, I can confidently say the most important lesson from this experience is, 'Now is the time.'" —Aya Medhat, CPTD
- "In my eyes, completing the APTD and CPTD gave me courage. In others' eyes, it gave me legitimacy—what an excellent combination for ongoing success." —Craig Engstrom, CPTD
- "Few of us said, 'I want to be a learning and development professional when I grow up.' We all come from different backgrounds in this field, which makes it beautifully diverse. We are a group of people, each with our own stories, who are passionately driven to help others succeed. I am now able to firmly say, 'I want to be a learning and development professional when I grow up.'" —Madeline Mbeh, CPTD
- "Pursuing the CPTD widened my perspective about the field. Learning and development is complex, yet simple at the same time. This field incorporates both art and science. The credential's impact on my own learning is a deeper hunger for knowledge, and it sparked my desire to contribute research." —Shermaine Perry Knights, CPTD

Questions (and Answers)

Still have questions about credentials? Here are a few more things to think about.

What Does It Take to Get a Credential?

The commitment depends on what kind of credential you pursue and from where. But here are some basic guidelines: When you go after a credential, you give two things and receive two. First, you give your hard work and money. In return, you receive an education and recognition—a certificate, certification, or degree. You can get an education anywhere—sitting on opposite ends of a log discussing things with a mentor is one example. But you go to an institution to get a credential. Certificates tend to be the easiest and least expensive, certifications are typically more expensive and more difficult, and degrees are the longest and most costly to obtain. But individual choices vary widely.

Which Kind of Credential Should I Get?

This is a complicated question. The kind of credential you pursue really depends on two things: your current professional experience and education, and what you want to do with the credential. So, why might you pursue each?

- **Certificates.** These are effective in getting highly specialized learning quickly—sometimes as short as a day or a few hours. Short certificates are helpful in consolidating your current work role, while longer ones are helpful in developing yourself for future roles and responsibilities. However, certificates are not always powerful as credentials go—employers and clients may not recognize them, or even know you have them!

- **Certifications.** Being a professional means knowing the profession's body of knowledge and participating in its activities, growth, and development. You get that from earning one of the profession's certifications. Because of that, employers tend to recognize and know about certifications in many industries. Earning one can be a powerful career booster, sometimes even as much as a degree.
- **Degrees.** These are the most widely recognized credentials. Although having a bachelor's degree might not have a strong impact on your career, the lack of one can really hurt. A master's degree, on the other hand, can really separate you from other practitioners. A doctorate? It's a mixed bag—the degree itself may or may not enhance your career prospects. However, the knowledge you gain and the work you produce in a doctoral program will help identify who and what you are for the rest of your career.

In general: If you don't have a bachelor's degree, get one. If you have one, consider obtaining a master's degree or your industry's certification. If you have a junior certification, consider going after the senior version. If you have specific learning needs, take a look at certificates offered by training companies, organizations, and universities. Finally, if you're interested in taking your place in your profession at the pinnacle of its practice, take a look a professional doctorate.

Who Will Pay for My Credential?

There are a number of possibilities for financial assistance when it comes to paying for credentials. Some employers have tuition reimbursement or payment programs. Colleges and universities are often able to provide financial aid (loans and grants). Each situation is unique—be ready to negotiate payment and support for your professional ambitions. You should also be willing to pay for your own credential. If you see the value, invest in yourself. It's something you should do. After all, if you won't invest in yourself, why should anyone else?

Final Thoughts

Talent development is a profession. To take your place in it and be as effective as possible, consider earning credentials—certificates, certifications, or degrees—that advance both your capabilities and the profession as a whole.

About the Author

Rich Douglas, PhD, CPTD, is a performance consultant and principle of Rich Douglas Consulting. He has extensive public- and private-sector experience in training, management, leadership, and delivering talent development solutions. Rich has served as a faculty member for several universities. He holds a PhD specializing in nontraditional higher education from Union Institute and University and a doctor of social science in human resource development from the University of Leicester. He also holds the Senior Professional in Human Resources (SPHR), Certified Professional in Talent Development (CPTD), and Professional Certified Coach (PCC) designations. Rich resides in Phoenix, Arizona, with his wife, Paula.

References

"Association for Talent Development." td.org.
"HR Certification Institute." hrci.org.
"International Coaching Federation." coachingfederation.org.
"Project Management Institute." pmi.org.
"Society for Human Resource Management." shrm.org.

Recommended Resources

Bear, M., and T. Nixon. 2006. *Bear's Guide to Earning Degrees by Distance Learning.* Berkeley, CA: Ten Speed Press.

Biech, E. 2021. *Skills for Career Success: Maximizing Your Potential at Work.* Oakland, CA: Berrett-Koehler Publishers.

Douglas, R. 2020. *Purposeful Leadership Development: Advance Your Leadership for Results That Matter.* Self-published.

Phillips, J., P. Phillips, and T. Elkeles. *Chief Talent Officer: The Evolving Role of the Chief Learning Officer,* 2nd ed. New York: Routledge.

Smith, N.-J. 2008. *Achieving Your Professional Doctorate: A Handbook.* Berkshire, England: Open University Press.

CHAPTER 7

Thriving in Your Career: Powerful Plans for Lifelong Learning

Catherine Lombardozzi

How often do you stop to consider how much of a privilege and challenge it is to be a learning professional? Our work consistently puts us in the center of important changes in people's lives—starting a new job, upskilling to stay current, learning new tools and practices, and honing needed skill sets. Our organizations count on us to deliver the capabilities necessary to successfully complete initiatives and meet important goals. Organizational leaders and employees depend on us to enable them to be the best they can be.

To effectively provide this support, we need to be the best we can be. Our role is to be experts in the dynamics of learning and in the tools and techniques of our trade. Given that learning theory, tools, and techniques are constantly being advanced, mastering our trade is a lifelong process. Just like the people we aim to serve, we must continue to learn every day in an environment that is often demanding.

> **IN THIS CHAPTER:**
> - Describe practices for lifelong learning for talent development professionals
> - Provide guidance on creating the kinds of self-development plans necessary for a diverse career in a rapidly evolving industry

We need to be exemplars in the techniques and activities of learning and lead the way in demonstrating how to manage a challenging personal learning agenda. To do that, we'll need to apply the learning expertise, design skills, and tools we employ in our work to the service of designing our own learning plans. This chapter will give you reminders and insight on how to do that.

Practices for Lifelong Learning

> Lifelong learning: The provision or use of both formal and informal learning opportunities throughout people's lives in order to foster the continuous development and improvement of the knowledge and skills needed for employment and personal fulfilment. —*Collins English Dictionary*

The practices for lifelong learning combine to make you the expert you need to be. Not surprisingly, they are reflective of the overall arc of an effective learning and development project, starting with defining goals and ending with improved performance.

These are the practices you'll want to put into play, and they will be elaborated on in the rest of the chapter:

- **Committing to professional excellence.** Making room for your own professional development requires deep motivation. You'll need to have a compelling vision of the kind of professional you wish to be, and you'll need to pledge your dedication to achieving that level of practice.
- **Identifying development goals.** The skill set for an exceptional learning professional varies widely, so you'll have to start by defining the development you need in your role and context. Making progress depends on focusing on specific knowledge or skills so you can strengthen the most important areas for you.
- **Designing learning plans.** How you go about developing your skills depends on the nature of the targeted skill, your projects, your work environment, and your time commitment. There are several approaches you may find useful for different situations (which are described later in the chapter). Regardless of the overall approach, you'll want to research and curate the best resources and activities for your need and organize how you will tackle working your way through them.
- **Applying learning skill.** As you work through learning materials, you need to activate learning processes that help you to translate those inputs into guidance for future action. Successful self-directed learners exhibit a specific set of qualities and skills that you'll want to cultivate.

- **Demonstrating mastery.** In the end, your goal is to employ your skills in the work of helping others succeed. As a professional, you should have some evidence of your mastery in the form of project artifacts, portfolios, and endorsements.

Committing to Professional Excellence

Working in a profession means you have a calling that requires a specialized body of knowledge. While many professions require deep academic preparation for entry, talent development does not. Still, those who work in talent development need to make a commitment to developing a deep understanding of the underlying theory and advanced techniques of the work. That's where lifelong learning comes in.

Most talent development professionals manage their own professional learning. They identify the knowledge and skill they need for their roles and seek out the training and development activities they need to ground their work. They also take pride in learning by doing and gathering experiences that allow them to claim certain skill sets. All that requires a certain amount of dedication and pride. Your first step in your own development is envisioning the level of knowledge and skill you need to be effective—to be the expert that your clients, business partners, learners, and peers need you to be.

What does professional excellence look like in talent development? Professional organizations in our field have invested energy in cataloging the necessary capabilities, and they have created comprehensive competency lists and standards. These analyses make it clear that experts need both the technical skills of talent development and core professional and business skills to be successful.

You can use these capability lists to self-assess your current skill set and define any areas that need further development. While individual professionals likely need only a subset of these skills to competently perform, these competency lists set out aspirational goals for expertise in a variety of areas in our field. Additional information and the URLs can be found at ATDHandbook3.org.

- **Talent Development Capability Model from the Association for Talent Development.** This model defines 23 capabilities in three domains: personal capability, professional capability, and organizational capability.
- **Learning and Performance Institute Capability Map.** This map defines 25 capabilities in five practice areas: strategy and operations, design and development, learning facilitation, performance and impact, and learning support. Each capability is behaviorally anchored at four levels of expertise: foundational, proficient, advanced, and strategic.
- **Learning and Development Capability Framework from the Asia Pacific Institute for Learning and Performance.** This framework defines key behaviors for 18 capabilities

across six dimensions: professional attributes, strategy and planning, design and development, execution and delivery, evaluation and feedback, and business smarts.
- **International Board of Standards for Training, Performance, and Instruction (ibstpi).** Ibstpi offers role-based competencies and standards for instructional designers, instructors, training managers, and evaluators.

Some professionals may also want to examine broader competency sets for human resource professionals. Here are a few to explore:
- **CIPD New Profession Map.** This map defines six core knowledge areas, eight core behaviors, and nine areas of specialist knowledge. These specialties include learning and development, talent management, and organization development and design, as well as people analytics, diversity and inclusion, employee experience, employee relations, resourcing, and rewards. Each of the knowledge areas, behaviors, and specialist areas are further defined by standards at the foundation level, associate level, chartered member level, and chartered fellow level.
- **SHRM Body of Competency and Knowledge.** This competency set recognizes behavioral competencies in three domains (leadership, business, and interpersonal), along with technical competencies in 15 HR functional areas, including learning and development, organization effectiveness and development, and diversity and inclusion. The body of knowledge identifies proficiency indicators at the core and advanced levels.
- **HR Certification Institute.** These competency sets cover five functional areas with different weights and specifics depending on the kind of certification desired: business management and strategic leadership, talent planning and acquisition, learning and development, reward systems, employee and labor relations, and engagement. HRCI certifies professional and senior professionals in human resources and other specialties.

Identifying Development Goals

If you explore published capability lists, quality review checklists, and job descriptions, one of the first things you'll notice is that the skill set in talent development is incredibly varied—and virtually impossible for one person to have. Your first task in managing your professional development then is to identify your personal development goals and ensure they're aligned with your situation and career trajectory.

Your goal selection is influenced by many factors, and often through more than one of these lenses:
- **Career intentions.** Consider the role you want to play or the kind of work in which you want to engage. Review job descriptions for the role or talk to hiring managers or people in the role to get a sense of what you'll need to be successful. Evaluate yourself against that set of criteria and note what you need to strengthen.

- **Feedback.** Refer to your appraisals or seek more detailed feedback from your peers, supervisors, and clients. If you are being derailed because you lack a specific area, that may need to be a priority. Otherwise, look for areas that are solid but need to be enhanced to take you to the next level.
- **Strengths.** Marcus Buckingham's work has shown that people grow the most in the areas that are their strengths—with *strengths* defined as skills that make you feel confident and put you into a flow state. Consider the activities that get your energy flowing and make goals that advance those skills so you can add more value when engaging in work activities.
- **Skill stacking.** One of the things that makes you unique is your particular set of skills and experiences. Consider strengthening your knowledge and skills in different areas that could give you a niche practice area. For example, you could cultivate a combination of skills (such as consulting and e-learning design) or practices for a particular industry or role (for example, training for nurses). Align your development goals to bolster these skills.
- **Competency development.** You can assess yourself against any of the competency frameworks cited in the previous section and select development goals based on that analysis. Your own organization may also have a competency model to guide your evaluation.
- **Trend analysis.** Keep an eye on where the profession is going. Perhaps you want to develop skills in designing learning experiences that use virtual reality or augmented reality or any of the other up-and-coming specialties. The field is constantly changing and there is always an opportunity to be on the leading edge.

Once you have a sense of the topic you want to pursue, it's useful to put together a short list of guiding questions for your learning project. You don't need to create formal learning objectives; in all likelihood, you won't have enough background in the topic to know what those formal objectives might be. Instead, decide what you want to explore and use that to guide your selection of learning materials and activities.

When pursuing a complex or long-term goal, there are two additional points to consider. One is to articulate why you are embarking on this journey: What do you hope to be able to do with the knowledge base or skill? And what is your driving motivation? To manage your own development, you'll need to have a compelling why to fuel your persistence. The other point is to put some markers down so you can track your progress. Imagine a long novice-to-expert continuum with a scale from 0 (no knowledge or skill at all) to 10 (expert), then make note of where you are currently and where you want to be once you've completed this project (note that this does not need to be all the way to expert level). Whenever it's time to reassess, you can use this scale to gauge your progress.

Designing Learning Plans

Once you know where your learning journey is heading, you can make a plan for exploring the arena you chose. The nature of your plan will depend on the nature of the learning project. In general, there are three types of plans:

- **Reskilling or upskilling plan.** This is an intense, focused effort for developing a new skill or substantially deepening a skill you have. The process of addressing a skilling need encompasses identifying a learning need, curating materials and activities, making a learning plan, learning, applying, and self-assessing progress.
- **Continuous professional development plan.** This is a longer-term, consistent pursuit that helps you keep a finger on the pulse of the areas of L&D that are important to you. Planning for continuous professional development involves first isolating a knowledge base or skill that you want to deliberately develop over time, then curating sources (who's putting out high-quality content in this area) and setting up feeds (journals, social media, internet alerts), and, finally, taking note of news and advances that enrich your perspective (continuous learning). This kind of plan usually contains more ongoing activities than a skilling plan; it's heavy on continuous learning sources, social learning, regular participation in professional gatherings, and consistent reflection and application activities.
- **Spot learning plan.** A quick search for resources, this plan can be immediately applied to your in-the-flow-of-work learning needs and curiosities. Spot learning is a relatively simple process of searching for material, vetting for credibility, learning from your found sources, and applying that learning to the work. This approach generally requires just a few well-chosen resources.

In truth, many professionals often wind up running these different plans simultaneously. You can imagine, for example, that a designer may want to upskill for e-learning design while still keeping core instructional design skills sharp and one day needing a quick refresher on the functionality of an e-learning course development tool.

The elements of these three plans are similar: you'll need a set of resources from which to learn; activities to process your learning and practice your new knowledge and skill; social supports in the form of co-learners, discussion partners, teachers, and feedback providers; and strategies for applying what you've learned and verifying that you're indeed grasping the concepts and skills. All the while you keep re-evaluating whether you are getting what you need so you can redirect your efforts if necessary.

Curating Learning Resources

When you go looking for learning resources and people with whom to network, look beyond the first few pages of your internet search. Seek specific kinds of resources to diversify and deepen your inputs and activities. It's important to have both inputs (readings, videos, and courses) and activities (people with whom to engage, assignments, and application projects).

When selecting resources and activities, consider where you are on the novice-to-expert continuum for the specific knowledge base or skill you are targeting. People on the novice-to-competent end are more likely to benefit from formal training or education, while people at the competent-to-expert end generally need more social and experiential learning. You should have diverse inputs and activities to be sure, but keep in mind what you hope to gain from each so you can prioritize finding the right kinds of resources.

Take the time to research options, but know that this will likely turn up substantially more options than you'll be able to complete. That's why curation is necessary. A worksheet that will help you decide which materials and activities are worth investing is available on the handbook's website at ATDHandbook3.org. To curate, evaluate the quality of the material, its depth, its relevance to your context, and the credibility of its sources. (Even if you are executing a spot learning plan, be sure to vet your sources! The internet is, unfortunately, full of bad advice too.) Use your professional network to get recommendations and help assess your options.

Table 7-1. A Guide to Curation

Type	Description	Advice
Learning materials	Books, articles, videos	• Seek out compelling long-form resources that provide nuance and detail • Check the credibility of authors
Continuous learning sources	Podcasts, professional journals, academic journals, social media	• Look for those that are frequently talking about your topic of interest • Check the credibility of authors • Build a professional learning network
Social learning	Peers, co-learners, collaborators, subject matter experts, role models, coaches, supervisors, teachers, feedback-providers, mentors	• Engage with people with whom you can have extensive, candid conversations and from whom you can learn a great deal • Consider the kind of social learning you need in this project and align people accordingly • Secure support from other professionals, arrange meetings, and follow their work on social channels • Be sure to have an accountability partner—someone who will urge you to stay on track

Table 7-1. A Guide to Curation (cont.)

Type	Description	Advice
Professional gatherings	Conferences, local professional meetings, vendor webinars	• Look for topics of interest, quality of speakers, and depth of content • Network to learn from others' experiences in those venues so you can select and engage in these gatherings wisely • Be sensitive to potential source bias (such as people who are focused more on positioning their products or services than on educating professionals)
Certifications and training	Workshops and extended development programs, some of which certify mastery of a specific knowledge base or skill	• Check professional organizations and offerings from well-known experts • Investigate reviews, credibility of instructors, and market value of credentials offered
Education	Academic degrees and certificate programs	• Network to learn the best academic programs for your needs • Check Coursera and other MOOC platforms for content you can access for free (you will likely need to pay for a certificate of completion from a MOOC)
Reflection activities	Actions you take to process what you've learned and prepare to apply it (e.g., discussion, journaling, coaching, and making checklists and job aids)	• Recognize that this is a critical part of the learning process • Make a habit of pausing for reflection!
Application activities	Projects or tasks you perform in context that use the knowledge and skill you are developing	• Start with small projects or specific tasks • Arrange for feedback if possible or develop quality criteria to check yourself

Making a Plan

Once you have an idea of all you want to include in your plan, you'll want to treat it like any other project and give yourself assignments and deadlines. Organize the activities into a general flow that stems from typical organizing principles (for example, moving from general materials to specific or weaving activities between various learning inputs).

Decide when and how much time you'll invest in these studies on a weekly basis and set goals and assignments for the reserved blocks of time. This will keep you from wasting time on just deciding what to do. Share your plan with your accountability partner and request any additional advice. Consider sharing it with your supervisor as well to gather support.

You'll know you have a good plan if you've described a clear goal, curated high-quality learning materials, identified dynamic social learning companions, integrated deep reflection and consolidation activities, and defined challenging, authentic practice and application opportunities.

Applying Learning Skill

The most important part of the project is to execute the plan. Keep your driving goal and guiding questions in mind as you engage in all the activities you have mapped out. Keep notes and notice progress at every step.

Your ability to navigate a self-directed learning plan requires a certain skill set and attitude. Research in self-directed learning consistently calls out these qualities (Lombardozzi 2020):

- **Motivation.** Planning for and attending to your own learning project in the midst of other demands requires dedication and commitment. The strongest motivations are internal, from your own desires and sense of self. You'll need this motivation to maintain persistence in the face of obstacles.
- **Self-efficacy.** The belief that you can learn is context and resource specific. You'll need your generalized growth mindset as a foundation, but then you'll want to nurture your conviction that your efforts will pay off and give you the outcomes you desire.
- **Self-assessment.** Managing your own learning requires candor and strength in assessing your own competency. You use that skill in defining your goal, and you'll use it again to assess progress. Note, however, that humans are particularly ineffective in judging their own performance, so be sure to request feedback and listen carefully to others' inputs.
- **Resourcefulness.** Despite how easy it is to search the internet or reach out to your network of peers, finding and vetting resources and activities is a tough job. You'll want to cultivate digital savviness and interpersonal networking skills to find and engage with the best resources. Hone your internet search skills, develop techniques for building your network, and always look for a window when a door closes.
- **Planning skill.** When putting together your schedule, use what you know about the dynamics of your own learning (and adult learning in general) to design an impactful flow of activities. It's critical that you reserve time and plan for how to use it. To ensure you don't waste time, make a plan before you begin. But you'll also want to be ready to adjust that plan as things come up, all the while keeping an eye on self-imposed deadlines.
- **Learning skill.** Learning under your own direction requires your full array of learning skills, including discourse, annotating, note-taking, reflection, retention, critical thinking, problem solving, and synthesizing. However, the most critical skill is your ability to translate what you've learned into guidance for future action.

As a parallel effort, you'll want to evaluate the degree to which you have these qualities and skills for your project. If you find that you're weak in some areas, you should include activities in your plan that shore them up along the way. For example, define behaviorally anchored criteria for self-evaluation. Or create reflection questions for a book or long article you plan to read and take the time to write down your thoughts. Or quickly review recommended practices for making a checklist (a spot learning project) as you set about creating one based on the information you've gathered.

While you are in the process of learning and taking notes, consider how you want to change your behavior going forward. It's useful to plan to make these new practices a habit if you can. Habituation requires you to:

- Clearly identify what you want to do and why.
- Set up a reminder about your commitment to that behavior.
- Make it as easy as possible to implement the behavior.
- Designate a positive outcome to the action (possibly rewarding yourself).

It's important to define exactly how you will integrate new knowledge and skills into your way of working to ensure that your new knowledge is not simply tucked away and never used.

The beauty of managing your own plan is that you have the luxury of rethinking it at any time. Regularly assess whether you are making progress. Notice potential side journeys and figure out where they fall in your list of priorities. If your curated resources and activities don't live up to your expectations, revise them to ensure you are getting the kind of depth and challenge you need.

If (read: when) your plan goes off track, evaluate causes. Shore up supports and mitigate barriers that ensure you can stay on plan. Get back into the flow as quickly as possible and evaluate how the delay will affect the plan going forward.

Demonstrating Mastery

Most adult learning projects are initiated to enable you to do something. The ultimate measure of success, then, is the degree to which you are able to demonstrate mastery of the knowledge and skill you've been pursuing. And the real proof of that is application in the real world.

As noted, your plan should include application projects. To start out, you could take on small parts of a project or specific tasks of a process, or you may ask to be assigned to a team of people who are sharing the work. If you aren't in a position to do the work, you can create mock projects to flesh out your portfolio. When you are practicing or applying, it's useful to get feedback from a knowledgeable party rather than rely on your own imperfect judgment of your performance.

As a professional, you should have a portfolio that demonstrates what you are able to do, and its elements can include exhibits beyond the obvious project artifacts and endorsements. These can include in-depth practice or demonstration projects as proof of concept for what you know how to do. You can also consider keeping a public blog or engaging in some other way of working out loud. These serve the dual purpose of contributing to the profession's common knowledge base and showcasing your growing expertise. Contributions to professional conferences and journals do the same. Overall, it's wise to have a digital presence that serves as a resume or calling card of sorts so that people can easily see what you have to offer.

Final Thoughts

Our profession puts primary value on outcomes and performance, too often glossing over the deep learning that enables exceptional work. As learning professionals, though, we should be expert learners and exemplars for our colleagues in other roles. We should apply what we know about adult learning, learning strategy, design, and quality learning products to the task when designing and executing our own learning projects.

The work of talent development breeds a huge array of roles and work products. Your specialization may change many times over the course of your career. The tools and techniques of the talent development field and the challenges we're encountering in our work are also constantly evolving, and that changing kaleidoscope of needs requires us to evolve our own capabilities as well.

Learning enables human flourishing, and it is no doubt a lifelong process. You can find inspiration and energy in the reinforcing cycle wherein your learning improves the learning and performance strategies you recommend to clients, which in turn improves the talent development initiatives that feed the capabilities organizations need to succeed. Learning starts with you, and it never ends.

About the Author

Catherine Lombardozzi is a lifelong learning and development practitioner and founder of Learning 4 Learning Professionals. Her work focuses on supporting the professional development of designers, facilitators, faculty, consultants, and learning leaders through coaching, consulting, workshops, and development programs. As an active workplace learning professional with nearly 35 years' experience, Catherine often contributes to professional conferences and journals, and she teaches graduate-level courses in adult learning, instructional design, digital learning, and consulting. She is author of *Learning Environments by Design* and holds a doctoral degree in human and organizational learning from George Washington University. Learn more at L4LP.com.

References

Lombardozzi, C. 2020. *Self-Directed Learning: Essential Strategy for a Rapidly Changing World*. Santa Rosa, CA: Learning Guild.

Recommended Resources

Biech, E. 2021. *Skills for Career Success: Maximizing Your Potential at Work*. Oakland, CA: Berrett-Koehler Publishers.

Cohen, D.J. 2016. *Developing Proficiency in HR: 7 Self-Directed Activities for HR Professionals*. Alexandria, VA: Society for Human Resource Management.

Lombardozzi, C. 2021. *Charting Your Course Workbook and Guidebook*. Wilmington, DE: L4LP.com.

McLagan, P. 2017. *Unstoppable You: Adopt the New Learning 4.0 Mindset and Change Your Life*. Alexandria, VA: ATD Press.

CHAPTER 8

The Irreplaceable Growth Mindset

Ryan Gottfredson

As a training and development professional, you have two primary jobs: to personally and continually learn and develop, and to help others learn and develop. Your ability to fulfill these jobs effectively is significantly influenced by something as small as your mindset—the mental lens you use to view the world. In this chapter I'll share a couple fascinating research studies that demonstrate this.

IN THIS CHAPTER:
- Describe what mindsets are and the foundational role they play in how people operate
- Discover the difference between fixed and growth mindsets
- Determine how possessing a growth mindset is essential to your success as a trainer and developer
- Explain the empowerment of developing a growth mindset and how to help others do the same

Let's start by examining a couple studies to find what you can learn about your growth mindset.

Study 1: Helping Yourself Learn and Grow

Several studies exist that provide insight into how you can help yourself learn. In one study, researchers had individuals take a mindset assessment (Diener and Dweck 1978). Those who scored low were designated as Group 1, while those who scored high were designated as Group 2. The researchers then gave them all the same task: an exam with eight easy questions and four really difficult ones. The purpose was to have them go from success to failure. They wanted to see if the participants would respond differently to failure depending on their mindsets.

Sure enough, that is what they found. They observed that those in Group 1 were rather pleased with themselves during the first eight easy questions, but as soon as they hit the four difficult questions, they quickly became depressed and engaged in negative self-talk. They also stopped applying themselves as they began guessing at the answers or even making attempts to avoid the task altogether.

Those in Group 2, on the other hand, responded in almost the exact opposite fashion. When they hit the hard questions, they dug in more vigorously, engaged in positive self-talk and remained optimistic, and continued to work hard to get the questions right.

Which group seems more likely to learn and develop? Group 1, who became disgruntled when faced with something they didn't understand? Or Group 2, who exerted greater effort when faced with something they didn't understand?

Study 2: Helping Others Learn and Grow

In another study, researchers engaged three different sample groups to see if mindset influenced the degree to which managers helped their subordinates learn and develop (Heslin, Vandewalle, and Latham 2006). In the first two groups, the researchers asked the managers to take a mindset assessment and then asked their subordinates to rate how well their managers engaged in effective coaching practices (such as providing clear performance expectations and constructive feedback, helping solving problems, and inspiring them to realize their potential). What they found across both studies was that the managers who scored higher on the mindset assessment were significantly more likely to engage in effective coaching practices.

In the third group, the researchers designed an experiment to see if they could help those who scored low on the mindset assessment improve their coaching practices after a mindset training. To do this, they divided a group of people who had scored low on the mindset assessment into two groups. One group was given a placebo training (which didn't deal with mindsets). The second group was given a training session on the desired mindset in question. Then, six weeks after the training, they watched two videotaped instances of poor negotiation performance and were instructed to list, in bullet-point format, suggestions for how the employees in the videos might improve their negotiation performance. The researchers found that those who had gone through the mindset training six weeks earlier were more likely to provide higher-quantity and higher-quality feedback than those in the placebo training.

Thus it was shown that people who either scored high on the mindset assessment or were provided training to improve their mindsets were more capable of helping others learn and develop.

Lessons to Be Learned From the Research

The studies focused on the difference between two mindsets: fixed mindsets (more negative) and growth mindsets (more positive). What they demonstrate is that your effectiveness as a training and development professional hinges upon your mindset—how you view the world.

Something that should stand out is that none of the people involved in these studies was likely conscious of whether they had a fixed or growth mindset. But each one likely believed they were seeing and reacting to their world in the best way possible.

If you want to elevate your effectiveness as a training and development professional, it is critical that you awaken to the quality of your current mindset. Then, if necessary, you need to work to improve your mindset so you're better internally programmed to learn and develop yourself and help others do the same. If you want to start this journey now, visit https://ryangottfredson.com/personal-mindset-assessment to take a free mindset assessment to determine whether you have a fixed or growth mindset.

The purpose of this chapter is to help you harness the power of the growth mindset so you can be more effective at fulfilling your two primary jobs as a training and development professional. By awakening to and improving your mindset, you will be both more willing and able to continually develop yourself and be more effective at developing others.

What Are Mindsets?

Most people consider mindsets to be akin to their attitude about something. But they are so much more than that. In fact, psychologists and neuroscientists have both independently identified our mindset as being the most foundational aspect of ourselves for why we do what we do.

Here is my favorite definition: Mindsets are mental lenses that selectively organize and encode information, thereby orienting an individual toward a unique way of understanding an experience and guiding one toward corresponding actions and responses (Crum, Salovey, and Achor 2007).

While mindsets are often described as "mental lenses," they are actually long-range neural connections that span across our brain's three major regions (the reptilian brain, mammalian brain, and human brain). These neural connections serve three primary jobs:

- **They filter unique information into our mind.** The reality is that our body sends our brain way more signals than we can process. So, we need a filter that allows in only the most salient signals. Our mindsets serve as this filter. In Study 1, when participants hit the four hard questions, their mindsets likely cued into the fact that the questions were more challenging than the questions before.
- **They interpret the filtered information in unique ways.** To respond effectively to the situations we encounter, we need a mechanism that quickly and automatically assigns meaning to things. Our mindsets serve as this meaning maker. When two different people assign different meanings to the same thing, we are able to get a sense of their mindsets (or their "meaning makers"). In Study 1, those in Group 1 interpreted their struggles with the four hard questions as a sign that they were less than, a failure, not very smart, or not of value; those in Group 2 interpreted their struggles with the four hard questions as an opportunity to learn and grow.
- **They activate other personal traits.** By engaging our personality traits or self-regulatory strategies, our mindset helps us best navigate the situations we encounter based on the information that's filtered in and how it is interpreted. In Study 1, those in Group 1 interpreted their struggle as an indication about their abilities, which then activated a defense response (give up or stop applying yourself) to protect them from feeling bad. Those in Group 2 interpreted their struggle as an opportunity to learn and grow, which then activated an approach response to dig deeper and continue to apply themselves.

Because our mindsets play these three initial roles in our mind's processing, they are our most foundational element (Gottfredson and Reina 2020). Understanding this has important implications for both our personal development and the development of those we work with. If we want to improve our behaviors or if we want others to improve their behaviors, we are going to be most effective if we go to the foundational aspect of ourselves—our mindsets. If we try to change behaviors without focusing on mindsets, what commonly happens is that the prevailing mindset resists the changes in behaviors we are trying to promote.

Fixed and Growth Mindsets

Researchers have identified different mindset sets based upon how different people interpret and respond to the same situations (Gottfredson and Reina 2020). Generally, these include two different mindsets that represent two poles of a continuum, with one mindset leading to more negative interpretations and responses and the other leading to more positive interpretations and responses.

The set that has received the most attention over the last 40 years is the fixed and growth mindset. This mindset set has been proven repeatedly to play a foundational role in a person's learning and development effectiveness (Gottfredson and Reina 2020).

Based on this research, we can confidently position a fixed mindset at the negative end of the continuum and a growth mindset at the positive end of the continuum. As you learn more about the differences between these two mindsets, the information is going to seem rather black and white, but the reality is that there is a spectrum of shades of gray. In other words, the mindsets people actually possess will fall somewhere along the continuum. Very rarely are individuals fully at one pole or the other.

Fixed Mindset

When someone possesses a fixed mindset, they believe that people are unable to change their talents, abilities, or intelligence. Their worldview includes the notion that they are who they are, and there is nothing they can really do about it. To them, who they are now is who they were five years ago; and who they are going to be five years from now is the same person they are now.

Because those with a fixed mindset don't believe that they can change their talents, abilities, or intelligence, they tend to see the world in terms of "haves" and "have-nots." If they fail at something, they interpret that failure as though they are a "have-not" and, because they believe they can't change, they won't be able to become a "have." To avoid feeling like a "have-not," research has found that those with a fixed mindset possess an internal operating system that is programmed to avoid failure. They always want to put themselves in a position where they will look good. Thus, they tend to avoid challenges and give up easily when the going gets tough. If something doesn't come naturally, it is an indication that they are a "have-not" in that thing, and thus they are not inclined to exert a lot of effort to improve or persevere.

Let me give you a personal example to bring this to life. During my freshman year of college, I wanted to become a medical doctor, so I signed up for the "weeder" pre-med chemistry class. At the end of the course, I got the lowest grade I had ever received: a "C." To me, this was a failing grade. With my fixed mindset, the way I interpreted this was that I was a "have-not" when it came to chemistry and that I could never become a "have." So, I changed my major—no sense continuing on the path to become a medical doctor if I was a "have-not."

Growth Mindset

When someone possesses a growth mindset, they believe that people can change their talents, abilities, and intelligence. To them, who they are now is a different, and hopefully better, version of who they were five years ago, and who they are now is only a shadow of who they are going to be in five years.

Because those with a growth mindset do believe they can change their talents, abilities, and intelligence, they don't see the world in terms of "haves" and "have-nots." If they fail at something, that doesn't preclude them from being a "have" in the future with some hard work and effort, even if they're a "have-not" right now.

With this outlook, they are not concerned about avoiding failure and looking good. They are concerned about learning and growing and improving themselves to better contribute to the people, groups, and organizations they serve. They may even see failure as the best way to learn and grow. And, they believe that effort, not natural talent, is what leads to success. Research has repeatedly found that because of these mentalities, those with a growth mindset exert greater effort and persistence than those with a fixed mindset, particularly in the face of adversity.

Now having learned about fixed and growth mindsets, I can't help but look back on my freshman chemistry class and wonder what might have been had I possessed a growth mindset instead of a fixed one. If I'd had a growth mindset, I believe that instead of seeing my poor grade as an indication of my inequities at chemistry, I would have decided that I didn't put forth enough effort and that my study skills were inadequate (which they surely were). With this interpretation, I probably wouldn't have changed my major and given up so easily on my dream of becoming a medical doctor. I would have chosen, instead, to be more willing to push and elevate myself to rise to the challenge.

Your Current Mindset

Did you take the mindset assessment? What did it say about the quality of your mindset along the fixed-to-growth mindset continuum relative to the more than 20,000 other people who have completed it?

How is your mindset influencing your life, perhaps without you fully recognizing it? As a college freshman, I responded to my situation in the way I thought was "best." Unbeknownst to me, my fixed mindset prevented me from seeing different, healthier, and more productive options and responses to a difficult situation.

Consider your current personal or career trajectory. How might it change if you developed more of a growth mindset? How could you better influence those you work with and serve with a stronger growth mindset?

Growth mindset experts repeatedly state that cultivating a growth mindset could be the single most important thing you ever do to help you achieve success. This is because success in life is achieved through working through challenges; a fixed mindset means we are more inclined to avoid the challenges we face as opposed to conquering them.

As a training and development professional, your job is to elevate your ability to learn and grow and ensure that everyone else elevates their ability to do the same. If you are not focusing on a growth mindset for yourself or the people you are developing, it's likely that you're not doing your job well.

Why Do People Develop a Fixed Mindset?

People with fixed mindsets aren't bad people—they simply developed a fixed mindset for a specific and justifiable purpose: to protect themselves.

Whether it comes from their upbringing, life experiences, or the culture that they currently operate within, the message they've been given is that they are not valuable if they fail or look bad. That messaging likely wired their mind to be sensitive to and filter in any information about a likelihood of failure or looking bad, to interpret that information as being an indication of danger, and to react self-protectively to any situation that might lead to failure or looking bad.

Somehow, during my upbringing and previous education experience, I had internalized the idea that success in life come by doing what you could most naturally succeed in. So, when the going got tough my freshman year, my fixed mindset stepped in to protect me from further failure and disappointment, and the increased effort it would take to improve my study skills and habits. This self-protection was justifiable and it felt "right" in the moment. However, because it felt so "right," it was hard for me to see that it was also limiting.

How Do We Shift to a Growth Mindset?

Shifting from a fixed mindset to a growth mindset requires, at a foundational level, a rewiring of the mind.

Shifting Mindsets in Theory

The wiring adjustments that need to be made are related to the first two jobs of mindsets: filtering in information and interpreting that information in unique ways. In the case of fixed mindsets, this means we need to decrease our sensitivity to signals of potential failure and improve our interpretation of challenges and failures to have a more positive connotation. For example, we need to believe that challenges and failure are opportunities to learn and grow.

This is a unique form of development called vertical development and differs from traditional notions of development, which are generally horizontal development (Petrie 2014).

Horizontal development is enhancing one's knowledge, skills, and capabilities. The focus is on helping someone to be able to do more. It is akin to downloading an app onto an iPad—the new app's benefit is that it broadens the iPad's functionality because it can do more than it could previously. But, the limitation of horizontal development is that it doesn't necessarily make the iPad operate any more effectively.

Vertical development, on the other hand, is elevating one's ability to make meaning of their world in more cognitively and emotionally sophisticated ways. For example, which interpretation of getting test answers wrong is more cognitively and emotionally sophisticated:

- It's an indication of your lack of ability (a fixed mindset).
- It's an opportunity to learn and grow (a growth mindset).

The focus of vertical development is helping someone be better. To use the iPad analogy, it is akin to upgrading the iPad's operating system. We may not be able to do more, but we can function much more effectively.

While both forms of development are valuable, shifting mindsets is the epitome of vertical development. In fact, when we focus on shifting mindsets, we are focusing on elevating our internal operating system.

While helping people vertically develop and rewire their mind may seem daunting, it is easier than we might think. Remember Study 2? The leaders with a fixed mindset who went through the training about fixed and growth mindsets gave higher-quality and higher-quantity recommendations for improvement six weeks after the training than those who didn't go through the mindset training. Other studies have also shown repeatedly that small interventions can move the needle on mindsets (Gottfredson and Reina 2020).

Shifting Mindsets in Practice

Shifting your mindset is not too different from learning how to count to 10 in a foreign language. Let's consider a native English speaker who wants to be able to count to 10 in Spanish at a fluent level. There are three primary steps:

- The English speaker needs to have the motivation to learn and the belief that they can develop the ability to count to 10 in a different language.
- The English speaker needs to put words to the numbers (uno means "one," dos means "two").
- The English speaker needs to spend five to 10 minutes per day practicing counting to 10 in Spanish. After several weeks, the native English speaker should be able to fluently count to 10 in Spanish.

When it comes to mindsets, the steps are essentially the same:

- The person needs to have the motivation to improve their mindset and believe that it is possible (admittedly, this is something that can be challenging for those with a fixed mindset).
- The person needs to learn the language of mindsets. They need to learn what fixed and growth mindsets are, how they cause people to process and operate differently, and how to assess the degree to which they possess a fixed versus growth mindset.
- The person needs to spend small amounts of time on a regular basis exercising their growth mindset neural connections. After several weeks, the person will have made significant progress in rewiring their mind.

It is helpful to think about the process of exercising our growth mindset neural connections in the same way we think about any muscle-building exercise. We are going to experience some benefits of a single workout, but those benefits won't be long lasting. The only way to truly increase our strength is to regularly work out. The same thing goes with our mindset. One workout may lead to short-term benefits, but consistent exercise is the key.

Growth Mindset Exercises

Across the body of mindset data, researchers have found that they can create significant mindset shifts through facilitated learning (for example, reading mindset content or participating in mindset workshops), watching short videos, engaging in journaling exercises, having discussions related to mindsets, and working to improve your self-talk.

Here are some specific examples of ways to develop growth mindsets:
- Read *Mindset*, by Carol Dweck, or *Success Mindsets*, by Ryan Gottfredson. Read Maria Popova's article "Fixed vs. Growth: The Two Basic Mindsets That Shape Our Lives."
- Watch the video of Carol Dweck's TED Talk "The Power of Believing That You Can Improve" or Eduardo Briceno's TEDx Talk "The Power of Belief: Mindset and Success."
- Use journaling exercises to ask yourself to:
  - Identify skills where you went from poor to proficient.
  - Identify a time when you took on a challenge and initially failed, yet persisted until you were successful.
- Work through these discussion questions:
  - Whom do you know with a fixed mindset? How does it limit them?
  - Are you more concerned about looking good or about learning and growing? What evidence do you have for either?
- Improve your self-talk. Instead of saying "I can't do it," say, "I can't do it, yet," "I can do anything I put my mind to," or "Mistakes are opportunities to learn and improve."

There's a more substantial list of growth mindset resources on my website or on the handbook website, ATDHandbook3.org.

Helping Others Develop a Growth Mindset

In our training and development efforts, we are frequently tasked with helping others learn new skills. For example, we might want to help managers improve their ability to provide effective feedback. If we are successful, the managers are going to have a more positive impact on their employees, and their employees will be more engaged and develop more quickly and effectively.

We may be tempted to organize a series of workshops that are designed to help managers learn the effective elements of feedback delivery and give them the opportunity to practice. This is largely a horizontal development approach. Essentially, you're asking the managers to download the "deliver effective feedback" app, which will result in them delivering effective feedback.

Unfortunately, horizontal development rarely works that way. Surely, some of those managers will improve in their delivery of feedback, but it might only be those who had a growth mindset to begin with. Those managers with a fixed mindset may believe that regardless of whether they deliver feedback effectively, their employees will not substantially improve. Thus, they might have downloaded the app, but their operating system isn't willing to run it.

If we want to be more effective in developing others, it is critical to start at the foundation, the key element of an individual's internal operating system, their mindset. And, in particular, we need to foster a growth mindset.

Final Thoughts

"The Irreplaceable Growth Mindset" is not just a gimmicky chapter title—it is substantive and based on decades of research. Individuals with a growth mindset are significantly more inclined to do things that will make them irreplaceable. They possess a mental wiring that pushes them to fulfill the two primary jobs of a training and development professional: to continually learn and develop themselves, and to help others learn and develop.

It is important for you as a TD professional to understand mindsets and the foundational role they play in everything we do. This will influence your personal growth and the growth of others. Once you see how you develop more of a growth mindset, you'll be able to appreciate the value of focusing on it when you are engaged in helping others develop.

Remember the three parts of helping others develop a growth mindset:
- Help them be motivated to develop a growth mindset and help them see that it is possible to develop a growth mindset.
- Help them learn the language of fixed and growth mindsets.
- Provide opportunities and exercises for them to regularly exercise their growth mindset neural connections.

About the Author

Ryan Gottfredson, PhD, is a cutting-edge leadership development author, researcher, and consultant. He helps organizations vertically develop their leaders primarily through a focus on mindsets. Ryan is the *Wall Street Journal* and *USA Today* bestselling author of *Success Mindsets: The Key to Unlocking Greater Success in Your Life, Work, and Leadership*. He is also a leadership professor at the College of Business and Economics at California State University–Fullerton. He holds a PhD in organizational behavior and human resources from Indiana University. Ryan has published more than 19 articles across a variety of journals, including *Leadership Quarterly*, *Journal of Management*, and *Journal of Organizational Behavior*. As a consultant, he has worked with top leadership teams at CVS Health, Deutsche Telekom, Circle K, and dozens of other organizations. You can connect with Ryan at ryangottfredson.com.

References

Crum, A.J., P. Salovey, and S. Achor. 2007. "Rethinking Stress: The Role of Mindsets in Determining the Stress Response." *Journal of Personality and Social Psychology* 104:716–233.

Diener, I.C., and C.S. Dweck. 1978. "An Analysis of Learned Helplessness: Continuous Changes in Performance, Strategy, and Achievement Cognitions Following Failure." *Journal of Personality and Social Psychology* 36:451–462.

Gottfredson, R.K., and C.S. Reina. 2020. "Exploring Why Leaders Do What They Do: An Integrative Review of the Situation-Trait Approach and Situation-Encoding Schemas." *The Leadership Quarterly* 31:101373.

Heslin, P.A., D. Vandewalle, and G.P. Latham. 2006. "Keen to Help? Managers' Implicit Person Theories and Their Subsequent Employee Coaching." *Personnel Psychology* 59:871–9902.

Petrie, N. 2014. *Vertical Leadership Development—Part 1: Developing Leaders for a Complex World*. Greensboro, NC: Center for Creative Leadership. antoinette555.files.wordpress.com/2015/10/nick-petrie-vertical-leadership-part1.pdf.

Recommended Resources

Dweck, C. 2007. *Mindset: The New Psychology of Success*. New York: Ballantine Books.

Gottfredson, R. 2020. *Success Mindsets: Your Keys to Unlocking Greater Success in Your Life, Work, & Leadership*. New York: Morgan James Publishing.

Nadella, S. 2017. *Hit Refresh: The Quest to Rediscover Microsoft's Soul and Imagine a Better Future for Everyone*. New York: HarperCollins Publishers.

CHAPTER 9

An Oath of Ethics for Learning and Development Professionals

Travis Waugh

Written fragments of the Hippocratic Oath date to 275 AD, and the concept was circulating in society for hundreds of years before that. The modern version, only 341 words long, continues to shape the medical profession we know today. It is used during medical graduation ceremonies, referenced in television shows and pop culture, and has been written into medical laws and regulations around the world. As a collection of simple principles to guide a profession, it has proven both enduring and useful.

As learning and development professionals, we need an oath of our own. Too often, our profession is misunderstood, misaligned, and misused by our organizations. This has been allowed because of a void that we have left open for too long at the center of our work. We have highly skilled wizards in our community today, colleagues capable of creating polished deliverables for virtually any subject you can imagine. But those are only our means. We have to decide, together, to what ends those means should be applied.

> **IN THIS CHAPTER:**
> ♦ Explain why we need an oath of ethics as L&D professionals
> ♦ Describe how to spread and reinforce a consistent oath of ethics in the L&D community
> ♦ Apply five key principles from the oath of ethics to your daily work

What does it mean to be a good learning and development professional? If it's defined only as someone who takes content and makes it looks pretty or facilitates killer discussion sessions or efficiently manages learning programs and curriculums, we are never going to reach the transformative potential of our craft. This chapter will explore a potential oath of ethics for our profession, along with practical applications of the oath in realistic learning and development scenarios.

A Proposed Oath of Ethics

We have the skills and position to help today's world change for the better, but to reach those lofty aims, we need to be more than simply what we do. We need articulated values to unite us as a profession and drive us forward through the hard conversations and inevitable dilemmas to come. We need an L&D Oath of Ethics.

> **A PROPOSED OATH OF ETHICS:**
> - I will only use learning and development to pursue real and meaningful improvements, while consuming the fewest resources possible.
> - I will treat my audience members how I would want to be treated.
> - I will use every project as an opportunity to reduce inequity and promote inclusive growth.
> - I will remove unnecessary barriers to learning and strive for universal accessibility.
> - I will lead by example in my organization and community.

Let's examine situations that all TD professionals experience and how the oath of ethics would come into play for each.

> **SCENARIO 1**
>
> You have been assigned to develop your company's approach to required sexual harassment training. The law requires that the course last at least two hours, and you will need to deploy the course as a self-paced online tutorial to reach the full required audience by the legally required deadline. *What would you do?*
>
> In these externally mandated situations, it may be tempting to focus on finding content and filling time. But it would be falling short of the oath to only pursue real and meaningful improvements. Instead, you should work with your SMEs and your community to identify real behavioral needs for your audience members. You might uncover a desire for bystander intervention training, for example. Or you might discover that your organization really needs an improved reporting mechanism to escalate concerns, or that your leaders need to be better prepared to respond to those reports. Instead of filling a course with obvious definitions and scenarios, we have to take time to understand our audience and identify what they really need from us. Then we can create training that makes a real difference.

Principle 1

I will only use learning and development to pursue real and meaningful improvements, while consuming the fewest resources possible.

Utilitarianism was first used as a formal term in the early 19th century by the English philosopher Jeremy Bentham. It was later advanced and refined by John Stuart Mill (2015), but it's a very old idea in the study of ethics. Simply put, an action is "good" if it is useful. Doesn't that sound like a good rule of thumb for learning and development?

Bentham and Mill were hedonists, so they defined *usefulness* in terms of pleasure and pain. An act was good if it maximized pleasure and minimized pain. More technically, an act was good if its net utility (the pleasure it would create, minus any pain it would create) was greater than the net utility of any other choices available to the actor at the time.

For our modern professional purposes, we will take a return on investment approach to usefulness. Our goal must be to maximize the behavioral benefits of each L&D initiative, while minimizing the cost of each project in time, money, and resources.

To put it in old ethical terms, we must ensure our end justifies our means.

How to Maximize Benefit

When we put out a long course that makes a subject matter expert happy but does no real good for our organization or our audience members, we are falling short. When asked to tackle a new project, we should all feel empowered and obliged to ask our stakeholders: *"How does this make our world (or our organization) better?"*

If it doesn't make the organization better, or if the benefit is too minor or theoretical to warrant real investment, we should say no. That might mean working harder to find new objectives that make a real difference *and* satisfy your stakeholders, but that extra work is worth the effort. In my book, *Fully Compliant: Compliance Training to Change Behavior*, I call this opportunistic analysis (Waugh 2019). It's the key to moving a project from a "check the box" exercise to a meaningful, ethical L&D experience.

How to Minimize Cost

If we are judging ourselves on the *net good* we create, we have to focus just as much on reducing the cost of our programs as we do on maximizing our benefits. If you can accomplish a worthy objective in 15 minutes, it would be a waste of time to tackle the same objective in an hour. That isn't just inefficient—by the proposed oath, it would be unethical.

Everything we do in life has an associated cost. Driving to work, for example, pollutes the environment, wastes our time, and burns through our money. And yet, for most of us, the good of keeping a job and connecting with our colleagues outweighs those costs. If you live close enough to walk to the office, on the other hand, you could begin to form an ethical argument that driving to work is "wrong." You would achieve the same benefits by walking to work (plus additional health benefits), with fewer overall costs. The net good of walking to the office would be higher, making it the best available action. To a good utilitarian, walking to work would be the right thing to do.

As we apply this principle to our daily work, it's important that we don't define costs too narrowly. There are many direct and indirect costs associated with modern talent development programs, which means we have many opportunities to cut costs and maximize our net good (Table 9-1).

Table 9-1. Sources of Direct and Indirect Costs for L&D

Audience Time	This is the most precious commodity we manage. Our organizations are busy; we owe it to our colleagues to keep every L&D experience as brief as possible.
L&D and SME Time	We should be careful which projects we take on and manage our workload efficiently to get the largest possible net gain from our finite resources.
Financial Costs	L&D budgets usually aren't the largest in an organization, but they are still worth managing carefully. In pursuit of our goals, we have an ethical responsibility to spend no more money than necessary.
Environmental Harm	Printing user guides is an obvious example of environmental harm. We've all seen old, unused guides gathering dust on our office shelves. If we can accomplish the same objectives while producing less waste (e.g., using electronic user guides), we are obliged to conserve those resources.

SCENARIO 2

A stakeholder tells you he has a $60,000 budget and wants an online refresher tutorial for his team. In your analysis, you notice that there are fewer than 100 colleagues involved, and they only need about 25 minutes of content. Because of changing systems and processes, all the content will have to be redesigned next year. *What would you do?*

Instead of investing $60,000 in an online course this year and spending the same amount next year to rebuild it, a lower-cost approach would be facilitating live virtual sessions for this relatively small audience. The stakeholder may have asked for a tutorial, but it's worth discussing a live alternative if you have capacity to host it. Spending $60,000 on a tutorial would violate the oath if a free virtual session would achieve the same results.

Principle 2

I will treat my audience members how I would want to be treated.

The often referenced "Golden Rule" appears in the Christian Bible as, "In everything, do to others what you would have them do to you" (Matthew 7:12). However, the idea is not unique to Christianity, and in fact predates the Book of Matthew by at least 600 years. Similar concepts can be found in the writings of Plato and Aristotle, and in the work of Confucius in the sixth century BC. Obviously, the idea has staying power, but it also has some limitations.

For example, if you are an avid military historian, you might get quite excited about an eight-hour symposium on an obscure battle from World War I. But that does not mean you are justified in requiring all of your colleagues to endure the same symposium. Just because you'd want it *done unto you*, there is no reason to believe they'd all want it *done unto them*.

Unfortunately, misapplication of the golden rule is a daily reality in our profession. "Of course, they can learn this way," a SME might argue for a bad, content-heavy program. "It's how I learned." Other stakeholders may argue for more and more courses on the grounds that they find the details interesting and important, implying that nonexperts should see value in it too.

Later philosophers, most notably Immanuel Kant, tried to tweak the golden rule to make it more resilient to such misuse. Kant called his version the Supreme Categorical Imperative: Never act for any reason that you wouldn't wish to become a universal law (Kant et al. 2020).

Taking this example back to learning and development, we should think of each project as a precedent for others to follow. If we launch a boring, four-hour lecture on a topic we deem to be worthy and important, we are endorsing the universal law that anyone should feel justified in mandating long, boring courses provided *they* think their content is worthy and important. Under that universal law, you and your colleagues would be subjected to a lot of bad L&D experiences.

So, here's a version of the supreme categorical imperative: Treat your audience how you would want to be treated *if you had no special interest or expertise in the subject*.

Be honest here. If you had no special interest or expertise, you would want every course to be as short and relevant as possible. You would want it to be not too difficult, but not insultingly easy either. You would want it to be honest and transparent in its design, with clear expectations. You would want the program's outcomes for success or failure to be fair, and not too severe. And you would probably want a choice of how to participate, or whether to participate at all.

These are the kinds of universal laws we would want other talent development professionals to follow for us. Thus, we should commit to follow them ourselves.

> **SCENARIO 3**
>
> You are working on a cybersecurity project, and one of your stakeholders would like to do a fake phishing campaign to identify vulnerable colleagues for added training. Another stakeholder is afraid that could be seen as manipulative and might offend colleagues who feel deceived by the exercise. *What would you do?*
>
> The dubious colleague is right to have concerns, but it could also be a useful learning tool if executed with empathy. Think of what you would want if such a program were targeted at you:
>
> - Simple, transparent expectations for how the campaign will work and what you are supposed to do when you receive a suspicious email
> - A chance to practice before the campaign
> - Clear and respectful feedback
> - The opportunity to try again if you fail
>
> All these things will help ensure the campaign is received as an interesting opportunity to practice and improve, not as a sneaky means to entrap and chastise our peers. We should treat the audience with the same respect we would want shown to ourselves.

Principle 3

I will use every project as an opportunity to reduce inequity and promote inclusive growth.

As L&D professionals, our job is to take the resources our organization has today and turn them into the resources our organization will want and need tomorrow. If we hope to succeed in that endeavor, we need the broadest possible pool of talent. We must ensure that every single colleague is given a fair, equitable chance to learn, grow, and succeed. Anything less would fail our organization's long-term needs and contradict the oath.

Sadly, equitable growth is not a given. Our organizations reflect our broader societies, and we still have serious issues to work through regarding our approach to race, gender, sexual orientation, and other dimensions of traditional oppression. Whether we work in the corporate world, government, or higher education, the people who get ahead tend to act like the people who have gotten ahead in the past. They tend to talk and look like them too.

In 2020, the *Wall Street Journal* reported that "out of the chief executives running America's top 500 companies, just 1 percent, or four, are Black" (Chen 2020). A similar review by the *New York Times* in 2015 of America's top 1,500 companies found that there were more CEOs named John than there were women CEOs of any name (Wolfers 2015). And gender and race are just two of many ways our colleagues can be held back from their potential by discriminatory or harmful policies and practice.

That's not just unfair—it's bad for business. The narrower our net of potential high performers, the fewer opportunities we have to find and develop the missing pieces we need. Instead of trying to train a small percentage of people to do everything, inclusivity gives us a chance to support and grow the innate skills and abilities that exist across our diverse communities, leveling up individual careers and evolving our business in the process.

But achieving real inclusive growth will take more than a single diversity and inclusion course. In a global environment in which inequity is still rife, every project we take on is either fighting inequity or allowing it to continue.

Whatever the subject, whoever the audience, we must ask ourselves: How will this project confront existing inequity and promote inclusive growth?

> **THERE ARE NO SHORTCUTS TO EQUITY**
>
> If we hope to have a real impact, we must listen to a broader set of stakeholders and be continuously willing to adapt. We need more diversity in our leadership teams, within the learning and development function, and in every stage of our projects, but real equity is more than numbers in a column. If our teams aren't willing to listen, change, and grow, any efforts to increase diversity are, at best, meaningless. At worst, they could promote assimilation and perpetuate harmful policy. Instead, we must remain humble and focus on how we can change what we have done in the past to work better for everyone. We aren't doing anyone a favor when we promote a diverse colleague or add a diversity component to a development program; we are simply giving our organization the opportunity it needs to evolve and survive.

To this end, L&D professionals should take principle 3 one step further and implement a holistic approach to our work: *We must use every course and project as an opportunity to fight inequity, in all its forms.*

Leadership Development

Inclusion skills should not be tacked on to leadership development programs as an extra lesson. They should be woven through every objective as a key part of what it means to be a leader. It's also important to ensure the participant selection process is equitable to build a diverse pool of future leaders.

Agile Project Management

Often, our organizations fail to benefit from diverse perspectives because they can't adapt quickly to feedback that challenges the status quo. If you have a course on Agile project management, add a project involving a case study based on fixing an internal process in response to feedback from a diversity and inclusion survey. Participants can practice their new skills and learn to think of inclusion as something concrete, like any other business deliverable.

Communications Training

There are well-documented gaps in how different races and genders are perceived in the workplace. Training on communication and personality styles too often reinforces this problem, placing emphasis on adjusting the speaker's style to better fit the expectations of the listener. Instead, focus at least as much time on training listeners to recognize and avoid potential bias in their perception.

> **SCENARIO 4**
>
> You work for a large social media company that has just invested in a brand-new suite of AI-powered software development tools. You've been asked to create an AI development curriculum to ensure all your coders can make the most of the new tools. *What would you do?*
>
> This is a perfect opportunity to broaden a traditional skills program with a strong focus on equity. Prejudice and bias in machine learning algorithms are well documented (Buranyi 2018). Adding that thread to your curriculum can create interesting scenarios that engage your audience, while also building real skills that acknowledge the limitations of AI and its potential blind spots. Such training could have a more long-lasting impact than a traditional IT skills course, decreasing inequities in your corporate culture and in the applications your company launches to the world.

Principle 4

I will remove unnecessary barriers to learning and strive for universal accessibility.

When we design learning tools and development programs, we have an ethical obligation to ensure those resources are available to *everyone*.

That might mean translating content for audience members who are more capable of learning in their native languages. It may mean making some online training and tools available as in-person learning for those who are too often ignored or neglected by the digital divide. It also means planning to ensure that individuals with disabilities can access and fully benefit from the experiences we create.

Captioning online videos is a good first step, but true universal accessibility requires us to rethink the fundamental ways we design and deliver content. For example, instead of an online multimedia course with accessibility features that were added during publishing, some individuals with disabilities may prefer an alternative method of delivery, such as a plain text document or an MP3 podcast. By designing those resources with the intended audience in mind from the start, you can create a much more engaging and effective experience.

As an added benefit, the alternative delivery formats we create offer more freedom for anyone to choose how they want to learn. It may also allow you to extend the reach of your content into new communication channels, like video boards in lobbies that play without sound.

Universal accessibility investment doesn't only benefit a few; it makes everything we offer more useful to everyone.

SCENARIO 5

Imagine you routinely host a four-hour onboarding session for new hires. One day, a participant arrives who is deaf. *What would you do?*

If you aren't prepared for this situation in advance, it may be almost impossible to welcome this colleague effectively. That's why it is so important to bake universal accessibility into every project from the start. If we consider all potential needs, we can plan the tools and resources necessary for equitable access.

For example, you could make sure you know how to turn closed captioning on for your PowerPoint deck and have a sign language interpreter on call if needed. You could also create some components for the session that are less dependent on speaking and listening, which could add welcome variety to the experience and benefit other members of your audience too.

Principle 5

I will lead by example in my organization and community.

NBA Hall of Famer Charles Barkley, amid frequent criticisms of his off-court behavior in the 1990s, famously proclaimed, "I am not a role model." As learning and development professionals, we can't afford to use the same excuse.

Regardless of our position in the organization, we must accept that learning and development is always a leadership role. We took on that responsibility when we joined a field that purports to help others improve. People expect us to have already improved ourselves.

The behaviors we model in our daily work are at least as important to our organizations as the content we write and the programs we develop. At a minimum, we should know and follow all applicable policies, processes, and legal requirements. We should also be honest and transparent, and own our mistakes when they happen. Finally, we should model the ancient ethical concept that Aristotle called the "Golden Mean."

Aristotle held that the right course of action is usually the moderate course of action between two extremes (Aristotle and Beresford 2020). In our profession, that balance is extremely important: We must be positive, solution-focused, and customer-service-oriented to succeed in our work. However, we must also be willing to point out flaws in an organization and stand up for our audience when a project isn't right.

We must be both kind and courageous, flexible and consistent, responsive and strategic. We must be willing to say yes, and able to say no.

The oath of ethics should help us strike that balance more confidently and consistently. If we all agree on the rules that govern our profession, we can all take strength from that commitment. It gives us a framework for knowing when to say no, and a shared vocabulary to explain why. It allows us to debate our concerns on shared terms and reach better solutions together. It helps us lead by example, every time.

"I took an oath of ethics," we can explain to our stakeholders during difficult conversations. "I have to do what I know is right."

How Should We Use an Oath of Ethics?

The more often we use the oath, the more powerful it will become. Adapt the oath as needed to fit your context, and then consider using it during:

- Graduation or orientation ceremonies for degree programs in talent development, corporate development, or instructional design
- Interviews for talent management roles—share the oath in advance and ask each candidate to tell you about a time in their career when they applied one or more of the principles to deliver an ethical result
- Team meetings and one-on-ones to help prioritize work, troubleshoot stakeholder requests, and build internal consensus
- Lessons-learned meetings to spot and explain opportunities for improvement

If we want the oath to help brand our profession and expand our potential, we have to share it often and follow it always.

You can find a copy of the proposed Oath of Ethics for TD Professionals on this handbook's website at ATDHandbook3.org. How would you change it? What would you add?

Final Thoughts

This oath draws on weighty and complex themes—including equity, inclusion, and accessibility—that warrant far more discussion than possible in a single chapter. I don't have all the answers on these subjects. Often, I don't even know the right questions. However, I did not want to exclude an important subject only for the sake of my own insecurity. Instead, I offer this oath as a humble draft.

You might wonder who am I to write an oath of ethics for our profession? That's a very fair question. My aim is to spark discussion and allow individuals with more expertise and intelligence than me to refine, expand, and improve the approach with time.

The Hippocratic Oath has changed often in response to shifts in society, technology, and individual expectations; I hope the learning and development community will change this oath too. It should be yours, not mine.

About the Author

Travis Waugh is the author of *Fully Compliant: Compliance Training to Change Behavior* (ATD Press). He studied English and philosophy at Ohio State University before earning a master's degree in instructional technology from Georgia State University. He has nearly 15 years of experience working in talent development, including positions at the Georgia Institute of Technology, Indiana University, and American Electric Power. He now works for Tech Data, one of the world's largest technology distributors, as their global manager for ethics and compliance policy, training, and communication. He is a frequent conference speaker on subjects including behavioral learning design, instructional technology, and behavior-driven compliance training. He lives with his family in York, England.

References

Aristotle, and A. Beresford. 2020. *The Nicomachean Ethics*. New York: Penguin Classics.

Buranyi, S. 2018. "Rise of the Racist Robots—How AI Is Learning All Our Worst Impulses." *Guardian*, February 14. theguardian.com/inequality/2017/aug/08/rise-of-the-racist-robots-how-ai-is-learning-all-our-worst-impulses.

Chen, T. 2020. "Why Are There Still So Few Black CEOs?" *Wall Street Journal*, September 28. wsj.com/articles/why-are-there-still-so-few-black-ceos-11601302601.

Kant, I., R. Stern, C. Bennett, and J. Saunders. 2020. *Groundwork for the Metaphysics of Morals* (Oxford World's Classics). Oxford: Oxford University Press.

Mill, J.S., M. Philp, and F. Rosen. 2015. *On Liberty, Utilitarianism and Other Essays* (Oxford World's Classics), 2nd ed. Oxford: Oxford University Press.

Waugh, T. 2019. *Fully Compliant: Compliance Training to Change Behavior.* Alexandria, VA: ATD Press.

Wolfers, J. 2015. "Fewer Women Run Big Companies Than Men Named John." *New York Times*, March 2. nytimes.com/2015/03/03/upshot/fewer-women-run-big-companies-than-men-named-john.html.

Recommended Resources

Cathcart, T., and D. Klein. 2008. *Plato and a Platypus Walk Into a Bar: Understanding Philosophy Through Jokes.* New York: Penguin Books.

Kahneman, D. 2013. *Thinking, Fast and Slow.* New York: Farrar, Straus and Giroux.

Kendi, I.X. 2019. *How To Be an Antiracist.* New York: One World.

Shafik, M. 2021. *What We Owe Each Other: A New Social Contract.* Princeton, NJ: Princeton University Press.

Watnik, R.-L. 2021. "Operationalize a Code of Ethics." *TD at Work.* Alexandria, VA: ATD Press.

Waugh, T. 2019. *Fully Compliant: Compliance Training to Change Behavior.* Alexandria, VA: ATD Press.

CHAPTER 10

What's EQ Got to Do With a TD Career?

Jean Greaves

How much of an impact does emotional intelligence (EQ) have on your professional success? The short answer is a lot! EQ is a powerful set of skills that will help you navigate your learning curve, meet the needs of the people you will train and develop, and ensure you are able to reach your long-term career goals. A deeper understanding of how people learn and interact will be necessary whether you want to design training programs, coordinate them, train and coach people, or scale learning initiatives. Investing in your own EQ skills will boost your performance, the performance of the teams you join, and the performance of the organizations you work for.

IN THIS CHAPTER:

♦ Discover what EQ skills have to offer TD professionals
♦ Learn why EQ is important to anyone in an organization
♦ Practice eight EQ strategies for guiding your own TD career

EQ skills enable you to connect with learners and guide them toward deeper insights and growth. Emotional intelligence skills will also help you face any fear or nerves you have about your career path. We all have them. *Can I master public speaking? What about audiences of more than 75 people or C-suite leaders? How do I handle a skeptic, especially when everyone is watching? What if I am not creative enough for curriculum design? And how about industry challenges on the horizon, such as competing priorities, virtual and e-learning dynamics, increasing workloads, or negotiating for resources?*

EQ skills can help you every step of the way if you begin your learning journey now and practice your EQ skills consistently.

What Is Emotional Intelligence?

First things first. Emotional intelligence skills were introduced to the world in the mid-1990s after magnetic resonance imaging (MRI) scans highlighted the areas of the brain that activate as people think and feel. Suddenly people could see the emotional center of the brain light up before and during mental tasks such as decision making or communicating. The business world embraced this scientific approach to behavior, and it opened new possibilities for tackling personal and interpersonal difficulties at work. Based on 25 years of research, along with training and development efforts across industries, this chapter presents a high-level briefing on what you need to know about emotional intelligence for a training and development career.

Emotional Intelligence Versus IQ and Personality

It may seem strange to begin defining emotional intelligence by clarifying what it is not. However, it is important to start here and address two of the most common questions learners ask: *Is my EQ influenced by my personality? Isn't EQ just part of my IQ?*

When you measure personality, IQ, and EQ in a single individual, each one offers unique insights into how people think and act at work (Figure 10-1).

Personality is made up of the stable "styles" that describe each of us. You may be more high energy, even-keeled, friendly, or intense, to offer a few examples. Personality traits appear early in life and remain prominent throughout adulthood. You might assume that some personality traits (for example, introversion) are associated with a lower EQ, but those who draw energy from being alone are no less emotionally intelligent than people who refuel by interacting with others. You can draw on your personality to assist in developing your EQ (and you will likely need to), but the latter isn't dependent on the former.

Figure 10-1. EQ + IQ + Personality = You

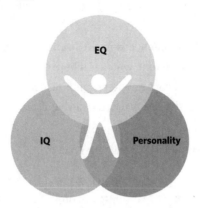

Your intellect is your ability to learn. Think of cognitive intelligence as the rate at which you can process new or complex information. It's not how much you know—you don't get smarter by learning new facts or information. Your IQ, short of a traumatic event such as a brain injury, is relatively fixed from birth, and it's the same at age 15 as it will be at age 50. EQ, on the other hand, is a flexible skill that can be learned. There is very little connection between IQ and EQ; you simply can't predict someone's EQ based on how smart they are.

> EQ offers unique insights into how people operate at work beyond personality and IQ.

People can be intelligent but not emotionally intelligent, and people of all types of personalities can have a high or low EQ. Of the three, EQ is the most flexible and able to change. Your emotional intelligence affects how you manage behavior, navigate social complexities, and make personal decisions that achieve positive results for you, other people, and the organization where you work.

The Biology of Emotional Intelligence

An MRI is a brain scan that uses strong magnetic fields and radio waves to produce detailed images inside the brain as people respond to stimuli. MRIs settled once and for all the notion that people can't leave their feelings at home when they go to work. Your brain is wired to process your emotions before you even think about them. The rational area of your brain (the prefrontal cortex) can't stop emotions "felt" by your limbic system (the emotional center of your brain), but the two areas do influence each other and maintain constant communication. The communication between your emotional and rational "brains" is the physical source of emotional intelligence.

The pathway for emotional intelligence is in the brain. Sensory information first travels along neural pathways through the limbic system, which is where emotions are processed. Then that information moves over to the prefrontal cortex, where thinking occurs. Emotional intelligence requires effective communication between the rational and emotional centers of the brain (Figure 10-2).

Figure 10-2. Sensory Information Movement Through the Brain

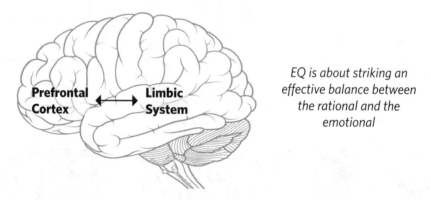

When Daniel Goleman (2005) introduced the concept of emotional intelligence to the business world, he was able to name a peculiar finding: People with the highest levels of intelligence outperform those with average IQs just 20 percent of the time, while people with average IQs outperform those with high IQs 70 percent of the time. This observation led researchers to look for another variable that explained success above and beyond one's IQ. The competencies of high performers pointed to emotional intelligence as the critical factor.

Because your mind is wired to give your emotions the upper hand, your first response to an event is always going to be an emotional one. You have no control over this. However, you do control what happens next. You can shape the thoughts you have following an emotion—if you are aware of it. When something someone says or does generates an intense emotional reaction in you, it's called a "trigger event." It triggers you because of similar experiences you've had before. When your emotions escalate to the point where your brain is unable to balance your emotions with rational options, you may find yourself saying and doing things you regret. Much of emotional intelligence is about learning to become more aware of your triggers and improving your reactions to them.

The Four Core EQ Skills

Emotional intelligence is a skill set that includes recognizing and understanding emotions in yourself and others, and your ability to use this awareness to manage your behavior and relationships.

Four skills make up emotional intelligence (Figure 10-3):
- Self-awareness
- Self-management
- Social awareness
- Relationship management

The first two skills, self-awareness and self-management, are more about you. The last two skills, social awareness and relationship management, are more about how you are with other people.

Figure 10-3. Emotional Intelligence Skills

	What I See	What I Do
Personal Competence	Self-Awareness	Self-Management
Social Competence	Social Awareness	Relationship Management

Self-Awareness

Self-awareness is the foundation of emotional intelligence. It includes your ability to accurately notice your own emotions in the moment and understand your patterns across time and situations. A self-aware person stays on top of their feelings about specific events, challenges, and people to quickly make sense of their reactions. Self-awareness requires tolerating some discomfort from focusing on emotions that may be negative.

Self-awareness is not about analyzing your deepest or unconscious motivations—rather, it comes from practicing a straightforward pursuit of understanding your needs, your habits, your style, and your strengths. Self-aware co-workers are remarkably clear about what they do well, what motivates and satisfies them, and which people and situations push their buttons.

Self-Management

Self-management is more than resisting explosive or problematic behavior. Self-management is the use of your awareness of your emotions to stay flexible and direct your behavior positively. This means managing your emotional reactions to situations and people. The process of self-managing includes tolerating uncertainty as you explore your emotions and options. Once you understand and build comfort with what you are feeling, the best course of action or inaction will show itself.

The biggest challenge that people face is managing their tendencies over time and applying their self-management skills across a variety of situations. Real results come from putting your momentary needs on hold to pursue larger, more important goals. Reaching such goals is often delayed, meaning that your commitment to self-manage and to tolerate waiting will be tested repeatedly.

Social Awareness

As the first component of social competence, social awareness is also a foundational skill. Social awareness is your ability to accurately pick up on emotions in other people and understand what is really going on with them. This means perceiving what other people are thinking and feeling even if you do not feel the same way. It's easy to get caught up in your own emotions and forget to consider the perspective of the other party. Social awareness ensures you stay focused and absorb critical information.

Instead of looking inward to learn about and understand yourself, social awareness is looking outward to learn about and appreciate others. Social awareness is centered on your ability to recognize and understand the emotions of others. Tuning in to others' emotions as you interact with them will help you get a more accurate view of your surroundings, which affects everything from anticipating what may come your way to communication and relationships.

Relationship Management

The difference between an interaction and a relationship is a matter of frequency. It is also a product of the quality, depth, and time you spend interacting with another person. Though relationship management is the second component of social competence, this skill taps into the first three emotional intelligence skills: self-awareness, self-management, and social awareness. Relationship management is your ability to use your awareness of your own emotions and those of others to manage your interactions and relationships successfully.

People who manage relationships well see the benefit of connecting with many different people, even those they are not fond of. The weaker the connection you have with someone, the harder it is to get your point across. If you want people to listen or care about you and your work, you must invest in every relationship, especially the challenging ones.

Why EQ Is Important for Anyone in an Organization

In addition to the widely accepted ideas that emotions influence people, and that organizations depend on their people, the business case for EQ continues to be supported by projections in the World Economic Forum's *Future of Jobs Report 2020*. The future for employees around the world involves major disruption and change in the workplace. Driving forces include rapid growth, uncertainty, remote and virtual learning, innovation, digital transformation, and the pursuit of inclusion, equity, health, and well-being for people at work. Because significant changes are in our future, and humans instinctually respond to change with emotion, it makes sense that emotional intelligence is central to two of the eight skill groups projected to be important. According to more than 90 percent of organizations who responded to the World Economic Forum's survey, Working With People and Self-Management skills will continue to be important or are increasingly important (Table 10-1).

Table 10-1. Critical Skills Required by Organizations

Relative Importance of Skill Groups	Decreasing	Stable	Increasing
Working with people	4%	32%	64%
Self-management	7%	43%	50%

Emotional intelligence was 11th on the list of the top 15 skills projected for 2025, which makes sense when you look through the other skills on this list. A person must be socially aware and able to manage relationships to lead others, have social influence, a service orientation, and the ability to persuade or negotiate (Table 10-2). People need self-awareness and self-management to take initiative, tolerate stress, flex to change, and be resilient.

Table 10-2. Top Skills According to World Economic Forum Survey

Top Skills for 2025	Corresponding EQ Skills
#5: Creativity, originality and initiative	• Self-Awareness • Self-Management
#6: Leadership and social influence	• Self-Awareness • Self-Management • Social Awareness • Relationship Management
#9: Resilience, stress tolerance, and flexibility	• Self-Awareness • Self-Management
#13: Service Orientation	• Social Awareness
#15: Persuasion and Negotiation	• Self-Awareness • Self-Management • Social Awareness

Some of the most challenging and stressful situations that people face are at work. Beyond workload or the pressure of deadlines, what can make tough times feel so challenging are the difficult emotions involved, such as feeling angry, resentful, disappointed, anxious, frustrated, overwhelmed, or disrespected. When people passively avoid problems at work—which typically happens if they lack the skills needed to initiate a direct yet constructive conversation—conflicts tend to fester. Emotional intelligence offers everyone the personal and social competence skills they need to self-manage and work with people through many nuanced interactions.

Can EQ Be Trained?

Let's review 17 years of research. While a single study exploring the trainability of EQ could never be definitive, looking at different studies across time, settings, and population can offer an emerging answer. Mattingly and Kraiger (2019) conducted a meta-analytical investigation of 76 published and unpublished research studies from between 2000 and 2016 on training for emotional intelligence skills. In their review, they found that 56 samples used a pre-post measurement design with 2,136 participants, and 28 samples from 26 more studies used a treatment-control group design with 2,176 participants. In all, the 4,312 participants in these studies included managers, nurses, police officers, sales professionals, teachers, and retail staff. In addition, the researchers reviewed student samples from undergraduate, graduate, and professional programs, with the most common being MBA students. EQ training in all cases was officially sanctioned by host organizations or academic programs and none of the participants were student volunteers for research credit. Both pre-post and treatment-control group designs showed a moderate, positive effect of training on the emotional intelligence scores of participants, regardless of gender. The effect was robust across emotional intelligence self-report measures. Overall, EQ training increased EQ scores, and the researchers concluded that EQ was trainable.

Progress Is Possible Within a Year

At TalentSmartEQ, we have investigated this question further. Hundreds of thousands of learners measure their baseline EQ using the Emotional Intelligence Appraisal, practice the EQ skills they need to improve, and then measure their progress. Learners in our databases see, on average, a seven-point increase in their EQ scores in a three-to-six-month timeframe (Figure 10-4). The average increase in scores grows to nine points for those who keep practicing several more months and then take a retest in the seven-to-10-month timeframe, which represents a marked increase in EQ skills in less than one year. This is more than double the increase anyone can expect from improvements and growth in their EQ over the normal course of life experience in similar periods of time.

Figure 10-4. Average Baseline EQ Score Versus at Average Retest Score

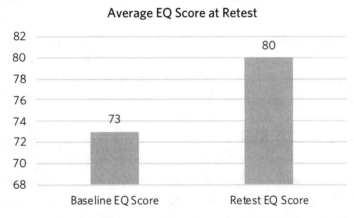

Note: 2020 self-report scores for a data set of 1,874 respondents on the Emotional Intelligence Appraisal are normed on a 100-point scale.

Seasoned working professionals frequently say they wish they'd learned about emotional intelligence earlier in life. For midcareer professionals and beyond, the wonderful news is that it is never too late to get started. People who are over 40 years old see an eight-point increase in their EQ score, on average, after practicing EQ strategies for six to nine months.

Understanding When Scores Don't Increase
Not everyone sees an increase. Among our data sets from working and student populations, 80 percent of learners see some type of increase, 3 percent see no change, and 17 percent find their EQ scores decrease.

Two possible reasons for the retest score to drop:
- If the person is engaged, they'll understand the importance of emotional intelligence and be more aware of the moments they slip back into low-EQ habits. Thus, when they take the retest, they rate themselves more realistically than the first time or hold themselves to a higher EQ standard.
- They may also hit a rough patch in life and discover that their high-EQ behaviors are less frequent than before.

Better EQ Takes Repeated Practice and Time
Your emotional habits have already been well exercised, so replacing them with high EQ habits will take repeated practice and time. You can't expect to change every facet of EQ within months, but you can work to change specific behaviors over several months. The length of time will vary. If you're attempting to reduce how often you interrupt people, you will likely have hundreds of opportunities to practice every month. If your EQ challenge is handling conflict or negotiating with confidence, you'll be able to practice EQ strategies only when the situation arises. It may take you a year or several years to master some EQ challenges. The goal is to keep at it, even after the inevitable setbacks that occur when you slip into an old habit or hit a rough patch in your career. Measuring your EQ scores periodically gives you an appraisal of how much progress you are making in your efforts to master emotional intelligence skills.

Develop Your Own EQ Skills
Would your EQ skills increase even if you never made an effort to develop them? It's likely that you would acquire constructive insights and behaviors that improve your work performance and relationships. Every training participant who completes an EQ assessment finds that they have some EQ strengths and other EQ development needs. The advantage of getting intentional about developing your EQ skills early in your career is that you will get farther, faster. You will also feel supported by proven EQ practice strategies. Following are eight of the 66 actionable EQ strategies from *Emotional Intelligence 2.0*, specifically applied to a TD career. They were selected to help you with the emotions, people, and situations you will encounter as a training and development professional. You will also find a tool to help you develop your skills on the handbook website at ATDHandbook3.org.

Develop Self-Awareness Skills

A training and development career places you in a front-row seat to watch and help people at work become more self-aware. Begin a similar process for yourself so you can speak authentically about the experience of becoming more aware of both painful and rewarding insights about how you operate at work.

You will soon discover that self-awareness is a pursuit that involves remaining open to learning about and observing yourself as objectively as possible as you interact with other people, face challenges, and experience the range of emotions that flow through you at work. You will never finish becoming self-aware because it is a continuous journey. Getting in touch with your emotions and tendencies takes courage. Be patient and give yourself time and credit for even the smallest steps forward. Noticing things about yourself that you weren't previously aware of (even insights you aren't always going to like) means you are making progress.

Table 10-3. Self-Awareness Strategies for TD Professionals

Quit Treating Your Feelings as Good or Bad (Self-Awareness Strategy 1)	Your emotions and feelings are signals. It's as simple as that. They're neither good nor bad. For example, frustration can play a constructive or destructive role in your words and actions, depending on how well you notice and manage it. Tell yourself now that you will quit labeling your feelings as good or bad, and instead, begin listening to your feelings to understand what they are trying to tell you.
Seek Feedback (Self-Awareness Strategy 14)	Asking those around you for feedback, both people you respect and those who are your critics, will provide the greatest leaps in self-awareness. Anticipate that it will likely sting. Give yourself adequate time to absorb and think through whatever they have to say, and then make your own decisions about what to do with their advice.

Adapted from Bradberry and Greaves (2009)

Develop Self-Management Skills

Everyone seems to think self-managing means learning to contain their emotions when they are about to explode or to refrain from saying or doing what they really want to say and do. It's true that self-control in these situations can be the best choice, but there is far more to self-management. Self-managing includes pushing through discomfort to speak up constructively or take action when you really would rather not.

Remember, you will experience emotions before you think or act on them. Self-management takes two steps to read your feelings accurately and then act on them constructively for both your benefit and the benefit of others. This is what sets the best self-managers apart. The self-management strategies recommended here will help you in the moment, over time, and over the course of your career.

Table 10-4. Self-Management Strategies for TD Professionals

Breathe Right (Self-Management Strategy 1)	Take deep breaths to allow your mind to begin calming down, lowering your heart rate and blood pressure. Breathe in slowly through your nose. Fill your chest and relax your belly to fill that too. Then slowly release all the air through your mouth before beginning again slowly. You'll get better on the second and third time. Apply liberally throughout your career and life.
Take Control of Your Self-Talk (Self-Management Strategy 9)	Turn your ear inward to hear the messages you are telling yourself. Are they kind and supportive? Or are they critical and self-defeating? The more situation-specific and encouraging you can be internally, the more you can keep trying when the going gets tough. Jot down more supportive phrases and practice saying them to yourself repeatedly until they replace your old negative self-talk.

Adapted from Bradberry and Greaves (2009)

Develop Social Awareness Skills

If you are working in the field of training and coaching others, you are already stretching your social awareness muscle to focus on the development of others. The question becomes, are you stretching and building this muscle to maximize the outcomes required of you? Take every opportunity to observe learners in all kinds of situations. You may watch a training participant fidgeting or looking lost, or you may be right in the middle of a coaching conversation feeling resistance from the person sitting across from you. Pick up on these types of body language, facial expressions, postures, and tones of voice. Looking outward isn't just about using your eyes and ears; it means tapping into all your senses. You can absorb deeper information through that sixth sense, your emotions. Your emotions can help you notice and interpret cues other people send you. These cues will give you some help in putting yourself in the other person's shoes.

Emotions, facial expressions, and some types of body language translate across cultures (Ekman 1971). These are mobilized by the biological aspects of emotions (such as sweating while feeling nervous and micro-expressions that appear on our face). How we express our feelings and body language is also driven by cultural norms, and this does vary depending on whether the culture is that of a team, department, company, or region of the world. Fidgeting while bored may not be visible if self-management skills are uniformly well exercised in the culture you are working in. You can use your social awareness skills across cultures if you work to understand the cultural norms you are operating in. The lens you look through must be clear, so you are able to read what is really going on, not just what you think is going on.

Table 10-5. Social Awareness Strategies for TD Professionals

Clear Away the Clutter (Social Awareness Strategy 7)	Clearing away the clutter means removing all the distractions in your head so you can be present and give your full attention to another person or a group. For a content developer, this means designing learning content for all learning styles, not just your own; or thinking through the rhythms of breaks needed to avoid learner fatigue. For trainers and coaches this means quieting your self-talk and refraining from forming your own response while the other person is still speaking. Shifting your head or body to focus more intently on a person's face and words can help.
Catch the Mood in the Room (Social Awareness Strategy 17)	In training and coaching spaces, absorbing the energy and emotions of learners requires seeing and hearing cues such as body language, sound, and tone levels. Notice how many people are participating, as well as their movements and volume, and be sure to tap into how you are feeling as a result. These signals will tell you when to speed up, slow down, take a break, or check in with what is really going on in the learning space.

Adapted from Bradberry and Greaves (2009)

Develop Relationship Management Skills

All relationships require an investment of attention and energy, even those that seem effortless. Thankfully, relationship management skills can be improved with practice, and they tap into the three other EQ skills. Your self-awareness skills help you notice your feelings and decide if your needs in the relationship are being satisfied. Your self-management skills help you communicate your feelings constructively and act accordingly to benefit the connection. Finally, your social awareness skills help you tune in to the other person's needs and feelings to better understand where they are coming from and how to meet their needs.

In the end, relationships are essential to fulfilling your career goals—guiding classrooms of people for a day or two; contributing on a team that is developing e-learning content, programs, or job aids; consulting with clients; or virtually coaching people. Because you are half of any working relationship, you have half the responsibility for building and deepening your working relationships over time. Here are two relationship management strategies that will help.

Table 10-6. Relationship Management Strategies for TD Professionals

Take Feedback Well (Relationship Management Strategy 5)	Feedback stings and learning how to absorb it, process it, and do something about it is one of the more important strategies for developing and deepening your relationships. When you receive feedback, consider the source, ask clarifying questions, and ask for examples to fully understand. Thank the person whether you agree or not. Take time to sort out your feelings and thoughts so you can decide what to do about the feedback.
Acknowledge the Other Person's Feelings (Relationship Management Strategy 10)	This strategy disarms the people who are skeptical or even resistant to you and your approaches at work. Lean through your discomfort with their skepticism or resistance, and instead acknowledge it with a statement such as, "I see how you're feeling this way," or "I want to understand more." Simple acts like this acknowledge their views or feelings as legitimate without making them a big deal or agreeing with them.

Adapted from Bradberry and Greaves (2009)

Final Thoughts

People operating with a high emotional intelligence take accountability for their thoughts, feelings, needs, and actions while also doing their part to understand and respond constructively to those of the people around them. Imagine if everyone in an organization was skilled in emotional intelligence. Resilience, adaptability, stress management, difficult conversations, change tolerance, and conflict resolution begin to read as reasonable expectations for everyone. Most people just need help understanding and managing the emotions that will surface along the way. That is where you come in. You play an important role in this TD profession by helping working people expand their EQ skills, know-how, and so much more as they help their organizations grow.

About the Author

Jean Greaves, PhD, has more than 25 years of experience as an author, speaker, master facilitator, and executive coach specializing in emotional intelligence in the workplace. She is the co-author of the *Wall Street Journal* bestseller *Emotional Intelligence 2.0*, and co-developer of the Emotional Intelligence Appraisal suite of assessments and TalentSmartEQ's Mastering Emotional Intelligence training programs. Additional books include *Leadership 2.0* and *The Emotional Intelligence Quick Book*. Her next book, to be released in 2022, was a team effort among the subject matter experts at TalentSmartEQ on team emotional intelligence skills and strategies. Jean holds a PhD in industrial and organizational psychology from the California School of Professional Psychology and a bachelor's degree from Stanford University. Questions for Jean can be sent to inquiries@talentsmarteq.com.

References

Bradberry, T., and J. Greaves. 2009. *Emotional Intelligence 2.0*. San Diego: TalentSmartEQ.

Ekman, P. 1971. *Universal and Cultural Differences in Facial Expressions of Emotion*. Lincoln: University of Nebraska Press.

Goleman, D. 2005. *Emotional Intelligence: Why It Can Matter More than IQ*. New York: Random House.

Mattingly, V., and K. Kraiger. 2019. "Can Emotional Intelligence Be Trained? A Meta-Analytical Investigation." *Human Resource Management Review* 29(2): 140–155. doi.org/10.1016/j.hrmr.2018.03.002.

Sault, S. 2021. "Davos Agenda: What You Need to Know About the Future of Work." World Economic Forum, January 24. weforum.org/agenda/2021/01/davos-agenda-2021-society-and-the-future-of-work-skills-gap-jobs-of-tomorrow-diversity-inclusion-worker-well-being.

World Economic Forum. 2020. *The Future of Jobs Report 2020*. Cologny, Switzerland: World Economic Forum.

Recommended Resources

Bradberry, T., and J. Greaves. 2009. *Emotional Intelligence 2.0*. San Diego: TalentSmartEQ.

Goleman, D. 2005. *Emotional Intelligence: Why It Can Matter More Than IQ*, 10th anniversary ed. New York: Random House.

Harvard Business Review. 2015. *10 Must Reads on Emotional Intelligence*. Cambridge, MA: Harvard Business Review Press.

TalentSmart EQ. "Articles." talentsmarteq.com/articles.

TalentSmart EQ. "EQ Trends." talentsmarteq.com/EQtrends.

SECTION III
TRAINING AND DEVELOPMENT BASICS

LUMINARY PERSPECTIVE

Train to Add Value and Make a Difference

Bob Pike

What is the purpose of training? To get results. Training is a process—not an event. It begins long before people engage in learning (whether face-to-face, virtually, or through e-learning), and it continues until we see results in the workplace. My goal as a trainer for more than 50 years has always been to empower, inspire, and equip my participants to build their confidence and help them get results.

One of the things I believe is important is understanding how people learn best. Instructional design is missing this link. For example, the ADDIE model (analyze, design, develop, implement, evaluate) is focused on content. Nowhere does it ask how to target how participants obtain the knowledge. How do they learn the best?

The Learning Preference Continuum

In the mid-1990s, I helped validate Inscape's Personal Learning Insights Profile (now part of John Wiley Company), which demonstrated how effective learning occurs. We have since assessed more than 70,000 participants in 25 countries and outlined three dimensions on the learning preferences continuum, which we focus on as we look at how they learn best. These three dimensions are learning purpose, learning structure, and learning activities.

Learning Purpose

Learning purpose represents why you want to know. You may want information to be practical and immediately usable, or perhaps you are more interested in new and informative content.

Think about where you find yourself on this continuum. An informative learner will learn anything! You may look at the back of a cereal box and think, "Whoa, I might use this information some day." Meanwhile, practical learners are thinking, "That was interesting, but who cares? Why bother reading all that trivia?"

Informative Learner ←————————————————————————→ *Practical Learner*

- **Informative learners** like to learn when the information is new and interesting.
- **Practical learners** prefer to learn things that they can use right now.

Are you a practical learner or an informative learner? Practical learners want to learn just what they need to know—no fluff, no fillers. Informative learners love information—at the extreme, everything is interesting. We've profiled people from all walks of life and about 50 percent are practical and 50 percent are informative. So how can you use information like this to improve your design and delivery?

I divide all my content into three buckets: need to know, nice to know, and where to go. Then, I make sure that 80 percent of the content in the need to know bucket is practical. That way, I engage both types of learners. The additional content in the nice to know and where to go buckets appeals to the informative learners.

Learning Structure

Learning structure represents how information is organized. It is either specific and step-by-step or flexible and more general. Maybe you like to have everything organized in a specific framework from the very beginning. An extreme example of this would be asking, "What do you want them to learn, by when, and what resources are available? How will we know they have learned, and how long will it take to learn?"

On the other hand, a general learner may ask, "What do you want them to learn?" And then they'll take it from there. The further you trend toward the general side, the more you believe in learner choice.

Specific Learner ←————————————————————————→ *General Learner*

- **Specific learners** want a clear path: What am I going to learn? How will I learn? Why am I learning? How will I know I've learned? How will I use what I've learned?
- **General learners** prefer to have information presented in a broader format. They want to create their own structure to make sense of information.

Are you a specific learner or a general learner? Based on our profiles, about 50 percent are specific learners and the other 50 percent are general learners.

How do you apply this to your design and delivery?

I develop a very specific structure. For example, I'll say something like, "You are going to work with a partner to do a case study. Here is a sheet that lists the steps and outcomes." This appeals to specific learners. Then I say, "Here are four case studies. Read through them with your partner and choose the one that you'll work on together." This appeals to the general learners, who want choices, not assignments.

Learning Activity

Learning activity represents how actively engaged a learner prefers to be in the learning process. It does not correlate with whether you are an extrovert or introvert. It is purely an engagement preference. You may like to actively participate with others, or perhaps you'd rather take in information and reflect on it independently. If you look at the extreme side, reflective learners would prefer to take all their classes online via e-learning programs so they don't have to interact or connect with anybody. In fact, they'd rather read a book. On the other hand, if a participative learner took that same e-learning course, they would take breaks every 15 minutes to run to the water cooler in hopes of connecting with someone.

Reflective Learner   *Participative Learner*

- **Reflective learners** want to think about new information when learning. They like learning on their own.
- **Participative learners** prefer to be more active and involved in the learning process. They like learning with others.

The interesting thing about the research is that more than 75 percent of the learners we profiled prefer to learn with others. I apply this to my design and delivery by creating exercises involving small groups—five to six people in a face-to-face environment or three people online. This appeals to the participative learner. Then I build in individual reflection activities, paired shares, and so forth, which falls into the comfort zone of the reflective learner.

These three dimensions will help you design and deliver training more effectively for your learners. You will find additional information about the learning preferences in chapter 2 and a grid on the handbook website at ATDHandbook3.org.

Now, let's look at three additional models that have shaped the way I design content to ensure retention and recall.

Model 1. The 90/20/8 (4) Rule

I always apply the 90/20/8 (4) rule. I learned from Tony Buzan (*Use Both Sides of Your Brain*) that while adults can listen with understanding for 90 minutes, they can listen with retention for only 20 minutes.

90/20/8 (4)

My daughter Rebecca inspired the additional eight minutes. High-school speech competitions were all eight minutes in length. When I asked her why, she said that TV programs break every eight minutes for a commercial. If you can't get it done in eight minutes, you've lost them. Did you know that in the US by the time a student graduates from high school, they've been in class 14,000 hours, but they've watched 19,000 hours of television? Imagine adult learners in your classroom that have 19,000 hours of programming that says you'll get a break every eight minutes! Every video game gives breaks. They are called levels. You play for a short amount of time and then, if you are successful, you level up and get the opportunity for a short break.

That's why I go a maximum of eight minutes before involving people in my face-to-face training sessions. For example, I may ask a question that learners can discuss with a partner, or I may ask them to write something down. When it comes to virtual delivery, the eight is replaced with four. I want to re-engage people every four minutes because there are more distractions in the virtual world.

Model 2. The CPR Rule

Based on the 90/20/8 (4) rule, I break all my content into chunks that last no more than 20 minutes, because I want participants to retain what they have learned. In fact, many of my content chunks are much shorter than that. For each content chunk I think about what the content will be, how I will get participants involved, and how often that content needs to be revisited.

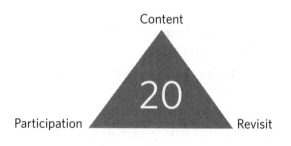

Notice I said revisited, not reviewed. Revisit is when the participants do it. Review is when the instructor does it again. Revisiting is far more powerful.

Model 3. The Social Model of Training—CIO

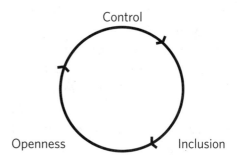

I adapted the CIO model from Will Schutz. Whenever someone comes into a learning environment, the first thing they want is to feel in control or safe. It is not that they want to control others. They just do not want to be controlled. Once they feel safe, they want to belong or feel included. When they feel included, they are willing to be open, and that's when they'll share and ask questions.

This is why I use openers in my training, not icebreakers. An opener will raise the *BAR*—it will *Break preoccupation* through involvement, *Allow for networking*, and will always be *Relevant to the content*. Remember our practical learner.

In an icebreaker, the trainer might pass out cards to everyone and say, "Find your match!" Then the participants will spend the next 10 minutes trying to match short with tall and salt with pepper and peanut butter with jelly. The practical learner won't see what this has to do with what they are supposed to learn for their job. And their first memory will be that we started with a silly game. That's not what we want.

Final Thoughts

I believe that one purpose of training is for participants to leave impressed with themselves, not intimidated by the trainer. They should be excited about what they now know and can do that they couldn't before. And they should have more confidence in their abilities. The masters that have written each chapter in this section have focused their content on helping you do this.

For my 50-plus years as a trainer my goal has been to add value and make a difference. May you be able to do the same.

About the Author

Bob Pike, CPTD Fellow, CSP, CPAE, is known as the "trainer's trainer." He is the author of more than 30 books, including the all-time bestselling train-the-trainer book, *Master Trainer's Handbook*. More than 150,000 trainers on five continents have graduated from his multiple-day train-the-trainer programs. Bob has keynoted, trained, and consulted in more than 25 countries and his "Training and Performance Forum" newsletter has more than 10,000 subscribers. He has presented at every ATD International Conference & Exposition since 1977 and has facilitated programs for more than 100 ATD chapters.

Recommended Resources

Buzan, T. 1991. *Use Both Sides of Your Brain: New Mind-Mapping Techniques*, 3rd ed. New York: Plume.

Meiss, R., and L. Wheeler, eds. 2016. *CORE: Closers, Openers, Revisiters, and Energizers: Activities and Games for Face-to-Face Training*, vol. 3. Eden Prairie, MN: Creative Training Productions.

Pike, B. 2015. *Master Trainer Handbook: Tips, Tactics, and How-Tos for Delivering Effective Instructor-Led Participant-Centered Training.* Amherst, MA: HRD Press.

Pike, B. 2017. *101 Games for Trainers: A collection of the Best Activities from Creative Training Techniques Newsletter.* Amherst, MA: HRD Press.

Pike, B., and L. Solem. 2000. *50 Creative Training Openers and Energizers: Innovative Ways to Start Your Training With a Bang!* New York: John Wiley and Sons.

Sousa, D. 2011. *How the Brain Learns*, 4th ed. Thousand Oaks, CA: Corwin.

CHAPTER 11

ADDIE: The Origin of Modern-Day ISD

Angel Green

Instruction is one of the earliest forms of documented human communication. Prehistoric drawings were likely used by tribal leaders to inform others of the location and type of animals to hunt, where to find freshwater sources, and how to perform religious rituals. The origin story of modern instructional design dates back over the past 100 years.

> **IN THIS CHAPTER:**
> - Explore the origin of ISD
> - Compare and contrast a selection of ISD models
> - Describe benefits and potential drawbacks of each ISD model

Why is an origin story so important? With the affordability and availability of historical archives and DNA testing, there has been a proliferation of people tracking their lineage and ancestral ties as far back as they can, scouring church records, government registries, and newspaper clippings to weave a story of those who came before them. Perhaps, in discovering our origin story, we feel like we're part of a community with a shared history. We uncover a lineage we never knew we had. Maybe the roots we uncover expose hardships endured by those who made it possible for us to be where, and who, we are today. And sometimes, we have the chance to learn lessons from mistakes that were made before us; with that knowledge, we have the opportunity to avoid history repeating itself.

The same reasons for why a personal origin story can be valuable—building a sense of community, understanding our shared experience, respecting those who paved the way for us, and learning from past mistakes—ring true for the origin story of instructional design and development models.

The Need for an Instructional Systems Development Model

Often, researchers, books, articles, and experts use the term *instructional design theories* interchangeably with *instructional design models*. However, for this chapter, we will draw a distinct line between the two:

- **Theories** provide instructional designers with evidence, research, conjecture, and criteria by which they can make design decisions (that is, the level of behavioral objectives, the setting and modality of training, the spacing and sequencing of instructional interventions, the appropriate evaluation method, and so forth).
- **Models** are processes that an instructional designer or team can use to create an instructional product.

Having a solid understanding of instructional theory will help in your design, but without a process to follow, you can't build an instructional product. On the other hand, simply using a model without an understanding of learning theory can push a product through to creation, but the product likely won't be appropriately designed (or instructionally sound).

Key learning theories that instructional designers should be familiar with before moving into design and development include B.F. Skinner's research on operant conditioning and programmed learning, Benjamin Bloom's taxonomy of educational objectives, Robert Gagné's Nine Events of Instruction, David Merrill and Charles Reigelueth's Component Display Theory, and the Center for Creative Leadership's 70-20-10 theory on executive success.

It is through these theories (and others) we begin to see instructional design become a process; gaining an understanding and taking these theories into consideration will be foundational to the creation of a successful training product. You'll need to think through these questions before you begin:

- Skinner: What behaviors need to be demonstrated and what reinforcement works?
- Bloom: To what cognitive level does the learner need to know the subject matter?
- Gagné: How can we design our program so that it meets the nine necessary events?
- Merrill and Reigelueth: How can we best sequence and chunk the content to scaffold the learning?
- 70-20-10: How does the work environment support the practical application of formal training?

Beyond these considerations, other design decisions need to be made, such as modality of delivery, which is seemingly endless and continues to expand as new apps and technology emerge. The rate of change expected is another factor to consider in design decisions. And, of course, budget, location, and time have a major influence on design and development.

Because of the number of considerations and decisions involved in a single training project, the US military implemented structured plans for the development, delivery, and evaluation of training, referred to as Systems Approach to Training (SAT) models. They were created, in part, to allow for decision-based trade-offs in design and development efforts. Their goal was to create instruction that aligned with the mission, the problem, the time to develop, and the cost and budget considerations. Each branch of the military created its own model, and divisions within each branch also created their own SAT models. In all, by 1973, more than 100 different models had been developed.

In 1973, the US Army began working with the Center for Educational Technology (CET) at Florida State University to evaluate the existing SATs and recommend one standard approach to training design. It quickly became evident that other divisions of the military could also benefit from this approach. So, they formed a joint committee of chief training officers from the army, navy, air force, and marines. The goal was to create a model that could be useful for improving *interservice* training design and development, thereby saving money and, where appropriate, combining training efforts.

This joint force would need to account for:

- A planning framework
- A suggested sequence of work
- The basis for a central management system
- The basic inputs, processes, and outputs
- The learning interfaces
- A feedback control

Instructional Systems Development: The Interservice Procedures for Instructional Systems Development (IPISD)

After two years and several iterations and revisions, Branson, Rayner, Cox, Furman, King, and Hannum documented the Interservice Procedures for Instructional Systems Development (IPISD) in 1975. This set of manuals was described for use as guidance in military ISD applications (Figure 11-1). The ISD model was based on the phases of systems engineering, which was a standard approach used across industries for the structured design and development of any product (such as auto manufacturing or satellite development).

Figure 11-1. Interservice Procedures for Instructional Systems Development Model

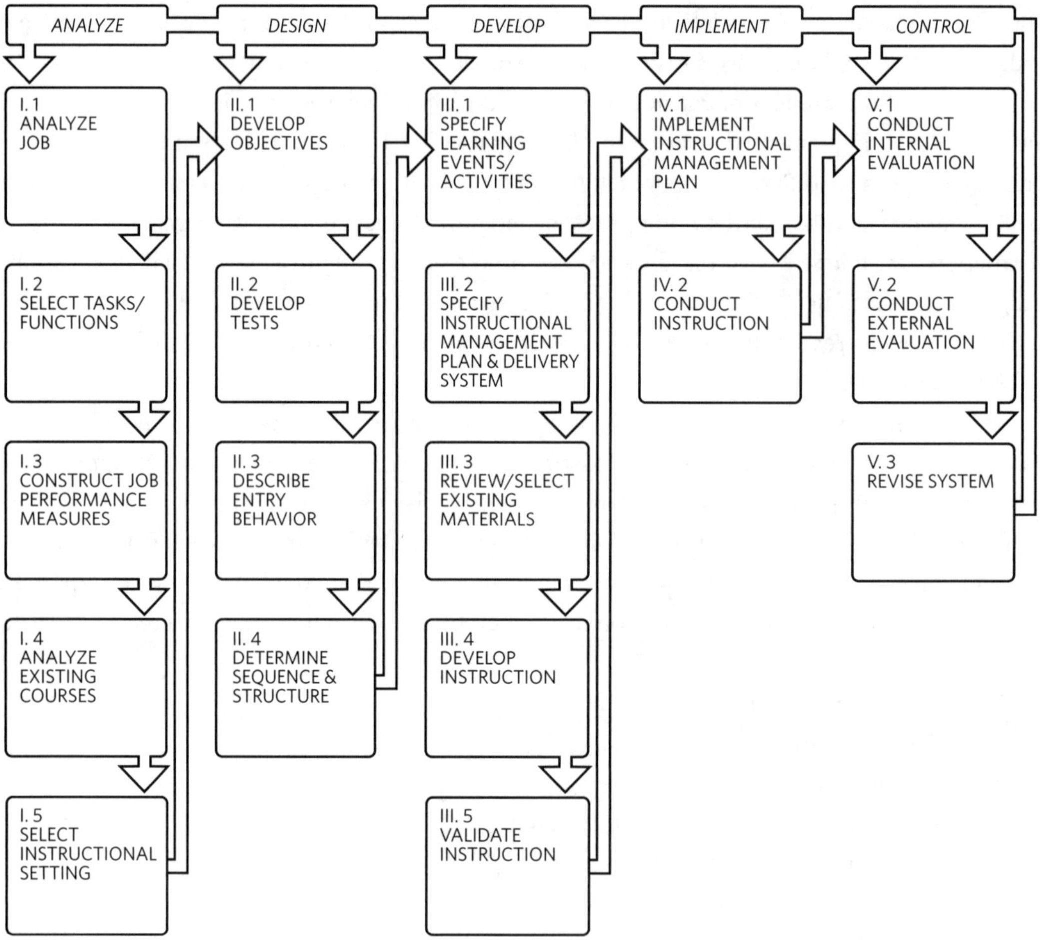

ANALYZE	DESIGN	DEVELOP	IMPLEMENT	CONTROL
I.1 ANALYZE JOB	II.1 DEVELOP OBJECTIVES	III.1 SPECIFY LEARNING EVENTS/ ACTIVITIES	IV.1 IMPLEMENT INSTRUCTIONAL MANAGEMENT PLAN	V.1 CONDUCT INTERNAL EVALUATION
I.2 SELECT TASKS/ FUNCTIONS	II.2 DEVELOP TESTS	III.2 SPECIFY INSTRUCTIONAL MANAGEMENT PLAN & DELIVERY SYSTEM	IV.2 CONDUCT INSTRUCTION	V.2 CONDUCT EXTERNAL EVALUATION
I.3 CONSTRUCT JOB PERFORMANCE MEASURES	II.3 DESCRIBE ENTRY BEHAVIOR	III.3 REVIEW/SELECT EXISTING MATERIALS		V.3 REVISE SYSTEM
I.4 ANALYZE EXISTING COURSES	II.4 DETERMINE SEQUENCE & STRUCTURE	III.4 DEVELOP INSTRUCTION		
I.5 SELECT INSTRUCTIONAL SETTING		III.5 VALIDATE INSTRUCTION		

The overall goal was to "train to specific job requirements, avoiding the expensive pitfalls of overtraining and undertraining" (Branson 1978). The complete executive summary of this model is available for download as an unclassified document from the US Army Combat Arms Training Board. The executive summary provides a detailed description of the goals of each phase, the activities that make up each "block" in the phase, the management decisions in each block, and the outcome of each block.

The model itself is a stage-gate, or waterfall, project management approach. As described in the summary, "Each of the phases is a separate and distinct function which could be carried out successively by one person, or each of the steps could be assigned to individuals." This does not mean, however, that iterations and revisions *within* the blocks are not conducted. As it is written, iteration or revisions are occurring within most, if not all the blocks in each phase of the IPISD model.

For example, the authors state in the develop phase that "a very lean approach to writing initial drafts is required. As the materials are tried with students, weaknesses and discrepancies can be identified, and, where necessary, materials can be expanded to overcome any shortcomings.... When a small amount of instruction on a learning objective has been developed, it is tried with a single trainee from the target population to see whether it is successful. Since these materials should have been prepared in the leanest possible form, the tryouts should reveal weaknesses."

Benefits of IPISD

The complete and full use of IPISD as it was designed should help those responsible for creating instruction to arrive at clear, data-based decisions about the product they create. In other words, IPISD helps instructional designers and managers resist the urge to develop training based on their own past experience, comfort with a modality, or desire to try something new or trendy. As described in Phase III, Block 2, "New delivery systems and techniques often become fashionable simply because they are available. In this block, procedures are defined for selecting one or more suitable media for specific learning events and activities. By using this approach, delivery systems can be selected on the basis of defined requirements rather than on the basis of availability or the appeal of currently existing fads" (Branson et al. 1975).

Limitations of IPISD

The IPISD model was designed for a very select audience using a unique use case: developing instruction for 1970s military personnel. Using the exact model as prescribed might work for an organization competing in the modern workforce, or it might not.

It is important to note that the creators of the IPISD model believed that whatever framework they developed would not be universally applicable. They stated that "the design of an efficient, effective, generic all-purpose model is no more likely than the design of an all-purpose drug" (Branson 1978).

This point is critical for readers today. From the origin of instructional systems development, it was never the expectation that any one model would be used for all instructional design and development efforts. And yet, immediately after its publication and in the decades following, we have seen organizations institutionalize a single ISD model for all their development efforts, professing that a standard model could and should apply universally.

Just as "two or more equally successful alternative solutions can be found for any instructional problem" (Branson 1978), there are likely two or more equally effective instructional design models that could be used in the creation of the solution. An instructional designer, therefore, should consider not just what to build, but also how to systematically approach the design and development.

Not long after the IPISD model was implemented, concerns began to arise regarding the practicality and consistency of adherence to a standard model throughout all branches of the military. By 1979, the Office of the Assistant Secretary of Defense Manpower, Reserve Affairs and Logistics (OASD MRA&L) engaged the help of Robert Vinberg and John N. Joyner from the Human Resources Research Organization (HumRRO) to answer the following questions:

- Do the current methodologies, as represented in the major guidance documents used in the services, provide the means for attaining the goals of ISD?
- Do current applications of ISD reflect these goals?
- How can ISD methodologies and applications be made more effective?

Vinberg and Joyner evaluated three ISD models in practice at the time:

- IPISD, which they referred to as ITRO
- Marine Corps Order P1510.23B, which was described as "a greatly reduced version of the ITRO model"
- Air Force Pamphlet 50-58, Handbook for Designers of Instructional Systems (1973–1975)

Additionally, they surveyed 209 units, agencies, and schools where instruction was developed and conducted detailed interviews of training developers to evaluate how they had designed and developed 57 courses.

In their summary report, Vinberg and Joyner (1980) stated that "ISD, a systems approach to training development, has many potential advantages, but it is demanding to carry out. It requires sustained commitment to a repetitive process of analysis, design, verification, and revision. Experience in attempts to institutionalize such a process has tended to reveal problems."

It is interesting to note that they described instructional systems development as "procedures for the development of training which are characterized by: (1) Rigorous derivation of training requirements from job requirements. Training requirements are to be selected so as to maximize the combined effectiveness of the training and non-training components of a total operational system. (2) Selection of instructional strategies to maximize the efficiency of training. (3) Iterative trial and revision of instruction during development until training objectives are met."

Again, it appears that from the early entry of ISD, iterations were anticipated. And, it is the iterative nature that they believed held the most potential, but also created the biggest obstacle to institutionalize. They went on to state that "its iterative and derivative character virtually assures that training will be relevant if available procedures are faithfully carried out. In practice, however, many of its components are omitted, and the close connection between components that is essential to make the process truly derivative is not maintained. Most important, the testing and revision necessary to insure job relevance generally do not occur. The potential of ISD to insure that training meets job requirements is not being realized" (Vinberg and Joyner 1980).

But perhaps the most impactful finding and recommendation from the study was the fault they found in the last phase, control. Training development and evaluation, they said, were "regarded as separate activities, which meant that the potential of the ISD process for improving the training was not happening." In other words, after a training initiative was live and in place, the instructional design team was no longer involved or engaged. The evaluation of the effectiveness of the training was instead observed and measured by the commanding officers. And the two were rarely in contact. In many cases, the instructional designer was a contract civilian, while those who witnessed the impact of the training (students, instructors, or officers of the students) were enlisted.

Through this perspective, we can now see why, the model changed shortly thereafter, with the name of the final phase changing from control to evaluation.

The Beginning of ADDIE

Around the same time that Vinberg and Joyner were engaged in their study, a doctoral candidate named Russell Wayne Watson was working on his dissertation, "The Analysis and Design of an Instructional Systems Course." In the dissertation, Watson described how, in the years following the 1975 launch of the IPISD model, it became increasingly difficult to meet the goal of developing all army training using the model.

After successful defense of his dissertation, Watson used his understanding of the challenges faced by the military to evolve the explanation of ISD in a paper he presented to the International Congress for Individualized Instruction. "The five phases of ISD are analysis, design, development, implementation, and evaluation and control," he stated. "The first four are sequential in nature, but the evaluation and control phase is a *continuous process that is conducted in conjunction with all of the others*" (Watson 1981). Watson's paper included a visual diagram of the ISD workflow, which shows how Phase V, evaluation and control, influences all other phases of ISD (Figure 11-2). This is in line with the changes to ISD recommended by Vinberg and Joyner.

Figure 11-2. Rendering of Watson's ISD Workflow Diagram

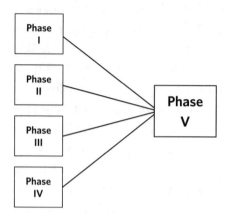

While the main phases of Watson's model also followed those of systems engineering, the supporting blocks in each phase differed slightly from the IPISD model (Figure 11-3). Obvious revisions that Watson made include renaming Phase V from control to evaluation and control, expanding the importance of task analysis during the analysis phase, and shifting the review of existing courses and materials from analysis to development.

The last two phases remained largely untouched, with the addition of the word *evaluation* and the removal of IPISD's revise system block. This removal is an interesting point, considering that Watson obviously understood the importance of evaluation throughout the process. Graphically, however, revision does not appear to be part of the model.

There are several iterations of the 1981 model; some involved shifting the graphical representation to a circular model in which evaluation enveloped all other phases. Added arrows indicate an iterative design.

In 1984, three years after the Watson paper was presented, the US Army published *A Systems Approach to Training*, which once again revised the model. This version shortened the name of Phase V from Watson's control and evaluation to evaluation. Thus, the acronym ADDIE was born (although the handbook still referred to the model as instructional systems development, ISD).

Although ADDIE is often accused of being a linear model, it is clear that the early users never intended it to be so. See, for example, the next iteration from the US Army Field Artillery School in 1984 (Figure 11-4).

Figure 11-3. Watson's Revised Model

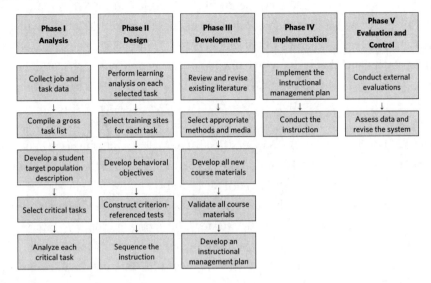

Watson (1981)

Figure 11-4. The ADDIE Process

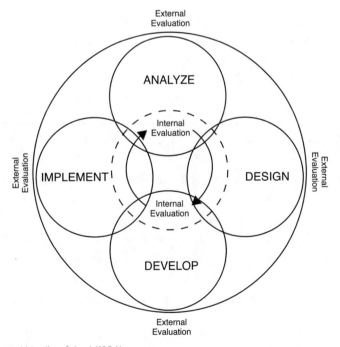

Adapted from U.S. Army Field Artillery School (1984)

ADDIE: The Origin of Modern-Day ISD | 175

The term *ADDIE* officially appeared nearly a decade later in *A Handbook of Instructional and Training Program Design,* by Michael Schlegel (1995). Within the abstract of the document he states, "This paper will utilize the generic Instructional Design Model of Analyze, Design, Development, Implementation and Evaluation (ADDIE) … and provide detailed job aids in the form of rating sheets and checklists (mechanically or hard copy) for each of the major steps." Whether others had used the term *ADDIE* to describe the ISD model before the publication of Schlegel's handbook is a question with a rich history of debate within the instructional design community.

Regardless of when or where the term was first used, ADDIE wins the prize in branding. It is an acronym that is easily remembered and aids in the communication of the phases of instructional systems design to those who aren't familiar with the process.

Even though the origin story is a bit unclear, ADDIE is the most well known or referred to of the ISD models. But, because there is no true "author," the acronym is open to interpretation and has been revised over the years to adapt to the needs of modern instructional systems design.

At this point, ADDIE has almost become an eponym for instructional systems design, as generic in use as Kleenex or Band-Aid. However, from person to person, the activities performed in each phase and even the order or sequence of the phase may vary widely.

There are many alternatives to IPISD or ADDIE, too many to include in this resource. Like the original IPISD authors stated, there is no all-purpose model that will work for everyone. Choosing which model to follow will likely vary over time, from project to project, or within different organizational structures. The rest of this chapter reviews some of these other models.

Systems Approach Model

Walter Dick, Lou Carey, and James Carey described a detailed process for the creation of instruction, which they referred to as the Systems Approach Model in their 1978 textbook, *The Systematic Design of Instruction*. While IPISD and SAT were popular in government, Dick and Carey's model gained popularity in educational institutions.

In the Systems Approach Model, Dick and Carey describe 10 components that are necessary for the creation of effective instruction. The model "is based not only on theory and research but also on a considerable amount of practical experience in application."

They also acknowledge from the outset that the model can be personalized, using an analogy of how a great cook first starts with a recipe and then uses intuition, experience, success, and failure to make a recipe their own, unique creation. Later, Dick and Carey (2021) go on to say that "the flexibility, insight, and creativity required for original solutions reside in experienced users and professionals—not in models."

In their model, they lay out these components involved in the creation of instruction:
- Identify instructional goals.
- Conduct instructional analysis.
- Analyze learners and contexts.
- Write performance objectives.
- Develop assessment instruments.
- Develop instructional strategy.
- Develop and select instructional materials.
- Design and conduct formative evaluation of instruction.
- Revise instruction.
- Design and conduct summative evaluation.

In the diagram of their model, Dick and Carey distinguish iterative cycles of evaluation and revision with dotted lines (Figure 11-5; Dick and Carey 2021).

Figure 11-5. The Dick and Carey Systems Approach Model

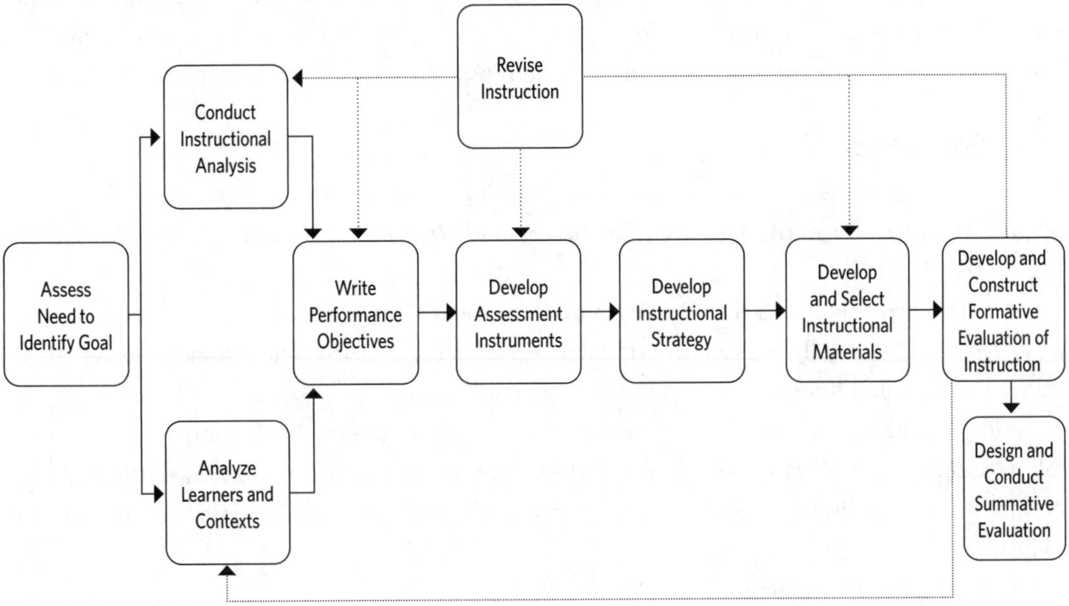

Dick and Carey (2021)

The explanation of each component describes, in detail, the activities that are involved within the broader component. For example, for identify instructional goals, the authors provide a decision tree for front-end analysis, the main steps in performance analysis, structure for conducting a needs assessment, job and task analysis, and guidance on writing instructional goals.

Benefits of Dick and Carey's Systems Approach Model

Probably the greatest benefit of the Systems Approach Model is how the original authors have evolved the process over the last 40 years to keep the model current. The descriptions and examples are relevant to today's instructional designers. It also has the credibility of decades of practical evidence, research, and theory that some modern ISD models may lack.

Potential Limitations of Dick and Carey's Systems Approach Model

The Systems Approach Model is a long process. There is little doubt that the instructional designer will be thorough, but the entire process may be unnecessary for some projects. And, while the authors encourage the reader to make it their own, for many instructional designers that takes a lot of courage and experience. With businesses continuing to compress training project timelines (anyone can make a YouTube video!), instructional designers who are still reliant on following the process as described might find themselves in an unfavorable position.

The Kemp Model

More than 50 years ago, Jerrold Kemp wrote, "Panning for a student's learning should be a challenging, exciting, and gratifying activity" in his textbook *Instructional Design: A Plan for Unit and Course Development*.

Kemp then introduced a circular diagram of his process in the 1985 textbook *The Instructional Design Process*. Originally referred to as the Kemp model, this process is now sometimes called the Morrison, Ross, and Kemp model or the MRK model (Figure 11-6).

Although Kemp died in 2015, his model and revisions to the textbook continue through his fellow authors, Gary R. Morrison, Steven J. Ross, Jennifer R. Morrison, and Howard K. Kalman. Now in its eighth edition, *Designing Effective Instruction* outlines nine elements that are essential to instructional design:
- Instructional problems
- Learner characteristics
- Task analysis
- Instructional objectives
- Content sequencing
- Instructional strategies

- Designing the instructional message
- Development of instruction
- Evaluation instruments

Figure 11-6. The Kemp Model

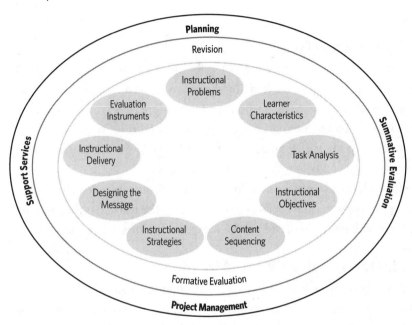

Kemp (1985)

Similar to other models, the Kemp model posits that "there is never one perfect approach to solving an instructional design problem." And the authors also reinforce the idea that "a design model must grow with the instructional designer." Additionally, each of the nine elements in the Kemp model has an accompanying set of activities and considerations for the instructional designer and project team to make. For example, the task analysis element provides guidance for preparing for a task analysis, advice on ways to extend beyond a typical procedural analysis, and techniques on gathering and recording your data.

There are, however, a number of differences between Kemp's model and the others. The most obvious is the graphical depiction of the model as a series of three concentric ovals, with nine independent ovals contained within the third. This is a visual departure from the series of lines and arrows connecting boxes in other ISD models.

The outer two ovals in the Kemp model represent ongoing factors that are present throughout the entire instructional design and development project. The first ring represents the managerial considerations (support services, project management, and planning) that an instructional designer and team will need to consider. The second oval contains the activities of evaluation (summative, formative, and confirmative) and revision. The third ring contains independent ovals representing each of the nine elements. The independence of these ovals is critical, as it is intended to visually represent the belief that each element can be addressed simultaneously, individually, or perhaps not at all.

Benefits of the Kemp Model

The Kemp model has received praise for its flexibility and nonlinear design. It is less prescriptive and allows for amplifying or downsizing the process based on a project or learner need.

The latest version includes a section on Lean instructional design, which describes the appropriate concessions to make when faced with limitations on time and resources. This guidance could help overcome potential trepidation of newer instructional designers who aren't ready to make it their own without advice on how to do so effectively.

The Kemp model is also often noted for its emphasis on a learner-centric design; for example, considering the personal and social characteristics of the learner, including culturally diverse learners, learners with disabilities, and adult learners in the corporate environment.

Potential Limitations of the Kemp Model

As with the Systems Approach Model, it's challenging to explain the Kemp model in a simple, concise fashion to non-instructional-design team members. And, while the authors attempt to address this in the textbook's introduction, the model still falls short of having a catchy, easy way to explain the process.

Another potential challenge is a by-product of its flexible design—when do you cut out an activity or element and when do you know you've done enough? While there are benefits to having a flexible model, an instructional designer might unintentionally miss key details that could result in a better design, had they not excluded one (or more) of the nine elements.

Successive Approximation Model (SAM)

Allen Interactions, the custom learning content company founded by Michael Allen, created the Successive Approximation Model (SAM), which followed an interactive design process. In an effort to help instructional designers create better quality instruction, faster, Allen along with Richard Sites published *Leaving ADDIE for SAM* in 2012. In the book, Allen described the iterative nature of SAM, directly comparing and contrasting SAM with a genericized ADDIE model. The term *ADDIE*, he believed, had become ubiquitous even though no one applied the model in the same way beyond dividing "tasks into analysis, design, development, implementation, and evaluation phases" (Allen and Sites 2012). Beyond that, the actual activities varied widely between organizations and even among departments.

While IPISD was inspired by the early 1970s systems engineering models, SAM was based on the Agile, or iterative, design models prevalent in the software industry. The goal was to be an effective and manageable process that allows teams to "complete projects within time and budget expectations, predict the impact of in-process changes, and produce a product that meets established criteria for quality." The nonlinear process was designed to help avoid a problem often encountered in more linear models—costly mistakes in design that are not caught until after the training is developed, and in some cases implemented.

SAM also attempts to simplify the process. There are two versions an instructional designer uses, based on the complexity of the project. SAM 1 is a very simple version that is most effective when there is a small design and development team and no complex media elements; SAM 2 is more robust.

SAM 1 is a three-stage iterative process of evaluate, design, and develop (Figure 11-7). Prototypes are revised through a series of three cycles, ultimately arriving on a final production quality training solution. Fewer than three cycles, Allen warns, may lead to sacrifices in design, and more than three may lead to perpetual cycling in the pursuit of perfection. SAM works on the principle that "good enough" is always better than nothing, and that no training product will ever be perfect.

Figure 11-7. SAM 1

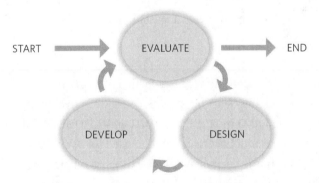

Allen and Sites (2012)

The model and diagram that most people associate with SAM is that of SAM 2, which is better suited for more complex teams and training projects. SAM 2 is divided into three phases: preparation, iterative design, and iterative development (Figure 11-8).

Figure 11-8. SAM 2

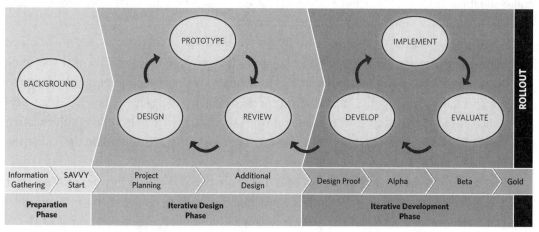

Allen and Sites (2012)

SAM 2 also requires the use of prototypes in design followed by a series of four review moments (design proof, alpha, beta, and gold) each time the product in development increases in fidelity and completeness. By reviewing a tangible product, rather than a written explanation, misinterpretations and incorrect assumptions can be caught early in the development process, when they are less costly to fix.

Like the Kemp model, SAM is focused on learner-centric design. Representative or actual learners are involved, not only at the beginning and end of the process like in many ISD models, but throughout the preparation, design, and development phases.

Benefits of SAM

Prototyping at each phase allows designers to get feedback along the way from learners and project stakeholders. While tangible learning products are not developed until later in linear ISD processes (such as the second D in IPISD's ADDIC and ADDIE), SAM designers immediately start developing tangible products, which are then used for evaluation.

Another benefit of SAM is how easy it is to describe to those outside the instructional design world, since many organizations use Agile and iterative design in their own product development. Even when not familiar, the model is simple to explain and SAM provides a simple, catchy, acronym (like ADDIE) that was missing in IPISD, the Systems Approach Model, and the Kemp model.

Potential Limitations of SAM

Perhaps the greatest risk of SAM is the temptation to continue iterating in a quest for unattainable perfection, which can start early in the process. Instructional designers, by and large, are not used to operating in the space of imperfection; however, overdesigning the prototype reduces, if not eliminates, the value of iteration. If colors and graphics are included in prototypes too early, the focus may shift from debating the effectiveness of the instructional interaction to how the graphic or color they chose was off-brand. Prototypes are intended to be imperfect because their value is found in how easy they are to discard.

There's also a risk of getting stuck in an endless cycle of development iterations. Organizations need to be comfortable with versioned improvements of training, similar to the versioned improvements in software or applications. Think about how a new smartphone release, a new software update, or a new version of our favorite video game improves the user experience based on actual data while addressing known bugs. Similarly, SAM encourages organizations to launch a product with the expectation that it will undergo revisions, sometimes quickly, after go-live.

Final Thoughts

There are many ISD models from which to choose, and this chapter presents only a few that have been implemented across educational, governmental, and private institutions. And there's also the option to create a custom process based on the unique needs of a business or institution.

Perhaps the biggest takeaway from this exploration is the affirmation that there is no standard model in instructional systems design. However, there is one similarity across all models: the intent to create training that helps learners and organizations perform better. How you achieve that will be up to you and can be limited, both in the design and process, only by your creativity, intuition, experience, and constraints (either real or imagined).

About the Author

Angel Green is a learner advocate who is passionate about driving business results through innovative solutions in organizational design, performance management, and learning programs. With nearly 20 years' experience in the learning industry, she has led the creation of numerous award-winning programs, each dedicated to improving employee performance. Angel is dedicated to sharing her knowledge and experience on the benefits of empathetic design, introducing tools and techniques that designers can use to help create learner-centered instructional products. She is the co-author of *Leaving ADDIE for SAM Field Guide* and has written and spoken extensively within the learning and development industry.

References

Allen, M., and R. Sites. 2012. *Leaving ADDIE for SAM*. Alexandria, VA: ASTD Press.

Branson, R.K. 1978. "The Interservice Procedures for Instructional Systems Development." *Educational Technology* 18(3). Special Issue: Military Training.

Branson, R.K., G.T. Rayner, J.L. Cox, J.P. Furman, F.J. King, and W.H. Hannum. 1975. "Interservice Procedures for Instructional Systems Development, 5 vols. (TRADOC Pam 350-30 NAVEDTRA 106A). Ft. Monroe, VA: U.S. Army Training and Doctrine Command, August. (NTIS No. ADA 019 486 through ADA 019 490).

Dick, W., and L. Carey. 1978. *The Systematic Design of Instruction*. Glenview, IL: Scott, Foresman, and Company.

Dick, W., and L. Carey. 2021. *The Systematic Design of Instruction*. New York: Pearson Publishing.

Kemp, J. 1971. *Instructional Design: A Plan for Unit and Course Development*. New York: Fearon Publishers.

Kemp, J.E. 1985. *The Instructional Design Process*. New York: Harper and Row.

Morrison, G.R., S.J. Ross, J.R. Morrison, and H.K. Kalman. 2019. *Designing Effective Instruction*. New York: John Wiley and Sons.

Schlegel, M.J. 1995. *A Handbook of Instructional and Training Program Design*. ERIC Document Reproduction Service ED383281.

U.S. Army Field Artillery School. 1984. "A System Approach to Training." ST-5K061FD92. Washington, DC: US Government Printing Office.

Vineberg, R., and J. Joyner. 1980. "Instructional System Development (ISD) in the Armed Services: Methodology and Application." Final Report, August 25, 1977, through March 19, 1979. (Report Number: HumRROLTR-80-1). Office of the Assistant Secretary of Defense for Manpower.

Watson, R. 1981. "The Analysis and Design of an Instructional Systems Course." A Dissertation Submitted to The University of Arizona.

Recommended Resources

Biech, E. 2017. *The Art and Science of Training.* Alexandria, VA: ATD Press.

Bloom, B.S., and D.R. Krathwohl. 1956. *Taxonomy of Educational Objectives; The Classification of Educational Goals by a Committee of College and University Examiners. Handbook I: Cognitive Domain.* New York: Longmans, Green.

Gagné, R. 1985. *The Conditions of Learning,* 4th ed. New York: Holt, Rinehart & Winston.

Lombardo, M.M., and R.W. Eichinger. 1996. *The Career Architect Development Planner.* Minneapolis: Lominger.

Merrill, M.D. 1983. *Instructional Design Theories and Models: An Overview of Their Current Status.* Hillsdale, NJ: Prentice-Hall.

Reigeluth, C.M. 1983. *Instructional Design Theories and Models.* New York: Routledge.

CHAPTER 12

Using Evidence to Assess Performance Gaps

Ingrid Guerra-López

Talent development professionals add measurable value to their clients and organizations when using a systems-oriented framework for assessing needs and opportunities. The framework can help clarify what questions should be asked to collect relevant data that defines the problem and appropriate solutions, and in turn, contributes to human and organizational performance improvement.

IN THIS CHAPTER:
- Discuss the importance of a systems approach in assessing needs and selecting solutions
- Describe a strategic alignment framework for ensuring needs and solutions are aligned to measurable value
- Examine key considerations and methods for collecting relevant and useful evidence

What would your stakeholders consider to be a valuable use of learning and talent development initiatives? What concrete organizational returns and benefits has your organization received for its investment in a recent talent development initiative?

To maximize worthy accomplishments, these questions must be answered prior to selecting solutions, rather than after implementing them. Much of the learning and talent development literature starts with a preimposed solution mindset, particularly a training mindset, and assumes that positive results will follow. Beginning with a solution in search of no known problem can take us down a dangerous path. Conversely, if we use performance data to inform the selection of solutions and actions, we have a much better chance of measurably contributing to organizational success and justifying our resource spending.

> We fail more often because we solve the wrong problem than because we get the wrong solution to the right problem.
> —Russell Ackoff, management science pioneer

The most successful talent development professionals view their roles as much more than mere deliverers of training and learning products. They work to nurture strong partnerships with managers and other organizational stakeholders to support human performance that is aligned with organizational priorities. To this end, they generate, share, and use timely and relevant performance data to support decision making and action.

A Systemic Approach to Assessing Needs and Improving Performance

A needs assessment has the greatest utility and impact when we take a systems approach because it provides a holistic view of reality, helps distinguish assumptions from facts, validates evidenced-based needs, and reduces the risk of wasting precious resources on solutions (particularly training) that will not address underlying issues or get us much closer to expected outcomes. Therefore, a performance improvement mindset requires a systems approach to assessing needs.

Assessment and Analysis in Human Performance Systems

The term *needs assessment* is often used interchangeably with other terms such as *performance assessment*, *front-end assessment*, *performance analysis*, and *diagnosis*. Fundamentally, a needs assessment process provides a framework for measuring gaps in results and generating the performance data you require to make sound decisions about how to close these gaps. It starts with asking the right questions so you can align the right solutions to the right problems and devise a plan for effectively implementing those solutions.

While it's necessary to define needs in terms of a results gap to solve a performance problem, it is not sufficient. In addition to defining the performance problem, we must also understand why these gaps exist. Organizational solutions must be thoughtfully aligned to the factors driving the problem you want to solve. To this end, we employ a causal analysis to break down a performance gap into its component parts and identify interrelated root causes that are driving or sustaining the problem. It's important to note that the overwhelming majority of performance problems are a product of circular patterns of events at the organizational level. For example, your data indicate a dip in sales for the sales team, so you quickly jump into solution mode and tackle the problem in two key ways: First, you retrain the sales team to make sure it has the best knowledge in the industry, and second, you enhance the incentives for meeting sales targets. However, you still don't see a noticeable improvement in sales.

Why not? Well, perhaps you never asked the "why" question. You should have done that immediately upon noticing the decreased sales figures. Asking why may have revealed that the trained staff do not have a chance to apply the "best industry knowledge" if their supervisors are communicating conflicting expectations, are not providing relevant feedback and coaching on the job, or are discouraging the sales team from applying those techniques once it is back in front of the customer.

In addition to causal analysis, talent development professionals are also engaged in conducting other types of analyses, particularly if we already have a compelling body of evidence to conclude that we have skills and knowledge gaps that are best addressed through training. These include audience analysis, task analysis, and environmental analysis:

- **Audience analysis** helps us better understand who our target learners are by collecting data related to relevant characteristics. These can include specific demographics and background information such as relevant prior knowledge and skills, work experience, and other characteristics that should be factored into the training design and delivery.
- **Task analysis** helps us clarify what trainees should be able to do. Concentrating on doing rather than knowing will help us focus the training activities and content on what is directly related to performance requirements, rather than what might be nice to know but not essential. Training is much more effective when it has direct relevance to a trainee's work requirements, and when this relevance is made explicit. Tasks are concrete activities that make up the duties of a given job role; in a task analysis, each one must be considered individually. The essential steps in task analysis include clearly defining the task that must

be performed, breaking it down into component subtasks, and breaking each component subtask into a clear, chronological, step-by-step process. While it is important not to make unfounded assumptions about what might be obvious to the learners, the trick is finding balance and providing just the right level of detail. Direct observation and expert interviews using out loud process protocols are particularly helpful data collection methods for task analysis.

- **Environmental analysis** helps us understand the learner's actual performance context (that is, the work setting) so we can design an instructional environment that resembles the performance context as much as possible. Various learning theories and sound instructional design practices support the importance of performance cues for helping individuals learn and perform effectively. Understanding performance cues is also critical for enhancing the transfer of training to the performance context. For example, if the work setting requires the trainee to perform a given task with the use of specific tools and under time constraints, the instructional activities included in the training should provide the same conditions. Environmental analysis can also be used to better understand the learning environment of the target audience, including what resources might be available to them during the training, the timing, their preferred training modality, and instructional strategies.

In summary, addressing skills and performance gaps requires us to understand the system, which is made up of interrelated factors and dynamics that create and sustain those recurring issues. A systems approach to needs assessment allows us to clearly define the outcomes that the system should deliver, the root causes or barriers that are getting in the way of achieving those outcomes, and the requirements that must be met by the solutions. This, in turn, gives us a strong foundation with which to judge the appropriateness of proposed solutions (Guerra-López 2018, 2021; Guerra-López and Hicks 2017; Kaufman and Guerra-López 2013).

The Strategic Alignment Process

The strategic alignment process integrates all these essential elements and considerations into a structured yet flexible process for ensuring that your talent development efforts clearly align to organizational priorities and generate useful feedback for decision making as well as hard evidence of your contributions to the organization's success. Therefore, the process rests on a performance measurement backbone and connects needs assessments to other evidence-generating processes such as analysis, monitoring, and evaluation. It offers a pragmatic way to establish effective partnerships with your stakeholders through a series of key questions and activities that help ensure you have the information required to make the best decisions possible.

The strategic alignment process comprises four phases, which are all equally important and require specific outputs to successfully complete the other stages (Figure 12-1; Guerra-López and Hicks 2017).

Figure 12-1. The Strategic Alignment Process

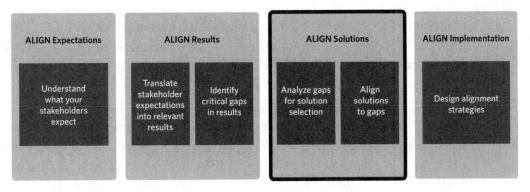

Adapted from Guerra-López and Hicks (2017)

Aligning Expectations

The initial phase, aligning expectations, helps us gain an understanding of the expectations, wants, and perceived performance needs from various perspectives. Stakeholders include the person who made the original request as well as those who will influence or be affected by the selected solutions, which could include top leadership, frontline supervisors, staff, or other relevant functional unit representatives. With a calibration of these perspectives, you will gain an understanding of what is or will be driving stakeholder decision making, assumptions, and satisfaction. In a sense, this step represents the beginning of creating and managing organizational change because it engages people in the process and, in turn, their views focus the improvement efforts. This helps generate a comprehensive picture of the issues and some of the factors that may affect the initiative's success.

Aligning Results

The aligning results phase helps identify measurable gaps in various levels of organizational results. Here, we work with stakeholders to translate their wants and expectations into the current and desired levels of results in skills, performance, value-added contribution to clients and community, and other strategic consequences that affect organizational sustainability. Many find it challenging to articulate their wants in terms of specific and measurable performance results, so we play an instrumental role in aligning their wants and valuable results. This is the foundation of the measurement framework and provides the focus of our data collection through relevant performance indicators. Data is collected to determine the critical gaps between current and desired results. These priority gaps are the foundation for further analysis, recommendation of solutions, and implementation plans.

Aligning Solutions

In the aligning solutions phase, we focus on the deliberate analysis of priority gaps. Now that we have defined the important problems to solve, it is critical to understand each one. What are the contributing factors? How do the contributing factors affect each other? What elements of the environment are perpetuating recurrent patterns? The answers will lead to a thorough understanding of the concrete changes our potential solutions should deliver.

The process of identifying alternative solutions should be collaborative; include input from stakeholders, beginning by identifying relevant and useful criteria for selecting solutions. This helps ensure that this process is not only driven by evidence, but also informed by the needs of the organization's culture and resources. The alternatives are then reviewed and the solutions are selected that most likely offer the best payoffs in the most resource-efficient ways.

Aligning Implementation

The aligning implementation phase deals with the critical success factors necessary to effectively implement the proposed organizational improvement initiatives to ensure successful execution, integration, and sustainability. Implementation leverages specific strategies for driving the transfer of results from training and development contexts to the performance environment. It's also important to consider thoughtful change management strategies that include defining who needs to be informed about what, when, and how, as well as how to gain useful input about other issues. In addition, we should define mobilization strategies that must be aligned to effectively implement our improvement initiatives. For example, should a core group or change coalition be formed to support the change? If so, who will be involved and in what ways? Mobilization strategies may also include defining implications for job descriptions, feedback mechanisms, performance evaluation, and process redesigns. Finally, a clear monitoring plan to track the progress of improvement initiatives must be articulated, including what data to track, how frequently to collect data, who should use it and when, and how to use data for corrective or improvement actions.

To help you identify objectives and activities for the alignment process, download the tool available on the handbook website at ATDHandbook3.org.

Collecting Relevant and Useful Evidence

A central premise of assessment is that we use relevant evidence to define needs and select appropriate solutions. Unfortunately, a common mistake is to force connections between easy-to-collect data, or data that the organization has already captured, and our definition of needs. In other words, people look at the available data and then ask questions they can answer with it. When this happens, they overlook important questions that do not naturally stem from the data—questions that they should ask and answer, but currently lack the data to do so. There is absolutely nothing wrong with using data that is already available (in fact, this can save time and other resources) if, first and foremost, it is relevant for answering the assessment questions.

Likewise, the data collection methods we use must be relevant for the type of data we seek. *Data* can mean any documented record of something—an event, a performance, a result—that took place during the period of interest for the assessment. It's typically driven by our selection of the relevant indicators for the results or phenomena we want to measure to answer our assessment questions. Examples of indicators could include account retention rates, turnover rates, net promoter scores, customer support tickets, employee satisfaction, salary competitiveness ratio, revenue growth, revenue per client, and customer lifetime value.

However, not all data carries the same weight in reaching conclusions, and some data may be misleading due to bias. Sound decisions are directly related to the appropriateness and quality of the data used to make them. Thus, data must meet four critical characteristics:

- **Relevant.** Data is directly related to the assessment questions (overarching and specific) that must be answered to clearly define and address important problems.
- **Reliable.** Data is rigorously measured, trustworthy, and consistent across various types of observations.
- **Valid.** Data truly indicates or relates to the results we want to measure; it measures what we say it measures.
- **Complete.** When systematically collected, analyzed, and synthesized, the data helps us generate an accurate and holistic view of reality.

Two related and essential terms that refer to both data and the techniques used to collect it are *qualitative* and *quantitative*. The qualitative technique requires careful and detailed observation and description, expressed through narrative rather than figures. Some appropriate ways to collect this type of data are observations, interviews, focus groups, open-ended questions on surveys, and reviews of existing documents.

Quantitative techniques are used to establish facts numerically, based on independently verifiable observations. Methods commonly used to collect quantitative data include Likert scale surveys and other validated scales, as well as a review of secondary data sources that could include a wide range of automated performance figures and statistics.

The distinction between qualitative and quantitative is not an either/or proposition. Typically, we gain a much better understanding of needs and problems when we use a mixed methods approach. For example, we may start with decreased employee engagement survey scores (quantitative), and subsequently use focus groups to help collect rich, in-depth narratives about employee experiences (qualitative). These provide a more complete picture of interrelated organizational climate issues and stronger evidence for making decisions about how to address those issues (or at a minimum, areas that require further inquiry and evidence).

Identifying Data Sources

Carefully considering from where or whom we collect data is a critical part of developing a useful data collection plan. This helps improve access to the data, ensure the appropriateness of data collection tools, and prevent unnecessary data gaps on the back end. Ongoing technology innovations are improving access and the timeliness of data on a continuous basis, both within and outside the organization, by linking reports, databases, experts, and other sources. As much as feasible, it is important to triangulate various sources to increase data confidence and subsequent conclusions and recommendations.

Selecting Data Collection Methods

The quality of the evidence we collect reflects the appropriateness and quality of our data collection methods. The type of data we seek and the sources we plan to use will inform the type of data collection methods we use. A common mistake is picking a data collection tool (like a survey) simply because it's familiar or what was used before. The data collection method should be chosen based on the function we want it to perform. For example, if you want to measure error rate across various sites or teams, you don't need a survey to collect attitudes about error rates. Instead you want to review quantitative data that is likely already being generated by automated performance reports. If you seek a deep understanding of low employee engagement survey scores (quantitative), you may want to select a data collection method that renders rich, in-depth qualitative data, such as focus groups or interviews. Many other resources provide detailed descriptions and steps for deploying data collection methods, so this chapter will not describe them at length. You will find a tool on the handbook website at ATDHandbook3.org that provides deployment tips to maximize the utility of several data collection methods, including observation, interviews, surveys, focus groups, and data reviews.

Data Analysis

Both qualitative and quantitative data are subject to rigorous analysis. Analysis involves organizing, summarizing, reviewing for quality, and synthesizing data to discover patterns or relationships, strengthen interpretations, and support conclusions and recommendations. Just as the type of data we want plays a major role in selecting data sources and collection methods, it also influences the type of data analysis techniques we select. Quantitative analysis techniques can be further subdivided into *descriptive* and *inferential* statistics. Common descriptive statistics include measures of central tendency such as the mean (average), mode (most frequent), or median (the middle) scores or responses, as well as measures of data variability such as the range of scores, standard deviation, or variance. Frequencies and percentages are also commonly used to represent quantitative data. Inferential statistics is a method that deduces a measure from a small random sample that represents the characteristics of a larger population. It allows you to make assumptions for a larger group based on the sample results.

Qualitative analysis can also be divided into major approaches: *deductive* and *inductive*. A deductive approach is based on a predetermined set of categories or domains selected by the assessor, which can make the analysis process quicker and easier. This is a feasible approach when we know enough about the subject matter to define logical categories of information that we can use to identify themes and patterns from the data. Conversely, an inductive approach can be more time consuming and is probably the best option when little is known about the subject matter and we have to take a more exploratory approach to identify themes. With this approach, we code and organize information around major emerging themes, and likely further subcategorize it into more specific themes.

Data Collection and Analysis Planning

One practical way to build your methodological plan is by using a data collection and analysis planning matrix, which you can find on the handbook's website, ATDHandbook3.org. Use the outputs generated during the initial phase (align expectations) to list each overarching needs assessment question (first column); then for each assessment question, work with stakeholders to gain consensus on the indicators to measure (the data you will collect). For each indicator, identify the data source and methods you will use to collect the data, as well as how you plan to analyze the data you collect. For larger or more comprehensive needs assessment projects, you might also consider adding two additional columns to define the timeline for collecting the data and the parties responsible for deploying the data collection methods.

Note that data collection in the context of performance improvement typically requires multiple rounds, with initial collection and analysis providing answers to initial assessment questions, as well as generating additional questions (which are typically related to why and how for gaps) for additional data collection and interpretation. These questions should be answered before you can prepare a report with well-supported conclusions and actionable recommendations.

The importance of effective communication cannot be overstated and should occur throughout the needs assessment process. Keeping key assessment stakeholders engaged throughout the process promotes transfer of ownership of the assessment findings and recommended actions. In addition to ongoing communication, a needs assessment report is a common way to share the assessment results. The report should be clearly aligned to stakeholder expectations and the decision-making needs to maximize the use of its findings and recommended solutions. It often includes an executive summary, an introduction, a description of methods, findings, conclusions, and recommendations. The executive summary is a good way to communicate key takeaways for leadership and should include essential highlights of the initial situation, opportunity, or presenting symptoms; aims of the assessment; findings and conclusions; and concrete solutions.

Oral presentations are another typical deliverable. As with any presentation, it is important to understand the audience in order to communicate effectively. Stories can be a powerful way to convey key issues and bring the data to life. The presenter should have a thorough understanding of the needs assessment process, the findings, and the recommended solutions; they should also be prepared to effectively address questions. The presenter's perceived credibility can influence the perceptions of the needs assessment's findings and recommendations.

Final Thoughts

It is important to reiterate that needs assessment plays a foundational role in the performance improvement process. Therefore, articulating concrete considerations for implementing recommendations, as well as suggesting which stakeholders or partnerships are best suited to support specific elements of solutions, will also improve success. Having a clear plan in place ensures the results you will require.

About the Author

Ingrid Guerra-López is a professor of learning design and technology and interim dean of Wayne State University's College of Education. She has held numerous leadership roles in a variety of prominent groups and organizations, including the International Society for Performance Improvement (ISPI) board of directors, editor in chief of the peer-reviewed journal *Performance Improvement Quarterly*, chair of ISPI's research committee, and various other key committees and task forces that set standards and future direction for the instructional design and performance improvement field. Ingrid has led major educational and institutional effectiveness initiatives for international development agencies, government, education, and private organizations, including strategic planning efforts, educational and workforce needs assessments, program design and development, and program evaluation and quality assurance projects. In this capacity, she has led and mentored diverse groups of students, work teams, and institutional leaders in more than 40 countries. Ingrid may be reached at Ingrid.guerra-lopez@wayne.edu.

References

Guerra-López, I. 2018. "Ensuring Measurable Strategic Alignment to External Clients and Society." *Performance Improvement Journal* 57(6): 33–40.

Guerra-López, I. 2021. "An Ounce of Good Assessment Is Worth a Pound of Analysis and a Ton of Cure: Revisiting Seminal Insights in Performance Improvement." *Performance Improvement Journal* 60(1): 26–30.

Guerra-López, I., and K. Hicks. 2017. *Partner for Performance: Strategically Aligning Learning and Development*. Alexandria, VA: ATD Press.

Kaufman, R., and I. Guerra-López. 2013. *Needs Assessment for Organizational Success*. Alexandria, VA: Association for Talent Development.

Recommended Resources

Dearborn, J. 2015. *Data Driven: How Performance Analytics Delivers Extraordinary Sales Results*. New York: Wiley.

Evergreen, S. 2020. *Effective Data Visualization: The Right Chart for the Right Data*, 2nd ed. Thousand Oaks, CA: Sage Publications.

Guerra-López, I., and A. Hutchinson. 2013. "Measurable and Continuous Performance Improvement: The Development of a Performance Measurement, Management, and Improvement System." *Performance Improvement Quarterly* 26(2).

Guerra-López, I., and A. Hutchinson. 2017. "Stakeholder-Driven Learning Analysis: A Case Study." *Journal of Applied Instructional Design*.

Phillips, P.P., and J.J. Phillips. *Measuring ROI in Learning & Development*. Alexandria, VA: ASTD Press.

CHAPTER 13

Design Thinking for TD Professionals

Sharon Boller

Design thinking is a problem-solving technique, not a design technique. It assumes we need to start by focusing on the people our solution is intended to serve. This approach to problem solving focuses on getting insights into the wants and needs, environment, thought patterns, and world of the people who will be the recipients of whatever solution we devise.

> **IN THIS CHAPTER:**
> ♦ Clarify what design thinking is and its value to you as a TD professional
> ♦ Explain what user experience means, how to distinguish a great one from a bad one, and how the concept of user experience relates to learning
> ♦ Identify six tactics and associated tools that enable you to apply principles of design thinking to create outcome-focused, meaningful learning experiences

Imagine that you and your friend Suzy decide to go on a vacation together. Suzy is all-in on the idea of a vacation, but she's not into planning. "No worries," you tell her. "I love planning trips. I'll take care of everything. All you have to do is show up." Because you want to ensure you both have a great vacation, you agree on the timing (summer), the climate (warm), the desired activity level (high), and a budget (medium). Suzy says she trusts you to take care of the rest.

You dive into planning. You find a perfect hiking trip for the two of you in Maine. Suzy and you have gone on several day hikes before and seemed to have fun, so you are confident she'll love what you are planning. Your week-long trip features daily long hikes, tent camping, and backpacking your supplies between each hiking destination. Your trip will be a fantastic respite from the frenzy of daily life.

The designated departure day arrives. You reached out to Suzy a few days prior to tell her what time to meet up at the airport and what to pack: shorts, hiking shoes, socks, t-shirts, and plenty of bug spray. You don't list any other type of clothing, which is when Suzy starts to get nervous. However, she gamely packs her suitcase without asking questions and meets you at the airport.

When she arrives, you excitedly share the itinerary. Suzy's crumpled face says it all: She's horrified. She lets you know she H-A-T-E-S camping. Her idea of a "high" activity level is more along the lines of the three-to-five-mile day hikes you've done in the past, not a 10-mile hike every day for a week. She had envisioned vacationing at lovely seaside resorts you could bike around, perhaps stopping for a bite to eat between bouts of pedaling. She wants a hot shower every night, along with a bed in a temperature-controlled room where no bug spray is required. Finally, she does not want to carry any food. She wants it all served in a restaurant.

What happened?

You both agreed on the generalities, and Suzy felt confident in your planning abilities. You thought you had good info on Suzy based on your past experiences together, but you made several assumptions fueled by limited facts. As a result, you planned a vacation that did not meet Suzy's wants or needs, leading to an unsatisfactory vacation for everyone. Neither of you got what you wanted or needed.

At this point, you are likely thinking, "I would never do this. This is a completely unrealistic scenario. Obviously, anyone going on a vacation needs input into the activities that go beyond a description of 'high' activity level. Otherwise, they risk a horrible experience that doesn't meet their wants or needs."

However, people inside companies are guilty of different versions of this kind of blunder all the time. It's called business-centered design. Businesses create solutions—particularly training solutions—that solve a business need but may not connect to the wants or needs of the people the solution is supposed to target. This creates a huge mismatch between the business's wants and needs (as well as complete lack of acknowledgment of the working environment) and the wants and needs of the people who work there. When this mismatch happens, the result is solutions that waste people's time and the company's money.

How Do You Prevent These Kinds of Oversights?

Principles from design thinking can offer you, the TD professional, as well as your company stakeholders, a way to prevent these oversights. Design thinking, in contrast to business-centered processes, is a human-centered approach to solving problems. It starts with a focus on people rather than the business's desire for profit and has been used since the 1960s to both resolve massive human challenges and design software solutions and consumer products. In its original form, design thinking consists of five steps: empathize, define, ideate, protype, and test (Figure 13-1).

Figure 13-1. The Five Steps in the Design Thinking Process

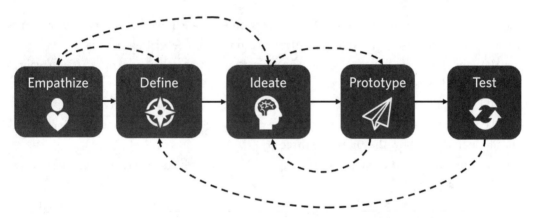

After we take time to empathize with our users, we can then better define the problem we hope to solve. Armed with a clear definition, we can then co-create with the targets we're solving for working as a cross-functional team to ideate possible solutions. These solutions get prototyped, and then we invite the people the solutions are intended to support to test them. This process of ideation, prototyping, and testing is repeated, sometimes with a return to the problem definition stage, until an optimal solution is reached.

How do you know when you've reached optimal? It's when you hit the sweet spot between what users want or need, what the organization needs to achieve, and any constraints that exist in the user's environment or within the business environment. The optimal solution is typically represented by a Venn diagram that looks like Figure 13-2.

Figure 13-2. Human-Centered Design Focuses on Finding the "Sweet Spot"

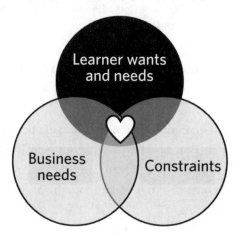

The User Sweet Spot

What makes a "sweet spot" in terms of user experience? The simple definition of a great user experience when discussing products or software is one that meets three criteria:
- It delivers value to the user (solves a problem they perceive they have or satisfies a want).
- It is easy to use.
- It is enjoyable to use.

Have you ever used a ride-sharing app like Lyft or Uber? Think about your experiences with them and then look at how they meet the three criteria:
- **Deliver value to the user.** Ride-sharing services solve a huge problem for many travelers: finding safe, reliable transportation when taxis are not easily located.
- **Be easy to use.** New or occasional users can intuit their way through the app even on their first use. I first download the Uber app in 2012 at ATD's International Conference & Exposition. My colleagues and I needed a way to get to and from a movie theater in the Dallas suburbs and our hotel downtown. Try calling a cab to come pick you up at midnight in a suburb 20 minutes from downtown. It was very hard to do in 2012, but Uber made it easy.
- **Be enjoyable to use.** When I first used Uber, I was delighted by my ability to see where my driver was, as well as watch the driver's route of travel to me. I liked being able to see approximate arrival time, the driver's name, car model and color, and customer ratings. All those things contributed to my "enjoyment" of the app and continue to drive my use of it as well, particularly compared with the alternative—hunting for a cab company, calling them, and then wondering when they might arrive.

The features embedded into these ride-sharing apps didn't happen by accident. The product teams behind Uber and Lyft didn't start out just knowing what users would want. They determined which features mattered most by starting their quest from the user's point of view. They put themselves in travelers' shoes, asking what challenges they faced when trying to navigate in places they visited. Product team members asked travelers to share what they thought about and felt as they attempted to use taxis or public transportation. Designers did ethnographic research to explore firsthand what it's like to be in a strange city and need or want to get places at different times of day or night.

Once they had a good perspective on travelers' wants and needs, the design teams could start ideating the optimal solution. By rolling out evolving versions of the apps and getting feedback from users with each, they could refine the apps based on that feedback. Travelers helped the teams recognize the value of including a street map showing an icon representing their driver's current location and their progress toward them. They also suggested other "wow" factors, such as knowing the driver's name, customer rating, and estimated ETA. And travelers let them know that pre-paying for the ride instead of having to fumble with cash or a credit card would be hugely valuable.

Now think about the typical workplace learning experience. What problem does it solve for the learner, as opposed to the organization? What value does it bring them? What components or features might delight them and create a feeling of enjoyment? And how is the learner involved in communicating their biggest pain points and optimal solutions? Most stakeholders and project clients focus exclusively or primarily on their own point of view and underestimate the benefit of considering things from the learner's point of view. This lack of awareness places you in an awkward spot because your direct client is the project owner or stakeholder, not the learner. You can get caught in the middle—trying to satisfy your client while also producing something learners will value. When the two conflict, you may be tempted to defer to the client requesting the solution, especially if there is a power imbalance between your role and the role of the client. But that could make you go in the wrong direction.

When clients don't understand the criticality of the learners' perspective, subject matter experts (SMEs) and stakeholders often indicate they will represent the learner. However, they are overconfident in their belief that they know what learners think and feel, as well as what they say and do in relation to a particular performance challenge. SMEs may also assume they understand the environment in which the learner must perform (and learn). Decisions get made based on the business's needs without factoring in the experience of the learner at all. They also get made based on the technology a company already has on hand or wishes to purchase, without regard to what learners might find most usable. Finally, SMEs may fail to consider the entire learning journey, often preferring to focus simply on creating an event for learners such as a workshop or an e-learning course.

Understanding the Learning Journey: The Key to Making Things Magical

The goal of user experience design is to optimize magical and eliminate miserable. The same should be true of learning experience design: We should seek to optimize what makes learning magical and avoid the things that make it miserable. To do that, we need to understand the journey learners are on and what makes each step magical or miserable. Figure 13-3 illustrates the journey; the table following it explains each step along with the potential positive or negative emotions that can occur in each step, depending on how well or poorly you design it.

Figure 13-3. The Stages and Steps of a Learning Journey

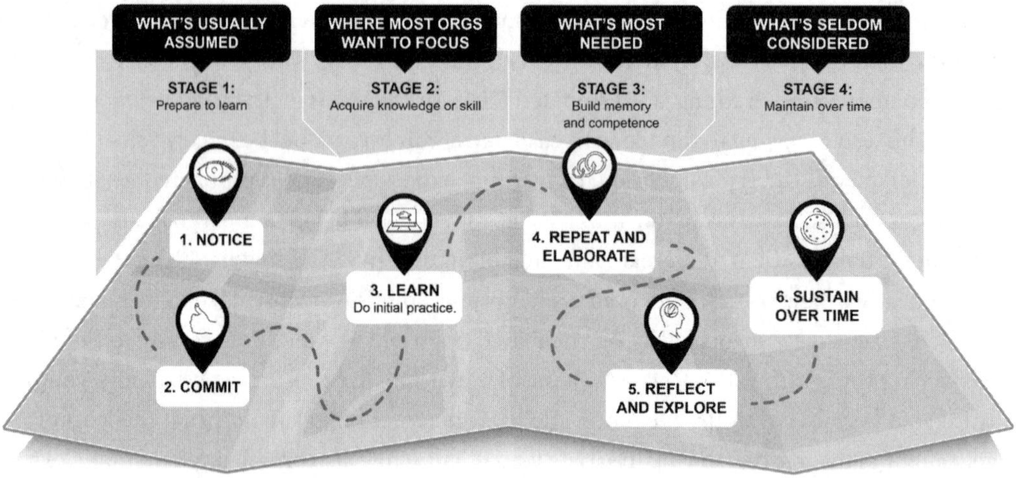

Diagram shows four stages across a map:

- **STAGE 1:** Prepare to learn — *What's Usually Assumed*
  - 1. NOTICE
  - 2. COMMIT
- **STAGE 2:** Acquire knowledge or skill — *Where Most Orgs Want to Focus*
  - 3. LEARN — Do initial practice.
- **STAGE 3:** Build memory and competence — *What's Most Needed*
  - 4. REPEAT AND ELABORATE
  - 5. REFLECT AND EXPLORE
- **STAGE 4:** Maintain over time — *What's Seldom Considered*
  - 6. SUSTAIN OVER TIME

Boller and Fletcher (2020)

Step	Best- and Worst-Case Descriptions	Learner's Potential Positive Thoughts and Feelings	Learner's Potential Negative Thoughts and Feelings
1. Notice	**Best case:** The learner notices a need or recognizes an opportunity to learn. There's some recognition that a gap exists between current knowledge or skill and optimal knowledge or skill. **Worse case:** Learner gets an email telling them they need to take a course.	Intrigued, interested, curious	Dismayed

Step	Best- and Worst-Case Descriptions	Learner's Potential Positive Thoughts and Feelings	Learner's Potential Negative Thoughts and Feelings
2. Commit	**Best case:** The learner makes space in their calendar to put time and effort toward learning. Time is set aside for learning. **Worse case:** The learner avoids scheduling time for learning unless forced to do so.	Motivated	Resistant
3. Learn The learner participates in a workshop, an online course, or an independent study that involves reading, doing activities, and discussion	**Best case:** Learner finds materials, content, and activities relevant and practical. **Worse case:** There is little relevance and no realistic context.	Curious, immersed	Bored, overwhelmed, uninterested
4. Repeat and Elaborate For learning to last it must be repeated and expanded upon. In this step, learners get reinforcement through additional practice opportunities coupled with feedback. Simple exercises presented in the previous step may be expanded upon and made more challenging.	**Best case:** Reinforcement and feedback are appropriately timed and provided. **Worse case:** Learning is lost because no reinforcement is provided.	Committed to improving and becoming proficient	Disengaged
5. Reflect and Explore Simultaneously with step 4, as well as beyond it, learners reflect on their performance or knowledge and seek ways to expand it or consider how well they are performing or leveraging new knowledge and skills. There is self-reflection and ongoing feedback from managers, peers, and customers.	**Best case:** Reflection and exploration are planned and encouraged. **Worse case:** This step is omitted.	Confident in their ability to apply new learning; belief in emerging proficiency	Discouraged or disillusioned; desire to avoid using
6. Sustain Over Time At this point, the learner has integrated new knowledge or skills and actively uses them to complete aspects of their role.	**Best case:** Learners complete all the prior steps and arrive here proficient and confident. **Worse case:** Learners never arrive.	Supported	Cynical

Design thinking principles can be integrated into a variety of instructional design models to help craft learning experiences that are magical. We define magical experiences as ones that:

- Deliver value to learners and the business; the experiences produce tangible outcomes for both learners and the business
- Are easy to use and integrate with the learner's environment and constraints
- Are enjoyable, which means they engage the learner and hold their attention (note that enjoyment doesn't mean edutainment, simply that a learner finds something interesting and useful)

Six Tactics to Integrate Design Thinking Practices Into Learning Experience Design

Design thinking tools can help you objectively navigate the tricky waters of effective learning experience design. They can enable you to find the sweet spot that meets learner wants and needs, satisfies business goals, and factors in environmental constraints. Although I co-authored an entire book on the topic of how to apply design thinking in TD, here are six steps to get you started (Boller and Fletcher 2020). Each step has an associated tool and most have examples as well. These tools, as well as completed examples when appropriate, can all be found at ATDHandbook3.org.

1. Get Crystal Clear on the Problem You Are Trying to Solve

This sounds like a "duh," but too often people start crafting solutions when they don't know what problem they need to fix. This situation is extremely common, especially when stakeholders, learners, and designers aren't unified on the problem being solved. By using a tool called a strategy blueprint, you can help everyone gain clarity on the challenges to be resolved (or opportunities to leverage) as well as how success will be measured. This blueprint also enables you to get clear (or recognize you are not clear) on what training can solve and what must be solved through another solution, such as process design, role changes, or environment adjustments. The content in a strategy blueprint includes:

- **Challenges stakeholders are seeing or opportunities people want to leverage.** These are in relation to something specific (for example, sale of a new product, ramping up employees, maintaining compliance with data security, executing a new process, or rolling out a new software system).
- **What success looks like.** If specific challenges are resolved, what will the stakeholders see and hear in the workplace? What will people be doing?
- **Focus areas.** To solve the problem, what areas must be addressed? (Note that training could be embedded into all focus areas or only one with other focus areas emerging as your design team starts analyzing the challenges and how they might be solved.)
- **Key principles to follow.** As you execute your strategy, what are key guide points you want to follow or values you want to uphold?

- **Activities.** What tactical steps enable you to solve your challenges? What focus area does each activity address?
- **Metrics.** How will you measure success? What quantitative measures will indicate you succeeded in resolving the challenges or leveraging the opportunities you identified?

2. Get Perspective From Your Learners via Empathy Mapping

A second tool you can use is empathy mapping. An empathy map is a powerful yet simple tool for getting perspective. Your map should focus on whatever task you are trying to get people to do or block of knowledge you are trying to get them to understand. There are many digital tools for creating empathy maps, which gives you the flexibility to generate them even if you cannot physically be in the same room with learners. A baseline map addresses questions in five areas:
- What is this learner **thinking** and **feeling** about X? ("X" represents whatever it is learners must do, learn to do, or know about as part of their job.)
- What does the learner **see** and **hear** from others as they do X or apply knowledge of X in their job?
- What does the learner **do** in relation to X? (For example, if the training is going to focus on selling a product, ask yourself what the sales rep [the learner] does in the job as they sell a product.)
- What are the learner's **pain points** in attempting to do the task or apply the knowledge?
- What are the **motivators** for doing the task or applying the knowledge?

3. Craft One or More Learner Personas

Use the outputs of your mapping exercise to create fictionalized representations of your learners. These personas help you focus on the learners' most critical challenges, motivators, and daily realities. Create a descriptive name for your persona that captures the flavor of the persona's needs and wants (for example, "Just Get It Done," "Show Me, Don't Tell Me," or "High Anxiety"). Use the persona throughout your design and development to keep you honest in your plan. As you build the solution, ask, "What would the Just Get It Done persona think of this? Would this satisfy their needs?" When a SME pushes you to include large amounts of content that would not resonate with a particular persona, you can refer back to that persona for some validation by asking, "Would our Just Get It Done persona find this useful or helpful?"

4. Recognize Learning as a Journey, Not an Event

Build a learning journey map to discuss and plan the entire learning process—not just what goes into a workshop or an e-learning course. Recall the learning journey stages and steps shown in Figure 13-3; the path to learning anything starts with Step 1: Notice the Need to Learn and ends with Step 6: Sustain and Use Knowledge and Skill Over Time. Learn the steps to the journey and help your client and project stakeholders understand the impact and criticality of each step in ensuring that you achieve the success metrics they define. Emphasize that without opportunities to elaborate on initial learning and have multiple repetitions, learners will forget. We execute only on what's reinforced multiple times. The smallest part of any journey is likely to be Step 3: Learn. It's the steps around it that make or break your endeavor.

5. Brainstorm Ideas for Solving Your Problem and Create Simple Prototypes

After you have successfully defined your problem, avoid jumping too fast to a solution. Don't move immediately to "We need an e-learning course." Allow yourself to brainstorm possible activities or solutions. Take time to formulate "learner stories," which can help you gain clarity on the solutions that will be most effective in delivering on the story.

Then create low-fidelity (that is, paper and pencil) prototypes and let four to six target learners give you feedback on what's delightful about the experience and what is miserable about it. Let learners (not just SMEs) suggest ways to improve it. You can prototype themes, activities, learning flows, and more. What's critical is learner input and consideration of all three elements that contribute to your solution: learner wants and needs, business needs, and environmental constraints.

6. Test—But Keep It Simple

Testing is too often skipped. We're not talking about fully building everything out and conducting a pilot. We're talking about testing early drafts or prototypes, which you can use to refine your concept instead of having to entirely rebuild things that don't work. When you test early prototypes, make sure your testers include people who are your target learners. Ask them to give you feedback on three things:
- How would you rate your engagement level as you went through the experience (low, medium, high) and why?
- How would you rate the clarity of what you tested (low, medium, high) and why?
- How would you rate the relevance of the experience to your work context (low, medium, high) and learning needs and why?

Final Thoughts

Design thinking principles can be used to add tremendous value to the learning experiences we create. They help us recognize that if we fail to factor in the learners' wants and needs—as well as their environmental constraints—we will fail to deliver business value as well. They also help us recognize learning as a journey rather than an event, which is key to producing changes in behavior and enabling learners to go the distance from noticing a need to learn to sustaining changed performance in their jobs.

About the Author

Sharon Boller is a former managing director and current affiliate consultant at TiER1 Performance. She retired from full-time consulting in December 2020 to shift her focus to philanthropy, launching Small Things Great (smallthingsgreat.com), an Indianapolis-based giving circle. Sharon has been a frequent speaker at industry conferences on topics such as performance-focused learning design, UX, technology and trends, learning game design, and design thinking. She is the author or co-author of three other books published by ATD Press: *Teamwork Training* (1995), *Play to Learn: Everything You Need to Know About Designing Effective Learning Games* (2017, with Karl Kapp), and *Design Thinking for Training and Development* (2020, with Laura Fletcher). Her industry interests are wide-ranging and include storytelling, emerging technologies, business strategy, leadership, learning, and experience design.

References

Boller, S., and L. Fletcher. 2020. *Design Thinking for Training and Development*. Alexandria, VA: ATD Press.

Kalbach, J. 2014. "UX Strategy Blueprint." Experiencing Information (blog), August 12. experienceinginformation.com/2014/08/12/ux-strategy-blueprint.

Kalbach, J. 2016. *Mapping Experiences: A Complete Guide to Creating Value Through Journeys, Blueprints, and Diagrams*. Sebastapol, CA: O'Reilly Media.

Recommended Resources

Boller, S., and L. Fletcher. 2020. *Design Thinking for Training and Development*. Alexandria, VA: ATD Press.

Brown, T. 2009. *Change By Design*. New York: Harper Collins.

Garrette, B., C. Phelps, and O. Sibony. 2018 *Cracked it! How to Solve Big Problems and Sell Solutions Like Top Strategy Consultants*. Switzerland: Palgrave, Macmillan.

Glynn, K., and D. Tolsma. 2017. "Design Thinking Meets ADDIE." *TD at Work*. Alexandria, VA: ATD Press.

"Interaction Design Foundation." interaction-design.org.

"Luma Institute." interaction-design.org.

CHAPTER 14

Innovative Design: Uncovering the Art of the Possible

Brian Washburn

Reel-to-reel movies in theaters eventually turned into Beta tapes (briefly), then VHS tapes for home entertainment in the 1980s, which turned into DVDs in the 1990s, which eventually turned into streaming videos that we can watch on our TV, computer, or smartphone, or embed into a PowerPoint presentation.

This simplified chronology of innovation in the way we have experienced film. While the end result of innovation and innovative design can be cool and useful and lead to other changes, it also requires time, iteration, the willingness to fail, the ability to pick oneself up and dust off the failure, the desire to figure out what lessons can be learned, and then more iteration.

> **IN THIS CHAPTER:**
> - Decide whether an innovative design approach could be appropriate for your situation
> - Discover transferable lessons from some real-life examples of innovative design
> - Identify potential sources of inspiration for creativity and innovation from outside the world of training and instructional design
> - Apply a process to ensure innovation isn't discouraged in the event a first attempt doesn't yield the desired results

What Is "Innovative Design"?

Innovation can oftentimes be synonymous with cool products that we may not have known we needed, but we sure like when we're exposed to them. (Think about the way Steve Jobs sold iPhones to us when our flip phones were perfectly adequate!) Sometimes we don't even realize that it is happening right in front of us, but the end result of innovative design can make life better, more convenient, and perhaps lead to more innovations in different fields.

Before we go too far into the question of why and how you may want to bring innovation into your learning program, let's first define the terms *design* and *innovative design*.

For the purposes of this chapter, the term *design* represents an intentional approach to a learning initiative that includes:
- A sequence and flow of learning activities intended to meet the learning objectives
- An appropriate delivery medium (such as in-person, virtual, self-directed, blended, a job aid, or a resource on a company-wide intranet)

Innovative design is using a new, unique, or unexpected approach in your design process.

When it comes to innovative design in the learning space, we're not always referring to the latest technology. As you'll see, innovative design can be the unexpected introduction of analog materials such as Play-Doh into a learning experience.

Can Anyone Be Innovative in Their Design?

"I don't know what you want me to say. Quality assurance is a boring topic. At the end of the day, the lab techs just need to know the information. I don't do 'touchy feely' with my training."

I had just finished an initial conversation with our organization's vice president of quality assurance (QA), who was preparing to deliver a new QA training program on inspecting and conducting a mock audit of our eye bank's laboratory. He had his own idea of what had worked for him in the past and wasn't very interested in my suggested changes or innovations on his program.

This wasn't the first time I'd heard an objection from someone I had been asked to coach and help create a more engaging training program. Any time a new or different approach to a task is introduced, especially when people think they've been doing just fine with their traditional approach, questions will arise. Questions *should* arise.

One of those questions is, "Can *anyone* be innovative when it comes to putting together learning programs?" What about subject matter experts whose primary roles have nothing to do with training or instructional design? What about people who want to create something using a unique or unexpected design, but just don't think they're very creative?

The answer is an unqualified yes, although it can take some time to get used to a different way of doing things.

In the example above, I spent significant time talking with and coaching our QA VP to move away from his traditional PowerPoint-based lecture and toward a session in which QA trainees were up and doing something. Even though we'd need to conduct this training in a hotel ballroom, there were ways we could re-create the lab environment.

As we talked more about this idea and what could be possible, he realized we could bring lab materials into the ballroom and have trainees inspect them for any items that were beyond their expiration dates. We could take photos of things in the lab that were out of place or just a little off, make posters out of these photos, and hang them around the training environment to simulate (as best we could) a lab inspection and audit.

When we finally launched this training program and the VP saw the engagement of the participants, listened to the questions they asked, and observed the behaviors of the trainees in the simulated environment, he completely bought in to this more innovative design approach. He would go on to write a blog post reflecting on this experience, saying:

> The process was painful as it was a foreign approach—foreign because it added activities to the structure of the course. I was no longer to be the expert that would do a data download by slides but would actually have to teach and challenge the students with activities and hands-on learning. With the lesson plans completed, I sighed with relief. I was done with the process.
>
> Then I was informed our process would include a multi-day walkthrough of the material—a sort of dress rehearsal. My idea of what went into a successful presentation was again being stretched.
>
> In the end I learned that by following this process, we were set up to deliver a session which was well-received by the attendees, evident by the learning that could be physically observed during the sessions. I plan to use this process again when invited to speak and I look forward to increasing my presentation prep proficiency.
>
> And to be honest, I guess I can do touchy feely.

While anyone *can* grow more innovative in their learning design, another question that needs to be asked is, *should* anyone be innovative in their design?

The answer to this second question is a more qualified yes.

In some instances, time is of the essence and good enough will have to be good enough. In other situations, there is a very good reason to continue to do things the way they've always been done and innovation just for innovation's sake won't add value. In fact, it can lead to resentment from those who originally created a program and have seen evidence of its effectiveness.

If an innovative approach to design can boost learner engagement, increase the possibility of accomplishing learner objectives, and improve training outcomes, then innovative design should absolutely be applied to the initiative.

What Does Innovative Design Look Like?

Innovative design comes in many shapes and sizes, including slight tweaks or major updates to existing programs, quick and easy solutions applied to new content, or even unique approaches brought into multiweek or multimonth courses that are built from the ground up.

Let's look at several real-world examples to help illustrate the range of innovative design approaches.

Example 1: A Minor Facelift With an Unexpected Material

A tire manufacturing company had been training sales representatives for years on how their tires were made and what made their tires unique by using a series of technical drawings that appeared on slides. Several experienced trainers and content experts agreed that the slides were critical because they very clearly explained the components of a tire. However, while the slides were conveying the technical tire information, even the trainers acknowledged that it was difficult to tell if the sales trainees were grasping or retaining it.

The information about how tires were constructed and what made them unique was only part of the multiday training program, but it seemed foundational to any practice sales conversations and role-play activities that took place later in the session. So the training team decided to try replacing the PowerPoint-based technical presentation with a shorter technical presentation and a hands-on activity in which participants were asked to use technical drawings to construct their own tires using Play-Doh (with different colors representing different layers in the tire). Participants were then asked to explain their models to the group.

This was initially met with skepticism by the tire manufacturing company. "Hold on a minute. You're trying to tell me you're going to ask a group of 50- and 60-year-old salespeople who have been in this industry for 30 and 40 years to play with Play-Doh during our training program?"

However, after taking part in a pilot version of this updated activity, skepticism gave way to an appreciation of the effectiveness of this approach. One member of the internal training team put it this way: "When I first heard that we were going to use Play-Doh, I was borderline offended. We're not preschoolers. But when I experienced that activity, I don't see how people wouldn't learn the components of our tires. They had to re-create a tire, and then they had to explain what each layer of their Play-Doh model represented. This is clearly one of the most effective training activities in our entire program."

Example 2: Circumstances Require Converting From In-Person to Virtual

A regional chain of skilled-care facilities used a popular leadership development program to bring executives and high-performing employees from across their locations together for a weeklong series of courses and networking activities. Visiting the headquarters and engaging with peers and organizational leadership was a high point for the participants. When the COVID-19 pandemic eliminated the possibility of bringing cohorts together in person, the learning team realized they needed to innovate on their delivery medium—they needed to take it from in-person to virtual—while maintaining the quality and popularity of the established program.

The content needed to remain exactly the same, but the design, sequence, and flow could not. Nobody had the stomach to sit through several back-to-back-to-back days' worth of online instruction, and it would be impractical given that situations would arise in their facility and they would likely need to respond. The first innovation in the design was to create a multiweek program in which leadership development sessions would take place in two-hour time blocks, several days each week. While the previous iteration of the program could be completed in just a few days, this new version required a commitment from participants and organizational leadership for up to two months.

The next area in which innovative design could be applied was in modifying activities for virtual delivery. Anchor activities were introduced at the beginning of each session to find ways for participants to quickly relate to the topic at hand, make connections with their peers, and limit the likelihood of participant boredom and multitasking. Virtual breakout rooms replaced small group table discussions. Some presentations from department heads were recorded and posted to the learning management system. Web-based game platforms (such as Kahoot and an online prize wheel) replaced traditional PowerPoint-based learning activities.

Of course, innovation doesn't yield perfect results every time and not everyone appreciates the changes that it brings. There were times during the initial launch of this program when the breakout rooms did not work, and the program organizers did notice some drop-off from participants. On the other hand, scores of new leaders were exposed to key leadership concepts that were central to the organization's intentional efforts at building a culture of leadership development, and post-training evaluation scores were on par with the in-person version of the program.

Example 3: A New Approach to a Conventional Handout Changed an Entire Training Program

An experienced group of salespeople was being asked to sell a service for the first time. While they were quite comfortable and had a lot of confidence in the products they were selling and had received a wealth of information about the new services, the salespeople were skeptical about whether selling a new service to their existing customers would ultimately be good for them.

To assess the needs of the learners, the program manager created a conventional checklist for trainees, asking questions such as, "Are you comfortable discussing services with your customers?" and "Do your customers like talking about their business?" The manager also compiled some information about the new service that could be used in the training program.

A team of instructional designers looked at the checklist and other existing materials and thought they could be useful. The real problem to be solved with this training program, however, was not increasing the team's knowledge about the new service, but rather addressing members hesitancy to sell a new service in addition to their conventional products.

To address this problem, the instructional design team chose to put the whole idea of selling a service on trial. It converted the checklist that the program manager had developed into a jury summons, complete with a questionnaire for the "jurors" (training participants) to fill out when they entered the room (Figure 14-1).

Figure 14-1. A Sample Learner Assessment

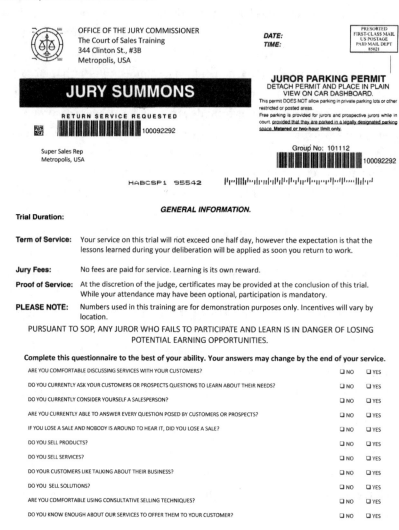

Continuing the court theme from this initial handout, the half-day training session was designed to allow the participants to determine if this new service they were going to be asked to sell was innocent or guilty of helping them as salespeople. Actors were hired and filmed to play the role of the prosecutor and the defense attorney, and the trainer for the session played the role of judge, facilitating the experience and laying out the parameters for the juror participants to render their verdict.

While it can be a challenge to come up with new or original ways to present material, finding an appropriate theme (in this case, putting an idea on trial and using a court theme throughout) can help give structure to your ideas and guide the design of a learning program from start to finish.

Example 4: A Major Overhaul to Existing New Employee Orientation

A rapidly growing global health organization found itself needing to orient an increasing number of newly hired employees to its culture and to the other departments of the organization. Hiring managers began to raise concerns about the existing new employee orientation program. They questioned the value to their new employees and the impression they received by the familiar formula of parading one department representative after another in front of new employees to talk at them for two hours at a time, for three straight days.

A small team of instructional designers wondered if they could turn their new employee orientation program into an immersive learning experience. What they came up with was a two-day program inspired by the original *Jumanji* movie. The first day and a half was used to introduce new employees to each department across the organization through a series of short games representing the work of each department and then a short Q&A session with a department representative.

For example, the department that handles sensitive communication (which needs to be edited or redacted before it can be shared) was represented by a game that used an e-learning authoring tool to challenge new employees to identify and try their hand at redacting sensitive or personal information. The department responsible for quick medical procedures featured an activity using a modified version of the board game *Operation* to give new employees a sense for how steady one needs to keep their hands while rapidly conducting the procedure.

Each small group accumulated points through successfully completing the games and challenges representing each department. For the final half day of this program, all participants came together in a cooperative game inspired by *Settlers of Catan*, in which they could exchange their accumulated points for resources and work together in a simulation representing the global nature of the organization's mission.

The revamped new employee orientation program was piloted, certain activities were adjusted, and then it was launched for all new hires. Hiring managers who had been reluctant to send their new employees to the previous version of new employee orientation were now not only sending their employees but also requesting that they themselves be their respective department's representative during the brief Q&A portion.

The new design also reduced the duration of the new employee orientation from three to two days.

What Do These Examples Have in Common?

By their very nature, the things that make design innovative cannot be prescribed or formulaic. There is no simple structure or algorithm that will allow you to replicate innovative design over and over again (otherwise it would just turn into something routine and mass producible, which is the opposite of innovative). There are, however, some common threads among these four examples that can be studied and can help with future attempts at innovation:

- **Begin with a challenge or a problem.** Innovative design is intended to find ways to boost the engagement and effectiveness of a learning solution.
- **Brainstorm possible solutions.** Whether you call it brainstorming, ideation, or simply thinking, the more ideas and possible ways to address a challenge or problem that you're able to generate, the more options you'll have at your disposal. As Nordgren and Lucas (2021) point out, "Prior research has shown that people's first ideas are rarely their most creative. Coming up with just one breakthrough idea typically requires a lengthy brainstorming process, in which you generate and iterate on a large pool of potential options before finally reaching your most creative idea." If you're stuck, it can be extremely helpful to talk with a colleague to help kick-start some new ideas. All the examples in this chapter involved more than one person coming up with ideas and possible solutions.
- **Pick one idea.** Coming up with ideas is the fun part, but narrowing in on one idea and honing it to a workable solution can be a lot of work. This is also where doubts can creep in. Is using Play-Doh with extremely experienced professionals a good idea? What if the cool feature on the e-learning module breaks? What if we try a learning game in front of a group and it isn't as well received as we'd hoped? When it comes to applying innovative design, you can't let perfect be the enemy of good, and you can't succumb to analysis paralysis. Choose a path, put it together as best as possible, then try it out. That's the only way you'll actually be able to answer any of these questions.
- **Test your idea** (ideally in a low-stakes environment). Getting your idea out of your own head and putting it in front of other people to use, poke holes in, test, break, or otherwise play with is an important step, and it's not for the faint of heart. You will get feedback, and that feedback may not always be positive. Ideally, you'll be able to test your ideas with a

small group in a low-pressure situation (such as bringing a few trusted colleagues into a conference room and doing a dry run with them). If you can focus on listening to feedback and avoid being defensive about your choices, the lessons you learn from this test will be invaluable in refining your innovative ideas.
- **Iterate.** Don't assume you'll have everything right the first time. The reason you test is to find out what doesn't work, not necessarily to prove that it does work. Having the mindset that changes, revisions, and iterations can make your ideas even better will be something you'll want to embrace.

How Can You Develop Your Innovative Muscles?

Just like going to the gym regularly can help you to build, tone, and maintain strong muscles in your body, you'll also need to work out your innovative design muscles on a regular basis if you want to be successful in this approach to learning program design. Be sure to check the handout on this handbook's website (ATDHandbook3.org), which provides a guide for developing an innovative learning event. In addition, here are several practices you can adopt to help build your innovative design muscles.

Look Around, With Intention

There's an old saying: There are no new ideas, just recycled ones. That rings particularly true for several of this chapter's examples of innovative design, which were inspired by experiences that happen to people in the course of their regular day. Using Play-Doh, receiving a jury summons, or watching the movie *Jumanji* led to some unique training applications. The potential for everyday experiences to turn into inspiration for innovative design might be lost unless you begin to walk through the world with an instructional designer's lens on.

For example, think about transferable design applications you can glean from any of the following routine activities:
- **Visit a museum.** Pay attention to the way curators organize exhibits in a museum (particularly children's museums or museums where there are more interactive exhibits).
- **Play a game.** Whether you're playing a card game, a board game, or a computer game, there are mechanics at play that keep players coming back time and again. Don't just limit yourself to games like *Jeopardy!* or *Trivial Pursuit*. Find some new games and compare the mechanics and player experiences in competitive versus cooperative games. Visit a thrift shop and buy several kids' games or pick games from your kids' shelves. Pay attention to how easy or hard the game is to play. What makes you want to keep playing the game? Keep in mind that complex games with lots of rules may prove less inspiring for a training session.

- **Have coffee.** Sometimes it's fun to simply connect with someone over coffee. Ask them what they're working on (regardless of their profession), and you may hear something that inspires a new solution to your latest training challenge.
- **Pay attention to signs and fliers.** Perhaps your innovative training solution is a resource, not a course. You can find examples of job aids being used without needing to formally train anyone at grocery stores (think self-checkout aisles and information about how to insert your credit card properly in the payment machine), at restaurants (QR codes that bring up the menu on your smartphone), and even in public bathrooms (signage that shows how to properly wash your hands).

Inspiration for innovative design is all around us as long as we're looking with intention.

Get Out of the Learning and Development Space

There are so many good resources within the learning and development community—this book certainly being one of them. Other resources include a membership with the national or local ATD chapter, attending conferences, reading industry publications, attending webinars, reading blogs, or listening to podcasts. If we rely solely on the learning and development community for our education and information, however, we'll be missing out on a whole world of potential inspiration.

Here are several other industries from which we can draw inspiration and creativity for innovative design approaches:

- **Marketing and advertising.** Experienced training professional Mike Taylor spends a lot of time advocating for L&D professionals to pay close attention to the world of marketing and advertising. Think of how difficult it is to motivate people to act based on what they see on a billboard as they drive 60 miles per hour in their car, or how difficult it is to persuade someone to buy your product in a 30-second message. Yet marketers and advertisers are extremely effective at doing this. Our slide design, our e-learning design, and the way in which we hook people into our content can stand to take a lesson or two from the world of marketing and advertising.
- **Art and fashion.** Perhaps you don't quite understand what a Jackson Pollock painting portrays or why someone would spend more than $3,000 on a Louis Vuitton *petite malle souple* (that's a purse), but many famous artists and designers got where they are because they pushed boundaries and tapped into the emotions of their audience.
- **Brain science.** This can be an intimidating area in which to stick your nose, but having a greater understanding for how people's brains are wired and how they learn goes to the heart of innovating effectively. Making sure our learning programs adhere to what the

science says works can limit our risk of creating something that's simply a fad or rooted in ineffective pseudoscience.
- **Business.** Learning and development doesn't exist in a vacuum; we're usually helping people do their jobs better and more effectively to improve business outcomes. Understanding more about the world of business in general is helpful, and understanding more about the industries in which we operate is essential. It's very difficult to respond to skepticism about the use of Play-Doh in a training program if we can't attach it to a business problem or goal. Learning theory can be important, but business leaders won't respond if you can only use the language of adult learning theory in the same way as do your L&D peers.

Final Thoughts

Many people design their own training based on the way they themselves have been trained. This too often has a heavy emphasis on PowerPoint-based lectures. When we're able to apply innovative design to training programs, we are not only finding unique and unexpected ways for our learners to discover new content and practice new skills, but we're also opening their eyes to what's possible when it comes to training design.

What's possible may include shiny new technologies, but it doesn't have to. You'll notice that none of the examples cited in this chapter involved mobile learning, augmented reality, virtual reality, artificial intelligence, or other cutting-edge technologies. To be sure, the appropriate integration of any of those would represent innovative design, but you shouldn't feel that innovation is synonymous with technology.

I often design train-the-trainer and presentation skills training sessions that intentionally avoid the use of PowerPoint to demonstrate that it's possible to conduct an effective and engaging training without the use of slides. A training program without slides? Now that's innovative!

Sometimes a new approach to training design works well. Those times should be celebrated. Sometimes a new approach will flop. Those instances should be examined, questioned, treated as a learning experience, and, if you're convinced that it's still the correct approach, iterated.

Thomas Edison didn't get the light bulb to work on his first attempt. Steve Jobs didn't pull off the Mac overnight. We won't get everything right the first time either, but when we apply innovative design (and iterate until we get it right), we unlock a whole new world of learning possibilities.

About the Author

Brian Washburn is co-founder and CEO of Endurance Learning, a boutique instructional design firm specializing in innovative solutions to all sorts of training challenges. He is also the co-creator of Soapbox, the first rapid design tool for instructor-led training. Prior to launching Endurance Learning, Brian spent most of his career in the nonprofit sector, finding ways to use engaging, effective learning to assist foster children in finding safe, permanent homes, to help youth achieve their GED credentials, and to eliminate corneal blindness around the world. Brian is the author of the book *What's Your Formula? Combine Learning Elements for Impactful Training* and hosts a weekly podcast called *Train Like You Listen*. Brian can be reached at brian@endurancelearning.com.

References

Nordgren, L., and B. Lucas. 2021. *Your Best Ideas Are Often Your Last Ideas*. Cambridge, MA: Harvard Business Review.

Recommended Resources

Duarte, N. 2010. *Resonate: Present Visual Stories that Transform Audiences*. Hoboken, NJ: John Wiley & Sons.

Linker, J. 2021. *Big Little Breakthroughs: How Small, Everyday Innovations Drive Oversized Results*. Nashville, TN: Post Hill Press.

Washburn, B. 2021. *What's Your Formula? Combine Learning Elements for Impactful Training*. Alexandria, VA: ATD Press.

CHAPTER 15

We Need It Personalized, Accurate, and NOW!

Lisa MD Owens and Crystal Kadakia

The term *modern learner* seems to pop up everywhere. But who is the modern learner, what do they want, and how do they affect talent development professionals and their work?

IN THIS CHAPTER:
- ♦ Describe the modern learner's wants and needs, as well as their "why" and influence on learning design
- ♦ Use new design practices to meet modern learner needs
- ♦ Personalize training design
- ♦ Improve the reliability, accuracy, and currency of content
- ♦ Provide immediate access to needed learning assets

When we hear about today's employees' desires for development opportunities, some wonder how and why we should cater to their demands. L&D is frequently overwhelmed by simply managing learning topics that are deemed mandatory for the organization—from onboarding to compliance. We know that the world around us has changed exponentially. Now is the time for L&D to radically change our training basics—how we design and deliver learning—so we can better meet the needs of the people and businesses we serve. With the explosion of new evidence about the science of learning and how the brain works, as well as the (overwhelming) profusion of digital tools, L&D is primed to make a gigantic leap to deliver learning products that drive change in employee productivity and skills in the workplace.

How do we in L&D do this without adding more to our already full plates? We go beyond webinars, computer-based e-learning, and blended learning. We go beyond creating one excellent learning pathway for each skills gap that needs to be closed. We start delivering contextual bites of learning in and out of the flow of work as different learner personas face their five moments of learning need. And, we upskill ourselves and set new goals based on newer learning design models, such as focusing on user experience or delivering learning clusters.

That's a mouthful! Let's break it down so you can be part of the growing movement of today's L&D organizations who are vital to business and employee success. First, let's define the modern learner.

Who Is the Modern Learner?

Based on work by Jane Hart, Josh Bersin, and others, we define a *modern learner* as someone who needs to learn fast in an ever-changing environment and will access a wide variety of resources to get answers.

Modern does not just mean millennials or Gen Z. Modern learners are defined both by their external environment and by their approach to learning. It's anyone in a job where things change quickly. And, especially since 2020, that seems to be all businesses. A modern learner is also someone who proactively seeks continuous learning through the best means for the challenge at hand. Because it is shaping up to be driven by the context and the learner, modern learning does not just mean introducing flashy new tools or following standard, fixed rules for every design (for example, "Everything must be micro!").

Modern learners need something fundamentally different from what L&D has normally provided, in part because of how many things have shifted in recent years—from the type of work being done to where and how it gets delivered. Time pressures have increased to grow capability, and the access to a wide variety of technology at home has increased demands for more options in the workplace, making it easier to meet learners where they are at work.

But it's not just generations or employees who are changing their expectations. The shifts in business have driven higher demands on employees (Figure 15-1). The pace of change has increased, as have the demands to work remotely, even globally, while fostering soft skills that build teamwork. The shifts in workplace demographics mean that employees, managers, and leaders have to learn more about one another's generational differences before they can effectively transfer their knowledge to others on the team or in the organization. And that flow of information is not a one-way street from older to younger; it's also going from younger to older. Add to all this that every job has become less hands-on and more digitally enhanced. We see it everywhere from Napa Valley vineyards, where field workers use electronic systems to manage the harvest, to the doctor's offices where physicians record our vitals on a laptop instead of a paper chart.

These shifts have driven leaders to change their business strategy to survive. L&D must shift too, or risk becoming the proverbial leader running after their group yelling, "Hey! Wait for me!"

Figure 15-1. Shifts for Business and Learners Drive L&D Evolution

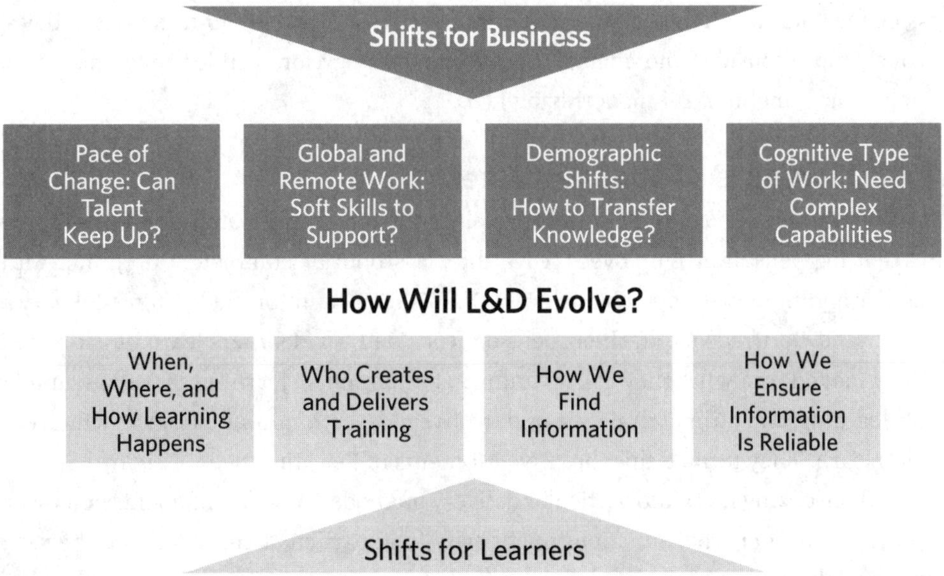

Shifts for Business

| Pace of Change: Can Talent Keep Up? | Global and Remote Work: Soft Skills to Support? | Demographic Shifts: How to Transfer Knowledge? | Cognitive Type of Work: Need Complex Capabilities |

How Will L&D Evolve?

| When, Where, and How Learning Happens | Who Creates and Delivers Training | How We Find Information | How We Ensure Information Is Reliable |

Shifts for Learners

Kadakia and Owens (2020)

Given these shifts, employees need a wider range of learning assets that offer a "both/and" approach so that they can learn and do their jobs (Figure 15-2). It's not as trivial as L&D simply meeting changing expectations; these pressures call for a fundamental shift.

Figure 15-2. The Dichotomy of What Learners Need

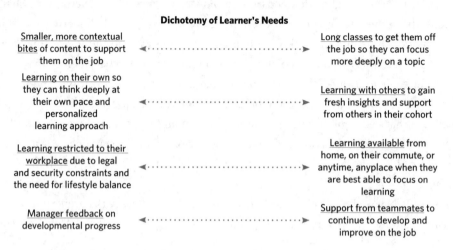

Today's L&D offers choices so employees, managers, and leaders can learn at the speed of business change. Rather than sticking to a formula or their standard go-to toolkit, today's L&D professionals must consider and change their design strategy for each learning challenge. Let's take a look at three methods for modernizing L&D.

The Five Moments of Learning Need

In 2011, Bob Mosher and Conrad Gottfredson elevated and brought attention to the amount of learning that happens after employees leave the classroom or complete a program. Although other models and frameworks, such as CCL's 70-20-10, look at informal learning delivery methods, Mosher and Gottfredson put their focus on *when* and *why* learners learn outside the classroom. They looked into what they called "informal intentional" learning as well as "unplanned informal" learning, and ultimately delineated the five most common situations in which employees need to learn. They termed this the "Five Moments of Learning Need" (Figure 15-3).

Rather than locking L&D into particular delivery methods, these five moments empower L&D to thoughtfully consider what situations might arise for a particular capability and then strategically choose the best way to meet the learner with learning material. In addition, this model helps give equal importance and weight to formal program design *and* what is provided afterward, both formal and informal. Whereas in the past L&D focused primarily on the "new" moment of learning need by elevating the importance of learner context, Mosher and Gottfredson helped empower a fundamental shift toward a more modern "learning in the flow of work" approach.

Figure 15-3. Mosher and Gottfredson's Five Moments of Learning Need

Nine Elements of Modern Learning

Even if L&D has followed all the prescriptions for modern learning, you may still hear negative feedback. Rather than including prescriptions, we suggest including nine elements or characteristics in a training program to make it feel better to participants. The elements are accessible, autonomous, chunked, current, experiential, "for me," hyperlinked, MVAK (multimedia/visual/auditory/kinesthetic), and social. L&D professionals can determine how to include these elements based on their learner research. You will find the upgrade tool on this handbook's website at ATDHandbook3.org.

These nine elements, based on Jane Hart's work, reflect the modern learner's need for personalization, up-to-date content, and the now of training delivery. By focusing on characteristics, rather than being prescriptive, they leave room for flexibility as new technologies are introduced. In addition, more traditional methods can be included, while still creating strong modern learning designs.

In L&D, we often think we have to add lots of technology to keep the training engaging. We all agree that technology-enhanced training is intrinsically more interesting. But in truth, even an old-school live training program or a training manual that is chunked, accessible, social, and personalized "for me" can be a big winner.

On the other hand, simply building a learning program around the latest technology can flop if the program lacks those same elements. For example, some designers have tried chatbots, only to fail. They may blame culture as the downfall, but a deeper dive can reveal other missing components. One might think a chatbot is, by definition, "for me" because it responds to the learner's comments. But is it really? Or is it simply delivering a predetermined set of branching options that don't meet the learner's needs? Or does the learner have to go to a different platform to engage with the chatbot? That would make it difficult to access in the flow of work. As with any training design, it's always best to do early testing on small parts of a new, digitally enhanced learning program to find out how your learners will respond.

The Learning Cluster Design Model

Building on the latest neuroscience and work like Mosher and Gottfredson's, the Learning Cluster Design (LCD) model was developed to address the shifts that are pushing L&D from a traditional approach into the digital age. While learning design models focus on designing excellent training, most assume that the goal is to design a single deliverable—be it a class, course, set of videos, e-learning program, or learning path. But modern learners and our businesses need more. Learning happens in a variety of ways, times, and places related to a particular need and based on learner choice in the moment.

The LCD model posits a new modern learning goal for L&D: to focus on making a difference back on the job through a new deliverable—a learning cluster (Figure 15-4). A learning cluster is a set of learning assets, selected with the business need and various learner personas in mind, that span the five moments of learning need. Rather than focusing on delivering and guaranteeing performance at the end of a single program, the model enables L&D to look at how a collection of learning assets can, together, contribute to performance where it counts—on the job.

It also comprises five Actions that L&D—not managers, IT, or recruiting—is best suited to do based on its expertise in how learning happens. The LCD model is nonlinear, and L&D practitioners can start at any Action, based on each unique situation.

Figure 15-4. Learning Cluster Design Model

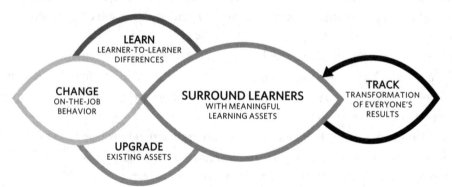

The Actions create a memorable mnemonic: CLUSTER. Here's a brief overview of each:
- **Change on-the-job behavior.** The Change Action sets the goal for the learning cluster (called a strategic performance objective). This goal articulates the connection between learners' on-the-job performance and the desired business results. This is one of three early Actions leading to the Surround Action.

- **Learn learner-to-learner differences.** The Learn Action identifies learner personas within the target learner group whose behavior change will have the greatest effect on the desired business impact. Persona definitions go beyond demographics and job type to explore contexts of when, where, and how each persona will most likely need to learn. This Action guides strategic choices in the Surround Action.
- **Upgrade existing assets.** The Upgrade Action applies the nine elements of modern learning to quickly improve current programs. As a bonus, the ideas for new learning assets identified here will jump-start the work in the Surround Action.
- **Surround learners with meaningful assets.** The Surround Action combines the work and insights from the other Actions to intentionally select social, formal, or immediate learning assets to build a learning cluster that meets the needs of each learner persona. Taken together, these learning assets should deliver both the desired behavior change on the job and the related business results.
- **Track transformation of everyone's results (TER).** The Track Action identifies those measures—qualitative and quantitative—that will indicate the impact of the learning cluster. Then it tracks these measures and turns the results into a story about the impact of learning. Use the results for further improvements.

Three Needs for Business and Learners

Let's take a closer look at personalization, up-to-date content, and the now of training delivery—the three needs for business and learners.

Personalized Training

Customization and personalization of training comes in many forms, but all center on being driven by learner choice—not L&D or SME wants and needs. David Rock, in *The Brain at Work*, described how to create a "towards" response from an individual by using the SCARF model to ensure that status, certainty, autonomy, respect, and fairness are included in the approach. Learner choice is all about building a sense of autonomy, creating magnetic learning experiences that draw the learner in and invite usage.

There are options for both complex and simple personalization, and you can improve personalization based on two compatible approaches: learner personas and social, formal, and immediate (SFI) learning touchpoints.

Simple or Complex Personalization

Customization and personalization can be simple or complex. For example, a more complex type of personalization may use artificial intelligence technologies to monitor what an employee is doing and offer up learning assets that can improve their performance. For this type of personalization, we suggest you talk with several software providers and run a trial on a small, but real project. These technologies are changing daily, so referrals, supplier interviews, and online reviews are your best bet for finding something that will work for you.

On the simpler side, personalization might be a personal invitation or nomination to participate in a learning program. Often, customizing can be as simple as giving learners a choice of what and how they want to learn, with some guidance on where to start to ensure learners are not overwhelmed.

Learner Personas

Typically, we define learners as a group, such as first-time managers. However, within that large group are several smaller subsets of people who have distinct differences based on things that go beyond demographics. There are many different approaches to developing learner personas. For example, the LCD model suggests that L&D consider these differences when developing three to five learner personas that then connect directly to the design of the learning cluster:

- Learning need differences (for example, loves to learn or not, is self-aware, or knows how to learn)
- Performance gap differences for the topic being taught
- Life-at-work differences (such as location, when they need to learn, time constraints on learning, and the availability of mentors or in-the-moment cohort coaches)
- Differences in their five moments of learning need

You can find the Learn Learner-to-Learner Differences Tool from the LCD model on the handbook website (ATDHandbook3.org). No matter the approach we use, by digging a bit deeper to better understand our learners, we can uncover what will truly help them change their behavior in the workplace so that they perform better, developing and growing on the way.

As you dig deeper to better understand your learners, consider how different learner personas will react when faced with their moments of learning need. Where will they be physically located when they learn the first time (new) or when they have to apply what they learned? What resources will they have on hand to solve a problem? How much time will they have to solve that problem or to learn more? Different groups need different things—by providing for their needs, people at your company will feel supported in their personal development.

Three Learning Touchpoints

Marketing managers look for touchpoints where, when, and how they can be visible to and reach customers. The LCD model reapplies this approach to L&D and identifies three learning touchpoints. Similar to the CCL 70-20-10 framework, LCD surrounds people with useful learning assets that support their learning: social, formal, and immediate.

- **A social learning touchpoint** involves other people and can range from training with others face-to-face to simply getting the opinions of others via the comments section on a social media platform. Learners are looking for anything from validation of content truthfulness or applicability to inspiration from others.
- **A formal learning touchpoint** is defined as something with a start and a finish, and for which L&D could provide a certificate upon completion if desired. This formal touchpoint tends to cover 90 percent or more of the products produced by today's L&D organizations. We hope to see that number change as L&D modernizes and provides learners with a broader range of learning assets that tap the social and immediate learning touchpoints.
- **The immediate learning touchpoint** is defined as a learning asset that is available 24/7 (or whenever in the workplace) without extensive searching. Typically, immediate learning assets include online jobs aids, wikis, searchable databases, active discussion boards, and e-learning programs that are both bite size and menu driven.

A unique concept in the LCD model is to create a strong tie between learner personas and the learning assets L&D chooses across the three learning touchpoints. The Venn diagram template gives a quick overview of the set of learning assets and the learner persona each asset will best serve (Figure 15-5). It's common for learning assets to fall into two of the three touchpoints. For example, a self-study online course is a formal learning asset, and, in this case, was designed to be chunked and menu driven so it could serve as a post-course job aid immediately. What learners find helpful is to have choices to meet their learning needs, using social, formal, and immediate learning touchpoints. You can find the Surround Learners With Meaningful Assets Tool from the LCD model at ATDHandbook3.org.

Staying Up-to-Date and Accurate

Keeping our training material up to date is not easy. Some L&D organizations schedule regular yearly or biannual reviews of programs. Others count on the training facilitators or an owner or a team to decide when a learning asset needs updates. Still others wait until learner ratings dip too low, and then rejuvenate the program.

However, these approaches all require L&D staff to be experts in the topic being trained. L&D is not always the expert, especially on technical topics and the capability to develop and maintain modern learning. Rather than doing it yourself, use approaches such as reusing, building an update infrastructure, crowdsourcing, and self-sourcing.

Figure 15-5. Example Venn Diagram of a Learning Cluster, With Learning Assets Selected Across SFI Learning Touchpoints

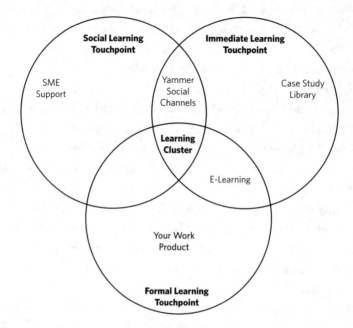

Reusing

Reusing takes advantage of each class to update materials. For example, SME instructors could update the materials as they prepare for the next delivery session. Or you could use the output from activities and exercises—have learners highlight out-of-date screenshots and instructions and give badges or awards to those who find them. Don't worry that out-of-date materials look bad; we all know how fast things change and most employees like to fix problems for the good of all. Another example is to use an open-ended activity where learners discuss issues from their day-to-day work and apply what they've learned. This can also provide material for case studies in future courses.

Developing an Update Infrastructure

Don't forget to take a look at your internal L&D processes. Do you have an avenue for feedback for the learning assets you put out there? A major telecommunications company we interviewed told us how they built a system of SMEs throughout the organization who were given a direct line to the L&D training team. People in the organization knew their training-connected SME contact and would feed all the change data to that SME, who then fed it to L&D. That's a strong update infrastructure.

Crowdsourcing

Are you still taking responsibility for developing all the content at your organization, only to find employees using external resources from an internet search? Crowdsourcing means working with the resources available, rather than inventing from scratch. When designing content or learning assets, explore what employees are already commonly referencing. If possible (within legal constraints or through purchasing), include these assets in your design. Another infrastructure approach is to internally crowdsource. Many organizations have internal informal experts and thought leaders that are underutilized. Social community platforms like Slack or Teams can help identify these experts as well as more formal means like establishing communities of practice. These experts are great for L&D to collaborate with to keep assets up to date. Develop a list of these informal experts as a go-to resource for your L&D team.

Self-Sourcing

An evolving system is to seek out people within the company who want to do more. There are always people who are temporarily underutilized who want to expand their network or continue to hone some skills. Tapping these people to monitor the current state of content—even if it is only to review the crowdsourced comments—is a boon to L&D staff and helps keep employees more fully engaged. There are also those who have strengths that can be beneficial for L&D to collaborate with. For example, marketing and communications talents can help build a newsletter or share communication ideas. IT can help develop searchability and accessibility solutions. Sometimes, individuals in these spaces are passionate and interested in using their talents in another avenue.

The key is that it is no longer normal or feasible to keep everything up to date without engaging others. What's counterintuitive is that the more people we engage in our learning work, the more others in the company appreciate what L&D offers.

Deliver NOW! Deliver More, Faster

With the new goal of modern learning shifting from delivering just a single class or course to delivering multiple learning assets or a learning cluster, you might be wondering how to keep up. Delivering more, faster has several angles. First, the business wants L&D to start delivering learning assets quickly when a need arises and to deliver more with less (that is, less staff and less budget). Second, when the moment of learning need arises, people want some learning assets to be available to them immediately, because they may not have time to wait for a class to be offered.

Deliver Learning Assets Sooner

If you have a great training program sitting on a shelf that meets the current business need, but is feeling a bit dated, don't throw it out! While a single learning asset, such as a course, is not the only thing learners need, you'll get a quick start by modernizing an existing asset. Although we have a lot of methods to design and deliver learning, we often struggle with a consistent approach to upgrade training initiatives fast. One solution is to look for ways to add two or three of the Nine Elements of Modern Learning to make it more interesting. (Do not add all nine elements—that would be overkill.) You can learn more about this process by referring to the LCD model.

A second idea is to construct a roll-out plan. Surround learners with multiple learning assets that will help them in the five moments of learning need. Determine which assets are a priority to deploy now and which can come later. Leadership will be pleased to see various learning assets rolling out over a planned schedule. Further, L&D, business leaders, and learners have greater confidence in the results because the learning is supported over time both in and out of the flow of work.

Deliver More to Solve for the Business Pain

The Change and Track Actions in the LCD model help L&D deliver more for the business and, ultimately, the employees. The Change Action starts with focusing on the desired end result in the workplace. The learning objectives for each learning asset seek to aid in delivering that workplace behavior change. The desired change is captured in the form of a strategic performance objective (SPO), which takes a form similar to Figure 15-6.

The key to success is to have in-depth discussions to discover the behavior change that is desired on the job. Often, people think they know what they want to see, but an L&D professional with good interviewing skills can uncover the real underlying issues and needed changes. This goes beyond defining knowing something or being able to do something. This approach drives doing something different in the workplace, and the multiple learning assets at each of the Five Moments of Learning Need support the modern learner as they develop. The difference on the job is what the business cares about the most, and by keeping our focus there, we orient our designs appropriately. You can find the Change On-the-Job Behavior Tool from the LCD model at ATDHandbook3.org.

Figure 15-6. Strategic Performance Objective (SPO) Template

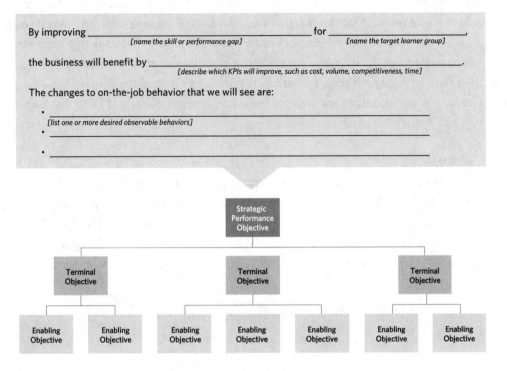

Note: if you are unfamiliar with terminal and enabling objectives, review "learning objectives," which are a foundational element of L&D and instructional design.

Deliver More for Learners

Learners face two big issues: The lack of time for training and learning, and the need for learning now when the moment strikes.

So many learners say they don't have time for training. One way to help them is to provide learning assets at the immediate learning touchpoint. Usually this means providing learning assets online in a place that is easy to find or search. Content is often chunked based on learners' most common moments of learning need on the job. This goes beyond formal learning assets and supports self-learning and learning in the moment of need. A nice shortcut is to take a formal e-learning program, chunk it, and use a menu-driven format with descriptive titles to help learners get to the one or two screens that they need right now.

Another way to help learners deal with their lack of time to learn is to make formal learning shorter. This doesn't mean to succumb to the pressure to take the wonderful one-day class and make it half a day. Instead, it involves reorganizing the content so that learners get only what they need. In other words, let's stop teaching them what they already know. We have to identify what 80 percent of the learners already know, cut that content out of the program, and provide an alternate means for the 20 percent to learn it ahead of time. Inevitably, this leads to a great strategy for chunking content for the learners. We might think of this content as remedial training, but in truth, it's a form of personalization that respects differences in experiences and knowledge. Be aware that within a single target audience, different groups of people will fall into that 20 percent category for different parts of the content.

Final Thoughts

Use the concepts in this chapter to make the fundamental shift toward modern learning design. Rather than a piecemeal approach, use them to help you build a comprehensive learning strategy that meets business and learner needs for a given learning gap. While the norm is to jump from new trend to new trend by considering and adopting a new thought process to designing learning, you will be prepared with a sustainable approach that gets you results for the future.

About the Authors

Lisa MD Owens is a learning expert who combines her engineering mindset with a deep interest in instructional design and learning sciences to create training that moves businesses forward. She is co-author of *Designing for Modern Learning: Beyond ADDIE and SAM* and the *Learners as Teachers Action Guide*. Her writing is based on new research, and her experience as president of Training Design Strategies, as well as serving as the dean of learning sciences emeritus at Procter & Gamble.

Crystal Kadakia is the leader of the LCD Group, as well as an independent organization development practitioner. The LCD Group offers workshops to upskill L&D on the LCD model and also consults on L&D initiatives. She is co-author of *Designing for Modern Learning: Beyond ADDIE and SAM* and the author of *The Millennial Myth: Transforming Misunderstanding Into Workplace Breakthroughs*. She spends most of her time as a consultant and speaker, helping organizations make sense of and determine strategy for complex changes related to culture and talent. She has a bachelor's in chemical engineering and a master's in organization development.

References

Davachi, L., T. Kiefer, D. Rock, and L. Rock. 2010. "Learning That Lasts Through AGES: Maximizing the Effectiveness of Learning Initiatives." *NeuroLeadership Journal* 3:53-63. blueroom.neuroleadership.com/assets/documents/AGES.pdf.

Davis, J., M. Balda, D. Rock, P. McGinniss, and L. Davachi. 2014. "The Science of Making Learning Stick: An Update to the AGES Model." NeuroLeadership Institute, August 15. neuroleadership.com/portfolio-items/the-science-of-making-learning-stick-an-update-to-the-ages-model.

Degreed and Harvard Business Publishing. 2019. "How the Workforce Learns." Degreed and Harvard Business Publishing. get.degreed.com/hubfs/HowWorkforceLearns2019_final.pdf.

Deloitte. 2017. "Deloitte Global Human Capital Trends: Rewriting the Rules for the Digital Age." Deloitte. deloitte.com/content/dam/Deloitte/global/Documents/About-Deloitte/central-europe/ce-global-human-capital-trends.pdf.

Greany, K. 2018. "Profile of a Modern Learner [Infographic]." Elucidat, August 15. elucidat.com/blog/modern-learner-profile-infographic.

Kadakia, C., and L. Owens. 2020. *Designing for Modern Learning: Beyond ADDIE and SAM*. Alexandria, VA: ATD Press.

Mosher, B., and C. Gottfredson. 2011. *Innovative Performance Support: Strategies and Practices for Learning in the Workflow*. New York: McGraw-Hill Education.

Mosher, B., and C. Gottfredson. 2012. "Are You Meeting All Five Moments of Learning Need?" *Learning Solutions*, June 18. learningsolutionsmag.com/articles/949/are-you-meeting-all-five-moments-of-learning-need.

Recommended Resources

Kadakia, C., and L. Owens. 2020. *Designing for Modern Learning: Beyond ADDIE and SAM*. Alexandria, VA: ATD Press.

Learning Cluster Design Group. "Learning Cluster Design Model." Blog. learningclusterdesign.com/blog.

Mosher, B., and C. Gottfredson. 2011. *Innovative Performance Support: Strategies and Practices for Learning in the Workflow*. New York: McGraw-Hill Education.

Williams, K.B. 2019. "Learner Personas: Beyond Demographics." *TD at Work*. Alexandria, VA: ATD Press.

CHAPTER 16

Delivering as if Learning Depended Upon It!

Hadiya Nuriddin

Delivery or implementation considerations may happen near the end of instructional design process models; however, the way learners will engage with a performance solution influences the entire design process. Design intends to support performance through authentic experiences, but how that support functions differs depending on how we plan to deliver it. Different delivery categories are often called modalities.

> **IN THIS CHAPTER:**
> ♦ Define the different delivery modality categories and how they are represented in workplace learning
> ♦ Describe how each delivery modality supports learning
> ♦ Identify key considerations for implementing delivery modalities within each category

How learners experience a solution is often referred to as a *mode*, which we define as how something occurs or is experienced, expressed, or done. It's often debated which learning modality is the best, fastest, or cheapest way to implement solutions. And truthfully, it's nearly impossible to compare them with one another, especially without a specific context. There is also the matter of selecting criteria for each measurement. For example, choosing a solution based solely on price now may result in higher costs down the line if shortcuts were taken.

The confusion comes from comparing the modalities with one another rather than assessing the qualities of each and determining whether it's a good fit for delivering the identified performance solution to the target audience. Consequently, choosing the most appropriate delivery strategy requires a clear understanding of how each type supports performance. The goal is not to choose the best modality; rather it's to choose the *right* modality for the *right* job.

Choosing the Right Modality for the Right Job

As much as we'd prefer to base our primary decision on how an implementation supports learning, the realities of the flow of business can, and should, influence our choices. Suppose we believe that the best way to teach managers how to give feedback to their team is to have them practice this skill in a face-to-face course. But if these managers are consultants who travel most of the time and can rarely attend a live course, a face-to-face delivery is not the best choice.

Decisions about which modality to use are often made based on four primary drivers:
- The modalities to which your learners have access
- The performance you are supporting
- The characteristics and work environments of your learners
- The modality that best supports the target performance

The Modalities to Which Your Learners Have Access

As Abraham Maslow wrote, based on a proverb, "I suppose it is tempting, if the only tool you have is a hammer, to treat everything as if it were a nail." Our primary goal should be to support shifts in performance; however, our options for delivering this goal are determined by the development and delivery means available within our organization.

Making modality choices based on access alone perhaps inevitably results in forcing a square peg into a round hole. We maneuver the class design to accommodate the delivery platform instead of selecting a modality that fits our preferred class design. Another possible consequence is creating logistical challenges that overshadow the design and delivery, like blending different modes, which could lead to confusion.

The Performance You Are Supporting

What you expect learners to be able do after engaging with the learning solution is a key driver in your delivery strategy. Creating an authentic experience, where the learner feels free to explore for better or worse in a safe, low-stakes environment, is essential.

Not all performances can be authentically reproduced in every modality. For example, while you can create customer interactions in asynchronous e-learning programs, the unpredictability of responses and gestures may be more realistically reproduced in a live role-play exercise with a classmate. If the risk of injury is high, e-learning may be the best alternative for encouraging learners to replicate the desired performance.

The Characteristics and Work Environments of Your Learners

Who your learners are influences the design and implementation strategy of any performance solutions you deliver. It's ideal to avoid encouraging learners to engage in activities that require a shift in performance while simultaneously asking them to learn a new method to access those activities. This contributes to extraneous cognitive load and may discourage your learners from using the solution and perhaps from engaging in the desired performance on the job.

Where, how, and when learners use a performance solution—such as an online course or a job aid—also influences its design. And this depends on the work lives of each participant. Here are some questions to consider:

- What technology can employees access on the job?
- What is their typical work schedule? When would they have time to engage with a performance solution?
- Where and how are employees completing most work tasks? (For example, are they on a sales floor with customers all day?)
- What policies specify what employees can use while working? (For example, employees may not have access to electronic devices on the job because of their work's physical location, the nature of their work, or corporate policy.)

The Modality That Best Supports the Target Performance

This final consideration is the focus of the rest of the chapter. Choosing a modality based on how it supports a performance is your primary goal. Using this lens to focus your modality decision requires taking all that we know about all the available modalities and understanding how they support learning and the desired performance.

Frankly, stakeholders often choose the delivery modality before they even request support from learning and development teams. Perhaps they may see it as a business decision because a primary driver is reducing or eliminating the expenses of financing same-time, same-place instructor-led training. In addition, a distributed workforce or high turnover may make traditional modes of training impractical. While these are just the realities of the businesses we support, learning and development teams should focus instead on which modality best supports learning and the desired performance.

We must make these decisions with the business in mind, but the learners' needs should be our priority—after all, the employees are the business. If employees fail to deliver the desired performance, the goals of the business strategy the solution is supporting will not be realized.

Terminology, Definitions, and Categories

It's challenging to define the modalities that are most prevalent in this space. In addition, different learning and development professionals often use different terms to describe the same modality. Have you had a discussion with a colleague about defining *e-learning* that turned out to be more frustrating than you anticipated? Some define it as a strictly asynchronous experience delivered using any digital device. That definition purposely excludes virtual learning (another debated term), but if virtual learning depends on a digital device and people are learning, doesn't that qualify as e-learning? The word *training* is also seen by some as an outdated and inaccurate way to describe an entire industry of performance solutions. However, because this chapter cannot resolve these universal debates, we'll use the most common definitions (and the word *training*) to explore each modality.

It's just as challenging to categorize these modalities as it is to define them. Because our definitions for modalities often overlap, so do the categories to which they belong. We are exploring the modalities by category, so we'll use the following delimiters and accept that overlaps may occur:

- **Instructor-led training (ILT)** is a synchronous (or same-time) learning experience facilitated by an instructor in the same location as the participants.
- **Instructor-led online training** is a synchronous or asynchronous learning experience led by an instructor. The participants and instructor may not all be in the same location.
- **Asynchronous online training** occurs when the trainer and the learner do not participate simultaneously. Training is done at different times and at different locations.
- **Performance support modalities or materials** are printed or digitized content designed to provide information when and where it is needed to support on-the-job performance.
- **Personalized support modalities** are one-on-one or small group targeted engagements. These standardized materials are also personalized to meet employee needs.

Let's explore these modalities further.

Instructor-Led Training

Instructor-led training modalities are synchronous learning experiences facilitated by an instructor who is in the same location as the participants. The typical implementation of ILT is a classroom-based experience in which the instructor is guided by course design and supports the participants in using course materials, like workbooks or handouts. In addition, the instructor often uses a facilitator guide and visual aids to explain the content and walk participants through activities that support the course's performance objectives.

Depending on the content and context, effective ILT can be designed and implemented quickly. The format is familiar to most learners and facilitators, so preparing people for the experience may take less time. However, implementation can also be a costly, logistical, and resource-heavy challenge. The quality of an ILT program may be compromised by inconsistent content delivery and learning experiences, especially when delivered by different instructors.

Here are three ways ILT modalities support learning:

- **The instructor can adjust the learning experience based on immediate feedback from participants.** Facilitators know that every group they teach has a unique collection of knowledge, experience, and skills. While a course is typically designed before it's delivered, instructors may alter its content, focus, or speed based on learner needs. Adjustments are more easily applied when facilitators can see learner body language or, as in software training, visually see how learners are progressing.
- **The instructor can provide hands-on experience for participants.** While learners can engage in hands-on activities in an instructor-led online training course, they may feel more supported if the instructor is physically in the room with them. Participants often judge the quality of a learning experience based on how quickly they receive personalized feedback because it provides insight into their performance and guidance for future behavior (Ambrose et al. 2010). ILT may provide learners access to that feedback during practice, which is when it is most beneficial.
- **Facilitators can provide opportunities for participants to quickly gain further insight into existing content or share and collect new ideas from other participants.** Learners benefit from exposure to various perspectives and feelings of connection if their classmates are also going through the same experience. While you can incorporate learner-learner interaction into other modalities, it is challenging to duplicate the experiences and interactions among participants in an ILT program. For example, participants in an on-the-job training program will learn from one another, but because they hold similar positions within the same department, they may miss out on the variety of perspectives they'd get from a mixed-audience ILT course. Also, the stakes are much higher during on-the-job training—training that their manager could be leading.

Here are some ways to implement ILT:
- **Lectures** are typically implemented as content-centric educational talks. This is a viable way to deliver content; however, it often leads to learning experiences stuffed with a lot of information and very little interaction. As a result, lectures are rarely authentic learning experiences for learners.
- **Workshops** are hands-on experiences designed to engage participants in targeted practice. Unlike lectures, workshops tend to be more learner centric. The primary goal of a learner-centric experience is to use the content to support what the learners need. The design encourages learners to draw on their own experiences and engage with the content while focusing on their individual needs. Experienced facilitators know that while learner-centric courses may vary from delivery to delivery, and are consequently more challenging to deliver, learners walk away with a more meaningful experience and new skills that they can use immediately. It's rewarding for everyone because learners will be more engaged and facilitators will put the focus on their participants, which is where it belongs.
- **Labs**, like workshops, tend to be hands-on, but they typically use a more self-directed approach. They feature less lecture and more practice and experimentation. While the assignments may be preselected, participants usually can use the time to go at their own pace and ask questions based on their immediate needs.

Instructor-Led Online Training

Instructor-led, online training is a synchronous or asynchronous learning experience led by an instructor who may or may not be in the same location as the learners. There are two primary differences when facilitating classes virtually: With some exceptions, no one sees one another in real time and everyone must communicate and engage with the content using technology.

The synchronous version of this modality is often called virtual training or virtual instructor-led training (vILT). Cindy Huggett defines virtual training as "a highly interactive, synchronous online, instructor-led training class, with defined learning objectives, that has geographically dispersed participants, each one individually connected using a web classroom platform" (Huggett 2017). In addition, vILT is typically conducted using software that allows everyone to simultaneously access the content and communicate in real time through voice and text. As of this writing, online tools such as Zoom, Adobe Connect, and WebEx are among the most popular.

In the *asynchronous* version of instructor-led online training, course administrators (or facilitators) post content in a central location, like a web portal, which participants access and read within a given window of time. Participants are also assigned work to complete, which a facilitator then reviews and grades. The facilitator is available throughout the length of the course to provide

FACILITATION IS LIKE A DANCE
Meghana Rajeshwar, APAC Faculty, Google

It all began with a conversation around dance. I was talking with a colleague about an upcoming blended learning session where participants complete self-paced content and then join live sessions for discussion and practice. During the live sessions we assess participants' understanding of concepts before they practice them. I mentioned a question I planned to ask when he said, "Meg, do you want to ask this question because it adds value, or because you want to show that you know this?

"You know," he continued, "like how some dancers do 10 backflips because they want to show they can do backflips, not because the music needs it. What if you just dance to the music instead?"

Like most professional facilitators, I certainly knew how to ask questions, but how could I take it to the next level? What if I could truly dance to the music?

The answer came to me with blinding clarity: Bloom's taxonomy. It has been around for decades and used by content designers to craft learning objectives at different levels. Bloom's original six levels of behavior are knowledge, comprehension, application, analysis, and synthesis. I realised that it also offered an elegant way to frame questions at six different levels, instead of the one or two questions I might normally have in my quiver for a given topic. I could use Bloom's action verbs to craft my questions more deliberately, calibrating them according to the level of discussion I wanted to drive:

- List the different types of.... (Knowledge)
- What is the difference between X and Y? (Comprehension)
- In situation X, what solution would you recommend and why? (Application)

Bloom's taxonomy can be used for both content and activity debriefs. Choosing the appropriate level depends on several factors, such as the knowledge level of participants or the level of discussion you want to drive. You might begin a discussion with simpler questions to get the group started, then gradually raise the level to challenge the group to think critically. Or you might want to have more complex questions ready if you're working with a more advanced group.

Many of us do this instinctively, but it is usually driven by our own facilitation style and preferences. Using Bloom's taxonomy to scaffold our questions brings more structure and intention, and most important, it puts learners' needs front and center. It taps into their motivation by giving learners meaty questions to chew on when they are ready. Additionally, it strengthens our facilitation muscle by helping us discover where we tend to operate in the spectrum and where we might need to add more conscious effort.

I realised that I tended to ask questions at either end, but not as many from the middle levels. This new approach helped me drive richer, more meaningful conversations with my learners and anchor my delivery in their needs. I am learning to dance to the music.

context to the content and answer questions. Some facilitators deliver content using prerecorded video or include occasional synchronous sessions in which they share new content, elaborate on existing content, or simply answer questions.

Instructor-led online training is often seen as an easy replacement when the "real thing" (that is, live classroom training) isn't possible or practical. But there are qualities about instructor-led online learning that make it a viable solution on its own.

Here are five ways instructor-led online training modalities support learning:

- **Participants engage in learning where the work happens.** Learning in a familiar space with easy access to all documents and tools you regularly use is valuable. In addition, learning where you are planted may help with learning transfer. The drawback is that this also comes with all the regular distractions.
- **Learning where you do the work integrates performance improvement into the flow of work.** This goes beyond the location of the training activities. Putting training in the flow of work supports the idea that learning isn't a separate activity that you access only in a training room on the fourth floor—it's part of your job.
- **Participants have options regarding social engagement during the learning experience.** Learning in a room with others is not desirable for everyone. Some people prefer to communicate through the online classroom tools instead of face-to-face. Also, when working in groups, there are fewer distractions in a breakout room than in a room full of multiple groups all talking at once.
- **Participants can benefit from spaced learning opportunities.** Asynchronous online learning experiences allow participants to engage in content and activities on their own time, over time. As Neelen and Kirschner (2020) write, "The effectiveness of spaced learning comes down to this: tackling learning in various short sessions works better than learning that same thing in one long session."
- **Spaced learning benefits everyone.** In addition to spacing, this strategy may also accommodate the individual needs of large, dispersed groups of people who prefer to experience and absorb content at different speeds. Most synchronous classroom tools allow for recording the experience so participants can review essential parts or the entire course once it's gone live.

Instructor-led online training can be implemented in a variety of ways:

- Full curriculums can be implemented via synchronous instructor-led online training. Most virtual training programs are no more than 60 to 90 minutes in length (Huggett 2017). Consequently, the design and the scheduling have to accommodate ways to include necessary content within that target timeframe.

- vILT is often blended with other asynchronous approaches. Learners may spend most of the time engaging at their pace and occasionally gather for an online session to learn new content or expound on existing content. Synchronous online ILT could also be part of a blend focused on question-and-answer instead of learning new content. It provides a way for participants to get immediate answers to their questions and feedback on their ideas and progress.
- To make synchronous learning experiences as concise as possible, designers offload content onto webpages, portals, or documents that participants can view on their own time. As part of course facilitation, instructors tell participants about the additional content and where to access it. With this approach it's important that participants know whether engaging with the content is optional or if it's a fully integrated (or required) part of the learning experience.
- While a typical implementation of asynchronous online ILT includes webpages on a portal tracked through a learning management system, asynchronous content can be delivered via any mechanism that participants can access. For example, content can be delivered by email, the intranet, or even social media.
- Both synchronous and asynchronous online training require technical support. Make sure you have a support model in place that includes instructions, documentation, and diagrams detailing how, when, and where instructors and learners can get support.
- Full courses using the asynchronous online ILT modality are more common in academic environments. If used in corporate environments, this modality may work better if the courses are multiday experiences where learners are kept engaged enough to work independently. However, most corporate courses range from one hour to two days.
- The common belief that asynchronous online ILT is somehow "easier" is a myth. The workload actually has the potential to be significantly higher for both facilitators and participants. The impression of increased work is due in part to the inclusion of ongoing learner-engagement activities. For example, facilitators and participants are required to engage on discussion boards in addition to their assigned homework.

Asynchronous Online Training

The asynchronous online training category consists of interactive learning experiences delivered digitally. Although there are many different implementations of this type of training, our focus in this chapter is on e-learning and mobile learning.

The definition of *e-learning* is frequently debated. Ruth Clark (2011) defines it as "instruction delivered on a digital device such as a computer or mobile device that is intended to support learning." I am adding to that definition that it is an asynchronous, interactive experience designed to support performance.

Defining mobile learning is a little more clear-cut—it's agreed that mobile learning is accessed via a mobile device. Chad Udell (2015) defines mobile learning as "the ability to move from place to place while using mobile devices to receive from and contribute to a variety of digital information sources." However, mobile learning should be specifically designed and optimized for access via a screen of mobile or tablet dimensions. For example, many interactions are impractical on a mobile device, and images intended to be viewed on a 15-inch laptop screen may not be legible on a six-inch smartphone. Avoid forcing learners to interact with e-learning on a mobile phone.

In addition to the convenience of anytime, anywhere access to content, asynchronous online training allows designers to create immersive experiences that may not be possible in the classroom. The tools developers use to create asynchronous online training allow them to get closer to creating authentic learning experiences, which ultimately support learning.

Here are a few more things to think about:

- **Learners get access to consistent messaging throughout the organization.** One of the challenges of live instructor-led training is that the organization is dependent on instructors delivering a consistent message to everyone. Unfortunately, instructors often fall short of that goal for a variety of reasons. Asynchronous online training, on the other hand, can deliver the same message to everyone. While this is more of a benefit to the organization, it helps increase learning transfer when employees can rely on others who have received the same message for support.
- **Learners can access the content at their own pace.** The most apparent way asynchronous online training supports learning is through spaced learning. But learners can also reaccess and reread content when needed.
- **Learners can engage with highly interactive modules that encourage skills practice in a safe environment.** Designers and developers can create interactive exercises that mimic, at least metaphorically, the performance expected of them back on the job. Authenticity is key.

As for implementation, e-learning is not instructor-led training on a computer, and mobile learning is not e-learning on a mobile device. Of course there are similarities among the decisions that need to be made, but the design, development, and implementation processes are not the same.

A typical implementation of e-learning is to use software to design and develop the modules. The course is then loaded onto an online system accessible to everyone who needs to access it (like a web portal); if participant engagement needs to be tracked the course would likely be placed on the organization's learning management system. These modules are ideally highly interactive to support the participant as they learn about and practice new skills. Courses range from short, targeted modules to long, multilevel experiences that take days to complete.

Two other implementations of e-learning are gamification and microlearning:

- **Gamification** is a popular e-learning design strategy that incorporates game elements into a learning experience. This could include creating levels of mastery or the awarding of points. Clark Quinn (2021) writes that "serious games are, perhaps, the ultimate learning experience. Putting people into the role of making contextualized decisions is an ideal practice for learning. We can approximate that fairly closely without having to build, or develop to, a full game engine."
- **Microlearning** is a strategy that provides the right amount of content and practice a learner needs to achieve a learning objective. *Micro* doesn't necessarily speak to the length of the course; rather, it speaks to how much the learner will be able to do after interacting with the module. For example, a 30-minute course with five learning objectives is not microlearning, but a 30-minute course with one objective could qualify as microlearning. Regardless of the length, a microlearning module must cover one complete task. It is not the same as "chunking," where you break one task into smaller chunks and then require the learner to engage with every chunk to learn how to complete that task. A microlearning course should be able to stand alone as a single task. For example, if you're creating a course on delivering feedback, you could build a microlearning module on how to deliver negative feedback. An experienced manager wouldn't have to go through an entire course on feedback just get to the part they need. Instead, they could take a 10-minute course on strategies for framing a poor performance.
- **Mobile learning,** or m-learning, is unique. When creating m-learning content, instructional designers should design an experience that's optimized for the mobile screen and refrain from simply building an e-learning module for a small screen. This goes beyond look and feel—it's the full learner experience, including how they will complete activities, engage with multimedia elements, and communicate with facilitators or other learners. An essential consideration is how, when, and where learners will access and interact with the course. Understanding that will influence the design, the implementation, and any communication strategies you have in play.

Many organizations have adopted a design strategy that allows them to "have it both ways" so that they do not need to create a course for e-learning delivery and another version for mobile delivery. That approach is often referred to as "mobile first." This means that most e-learning content can be accessed by mobile devices when the modules are built using a tool that interfaces with both small and large screens.

Performance Support

Performance support is any resource that supports a desired performance at the learner's moment of need. That moment of need is when the learner needs to demonstrate that performance. Bob Mosher writes that one goal of performance support is to move the solutions we provide "as far into the natural workflow of the organization as possible, so that we avoid, when we can, pulling people from their work for large periods of time to learn" (Gottfredson and Mosher 2011).

Performance support could take the form of literally anything that supports performance, particularly if it's easily accessible within the flow of work. In fact, some performance support even belongs more in the operations space than the learning and development department. Examples of performance support include:
- Printed or digitized documentation, such as job aids, reference guides, websites, and videos
- Process refinement or revamping processes and systems to accommodate the needed performance
- Social support for developing processes where teams or groups have dependencies in their responsibilities for groups and teams

Asynchronous varieties of training can also fall within this category, including e-learning and mobile learning, because while those modalities are formally referred to as training, they are often shorter and more targeted in a way that longer courses are not.

Performance support should be a vital consideration in any design strategy. Not including performance support would be akin to assuming that the learner would not need any additional support back on the job aside from what's provided in the learning experience. This is rarely the case. Yes, learners will have other means of support, but those mechanisms may not tie back to the objectives of the learning experience. Here are some benefits of performance support to keep in mind:
- **Learners may experience greater learning transfer.** Job aids and other documentation are typically guides, instructions, and memory aids readily available to help people accomplish tasks.
- **Learners will have access to information regarding rarely used skills.** When deciding which tasks may require additional performance support, it's often a choice between a task they often do or one that rarely happens and is consequently difficult to remember. There's no definitive answer to this question, but performance support certainly serves as a memory aid for difficult to remember tasks, whether the difficulty is due to time or complexity.
- **Learners can access updated information without having to be retrained.** You can update the performance support material and alert learners to the changes rather than having to retrain everyone.

Because performance support is defined so broadly, it's difficult to know where to begin. Resist the urge to create performance support based on the course's content and what you think could be helpful. The path to performance support requires designers to put themselves in the learners' shoes when they are back on the job and better understand how they engage with their work. For example, while the instructor may walk through a diagram of handoffs in the classroom, that doesn't mean that the same diagram will help them figure out whom to give reports to back on the job. Perhaps, instead, an FAQ document would work better.

Here are some strategies for implementing performance support:

- Gain a clear understanding of how and where people work back on the job and consider how you can incorporate the support into the flow of work. For example, if your learners work on a retail floor, they may not be able to pull out their mobile phones to find a job aid on how to upsell. However, reading from a sheet of paper in front of the customer may not work well either. Perhaps adhering small cards to the counter in a place that's out of the customer's line of sight is the answer.
- Ideally, performance support will not be buried in your learning management system under countless passwords. Post messages, tools, and documentation on the intranet or some other open place where they are easily accessible.
- Be creative about getting performance support to your learners. Websites are ignored. Documents are lost. Emails are deleted. You'll need to think of new and innovative ways to ensure that learners get what they need. Asking them and conducting a few tests using your best ideas will help. Unless you have experience doing the same job as your learners (in the same environment and using the same technology), do not assume you have a clear picture on which to base your decisions.

Personalized Support

Structured personalized support is the most broadly defined modality. The term *personalized learning* is more typically used in K–12 environments. *Instructional-Design Theories and Models, Volume III: Building a Common Knowledge Base* defines *personalized support* as "instruction that focuses on tailoring methods to target the particular learning needs of each student." We are broadening that definition by changing the "learning" to "support" and moving beyond gaining knowledge to including solutions that support actual performance based on the needs of learners when they need it.

Personalized support could include an experience that is:

- Tailored specifically to one individual learner's skill or knowledge level
- Designed to support individual learners and, while not necessarily catered to their personal needs, tailored to support self-directed learning

The options for personalized learning range from independent study, to one-on-one on-the-job training, to fully structured multiyear mentorship programs. Each type has benefits and challenges, but they are all designed with the intent of meeting the needs of individual learners. Here's a closer look at each:

- **One-on-one training.** The typical model for one-on-one training is a knowledgeable manager or peer teaching a person, such as a new employee, through job-related tasks specific to that person's role. While the tasks may be standardized, the training is personalized because the approach may differ depending on the learner's needs. The speed could be varied and tasks may be removed, added, or taught at different levels depending on the learner's experience. It's often information that will be used soon after (or while) the training takes place. This is often considered on-the-job training because it takes place in the work environment. It could also occur in a simulated environment or some other designated place, like a conference room. The trainer may be present during the entire training, or the learner may engage in self-study for part of the experience.
- **Self-study.** Learners are given content to explore on their own. The content could come as documentation, e-learning programs, videos, or some other asynchronous modality. Learners could also experience training using virtual reality technology where they can engage in on-the-job activities in an immersive, simulated environment. While the same content may be given to every learner, self-study is personalized because learners can go at their own pace and may have options regarding when, how, and where they engage in the learning experience. They do not need to wait for other learners to catch up or request that they slow down. Learners can also revisit content as needed.
- **Coaching and mentorship programs.** Personalized support programs can address immediate needs through solutions like on-the-job training and job aids, but they can also be used to support long-term goals and overall professional development. Coaching is a personalized support option for people who want to develop in specific areas. It's defined as a process in which a person provides a learner with constructive advice and feedback to help improve performance. Coaches could be professionals who've studied the craft and have coaching certifications or managers and peers with subject matter expertise and knowledge of coaching methods. Another option is mentoring, which is the practice of a more experienced individual sharing expertise with a mentee over a set period. Mentorships can be formal programs where mentoring relationships are assigned and the time is structured. They can also be informal, shaped and driven by the person's need or desire to get advice or perspectives on different aspects of their current or future career. Coaching and mentorships tend to be the most personalized types of support

because the one-on-one nature depends on learners being transparent about their needs and leaders responding in kind.

Organizations, teams, or individuals choose the personalized support modality for a variety of reasons. Group modalities such as ILT may be logistically impossible due to the learners' locations or the number of people who may need to simultaneously develop the same skills. E-learning may not be an option due to a lack of the expertise required to build the courses or the technology needed to support them. Personalized support is also often more economical than ILT or e-learning, although that may be seen only in short-term savings. In other words, having an asynchronous, consistently delivered, online solution that managers can point new hires to may cost less in the long run than taking a manager's time to walk through the onboarding basics for every new employee.

Here are some strategies for implementing personalized support:

- **Develop a formal coaching or mentoring program.** While it's true that many mentoring and coaching relations form organically, developing a formal program will help you facilitate connections, track the investment of time and expense, and continue to improve the program over time.
- **Blend with other modalities.** Personalized support is often blended with other modalities. For example, before and after training, give learners access to online resources, provide access to coaching, or assign a case study based on their current work role. The key is to avoid merely suggesting they complete these tasks, but to embed them as required elements. Refer to these elements as modules or units instead of pre-work or follow-up work so it's clear that they are part of the course.
- **Use technology to implement personalized support.** Technology is also influencing how personalized support is implemented. For example, in addition to the virtual reality technology mentioned earlier, augmented reality (AR) also exists. In her *TD at Work*, "Seeing the Possibilities With Augmented Reality," Debbie Richards (2019) describes AR as the use of "codes to overlay virtual elements—such as instructions or video that show users steps, processes, or directions—on real-world objects." She says that AR technology is accessible through devices already available to learners, like smartphones and tablets using the device's camera. The word *augmented* differentiates it from virtual reality in that AR technology overlays (or augments) the existing environment with information, rather than creating an entirely new environment with which the learner can interact. Other examples include chatbots, virtual personal assistant technology (like Alexa or Siri), and online collaboration tools like Slack and Teams. Learners can use these tools to get answers to their specific questions immediately.

Final Thoughts

This chapter provided a broad overview of some of the delivery options you can use to support learners. You're now better prepared to address the last of the four factors that contribute to choosing a delivery modality: The modality that will best support the target performance.

About the Author

Hadiya Nuriddin has more than two decades of experience in learning strategy, instructional design, e-learning development, and facilitation. She worked in corporate learning before founding her firm, Duets Learning. She frequently speaks at industry events and teaches courses for ATD. Hadiya holds an MEd in curriculum studies, an MA in writing, and the CPTD designation. She is the author of *StoryTraining: Selecting and Shaping Stories That Connect*.

References

Ambrose, S.A., M.W. Bridges, M. DiPietro, M.C. Lovett, and M.K. Norman. 2010. *How Learning Works: Seven Research-Based Principles for Smart Teaching*. San Francisco: Jossey-Bass.

Biech, E. 2008. *ASTD Handbook for Workplace Learning Professionals*. Alexandria, VA: ASTD Press.

Clark, R.C., and R. Mayer. 2011. *E-Learning and the Science of Instruction: Proven Guidelines for Consumers and Designers of Multimedia Learning*. New York: John Wiley and Sons.

Gottfredson, C., and B. Mosher. 2011. *Innovative Performance Support: Strategies and Practices for Learning in the Workflow*. New York: McGraw-Hill Education.

Huggett, C. 2017. *Virtual Training Tools and Templates: An Action Guide to Live Online Learning*. Alexandria, VA: ATD Press.

Knowles, M.S., E.F. Holton, and R.A. Swanson. 2015. *The Adult Learner*. New York: Taylor and Francis.

Metcalfe, J., N. Kornell, and B. Finn. 2009. "Delayed Versus Immediate Feedback in Children's and Adults' Vocabulary Learning." *Memory & Cognition* 37(8): 1077–1087.

Neelen, M., and P.A. Kirschner. 2020. *Evidence-Informed Learning Design*. New York: Kogan Page.

Quinn, C. 2021. *Learning Science for Instructional Designers: From Cognition to Application*. Alexandria, VA: Association for Talent Development.

Reigeluth, C.M., and A.A. Carr-Chellman, eds. 2009. *Instructional-Design Theories and Models, Volume III: Building a Common Knowledge Base*. New York: Taylor and Francis.

Richards, D. 2019. "Seeing the Possibilities With Augmented Reality." *TD at Work*. Alexandria, VA: ATD Press.

Udell, C. 2015. *Mastering Mobile Learning*. Hoboken, NJ: Wiley.

Recommended Resources

Anderson, H.H., I. Nelson, and K. Ronex. 2021. *Virtual Facilitation: Create More Engagement and Impact*. New York: John Wiley and Sons.

Biech, E. 2016. *The Art and Science of Training*. Alexandria, VA: ATD Press.

Bloomberg, L.D. 2021. *Designing and Delivering Effective Online Instruction: How to Engage Adult Learners*. New York: Teachers College, Columbia University.

Huggett, C. 2018. *Virtual Training Basics*, 2nd ed. Alexandria, VA: ATD Press.

LaBorie, K. 2020. *Producing Virtual Training, Meetings, and Webinars: Master the Technology to Engage Participants*. Alexandria, VA: ATD Press.

Nuriddin, H. 2018. *StoryTraining: Selecting and Shaping Stories That Connect*. Alexandria, VA: ATD Press.

Willmore, J. 2018. *Job Aids Basics*, 2nd ed. Alexandria, VA: ATD Press.

CHAPTER 17

21st-Century Media Skills: Put Learning Where the Work Is

Mhairi Campbell

People like to watch videos. We are now so used to taking in information onscreen that video is a vital part of a trainer's toolkit. According to Forrester Research (2019), "Employees are 75 percent more likely to watch a video than to read documents, email, or web articles."

> **IN THIS CHAPTER:**
> - Explore the power of video
> - Discover the value of bite-size learning
> - Recognise the benefits of hybrid learning

The training world is constantly evolving. There is now an expectation that training and learning need to reflect the changing nature of the workplace by applying the versatility that modern delivery methods allow. You will almost certainly find that blending a variety of media is the best way to get your message across most effectively and efficiently.

Using 21st-century media tools, you can engage your audience and deliver learning in a way that is appropriate for individual learning styles. Today it's no longer about spreading your message into the ether. The latest tools allow you to deliver learning in a much more personal and direct way with the ability to measurably track learning outcomes and progress.

Video and audio are still important, but the method of delivery has changed. Let's examine some of these tools and how you can use them. We'll consider important aspects of:
- Video, such as your target audience, equipment, content options, planning, shots and angles, and post-production
- Audio requirements for podcasting
- Bite-size or microlearning
- Hybrid learning delivery modes, such as social media and apps

Explore the Power of Video

So where to begin? Think carefully about the information you need to deliver and decide if video will suit your purpose. Video may be a total solution for the delivery of learning content to your audience, or it might be small part of the training experience. It may be delivered directly to your audience in a training room, over the internet, or even via an app. So what do you have to consider if you want to use video to its best advantage?

Your options are:
- **Using a previously made video.** It's always good when you don't have to reinvent the wheel and reusing material can be cost effective. However, just like other forms of media, your video may be dated and therefore not fit for purpose. (Updating a video is not as easy as changing a handout!)
- **Making a new video.** This is a lot easier than in the past and it does not have to be expensive. You can make top quality videos yourself without having to invest in a large amount of equipment.

Making a Video for Learning

To make a video to deliver learning you will need to consider your target audience, the equipment you use, the amount of time you have, your budget, and your delivery platform.

Target Audience

Knowing your target audience is vital, so find out as much as you can in advance. Using 21st-century media tools such as online questionnaires (I like to use Survey Monkey) is a fast way to do this. These surveys are easy to set up using freely available tools on the internet or your company's learning management system.

Try to find out your audience's learning preferences—we all believe we learn best in different ways, and your training should reflect this. Carefully phrasing questions in a pre-course questionnaire can tell you a great deal about the way people learn. Approximately 65 percent of the population are visual learners, so audiovisual tools will help create engagement.

Andrew Munden (2021), the general manager of Britain's North Norfolk Railway, uses hands-on training when instructing train drivers because he finds experiential learning works best for them. However, he states that "there's a time and a place for e-learning. It is particularly good for testing and assessing the theoretical elements of railway employees whether they are drivers, guards, or work the signals."

Video Equipment

Budget and time will both dictate the complexity of any video you wish to shoot. If you have a large budget, you may wish to employ a professional team. If you're making your own video, you'll need equipment, including:

- Camera
- Tripod
- Audio recorder
- At least one mic
- Headphones
- Batteries
- A separate power bank for back-up power
- SD cards
- Lighting kit (optional)

If a dedicated video camera is not available, many of today's smartphones produce very high-quality images and video. Cell phones also provide an excellent way to record high-quality sound. You will also need a simple editing package to edit the video. At the most basic level, Apple's iMovie and Windows 10's Video Editor do a pretty good job and are relatively easy and quick to learn. To make more complex videos you can invest in more advanced software, such as Apple Final Cut Pro, Adobe Premier, or Avid Media Composer.

Time and Budget

Time and budget play a large part in the type of video you can produce. It is nearly impossible to outsource the filming to a professional company if your timeline is short. If you produce the video yourself, make sure to plan for one that fits within your skill set. Budget also plays a part. Making your own video is obviously less expensive than hiring a production company; however, sometimes it is best to scale back your aspirations and pay for a professional team to deliver a professional product.

Delivery Platform

Consideration of the delivery platform is essential. You may want to use an app to deliver short, bite-size learning videos or upload your film to the company's learning management system. Your video could also be delivered via a streaming service such as YouTube or Vimeo. Think carefully about the video's format—should you shoot it in landscape or vertical? Landscape is best for delivery on television or computer screens, but vertical video is growing in popularity when delivery is on smartphones or social media channels.

Is your video going to be interactive? Will participants be able to click on the video and have an action take place? Interactive video (also known as IV) can be delivered on computers and smartphones. Trainees can click on a hotspot in the video, which makes an action take place. The smartphone app LifeSaver (available for Apple and Android devices) is a good example of using interactive video training to enhance a first-aid tool. LifeSaver is a free app that trains users to perform CPR through interactive scenarios. This form of self-directed learning is highly effective and allows the user to immediately apply what they have learned. It can also be used as just-in-time learning.

Video Content Options

It's also necessary to determine what type of video you're going to make. Four popular options are the talking head video, an interview-style video, use of screencapture, or animation:

- **Talking head.** In a talking head–style video, the viewer sees the presenter speaking directly to them (for example, a video of a TED Talk). This type of video is known as a piece to camera (PTC). To make a PTC more engaging the speaker may be set against an interesting background.
- **Interview.** In an interview-style video, the viewer is typically able to see both the interviewer and a guest or expert, because the camera records the conversation with an aim. (In other words, one camera is focused on each person, and the video is edited to cut between the two feeds.) If you have only one camera, this style of video can also be filmed as a two shot, with an over the shoulder angle. In this setup the camera would be placed

behind the interviewer with the shot focused on the guest (but keeping interviewers' the head or shoulder visible in the foreground).
- **Screen capture.** This style of video captures the action happening onscreen. Most computer and smartphone operating systems have the ability to do a video screen capture. It is very useful for demonstrating software applications.
- **Animation.** To make an animated video, you can use drawings (electronic or hand drawn) as well as figures and models. Kinetic typography, where moving type is used instead of static captions, can add speed and pace to a film. One of the benefits of using animation is the ability to record the narration in different languages to suit multiple audiences.

Planning Your Video

Careful planning is essential and leads to a successful outcome. You'll need to think about audience, your storyboard, types of camera shots, angles, and more.

Audience

You need to understand your audience and their needs. If you have no contact with your audience in advance, creating a persona is quite useful. Put yourself in the shoes of the trainees and build a picture of an average course participant.

Storyboard

A storyboard allows you to envisage your film and communicate its look and feel for pitching and delivery. A storyboard can highlight requirements regarding location, props, continuity, and any safety issues. It doesn't have to be a great work of art either—you can simply draw stick men using a free template. It's a good idea to talk through a storyboard with an informed colleague who may have useful suggestions.

Types of Shot

Use different camera shots to tell the story in a more interesting and engaging way.

A wide shot establishes the scene. It captures a complete object, view, or person and puts it in the context of its surroundings. This type of shot is used to set the context of the rest of the scene that follows.

 **A medium shot (also known as a mid shot or MS)** is used to develop the story. The screen is filled with the person's upper body, from the head to the waist.

In a close-up or extreme close-up shot the subject fills the film frame. For a person, this would include the top of the shoulders and the head (close-up) or just face or even part of the face (extreme close-up). This type of shot is used to create intimacy.

Camera Angles

The choice of camera angle can also affect the mood and style of the video.

 **A low-angle shot** frames the subject from below their eye-line, which conveys a sense of dominance of the subject.

An eye-level angle replicates how we see people in real life and conveys a sense of equality.

In a high-angle shot the camera looks down on the subject. This angle is ideal for practical demonstrations.

When your planning is complete, you are ready to go. Remember to consider any health and safety issues. Depending on where you are filming it may be a legal requirement to complete a risk assessment. Also check that you have cleared any permissions that may be needed for filming in certain locations.

Choosing the Right Equipment

You can use a smartphone or a dedicated video camera. If you are going to buy a camera it's best to choose one with a dedicated microphone input and adjustable audio level controls.

Always film in the highest quality your equipment will allow; 4K is excellent. Even if you intend to publish in a lower definition, filming the original in 4K gives you the ability to adjust and reframe your footage during editing without losing quality in the finished video.

In addition to the camera, there are a few other things to consider when choosing your equipment.

Tripod

Whatever camera you use, a tripod is essential. It will stop your film from being shaky and is useful for occasions when you need static shots. A monopod is similar to a tripod, but it has only one extendable leg. A monopod is useful if you need to steady shots but also have the flexibility to move locations easily.

Audio

No matter how good your film is, if the sound is poor you will not be able to get your message across. Use an external microphone plugged into the audio input of your camera or smartphone. This will produce superior results and give you the ability to get much closer to the sound source. There are a great number of microphones on the market, and choosing the right one for the job is important. As media producer Jeff Link (2021) says:

> Your choice of microphone will depend on the recording conditions. Choose between a directional mic or an omni-directional mic. If the recording conditions are less favourable and you are working in a noisy environment then a directional mic is the best choice. A directional mic picks up in a specific direction, which means you can favour the voice that you want to pick up and reduce the level of unwanted sounds. An omni-directional mic is useful if a number of speakers need to be recorded and the background noise is low, such as a quiet room or a quiet outside environment. Some directional mics can pick up sound in a "figure-of-8" pattern, which is useful for picking up two voices talking across a table. Different strengths of voice can be easily adjusted with a "figure-of-8," by simply moving the louder voice a few inches away from the mic. Whatever your choice of microphone,

always use a windshield (wind muff) as it will help to prevent voice pops and reduce wind noise when outside.

Other audio options include:
- **Small, personal lapel mics.** These work when doing interviews. They can be either wireless or connected via a cable. Wired lapel mics can remove the risk of unexpected interference, but they do limit movement to some extent.
- **Shotgun or gun mic.** A gun mic is an extreme version of a directional mic with a narrow field of pickup.
- **Handheld recording devices.** Using your cell phone as a recording device is a very easy way to record quality sound. You can plug a personal mic into the phone, press record, and pop the phone in a pocket. It's really useful to do this if you are filming yourself.

There are also a number of small handy recorders on the market that are relatively inexpensive but produce high-quality sound. These are mainly solid-state recording devices and are useful when recording sound for podcasts. It's even possible to use one of these hand recorders as a gun mic on a pole. I have done this when I want to record in a noisy environment where it was not possible to use a personal mic. I simply attached the hand recorder to a lightweight boom arm and held it close to the speaker but out of shot.

Incorporating Graphics

You may need to include a number of graphics in your movie. Graphics can reinforce your message, add context, and deliver information quicker than a long talk or pages of text. Whether you're adding tables, subtitles, diagrams, graphs, or photos, consider the following:
- **Appropriate.** Make sure your graphics are relevant to your audience.
- **Not overly detailed.** Too much information, which cannot be readily assimilated by the viewer, does not help learning.
- **Consistent.** When using multiple graphics, always use the same fonts, borders, and so forth.
- **Kinetic.** Moving graphics maintain pace and add interest.

Scouting Your Environment

Whenever possible, use natural light for your shoot. If you are filming outdoors the weather will play a crucial part. You might be filming in a noisy environment, such as a factory, or perhaps you are filming somewhere where the light is poor. It's important to take as much control as you can over where you are filming. You can do this by making sure to recce, or scout, the place in which you wish to film at least a day before you do so. Recce, derived from the word *reconnaissance*, is part of the planning process.

Check out the lighting, power source availability, and acoustics in the filming location. In addition, check for background noise and reflected sounds from walls and windows. This will help you determine which type of mic you want to use for the video recording.

If you are using cables, make sure they are secured to the floor with tape or cable covers so they don't become a tripping hazard.

Post-Production Techniques: Editing and Scripting

Once you have completed shooting your video, it's time for editing and post-production. You can do this using different software and apps on your smartphone, tablet, or computer.

Editing

The first thing to do after you transfer your footage to a computer is make a backup of your original files.

Using your editing package, import your footage. Begin by looking at all the material you have shot and referring to your plan. You can then decide how much of each shot to use in your final film, as well as the order in which you want to use your shots. Then use the editing software to arrange the shots in your chosen order and trim each clip.

Once your clips are edited and in the correct sequence, the rough edit is complete. Now you need to decide how you want to move from one clip to the next. Some clips may easily join seamlessly as a jump cut, but others may not look good spliced together. For these joins there are a variety of transitions available:

- **Fade.** You can fade in or out of a shot. This transition is usually a fade to black (or a blank screen), but you could also try a fade to white. This will create more energy across the scene change. Fade-ins can be used to show that a new scene is beginning, and fade-outs to black indicate a closure of some kind.
- **Dissolve (cross-dissolve or cross-fade).** In this type of transition, the first shot gradually fades and dissolves into the second shot.
- **Wipe.** In this transition, the shot on the screen is replaced by the clip that follows using an effect. For example, the outgoing shot could disappear to the left (wipe to the left) and the new scene could replace it, wiping in from the right. Most editing software packages offer hundreds of fancy wipes, but ask yourself if they are adding anything to the video before you use them.

This is also the time to add diagrams, photo stills, graphs, captions, and more.

The final considerations for your video are the addition of any voice-over, music, and sound effects. If you don't have a separate audio recorder, you can record a voice-over by plugging a microphone into your camera. When you import the footage into your computer, choose the option to import audio only. You can then add the voice-over to the soundtrack of your video.

If you're going to use music, choose it carefully. It can be a distraction to some learners, and music loops can be irritating. In addition, make sure the music isn't too loud or the voice will be difficult to hear. It's also important to check whether there are performing rights and royalty fees associated with the music you've chosen.

Scripting Hints and Tips

Writing is part of the planning process. You may have prewritten the words that are delivered in the video, but you may need to include a voice-over once you have edited your film. A voice-over is useful for introducing the video, linking scenes, and adding explanation where necessary. It can also end your video with a call to action.

When writing the script think carefully about your audience and what you are trying to say. Consider the:

- **Tone.** This must suit the type of video that you have produced. Be conversational in tone, but don't sound too intimate.
- **Clarity.** Record your voice clearly and in high quality. If you make mistakes you can use software to edit out any fluffs. There are programs freely available on the internet.
- **Sentence length.** Don't make your sentences too long and complex. Short sentences are best and are easily understood.
- **Word choice.** Don't use unnecessarily complicated words and jargon if it is going to get in the way of your message.

When your script is complete, read it out loud as you play your video. This will let you see if it fits in well and if it makes sense with the images. Finally, always remember not to put into words what your audience can already clearly see in the video footage.

According to author and trainer Jonathan Halls (2021):

Video is a show-don't-tell modality because people remember more of what they see than hear. As such, it's ideal for learning that might ordinarily be demonstrated in a class such as psychomotor skills, processes, or how things work. However, video is not as effective for narrative learning such as case studies, which might come alive as podcasts, or detailed topics, which are better conveyed by text and graphics.

Find additional tips to improve your video on the handbook website, ATDHandbook3.org.

Learning via Audio: Podcasting

An audio recording in the form of a podcast is a valuable asset in the training world. It allows you to deliver training anytime, anyplace, and anywhere. A downloadable podcast is a flexible and accessible method to deliver learning and can add to the learning experience for both pre- and post-course material. Podcasts are easy to update and can range in content from simple interviews to pre-meeting information.

For equipment, you'll need a mic, a recording device, and editing software.

Like a video, you need to plan your podcast. Writing for audio is a different skill than writing a script for a movie. Try to visualise your listener and remember you are engaging the audience on a one-to-one basis. Notes are useful because they allow you to break down learning objectives and order them so the ideas flow in a logical order.

If you have written a script, watch out for long sentences and words that are difficult to pronounce. A rehearsal will indicate where you need to pause for breath.

When you record, keep your tone conversational. Make sure the audio level is not too high or too low and that you are not picking up any background noise.

When you're ready to edit the recording, free audio-editing programs are ideal for use with simple podcasts. They allow you to remove any errors and tighten large gaps in the recording. Well-edited audio should flow and not sound as though it has been edited.

If your podcast is part of a series, you might want to brand it in some way with a musical introduction to each piece; the same goes for the end of your podcast. The music doesn't need to be very long and could be just a short "sting," as we say in England.

Discover the Value of Bite-Size Learning: Microteaching

Video is an extremely useful tool for training and can be used in a variety of ways. You don't always need to deliver a long and complex training package in one film. Small, bite-size chunks of learning form mini-modules that can be easily accessed online via a company's learning management system, delivered within a learning app, or even offered on your own website.

Microteaching is all about improving your own skills. You deliver a short session (up to 15 minutes) and invite analysis and feedback from your audience. It is a skill to be able to deliver training in these short bursts and requires you to plan effectively and really know your subject. You need to be able to engage your audience quickly and capture their attention.

Take these steps for a successful microteaching session:
- Create a short session plan (no more than a couple pages).
- Make sure you have a strong introduction, middle section, and summary.
- Include some interactivity.
- Leave a little time for questions.
- Ask for feedback.

Short bursts of learning can be quite effective. In a 15-minute session you can still use video and even give a short quiz. If you are going to use PowerPoint or Keynote, don't put too much information on one slide—only three to four bullet points.

Be careful that you don't run out of time or lose focus, which can happen if you take a lot of questions during your presentation. Practice is key!

Recognise the Benefits of Hybrid Learning

Hybrid learning is blended learning plus. It allows you to use 21st-century media skills and tools to deliver the best content for trainees using a blend of offline and online learning delivery.

When the COVID-19 pandemic began in 2020, many L&D professionals had to switch to using virtual platforms—such as Zoom and Microsoft Teams—to deliver learning content. We quickly learned that there are major differences between delivering live online training and delivering a face-to-face session in a training room. You cannot gauge the participants in the same way and building rapport may be harder. And even if you are practiced in live online delivery, your participants might not be and may find the technology a bit daunting at first.

Once again, a successful live online session comes down to planning. Webinars are useful for delivering training and information to a large audience and for public events. Zoom is better for training sessions that need interactivity or where you want to create smaller groups. Breakout rooms, where you separate online participants into small groups, allow for incorporating collaboration, discussion, and feedback into the session. You are effectively creating an online team!

Think carefully about the tools you are going to use. You can still deliver PowerPoint and Keynote presentations through Zoom and Teams, but too much detailed onscreen text can disengage the learner. Remember, when your learners are logging in from home or the office they may be more easily distracted. This is where knowing what these online delivery services can do is very useful.

A small group of participants is easier to manage than a large number. With a small group you can see people's faces more easily. Managing a large group is harder and it may be better to have an extra facilitator who is operating mics and monitoring breakout sessions.

You can use the built-in messaging tool for questions and answers, even building up a number of questions to be answered at a time.

Edward Scotcher (2021) of Agility in Mind, a leading business agility transformation consultancy, has this tip:

> When creating a virtual classroom, we make good use of an in-vision trainer and an interactive whiteboard. This allows greater participant engagement through interactivity. Our team of trainers uses Microsoft Teams, Zoom, and Mural.

Using Social Media and Apps

Using social media and technology is now second nature to many of us. Different social media platforms offer different opportunities for learning delivery. At its simplest level, you can create a Facebook page through which you can communicate to participants both before and after a course. You can also stream live training sessions and set up select groups. You can also use social media platforms for posting reminders, sending out the latest links to material, and even creating discussions. You can set up a blog and use your social media to deliver both video and podcasts.

Apps are good for accessing training modules when you are on the move. You can view them online as well as offline and they are particularly useful for just-in-time training. Apps can contain short video clips and microlearning modules and give instant access to diagrams and sets of instructions. Many of today's trainees are familiar with online games, and gamification within an app is a good way to deliver training. Marc Prensky (2001) coined the term *digital natives*, individuals who were brought up during the technology age and were familiar with computers and the internet from an early age. It is these digital natives that we are training today.

David Squire, creative director of Desq (Digital Learning Designers), states:

> Only digital learning that engages people and delivers memorable experiences will stick. We have been working with Fujitsu and the learning materials that we made for the company are delivered both online and via Hackathon style workshops. We created a virtual cityscape representing Fujitsu's operations, and staff were able to view and collect videos and animations on how Fujitsu is using pivotal technologies.

Final Thoughts

So what does the future hold? We are now in a world of lifelong learning and upskilling. Virtual reality allows us to practice skills before we need to apply them, and AI can be used to deliver greater personalised and differentiated learning.

The media technology of the 21st century truly put learning where the work is. We can build on the skills of the past using new delivery platforms. As trainers, we need to be aware not only of the tools we can use, but of our audiences and their expectations. Our work needs to be accessible to all learners, whether they have a disability or not. Producing mixed media for training purposes is essential for trainers. We need a good grasp of current media skills and to keep up to date with the ever-changing technology.

About the Author

Mhairi Campbell is an award-winning media producer and trainer. As an executive at the BBC, she spearheaded innovative online content for BBC Learning. After leaving the BBC in 2008, Mhairi set up her own production and training company, SqueakMedia. She has led projects for the Disney Corporation and Cambridge University Press. She has delivered training for NATO, the British Library, the World Association of Newspapers, and the Construction Industry Training Board. She has worked with the World Wide Web Foundation to produce a "Magna Carta" for the 21st century and continues to deliver master classes in journalism. You can email her at squeakmedia@btinternet.com.

References

"Agility In Mind." agility.im.
Desq. "Fujitsu: Tech & Me." Digital Learning Designers. desq.co.uk/work-project?clientid=4.
Forrester Research. 2019. "Video-Based Learning Facts You Can Use to Make the Case for a Video Platform." Panopto, August 19. panopto.com/blog/5-facts-you-can-use-to-make-the-case-for-video-in-your-learning-development-organization.
Halls, J. 2021. "8 Point Checklist for Video Production." The Learning Guild Publications Library, May 27. learningguild.com/publications/150/8-step-checklist-for-producing-engaging-instructional-videos.
Levy, D. 2021. *Teaching Effectively With Zoom*, 2nd ed. Self-published.
Link, J. n.d. "Broadcaster and Trainer Twitter Profile." @jefflinkradio.
Prensky, M. 2001. "Digital Natives, Digital Immigrants." *On the Horizon* 9(5). marcprensky.com/writing/Prensky%20-%20Digital%20Natives,%20Digital%20Immigrants%20-%20Part1.pdf.

Recommended Resources

Christopher, D. 2014. *The Successful Virtual Classroom: How to Design and Facilitate Interactive and Engaging Live Online Learning*. New York: Amacom.
Diefenbach, D.L., and A.E. Slatten. 2019. *Video Production Techniques: Theory and Practice From Concept to Screen*, 2nd ed. New York: Routledge.
Halls, J. 2017. *Rapid Media Development for Trainers: Creating Videos, Podcasts and Presentations on a Budget*. Alexandria, VA: ATD Press.
McLeish, R., and J. Link. 2015. *Radio Production*. New York: Routledge.

CHAPTER 18

Using Story Structure to Influence

Nancy Duarte and Jeff Davenport

Human beings are "storytelling animals" (Gottschall 2012). Our brains are wired for stories. They are how we process the world around us, giving us a lens through which we interpret almost all of life. According to Statista, "Consumers around the world spend an average of 463 minutes or over 7.5 hours per day with media. American consumers tend to average more time than most" (Watson 2020). Our thoughts, emotions, and actions can all be powerfully altered by stories. And yet, too often, training experiences are created without story in mind.

> **IN THIS CHAPTER:**
> - Define and employ the Seven Transformation Story Beats to see your learners' growth trajectories more clearly
> - Select and prepare stories intended to inspire learners
> - Prepare the right story, told in the right structure, to persuade decision makers

Built for Story

Lack of story-mindedness while building training programs creates learning that is centered on content, rather than the learner. The result is unmoved learners and decision makers who are unable to see the value in the training. But, when you use stories to focus the training, learners and decision makers can be moved and persuaded.

At Duarte, our hope is for learning professionals everywhere to realize the power of story and use it to create more empathetic, moving, and inspiring training that doesn't just teach—but transforms.

Story-mindedness will help:
- You empathetically see learners more clearly, so you know how to help them transform
- Your learners comprehend their own stories and apply frameworks to live better stories
- Decision makers discern the value of your strategy by seeing the powerful impact it will have

Let's begin by getting a better understanding of why story is so impactful on the mind of a learner.

Three Reasons Stories Matter

A significant amount of research has been conducted to gain a deeper understanding of how the human brain responds to stories. This research gives us insights into how the listener's (or learner's) brain is functioning when they hear information communicated to them in the form of a story. Let's look at three conclusions we can draw from this trove of research.

Stories Are How Humans Interpret the World

In 1944, in an effort to better understand how individuals made judgments of others, psychologists Fritz Heider and Marianne Simmel created a short, animated film. The crude, 90-second black-and-white piece showcased a large triangle, a small triangle, and a circle as they moved around the screen in and out of a rectangle shape (Kenjirou 2010; Figure 18-1).

Heider and Semmel showed their film to a group of test subjects. Afterward, they asked the respondents to describe what they saw. Almost every subject described the video in terms of a story, even though all they saw were shapes moving. Their stories varied, but the general idea remained the same: a "bully" (the large triangle) was mad at, or wanted something from, the "victim" (the circle). The smaller triangle stepped in and not only distracted the bully's attention from the victim but also locked the bully inside the large rectangle. As the small triangle and circle escaped, the bully broke apart the rectangle, smashing it to pieces in a fit of rage.

Heider and Simmel concluded that humans view the world around them through the lens of story, perceiving simple moving shapes in the form of a narrative arc.

Figure 18-1. Frame From Heider and Simmel's Film

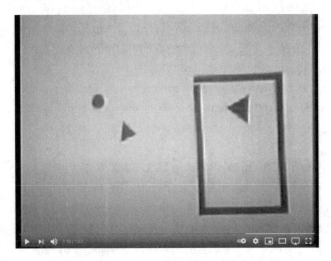

Humans unconsciously attach literal-minded things to narrative. If we're in a meeting and an attendee arrives late, covered in mud splatters and grease, we don't simply shrug and think, "Oh, they are here finally and covered in mud and grease." Our brains form a narrative around what could have happened. We will create or inquire about the backstory to comprehend what we're seeing.

As learning professionals, this means that even when you're not explicitly communicating via story, our learners' minds are trying to interpret the data and facts we're sharing through the lens of story.

Stories Stick

For learners to grow and change, they must be able to recall what they've been taught. Striking facts and data points may jar learners in the moment they're communicated, implying impact, but stories leave a much longer-lasting impression on learners.

In their book *Made to Stick: Why Some Ideas Survive and Others Die*, Chip and Dan Heath cite a study where Stanford students were asked to listen to presentations and then later report on what they could recall. The presentations included two types of content: statistics and stories. When asked what they remembered, only 5 percent of the respondents remembered a single statistic, whereas 68 percent remembered at least one story.

Because of the way stories engage listeners' brains, they stick in our memory longer than facts—even strong, powerful facts.

Think about the last three TED Talks you watched. The talks may have included a jarring statistic that, in the moment, made you sit up and take notice. But can you remember any with accuracy today? You may have a general impression of them, but did the numbers stick with you? Now, think about the stories those TED speakers told. Can you recall one of them? You may not be able to remember every beat, but can you remember the overall flow and point of the story? According to the Heath brothers, you're much, much more likely to remember the stories than the statistics.

It's the same with learners. The stories you tell while training will "stick" with learners much longer than the facts, data, or statements shared (Boris 2017).

Why does this matter? Because if learners can't remember the key points they learned, they'll be less likely to apply them in the moment. This in-the-moment application is the gold standard of training development—proof of long-lasting behavior change (Kay 2016).

Stories Release Powerful Chemicals Within Listeners

Stories help listeners focus, remember, and act because of the way they alter the brain's neurochemical processes. Studies show that when listeners are enthralled (or "transported," as story researchers describe the phenomenon), the hormone cortisol is let loose inside their blood (Smith 2016). As they experience the story, their minds take in the drama and tension of the various characters, resulting in nervous or anxious feelings. This is why we grip the arm of our chair when a character in a scary movie walks into a spooky house or grimace as the guy bumbles his efforts to get the girl to fall in love with him. As we watch, we're faintly experiencing the drama as if it were happening to us.

This release of cortisol (which normally gets a bad rap as the "stress hormone") actually helps listeners pay attention. That's why we focus more intently on stories with higher levels of drama. When we feel the tension, more cortisol is released, and our focus increases.

Stories also increase levels of the neurotransmitter dopamine in listeners' brains. Dopamine not only makes listeners feel good (which is one of the reasons we relax at the end of a taxing day by watching movies and television shows), but it also greatly increases memory (Shohamy and Adcock 2010). This is important because, as stated earlier, training programs can alter behavior only when the information they share is remembered.

Other chemicals are also released in a listener's bloodstream. For example, when a listener hears an emotionally laden story, their levels of the hormone oxytocin spike. This effect was most powerfully exhibited in a study performed by neuroeconomist Paul Zak (2015). Participants were shown a short film about a father dealing with his son, who had been diagnosed with cancer. Based on blood taken from the viewers after watching the film, they experienced higher levels of both cortisol and oxytocin. Zak observed that oxytocin moved listeners to action, compelling them to donate more based on the story they'd experienced.

In another study, participants who learned about the problems of starvation in Africa from factual information donated less than half the amount that was given by participants who heard a story about a struggling African child (Small, Loewenstein, and Slovic 2007).

Cortisol increases focus, dopamine increases memory, and oxytocin increases likelihood to act. These biochemical responses within a listener's brain all point to the power of story to not only engage listeners' brains but also influence behavior.

With a stronger understanding of the power of story to engage learners, help content stick with them, and move them to action, we arrive at the question, "How can I leverage story to benefit my learners?"

When crafting a new learning experience, it's a trap to start with the question, "What do we need to teach?" At first blush, this seems like a reasonable question because content often drives course creation and learning design. But what if you shifted your thinking? What if instead of starting with the content needing to be taught, you started by getting a better sense of the learners' stories? To some, such learner-centric thinking isn't new, but putting that philosophy into practice can prove challenging.

By considering learners heroes of a story, you can create more empathetic—and engaging—learning experiences that leave a longer-lasting impact on their journey of transformation.

The Seven Transformation Story Beats

The most powerful stories are stories of transformation. They describe a person (or group of people) who embark on an adventure, seeking something valuable, and, in the process, learning valuable lessons. They follow a similar three-act structure that includes a beginning, middle, and end. And they outline three ways to use stories: how you see your learners, how learners see themselves, and how decision makers see the value of your training.

After spending years analyzing dozens of story structure theories found in the works of Aristotle, Gustav Freytag, and Joseph Campbell (along with many other novelists, screenwriters, and playwrights), we at Duarte have identified the most important moments in any well-told story. We call them the Seven Transformation Story Beats. They provide the stepping-stones necessary to help story-minded people think through the critical stages of a powerful story.

We've created a worksheet based on the seven transformation story beats to help you guide your training development. It's available on the handbook website, ATDHandbook3.org.

The seven beats are:
- **Introducing the hero:** Who is the hero?
- **Looking toward the goal:** What does the hero want?
- **Sizing up the obstacle:** What is standing in the hero's way?
- **Encountering the mentor:** Who can help the hero overcome the obstacles?
- **Considering the tools:** What does the mentor offer that will help the hero?
- **Deciding to receive:** Does the hero accept or reject the tools the mentor offers?
- **Realizing the outcome:** What happens as a result?

These can be grouped in terms of the set-up beats (the beginning), the drama beats (the middle), and the resolution beat (the end):

- **The Set-Up Beats:**
  - *Introducing the hero* is when the audience meets the hero and discovers who the hero is—their personality, their strengths, their flaws, their desires, and the world in which they live.
  - *Looking toward the goal* is when the audience understands what the hero is chasing after. This is how the hero defines success. Every hero needs a goal, otherwise there is no story.
  - *Sizing up the obstacles* describes the roadblocks standing between the hero and the goal. If there are no obstructions in the hero's way, there is no drama or suspense and, thus (again), there is no story.
- **The Drama Beats:**
  - *Encountering the mentor* is the moment in the story when the hero meets a wise and experienced guide who can help them on their journey. The relationship with the mentor is valued because of what they offer.
  - *Considering the tools* is the mentor's extension of aid. The tools are the "just right" items the hero needs to continue on their journey, overcome the obstacles, and achieve their goals.
  - *Deciding to receive* is the hero's choice. Will the hero accept the tools the mentor has offered and use them? Or will they reject them? This decision point is the fulcrum of this simple story form.
- **The Resolution Beat:**
  - *Realizing the outcome* is the result of the decisions the hero makes. If the hero trusts the mentor and chooses to receive and use the tools, their outcome is positive. A positive outcome occurs when the hero uses the tools to overcome obstacles and reach the goal. If the hero said no to the mentor's offer and rejected the tools (or received them, but did not use them), then the outcome is negative.

All great stories include some form of this sequence of moments. Table 18-1 shows how the Disney version of *Pinocchio* aligns to the Transformation Story Beats.

The Learner Is the Hero on a Transformative Journey and You Are the Mentor

Now, imagine you're creating a training program to teach certain knowledge or skills to your learners. Let's look at how these Seven Transformation Story Beats can map to your learners' transformation journey.

Table 18-1. The Seven Beats in Pinocchio

Introducing the Hero	Who is the hero?	Pinocchio, the wooden puppet
Looking Toward the Goal	What does the hero want?	To become a real boy
Sizing Up the Obstacle	What is standing in the hero's way?	He doesn't know what it takes to become a real boy
Encountering the Mentor	Who can help the hero overcome the obstacles?	Jiminy Cricket arrives in the workshop
Considering the Tools	What does the mentor offer that will help the hero?	Jiminy acts as Pinocchio's conscience, guiding him toward what is right
Deciding to Receive	Does the hero accept or reject the tools the mentor offers?	At first, Pinocchio rejects Jiminy's guidance, but in the end, he listens to Jiminy and acts sacrificially
Realizing the Outcome	What happens as a result?	Pinocchio sacrifices himself to save his father, proving his character, and thus becoming a real boy

The Set-Up Beats

The introduction of the hero. The Hero is a single learner or group of learners. What are your learners like? In general, how would you describe them? What are their personalities? Strengths? Flaws? Deep desires? What keeps them up at night? What excites them? What is their world?

The articulation of the goal. Your learners want—or need—to achieve something. Otherwise, there would be no need to create a learning journey for them. What is their goal? Is it to rise in their career? Is it to influence their boss, a customer, or their team? Is it to communicate more effectively? Manage change? Work better with teams? Serve customers better? Consider this broad set of goals for your learners and try to avoid thinking of the goal as "learning something." What they will learn isn't the goal. As we'll see, it's the tool.

Understanding the obstacles. Again, if there are no obstacles standing between the hero and their goal, then there is no story. What's keeping your learners from achieving their goals? As you drill into this question, you'll uncover obstacles around lack of time and fixed mindset. That's good! That's why you're the one answering these questions on behalf of your learners.

You won't be able to help transform your learners if you don't truly understand their current state before creating or delivering a learning experience.

The Drama Beats

The encounter with the mentor. This is where you come in. Who is the mentor in a learning journey? You. You and your team are, in sum, the mentor archetype. You are the one offering the guidance and tools to help them get unstuck at the right moment so they reach their goals. You are the trusted guide. Ask yourself why learners should trust you and your team. Is it because you have experience reaching similar goals? Is it because you truly understand how to help others overcome obstacles like theirs? Is it because you have keen insights into what's to come for those learners and the new challenges they'll face as they try to apply what they've learned to their work?

You have to see yourself as valuable to your learners because they're going to rely on you to understand how best to navigate their future as they grow and transform. You'll also get a better sense of the value L&D brings to the organization and how it supports the larger corporate strategy.

Offering of the tools. This is the moment in your learners' story when you show them how to wield the tools they'll need to overcome their obstacles and reach their goals. These tools will likely come in the form of expert content, immersive training experiences, memorable job aids, or some other tool. The medium isn't what is important, however. What's important is how you articulate the tool's power so your learners choose to add it to their tool belt.

What are you offering learners that helps them overcome challenges? Is it a skill? Is it a mindset? Is it a more productive way of doing their job? Is it a more effective way of interacting with others? How will these tools help employees support the organization's overall mission? Think carefully about what these tools provide and how you would describe them in a single sentence. They become the bedrock of the learning experience. But, more than that, they're a way of realizing the value you, the mentor, are offering to the hero.

A decision to be made. This is the moment (or series of moments) when your learners either decide to accept and apply the skills, insights, processes, or mindset shifts you're offering them—or not. Crafting and designing experiences is all about making it easy for learners to say, "Yes, I believe these are the right tools for me to help me overcome my obstacles and reach my goals. Although it will cost me—leaving behind my old ways of doing things—these tools are clearly worth it."

The Resolution Beat

The final outcome. This is how it all ends. How do you envision learners flourishing after you've trained them? Learners may rave about the experience, but the final outcome is directly tied to the goals the learners set and whether or not they achieve them. Although many factors go into whether or not the learners' goals are achieved, it's important to ask whether the tools offered help the learner get closer to those goals. In a larger sense, how does the outcome positively affect the organization? The experience you design qualifies as a success if learners accept and apply the tools you've offered, and, in turn, the tools help them achieve their goals. Likewise, a learning experience could be considered a failure if the tools go unaccepted and unapplied, and, because of that, the learners miss their goals.

By thinking in terms of the Seven Transformation Story Beats, you can focus on more outcome-driven experiences with the unwavering aim of helping learners get past their roadblocks and achieve what they want (as well as your organization's needs). Beats help you create more empathetic, learner-focused training programs, rather than content-first experiences.

It's important to note that using this process doesn't just highlight how training can drive observable actions and behaviors. The beats also help point to a deeper, inner transformation they're experiencing as well.

Case in point, recall a memorable film or novel. More than likely, the protagonist experienced some sort of practical, physical journey, like getting the girl, saving the day, winning the battle, solving the crime, or stopping the bad guy. Those are all physical things—an outer journey. But if that story has endured for you in a deeper way, it's likely the main character also experienced an internal transformation—an inner journey. The shy, standoffish woman not only found romantic love, but also found a way to love herself. The headstrong detective solved the mystery, but also gained humility as he understood he didn't always see things clearly. The self-centered mogul who'd always done the right thing for the wrong reasons discovers that if they work for the common good, they gain an even greater reward.

Powerful learning experiences immerse learners in an outer journey of understanding material, gaining skills, or adopting new systems or processes. And the ones learners remember years later also lead them on an inner journey. This inner journey transforms them into more a confident, humble, brave, wise, team-oriented, vision-minded, strategic, and focused person. When creating and designing experiences with the outer journey and the inner journey in mind, learners don't just change, they transform, growing into a better worker, team member, or human being.

Table 18-2 presents an example of how we applied the Seven Transformation Story Beats when creating Captivate, Duarte's public-speaking workshop. (Note: We did a number of these to focus on a variety of learners, but this shows how we zeroed in on one type of learner.)

Try using the story beats to see the true value of the tools you're offering and how your training will help learners adopt them and, ultimately, achieve their goals. You can also use this structure to frame the broader learning trajectory as learners grow and transform.

Table 18-2. The Seven Transformation Story Beats of Captivate

Introducing the Hero	Who is the hero?	Software engineers who haven't been promoted like they'd expected
Looking Toward the Goal	What does the hero want?	Communicate in meetings with authority
Sizing Up the Obstacle	What is standing in the hero's way?	They're nervous; they either fail to speak up or overcommunicate with too many details
Encountering the Mentor	Who can help the hero overcome the obstacles?	Captivate facilitator-coaches who are trained in behavioral science
Considering the Tools	What does the mentor offer that will help the hero?	Training modules that help them see their value and how they're worth being heard
Deciding to Receive	Does the hero accept or reject the tools the mentor offers?	Reflecting on the value of workbook questions and practicing communicating confidently in coaching sessions
Realizing the Outcome	What happens as a result?	Delivering with a stronger voice and sharper sentences, indicating a deeper level of self-assurance; promotion opportunities are enhanced with improved confidence and communication skills

Motivating and Warning Stories Help Learners Commit to a Journey

As we've established, stories are an effective means of helping *you* see your learners; yet story can also help your learners see *themselves* better, which inspires them to continue along their path of transformation.

Many learners struggle to see how the training will help them get what they want. Your role is to help them decide to receive the tools. Telling the right story will help them see the value and inspire learners to apply them. Two types of stories can achieve this: a motivating story or a warning story.

- **Motivating stories are success stories.** They feature other learners (heroes) with similar goals and obstacles as your learners. They describe how those learners heard the mentor out, considered the tools, and ultimately decided to receive and use them. This resulted in a positive outcome—them reaching their goals. Learners see themselves in the story and ultimately say to themselves, "I want to be like that learner, so I'll do what that learner did."
- **Warning stories are the opposite.** They are cautionary tales designed to redirect learners from possible failure. Warning stories describe learners who heard the mentor's offer but rejected the tools. This resulted in them missing their goals. Warning stories help

learners see the peril in what could happen if they reject the tools. You want the learners to say to themselves, "I don't want to be like that learner. Because of that, I'm not going to do what they did."

In our presentation development workshop, Resonate, our facilitators often use both motivating stories and warning stories to help attendees better understand what's at stake and to inspire them to receive and apply the information. For example, they might share about a previous attendee who used the workshop content to build a presentation that not only got their ideas noticed but also got them promoted! Or how one attendee closed a $500 million deal. Or how a learner was able to motivate a team that was previously unable to get an initiative to move forward. They also share stories of clients who resisted adopting our methodology and, thus, ended up with less-than-compelling ratings on their keynote presentation, didn't close the deal, or failed to get the budget funding they needed.

These stories aren't told to brag about the value of the training. They're included to help learners see themselves in the stories of others and inspire them to emulate the positive stories and avoid the negative stories.

These motivating and warning stories can be told at any point during training. When told at the beginning they can give learners a lens through which to view the value of the tools. Stories can also be told at key points during the training in which you, as the facilitator or designer, anticipate resistance. They can help get participants over the hump of pushback and see how valuable these tools are. Tell stories at the end so learners leave feeling energized, inspired, and excited to apply what they've learned. We try to end all our workshops with a motivating story of how previous participants went on to great success so participants can see how they too can experience that same level of transformation.

Ask yourself these questions:
- When would stories help learners better understand their own experiences?
- When are motivating stories an appropriate means of helping them transform?
- When would a warning story be more apropos?

Carefully consider the moment to tell a story, and which one to tell.

Tell Stories to Move Decision Makers

Leverage stories as a means of helping decision makers understand the value of training so they continue to fund and offer training, increase the offerings, or trust you with the resources necessary to create more training content.

Your decision makers could be external clients who purchase training from you or your organization, or they could be internal stakeholders who look to you for the development of themselves and their team. Every decision maker wants to know about the return on investment in training so they can get a sense of the value the organization will receive in return. Story helps the ROI come to life.

Yes, it's helpful for decision makers to see the cold hard facts of the ROI—how it influences productivity, the bottom line, employee satisfaction, and so forth. But when you communicate the data points, along with a story describing real people who experience real transformations that result in achieving actual goals, the value of training sticks in their mind.

At Duarte, we organize our outcome stories so that it's as easy as possible for anyone to find stories that their customers will find relatable. If a buyer has learners (heroes) who struggle because their slides are too busy, we have stories about learners who overcame that challenge after taking our VisualStory workshop. They learned how to simplify their slide contents and their proposal got approved. When talking to a customer whose learners need help calming their nerves when presenting, we have stories of Captivate attendees who found the confidence they needed to deliver well, resulting in them being noticed and advancing their career.

Final Thoughts

Remember, humans are storytelling animals who are moved by stories. And decision makers are humans, which means they are just as likely to be moved to action by stories (especially stories accompanied by facts and data), as the rest of us.

Ask yourself these questions:

- How can you begin to leverage stories to communicate with your decision makers?
- What's your file of stories like?
- Do you have stories about learners who achieved the goals they needed?
- Are those stories organized in such a way that you can draw on them as each situation demands?

We've discovered that the more we center our training on a story mindset, the more we create empathetic, powerful, transformative programs. We hope the same for you. Challenge yourself to approach training with you as the mentor, who provides the right skills and information (tools) for your learners (the heroes).

Take every opportunity to tell stories about other learners who either achieved their goals or missed them because of accepting or rejecting your tools.

Consider also how you can tell stories to help decision makers see the training's true ROI and how you don't just teach, you transform.

By adopting a story mindset while building and delivering training, you'll begin to see your learners differently and see yourself differently, too. You'll identify as the wise, experienced mentor with a tremendous amount of knowledge to offer learners who cross your path.

How do you become that? By being a lifelong learner and seeker of wisdom yourself. Seeing yourself this way will increase your confidence as you understand the value of what you have to offer each learner. The very reason you went into this profession in the first place was to change lives and improve human flourishing. In the end, as you take on a story-first mindset, not only will your learners transform, but you and your culture will transform too.

About the Authors

Nancy Duarte is CEO of Duarte and the author of six bestselling books. Known as the Storyteller of the Valley, Nancy has worked with the highest-performing brands and executives in the world. She is a communication expert who has been featured in *Fortune, Time Magazine, Forbes, Fast Company, Wired, Wall Street Journal, New York Times, Cosmopolitan*, and the *LA Times*, as well as on CNN. As a persuasion expert, Nancy cracked the code for effectively incorporating story patterns into business communications. She has two grandsons and a grand-dogger.

Jeff Davenport is a content developer, executive speaker coach, and workshop designer at Duarte. He's coached dozens of Fortune 500 executives to help them leverage the power of story in their keynotes and everyday communications, while also authoring Duarte's Story Fundamentals Workshop and co-authoring the Captivate Public Speaking Workshop. An experienced public speaker and produced screenwriter, Jeff loves helping communicators everywhere experience the power of story. He lives in Colorado with his wife, Kristin, and their two daughters.

References

Boris, V. 2017. "What Makes Storytelling So Effective for Learning?" Harvard Business Publishing, December 20. harvardbusiness.org/what-makes-storytelling-so-effective-for-learning.

Gottschall, J. 2012. *The Storytelling Animal: How Stories Make Us Human*. New York: Houghton Mifflin Harcourt.

Heath, C., and D. Heath. 2007. *Made to Stick: Why Some Ideas Survive and Others Die*. New York: Random House.

Heider, F., and M. Simmel. 1944. "An Experimental Study of Apparent Behavior." *The American Journal of Psychology* 57(2): 243–259.

Kay, D. 2016. "Learning Theories 101: Application to Everyday Teaching and Scholarship." *Advances in Physiology Education* 40(1): 17–25.

Kenjirou. 2010. "Heider and Simmel (1944) animation." YouTube. July 16, 2010. youtube.com/watch?v=VTNmLt7QX8E.

Schomer, A. 2021. "US Adults Will Consume Almost as Much Media as Last Year, But TV Viewing Will Decline." *Business Insider*, June 7. businessinsider.com/us-adults-will-consume-almost-as-much-media-in-2021-2021-6.

Shohamy, D., and R.A. Adcock. 2010. "Dopamine and Adaptive Memory." *Trends in Cognitive Sciences* 14(10): 464–472. doi.org/10.1016/j.tics.2010.08.002.

Small, D.A., G. Loewenstein, and P. Slovic. 2007. "Sympathy and Callousness: The Impact of Deliberative Thought on Donations to Identifiable and Statistical Victims." *Organizational Behavior and Human Decision Processes* 102(2): 143–153.

Smith, J.A. 2016. "The Science of Story." *Berkeley News*, August 25. news.berkeley.edu/berkeley_blog/the-science-of-the-story.

Watson, A. 2020. "Media Use—Statistics & Facts." Statista, March 23. statista.com/topics/1536/media-use.

Zak, P.J. 2015. "Why Inspiring Stories Make Us React: The Neuroscience of Narrative." *Cerebrum: The Dana Forum on Brain Science* (2015): 1–13. ncbi.nlm.nih.gov/pmc/articles/PMC4445577.

Recommended Resources

Davenport, J. n.d. "These Screenwriting Principles Will Make Your Business Story More Engaging." Duarte. duarte.com/presentation-skills-resources/these-screenwriting-principles-will-make-your-business-story-more-engaging.

Davenport, J. n.d. "3 Situations That Demand a Story." Duarte. duarte.com/presentation-skills-resources/3-situations-that-demand-a-story.

Duarte, N. 2010. *Resonate: Present Visual Stories that Transform Audiences*. Hoboken, NJ: John Wiley and Sons.

Duarte, N. 2012. *HBR Guide to Persuasive Presentations*. Cambridge, MA: Harvard Business Review Press.

Duarte, N., and P. Sanchez. 2016. *Illuminate: Ignite Change Through Speeches, Stories, Ceremonies, and Symbols*. New York: Portfolio/Penguin.

CHAPTER 19

Implementing the Four Levels of Evaluation

Jim Kirkpatrick and Wendy Kayser Kirkpatrick

The purpose of all training is to enhance on-the-job performance through consistent application and to positively affect organizational results. The Kirkpatrick Model, often referred to as the Four Levels of Training Evaluation, is one of the primary methods used to ensure that training is being applied and contributing to results.

> **IN THIS CHAPTER:**
> - Define the four levels of evaluation
> - Describe why the four levels are used in reverse during the instructional design process
> - Explain why focusing on Level 3 creates the most training value

How do you best apply the Kirkpatrick Model? The most effective way is to consider all four levels during the training design and development process. Waiting until after the program ends to determine how learning will be applied on the job and how impact on the business will be measured generally means that these activities will not occur reliably.

In this chapter, you will learn about the four levels of evaluation and how they have been enhanced with the New World Kirkpatrick Model. Guidelines for their effective application are described using the Kirkpatrick Foundational Principles.

The Kirkpatrick Model

Donald Kirkpatrick (1924–2014) is credited with creating the Kirkpatrick Model in the mid-1950s while writing his PhD dissertation. His goal was to effectively measure the impact of the management development programs he was teaching at the University of Wisconsin Management Institute. His work became known and later published by a trade journal in the late 1950s, and worldwide use grew organically over the following six decades. Today, the Four Levels of Evaluation is the most highly recognized, used, and regarded method of evaluating the effectiveness of training programs (Figure 19-1).

Figure 19-1. The Four Levels of Evaluation

Level 4: Results	The degree to which targeted outcomes occur as a result of the training, support, and accountability package
Level 3: Behavior	The degree to which participants apply what they learned during training when they are back on the job
Level 2: Learning	The degree to which participants acquire the intended knowledge, skills, attitude, confidence, and commitment based on their participation in the training
Level 1: Reaction	The degree to which participants find the training favorable, engaging, and relevant to their jobs

In 2010, Kirkpatrick's son, Jim, and his business partner, Wendy, enhanced the Kirkpatrick Model to accomplish the following goals:
- Incorporate the forgotten or overlooked teachings of Don Kirkpatrick.
- Correct common misinterpretations and misuse of the model.
- Illustrate how the model applies to modern workplace learning and performance.

The resulting New World Kirkpatrick Model honors and maintains the time-tested four levels of evaluation and adds new elements to help people to operationalize them effectively (Figure 19-2).

Figure 19-2. The New World Kirkpatrick Model

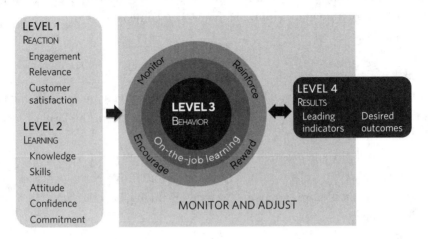

The New World Kirkpatrick Model—Levels 1 and 2

The first two levels of the New World Kirkpatrick Model are also known as *effective training*. These levels measure the quality of the training and the degree to which it resulted in knowledge and skills that can be applied on the job. The training function uses Levels 1 and 2 to internally measure the quality of the programs they design and deliver.

Level 1: Reaction

Level 1 is the degree to which participants find the training favorable, engaging, and relevant to their jobs.

In a 2016 study conducted by ATD, 88 percent of organizations evaluated Level 1 Reaction for their training. The current investment in gathering this type of data is far greater than the importance this level dictates, and occurs at the cost of measuring Levels 3 and 4, which would yield data more meaningful to the business (those levels were measured only by 60 percent and 35 percent of organizations, respectively). Sadly, these numbers have improved only a couple of percentage points during the preceding six years.

The New World Kirkpatrick Level 1 Reaction has three dimensions: customer satisfaction, engagement, and relevance.

Customer Satisfaction

Customer satisfaction refers to the degree to which participants find the training favorable. For example, did they find it enjoyable and free of distractions from the learning itself? Was it taught in a way that is comfortable and helpful for them? This dimension is the least important and tends to be overevaluated.

Engagement

Engagement refers to the degree to which participants are actively involved in and contributing to the learning experience. Engagement levels directly relate to the level of learning that is attained.

Personal responsibility and program interest are both factors in the measurement of engagement. *Personal responsibility* relates to how present and attentive participants are during the training. *Program interest* is more commonly the focus, including how the facilitator involved and captivated the audience.

Relevance

Relevance is the degree to which training participants will have the opportunity to use or apply what they have learned on the job. This is important to the ultimate training value because even the best training is a waste of resources if the participants have no application for the content in their everyday work.

Tips for Implementing Level 1

L&D professionals should remember that:
- Level 1 evaluation efforts should be matched to the degree of the course or program's importance to the organization.
- Level 1 is the least important evaluation measure to stakeholders, so keep it as brief and efficient as possible.
- A variety of methods is useful when measuring Level 1, including formative (that is, during the class) observation. Save surveys and interview questions for the higher, more important levels.

Level 2: Learning

The New World Kirkpatrick Level 2 Learning is the degree to which participants acquire the intended knowledge, skills, attitudes, confidence, and commitment based on their participation in the training program.

Knowledge and Skill

Knowledge is the degree to which participants know certain information, as characterized by the statement, "I know it." *Skill* is the degree to which they know how to do something or perform a certain task, as illustrated by the statement, "I can do it right now."

Many organizations make the costly mistake of inaccurately diagnosing poor performance as a lack of knowledge or skill. Underachievers are often returned to training with the belief that they do not know what to do, when the more common cause of substandard performance is a lack of motivation or other environmental factors.

Attitude

Attitude is defined as the degree to which training participants believe that it will be worthwhile to implement what is learned during the training program on the job. It is characterized by the statement, "I believe this will be worthwhile to do on the job."

Incorporating discussion about what is expected on the job and the why allows learners to develop the right beliefs about what you are asking of them.

Confidence

Confidence is defined as the degree to which training participants think they will be able to do what they learned during the training program once they're back on the job. It is characterized by the statement, "I think I can do it on the job."

Addressing confidence during training brings learners closer to the desired on-the-job performance. It can proactively surface potential application barriers so they can be resolved.

Commitment

Commitment is defined as the degree to which learners intend to apply the knowledge and skills learned to their jobs. It is characterized by the statement, "I intend to do it on the job." Commitment relates to learner motivation by acknowledging that even if the knowledge and skills are mastered, participants must still put forth daily effort to use the information or perform the skills.

Tips for Implementing Level 2

L&D professionals should remember:
- Measure Level 2 during formal training using quizzes, activities, demonstrations, and discussions.

- Use pretests and post-tests only when the program will be modified to fit the pretest results, or when stakeholders specifically request this information.
- Keep Level 2 measurement focused so resources stay in line with the relatively low importance of Level 2 when compared with Levels 3 and 4.

The New World Kirkpatrick Model: Levels 3 and 4

Levels 3 and 4, referred to as *training effectiveness*, encompass:
- On-the-job performance and subsequent business results that occur, in part, due to training and reinforcement
- Demonstration of the value that the training program has contributed to the organization

Level 3: Behavior

Level 3 is the degree to which participants apply what they learned during the training program when they are back on the job. The New World Level 3 Behavior consists of critical behaviors, required drivers, and on-the-job learning.

Critical Behaviors

Critical behaviors are the few, specific actions that, if performed consistently on the job, will have the biggest impact on the desired results. While there are thousands of behaviors an employee might perform on the job, critical behaviors are those that have been identified as the most important to achieving organizational success.

Required Drivers

Required drivers are processes and systems that reinforce, monitor, encourage, and reward the performance of critical behaviors on the job (Figure 19-3).

Organizations that use accountability and support systems to reinforce the knowledge and skills learned during training can expect as much as 85 percent application on the job. Conversely, companies that rely primarily on training events alone to create good job performance achieve around a 15 percent success rate (Brinkerhoff 2006).

Required drivers are the key to accomplishing the desired on-the-job application of what is learned during training. They also decrease the likelihood of people falling through the cracks or deliberately crawling through the cracks if they are not interested in performing the required behaviors.

Active execution and monitoring of required drivers is perhaps the biggest indicator of program success for any initiative.

Figure 19-3. Required Drivers

Support	
Reinforce • Follow-up modules • Work review checklist • On-the-job training (OJT) • Self-directed learning • Refreshers • Job aids • Reminders	Encourage • Coaching • Mentoring Reward • Recognition • Bonuses • Pay for performance
Accountability	
Monitor • Action learning • Interviews • Observation • Self-monitoring • Key performance indicators (KPIs)	• Action plan monitoring • Dashboard • Work review • Survey • Touch bases and meetings

On-the-Job Learning

On-the-job learning recognizes two facts of the modern workplace:
- Most learning takes place on the job. A 2017 study showed that 56 percent of learning came from job-related experiences, 25 percent came from social sources such as interactions with peers and managers, and 19 percent came from formal training activities (Training Industry 2018).
- Personal responsibility and motivation are key partners to external support and reinforcement efforts for optimal performance.

Creating a culture and expectation that individuals are responsible for maintaining the knowledge and skills to enhance their own performance will encourage individuals to be accountable and feel empowered. On-the-job learning provides an opportunity for employees and their employers to share the responsibility for good performance.

Tips for Implementing Level 3

L&D professionals should:
- Have a pretraining conversation with the managers of the people who will attend training. Jointly determine the critical behaviors that need to occur on the job for them to view the training as time well spent.
- Design learning objectives around critical behaviors.
- Create job aids that help participants perform these critical behaviors on the job. Introduce them during training and use them during hands-on activities.

- Design post-program follow-up when you create the training materials, which will ensure that this task gets accomplished. Take advantage of technology to schedule and automatically send reminders, refreshers, and encouraging messages.
- Make a note in your calendar (or set up automatic reminders) to check in with some or all of the training participants after they have had a reasonable amount of time to try their new behaviors on the job. Ask how it is going and if they need any additional resources or support to be successful.
- Make it part of your training design and development process to create the post-program implementation and support plan. Building this structure increases the likelihood that the resources that go into training will produce a measurable increase in performance.

Level 4: Results

Level 4 holds the distinction of being the most misunderstood of the four evaluation levels. It is the degree to which targeted outcomes occur as a result of the training, support, and accountability package.

A common misapplication occurs when professionals or functional departments define results in terms of their small, individual area of the organization instead of globally for the entire company. This creates silos and fiefdoms that are counterproductive to organizational effectiveness because the resulting misalignment causes layers of dysfunction and waste.

Clarity regarding the true Level 4 result is critical—it is some combination of the organization's purpose or mission and the financial reality of sustained existence. In a for-profit company, this means profitably delivering the product or service to the marketplace. In a humanitarian, government, or military organization that is not primarily focused on a financial outcome, it means accomplishing the mission within the available funding, allocations, or donations.

Every organization has just one Level 4 Result. A good test of whether the correct result has been identified is a positive answer to the question, "Is this what the organization exists to do, deliver, or contribute?" While this definition is straightforward, frustration with the seeming inability to relate a single training program to a high-level organizational mission is common. Business results are broad and long term. They are created through the culmination of countless efforts of people and departments, as well as environmental factors, and can take months or years to manifest.

Leading Indicators

Leading indicators help bridge the gap between individual initiatives and efforts and organizational results. They are defined as short-term observations and measurements suggesting that critical behaviors are on track to create a positive impact on the desired results. Organizations have several leading indicators that encompass departmental and individual goals, each contributing to the accomplishment of the highest-level results.

Common leading indicators include:
- Customer satisfaction
- Employee engagement
- Sales volume
- Cost containment
- Quality
- Market share

While leading indicators are important measurements, they must be balanced with a focus on the highest-level result. For example, a company with excellent customer satisfaction scores could go out of business if it did not maintain profitability, comply with laws and regulations, and keep its employees reasonably happy. Note that customer satisfaction is an example of a goal that does not provide an affirmative answer to the question, "Is this what the organization exists to contribute?" No organization exists simply to deliver customer service alone.

Tips for Implementing Level 4

L&D professionals should remember:
- At the beginning of any initiative or training program, start by considering the highest-level result your organization is charged with accomplishing. Use this as your target for each effort in the initiative. If you cannot describe how the intended training would in some way positively affect your overall result or mission, you are not on the right track.
- Every major training initiative should be tied to the highest goals and key directives of the organization. Here are a few ways to discover them:
  ○ Read the about us section of the organization's website.
  ○ Look at mission and vision statements, as well as what types of messages are posted on the walls of the office.
  ○ Ask your boss about the highest priorities or directives for each department that quarter or year.
  ○ If appropriate, request to attend strategy and planning meetings, even if just as an observer. Or ask for a summary of what was discussed.
- Once you are clear on the key initiatives and goals, look at the training programs that are consuming the most time, money, and resources. Is there a direct link between them? If not, re-evaluate whether training resources are being properly allocated.

The Kirkpatrick Foundational Principles

The Kirkpatrick Foundational Principles are the key beliefs underpinning Kirkpatrick evaluation:
- The end is the beginning.
- Return on expectations (ROE) is the ultimate indicator of value.
- Business partnership is necessary to bring about positive ROE.
- Value must be created before it can be demonstrated.
- A compelling chain of evidence demonstrates your bottom-line value.

Principle 1: The End Is the Beginning

Effective training and development begins before the program even starts:

> Trainers must begin with desired results (Level 4) and then determine what behavior (Level 3) is needed to accomplish them. Then trainers must determine the attitudes, knowledge, and skills (Level 2) that are necessary to bring about the desired behavior(s). The final challenge is to present the training program in a way that enables the participants not only to learn what they need to know but also to react favorably to the program (Level 1). (Kirkpatrick and Kirkpatrick 1993)

It is important that the results are at the organizational level and defined in measurable terms so that all involved can see the initiative's ultimate destination. Clearly defined results will increase the likelihood that resources will be used most effectively and efficiently to accomplish the mission.

Attempting to apply the four levels after an initiative has been developed and delivered makes it difficult, if not impossible, to create significant training value. All four levels must be considered at every step in the program's design, execution, and measurement.

Principle 2: ROE Is the Ultimate Indicator of Value

Return on expectations is what a successful training initiative delivers to key business stakeholders demonstrating the degree to which their expectations have been satisfied. When executives ask for new training, many learning professionals retreat to their departments and begin designing and developing suitable programs. While a cursory needs assessment may be conducted, it is rarely taken to the extent to which expectations of the training's contribution to Level 4 Results are completely clear.

Stakeholder expectations define the value that training professionals are responsible for delivering. Learning professionals must ask questions to clarify and refine stakeholder expectations on all four Kirkpatrick levels, starting with the organizational Level 4 Results and the leading indicators for the requested program. Determining the leading indicators upon which the success of an initiative will be measured is a negotiation process in which the training professional ensures that the expectations are satisfying to the stakeholder and realistic to achieve with the resources available.

Once stakeholder expectations are clear, learning professionals then need to convert them into observable, measurable leading indicators by asking the question, "What will success look like to you?" It may take a series of questions to arrive at the final indicators of program success.

Agreement surrounding leading indicators at the beginning of a project eliminates the need to later attempt to prove the value of the initiative. It is understood from the beginning that if the leading indicator targets are met, the initiative will be viewed as a success.

Principle 3: Business Partnership Is Necessary to Bring About Positive ROE

Research has validated that training events in and of themselves typically produce about 15 percent on-the-job application. To increase application and therefore program results, additional actions must be taken before and after formal training.

Historically, the role of learning professionals has been to accomplish Levels 1 and 2, or just to complete the training event alone. Not surprisingly, this is where they spend most of their time. Producing ROE, however, requires a strong Level 3 execution plan. Therefore, it is critical not only to call upon business partners to help identify what success will look like, but also to design a cooperative effort throughout the learning and performance processes to maximize results.

Before the training program begins, learning professionals need to partner with supervisors and managers to prepare participants for training. Even more critical is the role of the supervisor or manager after the training ends. They are the key people who reinforce newly learned knowledge and skills through support and accountability. The degree to which this reinforcement and coaching occurs directly correlates to improved performance and positive outcomes.

Principle 4: Value Must Be Created Before It Can Be Demonstrated

Up to 90 percent of training resources are spent on the design, development, and delivery of training events that yield the previously mentioned 15 percent on-the-job application. Reinforcement that occurs after the training event produces the highest level of learning effectiveness, followed by activities that occur before the learning event, yet each typically garners only 5 percent of the training time and budget.

Many training professionals put most of their resources into the part of the training process that produces the lowest level of business or organizational results. They spend relatively little time on the pretraining and follow-up activities that translate into the positive behavior change and subsequent results (Levels 3 and 4) that organizations seek.

Formal training is the foundation of performance and results. To create ultimate value and ROE, however, practitioners must focus on Level 3 activities. To create maximum value within their organizations, learning professionals must redefine their roles and extend their expertise, involvement, and influence into Levels 3 and 4.

Principle 5: A Compelling Chain of Evidence Demonstrates Your Bottom-Line Value

The training industry is on trial, accused by business leaders of consuming resources that exceed the value delivered to the organization. A chain of evidence includes data, information, and testimonies at each of the four levels that, when presented in sequence, act to demonstrate the value obtained from a business partnership initiative (Figure 19-4).

Figure 19-4. Chain of Evidence

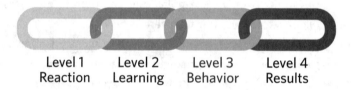

| Level 1 | Level 2 | Level 3 | Level 4 |
| Reaction | Learning | Behavior | Results |

Following the Kirkpatrick Foundational Principles and using the Kirkpatrick Model will create a chain of evidence that demonstrates the organizational value of the entire business partnership effort. It consists of quantitative and qualitative data that sequentially connects the four levels and shows the ultimate contribution of learning and reinforcement to the organization.

When L&D professionals work in concert with their key business partners, this chain of evidence supports the partnership effort and demonstrates the organizational value of working as a team to accomplish the overall mission. The chain of evidence serves to unify the learning and business functions, not to isolate training or set it apart. This unity is critical for Level 3 execution, which is where organizational value is produced.

When presenting a chain of evidence, keep in mind what is most important to the stakeholder audience. Data at Levels 3 and 4 is of most interest. Data related to Levels 1 and 2 should be limited unless a detailed report is requested specifically. Gather data and information to form your chain of evidence using the Kirkpatrick Blended Evaluation Plan tool found on the handbook website at at ATDHandbook3.org.

Final Thoughts

The Kirkpatrick Model, when implemented correctly, is an effective and time-tested way to support learning transfer and evaluate training impact on the business. Consider each of the four levels throughout the training design and development process. Determine what information is required to show that the training program improved job performance and key organizational results.

For mission-critical initiatives, create a strong Level 3 implementation plan and a Level 4 tracking and measurement strategy. Use evaluation time, money, and resources sparingly on Levels 1 and 2 for all programs.

Following these guidelines will maximize your training results and create the most organizational impact with the resources invested.

A MESSAGE FROM DON DURING HIS 90TH YEAR
Written in 2013

When I used what has become the four levels in my PhD dissertation in the 1950s, I honestly had no idea where it would all go. I am so pleased that they have come far since then. I am officially retired, but that doesn't mean that I have lost interest in where the Kirkpatrick Model is headed.

Over the past several years, I have proudly watched Jim, my son, and Wendy, his business partner, along with global ambassadors of the New World Kirkpatrick Model, take the four levels to new heights. New applications of the model have occurred in enterprise evaluation, key policies and procedures, and individual goal achievement. Powerful enhancements have been made to each of the levels.

Some have asked me, "Don, are you pleased about the new directions Jim and Wendy are taking the four levels?"

Well, let me save you having to ask. The answer is a resounding yes. Any way the four levels can be applied that will help more people in more powerful ways, I am all for it!

Learn, enjoy, and apply!
Don Kirkpatrick

About the Authors

Jim Kirkpatrick, PhD, is the senior consultant for Kirkpatrick Partners. He is a thought leader in training evaluation and the creator of the New World Kirkpatrick Model. Jim is passionate about assisting learning professionals in redefining themselves as strategic business partners to remain a viable force in the workplace. He co-authored three books with his late father, Don Kirkpatrick, and four books with Wendy Kayser Kirkpatrick, including *Kirkpatrick's Four Levels of Training Evaluation*. Jim can be reached at information@kirkpatrickpartners.com.

Wendy Kayser Kirkpatrick is the president and founder of Kirkpatrick Partners. She draws on experience in training, retailing, and marketing to make her programs relevant and impactful with measurable results. Wendy co-authored four books with Jim Kirkpatrick, including *Kirkpatrick's Four Levels of Training Evaluation*. She can be reached at information@kirkpatrickpartners.com.

References

ASTD (American Society for Training and Development). 2009. *The Value of Evaluation: Making Training Evaluations More Effective.* Alexandria, VA: ASTD Press.

ATD (Association for Talent Development). 2016. *Evaluating Learning: Getting to Measurements That Matter.* Alexandria, VA: ATD Press.

Brinkerhoff, R.O. 2006. *Telling Training's Story: Evaluation Made Simple, Credible, and Effective.* San Francisco, CA: Berrett-Koehler Publishers.

Kirkpatrick, D.L. 2010. *Evaluating Human Relations Programs for Industrial Foremen and Supervisors.* St. Louis, MO: Kirkpatrick Publishing.

Kirkpatrick, D.L., and J.D. Kirkpatrick. 1993. *Evaluating Training Programs: The Four Levels,* 1st ed. San Francisco: Berrett-Koehler Publishers.

Kirkpatrick, D.L., and J.D. Kirkpatrick. 2005. *Transferring Learning to Behavior.* San Francisco: Berrett-Koehler Publishers.

Kirkpatrick, J.D., and W.K. Kirkpatrick. 2016. *Kirkpatrick's Four Levels of Training Evaluation.* Alexandria, VA: ATD Press.

Training Industry. 2018. "Deconstructing 70-20-10." Training Industry, June. trainingindustry.com/Deconstructing_70-20-10.

Recommended Resources

Kirkpatrick, J.D., and W.K. Kirkpatrick. 2009. *Kirkpatrick Then and Now.* St. Louis, MO: Kirkpatrick Publishing.

Kirkpatrick, J.D., and W.K. Kirkpatrick. 2010. *Training on Trial.* New York: AMACOM.

Kirkpatrick, J.D., and W.K. Kirkpatrick. 2013. *Bringing Business Partnership to Life: The Brunei Window Washer.* Newnan, GA: Kirkpatrick Publishing.

Kirkpatrick, J.D., and W.K. Kirkpatrick. 2021. "Stumped on How to Measure DEI Training?" *TD,* October.

CHAPTER 20

Impact and ROI: Results Executives Love

Jack J. Phillips and Patricia Pulliam Phillips

Many TD professionals rarely think about the results their leaders want from the talent development department—but they should. Leaders depend on financial measures to define their organizations' success. TD professionals should develop the business acumen to understand what their leaders need and how to measure it.

IN THIS CHAPTER

- ♦ Define ROI
- ♦ Describe the importance of impact and ROI
- ♦ Ensure programs deliver positive impact and ROI

What Is ROI?

Organization leaders rely on financial measures. Financial measures describe how an organization is faring with a particular investment (Phillips and Phillips 2019). Each metric has its own use, and not all are suitable for evaluating training and development programs. Three financial measures are useful for any type of investment, allowing decision makers to compare results across a wide spectrum of programs and projects, including training and talent development. The measures are:

- Benefit-cost ratio (BCR)
- Return on investment (ROI)
- Payback period (PP)

Benefit-Cost Ratio (BCR)

The BCR is the output of cost-benefit analysis, an economic theory grounded in welfare economics and public finance. Economists in the United States adopted it in the early 1900s to justify projects initiated under the River and Harbor Act of 1902 and the Flood Control Act of 1936 (Prest and Turvey 1965). Today, BCR use describes the value of many types of projects. The BCR formula is:

$$\text{Benefit-Cost Ratio} = \frac{\text{Program Benefits}}{\text{Program Costs}}$$

Return on Investment (ROI)

The concept of ROI has been used in business for centuries to measure the success of investment opportunities (Sibbett 1997). While its initial use was in evaluating capital investments, it has become the leading indicator describing the value of other types of programs and projects. This growth in use, particularly in talent development and human resources, stems from the 1973 work of Jack J. Phillips, who began using it to demonstrate value for a cooperative education program. His use of ROI grew and was first formally recorded in *Handbook of Training Evaluation and Measurement Methods*, the first book on training evaluation published in the US (Phillips 1983). In the book, Phillips introduces an evaluation framework. More important, he provides a process and standards operationalizing the framework, something that had not been done with earlier training evaluation concepts. Over the years, his application of ROI has been adopted as a standard practice in talent development and HR evaluation, as well as marketing, project management, supply chain management, chaplaincy, and others. The ROI formula is:

$$\text{Return on Investment} = \frac{\text{Program Benefits} - \text{Program Costs}}{\text{Program Costs}} \times 100$$

> **SIMILAR, YET DIFFERENT**
>
> ROI and BCR provide similar measures of the financial benefit of investing in programs. BCR is typically used in public sector organizations, whereas ROI is used in business and industry. However, they're both applicable in all settings. BCR compares gross benefits to costs, while ROI presents the net benefits compared to costs reported as a percentage. A BCR of 2:1 means for every $1 invested, there is a gross benefit of $2. This translates into an ROI of 100 percent, which means for every $1 invested, $1 is returned after the costs are recovered (a net benefit of $1). Periodically, someone will calculate a BCR of 3:1, for example, and then calculate the ROI as 3 x 100 = 300%. This is incorrect. ROI is the net benefits divided by the costs. Thus, a 3:1 BCR is actually equal to a 200% ROI.

Payback Period (PP)

The third measure, payback period (PP), determines the point in time when program owners can expect to recover their investments. Those programs with a shorter PP are usually the more desirable ones. This measure does not consider the time value of money, nor does it consider future benefits. It simply indicates the break-even point, or a BCR of 1:1, which translates to an ROI of 0 percent. PP is used occasionally when evaluating training and talent development programs, particularly when forecasting the payoff prior to investing in a program. The formula for PP is:

$$\text{Payback Period} = \frac{\text{Program Costs}}{\text{Program Benefits}}$$

> **WHAT IS A GOOD ROI?**
>
> An ROI is only as good as that to which it is compared. Use the following guidelines to help establish your target ROI:
> - Set the ROI at the same level as other investments (for example, 18 percent).
> - Set the ROI slightly higher than the level of other investments (for example, 25 percent).
> - Set the ROI at break-even, 0 percent.
> - Set the ROI based on client expectations.

Why Impact and ROI Are Important

There are four basic reasons why impact and ROI data are important to an organization:
- ROI requires impact data.
- Impact and ROI are fundamental to resource management.
- ROI data answer a logical question: Was it worth it?
- Executives love impact and ROI results.

ROI Requires Impact Data

Whether you're calculating a program's BCR, ROI, or PP, the numerator of the formula requires the monetary value of the impact a program has on key business measures. Measures may be objectively based, such as output, quality, cost, and time, or they may represent more subjective measures such as customer satisfaction, image, and work climate. Attributing a program to improvement in business measures requires accounting for other factors that may have contributed to the improvement. Isolating the effects of the program is a requirement when describing the program's impact, and is a key step in the ROI Methodology. Omitting this step results in a baseless claim of business results, not to mention the overstatement of a program's financial value. Once you have credible proof that the improvement is due to the program, you can annualized it and convert the improvement to money. The annual monetary benefit is input into the numerator of the ROI formula.

For example, assume an organization suffers from too many employee complaints that meet a specific severity level. Experts in the organization indicate that each complaint of this type costs $6,500. Six months after a leadership program, the number of complaints decreased on average by 10 per month. Analysis to isolate the effects of the program found that it could account for seven fewer complaints per month (meaning that the other three fewer complaints were attributed to something else)—this is the impact of the program. Therefore, the annual change in performance was 84 per year, and the annual monetary benefit was $546,000. Assuming the fully loaded cost of the program was $425,000, the ROI was 28 percent.

Let's look closer at the steps to ROI using this example. (Note that Step 3 accounts only for the improvement due to the program, which was an average of seven fewer complaints per month.) Recall that the cost of the program was $425,000.

- Unit of measure: 1 complaint
- Value of a complaint: $6,500
- Change in performance due to the leadership program: 7 per month
- Annual change in performance: 7 x 12 = 84
- Annual monetary benefit: 84 x $6,500 = $546,000

$$\text{ROI} = \frac{\text{Program Benefits} - \text{Program Costs}}{\$425,000} \times 100 = 28\%$$

Impact and ROI Are Fundamental to Resource Management

When organization leaders fail to use financial resources optimally, it usually means one of two things:

- They are withholding opportunity.
- They are overextending their resources and using more than they have, which is not sustainable.

In either case, they are inefficient in their use of resources. This premise is based on an economic theory known as Pareto Optimality or Pareto Efficiency (Nas 2016). When optimal use of resources is occurring, leaders must take funding away from one program before they can increase funding for another. All too often opinion, intuition, and gut feel influence these funding decisions. Impact data and ROI are fundamental to resource management decisions because they reduce subjectivity and increase objectivity, allowing for better decisions while minimizing the risk of making the wrong one.

ROI Data Answers a Logical Question: Was It Worth It?

Almost any purchase requires weighing the benefits against the costs to answer the question, "Was it worth it?" The answer influences decisions about the value of the purchase and whether to purchase again or recommend to others. While impact data alone can answer this question to some extent, ROI answers it more clearly. ROI requires conversion of impact measures to money, normalizing them to the same unit of measure as the program costs. Doing so allows decision makers to compare benefits with costs mathematically. An even more compelling reason for using ROI is because it positions talent development as an investment, rather than a cost that can easily be cut. Training and talent development investments then rise to the same level of importance as marketing, supply chain, operations, and IT.

Executives Love Impact and ROI Results

Executives love to see the direct impact and ultimately the ROI of major investments. This includes expensive training and talent development programs that align with strategy and operational goals and involve a large number of people. In 2009, ROI Institute partnered with ATD to determine what organizations' CEOs thought about the learning investment. Results indicated a gap between the types of measures executives were receiving and the kinds of measures they believed would help them better understand talent development's value. Of least importance was data describing input, efficiency, and participant reaction to programs, yet that was the data most received. Impact (improvement directly attributable to training programs) and ROI were ranked the first and second most important data sets to CEOs, yet only 8 percent reported receiving impact data and only 4 percent reported receiving ROI (Phillips and Phillips 2009).

The call to talent development leaders to demonstrate real business value from these investments has grown even louder over the years, and talent development leaders are answering. In

2015, *Chief Learning Officer's Business Intelligence Board Measurement and Metrics Study* reported that 71.2 percent of 335 chief learning officers were either using or planning to use ROI as a measure of learning performance. In 2017, *Training Magazine's Top 10 Hall of Fame* report acknowledged that "ultimately, the success of any program is based on whether it improves business results." A 2019 survey of *Training Magazine's* Top 100 indicated that at least 92 percent of those responding used ROI as a measure of training's value to the organization (Freifeld 2021).

Progress with ROI is also evident in ROI Institute's 2019 benchmarking study. When comparing the suggested minimum percentage of programs that should be evaluated to impact and ROI, respondents reported that they evaluate 37 percent of their programs to the impact level compared with ROI Institute's minimum standard 10 percent. Respondents also indicated they evaluate 18 percent of their programs to ROI compared with the minimum standard of 5 percent. On the other hand, use of the lower levels of evaluation (reaction and learning) was lower than the recommended minimum (Table 20-1).

Table 20-1. Percentage of Use of Levels of Evaluation

Level	Recommended Percentage*	Current Percentage**
Input	100%	100%
Reaction	100%	80%
Learning	80-90%	70%
Application	30%	49%
Impact	10%	37%
ROI	5%	18%

*ROI Institute's minimum target percentage of programs evaluated at each level per year for the typical large organization.

**Current percentage of programs evaluated at each level per year by respondents to ROI Institute's 2019 benchmarking study.

MULTIPLE STAKEHOLDER VALUE

Shared value is an essential focus for many organizations, and it's also important to demonstrate impact and ROI for multiple stakeholders. For example, a major financial services company implemented a leadership development program, which ultimately was intended to drive value. However, a component of the program required participants to apply their newly acquired leadership skills to a project for a nonprofit organization and drive value for that organization as well. In the end, the program resulted in an ROI to the financial services company as well as the nonprofit, not to mention major intangible benefits for both.

Ensure Your Programs Deliver Positive Impact and ROI

W. Edwards Deming, the father of total quality management (TQM), has been quoted as saying, "Every system is perfectly designed to get the results it gets." Design begins with a problem or opportunity and ends with a solution that works and includes a feature that provides insight on the actions to take if it does not work. Figure 20-1 presents a process model that will help you design your programs to deliver positive impact and ROI. The methodology has four phases with 12 steps; it's flexible and appropriate for any type of program in any type of setting.

Plan the Evaluation

Planning an evaluation is a critical first phase in implementing and evaluating training programs, and it features three steps.

The phase begins with Start With Why: Align Programs With the Business, which addresses the business needs of the organization. Business needs include identifying the operational measures that need to improve and the value of improving them. This answers the question: Is this opportunity worth pursuing?

The next step begins to determine what is currently happening or not happening that, if changed, would address the business needs. Make It Feasible: Select the Right Solution is where having a mindset for curiosity is valuable. Doing the research that will lead to the most feasible solution includes quantitative methods and qualitative methods. Sometimes it is simply a matter of having a conversation with key stakeholders and asking a few pointed questions. You can download ROI Institute's alignment conversation toolkit on the handbook website at ATDHandbook3.org.

In the Expect Success: Plan for Results step you develop specific, measurable objectives, including application, impact, and an ROI objective. Using the objectives as the architectural blueprint for program design will increase the chances of delivering positive results. In addition, using the objectives as the basis for evaluation will make data more compelling and evaluation much easier.

Output of the planning phase includes two documents: the data collection plan and the ROI analysis plan. Developing these plans up front helps designers build data collection into the program design. It also offers evaluators an opportunity to get buy-in to the approach prior to execution, eliminating pushback on process during the reporting stage. ROI Institute's templates of these planning documents along with others are available for download on the handbook website at ATDHandbook3.org.

Figure 20-1. ROI Methodology Process Model

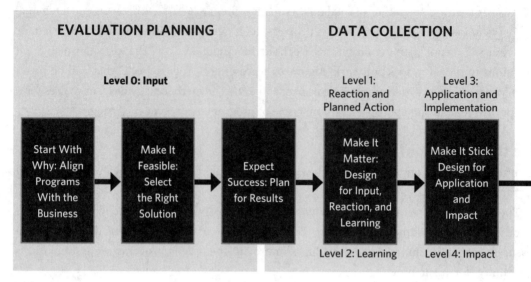

© ROI Institute Inc. Used with permission.

Collect Data

The data collection phase involves two steps that focus on designing for and measuring results at each level. To determine impact and ROI, positive results must occur at different timeframes.

The first step in this phase—Make It Matter: Design for Input, Reaction, and Learning—focuses on Levels 1 and 2. Collecting reaction and learning data is essential because the data can indicate the extent to which the program content matters to participants. Common data collection techniques at Reaction and Learning include end-of-course questionnaires, written tests and exercises, demonstrations, and simulations.

Make It Stick: Design for Application and Impact focuses on Levels 3 and 4. Follow-up data is collected after the program, when the application of the newly acquired knowledge and skills becomes routine and enough time has passed to observe an impact on key measures. A point to remember is that if you identified the measures that need to improve through initial analysis, you will measure the change in performance in those same measures during the evaluation. Therefore, it is feasible to believe that data collection methods used during the evaluation could be the same as those used during the needs analysis.

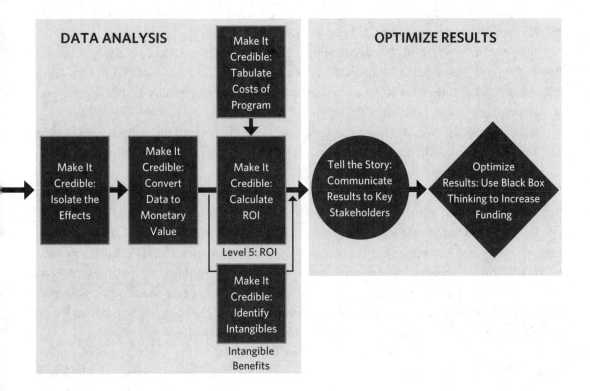

Analyze Data

Data collection is essential; the depth of analysis is even more so. When the data becomes available, analysis begins using the approach chosen during the planning stage. The data analysis phase involves five steps that focus on making the entire process credible.

Make It Credible: Isolate the Effects of the Program is the first step in this phase and occurs after collecting data at Level 4. Too often overlooked in evaluating the success of programs, this step answers the critical question, "How do you know it was your program that improved the measures?" This step isn't as difficult as some might suggest, and your results will have little credibility without it.

The move from impact to ROI begins with converting impact measures to monetary value. Make It Credible: Convert Data to Monetary Value is often the step that instills the greatest fear in training and talent development professionals. But, once they understand the data conversion techniques, along with the five steps to do it, the fear usually subsides.

The next step is to Make It Credible: Identify Intangible Benefits, which are the impact measures not converted to monetary value. Intangible benefits can also represent any unplanned program benefits that are not identified during the planning phase.

Fully loaded costs are also developed during the data analysis phase. Make It Credible: Capture Cost of Program includes calculating costs for needs assessment (when conducted), design, delivery, and evaluation. The intent is to leave no cost out of the analysis to ensure a credible and accurate accounting of the investment.

Make It Credible: Calculate Return on Investment is the last step of the analysis phase. Using addition, subtraction, multiplication, and division, the BCR, ROI, and PP are calculated.

Optimize Results

Optimize results is the most important phase in the evaluation process. Two steps are involved.

Tell the Story: Communicate Results to Key Stakeholders is the first step. Evaluation without communication and communication without action are mere activities with no value. If you don't tell anyone how the program is progressing, how can you improve the talent development process, secure additional funding, justify programs, and market your initiatives to future participants? There are a variety of ways to report data. Micro reports include the complete ROI impact study, while macro reports include scorecards, dashboards, and other reporting tools.

Regardless of the type of report, communication must lead to action—and that action requires stepping back and analyzing what is learned from the data. Optimize Results: Use Black Box Thinking to Increase Funding is the second step of this phase and the final step in the ROI Methodology. It's inspired by the aviation industry's safety system where each aircraft has black boxes that record technical flight data and pilot interactions. When an accident or near miss occurs, the black boxes are analyzed to understand what caused the incident and how to avoid it in the future. Black box thinking is all about learning from mistakes, which is essential if we want to learn why a program failed to succeed and how to improve it to ensure a positive ROI.

The job of talent development professionals is not to "train" people. Rather, the purpose is to drive improvement in output, quality, cost, time, customer satisfaction, job satisfaction, work habits, and innovation. This occurs through the development of others, and doing it well means assessing, measuring, evaluating, and taking action based on your findings. For more detail on each step in the ROI Methodology, download ROI Institute's application guide on the handbook website at ATDHandbook3.org.

Final Thoughts

The message for this chapter is simple. If you need more support, commitment, and funding for major training and talent development programs, report results executives want—impact and

ROI. Executives will begin to view talent development as an investment that yields a return, rather than a cost that can easily be curtailed, postponed, paused, frozen, reduced, or, in the worst case, eliminated. While executives may not explicitly ask for impact and ROI, in the end, that's what they'll want most.

About the Authors

Patti P. Phillips, PhD, is CEO of the ROI Institute. Since 1997, Patti has been a driving force in the global adoption of the ROI Methodology and the use of measurement and evaluation. Her work as a researcher, consultant, and coach supports practitioners as they develop expertise in evaluation. Patti serves as chair of the i4cp People Analytics Board; principal research fellow for The Conference Board; chair of the board for the Center for Talent Reporting; board of trustees member for the UN Institute for Training and Research (UNITAR); and board member of the International Federation of Training and Development Organizations. Patti also serves on the faculty of the UN System Staff College in Turin, Italy. Her work has been featured on CNBC and EuroNews, as well as in more than a dozen business journals. Patti is author, co-author, or editor of more than 75 books and dozens of articles focused on measurement, evaluation, accountability, and ROI.

Jack J. Phillips, PhD, is the chairman of the ROI Institute. He is a world-renowned expert on accountability, measurement, and evaluation. He provides consulting services for Fortune 500 companies and major global organizations. The author or editor of more than 100 books, he conducts workshops and presents at conferences around the world. Jack's expertise in measurement and evaluation is based on more than 27 years of corporate experience in the aerospace, textile, metals, construction materials, and banking industries. Jack regularly consults with clients in manufacturing, service, and government organizations in 70 countries.

References

Freifeld, L. 2021. "Training Magazine Ranks 2021 Training Top 100 Organizations." Training Magazine, February 8. trainingmag.com/training-magazine-ranks-2021-training-top-100-organizations.

McLeod, K. 2019. "2019 ROI Institute Benchmarking Study." roiinstitute.net/2019-roi-institute-benchmarking-report.

Nas, T.F. 2016. *Cost-Benefit Analysis: Theory and Application*, 2nd ed. Lanham, MD: Lexington Books.

Phillips, J.J. 1983. *Handbook of Training Evaluation and Measurement Methods*. Houston, TX: Gulf Publishing.

Phillips, J.J., and P.P. Phillips. 2009. *Measuring Success: What CEOs Really Think About Learning Investments*. Alexandria, VA: ASTD Press.

Phillips, P.P., and J.J. Phillips. 2019. *ROI Basics*, 2nd ed. Alexandria, VA: ATD Press

Prest, A.R., and R. Turvey. 1965. "Cost-Benefit Analysis: A Survey." *The Economic Journal* 300:683–735.

Sibbet, D. 1997. "75 Years of Management Ideas and Practice 1922-1977." *Harvard Business Review*, September 28.

Recommended Resources

Doer, J. 2018. *Measure What Matters: How Google, Bono, and the Gates Foundation Rock the World with OKRs*. New York: Portfolio.

Grant, A. 2021. *Think Again: The Power of Knowing What You Don't Know*. New York: Viking.

Sayed, M. 2015. *Black Box Thinking: Why Most People Never Learn from Their Mistakes… But Some Do*. New York: Portfolio.

Sinek, S. 2009. *Start With Why: How Great Leaders Inspire Everyone to Take Action*. New York: Portfolio.

Sunstein, C.R. 2018. *The Cost-Benefit Revolution*. Cambridge, MA: The MIT Press.

SECTION IV
ENHANCING AND SUPPORTING TALENT DEVELOPMENT

LUMINARY PERSPECTIVE

Talent Development Changes in a Changing Time!

Elliott Masie

I am deeply honored that ATD asked me to do the kickoff for the section on enhancing and supporting talent development. As a veteran of 50 years in the learning, training, EdTech, and innovation space, I should find it easier to predict the trends that are changing our field. I am excited, challenged, and confused about the future of work, the workplace, and talent development. I've distilled my thoughts into nine focus points that pique my curiosity about the future of talent development, as a field and a practice.

I challenge you, as a colleague, to use these topics for self-reflection and discussion with colleagues and neighbors:

- E-learning expands, explodes, and evolves
- Technology empowered: AI, machine learning, robotics, and ecosystems
- Where do our workers work?
- The learner is changing—self-engineering, curator, and nudges!
- Career shifts and chapters!
- Can coaching scale?
- Empathy is vital!
- New horizons: health, cyber, and cognitive
- Data, data, and more data!

Let's expand each topic and explore how your talent development might evolve significantly as business and the workforce changes.

E-Learning Expands, Explodes, and Evolves

When we started to use the term *e-learning* in the early 1990s, there was joy if we could deliver a few modules on a couple topics to a modest number of employees using the emerging internet. During the COVID-19 pandemic, billions of school-age students and millions of workers were pushed rapidly into an e-learning-only format. We wired the world together impressively—with sessions on Zoom and Microsoft Teams throughout the week. And there were new approaches to onboarding, compliance learning, leadership development, and more. It didn't work perfectly. But we passed through a change door. Talent development will need to create new designs that spike the levels of engagement, practice, assessment, and support for e-learning.

Technology Empowered: AI, Machine Learning, Robotics, and Ecosystem

Technology at work and in our lives is changing radically. AI and machine learning are driving more and more corporate work platforms. Robotics are changing manufacturing, distribution, and even retail settings. Our learning systems, talent systems, HR systems, performance systems, and customer-facing systems are integrating. Employees' desktops or mobile devices increasingly will blend technology with worker talents. This will require shifts in how we select, develop, support, and deploy our staff—with a new openness to work hand in hand with smarter tech.

Where Our Workers Work

Coming through the COVID-19 pandemic, organizations are actively shifting and experimenting with the right balance of work from the office or work from home on a hybrid basis. The location of our workforce has serious implications for our talent approaches. Imagine recruiting, onboarding, and managing workers who have never met another colleague in person. That happened around the world, and with some significant impacts. What are the retention or promotion differentials of home-based versus on-site workers? Does the home-based worker get equal or less support and workflow assistance from colleagues?

The Learner Is Changing: Self-Engineering, Curator, and Nudges!

Our employees, including yourself, are changing as learners. We want to be more in charge of the timing, format, and focus of our learning experiences. We have significant differences in how we optimize our learning—some want detailed video examples, others want bullet point processes, and others want conversations with experts. The learner is more of a self-engineer of their own content—they want to focus on what they need now and curate access to more for later. And, learners don't necessarily want to be branded learners or students. Many will resist going to a class or seminar, but want to gather with an expert to get assistance on a task. Finally, many of our learners need (or even ask for) nudges to remind and prompt them of newly acquired knowledge. The changing learner is pushing us to have more user experience approaches and have deeper experimentation with design formats.

Career Shifts and Chapters!

My chief learning officer colleagues have been reporting significant shifts in the career paths, expectations, and "chapters" for their employees. Days of recruit-to-retire may be gone for a large percentage of the workforce. In addition, length of stay in some industries is shifting downward, which creates more pressure to quickly get new talent to readiness. We need to build more transportability of the workforce credentials and incorporate a more accelerated role to develop leadership and collaborative skills from day one rather than at later points of promotion. Significant experimentation is needed here!

Can Coaching Scale?

When asked what would help their development, many employees request coaching. Working with my colleague Marshall Goldsmith during the pandemic showed me how enterprises have the opportunity to take the power of coaching and scale it from a few select executives to the wider employee population. Scaling coaching will require new systems, new development programs, and rethinking the length and format of coaching incidents. I have been coaching three colleagues with 10-minute phone conversations every week. Let's push these boundaries and traditions.

Empathy Is Vital!

Empathy is the powerful connection and acceptance that we have and demonstrate to colleagues. Empathy is not sympathy. Empathy is acknowledging our unique characteristics and opening the door to sharing our stories and acceptance. Talent development can make empathy a vital part of every program and project they deliver. During the pandemic, the MASIE Center hosted more than 35 free online Empathy Concerts with Broadway musical stars and learning leaders, exploring the role and need for empathy. We had thousands of colleagues participate from around the world. Empathy is vital!

New Horizons: Health, Cyber, and Cognitive

Talent professionals will need to up their readiness to deal with new horizons of employee and workplace disruptions. We will want to weave these topics into our roles and programs in the future:

- **Health.** The COVID-19 pandemic pushed our organizations to adopt health, wellness, and screening systems to support our populations. There will be ongoing health issues that will become part of our talent development agenda. We don't need to become experts on these issues, but programs focused on health at the workplace will expand in reach and scope in the years ahead.
- **Cyber.** The next pandemic may be a cyber-demic. The fully wired and online enterprise is also ripe for cyberattack and disruption. What if no one could get to any files? What if our customers could not reach us? What if payments could not be processed? Cyber threats and readiness to cope with a potential major cyber disruption are another talent development issue to consider.
- **Cognitive.** This is a tricky one to raise. A percentage of our workforce may have a cognitive challenge or uniqueness. In some instances, an employee may have early-onset dementia or another memory or processing disease.

Data, Data, and More Data!

This is one of the big trends that I consider almost every day, as the field of talent development evolves. How do we leverage the data in our systems to design, personalize, and accelerate talent development for our employees? How do we use evidence from our previous programs to continually adjust the mix, timing, and levels of engagement? How do we provide managers with actionable data about the skill levels (and gaps) of their team members? How do we create dashboards that reflect each employee's current knowledge status, and make sure it stays updated as business and their roles change? Talent development colleagues must grow their comfort and agility to use, understand, and leverage data to focus our programs and initiatives.

This piece is the appetizer to the wonderful stories and case studies in this section about growing and evolving our talent development skills and readiness. Our workers are changing. Our workplace settings are changing. Our technology is changing. Our own careers may be changing.

Let's stretch our own talent development skills to match these changes. Tomorrow's workforce will need our energy, competencies, and agility more than ever!

About the Author

Elliott Masie is a provocative, engaging, and entertaining researcher, educator, analyst, and speaker focused on the changing world of the workplace, learning, and technology. He is acknowledged as the first analyst to use the term *e-learning* and has advocated for a sane deployment of learning and collaboration technology to support the effectiveness and profitability of enterprises. He heads MASIE Innovations, a global "B" company focused on learning, talent, technology, Broadway theater, social change, and innovation. It includes the Learning COLLABORATIVE, Masie Productions, and Empathy Concerts. Elliott is the author of 12 books, including *Big Learning Data* and recent e-books on learning pivots and empathy. Over the past 35 years, Elliott has presented programs, courses, and speeches to more than 3.1 million professionals around the world. He lives in Saratoga Springs, New York, and is a Tony-nominated Broadway producer. You can reach him at elliott@masie.com.

CHAPTER 21

The Journey to Learning Experience Design

George Hall

While learning experience design (LXD) may appear to be an expression of a new definition for an evolved mindset, improved practices, and a broader perspective, it is not new. In fact, this evolved mindset, while not widely understood as a coordinated and integrated set of design principles by many people, has been recognized by some innovative educators for decades.

> **IN THIS CHAPTER:**
> - Explore how innovators pioneered human-centered design techniques decades before the field moved in this direction
> - Understand the roots of the LXD principles and techniques in use today

Some try to define LXD using well-worn phrases such as "LXD is learner centered," "LXD acknowledges that training is not always the answer," "LXD offers a meaningful user experience," or that "learning is a journey, not an event." But those platitudes have been around for 30 years. Others say that experiential learning is at the heart of LXD, but it has been valued since John Dewey advocated for it in the 1920s and others such as Bloom, Gardner, Lewin, and Kolb followed. LXD has received lots of attention as the new way to shape learning experiences. Is it new and where do the roots of LXD lie?

At a certain level of educational practice, we can agree that definitive prescriptions are not possible. Elliot Eisner (1998) has persuasively argued that:

> Education will not have permanent solutions to its problems, we will have no "breakthroughs," no enduring discoveries that will work forever. We are "stuck" with temporary resolutions rather than with permanent solutions. What works here may not work there. What works now may not work then. We are not trying to invent radar or measure the rate of free fall in a vacuum. Our tasks are impacted by context, riddled with unpredictable contingencies, responsive to local conditions, and shaped by those we teach and not only by those who teach.

Although a few ambitious talent development professionals claim to have invented LXD, several highly creative pioneers have been incorporating LXD design principles into their courses since the late 1950s.

Starting the Journey

Following Eisner, I started my journey not by identifying gaps in the literature, but rather by finding a real-world situation that seemed to be worthy of studying. I am a traveler on a lifelong journey, walking through fields and forests, looking at the scenery, and trying to decide what path to take next. I do not know exactly what the path will be like. I can see some places I would like to go—there, that mountain off in the distance—but I do not know exactly how to get there or if I will get there at all. And of course, when I get closer, I might decide it is not as appealing as it seemed, and another destination is more worthy.

Project Outreach and Wilbert McKeachie

In 1985, as an undergraduate student at the University of Michigan–Ann Arbor, I stumbled upon a particularly well-designed course called Project Outreach. This course provided thousands of Michigan students a unique service-learning experience unlike any other available at that time. I was able to simultaneously learn about psychology-in-action, explore myself and my interests, and provide a meaningful service to the Ann Arbor community. Clearly, someone was a master designer and ahead of the time. *What had I stumbled upon? How can I unravel this mystery?*

I began to research my professor and our program director, Wilbert McKeachie. In 1945—after serving in WWII's Pacific Theater as a radar and communications officer on a destroyer—McKeachie enrolled in graduate school at the University of Michigan to study psychology. At Michigan, he participated in a crucial formative experience as a teaching fellow in an introductory psychology course led by Harold Guetzkow. Guetzkow, who had also earned his doctorate at Michigan, was fascinated by the fields of psychology, sociology, and political science. A pioneer in education, he built simulations incorporating many of the learning experience design principles we now focus on as "new." He studied the pedagogy involved in designing such simulations and used what he learned to design new simulations. His most famous was the Inter-Nation Simulation, which uses simulation to study relations among nations, similar to war games, for chiefs of state and foreign ministers to learn skill from games.

The Project Outreach class was a crucial, formative experience for me—just as Harold Guetzkow's section had been for McKeachie. Project Outreach involved volunteering as a crisis counselor at Ozone House, a shelter for runaway teenagers, and then reflecting on the experience itself, guided readings, and the pedagogy behind the designed learning experience. This immersive class had it all and more. It was human-centered and inclusive, provided positive and meaningful learning experiences, emphasized that learning is a journey, relied on research-based findings to make design decisions, sought input from students and participants, used real-world metrics to measure performance improvement, emphasized sharing and social engagement, and was innovative and flexible. Ozone House, a nonprofit working with University of Michigan students, was a special place as well. It has won numerous awards since 1960. Project Outreach continues to thrive, currently delivering innovative training programs as well as a leadership institute.

McKeachie, a longtime faculty member at Michigan, taught until 2005. He was innovative and a true force at Michigan's famous School of Education (SOE). In 1950, he started to distribute a manual he had written to his teaching assistants to provide proven educational strategies and techniques. This informal manual of best practices evolved into *McKeachie's Teaching Tips: Strategies, Research, and Theory for College and University Teachers*. Initially published in 1951, the book's 14th edition was released in 2013.

McKeachie was later involved in the collaborative founding of a combined program in education and psychology that became one of Michigan's first joint PhD programs. These programs created select groups of outstanding scholars and researchers who studied, collaborated, and worked in interdisciplinary environments, such as psychology, education, sociology, anthropology, political science, and social work. McKeachie also established the Center for Research on Learning and Teaching (CRLT), which helped translate teaching and instructional design best practices across interdisciplinary environments.

Frederick Goodman and the ICS

Frederick Goodman was a colleague of McKeachie's and another education giant. He was later named a professor of education emeritus at the SOE and taught there until 2005. Goodman pioneered the design of teacher-training residency programs and internship models. He was deeply inspired by the work of John Dewey, who spent 10 years at Michigan (1880–1890) and left an indelible imprint on the SOE. Goodman worked to embody Dewey's idea that "experience is education."

Toward that end, Goodman was foundational in the creation of the Interactive Communications and Simulations (ICS) group at Michigan, which specialized in experiential education, game design, authentic assessment, and entrepreneurial education. The team designed experiential education, developed new game design principles, and gleaned insights from expertly designed service-learning projects that embodied modern human-centered design principles, obtaining thoughtful answers to questions such as:

- What are good problems for human-centered design?
- What problems do not require human-centered design?

They learned that human-centered design is most useful if you are working on problems that are open ended and ill defined, where cause and effect are not clear and have many interrelated components that operate as a complex system. Human-centered design is useful when the problem is new and you find myriad human perspectives.

Human-Centered Design

At ICS, Goodman's core team pioneered human-centered design techniques, philosophies, and methods decades before the field would begin to move in this direction. Essentially, they saw LXD as a variation of UR/UX (client-centric creation of user research and user experience), where the users are learners. What is the difference between UXD and LXD? Although these terms started to be used widely 10–20 years ago, this group was early to recognize the importance of UX for learning and education. When you are designing for learning and using human-centered design, they believed that you should consider the needs of the user from the users' perspective, asking:

- What sort of problem or challenge does the user have?
- How can learning design help them meet that challenge?

This group was quick to observe that learners may have many different needs. In other words, while learners have unmet needs, they might not be the only needs that matter. The learner, for example, might need to get a good grade, be placed on the dean's list, or get accepted into a graduate program, and these needs are not strictly learning related. There might also be other needs or even competing needs. For example, a company may believe that employees have a certain set of skills, yet because there are many different stakeholders, the actual learning need may be buried. The learners' primary goal may not be learning, despite their participation in a learning program.

Perspective Taking

The team at ICS pioneered learning experience design principles by intuitively practicing them, starting in the 1990s. Although the group now practices these principles more intentionally, they came to realize that the most important part of the design process was defining the problem or framing it in a way that looks at the world from the users' perspective. In that sense, the perspective-taking parts of the service learning projects they designed prepared them to embrace what we now see as the ideas of human-centered design, the design mindset, and design thinking.

The team discovered that you can create experiences that generate further experiences and encourage the practice of perspective taking. These experiences can even be artificial, taking form as a simulation, social simulation, or games. Although these scholars may not have even heard of LXD, they were already designing through perspective taking and designing for people's needs.

Story-Based Learning

The team's learning designs were typically grounded in well-conceived stories with a clear beginning, middle, and end. A recurrent theme was the notion of designed provocation. In the content they designed, in the characters selected, and in the kinds of exchanges fostered, one of the team's prime tasks was to keep it interesting by making the learning experience as interactive and provocative as possible. These designed provocations were enacted in a strategic and coordinated way. As a central aspect of the choice architecture, they empowered learners, altering their behavior in predictable ways without forbidding or foreclosing any options or significantly changing their incentives.

Rapid Prototyping

I believe that you are unable to reach great LXD from simply reading about the history of instructional design. It will not happen. A leap of imagination is required to bring all the necessary pieces and perspectives together with skill. Goodman, who was always able to attract talented people to his service-learning projects at ICS, was a famous connector. He liked to introduce two people by saying, "I do not know what you have in common, but you will figure it out; go talk." He was always right. He had a design mindset from the beginning. Such a mindset involves trying something in a low-stakes environment, prototyping it by taking your users' perspective into consideration, attempting to define your problem, and then identifying things to try.

A Radical Research Methodology

What was truly radical about the ICS group in the 1990s was its approach to conducting educational research. At that time, the classic way to do educational projects was to get a substantial grant from the National Science Foundation (NSF), build a piece of software, launch the project at a dozen schools, collect test data, write a paper, and then write your next grant. What this classic method fails to recognize is that the investment in the project's infrastructure influences the researchers' openness to feedback. Researchers want the feedback but cannot do much with it because they already built an infrastructure, and spent money, time, and human effort building this software. In other words, their ability to systematically apply design-thinking principles may be compromised by the structures they built, had invested in, and needed to maintain.

Agile Team Dynamics

By design, the ICS team was agile, nimble, and unencumbered by methods ill suited to their purpose. They mastered the process of rapidly prototyping learning experience designs. "Let's see if we can put together a website in a weekend," they'd say. "We acknowledge that it might not be that great, it might crash a lot, and maybe we'll have to do some behind-the-scenes-stuff, but let's try it, and see how it works."

This team rapidly prototyped their designs, did so at an extremely high skill level, gathered feedback, and then incorporated it into the design to improve it. They were incredibly modest and able to collaborate, and lacked any ego or intellectual investment in the designs they prototyped.

Ironically, one reason the group was able to last and flourish was because they were not funded by major grants. Instead, they work with minimal resources, which forces them to figure out how to design on a shoestring, advertise by word-of-mouth, and incorporate LXD service-learning projects into existing courses and programs. The courses they designed, however, became masterpieces, which were built over several years by a diverse team of learning professionals constantly prototyping new designs. Their skill sets covered a wide variety of areas including classroom teaching, online teaching, game design, pedagogical theory, instructional design, learning experience design, graphic design, and web design.

Brilliant—But Not Mainstream

Expertise in these areas is hard-won—the ability to integrate insights uncovered across disciplines is only the result of a lifetime spent focusing on these topics. That said, as powerful as these innovative LXD projects were, they did not easily fit into existing school structures or even appeal to the mindsets most teachers had at the time. They were more in the long tail of educational practice; in other words, they were amazing, but not mainstream. However, they were able to succeed despite the lack of strong institutional or financial support. The ICS team's primary focus was, and continues to be, to inspire more people in the world to run their own games or start their own projects or activities that incorporate these powerful LXD principles.

The Journey to Learning Experience Design

My journey to learning experience design has come full circle. After graduating from Michigan in the late 1980s, I went on to focus on a career as an instructional designer and project manager at Walt Disney and other companies. Most recently, I returned to Michigan—33 years after my enrollment in Project Outreach but still affected by it—to start a master's degree in learning experience design. Not surprisingly, I found a vibrant intellectual community and was quickly drawn to the evolved mindsets evidenced in the educational simulations designed by students and tenured faculty, many of whom were Goodman's and McKeachie's doctoral students.

Final Thoughts

Like so many of the "new" developments we see in learning and development, LXD isn't all that new. McKeachie and Goodman are undeniably seminal figures in LXD thinking. Fortunately, because they led and influenced generations of distinguished educators, it is still possible to follow in their footsteps and embrace the traditions they've established. LXD has evolved over decades to be embraced by all of us today.

About the Author

George Hall is a learning solutions architect and instructional designer with extensive experience leading the digital transformation of learning services, developing digital learning products, and managing education and learning services for global Fortune 500 companies, US government agencies, state governments, and nonprofits. In his spare time, he volunteers as a learning industry advisor to a nonprofit educational charity that actively supports schools, government organizations, and other nonprofits. When not teaching, writing, or developing his EdTech superhero skills, George loves spending time traveling, cooking, and laughing with his wife and wonderful family. He can be reached at george@driveontheocean.org. Learn more about George at driveontheocean.org.

References

Alter, A. 2018. *Irresistible: The Rise of Addictive Technology and the Business of Keeping Us Hooked.* New York: Penguin Books.

Anderson, S.P. 2011. *Seductive Interaction Design: Creating Playful, Fun, and Effective User Experiences.* Berkeley, CA: New Riders.

Brown, T. 2009. *Change By Design.* New York: Harper Collins.

Dean, J. 2013. *Making Habits, Breaking Habits: Why We Do Things, Why We Don't, and How to Make Any Change Stick.* Boston: Da Capo Press.

Eisner, E. 1998. *The Kind of Schools We Need: Personal Essays.* Portsmouth, NH: Heinemann.

Goffman, E. 1959. *The Presentation of Self in Everyday Life.* New York: AnchorBooks.

Goodman, F.L. 1992. "Instructional Gaming Through Computer Conferencing." In *Empowering Networks*, edited by M.D. Waggoner, 101–126. Englewood Cliffs, NJ: Educational Technology Publications.

Goodman, F.L. 1995. "Practice in Theory." *Simulation & Gaming* 26(2): 178–189.

Kupperman, J., G. Weisserman, and F.L. Goodman. 2001. "The Secret Lives of Students and Politicians: Online and Face-to-Face Discourse in Two Political Simulations." Paper presented at the Annual Meeting of the American Educational Research Association, Seattle, WA.

McKeachie and M. Svinicki. 2013. *McKeachie's Teaching Tips: Strategies, Research, and Theory for College and University Teachers*, 14th ed. First published in 1951. Belmont, CA: Wadsworth Publishing.

Ozone House. n.d. "Job Training and Leadership." ozonehouse.org/how-we-help/job-training-leadership.

Recommended Resources

Collins, A., and R. Halverson. 2009. *Rethinking Education in the Age of Technology: The Digital Revolution and Schooling in America.* New York: Teachers College Press.

Facer, K. 2011. *Learning Futures: Education, Technology and Social Change.* London: Routledge.

Turkel, S. 2017. *Alone Together: Why We Expect More from Technology and Less from Each Other.* New York: Basic Books.

Wesch, M. 2007. "A Vision of Students Today." YouTube video, October 12, 2007. youtu.be/dGCJ46vyR9o.

CHAPTER 22

Keys to Designing and Delivering Blended Learning

Jennifer Hofmann

When the last ATD handbook was published, in 2014, we were still trying to convince organizations that blended learning was worth the investment in time, money, and other resources. This chapter will explore why organizations resisted blended learning and how it can be a valuable part of your learning strategy.

> **IN THIS CHAPTER:**
> - Determine why designing effective blended learning is a critical part of your learning strategy
> - Examine 10 effective blended learning design practices
> - Evaluate how well your designs align with the effective practices

Why did organizations resist blended learning? There are several reasons:

Traditional classroom learning is easy to schedule, and it was readily apparent who "finished" class by simply tracking attendance. Blended learning, on the other hand, requires an LMS to track completion of individual components.

Blended learning requires multiple technologies and instructional approaches. With that comes investments in EdTech, and a commitment to teaching the instructional staff how to effectively develop and implement these technologies.

Blended learning can be complicated: Watch a video, take a 20-minute e-learning program, go to a classroom, and attend three virtual sessions. This is often viewed as logistically difficult to manage, and not worth the effort. Organizations found it difficult to implement, and learners simply didn't take it seriously.

When blended learning was attempted, it often wasn't successful. Learners and, if truth be told, facilitators, only seemed to pay attention to the "most live" portion of the program. If there was a face-to-face section, supported by e-learning and video and virtual classroom, many learners just assumed the "important stuff" would happen in the classroom. And trainers, concerned that learners wouldn't complete self-directed work, would find ways to insert the other content into the live sessions.

With all this complexity, it was easier to organize live training in a classroom.

So Why Blend?

As I mentioned in the 2014 edition of the *ASTD Handbook*, "The classroom has been used for so long (centuries!) not because it is the most effective means of teaching, but because it was the technology available at the time."

We've been trying to implement blended learning in organizations for decades. There are so many obvious advantages, including:

- **Cost reduction.** When learners are at their desks, there are real cost savings associated with travel expenses and infrastructure (classroom) investments. As teams become more geographically dispersed and workplaces become more virtual, bringing groups together for training is less economically feasible.
- **Flexibility.** While there are some fixed time commitments associated with live sessions, individuals have the flexibility to learn on their own schedules. Also, there can be many more enrollment options so learners can participate in a program when it is convenient and relevant for them to do so. In today's business environment, there is a real need for just-in-time training—when and where we need it. Blended learning helps solve that need.

- **Increased learner retention.** Since individual pieces of learning content are shorter in duration, learners have a chance to process the information and perhaps even practice a new skill in a real-work situation before moving on to the next lesson in the learning journey. This phenomenon is known as the spacing effect.

> **THE SPACING EFFECT**
>
> The spacing effect is based on the Ebbinghaus forgetting curve. It says that we're better able to recall information if we learn it in spread-out sessions. We can use spaced repetition or practice to help people learn almost anything. Theoretically, the practice of spacing content in such a way so that learners can process and apply it seems logical. In his post "Make the Spacing Effect Work for Online Students," Peter Seaman provides some helpful talking points we can use to gain buy-in:
>
>> The spacing effect is supported by more research than almost any other learning principle. One estimate says that there are at least 10 research studies per year on the spacing effect, and they continue to build support for and understanding of this principle. In general, the more space between learning events, and the more repetitions, the longer knowledge stays in long-term memory. What is the ideal amount of space? The jury (of researchers) is still out on this question, but there seems to be a sweet spot of about a week. The minimum amount of time seems to be one day, as researchers speculate that good things come from putting a night's sleep between two learning events.

These are great reasons for implementing blended learning, and most learning professionals would agree that a strong blended learning curriculum is their goal. But blended learning programs are not getting the traction you would expect—and that's because creating and implementing a blend is, simply put, hard.

Training programs delivered using a single format (such as face-to-face, virtual classroom, or e-learning) are easier to design, easier to implement, and easier for learners to complete.

And, there is a much more subtle and subconscious reason we aren't focused on blended learning: It's not exciting or new. It is more interesting to focus on emerging technologies, like virtual reality and chatbots, or developing instructional techniques like gamification, curation, and simulations, than it is to talk about blended learning. But by focusing on these individual pieces, we are losing the big picture. Blended learning can be the best of both worlds.

The Flipped Classroom

During the last decade, "flipping the classroom" became a popular concept for explaining how and why to create a blend. This concept is credited to primary education, when lectures and knowledge transfer activities occur during the traditional homework and self-study times. Then, when students interact with their instructors in the classroom, they are led through hands-on application, lab exercises, and other higher-order thinking activities.

As a baseline, the flipped classroom is what we're trying to achieve. This so-called webinar model of instruction, where we insist people get together virtually at the same time but only allow them to listen and ask questions via chat, is not a viable training approach. If learners can log on to a recording and have the same experience as attending a live event, it's simply knowledge transfer and not a training program.

If, however, we can develop an approach where learners see the value in completing self-directed work before coming to a live environment where they are challenged, have opportunities to practice, and are rigorously assessed, we can start to create a true blended learning mode.

When designing a blend, we are effectively trying to achieve a flipped classroom. We are determining what content needs to be live, what content can be self-directed, and what instructional strategies, techniques, and technologies should be used to create the most impactful experience.

What Is Blended Learning, Really?

A casual internet search for blended learning "types" or "models" often brings us to research by the Christiansen Institute. It's tempting to try to adopt the different models identified by the institute (such as the rotation model, flex model, à la carte model, and enriched virtual model) as a corporate training framework. The institute's research is based on educational experiences in schools (elementary, secondary, and so forth), not the corporate training environment. The definition used by the Christiansen Institute assumes that there is a brick and mortar (or traditional classroom) component to most learning experiences.

That is not the case for modern blended learning outside an educational institution. Especially in this post-pandemic economy, face-to-face experiences and corporate training are no longer the norm. Organizations are adopting a "virtual first" approach to learning and development and requiring a strong business case for more traditional programs.

In a corporate context, blended learning is the framework that connects instructional technologies with techniques, providing a solution that meets the needs of modern learners and a business climate that's increasingly mobile, global, and reliant on social, collaborative technologies.

When we say, "Connect instructional technologies with techniques," we mean that designers of blended learning need to identify every performance objective associated with the curriculum, including enabling objectives, and map each one to the most appropriate instructional technology. Blended learning doesn't have to begin and end with formal experiences.

Fundamentally, we need to make sure we start with a strong instructional design approach prior to selecting the delivery technology. We should base our selection on two considerations:
- How will you assess mastery of a particular concept during the formal training?
- How will the content be used after the training is complete at different moments of learner need?

Assessing Mastery

As mentioned already, stakeholders in a blended learning program, including facilitators, learners, and managers, tend to focus on the "most live" component of a blend and see the self-directed work as optional. And, because most self-directed work is not completed, facilitators find ways to address that content during the live events, at the expense of the time set aside for activities and practice. The result of this practice is often a series of (well-designed) related content that is not tied together by a narrative and is underutilized.

To avoid this, each individual component of the blend should have some way to assess completion and mastery. It could be a simple test, integration of the self-directed content into the live conversations, or some kind of encompassing case study that ties everything together. What we need to avoid is reteaching self-directed content in the live program.

Assessing Whether Learning Objectives Are Met

There is generally a direct correlation between the type of assessment to use and the type of technology used to deliver the content associated with that assessment. For example, if your assessment is a self-paced instrument that tests the learners' recall of content, you can probably deliver that in a self-paced format. If learners are required to collaborate with others to be assessed, you will probably need to deliver content using a collaborative technology, which can be live (traditional classrooms and virtual classrooms) or not live (discussion board postings and some forms of social media).

Remember, blended learning is not only about matching content to the most appropriate delivery technology, but doing it at the performance objective level. It's the assessment technique that marries these two concepts.

Meeting Learners at Their Moment of Need

Blended learning requires you to be even more specific when identifying performance needs and performer needs. (As a result, you may have more specific potential solutions.) That's because with modern blended learning design, you can be responsive not just when learners are learning something new for the first time; you can design and implement solutions that affect every moment of learning need.

Bob Mosher and Conrad Gottfredson (2012) identified five moments of learning need to help illustrate where performance support could supplement the formal learning process:
- When people are learning how to do something for the first time (new)
- When people are expanding the breadth and depth of what they have learned (more)
- When people need to act upon what they have learned, which includes planning what they will do, remembering what they may have forgotten, or adapting their performance to a unique situation (apply)
- When problems arise or things break or don't work the way they were intended (solve)
- When people need to learn a new way of doing something, which requires them to change skills that are deeply ingrained in their performance practices (change)

These same moments lend themselves to the entire blended learning process because different training solutions support different moments of need.

From Push Training to Pull Learning

The COVID-19 pandemic has accelerated our movement from an industrial economy to the new knowledge economy. Learning and development models have been slow to change. We know that classrooms and week-long sessions are not efficient, and people don't remember most of what they learn in those contexts, but we were still using them until recently. We always meant to move content online and create better blends, but the impetus wasn't there to make it happen.

Now, our training has gone virtual and it will be staying there.

The pandemic and other economic factors (such as globalization, digitalization, and a younger generation accustomed to on-demand learning options and social networks) are forcing us to change our approach. Organizations are moving away from delivery-focused, instructor-centered events based on centralized and siloed content. Instead, they are moving toward ongoing, learner-centered, decentralized learning solutions that focus on results.

This evolution perfectly describes push training versus pull learning. Push training comes to the learners whether they're ready (and willing) or not. In comparison, pull learning is made available to learners when they need it. This is a major change in culture that companies are just beginning to manage. And we can help by working to prove the value of including more pull learning opportunities. To meet the needs of modern learners, you need to focus on the pull learning model as a significant part of your blend, where people can connect and learn from one another.

Incorporating blended learning will be a big change for most organizations. Part of the change strategy requires contemplating how to influence the mindset of your learning organization, changing from a "push training environment" to a "pull learning environment."

Blended Learning Effective Practices

To help you make this transition, let's examine 10 effective blended learning practices. You can evaluate how well you are doing using the Blended Learning Scoring Tool on the handbook's website at ATDHandbook3.org.

Effective Practice 1

Instructional goals are established and communicated, including clear definitions of what will be taught, and why it will be taught within a blended solution.

When instructional goals are established for a blended learning solution, the entire team needs to be made aware of what materials will be taught and why the learners would benefit from a blend of delivery methodologies. Once this information is defined and communicated, the team can begin to determine the best way to design a blended solution.

Blended learning solutions are just that—a blend of the best delivery methodologies available for a specific objective. It is less about the technology available, and more about the needs and priorities of the learning community as framed within established instructional goals. Asking "What?" and "Why?" will guide the design process and help determine which elements work best for online, classroom-based instruction, electronic performance support, paper-based, and formalized or informal on-the-job solutions.

Recommendations:
- Clearly communicate the instructional goals of the learning solution.
- Remember to ask "Why?" along with "What?"
- If this is your first blended learning instructional design project, reframe the needs analysis to focus on the "why" to better inform your design.
- Create an executive summary that expands on what will be taught and why it will be taught within a blended solution.
- Ask for feedback on the summary from key stakeholders to be sure that you are on track.
- Share the summary and feedback with your learning designers, developers, facilitators, and producers.

Effective Practice 2

A needs analysis is conducted to determine if a blended learning approach is appropriate for the learning program.

The needs analysis phase is critical to the design, development, and delivery of learning solutions, and it will benefit the entire learning team (and learners) to consider if a blended approach is appropriate.

Needs analyses are tied closely to instructional and organizational goals. As you craft your needs analysis, consider what solutions have been effective in the past, and research, as best you can, where the organization as a whole is headed.

If the results tell you that a blended learning solution is not the right fit, consider going back to the instructional goal and ask the "what" and "why" questions again.

Recommendations:
- Review past, current, and future instructional approaches before you conduct a needs analysis.
- Consider how, where, and when people work and learn.
- Refer back to the "what" and "why" of the instructional goals before you conduct your needs analysis.
- Compare results with current and future instructional goals and performance objectives.

Effective Practice 3

Measurable performance objectives are developed to support learner success.

Performance objectives indicate what learners will be able to do at the end of the training. Taking the time to craft meaningful performance objectives will guide learner success and ensure that the blended learning solution will support the overall instructional goals.

Focus on the audience, behavior, condition, and criteria for success when creating learner-centered objectives.

To create measurable performance objectives:
- Identify the learner.
- Describe what the learner will be able to do when learning is complete.
- Specify the conditions under which the performance will occur.
- Detail the criteria used to evaluate learner performance.

Measurable performance objectives provide a road map for designing a successful blended learning program. They provide guidelines on how to assess knowledge gain and establish the pathway for learners to explore throughout their learning journey.

Recommendations:
- Review your learning objectives as a whole to be sure that they create a learning pathway.
- If applicable, create objectives that guide the scaffolding of learning from lower-order to higher-order thinking.
- If you are converting to a blend from a face-to-face environment, take this opportunity to review your performance objectives to ensure that they are still applicable within the blended solution.

Effective Practice 4

Modes of delivery and technologies are selected in alignment with performance objectives.

Performance objectives should drive the consideration, evaluation, and selection of technologies and delivery modes. Once you identify the performance objectives, you should decide how you will know whether a learner has mastered each objective.

Following these simple steps can help guide your selection of delivery modes throughout the blended learning design process:

- Determine what needs to be taught and what associated objectives are included in that topic.
- Establish if the associated objectives can be assessed online. If the answer is yes, then the associated learning can also be taught online.
- Decide whether collaboration would enhance learning associated with the objective by asking:
    - Is there a purpose to bringing learners together?
    - Does mastery of this objective require the synergy of a group?
    - Will the outcome for learners be better because we have brought them together to learn?

By taking the time to step through this process, you can design a blended learning program that best achieves your performance objectives.

Recommendations:

- Take the time to review each individual learning event and all associated performance objectives before you start the conversation about delivery modes.
- Create a curriculum map to illustrate the relationship between learning objectives, learning content, and selected modes of delivery.

Effective Practice 5

Methods and approaches for assessing learner mastery are designed in alignment with performance objectives.

Blended learning is not only about matching content to the most appropriate delivery medium but also doing it at the learning objective level. It's the assessment technique that marries these two concepts.

Learning activities and assessments should be designed to support the mastery of performance objectives. Activity and assessment types are typically discussed and designed alongside the delivery mode review process.

As there is generally a direct correlation between the type of assessment and the type of technology you will use, it is important to loop back to the performance objectives on a regular basis to be sure that your design stays on target, with learner success always in mind.

Recommendations:
- List all performance objectives associated with each activity and assessment to be sure that learners can achieve all objectives.
- If scaffolded learning is part of the instructional goal, create a curriculum map to illustrate the alignment of the lower- and higher-order thinking levels to the assessment approaches.
- Loop back through the delivery mode selection process to be sure that the selected delivery modes are appropriate for each activity and assignment.

Effective Practice 6

Learning material that supports knowledge-based objectives is designed to be delivered through self-paced technologies.

Knowledge-based objectives, such as remembering and understanding, are well suited for self-paced learning. Learning objectives that use keywords such as *recognize, list, identify, define,* and *locate* fit within that scope.

When designing blended learning solutions, consider technologies that focus on disseminating information and require little or no connection or collaboration with other learners (or the instructor).

Recommendations:
- Focus on the design of interactions between learners and content for knowledge-based objectives.
- Ensure that learners have detailed instructions on how to access and complete all self-paced materials.
- Provide opportunities for learners to reflect on or share their self-paced learning experiences within the blended learning solution.

Effective Practice 7

Live learning events are designed to encourage learners to collaborate, solve problems, answer questions, and pose solutions.

The time set aside for live events in any blended learning solution should focus on collaboration, not information dissemination. Real-time events (face-to-face or virtual) can be designed to review key concepts, provide feedback, and create the opportunity to work in groups to solve a learning challenge.

Loop back to the blended learning delivery mode selection process, where we asked if collaboration would enhance learning associated with the performance objectives. The live events are where we establish the purpose for bringing learners together, harness the synergy of the group, and achieve better outcomes based on input from and interaction among learning peers.

Recommendations:
- Delivery approaches should be designed to promote the instructor as a facilitator, not lecturer, within all live learning events.
- Provide and promote options for co-creating and sharing learning assets.
- Include opportunities for learners to reflect on or share their live learning experiences within the blended learning solution.

Effective Practice 8

A course map is created to illustrate the balance of learning elements within the blended curriculum.

The course map provides an overview of the entire blended learning curriculum by explaining the sequence of events, the types of learning activities, the anticipated length for each activity, and an indication of when the activity will take place.

Course maps provide details of the journey for learners, helping them get started, find their learning pathway, and determine what it will take to complete the journey. While the map details the phases of the learning journey for the learner, it also provides an overview of the balance within the blended learning solution for the designer. Reviewing the course map will better enable designers to determine if there is a correct balance and application of content, interaction, and assessment modes within the blend.

Recommendations:
- Create a checklist to go along with the course map to help guide learners on their learning journey.
- Include time management tips and tools (or link to them) within the course map.
- Integrate the course map into every learning event within the blended learning solution to be sure that learners know how they are progressing within their learning journey.

Effective Practice 9

Communication channels and tools are designed to support learner progress and reporting throughout the blended learning schedule.

Communication channels allow instructors and learners to connect and collaborate within the blended learning environment. As learners work on their own or in groups, these communication channels provide value by enabling the exchange of information and ideas, as well as the creation of new knowledge.

Communication channels provide a means for instructors to keep learners on track, and for learners to report on their progress. These channels need to serve a purpose and be associated with performance objectives. This association will ensure that learners keep progressing, learning, and sharing.

Recommendations:
- When creating a communication channel, remember to focus on the associated learning objectives.
- Design communication channels to include feedback mechanisms that guide learners as they progress through the learning curriculum.
- Provide a means within the channel to communicate milestones and achievements within the learning community.

Effective Practice 10

An evaluation plan is in place to determine the effectiveness of the blended learning solution.

Evaluation of all learning events leads to informed decisions to review, revise, and renew materials and modes of delivery. When conducted throughout the blended learning experience, evaluation can help better define performance objectives, refine learning materials, and ensure that learner needs are being met.

Designing and planning the evaluation process in advance will guide the development of learning materials and blended delivery methods. It will ensure that learners are satisfied with the curriculum, as well as determine what they have learned and let you know if they are able to apply the skills they have obtained.

Evaluation results also provide stakeholders with information to guide future planning for learning solutions within the organization.

Recommendations:
- Clearly state (and continuously refine) the purpose of conducting any evaluation in advance.
- Share the purpose of the evaluation along with the results.
- Ask for feedback from stakeholders and continuously refine your evaluation methods.

Final Thoughts

There have always been good reasons for choosing blended learning over a single virtual or live program, but resistance to implementing a blended solution is common. In this chapter we discussed the challenges to creating blended learning solutions and how a well-designed and implemented program can offer the best of both the virtual and live worlds. Following the 10 blended learning design practices and making them part of every design strategy ensures that your design will be effective. An effective blended learning design ensures a reduced cost, more flexibility, and increased learner retention.

About the Author

Jennifer Hofmann, virtual classroom and blended learning pioneer, is founder and president of InSync Training. Her virtual consulting firm specializes in the design and delivery of engaging, innovative, and effective modern blended learning. Jennifer has written and contributed to a number of well-received and highly regarded books including *The Synchronous Trainer's Survival Guide: Facilitating Successful Live Online Courses, Meetings, and Events, Live and Online!: Tips, Techniques, and Ready to Use Activities for the Virtual Classroom*, and *Tailored Learning: Designing the Blend That Fits* (co-authored with Nanette Miner). Her latest book, *Blended Learning*, introduces a new instructional design model that addresses the needs of the modern workplace and modern learners. She frequently presents in person and online for leading learning organizations around the world. Subscribe to Jennifer's blog virtually at blog.insynctraining.com or connect with her on LinkedIn (linkedin.com/in/jennifer-hofmann-dye) for new content and timely insight.

References

Biech, E., ed. 2014. *ASTD Handbook*, 2nd ed. Alexandria, VA: ASTD Press.

Christensen Institute. n.d. "Blended Learning Definitions." Christensen Institute. christenseninstitute.org/blended-learning-definitions-and-models.

Hofmann, J. 2014. *Blended Learning Instructional Design: A Modern Approach*. InSync Training, August 19. blog.insynctraining.com/modern-learning-resource-library/blended-learning-instructional-design-a-modern-approach.

Hofmann, J. 2018a. *Blended Learning*. Alexandria, VA: ATD Press.

Hofmann, J. 2018b. *Blended Learning in Practice*. The Learning Guild Research Library, May 9. learningguild.com/insights/221/blended-learning-in-practice.

Mosher, B., and C. Gottfredson. 2012. "Are You Meeting All Five Moments of Learning Need?" *Learning Solutions*, June 18. learningsolutionsmag.com/articles/949/are-you-meeting-all-five-moments-of-learning-need.

Seaman, P. 2017. "Make the Spacing Effect Work for Online Students." Portland Community College Online Learning, August. pcc.edu/online/2017/08/make-the-spacing-effect-work-for-online-students.

CHAPTER 23

The Many Aspects of Accessibility

Maureen Orey

Designing accessible learning goes beyond creating learning content that is fun, engaging, and meaningful. Fully accessible content challenges the designer to explore the learning experience from all possible angles. Consider the multiple ways that learners access content, including visual, auditory, physical, and cognitive. However, when viewed through the framework of accessibility, old-school learning styles truly don't do justice to the real need for access.

> **IN THIS CHAPTER:**
> - Explore the mindset for inclusion
> - Create accessible learning environments
> - Design for specific access needs

The Mindset for Inclusion

Accessibility requires us to carefully examine the need for access when learners cannot see, hear, or physically interact, as well as account for any learning or psychological differences that affect their ability to process content cognitively.

A word of caution—the particular challenge for talent development professionals is to consider accessibility during the needs assessment and design process. If you wait to think about accessibility until after a program is designed and developed, it's too late and you will likely need to redesign your content. If you begin with the mindset of inclusion and accessibility, you set yourself up to build inclusive content from the very beginning.

Note that in an effort to be respectful and inclusive, this section purposefully minimizes the use of the terms (labels) *disabled, disability*, and *impaired*. Instead, the language focuses on the specific way individuals must access learning content differently due to a medical or cognitive condition. The language we use reflects and influences our mindset.

So, What Does "Accessible" Really Mean?

In the context of learning design, *accessibility* does *not* mean internet bandwidth or passwords—in other words, it's not about the technical side of the computer system, although ultimately all public-facing websites and learning management systems must also be accessible to individuals with disabilities. In the context of designing learning, talent development professionals and instructional designers must become familiar with designing content to meet every major access need of the learner.

According to the Web Content Accessibility Guideline (WCAG 2.1), content should be perceivable, operable, understandable, and robust. The acronym frequently used in this approach is POUR; each aspect is summarized here:

- **Perceivable**
    - Provide text alternatives for nontext content, such as pictures and graphics.
    - Include captions and audio descriptions for multimedia content.
    - Design content that can be presented in multiple ways and include assistive technologies while retaining all relevance and meaning.
    - Enable easy ways to see and hear course content.
- **Operable**
    - Ensure all navigation is functional and available from a keyboard.
    - Give users enough time to read and interact with the content.
    - Do not use content that flickers, flashes, or blinks excessively, which can trigger seizures or other physical reactions.

- Consider the ease of course navigation and finding content.
- Design multiple inputs in addition to the keyboard, such as the ability to use a mouse, touchscreen, or voice interface.
- **Understandable**
  - Ensure that text is readable and understandable.
  - Make content appear and operate in predictable or standard ways.
  - Help users avoid navigation and interface mistakes or to correct them with ease.
- **Robust**
  - Maximize current and cutting-edge user tools for long-term compatibility.
  - Maintain quality content while ensuring accessibility.

Then There's the Legality Mindset

Disability laws have been evolving for many years. In the United States, they came on the heels of the civil rights laws of the 1960s, and represent an awakening of deeper awareness to the rights and needs of a population of people who have been marginalized by limited access over the years. The spirit of these disability laws is to provide access to information and, in turn, access to the opportunity to learn content that was previously not available to disabled individuals.

Title III of the 1991 Americans With Disabilities Act (ADA) requires educational and instructional videos to be accessible to hearing impaired and deaf individuals (this is where learning programs enter the scene). The law applies to state and local governments and some private organizations and mandates the provision of appropriate auxiliary aids and services where necessary. More information can be found in the *ADA Title III Technical Assistance Manual Covering Public Accommodations and Commercial Facilities*.

On January 18, 2017, the US Access Board published an updated set of requirements for information and communication technology (ICT) as covered by Section 508 of the Rehabilitation Act and Section 255 of the Communication Act. Section 508 requires access for both members of the public and federal employees to electronic and information technologies when developed, procured, maintained, or used by US federal agencies. The standards also apply to electronic and information technology procured by the federal government and in the public domain, including computer hardware and software, websites, phone systems, and copiers. In other words, if you work for a US federal agency, have a client who is a federal agency, receive funding from the US government, or have learning programs and content in the public domain, your content and learning programs must be compliant with the law.

The final published rule jointly updates and reorganizes the Section 508 standards and Section 255 guidelines in response to market trends and innovations, such as the convergence of technologies. The refresh also harmonizes these requirements with other guidelines and standards both in the US and abroad, including standards issued by the European Commission and with the Web Content Accessibility Guidelines (WCAG), a globally recognized voluntary consensus standard for web content and ICT.

The new standard for Section 508 is expected to require conformance to the WCAG 2.1 Level AA. But what does this mean? The WCAG 2.1 Success Criteria are categorized according to three levels that provide successively greater degrees of accessibility:

- **Level A** (minimum) provides the most basic web accessibility features.
- **Level AA** (midrange) deals with the biggest and most common barriers for disabled users.
- **Level AAA** (highest) gives the highest level of web accessibility.

Conformance at a higher level indicates conformance at lower levels; that is, conformance to Level AA necessarily implies conformance to Level A.

Level A sets a minimum level of accessibility and does not generally achieve broad accessibility for many situations. Level AA is proposed as the new standard for the anticipated refresh of the Access Board Standard for Section 508. WCAG does not always recommend requiring Level AAA conformance as a general policy, because it is not possible to satisfy all Level AAA success criteria for some content.

Creating Accessible Learning Environments

Learning and development programs that are designed and delivered in organizations around the world can be broken down into three basic categories of learning environments:

- Brick and mortar (in person, instructor led)
- Online, instructor led (vILT)
- Online, asynchronous e-learning

Each category requires its own set of design considerations for accessibility. Preliminary scenarios regarding program design and development considerations are shown in Table 23-1. As you review them, you will notice that some of the development opportunities focus on the people aspect, not just instructional design and technology. For example, when considering a culture of inclusion (not just compliance), one of the most important aspects of employee development and learning is on-the-job training (OJT). When training a new employee, their supervisor or manager may work directly with the individual and can have a significant impact on their learning experience—for better or for worse. Individuals who conduct on-the-job training must be educated not only on the legal requirements but also on how to handle the human components of an employee with disability-related needs.

Table 23-1. Accessibility Considerations for the Categories of Learning Environments

	In Person, Instructor Led	Online, Instructor Led	Online, Asynchronous
Scenarios	• Classroom training • Coaching and mentoring • On the job	• Webinars • Webcasts • Conference calls	• E-learning (all forms) • Websites and wikis • Learning management system
Considerations	• Physical access to the facility • Designing accessible curriculum and materials • Prepare the trainers so they're aware of any access needs of participants • Supervisor preparation and awareness	• Verify software accessibility • Designing accessible curriculum and materials • Prepare presenters and SMEs so they're aware of any access needs of participants	• Verify software accessibility • Designing accessible curriculum and materials • Provide easy access to assistance when help is needed

Instructional Design Strategies for Access and Inclusion

Sir Francis Bacon is known for saying that knowledge is power, yet the opportunity to learn can be disempowering to a disadvantaged group in ways that are invisible to the advantaged group. It seems that some learning professionals are hesitant to embrace the importance of designing accessible learning programs because they are viewed as complex, cumbersome, and time intensive. Instructional design has evolved over the years; new and creative ways have emerged to implement fun, interactive games and methodologies that we hope enhance the learning experience. However, it often seems that most initial design approaches assume the participants have no barriers to learning. To design accessible learning, begin with a positive, inclusive mindset and a willingness to accept the challenge.

Let's explore five instructional design strategies for access and inclusion.

Use Design Thinking to Discover Creative Approaches

According to IDEO CEO Tim Brown, "Design thinking can be described as a discipline that uses the designer's sensibility and methods to match people's needs with what is technologically feasible." Design thinking is solution-focused, not problem-focused, and instructional designers need to draw upon logic, imagination, intuition, and systematic reasoning to explore the possibilities of creating the best outcome that will benefit the learners. At first, it may be helpful to work with colleagues to explore each aspect of design thinking. For example, assign one aspect of design thinking to each team member, then talk through the course design together—similar to Edward DeBono's "Six Thinking Hats." This approach can be helpful because you really can't make a course accessible until you have envisioned how best to communicate a concept using different methodologies. Begin with a mindset for inclusion and the job will go more smoothly than if you try to redesign it after the fact—508 or WCAG compliance is not an "add in."

Write Clear and Concise Learning Objectives

Well-written learning objectives provide a clear picture of the performance you expect from learners as a result of the lesson. Robert Mager said that learning objectives should be specific, measurable objectives that guide instructors and aid students in the learning process. His ABCD model for learning objectives includes four elements: audience, behavior, condition, and degree of mastery needed. This is no different when writing learning objectives for participants with or without disabilities. Each aspect of the model is important; however, when designing accessible learning, the needs of your audience and the behavior to perform on the job are critical to keep in mind.

Instructional designers frequently make two mistakes when writing learning objectives:
- The objective is too vague and does not focus on the particular behavior expected. For example:
  - Vague objective: Participants will learn the key aspects of essential communication.
  - More specific objective: Participants will demonstrate the four steps to having a difficult conversation.
- Too many behaviors are included in one objective. Each objective should be written to support one behavior, such as demonstrate, identify, discuss, or explain. Bloom's taxonomy is a great resource for active verbs to describe the specific behavioral change desired.

Create a Course Structure That Makes Sense

Have you ever been a participant in a poorly designed course? Or tried to complete an activity that had incomplete or confusing directions? A course structure that flows well and integrates all key concepts of the content creates a positive learning experience, reduces confusion, and presents the content in a digestible format. When designing for asynchronous e-learning courses, the flow is typically in this order: welcome, instructions, objectives, course content, assessment, summary, next steps, and exit instructions. Always consider the content—is it linear and does it have to be presented in a particular order? Or are you starting with the least important topic and leaving the most important for the last part of the course, when participants have less stamina for focused learning?

Provide Both Content and Context

Simon Sinek is known for his book *Start With Why* (2009), in which he explores the importance of helping people understand the reason behind what we do. Learning professionals can take a page from his book and add more context to the training programs we develop. You can do this by incorporating meaning or emotion into your content through pictures and graphics. It's also important to add "alt text" (alternative text) that effectively describes all visuals, such as pictures, icons, and graphics. *Alt text* is described as a word or phrase that can be inserted as an attribute in an HTML (Hypertext Markup Language) document to tell website viewers the nature or contents of an image. Alt text appears in a text box and should be readable by screen reader software.

Another way to add context is through audio description of videos. Audio description provides a vocal summary of what is happening on the screen for people who are visually impaired; it is similar to how closed captioning adds context to the background sounds for people with audio access needs.

Design for Specific Access Needs

The next aspect to consider is the learner's individual learning needs based on their medical or cognitive condition. Talent development professionals are not new to needs assessment in learning and development; however, the focus has traditionally been centered on the learner's topical or competency needs, as well as how to design and deliver the content most effectively. Essentially, the 508 and WCAG requirements ask us to add another layer of complexity to the needs assessment considerations.

The four main conditions to consider in every learning environment are shown in Table 23-2.

Table 23-2. Four Main Needs Assessment Conditions for Every Learning Environment

Auditory	Visual	Physical	Cognitive
• Deaf • Hard of hearing • Hearing impaired • Cognitive processing • ADHD	• Blind • Limited vision • Dyslexia • Color-blind • Cognitive processing • ADHD	• Mobility • Ambulatory • Motor coordination • Hand/eye coordination	• Ability to focus • Learning differences • Cognitive processing • Attention deficits • Stress or anxiety

Perhaps the most interesting thing to notice in the conditions table is that there are overlapping access concerns. For example, someone who is deaf or hard of hearing will have an auditory access concern; however, some learning differences also have an auditory processing component. Similarly, someone who is blind or has limited vision has a visual impairment, while some learning differences (such as dyslexia) have a visual processing aspect that would be accommodated in a remarkably similar way. In many ways, this is like the physical and architectural changes that were made in the early 1990s after the passage of the ADA, which regarded physical curb cuts at intersections for people who use wheelchairs. One unexpected benefit of accommodating people using wheelchairs was that delivery personnel and parents with children in strollers immediately found a benefit too! In a nutshell, accommodating one learning need will benefit more than one type of condition; in fact, you may find that accommodating the different learning needs may also benefit individuals with language or literacy needs.

Let's Put This All Together

Our concept matrix pairs the three different learning environments with the four main access needs. This matrix can be used as a big picture tool to identify accessible design strategies. Across the top are the three main learning environments and down the left side are the four main learning access needs. Each box in the chart provides some preliminary ideas for accommodating the learning needs in each learning environment. Note that this matrix is not a comprehensive list; it is designed to provide basic initial design considerations. You can download a copy of this matrix from the handbook website at ATDHandbook3.org.

Final Thoughts

Be sure to test your assumptions about accessibility. Never assume the program works like you imagined it will. A designer once told me that if we simply designed a course using HTML 5.0, it would automatically be accessible. Six months later, after testing for accessibility, we were still redesigning the program to be compliant with the law. Test your process and your design along the way to ensure that it is working as you intended it to in the design process.

About the Author

Maureen Orey, CPTD, is an expert in designing, developing, and delivering high-impact, inclusive learning solutions. She founded her boutique corporate training and consulting firm in 2009. Her mission is simple: to help organizations develop strong and resilient leaders and employees. She can be contacted at maureen@wlpgroup.com.

References

Americans with Disabilities Act. *ADA Title III Technical Assistance Manual: Covering Public Accommodations and Commercial Facilities.* ada.gov/taman3.html#III-4.3500.

Bono, E.D. 2010. *Six Thinking Hats.* New York: Little Brown and Company.

Brown, T. 2008. "Definitions of Design Thinking." IDEO blog, September 7. designthinking.ideo
.com/blog/definitions-of-design-thinking.
Orey, M. 2017. "Designing Section 508 Compliant Learning." *TD at Work*. Alexandria, VA:
ATD Press
Sinek, S. 2009. *Start With Why*. New York: Penguin.

Recommended Resources
Lindstrom, C. 2017. *What's Missing? Best Practices for Teaching Students With Disabilities*.
Lanham, MD: Rowman & Littlefield

CHAPTER 24

Learning Transfer: The Missing Link

Emma Weber

One of the biggest challenges that businesses have always faced in the development and delivery of training relates to what happens after the training course is complete; is the company going to see a real change in employee behaviour?

The answer most often is no. Achieving truly lasting change requires the most robust training reinforcement approaches, an approach that creates and measures learning transfer.

IN THIS CHAPTER:
- State the missing link in learning and why it has been missing for so long
- Name the fundamental principles of successful learning transfer
- Discover the steps to a transfer journey that delivers and demonstrates business outcomes

There have been many debates around the concepts of making training stick and the organisational benefits of embedded learning and the like. These, of course, have merit, but they are predominantly about people being able to remember or recite what they were taught. Retention of learning in terms of what people actually remember is rarely the issue. This should not be confused with learning transfer, which is about changing, in a very practical way, how individuals operate in the workplace after a training program.

Study after study shows that learning approaches are typically only around 10 to 20 percent effective. This means that the return on financial and time investments in training is rarely, if ever, fully maximised. Employers are often unsure how to hold people accountable to change after training, and thus they are unable to ensure effective learning transfer; in essence, people follow a strategy of hope!

Meeting the learning transfer challenge isn't helped by the fact that one of the key metrics of evaluating an L&D team is "training days delivered." This means that if participants leave a training event, in theory, knowing what to do and demonstrating the desired new skills or behaviour in the classroom, this metric is satisfied regardless of whether that knowledge is ever actually implemented back in the workplace. Even when the intention to transfer is captured, this still isn't a measure of whether an outcome happens. As a profession, we have the opportunity to hold ourselves to a higher standard and start creating and demonstrating real behaviour change.

Whenever L&D professionals have a "light bulb moment" and recognise this flaw in the evaluation of training, they realise that providing training is only half of their job. They also need to ensure that what they taught is transferring to the workplace to demonstrate real business benefit.

Learning's Missing Link

Clearly, for the learning transfer problem to have been evident for so long, there has to be something missing in the instructional design process (IDP). The acknowledgment that behavioural change is the key to massively improving business results and learning transfer will close that gap. If there is no robust learning transfer after training, it doesn't matter how well the rest of the process—analysis through to evaluation—has been implemented.

Why It's Been Missing for So Long

The individual elements of the IDP have been perfected over the years, but because training still falls short of meeting goals, there must be a missing link. But why is this link missing? Let's review a few causes:

- **No ownership.** Too often, the different parts of the IDP are divided up across resources, and there is no common finish line for each stage. This simply means there is no ownership present.

- **Wrong objectives.** When planning a program, the wrong objectives are often mistakenly set. From the beginning, the objective is set to gauge what people *intend* to do and what they demonstrate they *can do* in the classroom. Rarely are they set to deliver results after the training is complete. With these loose objectives, there's limited chance that learning transfer can occur because it wasn't included or prioritized within the objective stage. You cannot hit a target without having one to aim at. The ROI Instrument Alignment Model can help you consider learning objectives in addition to preparing for evaluation. *Beyond Learning Objectives: Develop Measurable Objectives That Link to the Bottom Line*, by Jack and Patti Phillips, is a great resource for helping identify the difference between learning objectives and behavioural objectives.
- **Obsession with content.** L&D functions have become obsessed with finding new and innovative ways of getting content delivered, especially through the avenue of technology. While the intention is good, it has also allowed people to believe that improving the content and delivery will create a behaviour change when this simply isn't enough.
- **Obsession with evaluation.** Level 1 evaluation, Reaction, represents the Holy Grail of learning and development, but it does not *create* change; it only measures the extent of it. Forget the happy sheet!
- **Focus on learning, not on change.** Effective learning transfer needs strategies to promote change. If the training program's primary goal isn't to create behavioural change, then how can we expect this to be the result?

At the very beginning stage of the IDP process, when analysing the business situation and identifying if learning could be the solution to the problem, you also need to ask the question: Do I need to supplement the learning with a learning transfer solution?

In most cases the answer will be yes, and this is when you come to grips with the concept of near and far learning transfer. Patti Shank (2004) captures this beautifully in her article for *Learning Solutions* magazine, "Can They Do It in the Real World? Designing for Transfer of Learning":

This concept is called near and far transfer. That's a bit of a misnomer because it's a continuum from near(er) to far(ther) transfer, with potentially higher degrees of transfer along the way. Near(er) transfer is transfer between very similar contexts.... Near(er) transfer is generally what is needed for tasks that are routine and consistent.

Far(ther) transfer refers to learning applied in real life situations that are somewhat to greatly different than the learning contexts. This is most needed for tasks that are executed differently depending on the situation. The hallmark of far(ther) transfer is the need to adapt actions based on judgment.

In my book, this pretty much means anything that involves people or situations that change!

It's perhaps easier to confirm when you don't need a specific learning transfer solution or when it won't add value. Ask yourself, is this training program taking the form of a performance support tool? Imagine the program is a piece of content that the individual has sought out to solve a particular issue at a moment of need. In that case, it is less likely that a transfer strategy would be required, as it's highly likely that the information would be applied because the person has an immediate need for it.

Some may think, "Perhaps all learning should be like this: We should always learn in the moment of need." I would argue that for some skills, particularly technical skills, that is ideal. However, with many learning programs we are talking more about developing softer skills (or the human skills, as I now like to call them!)—things like listening, leadership, and communication. These skills are ingrained as part of who we are. Judgment is required. They go beyond an immediate, specific need (like having a performance conversation), to helping individuals grow in who they are.

In this chapter we are exclusively talking about the problem of scrap or waste learning, where learning isn't applied back in the workplace, and how this can be resolved. Our discussion assumes that you have a training program in place that is designed for transfer. Ask yourself:

- Have I designed the learning program to a point that it can be applied?
- Do people know how to apply what they learn?
- Have I given time for reflection in the training and given people the opportunity to work out how it is relevant to them?
- Fundamentally, have they reached the stage where they can then apply what they've learned?

If the answer to these questions is "yes," then transfer is the next step supporting them to apply it. But the training has to get them to a point where they can do what they *actually* need to do.

In addition to the program being designed for behavioural change for a whole host of people, it needs to be able to be applied back in the workplace at an individual level. If you find yourself or the participant saying, "This isn't relevant to my role" or "I can't apply this for another six months," then a transfer strategy isn't going to produce positive outcomes. Additionally, if it's a behaviour that will be used by the individual only once every few months, rather than on a weekly or daily basis, it is much harder to create transfer, and a different strategy could be required. An example of this would be focusing on presentation skills training for someone who rarely presents as part of their role.

Learning transfer can also be difficult for something like a Preparing for Tough Communications program. I was recently speaking with a client about a program they were creating to help upskill leaders in having tough communications. The transfer challenge was that in attendees' minds this was a skill they would need infrequently, because they may have a tough conversation only once a quarter or even less. I suggested they switch the program to a focus on meaningful conversations and cover the types of conversations that can happen all the time at different levels.

Think of it this way: The tough or "high stakes" conversation can be compared to lifting 200 pounds. You can't walk straight into a gym and begin by lifting that amount. You need to work your way up over time and with repetition using smaller weights. With time, practice, and experience, you'll eventually reach your goal of lifting 200 pounds. You can't expect to go from lifting 20 pounds to 200 pounds immediately. And comparatively speaking, if you haven't been practicing with 50-pound or 100-pound "situations," lifting the 200 pounds straight away would be extremely challenging. If you have identified what a 50-pound situation looks like and are managing it on a daily or weekly basis, then the 200-pound situations won't seem like such a challenge.

Key to transfer success in this case was shifting the focus from a program that would be applied in rare situations to one that could be applied weekly. And how do we set up people to decide what a 50-pound conversation is for them? We ask them! They need to identify it themselves to promote accountability and ownership. Then, throughout the transfer period they could track how they are doing with these different weights of conversations.

The Principles of Learning Transfer

Knowing the three fundamental principles of good learning transfer—reflection versus reminding, ownership, and accountability—is a great place to start when you are deciding your learning transfer strategy. Let's look at each of these individually.

Reflection Versus Reminders

You can't nag someone into long-term behavioural change. We all know from our own personal experience that when we are reminded of behavioural change, it becomes more about the person who is reminding or nagging than the person hoping to change themselves. Regardless of how the message is worded, reminding someone to take action on what they have learned isn't an effective way to create that change and make it stick.

It's easy to fall into the follow-up trap of pushing additional learning content out to participants to deepen the message. This provides little value when creating and measuring learning transfer and change—and can even be a bit of a red herring. The Ebbinghaus forgetting curve and discoveries in neuroscience have educated us in the importance of spaced learning for memory and recall. In reality, however, the learning transfer phase is about promoting behavioural change and not about pushing more content for retention. For adult learners, it's rarely because people don't know what they've learned that they fail to apply it. At worst, if learners can't remember content, they typically have very easy access to tools where they can reference it. It's much more likely to be our own thoughts, values, feelings, beliefs, fears, and needs that control our behaviours and are either a barrier or a doorway to effective behavioural change. Our internal dialogue ultimately controls our behaviours, so the goal should be to encourage people to reflect on what is actually happening with the application of learning, rather than reflecting on the learning content.

The key to effective reflection is to use an intrapersonal approach, including internal dialogue and imagination. When people reflect, they are opening up a conversation with themselves. This is one of the key reasons that chatbots can be so valuable in this realm. This rich, reflective state is easier to achieve one on one rather than in a group—or solo if you are using technology. Often the higher the psychological safety, the easier it is for a person to reflect. This could be one of the contributing factors as to why it's harder for a manager to help an individual with learning transfer conversations than an external or uninvolved person.

Note also that we aren't talking about reflection on the learning itself but specifically a reflection on the application of the learning. This includes application in the real world in real time. Learning within the flow of our work has become a buzz phrase; learning transfer requires learners to reflect on how they apply what they learned to their work.

Ownership

The work of Daniel Pink in *Drive: The Surprising Truth About What Motivates Us*, supports the idea that autonomy is critical in adult learning. Self-determination theory, developed by Edward Deci and Richard Ryan, highlights the importance of intrinsic motivation for behaviour change, with the drivers being autonomy, competence, and relatedness. Giving people ownership of what they are putting into place is therefore key to successful outcomes.

Anne Bartlett-Bragg talks about "scaffolding" for technology adoption, which is a form of guiding and shaping that ultimately leaves the final decision to the learner. In learning transfer, this principle can be applied to scaffolding autonomy. An example in the learning transfer context could be to allow learners to decide when to conduct a reflective conversation about their learning. A second example is to allow people to determine which goals in their action plan to address first. The scaffolding is the framework for the conversation; the autonomy is allowing people to decide what they use the time to work on.

Likewise, we can help learners create ownership by trusting them to choose their own goals for an action plan rather than suggesting what their organisational goals should be. Empowering people to take ownership over what they choose to change will lead to more effective and sustained growth.

Accountability

Although accountability has historically been viewed through a negative lens, this likely stems from a legacy of command and control leadership styles, where people are used to being told what to do. For adult learners, being told what to do isn't an effective way to create behaviour change. That being said, there is an opportunity to create an environment where accountability looks more like empowering people to keep themselves accountable to themselves rather than being pushed by a manager. Accountability can be achieved by asking questions about how the learners will follow through.

"How will you hold yourself accountable for following through?" can be a really good question to ask (just make sure to use the right tone!). Many learners will immediately know what they can do to hold themselves accountable. If they need a prompt, three areas to consider could be rewards, reminders, and relationships. See the resources section for an animated video that shares ideas for each area.

The most effective way to intertwine these three principles of reflection, ownership, and accountability is with a conversation. That will, in most cases, be with another person who is able to support someone to have a conversation with themselves. As described, if you can tap into a person's internal dialogue, it's the fastest and most permanent way to shift behaviours.

Where to Begin Your Journey?

What can you do now to start bridging the knowing-doing gap and creating true business outcomes from learning? Choose your methodology, adjust the finish line, and get to grips with action planning, and you will be well on your way! When you are beginning your learning transfer journey, get clear on the conversation methodology that you will use for transfer, focusing on driving ownership and accountability.

One example of a learning transfer conversation methodology is the TLA (Turning Learning Into Action) Conversation model. The TLA model recommends holding conversations over a period of weeks while the participant is embedding the learning. As a rough guide (which will depend on the type and depth of the changes being made (these are three 30-minute conversations over a 10- to 12-week period). The TLA model expresses the interplay between structure and flexibility that creates enhanced coaching and differentiates TLA.

ACTION is an acronym for the stages that the conversation must pass through to successfully facilitate transfer of learning and behaviour change back in the workplace:

- **Accountability.** Establish the process context and the learning transfer conversation parameters.
- **Calibration.** Create a score for where the learner is now, as well as their future target.
- **Target.** Where the individual is trying to go for the session.
- **Information.** Gather information about what occurs in the workplace and highlight the context with the learner.
- **Option.** Define the options that are available in this situation.
- **Next steps.** Plan for how the individual is going to commit to action and move toward their target.

Having a methodology means it is replicable across cohorts and programs. It is program agnostic and doesn't rely on adding more content in. The only content of the conversation is the action plan, which is driven by the individual. Whatever conversation methodology you choose or whether you create your own, ensure that the driver is helping the individual have a conversation with themselves to drive accountability and ownership.

A next key step is to educate the learner by identifying their new finish line and setting expectations up front.

Learning transfer can't be presented as a surprise or as optional! When given the choice of being held accountable or not, it's human nature that we would rather not change—change is easy; it's just a whole lot easier not to change.

In their book, *The Six Disciplines of Breakthrough Learning*, Calhoun Wick, Andrew Jefferson, and Roy Pollock talk about the importance of the finish line. Educating the learners that the process of learning isn't focused exclusively on receiving the content or instructional aspect is key. We have historically set the expectation that learning happens in a classroom. As we have shifted more toward virtual learning, this has started to change the notion of the classroom being at the heart of learning, but the idea that content and instruction are the crux of learning still remains. Helping people see that the learning doesn't finish when they leave the learning environment—be that virtual or face-to-face—is essential in shifting the finish line of learning and creating behavioural change and program outcomes. The true finish line is back in the workplace, where the new information is applied to consistently improve business outcomes.

Finally, connect the bridge between the program and the behavioural change with meaningful action planning.

Action plans are the bridge between learning and behaviour change. Yet they are often rushed, ignored, or pushed off the learning agenda to allow time to cover more content. Once someone has left the learning environment, their perspective shifts on what is possible to implement. Despite the best intentions, unless people commit to an action plan as part of a learning event it is rarely completed afterward, let alone followed through with. It is essential for actions to be captured during the instructional phase.

Most important, don't leave developing action plans till the end of a program. This is a bit counterintuitive because how can people complete action plans when they haven't completed the learning? It's a trade-off. The upside of completing more thoughtful action plans during the learning program outweighs the benefit of having rushed plans at the end of the program.

For a free action planning tool, visit turninglearningintoaction.com or turn to the handbook's website at ATDHandbook3.org.

Many facilitators are walking away from the humble action plan because they worry about what will happen to it afterward. And of course, what happens to the action plan is the crucial question in ensuring success from the process.

In a robust transfer environment, the action plan becomes the document that is used as the basis for the learning transfer conversations, hence the quality of the action plan is crucial to successful learning transfer outcomes.

The Powerful Combination of Data and Learning Transfer

Your learning transfer strategy and learning data strategy will be closely linked. Transfer will create the outcomes, while the data captures them. And of course, data can also be used throughout the learning transfer process to identify and minimize the risks of program outcomes not being met.

In the ACTION methodology, you'll notice references to calibrating scoring goals on a scale of 1–10. The specific number isn't important, but that people are moving in a direction of improvement is key. As a basis of data collection, these numbers can be used to track progress as they are captured in the learning transfer conversation. Tracking these action plan progress numbers can be supplemented with outcome-based questions.

When this data is captured 10 to 12 weeks after the program's content phase is complete, a picture can be created of the benefits and the impact of the learning implementation. This process is far superior to a happy sheet capturing Level 1 data at the end of a learning initiative and it opens the opportunity to capture data reflecting both behaviour change and business impact—data that can then be used to calculate the ROI of the learning. One practical tip when capturing summative data is to label the tool a Progress Review Form rather than a Feedback Form. The Progress Review Form, which is an opportunity for learners to share their progress with the organisation, has a much higher perceived value than completing a feedback form and therefore a much higher response rate. Typically, 80 percent plus of learners share progress review data with their organization 10 to 12 weeks after a training program.

Trish Uhl from Owl's Ledge challenged my thinking about data and learning transfer, highlighting the power that using technology in transfer can bring to data capture. In conversation with Trish, while I was insisting that working with chatbots in learning transfer had created a whole new opportunity to scale a person-centred approach to transfer, Trish saw the potential that chatbots created for generating rich data about the progress and outcomes of learning. While valuable, it's essential that this data is treated within the legal and moral bounds of data privacy frameworks, including aggregating and deidentifying data, holding it securely, and deleting it appropriately.

The data captured can be used to improve the learning design and, in due course, learning outcomes. Leveraging AI, text analysis, trend analysis, and factor analysis to unpack that data can provide valuable data insights for the learning team. It can also be used to identify what outcomes have been generated and provide actionable insights for the organisation.

> **COACH M AND LEARNING TRANSFER**
>
> Learning technology is a fast-moving arena. Solutions using technology are inherently more scalable and repeatable than a people-based approach. When choosing which technology to use for learning transfer, consider whether the technology aligns with the principles of successful transfer. In pursuit of a technology that supports conversations, experiments showed that chatbots were a tool that could be used effectively in learning transfer. Participants on average spent 20 minutes having a conversation with "Coach M," the Lever-designed chatbot. When chatting with Coach M, participants slowed down and reflected on the action plans they created, shared progress, and strategized how to overcome barriers that could derail the behavioural change process.
>
> A learning transfer chatbot requires you to forget everything you know about chatbots. Most people have had experiences with customer service chatbots that are designed to help answer your questions. A learning transfer chatbot works in the reverse—it is designed to ask the participant questions. The chatbot offers a high level of psychological safety due to its inability to judge. This can help learners slow down, reflect, and have a powerful conversation with themselves.
>
> Coach M learnt from the nuances of the Turning Learning Into Action methodology based on the 120,000 human conversations Lever had over a 12-year period. Coach M can simulate a learning transfer conversation to truly leverage what's possible using emerging technology in learning.
>
> (For more on chatbots see "Bayer: Chatbot Coaching for Learning Transfer" from ATD's 10 Minute Case Study Series, which is referenced at the end of this chapter.)

Final Thoughts

Consider learning's missing link through the lens of learning transfer. This should encourage you to ask even more questions about transfer—more than one chapter can answer. Engage your colleagues in these discussions, experiment, collect evidence of behavioural change, and continue to stretch your thinking beyond the traditional context and confines of the learning environment.

Get curious about what happens when learners leave the classroom, whether that classroom is virtual or in person. How do they integrate the behaviours into their day-to-day role? How can you support, challenge, and capture the outcomes for continued learning and improvement for all? How can you embrace this as part of your role and remit to get even closer to the outcomes that drive business results?

The great news is that for most organizations it doesn't mean learning programs need to be redesigned or rewritten from scratch. In fact, organizations generally have an extremely high quality of learning design and execution. There is little to improve on in learning design—the race for learning excellence, and indeed organizational excellence, will now be won by those who develop and deploy effective learning transfer strategies. Those who realise the tools that can aid learners to slow down and reflect, develop their meta cognition, and provide data along the journey will have a true advantage. Developing leaders and organisations fit for tomorrow will require us as learning professionals to drive accountability and ownership in both our learners and ourselves. Are you up for the challenge?

About the Author

Emma Weber, CEO and founder of Lever—Transfer of Learning, is a learning transfer authority. She makes it her mission in life to make a difference in learning transfer worldwide. Frustrated by the amount of learning that is wasted, Emma created the Turning Learning Into Action methodology in hopes of solving this problem. This methodology is deployed in 20 countries and 12 languages thanks to her talented team and Coach M, a conversational intelligence program. Coach M is challenging the industry's thinking of what's possible in learning transfer. Emma shares her passion and expertise through conversations with others and her writing, including her first book, *Turning Learning Into Action: A Proven Methodology for Effective Transfer of Learning*, published by Kogan Page in 2014. Reach out to join the conversation through email (emma@leverlearning.com) or on her website (transferoflearning.com).

References

Phillips, J.J., and P.P. Phillips. 2008. *Beyond Learning Objectives: Develop Measurable Objectives That Link to the Bottom Line.* Alexandria, VA: ASTD Press.

Pink, D. 2011. *Drive: The Surprising Truth About What Motivates Us.* New York: Riverhead Books.

Shank, P. 2004. "Can They Do It in the Real World? Designing for Transfer of Learning." *Learning Solutions Magazine*, September 7. learningsolutionsmag.com/articles/288/can-they-do-it-in-the-real-world-designing-for-transfer-of-learning.

Weber, E. 2014, *Turning Learning to Action: A Proven Methodology for Effective Learning Transfer*. London: Kogan Page.

Wick, C., A. Jefferson, and R. Pollock. 2010. *The Six Disciplines of Breakthrough Learning.* San Francisco: Pfeiffer.

Recommended Resources

ATD Case Study Team. 2019. "Bayer: Chatbot Coaching for Learning Transfer." ATD Case by Case, November 20. casebycase.td.org/bayer-chatbot-coaching-for-learning-transfer.

Dirksen, J. 2016. *Design for How People Learn*, 2nd ed. Indianapolis, IN: New Riders.

Turning Learning Into Action. n.d. "Online Action Planning Tool." turninglearningintoaction.com.

Weber, E. 2021. "Accountability Video." YouTube video, June 1. youtu.be/Bkeb79rEaWg.

CHAPTER 25

Critical Tools to Support the Fundamentals of E-Learning

Diane Elkins

A plethora of e-learning tools is available. How can you make strategic decisions about which ones you need to create e-learning content? While we can't cover all of them, let's focus on those that seem to be in greatest demand by TD professionals—specifically those related to self-paced e-learning. You'll need to start by assessing the technology required for e-learning development and then determine how to choose the right tool for you.

IN THIS CHAPTER:
- Evaluate your technology needs for e-learning development
- Create a wish list of the types of tools you'll need
- Establish criteria to help select the right tools

If you've ever looked on YouTube to learn how to fix a toilet or bake a potato, you've experienced e-learning. In the broadest sense of the word, e-learning can be created with nothing more than a keyboard or a smartphone camera.

But to create engaging, interactive e-learning content that meets an organization's talent development needs, you'll probably want a few more tools in your toolbox.

There are three main types of e-learning and each one requires a slightly different combination of tools:

- **Self-paced.** Self-paced e-learning, often referred to as asynchronous learning, can be taken by a learner at any time. It can be as simple as a series of text webpages or a single video, and as complex as branching or gamified simulations.
- **Virtual classroom.** Often called a webinar or virtual instructor-led training (vILT), this is a live web-based event with an instructor and participants who all go through the session together. Communication may be one-way or it may be interactive. vILT programs can be recorded and played on-demand as self-paced e-learning. Check chapter 26 for more information on this type of content.
- **Cohort based.** With a mix of synchronous and asynchronous features, cohort-based training has an instructor and participants who all go through the e-learning program at the same general time. There is a start and end date with weekly content and activity assignments (the synchronous aspect). However, each participant can review the content and complete the activities at any point during the week (the asynchronous aspect).

This chapter will help you make strategic decisions about what tools you might need to create e-learning programs, focusing primarily on self-paced e-learning.

It's important to note that products are born, get rebranded, get updated, and go away. Companies start, merge, rebrand, and end. Thus, while the names and descriptions of specific products in this chapter are current at the time of publication, they will likely change over time.

E-Learning Authoring Tools

An e-learning authoring tool is software used for primary course creation. You would use this type of tool to build course pages, add media and interactions, and publish your course.

Just about every e-learning authoring tool has the following capabilities:
- Add text and graphics.
- Add audio and video.
- Create simple quizzes.
- Publish the course to HTML5.
- Communicate with a learning management system (LMS).

Tools tend to differentiate themselves in the following areas:
- Price
- Learning curve
- Ease of use
- Feature set
- Authoring environment

The more you know about what you want your finished e-learning program to look like and how you want it to function, the better you can select the tools that are best for you.

> **DO YOU NEED AN AUTHORING TOOL?**
>
> No, you don't. Most e-learning authoring tools generate HTML5 for the published course output. The authoring tool makes it so that you don't need to program your own code (such as HTML5, JavaScript, or CSS). But you could—you can create an engaging, interactive e-learning course by coding it yourself.
>
> Advantages of programming a course include the ability to create exactly what you want, not being tied to a specific tool that may or may not be around in a year or two, and possibly future-proofing your course. (Custom-programmed courses tend to have "cleaner" code than those that use the auto-generated code from an authoring tool.)
>
> However, programming is a time-consuming task performed by often expensive resources. Hand-coded courses require more decisions (since nothing is built in) and perhaps more quality assurance testing (since everything is made from scratch).

Price

Authoring tools can range from completely free to several thousand dollars. Some tools you purchase outright, and others use a subscription model. Others (such as Adobe Captivate), let you choose between the two pricing models.

Free Tools

Some authoring tools are available completely for free. Some are open source (such as H5P), some are limited (freemium) versions of fee-based tools (such as iSpring Free), and some are from individuals or private companies who just want to share what they've created.

However, just because they don't cost anything to use, doesn't mean that they are free—you may still need to budget for IT infrastructure requirements. For example, Adapt is a free, open-source authoring tool, but it needs to be installed on your own servers. If you don't have servers to install it on, you can pay a third party (such as Learning Pool) to host it for you.

Another way to author your courses for free is to use tools you already have. If you don't need something complex, for example, you might be able to:
- Create what you need in PowerPoint.
- Assemble a collection of existing assets on an intranet page.
- Use the authoring capabilities built into your learning management system.

Tracy Parish maintains a great list of free tools for e-learning development; you can find a link to that in this chapter's additional resources.

One-Time Purchases

For tools you purchase outright (which are usually installed software versus web-based software), you pay your money once, install the software, and use it as long as you want. At some point, an update will likely be available, and you can choose whether you want to pay for the upgrade (often with a 50 percent savings off the original price) and get the new features or stay with the version you have.

Some purchased tools have an optional annual service fee that provides ongoing customer support and all software updates.

One-time purchase agreements are especially helpful if you have limited funding. For example, you have grant funding this year but might not have funds next year. If you buy your authoring tool outright, you can continue to use it even though your money has run out. However, you will need to update the tool eventually once the technology becomes outdated.

Subscription-Based Tools

Subscription-based tools (also known as Software as a Service, SaaS) can be web-based or software you install on your computer. You pay a monthly or annual fee and can use the software as long as you keep paying for the subscription. When your subscription runs out, you lose the ability to create or edit your work. In most cases, you can continue to use the published e-learning content after your subscription ends, but you wouldn't be able to update it. Software upgrades are generally included in the subscription price.

If you want to always have the latest and greatest features, the subscription-based tools will likely be the best choice. But you do have to plan for the ongoing subscription costs.

> **HOW IMPORTANT IS PRICE?**
>
> It's tempting to choose the least expensive tool. With authoring tools as with cars, it's helpful to think about the total cost of ownership. Bigger than the cost of your software is the time it takes you to create e-learning content. If a tool lets you create e-learning content more quickly, it might cost less in the long run, even if it costs more up front. The bigger cost still is the impact to the organization for effective versus ineffective training. If a less expensive tool doesn't let you create high-impact training, then it isn't worth the price.

Learning Curve and Ease of Use

The learning curve describes how easy or hard it is to learn how to use the tool initially. Ease of use is how quickly and easily you work in the tool once you know how to use it. For example, you might have a tool that takes a while to learn, but once you know what to do, you can work very quickly (and vice versa).

In general, tools that are easier to learn and use are less robust, and tools that take longer to use are more robust. For example, some tools are based on templates where you select from certain content blocks or layouts, and you fill out a form with your content. You don't have to figure out how to set up what you want, and the graphic design is often done for you. However, you can only make something if there's a template for it. Articulate Rise 360 and Gomo are examples of this type of tool (Figures 25-1 and 25-2).

Figure 25-1. Adding a Content Block in Articulate Rise 360

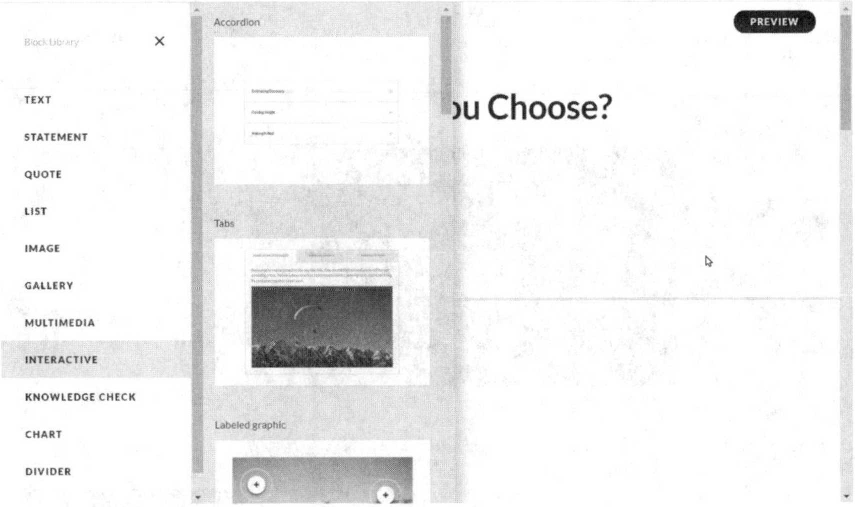

Figure 25-2. Configuring the Tabs Content Block in Articulate Rise 360

More robust tools (such as Adobe Captivate, Articulate Storyline 360, and Lectora) let you create just about anything you can imagine (with some limits). However, you'll need to determine how to mix and match the software features to construct what you want, and you'll need to make it look nice (Figures 25-3, 25-4, and 25-5).

Figure 25-3. Time Management Interaction Created in Articulate Storyline 360

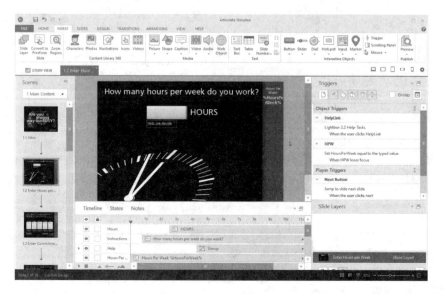

Figure 25-4. Branching Scenario in Adobe Captivate

Figure 25-5. Meeting Expense Calculator Created in Lectora

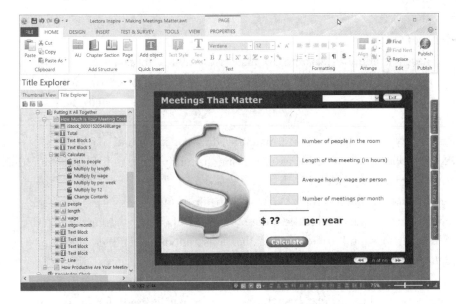

You don't necessarily have to give up power to gain ease of use. When selecting an authoring tool, look for time-saving features such as:
- Keyboard shortcuts and customizable toolbars
- Built-in templates
- Master slides
- Built-in media libraries and editing tools (so you don't have to go to third-party tools and platforms)
- The ability to easily reuse assets
- Intuitive user interface and similarity to tools you already know (for example, the Adobe Captivate interface will feel familiar to Adobe users, while the Articulate Storyline 360 interface will feel familiar to Microsoft PowerPoint users)
- Available training (free or fee-based)
- Customer support and online community

Feature Set

When selecting an authoring tool, you'll want to be clear about the types of courses you want to create, as well as what instructional, administrative, and technical requirements you'll have. Then you can match up the tool's feature set with your needs. Here are some of the major categories to evaluate.

Questions and Quizzing

Many organizations adopt e-learning because of the ability to easily test and track learners. While just about any tool can create a multiple-choice quiz and track to an LMS, some tools have much more robust features. Consider how important these features might be when evaluating different tools:
- Question types (multiple-choice, matching, drag-and-drop, and so forth)
- Feedback logic (per question versus per option, multiple attempts for each question, branching feedback, and so forth)
- Question formatting (text only versus rich media on questions and on feedback)
- Randomization (randomize the order of question choices, randomize the order of the questions, pull from a bank of questions, randomized pulled questions with each attempt)
- Test-out capability (letting learners get credit for a course by passing a pretest)
- Special scoring logic (such as weighted questions, partial credit for answers, multiple attempts at the overall quiz)

Published Output

Authoring tools help you create a course, but the real goal is to get it out to your learners. You'll want to make sure the finished, published product meets your organization's and learners' technical needs. Consider tools with these features:

- Interoperability standards (Does the tool use an industry standard to talk to your learning management system?)
- Browsers and devices (Will the course play well on different browsers and devices, such as phones and tablets?)
- Need for proprietary players (Can the course be played by your learners without having to download any proprietary plug-in or players?)
- LMS app (If your LMS has a mobile app, will the course play properly in it?)
- Player features (Does the course player have the structural components you want, such as a menu, a glossary, and volume control?)
- Restricted navigation (If needed for compliance purposes, can you lock navigation so learners must complete each slide before continuing?).

> **WHAT ARE THE SCORM AND XAPI STANDARDS?**
>
> When you buy toilet paper, you probably don't look at the measurements to make sure it will fit on your toilet-paper holder at home. You know it will. Why? Because the people who make toilet paper and the people who make toilet paper holders have agreed to some specifications, often called standards. The e-learning industry also has standards to ensure that courses created with an authoring tool will interact properly with a learning management system.
>
> Over the years, there have been many different standards. SCORM has been around for more than 20 years, and it is still widely used. xAPI is a newer standard and allows for tracking of much more learning data than SCORM. Work with your LMS provider to determine which standard is best for you, and how to take best advantage of the tracking and reporting capabilities.

Accessibility

One of the business benefits of e-learning content is to be able to reach more learners. If you really mean all learners, then you'll need to consider how your e-learning courses function for individuals with disabilities, especially those who use assistive technology. Not everyone can see your slides, hear your narration, or use a mouse. (Check chapter 23 for more information.)

To ensure your courses can be accessed by everyone, look for the following accessibility features:

- Closed captions (manually created within the tool, imported using an industry-standard format, or auto-generated with the ability to edit)
- Adequate color contrast (especially with the design features that you are unable to modify)
- Alt text (the ability to add a text description to visual media for someone who can't see it)
- Focus order (the ability to put objects in a logical order, such as putting instructions before a question, as well as the ability to remove decorative objects so they are not picked up by assistive technology)
- Keyboard-only navigation (the ability for a learner to use a keyboard instead of a mouse to move through the course and access all content)

Translation

If you'll be translating your courses into several languages, you'll likely want a tool that makes it easy. Many authoring tools let you export all text contained in the course. Then you translate that content and reimport the text into the tool (Figure 25-6).

When evaluating a tool's translation capabilities, consider:

- Use of industry formats for export documentation (such as XLIFF)
- Export of *all* text (including system-generated text and accessibility features)
- Support for right-to-left languages

Figure 25-6. Translation Export From Articulate Storyline 360

ID 🔒	Type	Source Text	Translation
VBc	Slide name	What Would You Do With Extra Time?	What Would You Do With Extra Time?
YRE	Text Box	What Would You Do With Extra Time?	What Would You Do With Extra Time?
lyw	Text Entry	Type your thoughts here.	Type your thoughts here.
gck	Text Box 1	What would you do if you had an extra two hours at work each week?	What would you do if you had an extra two hours at work each week?

Interactions and Custom Logic

How creative and flexible do you want to be with your designs? If you are working with a template-based tool, you'll want to evaluate the collection of interactive templates to determine if they meet your needs (Figures 25-7 and 25-8).

Figure 25-7. Adobe Captivate Scenario Using Variables to Calculate Allowable Expenses

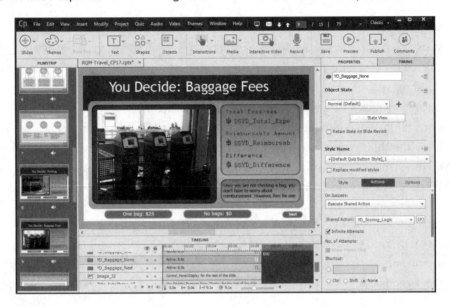

Figure 25-8. Articulate Storyline Scenario Using States and Variables to Customize an Avatar

If you are considering a more robust authoring tool that lets you design your own interactions, look for these features:

- Branching (such as with a choose-your-own-adventure interaction)
- Types of actions (such as the different functions you can add to a button, like play/pause media, jump to a slide, jump to a certain point on the timeline, show something, and hide something)
- Conditional logic (the ability to create if/then statements)
- Mathematical functions (such as adding points to a total)
- States (the ability to make a feature, such as a button, look different in different situations)
- Variables (the ability to store information—such as the learner's name, the answer to an earlier question, or points in a game—and use it elsewhere in the course)

Media

Many e-learning courses have richer media than classroom-based training, so it will be important to select an authoring tool that gives you the media options you want. Table 25-1 can help you decide what to consider.

Table 25-1. Media Options to Consider for E-Learning

Type of Media	Features to Consider
Photos and illustrations	• Import various graphic file formats • Access a built-in library of graphics • Access a built-in library of characters to use in scenarios • Crop and resize images • Easily edit images in other applications using round-trip editing • Add 360-degree images
Animation effects	• Synchronize elements to audio and video • Add entrance and exit animations • Add custom motion paths • Add logic based on the position of items on the screen
Audio	• Import various audio file formats • Record audio directly in the tool • Edit audio • Process audio, such as removing noise and leveling volume • Access a built-in library of sound effects and intro music • Generate audio using text-to-speech
Video	• Import various video file formats • Record video (webcam) directly in the tool • Edit video • Create picture-in-picture effects • Access a built-in library of video clips • Add 360-degree video
PowerPoint import	• Import PowerPoint slides as-is • Import PowerPoint slides and manipulate the slide objects in the tool

> **SHOULD YOU IMPORT YOUR CLASSROOM SLIDES?**
>
> Many e-learning authoring tools make it quick and easy to import existing PowerPoint slides. That might feel like great news if you've got hours of classroom training that you'd like to convert to e-learning. But should you? It all depends on the quality of your slides and their fitness for the e-learning medium.
>
> Few people enjoy attending a classroom training program where the slides are nothing but walls of words. However, a good instructor can carry a bad PowerPoint in the classroom—the instructor is the primary visual. In e-learning, especially self-paced e-learning, the slides are often 100 percent of the visual. In the classroom, a good instructor can easily present on a single slide for five or more minutes. In self-paced e-learning, five minutes is an eternity to be looking at the same visual.
>
> So yes, you can import your existing PowerPoint slides, add a quick quiz, and be on your way. But just because you can doesn't mean you should.

Screen Simulations

If you are creating e-learning content to teach learners how to use a software application or website (such as conditional formatting in Excel or your new expense reimbursement system), any authoring tool will let you import screenshots you've taken of the software. Some tools also let you create more robust software simulations, such as sit-back-and-watch videos of the software in action and interactive try-it-yourself practices.

Authoring Environment

Authoring tools are either installed on your computer or cloud-based. PowerPoint plug-ins can be effective for newer users, and your LMS can be helpful for gathering assets. A few authoring tools offer a suite of tools that might be useful in combination.

Installed Software

Some authoring tools are designed to be installed on your computer. Make sure they will work with your computer configuration. For example, Adobe Captivate has a PC version and a Mac version, whereas Articulate Storyline 360 has only a PC version, and Mac users need a Windows virtual environment such as Parallels to run the software. Most software license agreements let you install the software on a primary and secondary computer for a single user (such as one at work and one at home or a desktop and a laptop computer).

Cloud-Based Tools

Other authoring tools, including most subscription-based tools, are accessed via a web browser. This means you can access them from just about any computer, including Mac versus PC. Some, but not all, of these tools also let multiple authors work on a single course at once (which is not true of installed software tools). Some tools offer both an installed and an online version (such as Lectora), but you may need to license them separately if you want to use both.

PowerPoint Plug-Ins

Programs such as iSpring and Articulate Studio 360 let you use Microsoft PowerPoint as the base authoring tool (Figure 25-9). Presentation (noninteractive) slides are built as PowerPoint slides. Then, e-learning-specific features—such as click-to-reveal activities, quizzes, and publishing—are housed on an extra ribbon that is added to PowerPoint once you install the tool.

This type of tool can be great for designers just getting started who aren't particularly software savvy, because much of the authoring is done in a tool they are likely already familiar with.

However, the feature sets are somewhat limited in this type of tool.

LMS Assembly

Many learning management systems let you assemble assets into a course. These tools may or may not let you create the content in the LMS, but you can often gather videos, articles, imported lessons created in an outside authoring tool, quizzes, assignments, and discussions, and arrange them on a webpage with a course structure.

Combinations

A few authoring tool providers offer a suite of tools. For example, Articulate 360 includes three authoring tools as well as some supplemental tools. dominKnow|ONE includes a simpler template-based tool called Flow and a more full-featured authoring tool called Claro.

Figure 25-9. The Articulate Studio Ribbon in Microsoft PowerPoint.

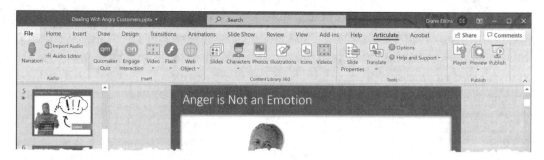

WHAT'S THE MOST POPULAR E-LEARNING AUTHORING TOOL?

In June 2021, the Learning Guild surveyed 808 e-learning professionals about their use and preferences around e-learning authoring tools. When asked what tools they used frequently (at least a few times a month), more than half chose Articulate's Storyline 360 and Rise 360. Techsmith Camtasia and Adobe Captivate were also extremely popular.

Figure 25-10. Frequently Used E-Learning Tools

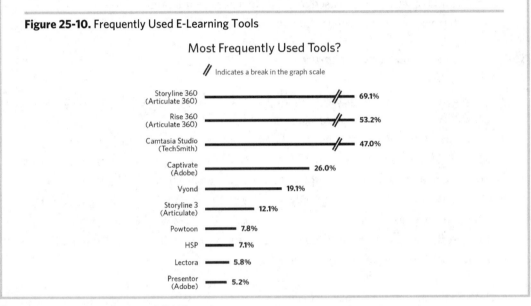

Used with permission fron Jane Bozarth (2021)

Supporting Tools

Your main authoring tool is where you'll likely spend most of your effort, but you can supplement its capabilities with other tools.

Interaction Tools

Your e-learning design choices may include special features such as simulations, branching, gamification, and software simulations. You may be able to build what you need within your primary course-authoring tool. However, template-based tools (such as Articulate Rise 360) and PowerPoint import tools (such as iSpring) may not provide many options. More robust tools, such as Adobe Captivate and Articulate Storyline, do have features that let you create these types of course features. You can even find templates to help you get started.

In addition to the built-in options, there are stand-alone tools specifically designed for creating one or more of these course features. They can be helpful even if you do have the ability to create them in your course-authoring tool. Why? Specialty tools can make it easier to create the features you want (more templates and built-in logic) or give you more options than the authoring tool provides.

Simulation and Branching

Some tools are specifically designed to help with the complex logic required for simulations and branching scenarios. For example, tools that can do this include:
- SmartBuilder, which can be used to create business simulations
- BranchTrack, which lets you visually map out complex branching scenarios

Software Training and Screen Capture

Tools that can do this include:
- Articulate Storyline and Adobe Captivate, which both come with robust screen simulation capability for both lessons and practices.
- TechSmith Camtasia is the most popular stand-alone tool for recording and editing software videos (Figure 25-11). It includes options for adding audio, transitions, captions, zooms, and more. However, its options for interaction are limited.
- TechSmith SnagIt is more commonly used for static screen captures, but you can also do simple recordings of your desktop.
- Microsoft PowerPoint can be used to create a simple recording. You can choose the option right from the Insert tab in PowerPoint.

Figure 25-11. Editing Interface in TechSmith Camtasia

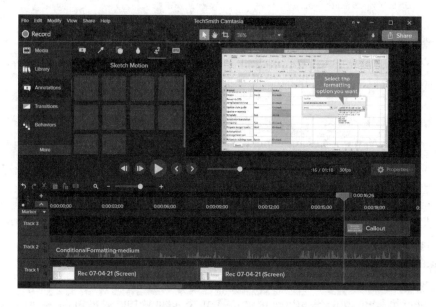

Gamification

Gamification means integrating game mechanics into your training, such as adding one or more game elements including rewards (points and badges), levels, storytelling, and game themes. A table of common game elements is located on the handbook's website at ATDHandbook3.org.

Games created with specialty game software can be either embedded into a larger course or published and posted as a stand-alone learning unit. Gamification software options include:
- Raptivity, which is a collection of template-based games (primarily gamified quizzes) and other interactions
- The Training Arcade, which provides template-based games, including officially licensed *Jeopardy!* and *Wheel of Fortune* games, that can be used in live or self-paced training

Quizzing and Assessment

Just about every course-authoring tool lets you create questions and track the score to a learning management system. You can also use your LMS or stand-alone tools to create the quiz:
- LMS quizzing tools. Built-in quiz tools don't usually have as many design options as course-authoring tools, but they usually provide more detailed tracking options. For example, an LMS might report only on the final score and number of attempts on an externally created quiz, but offer detailed question-level data on a quiz created with its own built-in tool. (Note that LMSes can provide detailed tracking on externally created courses, but that doesn't mean yours will.)
- Gamification tools typically offer gamified quizzes.
- Assessment-specific tools. If you have very formal testing requirements, you may benefit from stand-alone tools (such as Learnosity's Questionmark). Some provide extremely robust options for design, delivery, and reporting.
- Survey tools. If you don't have an LMS for tracking quiz results, you can always create quizzes in an online survey tool (such as Survey Monkey).

Media Tools

E-learning content can be as simple as text-only, but it usually includes rich media. You can often make your e-learning more engaging and more instructionally sound with well-crafted media. Having the right tools helps too. As with the interaction tools, your primary authoring tool may give you what you need, but third-party tools might give you a wider range of capabilities.

Graphics

Tools that can enhance your graphics include:
- SnagIt. Although it's primarily known for its screen capture ability, you can actually do quite a bit of image editing in SnagIt, such as cropping, resizing, adding callouts, and correcting color.
- Canva. Canva lets you create layouts (such as infographics) using a large library of templates and images.
- Adobe Photoshop. Photoshop is the gold standard for photo editing. You can also use it for illustration and layout.
- Adobe Illustrator. Whereas Photoshop is designed primarily for photo work, Illustrator is designed for illustrations.

Audio

Tools that can enhance your audio include:
- Audacity. This free software lets you add and edit audio files as well as run helpful filters and effects, such as noise removal.
- Descript. This audio- and video-editing tool uses artificial intelligence (AI) to automate a number of functions, including transcription or creating a text-to-speech profile of your voice.

Video

Tools that can enhance your video include:
- TechSmith Camtasia. In addition to its screen simulation capabilities, you can use Camtasia for editing any type of video.
- Adobe Premiere Pro. For more robust, professional-level video work, consider this tool from Adobe.
- Vyond. This tool lets you create whiteboard-style animated videos (Figure 25-12). Using Vyond's built-in library of characters, wardrobes, settings, and props, nonartists can create extremely custom scenarios.
- Adobe After Effects. This program is the industry standard for high-end motion graphics and animations.

Figure 25-12. Still From an Animated Vyond Video on Delegation

Illustration used with permission from Pryor Learning

Other Helpful Tools

These range from storyboarding, prototyping, and project management tools to those with review features. Lastly, there are tools to help you manage your course files and assets, as well as host and track your courses.

Storyboarding Tools

Storyboards are where you plan out your course (and get stakeholder input) before you build it. You can create high-level storyboards to plan out the overall flow, as well as detailed storyboards that describe every single word, image, and interaction to be included. Here are a few tools that might help:
- Microsoft Word or Google Docs. These tools make it easy to manage feedback using comments and tracked changes. Cloud-based tools make it easy for several people to work on or comment on a document at once.
- Microsoft PowerPoint or Google Slides. Some people prefer these tools so they can better plan and communicate the look of their slides. Others find the visual aspects distracting and choose to focus on that only after the written content has been approved.

- Outlining and mind-mapping tools. If you'd like help organizing your thoughts, there are many tools available to help you with your initial outline and design plan (such as MindMeister).
- Storyboarding-specific tools. Storyboarding isn't unique to e-learning, meaning you can easily use tools created for other industries, such as advertising or video development. Consider programs like Twine or Boords.

Prototyping Tools

While storyboards let you plan out the content, a prototype lets you try out how the course will look or function. You can create a prototype directly in your course-authoring tool by building out a few slides with placeholder graphics, or you could simply create a mock-up in PowerPoint. You could also consider prototyping, sketching, and wireframing tools (such as Microsoft Visio or Adobe XD).

Project Management Tools

Project management tools can be an important part of any training development initiative. E-learning development typically takes more hours, involves more people, and has more moving parts than developing classroom-based training. Because of this, you may benefit from a more formal project management process:

- For your project administration, you can use something as simple as Microsoft Excel or Google Sheets. If you want to use more formal project management methodology, consider tools like Microsoft Project, SmartSheet, or Trello.
- Email is where information goes to die! With so many moving parts and stakeholders, you may want to formalize communication with tools such as Slack or Microsoft Teams.

Quality Assurance and Reviews

Storyboard feedback can often be managed in whatever software you use to create them, such as comments and tracked changes in Word. Once you move to the online draft, you'll want a system that makes it easy to capture and manage internal and stakeholder feedback. That system could range from a Google Sheet, to bug-tracking platforms used in software development, to a review tool specifically designed for e-learning content.

More and more authoring tools now come with a built-in review feature (such as Articulate Review 360). You can post a published version of your course on a review platform hosted by the authoring tool provider. (This solves a big problem for organizations that have a place to host finished courses but not in-progress courses.) From there, you can send out a link for reviewers to comment on any given slide. Reviewers can read each other's comments and respond. On the back end, you can manage the comments, such as exporting lists, adding updates, and closing them out. If your authoring tool doesn't have such a feature, you can purchase third-party tools such as Review My eLearning or TechSmith's Video Review.

Asset and File Management

E-learning courses involve a lot of files, and they can be very large. You'll want to think about:
- How to organize your files so everyone on the team can find what they want
- Where to store files for safe backup
- How to transfer large files to stakeholders or co-workers as needed

The answer could be as simple as using an existing shared network drive or may require a third-party tool (such as Dropbox).

If you have or expect to create a large training library, you may want to consider an asset management platform. Such platforms might manage version control, let you tag and search for specific images, make it easy to reuse images, let you reuse content in different training modalities, and even update content in one place and have the change trickle down to every course where that content appears.

Some authoring tools (such as Xyleme) and some learning management systems offer asset management tools. These are sometimes referred to as learning content management systems (LCMS), although that term can have many different interpretations.

Hosting and Tracking

You can share your e-learning content with your audience from a learning management system, an intranet page, a public-facing website, or even a USB drive. Your overall technology ecosystem should include the tools you need to host, assign, and track your e-learning content. (Read more about ecosystems in chapter 34.)

Final Thoughts

With more than 30 different tools featured by name in this chapter (and many, many more that weren't mentioned), you have a wide range of choices to help you build engaging, effective e-learning. It can be easy to get caught up in all the choices available. However, rather than being swayed by a cool example or slick demo, start with the fundamentals. Be clear about what's important for your organization to achieve its goals, and then select the tools based on what you learn.

About the Author

Diane Elkins is the co-owner of Artisan E-Learning, a custom e-learning development company specializing in Articulate Studio, Storyline, Lectora, and Captivate. She has built a reputation as a national e-learning expert by being a frequent speaker at major industry events such as ATD's International Conference & Exposition, ATD TechKnowledge, DevLearn, and Learning Solutions. She is also the co-author of the popular E-Learning Uncovered book series as well as *E-Learning Fundamentals: A Practical Guide* from ATD Press. She is a past board member of ATD's Northeast Florida and Metro DC chapters. Reach Diane at dpelkins@artisanelearning.com and learn more about her work at artisanelearning.com or elearninguncovered.com.

References

Bozarth, J. 2021. "Authoring Tools 2021." The Learning Guild. learningguild.com/insights/264/authoring-tools-2021.

Recommended Resources

ATD. "Technology Application." td.org/topics/technology-application.

Elkins, D., and D. Pinder. 2015. *E-Learning Fundamentals: A Practical Guide.* Alexandria, VA: ATD Press.

Learning Solutions. "List of Authoring Tools." learningsolutionsmag.com/authoring-tools.

Parish, T. "E-Learning." e-learning.zeef.com/tracy.parish.

CHAPTER 26

Designing and Delivering Virtual Training

Cynthia Clay and Cindy Huggett

Virtual classrooms have been around for more than two decades and have been increasing in popularity every year. According to the annual ATD *State of the Industry* report, virtual training made up approximately 7 percent of all formal training in 2010, rising to 19 percent in 2019. And in 2020, when the global pandemic forced organizations to operate remotely, virtual training jumped to 35 percent (ATD 2018, 2021).

Trainers around the world needed to quickly adapt to virtual training whether they were ready for it or not. Traditional, in-person classes were rapidly converted to the virtual environment. And while some learning experiences will likely return to the traditional classroom, virtual training is here to stay.

> **IN THIS CHAPTER:**
> ♦ Design effective, interactive virtual training
> ♦ Deliver interactive virtual training

Because there are many definitions of virtual training, we want to be clear about our meaning. For the purposes of this chapter, *virtual training* is:

> A highly interactive, synchronous online, instructor-led training class, with defined learning objectives, with participants who are individually connected from geographically dispersed locations, using a web classroom platform. (Huggett 2013)

In other words, virtual training is a live, online, and facilitated learning experience. It's more than a presentation or a recorded webcast. It expects dialogue among participants, engagement using platform tools, and performance feedback from a skilled trainer. It's a program that leads to on-the-job results.

The most common length of a virtual class is 60 to 90 minutes, and more often than not, the class is part of a series (Huggett 2020). Participants might attend part 1 on a Tuesday, part 2 on a Wednesday, and part 3 on a Thursday, while completing asynchronous, self-directed assignments between each session.

To be successful, virtual training requires an interactive design and an engaging facilitator. Design and delivery go together as inseparable components of effective virtual training. You can't—and shouldn't—have one without the other.

Designing for Interaction

Effective virtual classes engage participants, create a comfortable space for learning, and provide opportunities to apply new skills. They do this through well-thought-out, intentionally planned designs. That means it's more than just clicking through slides while someone talks. It takes intentional design decisions to create a high-quality virtual learning experience.

Whether you are converting a traditional class to the virtual environment, or starting from scratch with a new program, here are five tips to design an interactive virtual class:
- Set expectations.
- Start strong.
- Structure for variety and engagement.
- Seek social interaction.
- Strengthen slide design.

Design Tip 1. Set Expectations

Because there are several different types of online events—with meetings and presentations being the most common—participants may be surprised if they're asked to actively engage in their online class. So, it's important to set expectations well before an online workshop begins. An interactive virtual class should be engaging from the moment participants register for it.

This means designers should carefully craft the program description to emphasize interaction. They should also write course communications—such as custom registration and reminder messages—that clearly establish these expectations. Designers could even draft a scripted email that the trainer of the virtual session could send that begins to build rapport and relationships before the class start time.

This is important because the more participants get involved in the learning experience, the more likely the training outcomes will be reached. In other words, if participants will need to collaborate on a case study and practice new skills with a partner, then they need to come prepared to actively contribute. Don't leave this to chance. Let them know at every opportunity that it will be an active workshop instead of a passive presentation.

Design Tip 2. Start Strong

At the start of your virtual training class, get everyone involved by beginning with an interactive exercise. Instead of starting with a slew of administrative slides or string of facilitator announcements, start with a spotlight on the participants. Get everyone interacting with the tools and with one another within the first three minutes, or you will be less likely to have an engaged audience.

For example, have a call to action activity when participants first log in to an event. This can be an icebreaker question, or a content-related question that sparks interest and discussion.

Then, at the official start time, plan an opening activity that engages the entire audience. It could be asking everyone to introduce themselves via chat, or it could be asking everyone to respond to a poll question about their experience with the topic. The point is to get everyone typing, clicking, or talking within the first few minutes.

Design Tip 3. Structure for Variety and Engagement

Once you begin your virtual class with engagement, it's important to continue with it. Fortunately, virtual classroom platforms provide an abundance of ways to involve a remote audience. By using these tools creatively, you can involve participants in the content, which leads to deeper learning. And deeper learning leads to better learning outcomes.

For example, use:
- Polls for conversation starters
- Chat for group conversations
- Webcams for deeper dialogue
- Whiteboards for team collaboration
- Breakouts for practice and feedback

Keep in mind that it's not about using the platform tools just to use them. The tools should be used to further the learning outcomes. For example, if participants have to learn a new job-related technique, then they could respond to a poll about their experience with that technique, see a short demonstration via video, brainstorm application ideas with their peers on a whiteboard, and then go into breakout rooms to practice the new technique in small groups.

It's also important to maintain interest by not using the same activity over and over again. Participants will get bored quickly if the only activity is "type your response in chat." Designers should get creative with the available tool set in ways that keep the content fresh and exciting. For example, creating a competition to see who gets the most poll questions correct, or asking participants to write a response on paper and then hold it up on camera for all to see, or coming up with some other unique way to use the platform tools.

You can download a sample virtual class outline on the handbook's website at ATDHandbook3.org.

Design Tip 4. Seek Social Engagement

Remember that we're talking about synchronous virtual training, which means that participants are joining at the same time to learn. If you're going to bring them all together, then make the most of that opportunity.

The very nature of virtual training means that participants are remote and isolated from one another. But as we've already established, engaged participants are more likely to learn and apply the new knowledge. Therefore, design virtual training classes that allow for, and even emphasize, participant-to-participant interaction.

There's another benefit to social engagement: Participants learn from one another through shared experiences and robust conversation. They also feel less isolated when they realize they're part of a group. By integrating conversation and teamwork into the workshop, participants become part of a community and are more likely to participate. On the other hand, if a participant stays anonymous, then they are more likely to tune out and multitask. We want engaged participants who learn.

Simple ways to include social engagement include:
- Encouraging small talk between and among participants
- Using polls to gather input, sharing those results for all to see, and then commenting on the group's responses
- Using breakout groups for deeper discussion and dialogue
- Allowing time for conversation throughout the session (that is, don't cram too much content into a session)
- Assigning participants to teams at the start of a session and encouraging the teams to work together
- Asking participants to choose a learning partner with whom they can privately chat throughout the session to share insights

Design Tip 5. Strengthen Slide Design

Most virtual classroom platforms emphasize document sharing, which means your slides take center stage. Therefore, you should intentionally design slides to fit an interactive virtual class.

Slides should enhance the content and provide activity instructions. When used during short teaching sections, they should be visually appealing and follow these generally accepted design best practices:
- Include only one thought per slide (not text-heavy or filled with bullet points).
- Use san serif fonts, which are easier to read onscreen.
- Choose photos or vector graphics for slide imagery (not clip art).

As a general rule, virtual classes have more slides than their in-person counterparts because you'll want to keep the screen moving for visual interest. In other words, if the same slide stays on the screen for a long period of time, participants will grow tired of it and look away. But every time the screen changes to a new visual, it attracts their attention.

Also, remember the difference between visual aids and reference material—the best slides make the worst handouts. For technical content, provide separate job aids or other documentation, using the slides to highlight key content.

Finally, because your participants may join from many different device types, each with a different screen size, pay attention to the selected font sizes. The smaller the screen, the larger the font needs to be for readability. As a general guideline, fonts should be at least 34 point to be read on most screens.

CONVERTING CLASSROOM TRAINING TO VIRTUAL TRAINING

Avoid these common mistakes when converting in-person classes to online ones:
- Including too much content. Just because you can teach it online doesn't mean you should. Be choosy about what content you include in a virtual class versus the topics you put into an asynchronous learning program.
- Inviting too many people. Just because you can have hundreds of people in a virtual classroom doesn't mean you should.
- Ignoring good design principles. Just because you have a remote audience doesn't mean that there isn't opportunity for interaction. Don't take an interactive in-person class and turn it into a boring online lecture.
- Forgetting the virtual classroom tools. There's more opportunity to interact online than in the in-person classroom. Take advantage of it!

Delivering Engaging Virtual Training

Once an instructional designer has created an engaging, interactive learning design, it is up to the virtual trainer to bring that program to life in the virtual classroom. Assuming that the design includes compelling interactive activities, a skilled virtual facilitator has the responsibility to ensure that their mastery of the content is combined with meaningful engagement, peer-to-peer collaboration, and long-term learning retention.

There are five areas of focus that support excellent virtual delivery:
- Set up for success.
- Establish social or virtual presence.
- Develop a synergistic style.
- Support shared conversation.
- Tell engaging stories.

Delivery Tip 1. Set Up for Success

Engaging virtual training begins well before the start time. To get a strong start in a virtual training session, the facilitator must log in to the platform at least 20 to 30 minutes before the class begins. In a virtual workplace, it can be tempting to schedule back-to-back meetings that run right up to the start of your virtual training event. However, rushing in at the last minute only to discover your laptop needs to be rebooted or that you need to download the latest version of the virtual classroom software is a recipe for a bumpy beginning.

The best facilitators know that signing in early allows them to address technical issues, review the learning objectives and program content, and create a welcoming environment as participants arrive in the virtual classroom. The facilitator can also create warm connections and have informal conversations a few minutes before the formal program begins. If you are partnering with a producer or co-facilitator, use this time to review last-minute logistics. Use the call to action described earlier or consider posing a starter question in chat as people arrive to keep them engaged before the official start time.

By being prepared and ready, instead of being anxious and irritated, the virtual trainer can be warm and focused.

Delivery Tip 2. Establish Social or Virtual Presence

In the virtual environment, social or virtual presence is demonstrated by how real a facilitator feels to the people attending the session. Participants respond well to a facilitator who turns on their webcam and greets them warmly, making it feel as if they are attending a training class in the physical workplace. The more "real" you feel to the participants, the easier it will be to create an energized, personal learning environment. As participants hear your voice, observe your facial expressions, and see your body language, they will experience your virtual presence fully.

Your virtual presence demonstrates a brain-based learning principle: Social learning fires mirror neurons. Simply put:

> When you watch someone experience an emotion, your brain fires mirror neurons in the same pattern. If they feel happy, your brain mirrors happiness. If they feel disgust, your brain mirrors disgust.... Showing up on web camera with positive, enthusiastic virtual presence can help you create a lively, engaging virtual learning session. (Clay 2019)

Place your webcam either at eye level or slightly above. If you present using a laptop, place a box or a stack of books beneath it to lift the webcam to the ideal position. This will allow you to easily look into the lens and it frames your head and shoulders in the display. If you are too close to the webcam, your viewers may feel as if you are invading their personal space. If you are too far away, they may have difficulty reading your facial expressions or they may see too much of your background instead of you, their facilitator.

Make sure that you sit in front of a wall rather than in front of a window and that your face is well lit by diffuse light from above and in front. The harsh light from a window with open blinds may not give you the best appearance. And avoid any bright lights behind you, which might throw your face into shadow. In addition, choose your background carefully. The wall behind you might have a bookshelf with a tidy row of books, a painting, a lush plant, or photographs. Ensure that there's nothing in the background that could be distracting to participants. For example, a door in the frame behind you sets up the expectation that someone might open it and walk into the space. That can be oddly distracting. Experiment with your lighting and background until you achieve a professional look.

If you don't have an ideal setup, most modern virtual classroom platforms allow you to blur your background. If needed, use that option instead of selecting exotic or unusual backgrounds. A real background increases the sense of warmth and trust between you and your audience. If you must use a virtual background, choose a simple brick or paneled wall, rather than an eye-catching landmark, a beach scene, or a fancy conference room.

As you present content or facilitate discussion, try to create the illusion of eye contact by looking directly into the camera lens when you are speaking. Of course, you may need to look away at times to check your notes or look at the chat discussion. Those changes in your focus create the experience of a natural conversation. You should also look into the camera lens when a participant is speaking out loud. They will experience the illusion of eye contact as evidence that you are listening. Allow your face to reflect your thoughts as you listen. Nod, smile, frown, or shake your head, as appropriate. Looking directly into the camera lens may at first feel awkward, but it will become second nature as you use the webcam to increase the experience of your social or virtual presence.

Delivery Tip 3. Develop a Synergistic Style

When you first begin delivering virtual training, it can be tempting to simply deliver a lecture. Remember, virtual training is different from a presentation. A lecture-style delivery approach leads to participants multitasking or tuning out the virtual session. Many treat the virtual training as a video they can simply play in the background while they work on other projects. They may be logged in, but they are likely checked out.

A well-designed, interactive program will provide plenty of opportunities for participant involvement. Strive to capture their attention by calling for interaction every few minutes. Ask a juicy question and have people chat their responses. Pose a polling question and have them compare their responses. Ask for a show of hands or use thumbs up/thumbs down to see whether people agree or disagree with a point that's been made. Ask for a pulse check to see if you should spend more time on a question or move on to the next topic. Or give people the opportunity to have small group conversations in a breakout room. Get comfortable releasing control, opening up the discussion, and sharing airtime with participants.

The goal of a synergistic delivery style is to encourage participants to co-create the learning experience with you. It would not be the same experience without them present in the virtual classroom on this day at this time, responding to questions, participating in discussion, sharing their opinions in breakout sessions, and asking questions that occur to them. You know you've achieved synergy when your participants have been just as active as you have throughout the program.

The Buddhist term *Beginner's Mind* describes a person open, eager, and willing to put aside preconceptions. When the facilitator brings a Beginner's Mind to the virtual classroom, they are well prepared but curious about what learners will bring to the workshop. They recognize that there is a wealth of experience in the virtual classroom, not just their own expertise on a particular topic.

Being fully prepared and comfortable with the content allows the virtual trainer to relax and make space for the opinions, experiences, and examples provided by participants. A richer learning process can then emerge as synergy is developed between the skilled facilitator and engaged participants.

Delivery Tip 4. Support Shared Conversation

One mental model that increases the effectiveness of virtual training is seeing it as a shared conversation rather than a presentation. For discussion to flow freely and comfortably, the facilitator needs to create a safe learning environment in which people can add their ideas, opinions, or guesses. This is especially important when there is no right or wrong answer. But even with concrete topics that have clear black and white answers, the virtual trainer can make it safe to choose the wrong answer. Try making a comment like, "Thank you for those insightful opinions. For this particular question, there is a right answer, according to the law. Let's explore that law now." This kind of comment welcomes input and yet directs the flow of discussion when the right answer needs to be presented.

A strong virtual facilitator poses thought-provoking questions that invite participants to jump in and offer their thoughts. You can capture a variety of opinions and observations both by having people speak aloud and by having them type their comments in chat. If using the chat function, strive to acknowledge a variety of viewpoints, using people's names as you ask them to elaborate on their comments. If several people have made similar points in chat, you may choose to summarize a key theme but acknowledge that Katy, Allen, and Marcy are making a similar point. You'll grab the participant's attention by speaking their name out loud or giving them affirmation or validation for their contribution to the discussion.

To avoid the curse of silence after asking a question, be thoughtful about how your questions are worded. Start a conversation by asking a specific question and provide clear instructions on how to respond. For example, ask, "Who has experienced a similar situation? Raise your hand." And then invite those with raised hands to share their experiences. Or ask participants to respond to a multiple-choice poll question, and then ask those who selected choice A to share reasons why. By using the tools to help you ask questions, you're more likely to generate conversation.

As you strive to build a shared conversation, your spirit of curiosity should lead you to ask probing questions. If someone makes a pithy comment in chat, and you think they have a good example to share, call on them by name and ask them to explain their comment. For example, if a supervisor in a management course types the comment, "Trust but verify," you might probe for more by asking them if they have an example of a time when it was important to verify and not just trust what they heard in a performance meeting. Let them know whether you want them to unmute their microphone and speak aloud, or whether you want them to type more in chat. Your willingness to go deeper to bring out people's lived experience may create a more robust learning experience for everyone.

If you are concerned about confidentiality, consider using polling as a safe way to allow people to express their opinions. The polling tool can be used to:

- **Pose self-assessment questions.** (How would you rate your effectiveness as a project manager on a scale of one to five?)
- **Ask agree or disagree questions.** (Use a Likert scale of strongly agree, agree, neutral, disagree, or strongly disagree.)
- **Make a decision.** (Which of these four software packages is your preferred option?)

Most virtual classrooms also have whiteboards that can be used to gather opinions. You could ask a scribe to type comments on the whiteboard, or direct participants to type their own ideas. The visual appeal of a whiteboard can be mimicked by formatting a slide in the slide deck and allowing people to type directly on that slide. This approach prevents someone from inadvertently clearing the formatting when they are simply attempting to erase one comment.

Chatting, polling, and whiteboarding are all virtual training tools that create shared conversation and collaborative learning. Measure your effectiveness as a virtual trainer not by how well you performed or how smoothly you delivered the content, but by how engaged your participants were in the shared conversation and how much everyone learned as they co-created the learning experience.

Delivery Tip 5. Tell Engaging Stories

Our brains are wired to remember narrative or stories. If you think back to the most memorable learning experience you've ever had, the chances are good that memory comes wrapped in a captivating story. Stories create patterns that allow our brains to store and retrieve information effectively. Human beings are meaning-making machines, and we have been telling stories about how the world works since we were babies.

The skilled trainer uses storytelling to frame the key concepts and points they want participants to remember. They also ask questions to stimulate the recall of stories from participants' experiences. These story frames create the context for new information. John Medina states that "information is remembered best when it is elaborate, meaningful, and contextual" (Medina 2014).

A good story features a lead character (a hero), a clear place and time, a challenge or problem tackled, and an outcome (success or failure), followed by the moral of the story or the key point you want people to take away. When you write that story, the hero needs to be familiar to the listeners, who need to recognize aspects of the hero in themselves.

Ideally, the challenge faced by the hero stimulates an emotional response (they root for them to succeed). The tools the hero uses to tackle the challenge are the same tools the participants might be learning in this training program. Alternatively, the hero may not have access to the tools participants are gaining in the training program, and therefore fails to defeat the challenge. In either the success scenario or the failure scenario, the key point should be summarized in one sentence at the end (for example, "And that's why we always have two signatures on every check").

In the virtual training environment, you may introduce a specific objective by telling a story about someone who successfully tackled a workplace challenge. Be sure to state a clear moral or learning point at the end of the story. Then you might ask participants to recall a similar situation in which they faced that same issue. You might invite someone to describe their experience out loud and explain how they handled that tough situation. Or you might send them into breakouts to discuss and share. Your job is to guide them to put into words specifically what they learned that has made them a more effective manager, team leader, or collaborator. As an alternative, you might tell participants listening to a colleague's story to type into chat what skills and abilities they hear the speaker using to successfully resolve the situation. You might ask listeners to identify the moral or key learning point of the speaker's example. This active listening with analysis captures their attention and anchors their memory.

Does Audience Size Matter When It Comes to Engagement?

No matter the size of the audience, a great virtual learning experience is always engaging and interactive. Whether you are facilitating a group of 15 participants or presenting to 1,000 people, leverage the right interaction tools in your web conference platform. A useful rule of thumb is to strive for interaction every three minutes to keep people contributing and participating throughout the virtual session. Table 26-1 takes you through ideal tools to use with different audience sizes.

Table 26-1. What Tools for What Audience?

Audience Size	Tools to Leverage	Purpose
Small (< 25)	• Chat • Polling • Webcam • Annotation tools • Audio	• Share opinions and ideas. • Compare opinions and make decisions. • Build strong virtual presence for participants. • Brainstorm ideas on a whiteboard. • Discuss ideas and share examples aloud.
Midsize (25-100)	• Chat (directed) • Polling • Thumbs up and down • Webcam • Breakout rooms	• Have specific people or groups answer questions. • Compare opinions and make decisions. • Quickly check for agreement or disagreement. • Strengthen facilitator's virtual presence. • Solve problems and discuss case studies.
Large (100+)	• Polling • Q&A • Chat (directed) • Thumbs up and down • Webcam	• Compare opinions and make decisions. • Respond to selected, relevant questions. • Have specific people or groups answer questions. • Quickly check for agreement or disagreement. • Strengthen the facilitator's virtual presence.

SHIFTING THE RULES OF TRAINING AND DEVELOPMENT TO ACCOMMODATE THE NEW NORMAL
Jennifer Linch, Director, Training and Development, American College of Education

As working from home evolves from being a once-in-a-while break from the office to the new normal, talent development professionals must be prepared for the evolution. The platforms for training delivery may change, but the expectations of delivering high-quality learning opportunities do not. The same rules apply for the development and delivery of training: Know the audience, engage with learners, and take into consideration prior knowledge. Transitioning from in-person training to virtual training requires an intense focus on these guidelines.

Consider the Learners

Seasoned TD professionals understand what it means to consider the learners: ensuring the training is designed for and delivered to the right individuals. However, with the transition from in-person training to virtual training, learners are no longer sitting in a classroom. It's a mom trying to juggle family life or a husband calming a barking dog because the repair technician is at the door. The learners have laundry piling up, dinner in the oven, and three meals a day to plan. The audience's challenges have shifted to juggling home life with work responsibilities. TD professionals keep distracted learners engaged with short, collaborative, focused training.

Engage With Learners

My department recognized the importance of incorporating more interactions in our asynchronous trainings. As we develop content delivery, we consider how engagement occurs in the virtual environment. Often, participants have difficulty focusing on virtual learning. TD professionals can create an engaging environment where the distractions of home—piles of laundry and barking dogs—are momentarily set aside. We use available tools—such as polls to explore opinions, breakout rooms to facilitate collaboration, and whiteboard features to encourage brainstorming—to help bring engagement to the next level. In addition, engagement increased when our department decided to focus on developing microlearning opportunities.

Consider Prior Knowledge

Participants, in any environment, enjoy sharing what they know. In a virtual environment, TD professionals must consider the prior knowledge participants bring to the learning session. Recognizing this knowledge is a strategy that focuses the session and engages participants. The TD professional can review and check for learners' current understanding and use this base to introduce new content. Recognizing prior knowledge first keeps learners engaged and focused on the new information.

> **SHIFTING THE RULES OF TRAINING ...** *continued*
>
> **The Key to Successful Virtual Learning**
>
> I am a director of training and development for an online college with a remote workforce already in place, and the task to develop training during the COVID-19 pandemic changed little for my department. However, we now had to consider all the added distractions and layers to what was going on at home for our audience. We had to ensure our levels of engagement were higher than ever. Each new training initiative we developed had to be focused, concise, and relevant; we had to decide if it should be live or asynchronous. We collaborated with other departments to take meetings and training sessions from live, recorded Zoom sessions to asynchronous videos.
>
> TD professionals are challenged with delivering effective training as distracted learners work from home. They must understand the learners' challenges, engage them, and recognize their prior knowledge. The expectations of delivering high-quality learning opportunities do not change just because the training delivery changes.

Looking Ahead: The Future of Virtual Learning

People have been predicting the demise of instructor-led training for decades as innovative digital tools have been developed and adopted. The pandemic response in 2020 led many organizations to rapidly pivot to virtual instructor-led training that integrated video- and web-conferencing technology to reach employees working from home. The future now appears to be hybrid—face-to-face training delivered to co-located people and virtual training provided when some or all of the workforce is remote.

Besides the obvious cost and time savings, there are other benefits to having a facilitator in the virtual mix of training modalities. The dynamic interaction between a skilled virtual trainer, individual learners, and collaborative colleagues can result in more robust learning experiences. Subject matter experts may join live virtual training classes to add their expertise to the dialogue. Role play with instant feedback can help people modify their behaviors. Breakout rooms can encourage greater collaboration and practical problem solving among peers. Guidance from a live coach or expert can increase long-term retention of new knowledge and skills.

The widespread use of webcams has led to the development of new norms of virtual etiquette. To reduce the fatigue of being on webcams throughout the day, groups may need to develop norms about when to have people on camera or off camera, how to ensure the best audio experience for everyone participating in a training session, and the right uses of virtual or physical backgrounds to enhance trust in virtual relationships. Immersive backgrounds, in which everyone appears to be sitting at the same conference table, for example, may contribute to a stronger feeling of belonging in virtual meetings and digital training.

Augmented reality (AR) combines real and virtual worlds in real-time interaction, allowing users to manipulate 3-D virtual objects or review information overlaid on a real object or situation. Virtual reality (VR) replaces the physical world with a fully virtual simulated environment. Both AR and VR provide opportunities to safely train users who might not otherwise be able to practice a new skill in a real, physical environment. Because most people now perform at least a portion of their work on a mobile device or tablet, you likely hold an AR device in your hand every day. AR applications range from filters in web conferencing, messaging apps, and gaming systems to navigation systems, photography tools, and medical applications. While the adoption of AR and VR for corporate training has been slow, the steady growth of new applications will continue, as on-demand applications support the skills development of people on the job.

When higher-order thinking skills are important to the learning process, virtual instructor-led training may be the ideal delivery method. But facilitated training should not stand alone. The future of virtual learning will combine many elements of compelling, blended solutions, including the use of AR, VR, microlearning activities, and short videos. Blending these asynchronous digital elements with focused, instructor-led learning experiences has the potential to deliver compelling learning content that can be integrated into the workday for learners on the go. This social, facilitated aspect of online learning meets people's need for human interaction and connection.

The future of virtual learning requires experienced instructional designers who can integrate a variety of digital and interpersonal solutions. It also preserves skilled virtual facilitators as a critical component of results-oriented training. The combination of interactive design and engaging facilitation will continue to be essential components of effective learning experiences.

Final Thoughts

Whether you are designing or delivering virtual training, you will want to continue to develop your skills, and your competencies go beyond what we mentioned in this chapter. For example, you will want to develop skills in how you communicate in a virtual setting and how to be most effective using a webcam. You can download a virtual facilitator competencies checklist on the handbook website, ATDHandbook3.org, which addresses the skills you need for effective design and delivery of virtual training.

About the Authors

Cynthia Clay is the founder and CEO of NetSpeed Learning and the author of *Great Webinars: Interactive Learning That Is Captivating, Informative, and Fun*. She works with clients to build thriving virtual and hybrid workplaces. The company partners with clients to develop the management skills of leaders who want to motivate, communicate with, and resolve conflict masterfully for employees and teams. She develops the skills of virtual facilitators, designers, and producers who are committed to delivering high-energy, engaging virtual learning. Cynthia is a passionate advocate of brain-based learning principles and leads her team to design, facilitate, and produce compelling online learning experiences.

Cindy Huggett, CPTD, is the author of four books on virtual training, including *Virtual Training Tools and Templates: An Action Guide to Live Online Learning* and *The Virtual Training Guidebook: How to Design, Deliver, and Implement Live Online Learning*. Cindy partners with organizations to help them transition to online learning and teaches trainers how to effectively facilitate online. She facilitates, designs, writes, and speaks on topics related to leadership, learning, and technology. Cindy is a past member of the ATD National Board of Directors and was one of the first to earn the Certified Professional in Learning and Performance (now CPTD) credential.

References

ATD (Association for Talent Development). 2018. *2018 State of the Industry*. Alexandria, VA: ATD Press.

ATD (Association for Talent Development). 2021. *2021 State of the Industry*. Alexandria, VA: ATD Press.

Clay, C. 2019. *Great Webinars: Interactive Learning That Is Captivating, Informative and Fun*. Seattle, WA: Punchy Publishing.

Huggett, C. 2013. *The Virtual Training Guidebook: How to Design, Deliver and Implement Live Online Learning*. Alexandria, VA: ASTD Press.

Huggett, C. 2020. "Secrets of Master Virtual Trainers: 5 Keys to Online Classroom Success." ATD 2020 Virtual Conference Recording, May 11. td.org/videos/secrets-of-master-virtual-trainers-5-keys-to-online-classroom-success-2.

Medina, J. 2014. *Brain Rules*. Seattle, WA: Pear Press

Recommended Resources

Christopher, D. 2011. "Facilitating in the Global Virtual Classroom." *Infoline*. Alexandria, VA: ASTD Press.

Christopher, D. 2014. *The Successful Virtual Classroom: How to Design and Facilitate Interactive and Engaging Live Online Learning.* New York: AMACOM.

Clay, C. 2019. *Great Webinars: Interactive Learning That Is Captivating, Informative and Fun.* Seattle, WA: Punchy Publishing.

Huggett, C. 2013. *The Virtual Training Guidebook: How to Design, Deliver and Implement Live Online Learning.* Alexandria, VA: ASTD Press.

Huggett, C. 2018. *Virtual Training Basics*, 2nd ed. Alexandria, VA: ATD Press.

LaBorie, K., and T. Stone. 2015. *Interact and Engage!: 50+ Activities for Virtual Training, Meetings, and Webinars.* Alexandria, VA: ATD Press.

Pluth, B.P. 2010. *Webinars With WOW Factor: Tips, Tricks and Interactive Activities for Virtual Training.* Minneapolis, MN: Pluth Consulting.

SECTION V
REQUIRED FORWARD-FOCUSED PROFICIENCIES AND ATTITUDES

LUMINARY PERSPECTIVE

Slowing Down to Go Fast

Rita Bailey

How often have you wanted to slow down, take time to think, regroup, and recharge? With the demands and fast pace in which life and business move, there just never seemed to be enough time—until the COVID-19 pandemic hit with a hurricane-like impact and forced us to pause, slow down, or even stop. We learned to pivot, transition, reassess our priorities, and eventually redefine our *next normal*. Additionally, how we work, where we work, and our work priorities were drastically altered. As our profession enters the aftermath of the pandemic, we have an opportunity to reinforce the foundational elements that have sustained our industry, while also examining the proficiencies and mindsets required to move successfully into our future.

This reminds me of the movie series *The Expendables*. In the first two installments, the core group carried out the missions, but in the third sequel, new and younger-generation members were recruited to work with the original team. Old traditions gave new meaning to innovative practices, compromise, and adaptation as the team worked collaboratively to create new approaches and overcome the enemy.

It is an honor to be invited to contribute my thoughts as a luminary. My perspective from years of experience is fraught with memories of the many disruptions I've experienced and the necessity to change my thinking to make way for different attitudes, approaches, and skills. The pandemic allowed us a glimpse of what transformational, unexpected change looks like, and now we can, with eyes wide open, proactively focus on the changes necessary to navigate this new frontier.

Imagine receiving a dollar for every time you've heard or seen the phrase "In these uncertain, unprecedented times!" As learning professionals, we've heard it a lot, and it's our duty and obligation to be the change agents we expect others to be, regardless of our role or position. Bottom line, it's time to step up our game.

Eighteen months ago, I had never delivered a virtual class or conducted a strategic retreat on Zoom. My core content was primarily focused on culture, leadership, and learning strategies. Through client demands and challenges faced by changes in the learning community, I have now shifted most of my activities toward research, content, and facilitation on humanity and civility themes with an emphasis on diversity, equity, and inclusion. As a result, my network has expanded significantly; I've attended virtual conferences, workshops, groups, book clubs, and discussion groups without leaving my home office.

How was this possible while being isolated at home? My options were to mourn the loss of my active lifestyle centered on travel and social interactions, or to shift my mindset and attitude toward future possibilities. And that mindset helped me take myself, my business, and my relationships to a much higher level than before.

My hope is that you've had a similar experience and found that silver lining amid the crises endured by so many. For me, the past two years have been a real opportunity to reset, rejuvenate, and heal.

My goal in this section is to stimulate and challenge you to think about how we as talent and L&D professionals face this new future and lead the way as we develop new proficiencies and mindsets that help us meet the current and future needs of those who are depending on our expertise, guidance, and support.

Change at Warp Speed

While we know that change is constant, we're now experiencing change on steroids. For example:
- How we work, learn, and interact has led to a more virtual existence, both personally and professionally, so there is a need to adapt training access, tools, and technology.
- More awareness around mental health issues and challenges—including depression, social isolation, and stress—creates the need for an emphasis on wellness and well-being, empathy, safety, mindful training, and resources to accommodate employee emotional and physical needs.
- Some work roles are being replaced with technology and require retraining and rapid reskilling.
- Training and resources must meet changing customer needs and expectations.
- DEI practices are being integrated into TD processes, curriculums, and systems.
- People are taking greater ownership of their skills and learning opportunities through mobile, immersive technologies (AI, AR, VR), microlearning, videos, podcasts, and game-based learning.
- There is a growing influence of Gen Z and TikTok-type learning content.

There are obviously upsides and downsides to remote working. Every organization must determine how to accommodate the needs and desires of their workforce while also doing what's best for the business. These changes are causing an urgency to expand our thinking about ways to create a more personalized learner experience model. A recent Accenture report, *The Future of Work: Productive Anywhere*, emphasized that "it's less about a place and more about people's potential."

Several years ago, on a dare, I stepped out of my comfort zone and found the courage to go skydiving with friends. After a brief, just-in-time training session, we ascended to 10,000 feet and I found myself standing in the door of the plane, heart racing, breathing labored, and fear mounting as the countdown to my ejection neared. Upon descent, the free fall felt like it would never end and as the ground rose to meet me, I took control and pulled the cord to open the chute. In that moment I was laser focused, armed with the new skills I had just acquired in the pre-jump training, which allowed me to center my mindset on the peaceful journey and ultimately landing on the designated drop-zone target. I share this story because that's what it currently feels like to be a TD professional. We are in a seeming free fall and our very survival requires courage, a shift in attitude, and acquisition of new skills—we're being called upon to step out of our comfort zone.

In this section of the handbook, my colleagues provide details on required forward-focused proficiencies and attitudes necessary to remain relevant in this new training and TD environment. Heed these lessons and you will have a much smoother transition.

Have the Courage to Jump

There are several resources that support the notion that the time is now for TD and L&D professionals to go beyond the status quo and leap to the future:

- Skillsoft's *Mind the Gap* report states that 48 percent of L&D professionals believe their team is currently under-skilled to deliver what is needed for their business today.
- Emerald Works's *2020 Back to the Future* report finds that 39 percent of the L&D profession is overwhelmed and under-equipped, up from 29 percent in 2019.
- LinkedIn's *Workplace Learning Report* finds that 79 percent of CEOs are concerned that a lack of essential skills is threatening the future growth of their organization.
- McKinsey believes that by 2030, "375 million workers—or roughly 14 percent of the global workforce—may need to switch occupational categories as digitization, automation, and advances in AI continue to disrupt the world of work" (Illanes et al. 2018).
- Deloitte predicts the future of work will involve "superjobs," making upskilling and reskilling even more critical (Volini et al. 2021).
- A common theme from multiple reports confirms that soft skills are booming. For talent and TD professionals to succeed in the now and beyond, developing and honing soft skills should be a key focus.

Before you jump, do a preliminary assessment using this checklist:
- ❏ I have the essential skills and tools necessary to navigate workplace changes and new challenges, including analytical research, communication, problem solving, adaptability, empathy, and listening skills.
- ❏ I have the mindset to embrace courage, confidence, and collaboration.
- ❏ I know what role I should play in various situations (such as an expert, a pair of hands, or a collaborator).
- ❏ I have the capability to start, influence, or lead new and innovative initiatives that advance the learning function and align with organizational objectives and strategies.
- ❏ I am effective in recruiting, influencing, and directing SMEs and other key resources necessary to get desired results.
- ❏ I am proficient at facilitating content and messages that engage learners and leaders.
- ❏ I consider and integrate ongoing DEI principles and practices into all current and new initiatives and curriculums.
- ❏ I am current and confident about my knowledge of digital literacy and technology changes relative to talent development and L&D.
- ❏ I can contribute insight, knowledge, or creative considerations that affect the organization's tech strategy or ecosystem.
- ❏ I have a thirst and an enthusiasm for lifelong learning.

What Happens When You Land on the Designated Target?

One question I ask when facilitating the ATD Managing Learning Programs Certificate course is how the learning function's strategic plan aligns with the organization's plan. Most of the course participants report that they have an annual business or budget plan, but very few have an actual strategic plan. How can we focus on the future if we don't have a vision of what the future looks like? There are numerous benefits to investing the time and effort in developing a strategic plan even if it's not a required document in your organization. Here are just a few:

- A stronger partnership with senior leaders and clarity of mutually agreed upon outcomes. The need to prove value or ROI is no longer a debate because all decisions are aligned to the business.
- Leadership skills gaps are closed at every level by redesigning the skills and capability frameworks that support working with virtual, hybrid, and individual contributors. There are no more one-and-done, one-shoe-fits-all solutions.
- Learning becomes an active, participative, and rewarding experience as individuals process information into knowledge, values, and skills at their own pace.

- Authentic conversations are facilitated at all levels, addressing individual and organizational bias and creating strategies and processes that support cultures of inclusion.
- Data collection provides insights that lead to action by informing leaders about when and where to invest in people, programs, and projects.
- The organization will have more diverse representation. Training will be instrumental in preparing and enabling necessary skill opportunities for all, not only race and gender, but also other demographics such as age, disabilities, and military veterans.
- The succession bench is developed for the next generation of leadership.

Are You Willing to Shift?

Our real value and leverage come from our willingness to shift our mindset and attitudes. The *2020 Emerald Works Learner Intelligence* report shows the disconnect between L&D's mindset and the practical, on-the-ground practice and outcomes. Our industry is declining in impact while consuming more investment.

According to research by Gallup, the number 1 reason people change jobs is lack of career growth opportunities (Hoogerhuis and Nelson 2018). There is an even greater war for talent as people are considering other factors post-pandemic. If organizations, leaders, and talent professionals don't change the way they approach learning and development, they cannot expect to attract, retain, or sustain top talent or performance excellence.

Mindset and attitude are fundamental to everything we do—both good and bad. Those who create the most value relinquish control and share responsibility for learning with others. They see others as connected contributors to learning rather than passive recipients of content and training.

Our attitudes drive outcomes, so if your belief is that your purpose is only to fulfill compliance requirements or employee engagement rather than being a critical business function with measurable performance impact, then that becomes your reality.

But if we make the shift and allow the old to make way for the new, we can also align learning with the business.

Let's be real. As talent and learning professionals, we promote certain principles, but how often do we take the time to personally develop practices that shift our mindset and attitudes? For example, consider Stephen Covey's seven habits of highly effective people:

- Be proactive.
- Begin with the end in mind.
- Put first things first.
- Think win–win.

- Seek first to understand, then be understood.
- Synergize.
- Sharpen the saw.

Marshall Goldsmith reinforces this concept of continuous improvement in his book *What Got You Here Won't Get You There*. A forward-focused attitude is nonnegotiable if you're going to stay in the game.

Although we can't predict the future, certain attitudes will help us feel better prepared when facing it. An attitude can be defined as a predisposition to respond in a favorable or unfavorable way to objects or people in one's environment. Let's consider four different types of attitudes and what you might hear:

- **Passivity**—Status quo until change is imposed.
  - Our curriculum has been effective for several years, so why change now?
  - No one is requesting changes, so they must be satisfied.
  - A needs analysis is very invasive and uncomfortable, so do we really need to do it?
  - We tried that several years ago and it didn't work.
  - I am comfortable in my job and have no desire to change.
- **Reactivity**—Waiting for fires before acting.
  - I wish I had more time because there's no way to get everything done.
  - It's policy so there's nothing I can do.
  - They really make me mad.
  - I need … I must … I can't …
- **Pre-activity**—Anticipating what can happen before it happens and mitigating the risk factors.
  - We need to establish a policy to address that before it happens to us.
  - We need to develop a plan based on what happened with a competitor.
  - What are some of the obstacles or challenges that we need to consider?
  - Let's consider how other organizations are addressing training after the pandemic.
  - We can learn from others' best practices.
- **Proactivity**—Acting before something happens.
  - A strategic plan will help us achieve our vision and goals.
  - Let's assign individuals as project leads to execute our plan.
  - Let's enroll the support of senior leaders, SMEs, or other departments.
  - I take full responsibility to get it done.

- We need to work on our organization skills, priority management, being present, and planning ahead.
- Let's look at the alternatives.

After realistically assessing your proficiencies and attitude, are you ready to move into the future of talent development and L&D? How do you need to slow down to go fast?

About the Author

Rita Bailey is the founder and owner of Up to Something, a strategic consulting network focused on humanity, civility, and DEI. She has been actively involved in L&D leadership for more than 25 years as a former head of Southwest Airlines Corporate University, an ATD past chair, and a thought leader, author, speaker, and coach. She has traveled to more than 40 countries, speaking and helping organizations create more people-centric workplaces. Learn more at uptosomething.com or linkedin.com/in/ritabaileyuts.

References

Accenture. 2021. *The Future of Work: Productive Anywhere.* Accenture. accenture.com/_acnmedia/PDF-155/Accenture-Future-Of-Work-Global-Report.pdf.

Bersin, J. 2020. "The Big Reset Playbook: What's Working Now." Josh Bersin, Business Trends, August 26. joshbersin.com/2020/08/the-big-reset-playbook-whats-working-now.

Covey, S.R. 2004. *The 7 Habits of Highly Effective People.* New York: Free Press.

Emerald Works. 2020. *Back to the Future: Why Tomorrow's Workforce Needs a Learning Culture.* Mind Tools.

Hoogerhuis, M., and B. Nelson. 2018. "Why It's Time to Disrupt the Traditional Approach to L&D." Gallup, November 8. gallup.com/workplace/244628/why-time-disrupt-traditional-approach.aspx.

Illanes, P., S. Lund, S. Rutherford, and M. Tyreman. 2018. "Retraining and Reskilling Workers in the Age of Automation." McKinsey Global Institute, January 22. mckinsey.com/featured-insights/future-of-work/retraining-and-reskilling-workers-in-the-age-of-automation.

LinkedIn Learning. 2020. *2020 Workplace Learning Report.* LinkedIn. learning.linkedin.com/content/dam/me/learning/resources/pdfs/LinkedIn-Learning-2020-Workplace-Learning-Report.pdf.

Skillsoft. 2019. *Mind the Gap: Upskilling Asia Pacific Employees for the Digital Workplace*. Skillsoft. skillsoft.com/wp-content/uploads/2019/06/Bench-Skillsoft-APAC-executive-summary.pdf.

Volini, E. et al. 2021. *The Social Enterprise in a World Disrupted*. 2021 Deloitte Global Human Capital Trends. deloitte.com/content/dam/Deloitte/lu/Documents/human-capital/lu-hc-trends-2021.pdf.

Recommended Resources

Goldsmith, M., and M. Reiter. 2007. *What Got You Here Won't Get You There*. New York: Hyperion.

CHAPTER 27

Essential Skills for TD Professionals

Wendy Gates Corbett

The label "talent development professional" implies that we've achieved a level of competence or proficiency in the skills we use to do our work. More basic skills such as collaboration and agility support specialized skills like designing learning. And skills such as influence and global perspective enable us to better partner across our organizations, communicating how talent development practices can help achieve organizational goals.

> **IN THIS CHAPTER:**
> - Define the skills that are essential for talent development professionals
> - Examine where these skills are applied in the workplace
> - Consider strategies for developing essential skills

To create a world that works better, we use a combination of our own unique powers and a set of essential skills all talent development professionals employ to develop the people in our workplaces. Building these essential skills is vital for our successful contributions to our organizations. This chapter focuses on seven skills that are essential for talent development professionals and provides suggestions for how to build them. These skills are:

- Agility
- Global perspective
- Influence
- Collaboration
- Integrity
- Responsibility and accountability
- Resilience

Of course, there are other skills that all professionals need to succeed. The seven skills outlined in this chapter were selected after reflecting on my own career experience and talking with a broad cross section of TD professionals in a variety of work settings. They serve as the foundation for the other, more specialized skills outlined in other chapters of this book because they contribute substantially to our ability to empower others.

Where Essential Skills Show Up at Work

The essential skills outlined in this chapter are used throughout our everyday work routines. Let's review a few examples of where these skills show up in a typical talent development professional's day.

- David's learning and organization development team used *agility* and *collaboration* when it had to transition all scheduled in-person training programs to virtual delivery in a period of three weeks after the company froze all domestic and international travel.
- In a meeting with her senior leaders, Bonita used her *influencing* skills to make her case and successfully get buy-in for a new employee well-being initiative.
- Terry drew on her *integrity* and strong sense of *responsibility* as she led her team through a challenging reorganization process.

Whether we are employed by a large global company, a regional organization, or run our own business, the essential skills described here are key to our success. For example, Sharon Wingron has a small, family-owned talent development consulting and supplier business. She started out in 2002 as a solopreneur—a one-woman shop. But as her business evolved and the world of work changed, so did her needs. She now leads a small team of full- and part-time employees and contractors. Collaboration, communication, agility, and accountability come into play in every aspect of their work. She relies on and holds her team members accountable for completing all tasks on time and with the quality their clients require. She expects them to work well together on their tasks and projects so that her company can deliver as promised to their clients while continuing to evolve the business.

Essential Skill: Agility

> Agility: The ability to swiftly adapt to new circumstances, whether internal to the organization (such as a realignment or restructuring of department functions) or external to the organization (such as advancements in technology that affect the business)

Organizations need to be agile to quickly respond to today's ever-changing business environment. Talent development professionals need to steer confidently and competently toward goals with a clear direction, steadfast focus, and determination. However, unexpected circumstances can require us to quickly adapt, to change strategies for reaching a goal, or to change direction entirely and steer toward a new goal. With agility, we can make these changes quickly, smoothly, and successfully.

How and where people work is changing at a faster pace, and TD professionals need to provide flexible learning opportunities to meet the evolving needs of the workforce. If we're unable (or unwilling) to adapt, we run the risk of losing our seat at the table, our ability to influence, and our capability to contribute to the organization's success.

For example, Bernadette Costello is an instructor who was used to delivering live, face-to-face classes. With little warning, the university where she worked transitioned to live, virtual classes in the middle of a semester. While initially not a fan of virtual delivery, Bernadette adopted an agile mindset and experimented with interactive technologies that could mimic (and sometimes even improve upon) the face-to-face classroom experience. This introduced her to a variety of applications that allowed her to continue contributing to the university and the students' ability to learn.

Many of us exercise or build our agility daily. It can be applied in situations as simple as adjusting the start time for a training program to accommodate participants in a different part of the world or as complex as transforming a team member's job responsibilities to take on a new role in response to changes in the marketplace.

Humans are wired to fear change. Most of us don't like change, so being agile takes practice. Often our initial response to any change is negative, which doesn't serve us well. Here are three ways to practice expanding your willingness and ability to pivot and cultivate your agility:

- **Pause.** When presented with a pivot, pause before responding and take three deep breaths. Interrupting a conditioned response with a pause offers an opportunity to choose a different response.
- **Embrace the new.** Take advantage of situations away from your work environment and intentionally practice embracing the opportunities brought by an unexpected or sudden shift. Try looking at it as an opportunity for a new, novel chance at discovering something new.
- **Step outside your comfort zone.** Look for opportunities at work to try something completely different and outside your comfort zone to elevate your comfort level with the unfamiliar.

Essential Skill: Global Perspective or Mindset

> Global mindset: A set of attributes that helps people work better with individuals and organizations unlike themselves. It is the ability to understand the similarities and differences among cultures and not be paralyzed by the differences. It is about being comfortable with being uncomfortable in different environments. (Thunderbird School of Global Management 2021)

The workforce is becoming increasingly global—from multinational companies to organizations that do business around the world. The ability to embrace and understand differences among cultures serves us well as TD professionals regardless of our role. It enables us to have a deeper impact in our organizations by working effectively with people across borders, cultures, and generations and preparing others to do the same. Embracing a global mindset goes beyond appreciating similarities and differences in cultures and generations. It includes truly integrating them into our strategies, initiatives, and programs. Table 27-1 provides examples of where a global perspective can appear in a talent development professional's work.

Table 27-1. Using a Global Mindset Across TD Roles

Role	Global Mindset Influence
Talent development leaders	• Setting talent strategies • Defining policies that respect cultural and generational differences
Instructors	• Being aware of and respectful of different cultures while setting class expectations
Content developers	• Ensuring media, such as images and videos, include an array of diverse people

A global mindset can influence many aspects of your day-to-day work experiences (Ratanjee 2019). One part of adopting a global perspective is an increased awareness of how varied cultural and behavioral norms are. For example, on a geographically dispersed team with members in different countries, which culture's norms are adopted by the team? Another cultural aspect to be aware of is norms related to classroom behavior. For example, in a virtual class with participants from around the globe, is it acceptable to ask questions? Is it respectful to expect participants to have their web cameras on during class? These questions can be addressed effectively and fairly when you have an understanding of a global perspective.

For example, one company I worked for was based in the United States, with employees from India, Venezuela, Ireland, Canada, and the United States. Our office hosted a monthly potluck lunch where employees brought food dishes from their home countries or states, allowing us all to learn more about one another's cultures and customs.

Develop a global mindset by focusing on:
- Increasing your self-awareness
- Cultivating curiosity about people and cultures
- Expanding your flexibility and open-mindedness to include all options

Essential Skill: Influence

> Influence: The ability to transform and shape others' opinions and actions (Adapted from CCL)

We use influencing skills throughout our workday to get our point across in conversations, emails, presentations, reports, and the learning environment.

For talent development professionals to provide maximum value, we need to be able to influence the organization and its leaders. In fact, the ability to influence is an important trait for identifying leadership potential (Nielsen, Niu, and Meng 2016). Providing a convincing explanation for investing in programs that develop skills and drive employee success, employee engagement, and retention of top talent is a key opportunity for TD professionals. To influence business leaders, we need to have a clear understanding of the business needs and the ability to communicate using language that they understand and respect. We also need to be able to quantify the expected impact for the programs and provide relevant metrics related to the work.

For example, when Dawn Sander was a talent leader at a large global medical device company, she invested time learning the business of the division she supported. She took ride-alongs with sales reps so she could see the skills they used and those they needed. She also participated in business meetings to better understand their work and conducted focus groups to get a clear understanding of the sales reps' needs. As a result of her investment, she gained valuable insight about the business and was able to influence the leaders she partnered with by showing that she clearly understood their needs.

Here are a few examples of where influencing might appear during your day:
- Generating buy-in for your proposal for a new training program
- Deciding as a team which projects should get top priority
- Encouraging learners to adapt new behaviors as you facilitate a training program

Influence is built on genuine trust, connection, and integrity. Build your influence skills by:
- Consistently communicating with others clearly, honestly, and transparently
- Providing thorough, well-thought-out information that is backed by data and facts
- Following through on your commitments
- Creating genuine connections with others by listening, showing interest, and asking thoughtful questions

Essential Skill: Collaboration

> Collaboration: Behavior in which two or more individuals work together toward a common goal with equal opportunity to participate, communicate, and be involved (ATD 2020)

We don't empower others to develop talent in the workplace by ourselves; we do it by working with others. Today more than ever before, at all levels in the organization, our work as TD professionals requires collaboration. When collaboration is missing it slows or stalls projects, creates frustration among team members, squashes motivation, and leads to disengagement.

Collaboration skills include:
- Clearly and diplomatically communicating information in written and verbal forms
- Being open-minded with the ability to hear others' perspectives without judgment
- Empathizing to understand and be aware of and sensitive to others' feelings and experiences
- Demonstrating trustworthiness or the ability to be relied upon consistently

Whether we're collaborating within our own department or with multiple divisions that span the organization, we can use these guidelines to collaborate effectively:
- Create a shared vision or purpose and identify clear goals as a team-building exercise—this will offer a sense of team identity, unity, and shared purpose.
- Establish a team or project charter regarding communication, accountability, and responsibilities, as well as how decisions will be made and conflicts will be resolved.

- Develop trust and rapport among team members by providing opportunities to get to know one another as people.
- Keep the team goals front and center.
- Meet or communicate regularly, discussing timelines, progress, challenges, and decisions, as well as providing the opportunity for connection.
- Celebrate wins, big and small.

Use these three strategies to build your collaboration skills:
- Practice open-mindedness in how you respond to outcomes, comments, or ideas you don't like—look at them with curiosity.
- Use active listening in conversations and meetings.
- Ask for help from team members to get comfortable receiving it and ask your team members how you can help them.

Essential Skill: Integrity

> Integrity: Consistently acting in firm adherence to moral and ethical principles. Knowing and doing the right thing, even when no one is watching. Acting with integrity involves using morals as your beacon for decisions and direction.

Has anyone ever taken credit for something you did? That's what it feels like when someone does not act with integrity. How much do you trust that person now? How eager are you to collaborate with them or to offer your assistance? There are far-reaching consequences for not acting with integrity.

You want to trust your colleagues and leaders unequivocally, and to have no fear in their moral compasses. Similarly, your team, your leaders, and your learners need to know they can count on you to act with integrity.

Examples of integrity include:
- Committing to writing your own training material and not searching the internet to find content written by someone else.
- Acknowledging to your manager that your team member was largely responsible for a project's success.
- Not sharing a copyrighted handout from a conference presentation without approval from the author, even if the author would never know.

Build your integrity by striving to consistently act within your morals and values.

Essential Skill: Responsibility/Accountability

> Responsibility: Honoring your commitments, following through on your duties, and being reliable and trustworthy
> Accountability: Accepting responsibility for your actions
> (*Merriam-Webster Dictionary*)

Responsibility and accountability are closely related skills that professionals in every industry must have. Being regarded as irresponsible will have a significant limiting impact on your career because when your team can't trust that you will do what you committed to, they'll stop relying on you. Your leaders will lose trust in your ability to complete projects on time or at the quality level that meets their expectations. Conversely, when your team and leaders know you are responsible, their trust in you grows and your ability to influence them (and the organization) does as well.

Examples of responsibility include:
- Responding to phone calls and emails in a timely manner
- Completing projects on time, thoroughly, and without mistakes
- Attending team meetings and being fully present, attentive, and engaged

Being accountable means you meet all deadlines to provide exactly what's expected. And if you miss a deadline, you accept responsibility for your actions, don't make excuses, and apologize for the delay. It may mean that you submit a project update ahead of time and arrange for a colleague to share your report if you have to miss a meeting. Accountability also involves holding others accountable. While leaders are responsible for holding their team members accountable, strong teams empower team members to hold one another accountable as well. That means addressing behavior that is out of line or doesn't meet expectations.

Let's review a few examples of accountability:
- Maura couldn't go to a meeting, so she sent her project update in an email ahead of time and agreed to follow up with George, the project lead, for any new tasks she was assigned.
- Marcelo rescheduled his doctor's appointment for later in the day so he would be available to facilitate the new employee orientation program as his team expected.
- Rashad contacted a support team to find the answer to a question a participant asked during a training program and followed up with the answer before the agreed upon date.

Build your responsibility and accountability skills by making commitments to yourself and others that you can honor and then honoring them to the best of your ability. Be proactive and inform others as soon as you're aware of a change in schedule. Accountable TD professionals under promise and then overachieve.

Use these three strategies to build your accountability skills:
- Ensure that you schedule realistic due dates for all projects and tasks; if you can't meet a requested deadline, say so immediately.
- Clarify by ensuring that you know what result is expected on which date, at what time, in which time zone.
- Set high expectations for yourself by taking ownership of tasks that need to be done, accept personal responsibility for doing it on time every time, and then ask, "What else can I do?"

TD PROFESSIONALS MUST LEAD WITH COURAGE
Bill Treasurer, Chief Encouragement Officer, Giant Leap Consulting; Author, Courage Goes to Work *and* Leaders Open Doors

As TD professionals we must be leaders, even if we have high and often contradictory expectations of a leader's role. We wrestle with leadership conflicts knowing that leaders must be reasonable but passionate, strategic but tactical, decisive but inclusive, and confident but humble. As a TD professional you must be all those things too! You might be thinking, "Where on earth do I start?"

The starting point is courage. Aristotle called courage the first virtue, because it makes all the other virtues possible. Courage is what steels the backbone that leaders like you need to forge the future, set bold development priorities, face challenges, inspire others, provide candid feedback, confront ethical breaches, and support the bottom line. Sound familiar? It's what you do every day. Courage must be woven into everything you do. Thus, at the start of your leadership journey, you should first commit to nurturing, developing, and strengthening your courage.

My firm, Giant Leap, is a courage-building consulting firm. Our mission is to build workplace courage. The richest part of our workshops is the insightful discussions about the central role courage plays as it relates to leading and developing others. Four insights from my book *Courage Goes to Work* may provide you with a starting point:
- **Look for courage opportunities every day.** Small acts of courage make a big difference. Examples include pursuing big goals that stretch your skills, proposing ways your leaders can champion learning, giving candid feedback to your participants or peers, coaching managers about how to develop their people, or recommending that a favorite training program be cut because it doesn't support the organization's goals.
- **Set a bold future.** As a trusted advisor to your C-suite, you can partner with them to develop a workforce that supports the organization's strategic imperative. You can be at the forefront and take a courageous approach to offering an innovative and bold, yet effective and practical approach to upskilling the workforce. Help your leaders determine how they can establish a hybrid workforce that engages employees, manages equity issues, fosters teamwork, and achieves organizational goals. That kind of TD leadership takes courage!

> **TD PROFESSIONALS MUST LEAD WITH COURAGE** *continued*
>
> - **Practice three expressions of courage.** We believe that courage falls into one of three behavior expressions: tell, try, and trust courage. You show *tell courage*, for example, when you provide feedback, even if it's negative, to your leadership about why engagement scores are low. You demonstrate *try courage* when you volunteer to deliver a topic that you've never facilitated before. And you display *trust courage* when you let IT take the lead to develop the best cyber approach for your TD department.
> - **Start with you.** As a TD professional, you're required to model the values you expect others to uphold. If you want others to be courageous, you must be the first one to go up and jump off whatever high dive you're asking others to jump off. Here are some self-development questions to consider: *Where am I playing it too safe? What big goals am I pursuing that warrant my courage mojo? What tasks have I outgrown that I need to delegate to others? What actions can I take to be a better role model of courage behavior?*
>
> One of your primary TD goals should be to clarify your organization's readiness to create a learning culture. That means you need to ensure your leaders champion learning, your employees value learning, and everyone has a learning mindset. It's a big task but you can lead the way—especially if you let courage guide you. Courage can be the lifeblood of talent development, causing your department to step up to challenges, offer innovative ideas, be more productive, and ensure a measurable ROI. Make courage your department's essence, so all TD professionals get involved, embrace change, seek out leadership opportunities, and help the organization achieve its vision. Courage is the first virtue of development and leadership!

Essential Skill: Resilience

> **Resilience:** The ability to keep going, to recover, and to adapt well and quickly in the face of adversity, change, or stress

Resilience is the ability to keep going when the journey is longer than expected, or you've hit potholes and speed bumps along the way. Talent development professionals always have the next training program to develop or facilitate. Our work is never done because there is always another exciting new initiative around the corner. Constantly changing or competing priorities are the norm. Our ability to bounce back from these challenges helps us maintain our influence, trusted status, and reliability. It contributes to being seen as diligent, reliable, successful partners who rise to each challenge. Resilience is the refueling of our courage and wherewithal to get back up and keep going. If we're not resilient, we will struggle to persevere when our personal fuel gets low.

In February 2020, I finally finished shifting the focus of my business from one professional passion (slide design and presentation consulting) to my other passion of building belonging in organizations. But when the COVID-19 pandemic hit a month later, businesses shifted their focus from diversity, inclusion, and belonging to establishing remote work environments. Once their employees were set up to work from home, organizations turned their attention to helping employees present more effectively in a virtual setting. So, while I wanted to do more organization development and culture projects, my clients needed help with presentations. To feed my desire to move forward with my belonging work, I was resilient in that I continued to read, research, and attend training programs to develop my own knowledge and expertise while meeting my clients' immediate needs.

Here are three simple ways to build resilience:
- **Take a break.** Standing up from your desk or taking a 10-minute walk outside (with or without a colleague) can recharge your focus, attention, and motivation.
- **Sleep.** Getting the right amount of nightly sleep for you and taking a short nap when you are tired can refresh your alertness.
- **Enlist anxiety- and stress-reducing strategies.** Citing affirmations, meditating, practicing breathing exercises, using calming essential oils, and listening to music are all helpful.

Final Thoughts

We employ a broad range of skills as talent development professionals. The ones outlined in this chapter empower us to excel in our roles. Investing our time and energy in developing these skills is essential for our own success, as well as our ability to contribute to our organization's success. ATD's Talent Development Capability Model self-assessment is a valuable tool for evaluating these essential skills, as well as the others in this handbook. You can find that assessment on the ATD website. In addition, use the checklist on the handbook website at ATDHandbook3.org to identify which skills you need to develop. Then develop a plan to learn and practice the essential skills that will make you a better TD professional.

About the Author

Wendy Gates Corbett, CPTD, believes in the power of building belonging within people and places. She champions this through her speaking, training, and consulting work as the president of Signature Presentations. Wendy guides organizations in taking the difficult, yet necessary steps to create embracive spaces where people have no doubt that they belong. She's an experienced international speaker, award-winning consultant, and executive-level facilitator who has trained more than 100,000 people over the past 20-plus years. Wendy is a recognized leader in the training industry and a past member of the Association for Talent Development's board of directors. She speaks globally on building belonging, confidence, clarity, and powerful presence. You can learn more about her work at signature-presentations.com.

References

ATD (Association for Talent Development). 2020. "Collaboration." *Talent Development Body of Knowledge.* Alexandria, VA: Association for Talent Development.

Nielsen, C., D. Niu, and S. Meng. 2016. "Measuring Your Employees' Invisible Forms of Influence." *Harvard Business Review,* November 7. hbr.org/2016/11/measuring-your-employees-invisible-forms-of-influence.

Ratanjee, V. 2019. "The Future of Leadership Development: A Global Mindset." *Gallup,* February 8. gallup.com/workplace/246551/future-leadership-development-global-mindset.aspx.

"Responsibility." *Merriam-Webster* Online. merriam-webster.com/dictionary/responsibility.

Thunderbird School of Global Management. 2021. "Developing a Global Mindset." *Thunderbird School of Global Management; Arizona State University,* April 9. thunderbird.asu.edu/knowledge-network/developing-global-mindset.

Recommended Resources

Biech, E. 2021. *Skills for Career Success: Maximizing Your Potential at Work.* San Francisco: Berrett-Koehler Publishers.

Changcoco, R., M. Cole, and J. Harlow. 2018. *Focus on Them: Become the Manager Your People Need You to Be.* Alexandria, VA: ATD Press.

Tobin, T. 2019. *Peak Leadership Fitness: Elevating Your Leadership Game.* Alexandria, VA: ATD Press.

CHAPTER 28

Initiating a Talent Development Effort

David Macon

Initiating a talent development effort is a challenging and gratifying endeavor. Navigating all the twists, turns, and obstacles can be daunting. This chapter includes practical guidance to help TD professionals prepare for this exciting journey and traverse difficulties along the way.

IN THIS CHAPTER:
- Explore a practical framework for initiating a new talent development effort
- Address realistic examples of challenges that may occur during the initiation of a TD effort

Have you been asked to start a talent development program or department in your organization? Are you wondering where to begin? This chapter explores the five factors of an effective launch: purpose, planning, people, procurement, and production.

Purpose: Understand Your Organization's Vision

Organizations are diverse, unique, and constantly changing. Even organizations within the same sector or industry can have vastly different cultures, strategies, and processes. With so many intricacies to consider, it is critically important to kick off any talent development effort with a strong focus on the organization's purpose. If this is not already clearly outlined in a vision statement or some other company ethos, TD professionals will need to uncover, identify, and crystallize it themselves. By understanding the purpose of the organization, TD professionals can better understand how they contribute to that overall vision.

TD professionals should also identify strategic organizational objectives during this discovery process. By understanding both purpose and strategy, TD professionals should be able to recognize how they are expected to fit into the big picture. If an organization does not have explicit strategic objectives, it may be necessary to interview senior leaders and ask a few simple questions, such as:

- Why did they approve the launch of this talent development initiative?
- Why now?
- What impact are they expecting this launch to have on organizational performance?
- How will success of the launch be measured?

By clearly understanding both purpose and objectives, TD professionals can begin focusing on other factors that may affect the launch of their talent development effort. An effective talent development strategy focuses on *why* in addition to *what* and *how*. These core elements must remain at the vanguard during planning and execution. This is essential to developing an effective learning culture.

Management consultant and author Peter Drucker brilliantly and famously said, "Culture eats strategy for breakfast." This is absolutely true when evaluating learning within an organization. Organizations with a strong learning culture understand the importance of ongoing learning and the impact this has on human capital. An effective talent development strategy must address learning culture, and an effective learning culture stems from a deep understanding of the learners and their needs. It's important to note, however, that TD professionals may focus too heavily on the brain (neuroscience and cognitive psychology) and perhaps not enough on the heart (values, desires, dreams). This is why many organizations struggle to create or maintain a learning culture—they focus too heavily on delivering information and too little on meeting needs.

Learning happens continually within individuals and organizations, and it often goes unnoticed. However, by not recognizing the impact of ongoing learning, it is challenging to appreciate the effect it has on an organization. Unrecognized and underappreciated aspects of an organization seldom make their way into the cultural consciousness of leaders and employees. This is precisely why cultivating a culture of learning is so challenging. To combat these challenges, TD professionals must align the purpose and objectives for all three entities: the organization, department, and individual (Figure 28-1).

Figure 28-1. Aligning Purpose and Objectives Across the Organization

Example 1

	Organization	TD Department	Employee
Purpose	Enrich customers' lives	Improve skills	Meaningful work
Objectives	Profitability	Positive ROI	Greater compensation

Example 2

	Organization	TD Department	Employee
Purpose	Rewarding employment	Empower learners	Valued and appreciated
Objectives	Scale	Additional resources	Career advancement

By weaving a thread of shared purpose, TD professionals can highlight the ways in which ongoing learning benefits employees individually and the organization overall. By framing learning as the catalyst for fulfilling purpose and accomplishing objectives, it is more likely to be elevated within the organization's cultural consciousness.

Planning: Begin Crafting for the Long and Short Term

Having carefully considered the core elements of their organization's purpose, objectives, and learning culture, TD professionals should begin crafting a long-term strategic plan and a launch plan. Long-range planning is useful for shaping the core elements of how the TD department will operate. A launch plan is useful in establishing the short-term strategy and objectives that can be quickly executed within the first 30 to 90 days. Aligning a carefully structured long-term strategy with a well-thought-out launch strategy drastically increases the likelihood of success.

The foremost focus of a long-term TD strategy should be to support the organization's strategy. Failing to support the organization's strategic objectives is a recipe for conflict or even disaster. Beyond this primary concern, an effective TD strategy should address these basic questions:

- How will the department improve the organization? (Vision)
- How is the department going to operate? (Mission, values, and culture)
- What will the department accomplish? (Objectives)
- How will progress toward the objectives be measured? (Benchmarks)
- What specific outcomes must be achieved? (Milestones)

The questions are simple, but their answers may take significant time and thought. The initial creation of a long-term strategy is just a starting point. It is normal, even healthy, for objectives to evolve and change over time. Whenever possible, it is recommended to include TD personnel and stakeholders in the strategy development process. Inclusion and diversity of thought not only improve the outcome but also increase buy-in to the plan.

With a long-term strategic plan drafted, TD leaders should shift their focus to the first 30 to 90 days. Think of space explorers: Mapping the trajectory of a rocket from Earth's atmosphere to the surface of Mars is a clear goal, but it is just a plan if they cannot get the rocket off the ground. This is analogous to the relationship of the long-term strategy and the launch strategy for a TD effort. Creating and executing a detailed 90-day plan will create momentum.

To kick off the development of a 90-day plan, it is wise to begin the planning process with a stakeholder meeting. This can be useful because you'll review and select the most immediate needs for the organization, which may or may not align with the organization's strategic objectives. For example, improving the organization's net promoter score may be an urgent strategic objective, but launching a learning management system may be the most immediate need within the first 30 to 90 days. By involving stakeholders in the prioritization and planning process, they will be more invested in the initial effort and more understanding if high-priority objectives are delayed.

A formal needs assessment and learner evaluation can also help direct the initial effort. Unlike the stakeholder meeting (a top-down approach), a needs assessment and learner assessment can identify less visible needs within the organization (a bottom-up approach). Accounting for the needs, challenges, and experiences of learners can lead to more impactful learning solutions, which is critical in the development of a learning culture. Combining insights from stakeholders and learners will help narrow the TD effort's 90-day focus. Visit the handbook website (ATDHandbook3.org) to download a template for developing your 90-day plan.

As a general guideline, avoid tackling more than one major milestone per month when developing a 90-day plan. Major milestones are generally cost, labor, or change intensive, and they may span multiple months. A change-intensive milestone could be a specific outcome that requires learners to behave in a manner that is significantly different from how they are currently operating. Rolling out a new sales process, launching a new software platform, or changing a manufacturing process would all be examples of a change intensive milestone. Major milestones should be evaluated critically to ensure timelines are realistic.

Minor milestones should be limited to three per month. The delineation between minor and major milestones is dependent on cost, labor, and change intensity. If it seems like three is not enough, chances are the milestones are too small and should be reclassified as projects or tasks.

Milestones may involve three or more projects; however, remain cautious to avoid overcommitting. A task is a specific, measurable outcome assigned to a person or group, while a project is a collection of three or more tasks. An example of a task could be: "Raja will contact the LMS vendor and set up a meeting to review pricing before the end of next week." In contrast, a project might be: "Group A will identify the top three LMS vendors and develop a comparison matrix by the 15th."

Armed with a prioritized list of key outcomes based on stakeholder and learner insights, TD professionals should work backward to develop the 90-day plan. This is accomplished by deconstructing outcomes into milestones, then milestones into projects, and projects into tasks. In practice, this is often done with a whiteboard, a flipchart, or brainstorming software. It may seem daunting, but many complex challenges can be solved with a group of people, a stack of sticky notes, and a couple pizzas. Technology even allows for this process to be completed remotely through virtual workspaces. It may take several sessions to develop and refine the 90-day plan, but the time and effort invested should expedite and enhance execution of the plan later on.

During the process of deconstructing milestones (and subsequently projects and tasks), the key is specificity. A plan without details is an idea. Critically evaluate each step to determine if it could be more specific or concise. Once a plan is developed, each team member should have a specific list of tasks that need to be accomplished with clear deadlines and outcomes. It should also be clear what resources and approvals are needed for completion of the task, project, or milestone. This creates immediate accountability and prevents ambiguity paralysis. It is also recommended to keep a list of resource needs that can be discussed and evaluated with stakeholders and leaders that is independent of the task list.

When drafting a launch strategy, pragmatism is key. A common pitfall many TD leaders make is drafting an overly ambitious plan because they don't realize they have set unrealistic expectations until it is seemingly too late to modify them. At this point they often make the even bigger mistake of doubling-down instead of adjusting their plan. The pursuit of unrealistic goals often leads to burnout, inadequate work product, and poor communication. Additionally, the first 90 days sets the tone of your organization's TD function. If the department produces substandard training, it negatively influences the department's reputation and hurts the organization's learning culture.

In fairness, it is possible to execute a highly ambitious launch plan. The question is, at what cost? If TD leaders aren't careful, they can quickly burn through their resources in the first 90 days, leaving the department lean for the remaining nine months of the year. Also consider the ramifications of driving team members to operate at maximum effort to deliver unreasonable outcomes. Unreasonable outcomes can spring from a healthy focus such as striving to demonstrate value or

ROI. In some cases they are heaped upon the new department by senior leaders, stakeholders, learners, or supervisors. Unreasonable expectations can detrimentally affect mental and physical health and set an unhealthy standard. Senior leaders and executives may expect the department to continue operating at an unsustainable pace, for example. The first 90 days will set the precedent for how others expect the TD department to function after launch.

Theodore Roosevelt said, "Do what you can, with what you have, where you are." This simple thought embodies the mindset needed to successfully launch a TD effort. Adapting these famous words can provide a pragmatic framework for developing a launch plan: "What can I accomplish in the next 90 days, with the personnel and resources available, to achieve maximum strategic impact?" By focusing the launch plan on strategic impact, TD professionals set themselves up for a quick victory. This builds momentum, fosters goodwill, and demonstrates value. To achieve that impact, leaders need to carefully assess the people and resources available. Ideally, they will be able to negotiate headcounts, skill sets, and budgets, but that isn't always the case. Whatever the circumstances, TD professionals must maximize every asset and operate within their constraints. Finally, leaders must set realistic objectives, benchmarks, and milestones to guide all activities in the first 90 days.

Once the long-term strategic plan and launch plan are drafted, it is important to get feedback on each one. It is also wise to bounce ideas off trusted advisors within the organization throughout the process, and it is absolutely essential to do so at the end of the process. Specifically, TD professionals should seek the counsel of someone who can provide objective and analytical feedback. This can be anyone who is not directly involved in the TD effort and can be trusted to think critically, ask questions, and provide honest feedback. Consider leaders or peers in other departments, mentors, or an outside consultant. Even if the plan is solid, their feedback may help the TD professional prepare for questions and concerns that they may encounter from other leaders within the organization. It can be challenging to hear critical feedback, but if it prevents costly mistakes or improves outcomes, the feedback is worth hearing.

Once the plans have been reviewed and revamped, it is time to communicate the plan. In her book *Starting a Talent Development Program*, Elaine Biech creates a compelling case for the importance of this step: "This strategy is a tool that allows you to be proactive in your approach to starting your organization's talent development program." She also notes that "it leads to buy in, prepares you to make better decisions, and ensures that you will get better results." Transparency and effective communication are essential to a thriving learning culture. Sharing and discussing long-term plans and the launch plan can be a catalyst for ongoing talent development conversations within the organization.

BUILD A BUSINESS CASE
Elaine Biech, Author, Consultant, Lifelong ATD Volunteer

Your senior leadership team has requested a talent development program. You have uncovered the purpose for initiating a TD effort and gathered data for your 90-day plan. You can use the same information to create a document—a business case—to share with individuals in your organization. Why should you make a case for the TD program? A business case will be helpful in several situations (Biech 2018):

- Although your senior leadership team may have requested that you develop a TD effort, some may not have "agreed" as enthusiastically as others. Making the case requires you to gather data, define a rationale, and deliver supporting arguments.
- All members of today's senior leadership team may not be there when you are ready to roll out the program. Having a well-designed business case is an easy way to share the rationale as you educate the new arrivals.
- Even if senior leadership is supportive, the program will require approval from the next levels of management and employees. Building a business case prepares you for those discussions.
- Finally, do it for you! A well-thought-out case puts you in the driver's seat when you are quizzed by others about why the organization is investing in talent and development.

So, how do you start to build a case? Following these five steps will inform, prepare, and enlighten you at this stage.

- **Refer to your organization's strategy.** Training, learning, development, talent, and HR departments are seldom viewed as strategic because they are often putting out daily fires. This is a chance to start strategically—review your strategic plan, learn more about the organization's customers and competitors, and determine how your organization is viewed from the inside and the outside.
- **Describe how talent development can contribute to organizational priorities.** Does the organization have new priorities? Is it having difficulty with current priorities? What skills, knowledge, and attitudes do employees require to ensure efficient attainment? You may need to expand your thinking to several layers, so get others involved. For example, several years ago, my company helped a client move into the European market. We knew that employees would need certain traits to succeed, including cultural sensitivity, flexibility, emotional stability, and openness to adventure. They also needed to learn about the traditions and customs of the area. The learning department started researching and created learning events for the employees who were moving abroad as well as those remaining in the Minneapolis area who would interact with the company's new European employees.

BUILD A BUSINESS CASE *continued*

- **Determine the metrics that support the effort.** To demonstrate the effect on the organization's top and bottom lines, you will need to measure outcomes. No single set of metrics will apply every time, so talent development professionals need to consider a variety of possibilities. Some metrics are easy to measure, such as increasing retention, while others are more difficult, such as ensuring employees are agile learners. The difficult ones require you to dig down into the layers of results. Research other organizations to gather valid data to predict improvements for your organization.
- **Create a big picture budget to balance the success metrics.** Design it as a case study, so no one will expect exact numbers. Again, tap into your network to research other organizations. Obtaining data and examples will be valuable.
- **Create a pitch your CFO will buy.** The key for every organization, whether for-profit or not-for-profit, is return on investment. This means that your mindset needs to focus on how you will create organizational value. Show how a talent development effort is an investment—not a cost. If you can make a strong business case and have measures in place to show how talent development could contribute to the bottom line, you'll have a much better chance of getting support from your senior leaders. If you've developed a 90-day plan, you have most of the information you need to build a case that clearly shows how your talent development program offers a return on investment.

People: Surround Yourself With the Right Team

Of all the factors that affect the success or failure of a new initiative, people have the most disproportionate influence. A great leader and a great team can prevail against inconceivable challenges. Conversely, inept leaders and ineffective teams can easily squander the ripest of opportunities. Some individuals may decide to bypass assistance altogether and adopt a lone-wolf mentality, often succumbing to burnout in the process. An old proverb provides a noteworthy caution against this: "If you want to go fast, go alone, but if you want to go far, go together." Surrounding yourself with the right team will determine how fast and far your initiative progresses. In general, there are three broad people-growth strategies to consider when assembling a team: build, buy, or borrow (Ulrich 2009). Assessing each strategy is important and your preferred strategy may change as your department grows.

- **The build strategy** refers to developing talent internally. This can be highly effective when deep organizational knowledge is required. For example, if an organization uses a highly complex and proprietary software for customer relationship management and order fulfillment, it may make sense to develop the talents of a tenured employee who has significant experience with the software. This is because it may take less time and money to teach someone how to train than it does to teach an experienced facilitator how to use the software. The build strategy is also popular in organizations with a strong focus on workplace culture and values. Many of these organizations fear that external hires might dilute the company's culture; this is especially true if the new employee is responsible for the organization's learning function.

- **The buy strategy** refers to hiring skilled employees from outside the organization. Organizations that follow this strategy often do so to hire people with greater experience or specialization, or because it requires less employee development time. To secure more experienced and specialized employees, organizations should be prepared to spend more to acquire talent. Buying talent often leads to the infusion of fresh ideas into the organization, accelerating the growth of the TD department.
- **The borrow strategy** refers to leveraging freelancers, contractors, or consultants. Many organizations choose this strategy on a short-term basis, and it can prove very beneficial at the start of a TD initiative to create rapid momentum. It is also common for long-term partnerships to form with contractors and consultants, especially those with specialized skills. If the perceived benefit outweighs the cost, "borrowing" talent can be highly advantageous.

When selecting the talent strategy that best aligns with your initiative, consider these four factors: time, resources, specialization, and evidence. Once the TD effort has been initiated, the clock is ticking, and leaders within the organization will be expecting rapid progress and results. As such, factoring time into your talent selection is critical. Ideally, the organization may already have people with a TD skill set that could easily transition into a new role. If not, consider the time required to interview, train, coach, and develop an employee. If it appears that building talent will take months instead of weeks, TD professionals may want to assess other options.

Another important consideration is resources (such as salaries, bonuses, benefits, and other talent costs). Adapting the TD department's talent strategy to meet budgetary constraints is always wise. Specifically, TD leaders and organizations need to evaluate if they can afford the expertise of a specialist or consultant. Resource considerations might also include hardware and software investments. For example, the cost associated with producing studio-quality training videos in-house may be prohibitive for a startup or cash-strapped organization. Leveraging a videographer instead of purchasing equipment may provide a cost savings in the first year.

Balancing resources and talent specializations can be tricky. Organizations might discover they cannot afford to advance a TD effort without a specialist. For example, in highly regulated industries or highly technical fields, the potential risk of developing inferior or noncompliant training may be too costly a gamble. Additionally, a specialist may be able to produce a specific type of work product in a fraction of the time it would take a less experienced employee. In several scenarios, it may make sense to ask for more resources to secure the right talent.

Regardless of the organization's or department's talent strategy, always consider the evidence. What evidence exists to prove the employee, applicant, freelancer, contractor, or consultant can deliver on their commitment to your organization? Calling references, reviewing testimonials, and evaluating portfolios takes time but it is worth it. It is always better to prevent a problem than it is to manage it later. This is especially true when launching a new TD effort that will likely be scrutinized and evaluated. Making a poor talent selection can waste resources, damage your reputation, undermine your new department, and leave a bitter taste with executives.

When considering the impact of people on a TD effort, look outside the TD team as well. All organizations develop invisible networks of relationships, along with formal and informal hierarchies, which combine to form the political landscape. This landscape also functions like a microeconomy in which trust, influence, and goodwill are continually exchanged. Amassing large quantities of political capital is perhaps the most important asset for TD professionals to acquire. Maintaining relationships at all levels throughout an organization helps create buy-in for new training programs and other initiatives. It's also good to have a few fans and champions in positions of authority who can assist in securing approvals or increasing budgets. However, exercise caution when navigating office politics and always endeavor to give more than you take.

While political capital can help TD professionals accomplish their objectives, it is equally important to develop a network of subject matter experts (SMEs) and critics who can be called upon both formally and informally. SMEs can help ensure your training materials are accurate, relevant, and audience appropriate. Contrarians, on the other hand, can help uncover gaps, challenges, and shortcomings, which will improve TD solutions. This network is particularly helpful when initiating a TD effort because it increases its quality, buy-in, and impact, which is critical for demonstrating early success.

Relationships require a constant investment of time and energy, especially as organizations hire, fire, and restructure. In the whirlwind of emails, meetings, calls, and distractions it is easy to push relationship building to the back burner. However, it is impossible to effectively lead an organization's talent development function without a sharp emphasis on people. This includes TD personnel, stakeholders, SMEs, learners, supervisors, contractors, and peers. Developing relationships before, during, and after the initiation of a TD effort will open doors and amplify the TD department's impact.

Procurement: Understand Your Asset Needs

Procuring assets in advance of a launch is critically important. Assets come in all shapes and sizes—from five-story buildings to data-rich hard drives—and can include anything useful or beneficial to the TD effort. Think outside the box. For example, print and digital assets already in circulation within the organization can be quickly and easily leveraged as part of a learning library or be repurposed into an interactive e-learning course. A few hours spent collecting and categorizing could save days of development time.

One of the most important but often overlooked assets is information regarding organizational health and performance. Whenever possible, it is prudent to analyze how well the organization is advancing toward its strategic objectives. It is important to determine which metrics should be measured in addition to those used to evaluate strategic objectives. As they work to collect and analyze data, TD professionals may find complementary metrics that indirectly correlate to strategic objectives. For example, if an organization identifies reducing employee turnover as a strategic objective, a TD professional might find that new employee performance is the largest factor contributing to employee turnover. These insights can inform the direction of the TD effort, so it is wise to cast a wide net and let the data guide you.

Part of the data collection effort should include learner data because understanding the roles and responsibilities of learners is critical. Taking time to comprehend their capabilities, preferences, and constraints is also important, and helps avoid the creation of impractical learning solutions. Consider formal versus informal learning. Mobile learning or PC? Instructor led or self-paced? These are all questions that should be answered as you strive to collect learner data and insights. In some organizations, your learners may even be external (customers, contractors, vendors, or even community groups). Additionally, learner groups, demographics, and needs may change over time and should be evaluated often (quarterly or annually in most organizations).

After procuring all relevant and helpful information, TD professionals should move on to procuring more tangible assets like software, hardware, facilities, supplies, and any other resources they may need to conduct operations within their department. It is advisable to manage resources and spending carefully before, during, and after launch. Many organizations are hypersensitive to resources spent on training, and this is especially true in organizations with fledgling learning cultures. In these organizations, training is often seen as a cost center to be reduced or eliminated. Expect additional scrutiny during the first three years as senior leaders and executives evaluate the efficacy and impact of the new department. Running a lean but highly effective department will provide the greatest opportunity for future growth.

Procuring the right information, software, hardware, facilities, and relationships will streamline the launch of the TD effort. Maintaining each element is important to maintaining momentum. Information and software become outdated. Hardware and facilities require maintenance and updating. Preserving each asset is generally less costly than replacing it; as such, maintaining awareness and addressing issues early on can pay huge dividends in the long run.

Production: Transform Your Ideas Into Learning Solutions

With a clear purpose, carefully crafted plan, the correct people in place, and procurement complete, it is time to start producing results. Delivering learning solutions that improve performance should be the aim of all talent development efforts. However, you don't need to develop every course. Turn to the handbook website (ATDHandbook3.org) to download a table that will help you make decisions about whether to use internal or external resources to produce and deliver courses.

Performance criteria and measurements vary from organization to organization. At this stage in the process, it should be clear what results the organization is expecting the TD function to deliver in the first 90 days. Producing solutions that deliver tangible results is incredibly important, and failing to do so could cause the TD effort to end as quickly as it began.

The transition from planning to production is where TD departments begin to gain traction by transforming ideas into solutions. While many of the objectives, milestones, and projects that occur within the first 90 days may not directly correlate to learning solutions, it is likely that several will. For example, furnishing a training room or securing a contract with a webinar software provider might be important, but these are administrative priorities, not learning priorities. It is important to zero in on learning solutions and treat them with extra care and attention. After all, producing effective learning solutions is the predominant and unique purpose of an organization's TD function.

To transform an idea into a learning solution, TD practitioners need to start with clear and concise objectives. However, in this process, the objective is either a program objective or a course objective, based on the length and complexity of the desired solution. Courses can range from half-day workshops to multiple sessions over many months. A program, on the other hand, is a group of multiple courses. Course and program objectives should clearly align with business objectives and desired outcomes. For example: Upon successful completion of this course, learners will be able to resolve the five most common customer billing issues in less than 10 minutes without supervisor assistance, resulting in a 5 percent increase in customer net promoter scores.

With a clearly defined course objective (potentially culminating into a program objective), the next step is to develop terminal objectives. These are the requirements that must be met for learners to successfully complete a course. Terminal objectives should support the course objective; for example: Learners must navigate to the correct billing credit request form and fill out all 10 fields with 100 percent accuracy in less than five minutes when presented with 15 sample billing issues.

Finally, learners will need some prerequisite information or practice before they can accomplish each terminal objective. Enabling objectives should be crafted to support terminal objectives.

For example: Once given credentials, a computer, and internet access, learners must successfully log in to the company intranet site and navigate to the billing portal without assistance 10 times.

Enabling objectives are like breadcrumbs, leading learners toward terminal objectives. Terminal objectives allow TD professionals to assess if learners have the skills and knowledge needed to succeed in real-world environments. Course objectives provide measurable outcomes that can be used to determine if the learning solutions are truly improving performance.

The benefit of this process is that it simultaneously outlines the major components of a course or program while also aligning classroom activities and business outcomes. Creating objectives is a major component of learning solution development, but there are other factors to consider as well. In many organizations, learning is seen as an event. However, in an organization with a strong learning culture, learning is viewed as a process. When developing learning solutions, it is important to view learning as a process and consider the learner's journey, and blended learning can play an important role in this. TD professionals must consider methods of preparing learners for their involvement in a course (such as surveys, pre-work, or self-paced learning). Additionally, it is important to consider how they will be supported after they've completed the course material (for example, through evaluations, coaching, or performance reviews). Viewing these elements as part of the learning solution will lead to greater outcomes. The handbook website (ATDHandbook3.org) has a downloadable template to help you develop program, course, terminal, and enabling objectives.

If an organization has not had a formal TD function in the past, leaders may inundate it with requests for instructor-led training, self-paced training, quick reference guides, microlearning, and more. It is critical to balance these requests with the larger strategic objectives of the organization. Developing an intake process for requests can help. In the infancy of a TD department, an intake process may be as simple as an online form that employees are required to fill out when requesting new learning content or instructor-led training. Additionally, a formal review and approval process can aid in request management and prioritization. The formal review process might include a monthly call with senior leaders and select TD personnel to discuss recent requests. Balancing emerging requests and strategic objectives takes thoughtful consideration and practice, so exercise caution to avoid extremes in either direction.

As the TD effort takes shape, constantly review the performance of all newly formed learning solutions. From exit surveys to impact analysis reports, there are several factors to consider when evaluating learning impact. And if learning solutions are not having the desired impact (improved performance), TD professionals need to reassess every element of the learning solution. It is equally important to avoid hasty reactions. For example, if a new onboarding program is not improving new employee performance immediately after the first month, it probably is not necessary to scrap the program and start fresh. Instead, try a more metered approach that includes fact-finding, interviews, and experimentation.

The never-ending loop of execution and evaluation should allow for high productivity and performance. This is paramount during the first 90 days. When initiating a TD effort, time is the most precious resource. Leveraging agile development practices can maximize both effort and impact, and an iterative approach creates opportunities for minor course corrections early in the process. This approach often saves time and money, which can then be invested into other value-producing initiatives.

Organizations, like living organisms, constantly change, grow, and adapt. Internal and external factors are continuously reshaping organizational priorities. TD professionals must become adept at monitoring these changing conditions and pivoting with the organization to maximize impact. Developing this awareness with an organization can help TD professionals react to changes or even proactively identify changes that need to occur. Taking time to assess the impact at different levels within the organization will help TD leaders determine the most effective way to pivot and support the organization through the change. Failing to change at the right time can create challenges for learners and undermine the learning culture that TD professionals work so hard to foster. Adapting to changes ensures that the TD function continues to produce results and value.

Many organizations are continuing to wrestle with the changing nature of work. Hybrid offices and remote workforces require innovative learning solutions. Talent development leaders also need to keep a pulse on emerging trends in learning, which might include technological enhancements (such as virtual reality, augmented reality, and machine learning) or new research on the science of learning. New research and breakthrough technologies can help all TD practitioners craft more effective and efficient learning solutions. TD professionals should also exemplify a lifelong learning mentality by seeking out new information and insights. One of the most effective means of building a culture of learning is to lead by example. Constantly evaluate, discuss, and share new information with employees throughout the organization and encourage others to do the same. New does not always mean better, but thoughtful experimentation often leads to improved performance.

Final Thoughts

For talent development professionals, few experiences are more difficult or rewarding than initiating a new TD effort within an organization. However, these difficulties can be tempered with a few practical steps:

- Gain a clear understanding of how the TD function fits into the overall strategic framework of the organization.
- Align and refine this purpose through sensible planning to create structure and direction.

- Select the right talent management strategy, assemble a team, and develop relationships to set the plan in motion.
- Procure the necessary assets and resources to create momentum and push the team into action.
- Balance strategic and nonstrategic priorities with a relentless focus on performance to continue to propel the TD function closer to its stated vision and purpose.

Tackling this arduous effort step-by-step can provide clarity and a sense of progress. Take the first step on this rewarding journey and keep moving forward. It does not matter if the steps are big or small. Taking the right actions at the right time will advance the new initiative and catapult talent development within the organization to the next level.

About the Author

David Macon, CPTD, is a facilitator, learning designer, and consultant with more than 15 years of experience in the field of talent development. He specializes in launching agile L&D departments that affect organizational objectives. Through his consultancy, David works with clients to develop highly effective learning programs with an emphasis on employee onboarding, sales training, and leadership development. He also helps TD professionals enhance their skills and transform into strategic leaders within their organizations. Learn more at trainleadgrow.com.

References

Biech, E. 2018. *Starting a Talent Development Program*. Alexandria, VA: ATD Press.
Lauby, S. 2018. "How to Create a Recruiting Strategy: Buy, Build, and Borrow." SHRM, May 11. shrm.org/resourcesandtools/hr-topics/talent-acquisition/pages/how-to-create-a-recruiting-strategy.aspx.
Ulrich, D., J. Allen, W. Brockbank, J. Younger, and M. Nyman. 2009. *HR Transformation: Building Human Resources From the Outside In*. New York: McGraw Hill.

Recommended Resources

Biech, E. 2018. *ATD's Foundations of Talent Development: Launching, Leveraging, and Leading Your Organization's TD Effort*. Alexandria, VA: ATD Press.
Kirkpatrick, J.D., and W.K. Kirkpatrick. 2016. *Kirkpatrick's Four Levels of Training Evaluation*. Alexandria, VA: ATD Press.
Macon, D. 2021. "Successfully Build an Essential L&D Department." *TD at Work*. Alexandria, VA: ATD Press.

CHAPTER 29

Working Effectively With SMEs

Greg Owen-Boger and Dale Ludwig

Your career as a talent development professional will, at times, require collaboration with subject matter experts (SMEs). SMEs enrich the training process in many ways. Through their experience and insight, they bring a depth of knowledge impossible to find anywhere else. On the most fundamental level, SMEs deliver information, but it is the business context and practical application of that information that really matters.

IN THIS CHAPTER:
- Define SMEs' role and responsibilities to facilitate learning
- Help SMEs understand their role and responsibilities to facilitate learning
- Initiate and manage effective and efficient learning conversations with SMEs
- Support SMEs to initiate and manage effective and efficient learning conversations

When SMEs succeed in the classroom, whether face-to-face or virtual, they serve not only as experts in their content, but also as brand ambassadors, company historians, and color commentators.

As important as their role is, bringing SMEs into the learning and development process is challenging. No matter what their expertise, communicating it to learners in a way that leads to understanding and application on the job is not easy. So, it's the TD professional's job to help SMEs in three ways:

- Help them understand their role as a facilitator of learning.
- Create support material that works for learners and SMEs.
- Coach them to manage the training process effectively and efficiently.

Before we get into the details of these responsibilities, let's talk a bit about selecting SMEs.

Selecting SMEs

Broadly speaking, the SMEs you work with need to have the communication skills—or be able to develop them—to deliver content to ensure what's said is learned and can be applied back on the job. Ideally, they should be selected based on their subject matter expertise, communication skills, and willingness to learn how to become an effective trainer.

Unfortunately, this is not always the case. Many SMEs are selected based solely on their experience or availability. In addition, as we wrote in *Effective SMEs* (2018), "in our experience, there is sometimes a degree of mistrust between instructional designers and SMEs. SMEs may doubt that instructional designers know what they're doing, and instructional designers often don't trust SMEs to follow the plan they've created. Trust, openness, and a willingness to learn must be present on both sides."

The decisions that go into selecting SMEs for the training room are often outside the TD function's control. This is unfortunate. We believe the stakes are too high for selecting the wrong people. The SME's reputation is at stake and could be harmed if they are ineffective in the classroom. Over time, that can have a negative impact on talent development. In *Effective SMEs* we created a job aid called Criteria for Selecting Instructional SMEs to help you influence SME selection decisions. You can download it on the handbook website (ATDHandbook3.org).

Getting Started With SMEs

Let's begin with two assumptions: The SME selected is a willing and able partner, and everyone involved in the design and delivery of the learning program is an expert in their own area. This second idea is put forward very persuasively by Chuck Hodell in his 2013 book, *SMEs From the Ground Up*. Hodell says that while the SMEs you're working with may be experts in their field, you should remember that you are an expert in yours. You and your TD peers bring knowledge of learning design, virtual delivery platforms, adult learning, and coaching, which is crucial to the learning process.

The challenge you face, of course, is finding the best way for people with different types of expertise to work together. This begins by assuring the SMEs you work with that it is your job to help them be successful in the classroom and focus your attention on efficiency and ease for both them and their learners.

Here are the three fundamental challenges you face.
- There is always a tension between the work that is done in advance of a training program and the work that is done during its delivery. What is prepared—the content and structure—must be delivered in a way that is spontaneous and interactive. The interaction that takes place between SMEs and learners is a conversation, and it needs to feel that way on both sides.
- When SMEs are involved, there is also a tension between possessing a high level of expertise and the ability to help others understand that expertise. In his *New York Times* article "Those Who Can Do, Can't Teach," Adam Grant writes that Albert Einstein was a poor teacher, famously delivering uninspiring and disorganized lectures. However, Einstein wasn't alone in this struggle; as Grant points out, the more expertise someone has, the more difficult it is for them to help others understand it.
- Another challenge is that "training," which often takes the form of a PowerPoint deck, looks like, well, a PowerPoint deck. As a talent development professional, you know otherwise. You know the research that went into organizing the content in a particular way. You know the thinking and rationale for when and why to include an activity, facilitate a discussion, conduct a role-play exercise, allow time for reflection, and so on. What the SME sees, though, is a presentation. Adding to this misconception is the SME's past experience as a learner. They likely sat through endless lectures in school. This is what they know, so their inclination is to emulate that.

How do you overcome these challenges?

The Learning Conversation

In our work with business presenters and trainers, we've found it helpful to begin with a clear definition of the type of communication we're dealing with. We wrote about this in *The Orderly Conversation: Business Presentations Redefined* (2014). An "orderly conversation," or a learning conversation that occurs in the classroom, is an outcome-oriented communication that is prepared and well organized, and that takes place in a responsive, conversational way. While it is not scripted, it is not entirely free flowing either.

By defining *training delivery* in this way, we're able to focus on its essential characteristics. On the one hand, we have purpose, planning, and structure. On the other hand, we have a spontaneous, engaging conversation. Both characteristics are required for efficient, relevant, learner-focused training.

The connection between the trainer and learners that results from this conversation helps the trainer in important ways. It shifts their attention away from thinking solely about the content they're delivering and toward the needs of the learners receiving it. In effect, this lets learners drive the conversation. When this happens, the trainer's work is no longer a one-directional delivery of content, but an extended response, a series of adaptations and adjustments, made in the moment for the benefit of learners. While this may seem like a hair-splitting distinction because many of these adjustments are small, it is not. It is, instead, what separates mediocre from vibrant training.

Through these adaptations, which are called immediate instructional adjustments in the field of primary and secondary education, effective trainers speed up or slow down the delivery of content to meet the needs of learners (Popham 2011). They are also able to enhance the content through examples, personal stories, and experiences, which is why SMEs are so valuable in the training room.

Adult learners are primed for this type of conversation, and their need for efficiency and relevance requires it. Maybe Einstein would have been a more effective teacher if he had given up on lecturing and engaged his students in a learning conversation.

How Individual SMEs Respond to the Tensions of Orderly Conversations

Because an orderly conversation is a process that is both planned and spontaneous, it's important to think about how individual SMEs respond to the tension between the two. It will be useful for you to know that habits, assumptions, and a personal preference for the orderly part of the process or the conversation itself are at the root of a SME's strengths and weaknesses.

To illustrate this point, let's look at a couple of examples.

> Michaela is a director of finance at her company. She takes on SME responsibilities when she trains the accounting staff on policies and procedures. Michaela was a natural pick to deliver this training because of her broad experience and long tenure with the company. She is also highly organized and detail oriented. Because of this she likes to develop her own training deck, practice it extensively before delivery, and deliver it without interruption from her learners. Questions are reserved for the end because she believes that will cause less confusion and mean fewer questions. "Besides," she says, "I'm training accountants. They get me."

Michaela's comfort with the orderly part of the process is clear. Her challenge is that her approach to training delivery might frustrate learners who feel intimidated, bored, put off, or shut down by her lecture-style preference.

Anthony works for a company that makes telemedicine equipment. He is one of the leading salespeople on his team. He is outgoing, charming, and able to strike up a conversation with anyone. His manager, Enrique, asked Anthony to lead the New User Training because his personality and product knowledge seemed perfect for it. This training, which is delivered to customers who have recently purchased products, provides an introduction for people who may not have been involved in the buying process. It's meant to be informational, focusing on what the products can do and how they work. A week before the first training session was to take place, Enrique asked Anthony if he was ready for the workshop; Anthony said, "I haven't really done any planning. It will be like a product demo, and I can do those in my sleep."

Anthony's approach is to play to his salesperson strengths in the classroom. While he clearly has the knowledge and personality to succeed, he's ignoring the fact that he's delivering training, not selling. The audience is a group of users, not buyers. Plus, while the sale has been made, there's a good chance that some of the people he's training wanted their company to purchase a different product. Anthony's approach may not be successful with them.

We'll talk more about what you can do to help Michaela and Anthony succeed as we move forward.

From Expert to Trainer

A good way to help SMEs understand their role is to explain that when they deliver training content, they wear two hats. They have two distinct but equally important responsibilities. The first hat, we'll call it the SME hat, is about their knowledge, experience, and insight, along with the wisdom they've developed over time. Their ability to wear this hat is the reason they were brought into the learning process. This hat fits comfortably.

When wearing the SME hat, a SME can effortlessly:
- Deliver content showcasing their expertise.
- Use examples.
- Tell personal stories.
- Demonstrate using the tools of their trade.

The second hat is the trainer hat. This hat is less comfortable for SMEs because it's about managing the learning process as it takes place. As you work with SMEs, assure them that it's normal to feel uncomfortable with the trainer hat. It involves skills and techniques they may have never used or, in some situations, been exposed to.

By switching to the trainer hat, we add more value to the learning experience because the SME now:
- Delivers content showcasing their expertise clearly and concisely
- Uses examples to make complex information understandable
- Tells personal stories to enrich training content
- Demonstrates using the tools of their trade so that others become proficient

When wearing the trainer hat, a SME will also:
- Engage learners in fruitful learning conversations.
- Be open and curious about learners' experience.
- Set context to communicate relevance.
- Communicate why training content is important to the learners' work.
- Connect the dots between learning points.
- Facilitate discussions that enrich learning for everyone.
- Set up, run, and debrief activities efficiently.
- Make learning easy.
- Ask questions and encourage discussion.
- Create thinking opportunities.

When SMEs are comfortable wearing both hats, they will manage the learning conversation well and use this to meet their learning goal.

Do SMEs Have to Go It Alone?

Considering how high the stakes are and the steep learning curve a SME may face, you may want to consider co-facilitating with them to ensure success. The team approach can take a few different forms. Here are some examples:
- Allow the SME to shine by letting them wear only the SME hat. This means that the talent development professional is wearing the trainer hat to ensure context is set, dots are connected, activities are run well, discussions are fruitful, and knowledge can be applied back on the job.
- Have a talent development professional deliver most of the training and invite the SME to provide color commentary by sharing experiences, stories, and cautionary tales derived from their years on the job. Depending on how often the training is delivered, capturing their stories on video for future playback can further lighten the SME's load.
- Design training events that feel like panel discussions. Having a few SMEs answer questions facilitated by a talent development professional can be extremely interesting to

learners. Taking this approach also relieves the SMEs of having to spend their precious time preparing.
- Break large training modules down into smaller pieces and spread the content delivery across multiple SMEs.

Playing to the SMEs' strengths allows them to shine, which, as we've established, is one of your primary responsibilities.

How to Help SMEs Initiate and Manage a Learning Conversation

While a successful learning conversation takes place in the moment of delivery, there are things you can do during the design phase to make that easier. In this section, we'll talk about three:
- Framing the learning conversation
- Creating facilitator guides and slide notes that are in-the-moment job aids
- Designing slides for easier delivery and understanding

Framing the Learning Conversation

Informal conversations always happen prior to a training event as people file into the room. Encourage SMEs to participate in these by greeting people as they arrive, maybe even striking up a casual conversation. Then, when it's time to start the session, use a framing strategy to formalize the conversation and get things started on the right foot.

Every learning conversation requires a strong frame. While the primary frame is delivered at the beginning of the training session, it is more than a traditional "introduction." The frame assures learners that the training they are about to receive is important and relevant to their work. It also communicates a specific goal and an easy-to-follow structure. Build the frame using four components: current situation, goal, agenda, and benefits (Table 29-1).

Table 29-1. The Four Components of a Frame

	What This Component Does	Answers These Learner Questions
Current situation	Sets context and helps the SME meet learners where they are	• "Why am I here?" • "Why do I need to learn this?"
Goal	Communicates a sense of purpose and helps the SME set clear expectations	• "What will I be able to do or understand when this is over?"
Agenda	Communicates structure and a sense of direction and efficiency	• "How is this organized?" • "Is it going to be easy to follow along?"
Benefits	Communicates how learners and the business will benefit from this learning experience	• "What's the takeaway from this?" • "How will this help the business?"

If your training program involves PowerPoint slides, it's a good idea to use a few slides to support the frame. You may want to use four slides, one for each step, but you can use fewer by combining steps on a single slide or eliminating steps from the slides but including them in the facilitator guide.

Let's imagine that you convinced Anthony, our telemedicine salesperson, to put some energy into developing his training content. The two of you came up with a frame to help him wear his trainer hat and lay the groundwork for an effective training event.

Table 29-2 shows what Anthony might say when delivering the frame for his training.

Table 29-2. Example of Proper Framing

Component	Anthony's Script
Current situation	Good afternoon, everyone. I'm excited to be working with a new group of users as you begin to roll out your new equipment.
Goal	My goal today is for you to be comfortable with the basic operation of the equipment so that you'll be ready for tomorrow's hands-on practice.
Agenda	We'll be focusing on three things today: • The basic function of each piece of equipment • How each individual product functions within the network • Three types of user support: how to use the help feature built into each piece of equipment, how to find support online, and how to contact a live user-support professional
Benefits	When we're finished, you will walk away with: • Greater comfort with your new equipment's functionality • Confidence using the new equipment, knowing that there is a wide range of user support available to you going forward

Articulating the frame will bring learners into the training conversation and give them a sense of relevance and efficiency. It will also help the SME keep their expertise in the context of the learning process, not as something that exists apart from it. You will find a worksheet to frame a training session on the handbook website (ATDHandbook3.org).

In this scenario with Anthony, he went along with your recommendations and support. However, let's imagine for a moment that he resisted. You could support Anthony by delivering the frame. Once you're done, you can hand things over to him.

While the frame needs to be strong, it also needs to be adaptable. For example, if training is delivered multiple times to different groups of learners, the frame should be slightly different for each delivery because the learners will be different. They may have different levels of experience or knowledge, which may lead to slightly different goals or benefits for each group. These adaptations may be made naturally by your SME, but the fact that they are being made needs to be communicated to learners so they think their perspective is being considered.

You'll notice that the goal in each frame is related to, but different from, the learning objectives. In our experience, eyes start to glaze over if learning objectives are brought into the training room. It's not that learning objectives aren't useful; they are. As TD professionals, we need learning objectives to get the design right. However, they tend to be written in a way that isn't useful to learners because they're too formal and usually very specific.

For example, the learning objectives for the program we framed in Table 29-2 might be:
- Learners will be able to list the function of each piece of equipment.
- Learners will be able to explain how each piece of equipment functions as part of a larger system.
- Learners will be able to access three types of user support.

Instead, we should think of the goal as a broad statement that all the learning objectives fit into, and have the SME focus on that.

Framing doesn't only function at the beginning of a session or module. You can use a new frame when you move from module to module, when coming back from a break, or when setting up an activity. Learners will appreciate a new frame whenever the context shifts.

You may also ask the SME to develop their own content. In these situations, we recommend that you help them create the slides for the frame because it may not come easy for them.

Designing Facilitator Guides and Slide Notes

One way to help SMEs move away from the idea that the training they're delivering is essentially a presentation is to create a useful facilitator guide or slide notes (if slides are being used in the training session). With either option, remember that both the guide and the notes should be designed to support your SMEs in two ways. They will use them to prepare for the training session to gain familiarity with the content. SMEs will also use them as a job aid during delivery.

In addition, make sure that you focus not only on the intent of the design, but on its structure as well. Doing so will help your SME in two ways:
- It answers the question, "Why is this laid out this way?" This helps the SME understand the overall structure of the training, how the design flows, what the design is intended to do, and, sometimes just as importantly, what it is *not* intended to do. This will increase their comfort level.
- It gives SMEs flexibility. If they can focus on the learning that should take place, not just the content being delivered, they'll have the freedom they need to deliver content in their own way.

No matter what type of support you offer your SMEs, always avoid scripting. Even if your goal is to communicate the meaning of a slide or simply a *possible* way to deliver its content, scripting it will make things more difficult. When given a script, SMEs might rely on it too much—trying their best to follow it, reading it, memorizing it, and even asking questions exactly as they are written. Or, and far more common, SMEs will ignore the script altogether, treating it as a hindrance. In both cases the learning designer is failing to supply what SMEs need during delivery.

When the design allows for it, give SMEs options. You may be able to provide a range of examples that support a learning point. Let the SME decide which one to use or give them permission to use their own. You may also offer optional slides. There may be slides the SME may choose to use or not, given their preferences. You could also include a couple slides that are intended to make the same point, which the SME could choose between. For example, one SME may prefer a drawing of a piece of equipment because it's very accurate. Another may prefer a photograph of the device instead. Either slide is fine because both would work from the learners' perspective.

Encourage SMEs to share their experiences and stories. Stories can make otherwise dull training come to life. You may want to insert story reminders into the facilitation guide from time to time.

Designing Slides

When we're working with SMEs and there are slides involved, the most pushback and frustration always concerns slide design. The frustration is understandable because no one—trainer, SME, or anyone else—feels immediately comfortable delivering slides designed by someone else.

Sometimes the issue stems from slides that are overdesigned. They may include too many colors, too many highlighted or bolded words, overuse of slide animation, redundant graphics, or wordy bulleted lists. The design decisions were likely intended to make the meaning of the slide clearer. However, they usually don't.

On the other side of the spectrum, some slides are confusing because they don't include enough information to be helpful. This may be due to vague slide titles, poorly labeled graphics, metaphors that don't quite work, or jumbled or confusing bulleted lists.

When designing slides, focus on ease of delivery as well as ease of understanding. Once you've determined the content of the training program and organized it into a slide deck, adjust the slides in these ways:

- Create slide titles that are meaningful to learners and helpful to the SME. Too often, slide titles simply refer to *what* is on the slide. Adjust them to communicate *why* this information is important or *how* learners will use it back on the job. For example, "Speed and Accuracy of the Production Line" is a more effective title than "The Production Line."
- Streamline bullet points to make them concise, readable, and parallel in structure. Parallel bullet points each start with the same part of speech, noun, verb, or adjective.
- If slides are being delivered in a live, face-to-face setting, it's probably a good idea to decrease the amount of animation you use. For virtual delivery, use more animation to

help virtual learners stay focused. Always encourage the SME to run through the deck in slide show mode so they're not surprised by animations later.

It's not realistic to assume that the SME will be fully prepared to deliver the training in the same way an expert facilitator would be. This isn't because they're lazy. It's because they lack the training and practice talent development professionals have. They also don't have the time or bandwidth to think through every single "what if." Because of this, think of the slides and facilitator guides as in-the-moment job aids. The SME should be able to look at a slide title or page in the facilitation guide and be reminded immediately of what they should say. This is very different from developing materials for talent development pros.

How to Coach SMEs on Training Delivery

As shown throughout this chapter, part of working with SMEs as a TD professional means demonstrating how to deliver training effectively. Often this requires coaching them as they progress from lecturer to facilitator of learning.

During training, SMEs need to be highly aware of how information is being received. They need to express empathy and check in frequently to see if learners are understanding. This is because learners may be overwhelmed or distracted by work or worried about how they will be judged by the SME or their peers if they don't understand. They don't want to seem confused in public.

It's the SME's job, therefore, to normalize confusion and make it OK to be unsure, frustrated, or resistant about the content. It's important to make these feelings and concerns part of the learning conversation. This is one of the primary ways SMEs can demonstrate their concern for learner understanding, not merely demonstrate expertise.

To help your SMEs demonstrate empathy for the learner, help them to:
- Be curious about the learner experience and concerns.
- Listen without judgment and probe for more information when necessary.
- Connect the dots; take responsibility for helping learners see both the forest and the trees.
- Treat wrong answers or learner confusion as a learning opportunity to uncover the thinking behind the answer.
- Understand the power of admitting their own past errors. Doing so will build trust and empathy.

Engaging Learners in the Conversation

One of the most fundamental and sometimes most challenging things for SMEs to do is to initiate a genuine conversation with learners. When a genuine conversation is achieved, we call it being engaged. When SMEs are engaged with learners, they are in the moment, focused on others, and connecting. In other words, they're able to think on their feet just as they do in everyday informal conversations.

We recommend that SMEs focus on engagement from the very beginning of the training session, specifically when the frame is delivered. The reason for this is that the frame is, in its broadest sense, a conversation starter. It's focused on learners and their needs. It provides the headline for what's to come through the "We're all here; let's get started" nature, almost as if it's an invitation to begin. Because of this, SMEs should focus on the skills that help them connect with learners and get focused. Two skills are required:

- Eye contact, a natural part of face-to-face communication, should be used intentionally at the beginning of a training session. Having good eye contact allows trainers to read each learner's facial expressions and attitude. This insight helps them respond appropriately to the feedback they're receiving. And this, in turn, pulls the SME out of their head to focus on the conversation taking place. There is no magic length of eye contact that is necessary. And approaching it from that direction is really missing the point. What's important is that each individual learner feels like they are being addressed. If the SME avoids eye contact or merely scans the room in a scattershot sort of way (something they may have heard was a good idea), encourage them to slow down and hold eye contact a bit longer than feels necessary. This will make their use of this skill more intentional and effective.
- Pausing provides the SME time to think, stay focused, and respond to what someone else has just said. From the learners' point of view, pausing gives them time to take in information and an opening to ask questions if they need to.

Both skills may feel exaggerated to SMEs—that their eye contact is too intense or a pause is too long. If this happens, assure them that they are not. This is easy to point out if you're using video recording to help your SMEs prepare.

Facilitating Activities

Facilitating activities is one of the more challenging aspects of facilitating learning events. When training programs fall apart, it's usually due to an unclear or confusing setup. "Wait.... What are we supposed to do?" is a common question trainers hear after sharing the activity instructions with table groups. This is true for experienced facilitators, and it's especially true for SMEs. For this reason, you need to be extra careful when asking SMEs to conduct learning activities or role-play exercises.

The purpose of learning activities is to assess understanding and reinforce learning. Help SMEs do this by encouraging them to:

- Frame each activity for relevance and context.
- Debrief the activity to reinforce learning; uncover and discuss any confusion that may have been experienced.
- Trust the activity to achieve its goal, which sometimes takes patience.

Remember that the SME doesn't have to go it alone. Assuming you have the resources to do so, plan to conduct the activity yourself and allow the SME to provide guidance during activities and commentary during the debriefs.

Conducting Dry Runs

We encourage all training facilitators to conduct dry runs as part of their routine when launching new training initiatives. They need to realize before the learners are present if the activity is too complicated or they don't understand how a series of slides is organized. The purpose of a dry run isn't to perfect delivery; rather, it's about:

- Understanding how each module or element helps meet learning objectives
- Getting clear on the flow and timing
- Finding multiple ways to explain content so that you can be learner focused and flexible during delivery
- Identifying trouble spots that need extra attention
- Identifying trim points in case you're running behind time

The dry run is also your opportunity to provide gentle coaching to the SME.

Planning for Virtual Delivery

If your SME is delivering training virtually, a dry run is absolutely necessary. Remind them that the purpose of a dry run is not to perfect training delivery; rather, its purpose is to get comfortable with the virtual platform, iron out technical problems, fit the training into the time available for it, and develop flexibility. We strongly recommend that you use a virtual host (or producer) to support the SME during delivery. With the host focusing on virtual technology, the SME can focus on learning.

Delivering Feedback to a SME

You may have the opportunity to coach your SME during a dry run or offer feedback after they've delivered the training. No matter when it's delivered, giving a SME feedback can be a challenge. Defensiveness, impatience, lack of time, and ego can all affect a SME's willingness to accept even the most well-intentioned feedback.

Here are some recommendations to make the process easier and more effective for everyone:
- Coaching and feedback are always about building self-awareness. It's better to point out what you have observed rather than evaluating their performance. "You got a bit lost in the customer safety protocols section" is more useful feedback than, "You speak too fast."
- Be sensitive to the fact that some SMEs will follow the plan too strictly (Michaela from the scenario we outlined earlier in this chapter), while others tend to improvise too much (Anthony). The first type needs to work on being more flexible, while the second needs to trust the learning design to keep training focused. There is nothing wrong with either approach, but understanding what each SME prefers is useful.
- Begin every coaching session with self-assessment. Ask the SME what they think of the training they delivered. They may feel good or bad, effective or not, or they may even be unsure. No matter their response, use that as the starting point to build your feedback. This will help you avoid prescriptive, rules-based guidance and focus on building self-awareness and reinforcement instead. As an example, let's say you are working with Michaela in a dry run. You've been helping her let go of her strict adherence to her script and improvise a little. You just asked her to deliver a slide a second time, but this time to acclimate the learner to the graphic before diving into any details. After she does, ask her, "How'd that feel?" If she says, "Pretty good," you know that her flexibility is growing. If she says, "Not good," you know you need to try a new tactic.
- Keep your recommendations simple and actionable. This is important whenever you're coaching someone, but with SMEs in the training room, it's especially necessary. Asking your SME to pause a bit more or pose more open-ended questions is much better feedback than, "Your speaking pace was fast and some of the learners looked confused."

Final Thoughts

While SMEs bring a level of insight and experience to the learning process that is impossible to find anywhere else, they need our support to succeed in the learning environment. As talent development professionals, it's our job to make SMEs comfortable and effective in their training role. We do that when we:
- Help SMEs understand that training delivery requires skills outside their own area of expertise.
- Help SMEs frame the training they deliver, and each module contained in it, to communicate a sense of relevance and efficiency for learners. It's the SME's job to bring learners into the learning conversation.
- Create facilitator guides that are in-the-moment job aids for SMEs. Avoid scripting, focusing instead on the intent of each module.

- Design slides that are easily delivered and understood. Use meaningful slide titles, clear graphics, and concise, parallel bullet points.
- Avoid prescriptive, rules-based feedback when coaching SMEs; base recommendations on what you've observed, not what you assume; and provide feedback that is specific and actionable.

Following these guidelines will help you help SMEs succeed and make working with SMEs a much more enjoyable experience.

About the Authors

Dale Ludwig and **Greg Owen-Boger** are the owners of Turpin Communication, a communication training firm based in Chicago. Along with their colleagues, they provide training and coaching to business presenters, meeting facilitators, and trainers. Dale founded the company in 1992 to provide the best business communication skills training available. Their work continues to be based on the idea that effective, efficient workday communication is possible for everyone. In the training room, Turpin trainers are tireless in their desire to understand the unique challenge each learner faces and find the simplest, most practical path to improvement. Their expertise with subject matter experts has been built over years through countless engagements with groups of SMEs, helping them be successful in the classroom. To learn more, visit turpincommunication.com.

References

Grant, A. 2018. "Those Who Can Do, Can't Teach." *New York Times*, August 25. nytimes.com/2018/08/25/opinion/sunday/college-professors-experts-advice.html.

Hodell, C. 2013. *SMEs from the Ground Up*. Alexandria: ASTD Press.

Ludwig, D., and G. Owen-Boger. 2014. *The Orderly Conversation: Business Presentations Redefined*. Minneapolis: Granville Circle Press.

Ludwig, D., and G. Owen-Boger. 2018. *Effective SMEs: A Trainer's Guide for Helping Subject Matter Experts Facilitate Learning*. Alexandria, VA: ATD Press.

Popham, W.J. 2011. *Transformative Assessment in Action*. Alexandria VA: ASCD

Recommended Resources

Owen-Boger, G., and D. Ludwig. 2016. "Dual Role." *TD*, April 1. td.org/magazines/td-magazine/dual-role.

CHAPTER 30

Perfecting Your Facilitation Skills: The Facilitative Trainer

Michael Wilkinson

People have known for decades that training is *not* about being able to present a set of PowerPoint slides in an engaging way. To the contrary, the key to being an impactful trainer is in your ability to facilitate a learning experience that translates into action outside the classroom.

> **IN THIS CHAPTER:**
> ♦ Explore the mindset and approach of a facilitative trainer
> ♦ Practice strategies to encourage your participants so they're grabbing for the content right from the start
> ♦ Learn techniques to maintain high levels of interaction and engagement throughout the training session
> ♦ Identify methods for closing to help ensure learning transfer

We have all been there.

The title for the training class was exactly what you were looking for. Every one of the course's learning objectives aligned with what you wanted to learn. Even the instructor's bio reinforced your belief that the class was going to deliver the goods.

But instead, the class was a dud. You were suspicious from the beginning when the first 15 minutes were spent in a trivial activity that had nothing to do with the content. Your concerns increased when nearly every question the instructor asked was rhetorical: She'd ask the question and then proceed to answer it herself. And although the course description said "interactive," you soon realized that meant the instructor would ask for questions and every so often put the groups into dyads.

It was another waste of money, and, worse, your time. And yet, the course sounded so good!

But note: The problem had nothing to do with the content of the class—the content may have been just what you were looking for. The problem was the delivery: It was low on engagement and low on interaction, which likely meant it was low on learning transfer from the classroom to your everyday working experience. And this generally leads to poor impact on results.

> Better Facilitation = Better Learning Transfer = Better Results

So how do you do it? How do you create a learning environment where people are grabbing for information, where the atmosphere is charged with engagement, and where people walk away anticipating the opportunities to put their new skills to work? That's what this chapter is about.

Much of the content in this chapter comes from the principles and practices we teach in our three-day workshop called The Engaging Trainer, as well as my book *The Secrets of Facilitation*. We'll focus on four critical areas of facilitation in training:
- The facilitative trainer mindset
- Starting with impact
- Engaging throughout
- Closing for results

Successful facilitation starts with preparation. As a facilitator of training, your preparation must include making sure your client has a full understanding of the *6 Ps:* purpose, product, participants, probable issues, process, and place. Successful facilitation also requires a keen understanding of group dynamics and strategies for preventing, detecting, and resolving dysfunctional behavior. However, these two topics are beyond the scope of this chapter.

The Facilitative Trainer Mindset

The instructional design framework we use is based on a simple formula: PDI (practical, dynamic, interactive). We use documented methods, coupled with our own field experience and research, to isolate and package best practices in a way that is easy for people to understand and apply. We then employ adult learning principles to design highly dynamic and interactive modules that keep people interested and engaged. We use the term *facilitative trainer* to describe how an instructor creates a PDI experience. Facilitative trainers have four major responsibilities inside the classroom:

- Sell the why.
- Focus on the what, the how, the why, the engagement.
- Maintain your energy level.
- Engage, engage, engage.

Responsibility 1. Sell the Why

Your students should leave the training ready to apply as much as possible of what they have learned. And they will do this if they have the opportunity, the skill, and the will.

- **The opportunity** comes in their professional and personal environments. To aid them in application, continually suggest ways they can use what they've learned and describe situations where they can apply the tools.
- **The skill** comes from ensuring they understand the concepts and techniques and are able to practice and gain valuable feedback to improve.
- **The will** is the critical piece. If they have opportunities and learned the skills, but don't believe the skills are valuable, they will leave the learning in the room. Very little knowledge transfer to the workplace will occur.

Clients don't engage trainers to teach a class to their people. They engage trainers to bring about change by providing their people with new skills *and* the will to put those skills into practice. Trainers inspire! Accordingly, instructors first and foremost understand the critical role they play in inspiring people to have the will to put their new skills to use.

> We inspire! Accordingly, instructors first and foremost understand the critical role they play in inspiring people to have the will to put their new skills to use.

How do you do it? How do you inspire change? The key is to spend nearly as much time persuading people why they should employ a tool as you do instructing them how to use it.

Let's look at an example. Have you ever asked a question and gotten complete and utter silence? It's uncomfortable, isn't it? And a little embarrassing too, especially for the participants because they feel they should know the answer. Well, did you know that when you ask a question and get silence, it may be because you asked the wrong type of question? Table 30-1 shows what I mean. Look at the two questions. Which is better?

Table 30-1. Ask the Right Question Type

Type-A Question	Type-B Question
The first thing we want to talk about are inputs. What are the inputs to the scheduling process?	If you were about to develop the training schedule, think about the things you would need to have close by. Think about the tools and information you would have to have. What are the things you need to develop the schedule?

Why is the type-B question better? You can probably see that it draws a visual image of the answers ("They are on the desk in front of me") while the type-A question doesn't.

Type-A questions represent what you want to know, and type-B questions create an image of the answers. And when you draw an image of the answer, people can begin answering right away. When you ask a type-A question, you'll get silence; your learners are trying to draw the image in their minds *because you didn't draw it for them*!

So, if you facilitate a discussion about your topic and the participants understand why the skill is important, you can continue with your facilitation. Now that your participants have the will (why), you can provide the skill (how). You could do this by demonstrating the skill, practicing it together, identifying how to recognize the good elements, demonstrating the wrong way to do it, practicing in teams, or doing any of the other techniques that you use.

Spend more time on selling the why and only then provide the skills.

Responsibility 2. Focus on the What, the How, the Why, the Engagement

In your training delivery, focus on four elements:
- **The what,** which is the concept or skill you are teaching
- **The how,** which is how participants put the concept into use
- **The why,** which is why this concept should be important to the participants
- **The engagement,** which is how you will engage the participants to use and recognize the power of the concept

As you prepare to explain the major concepts, review Table 30-2 for more information.

Table 30-2. Four Main Elements Framework

The What	The How	The Why	Engagement
Checkpoint	Prior to every new module, take a checkpoint: • Review what we just did • Preview what we are about to do • Explain how what we are about to do fits into the training session's overall objective	Communicate that we are about to transition and get everyone clear on what we are about to do and why it is important.	Provide an agenda and have at least one person from each team execute a checkpoint with an agenda item.

These four responsibilities allow a facilitative trainer to create and maintain a highly engaging and stimulating environment that delivers a PDI experience: practical tools and strategies delivered in a dynamic way and in an environment that is highly interactive and engaging.

Responsibility 3. Maintain Your Energy Level

Your energy level is critical. It is important that you start your sessions at your highest energy level and then return to that energy level after each break to help spark the group's energy. I am not suggesting that you be a game show host. Instead, consider recognizing and capitalizing on what high energy typically does. We call this the *3 Es* of energy:

- Your high energy **engages** the group. It is certainly more interesting to listen to someone with high energy than low energy.
- Your high energy **energizes** the topic. It subtly says to the group that this topic must be interesting because the facilitator seems to think so.
- Your high energy **elevates** you as the facilitator. High energy makes you look confident and encourages people to follow you.

Responsibility 4. Engage, Engage, Engage

To keep people alert and learning in multiday classes requires a high level of interaction and engagement. Therefore, the fourth major responsibility of instructors is to create and maintain a highly engaging and dynamic classroom environment. More about this in a bit.

Starting With Impact

In the last section I focused on the mindset of a facilitative trainer. Now let's get into some specific strategies, beginning with how to start with impact. The first 15 minutes of a training session sets the stage—the tone and pace—for what participants can expect going forward. Through the opening, you convey your vision of the training session and the benefits to be gained. Therefore, be very intentional about what you do in your opening; you need to plan it carefully and execute your plan skillfully.

Facilitative trainers recognize that they must execute four things extremely well at the start of a training session:

- Inform participants about the overall purpose of the session.
- Excite them by identifying the benefits specifically to them of being in the session.
- Empower them by sharing the authority they have during the session.
- Involve them right away in an activity that contributes to the success of the session.

Let's take a look at an example of a trainer starting a training session for managers and supervisors to learn how to run masterful meetings.

> Good morning. My name is Michael Wilkinson, and I have the pleasure of facilitating this class with you. Let's start with purpose.
>
> The overall purpose of this session is to provide strategies for transforming meetings into highly effective, highly engaging, and highly productive gatherings. (Inform)
>
> What's exciting about this? Think about the number of meetings you or your people attend on a weekly basis. Think about how much of your time is spent in useless, unnecessary meetings, or how much time is wasted in meetings that are poorly run and executed. This is your opportunity to learn strategies that you can use, whether as a meeting leader or participant, to transform the meetings you are a part of. And when your people see how truly masterful meetings can be, they'll want to use these same strategies to transform the meetings they attend. Over time you can ignite a meeting revolution that changes the way your organization meets every day. But it starts with you. It starts with you learning and applying key strategies that can become transformational. (Excite)
>
> There are quite a few tools and techniques that I want to share with you. However, this is your workshop. Each of you has chosen to be here so I want to make sure this class answers the questions and covers the issues most important to you. I will discuss the eight modules, but how much time we spend on each is up to you. So, if you sense that I am spending too much time on a topic that is not as relevant to the group, raise your hand and say, "Michael, I think we can speed through this." I will then check in with the group, and if the group agrees, we will speed through it. Or if I am going too fast, bring it to my attention and I will check in with the group. Why? Because this is your workshop. I am committed to doing my best to ensure each of you gets exactly what you need to start your group's meeting transformation. (Empower)

Before we jump in, I need to understand exactly what you want to cover. What problems have you experienced in meetings and which issues do you want to make sure you have strategies for? Given the size of the group, let's use breakout groups for this. Let me explain how....

Let's focus on the key question. Think about the meetings you have attended in the last month or two. What problems frequently occur in those meetings and what challenges prevent those meetings from being highly productive? (Involve)

We find that "excite" is most often overlooked by trainers. Here's the key: Did you notice the number of times I used *you* or *your* in that section? I used them 11 times in that one paragraph! When you excite, use the words *you* or *your* frequently because it helps ensure that you are describing what is in it for them.

Facilitative trainers use the inform-excite-empower-involve (IEEI) format to start every training session with impact.

Engaging Throughout

While IEEI drives an engaging opening, the engagement can't stop there. Begin each training module with an interactive activity to get participants engaged right from the start. Then follow up with some type of participant engagement for every 20 to 30 minutes you are training.

Note: The activity should not be a randomly selected icebreaker intended to engage; instead it should be associated with furthering the topic of the module. For example, a beginning activity in which you asked participants to share their last vacation would be unhelpful if your training session was related to running masterful meetings. Instead, a better suited engagement topic might be to identify best practices for running masterful meetings or identifying root causes for why meetings are frequently so bad.

Along with the typical engagement approaches such as question and answer, role play, small group work, and brainstorming, have a full stable of engagement strategies that you can employ as needed.

Table 30-3 lists engagement strategies you can use in your next training session. You will also find a corresponding job aid on the handbook website at ATDHandbook3.org. Space doesn't permit detailing each engagement strategy, so let's take a look at just one of these in detail: dump and clump (Table 30-4).

Table 30-3. Engagement Strategies for Your Next Training Session

Name	Type	Purpose
Brainstorming (basic)	Generating ideas	To generate a large number of ideas
Brainstorming in teams	Generating ideas	To generate a large number of ideas
Breakout groups	Generating ideas	To increase engagement and reduce time by having groups work on different parts of an activity
Brief encounters	Inquiry	To allow participants to get input from others on a question they have
Dot voting	Decision making	To narrow a list or select items from a list
Dump and clump	Generating ideas and categorizing	To gather information and then categorize that information
Dyads and triads	Generating ideas	To generate ideas or answers in groups
Forced analogies	Generating ideas	To provide a creative approach for a group to identify potential solutions to a problem
Gifts and hooks	Introduction	To get participants familiar with one another at the beginning of a series of facilitated meetings
Group questioning	Inquiry	To increase engagement during a Q&A period and help ensure that the most important questions are asked
Grouping	Categorizing	To categorize information into groups
Informed majority	Decision making	To make a decision about wording or other items where full consensus is not needed
Introductions	Introduction	To have people become more familiar with one another
Last person standing	Generating ideas and categorizing	To identify the most unique information or ideas in a short and energy-filled period
Lobbying	Decision making	To build consensus around a few sets of ideas and to increase the level of commitment people feel to participate in implementation
More of or less of	Generating ideas	To help participants identify what is needed more of and less of from an organization in response to a likely change
Rotating flipcharts	Reviewing	To review information that has been developed in breakout groups and have teams provide detailed feedback
Start, stop, continue	Generating ideas	To help participants identify what they should start, stop, or continue in response to a likely change
Think, pair, share	Generating ideas	To gather information in groups of two and share the information in a crisp, concise manner

Table 30-4. Dump and Clump Details

Name	Dump and Clump
Type	Generating ideas and categorizing
Purpose	To gather information and then categorize that information
General description	Each team records their responses to a listing activity (e.g., what are all the steps in the hiring process? What are my objectives for this session?) or a brainstorming session (e.g., where might we plan our company outing?). These items are collected (dumped) and organized in categories (clumped).
Benefit	Provides an approach to have many people involved in developing and categorizing a large amount of input in a relatively short timeframe.
Preparation	In advance, create either a four-cell or six-cell matrix for placing sticky notes on two charts.

Sample words (purpose, example if necessary, general directions, specific exceptions, questions, starting question)	• **Clearly describe the purpose:** Let's build a list of the key issues that need to be addressed in this session if we are going to achieve our objective. To do this, let's use our teams. We have divided the group into three teams. We have the Red team over here (Red, are you there?), the Blue team...
	• **Select leaders:** To help the team process, I need a volunteer from each team to stand. Volunteer, please grab the pad and colored marker in one hand and, with your other hand, touch the shoulder of one of your teammates. Please hand this person the pad and marker. The person you are touching is the team leader for this exercise. Volunteers, you can sit down, thank you.
	• **Provide instructions and the starting question:** I have instructions for team leaders and team members.
	  ○ Team leader instructions first—you and your team will have two minutes to identify as many issues as you can related to our objective. There are only three rules:
	    – You must use the pen you have been given and the pad you have been given and only these.
	    – Only one item per sticky note. You can have as many items as you want.
	    – When the two minutes is up and the clock rings, your pen must be capped; otherwise, you will lose two issues.
	  ○ Team member instructions—your job is to contribute. So, think about our objective for a minute, the things we are doing well, and the things we need to do better. If we are going to improve things in this area, there are many issues we will have to address. We want to list these. Any questions? Remember both quantity and quality count. What are the key issues we need to address? Team leaders, the clock is ticking...
	• **Give the quantity awards:** Now, let's see how many responses we have from each team and, at the same time, do introductions. Each team member should share their name and organization. Let's go first with the Red team starting with the person on the team leader's left and moving through the group until we reach the team leader. Then the team leader can let us know how many issues your team came up with. [Pause for teams to respond.] So, it looks like our quantity award goes to the [insert team name] team. Let's give them a hand!
	• **Give the quality awards:** That's the quantity award; now, let's check the quality award, shall we? Let's start with the winning team. Their first issue is [insert issue]. Let's put that in a category. What is a broad name for this that might include other similar issues? Let's move on to the next item. [Go through each item in the winning team's list.] Now that we have finished with that team, let's move on to the next team. [Repeat the process.] Now that all the sticky notes have been grouped, it looks like the red team shows up in [insert number] groups, the BLUE team in ___ groups... So, the QUALITY award goes to the ___ team. Let's give them a hand!

Closing for Results

The last section focused on strategies for engaging during the session; now, let's focus on strategies for closing the session. How do facilitative trainers close to help ensure results are achieved? Imagine this:

> You have had a great training session. Participants demonstrated enthusiasm for the topic; they were asking questions that showed that they were digesting the tools and strategies, and during the practice sessions they were able to successfully put their new skills to work.
>
> Now it's time to wrap up the training. You want to close in an impactful way. You want it to be engaging, yet make sure that what they learned will translate from the training session to the workplace. How do you do it?

Table 30-5 outlines six wrap-up strategies that I use with groups. Each one has a slightly different purpose, so pay close attention because you should select the wrap-up strategy that best serves your purpose.

Table 30-5. Six Wrap-Up Strategies for Groups

Name	Purpose
Appreciations	To close a session on a high positive by giving participants the opportunity to express appreciation
Future letter to myself	To encourage commitment to action
Elevator speech	To have participants develop a short statement that summarizes the results of a session or other information
Journaling	To encourage individual involvement, engagement, and learning transfer
Talking stick	To promote deeper discussion and listening
Whip around	To give participants an opportunity to briefly share their thoughts or feelings about something

Let's go into detail on one of my favorites, the elevator speech.

The Elevator Speech

Purpose
- To have participants develop a short statement that summarizes the results of a session or other information. An elevator speech is designed to last the amount of time it takes an

elevator to go from the first floor to the top floor of a building—about 30 seconds. It should grab attention and deliver the key points in very few words.

Process
- Clearly describe the purpose. We are nearing the completion of our training session. When you walk out the door, people will likely ask you, "How was the class?" Here's your opportunity to develop a 30-second elevator speech.
- Introduce the elevator speech. An elevator speech is a short statement presented in the time it takes an elevator to go from the first floor to the top floor of a building—about 30 seconds. It should grab attention and deliver your key points in very few words. We will each create our own elevator speech.
- Define the key points. Before working individually, let's define key points to include in the elevator speech. Keep in mind that it should do two things: inform and excite. In this case, we should inform by telling people what happened and excite by communicating what excites you most about it.
- Give instructions. Consider using the O WOW format for your elevator speech:
    - Overall. Overall it was…
    - What we did. During the session we…
    - One thing. One thing that stood out for me…
    - What's next. Going forward, I will…
- You will have four minutes to jot down bullets for your elevator speech using O WOW as your guide. Keep in mind that it should be only about 30 seconds. So, imagine that it's Monday morning, you get on the elevator, and someone asks you, "How was the class?" What would you say to that person and how would you convey those points? Go ahead and write your bullets now.
- Share the elevator speeches. Now that we have written our elevator speeches, let's review them in teams of four. Have all your team members read their elevator speech and pick one of the four to share with the entire group.

Suggested Timing: 20 to 25 minutes for a group of 16
- Four minutes introduction, four minutes writing, four minutes small group sharing, four minutes large group sharing, and four minutes wrap-up

Additional insights
- It always amazes me how much people really get into creating and sharing their elevator pitches. Often more than one person at a table insists on sharing theirs too. I believe that there is something about the simple format that provides the minimum structure needed to spark creativity.

- As an alternative to small groups, you can have each participant stand in front of the group to give their elevator speech.
- Be sure to have the group clap after each participant shares to keep the energy up.

Final Thoughts

Facilitative trainers know the importance of creating and maintaining a classroom environment that not only maximizes learning, but also maximizes learning transfer. Key takeaways from this chapter:

- Sell the why to influence your participants to have the "will" to transfer their learning from the class space to the workplace.
- In your instruction, focus on the what, the how, the why, and the engagement approach.
- Use your highest-level energy to engage the group, energize the topic, and elevate you, the facilitator.
- Engage at the beginning, in the close, at the start of each module, and every 20 to 30 minutes using a variety of engagement strategies.

Over the next several months, consider trying one or more of the strategies covered to multiply your impact and your results even more.

About the Author

Michael Wilkinson is CEO and managing director of leadership strategies at The Facilitation Company, an organization that specializes in group facilitation training, effective training techniques, consulting skills, leadership skills, and meeting skills. His team also provides professional facilitators to help organizations with strategic planning, issue resolution, focus groups, and a variety of other business activities. Michael is the author of six books, including *The Secrets of Facilitation* and *The Eight Core Practices of Facilitative Leaders*. He is the founder of the FindaFacilitator Database and serves on the board of the International Institute for Facilitation. He is a Certified Master Facilitator and was inducted in 2016 into the International Facilitation Hall of Fame for his achievements and contributions to the field. You can find more information about Michael's company at leadstrat.com or connect with him directly at michaelthefacilitator.com.

Recommended Resources

Kaner, S. 2014. *Facilitator's Guide to Participatory Decision-Making.* Philadelphia: New Society, 1996.

Pike, R. 2003. *Creative Training Techniques Handbook: Tips, Tactics, and How-To's for Delivering Effective Training.* Amherst: HRD Press.

Schwarz, R. 2002. *The Skilled Facilitator: A Comprehensive Resource for Consultants, Facilitators, Managers, Trainers, and Coaches.* San Francisco: Jossey-Bass.

Wilkinson, M. 2012. *The Secrets of Facilitation,* 2nd ed. San Francisco: Jossey-Bass.

CHAPTER 31

Communicating With Executive Leadership to Gain Buy-In

Dianna Booher

What's the secret to getting buy-in from senior leaders? After more than 30 years of hearing leaders critique their briefers, I have a long list of dos and don'ts for HR professionals as they head into a meeting with executives—whether at their own organization, at a supplier's site, or at an industry conference.

> **IN THIS CHAPTER:**
> - Identify 14 practical ways to engage in a persuasive conversation with executives
> - Deliver persuasive proposals to an executive team with the proper structure, detail, timing, tone, phrasing, and facilitation skills
> - Ask and respond to tough questions in the C-suite

How often have you heard or even said things such as, "I never got a response to my email." "They never followed through on my recommendation." "I'd definitely like to have a seat at the table when that issue comes up next time!" You hear these common sentiments from those who've had their time in front of executive decision makers—and for some reason left disappointed and ultimately defeated.

Whether you're delivering a formal presentation or just engaged in conversation around the conference table or in the hallway, consider what it takes to gain buy-in and get the go-ahead at the executive level.

Talk About ROI

Your sales team tends to focus on revenue because that's what counts toward their commissions. Your marketing team focuses on growth because that's easy to measure; they create a three-week campaign and count the leads and conversions. Your operations people count widgets produced per hour or the cost of rejects because of a quality defect.

But top executives concern themselves with expenses as well as revenue and growth. That ratio translates to overall profitability and the ROI. In fact, increased revenue and growth—with no control on related expenses—can drive an organization into bankruptcy!

So, if you are an HR partner who wants to speak the language of executives, you'll need to be able to talk about profit margins on services provided, discuss overall head count cost compared with productivity, or relay the overall value in dealing with a strategic partner versus simply the cost. It's all about the return on investment.

State the "So What?"

Some technical professionals are so steeped in their functional roles and related jargon that they expect the facts to speak for themselves. However, they rarely do. A savvy communicator adds the "so what" to the conversation. For example, "We've had a turnover rate of less than 2 percent during the last year, so what that means is we should be able to shave more than $XXX off our projected training costs."

The formula is:

"Our data shows that X is happening, so what that means for our organization is that...."

Turn Topics Into Persuasive Takeaways

Simplify any charts and graphs. Cut the verbiage. Executives have many problems and projects in their pipeline. They don't have time to decipher the meaning of a slide with a heavy load of data. So, use a slide title that captures the key takeaway, not just a vague topic like "Staffing Costs." It should state the point you're making.

Ditto with graphics: Don't dump all your related data into one slide. You'll do far better to prepare three slides that make three key points than to make one complex slide that takes viewers three minutes to digest.

Have Data at Hand, But Never Depend on It

Executives expect you to have metrics to support what you say or recommend. But that doesn't mean they always want to *hear* that data. Taking executives through all your evidence can try their patience. They consider it your job to draw and share conclusions from your research—they don't want to hear a recount of your trouble in getting and validating the data.

Always have support for your recommendations, proposals, and opinions—but never expect data alone to build your case. Explain the impact. What's the story you're telling? What's the long-term effect or the potential missed opportunity? How might this change policy? How might this budget decrease or increase affect employees or suppliers? How would this change alter the general public's perception?

Add the human dimension—an analogy or a story that drives home the real impact on morale, productivity, retention, recruitment, or compliance.

Consider Timing

Even military generals try to avoid fighting on all fronts at once. If crises are occurring almost daily or weekly in your organization, consider the best time to approach the leadership team with your recommendations so you have their full attention. Remember, no matter how hungry people are, they'll have difficulty thinking about a gourmet dinner with flames shooting up around their head.

Understand the Impact of Your Personal Presence

For more than three decades, I've polled large audiences about skills, traits, attitudes, and habits that, in their opinion, contribute to someone's executive presence. During that same period, I've talked with client CEOs and senior executives who were sending team members to me for what they often referred to as "polish."

All the characteristics they've mentioned through the years fall into these four buckets:
- How someone looks (body language, dress, movement)
- How someone talks (vocal qualities, word choices, speaking patterns)
- How someone thinks (the ability to communicate clearly and persuasively under pressure)
- How someone acts (character traits, values, skills, and general competence)

By the time someone reaches adulthood, their character, values, and competence are typically well established. So, they generally need to address only their body language and communication

or "thinking" habits. Here are a few quick tips for transforming the visual (body language) and vocal aspects of presence:
- Stand as tall as possible—as if you're pushing your head through the ceiling.
- Relax, but keep that "tall" posture; don't be rigid.
- Stop any random, jerky gestures. Use your hands naturally, but with purpose.
- Gesture from your shoulder, not your elbow or wrist.
- If there's a group, select three or four people and have a conversation with them. (The rest of the audience will also feel connected and included.)
- Slow your speech. Talking too fast conveys nervousness.

That's it. Employing these few body language and vocal principles will make a dramatic difference in creating an impression of confident competence—exactly what you need when engaging with an executive team.

Present Your Ideas Concisely—Whether Speaking or Writing

Executives are impatient. If you can't *write* your bottom-line message in a sentence, you can't *say* it in an hour. So, make your bottom-line message your top-line message in emails, feasibility studies, proposals, and executive reports.

Think *before* you write—not *as* you write. Consider the readers' interests: what they want to know, what they need to know, what they already know, and how they may react. Then include and organize the appropriate details accordingly. Never tell executives something they already know.

And when the situation calls for an oral presentation, prepare thoroughly. Deliver information or recommendations with confidence and credibility rather than in a monotone accompanied by nervous fidgeting.

In the past three decades of communication coaching, I keep hearing a few of the same complaints from executives about those who present to them—whether presenting status updates, budget requests, or employee survey results. Let's look at these complaints more closely.

People Struggle to Get to the Point

Executives want to hear your point—fast. Not your topic, but your point. Don't promise that you're going to cover topics X, Y, and Z in the next 20 minutes. Take 30 to 60 seconds to state your case (debaters do this routinely). Then spend the rest of your time filling in the details.

Presenters, of course, wish executives had more patience. They've done the research and understand their subject or the problem to solve. So they feel constricted to have to "say it all" in a few short sentences. It feels far easier to add background, caveats, and data before presenting conclusions because they believe it will stave off potential challenges from opinionated listeners.

But don't be tempted to wade through the background before you give your conclusion. Start with your key message!

They Deliver Monologue

Many high-potential briefers receive a budget to fund research and work on a hot initiative. These smart people with great ideas polish their presentation to perfection. It's their big chance for visibility across several functional areas of the organization. Their excitement feels palpable.

They plan 25 minutes of formal presentation to fill their 30-minute slot, leaving five minutes for questions. Then they're surprised—and disappointed—at only polite applause at the end.

The problem? Executives expect a dialogue, not a monologue. In fact, some briefers get visibly ruffled when questions "interrupt" their flow. Big mistake. Plan to engage these strong executive personalities *throughout* your briefing—not just at the end in a Q&A session.

They Get Too Technical

The C-suite audience wants you to understand the technical details of your project or idea. They just don't necessarily want to hear about it in detailed technicolor. In fact, they rarely want to hear the finer details (legal, compliance, and so forth) unless they are equally as specialized as you are.

If they ask you a technical question, however, you better be able to answer it accurately and convincingly. Try to fake it and chances are you'll never make another presentation in the C-suite.

But senior leaders do expect you to have the skill to translate your technical expertise to a wider audience outside your specialized field. Yes, use your charts, graphs, KPIs, and flowcharts inside your department. But when you get to the C-suite, upgrade the language a few notches so that those outside your specialized field can understand what you've done, how it contributes to overall initiatives, and why it matters.

Take a Stand—While Listening to What Executives Say to You

Take a stand on important issues in your area of expertise. Your job in the executive suite is not simply to inform, but to persuade. But take care when and how you deliver a counterpunch: You're loaded with information. So why not unload it on your executive team at every opportunity?

A persuasive communicator often mimics the role of narrator Nick Carraway in *The Great Gatsby*, hearing what the frivolity, leisurely pastimes, and disjointed conversations around him reveal about character and motivations. As one of these master listeners, you'll at times find it advantageous to sit quietly at the periphery of a conversation, encouraging others to speak up with their opinions. These will become your data points for further strategizing about how to gain the support of your executive team—especially those members reluctant to engage.

Ask Tough Questions With Intention

Attorneys live by this axiom: "Don't ask questions in court if you don't already know the answers." Weak corporate leaders model this same principle when they question staffers, intending to put them on the spot and embarrass them. But persuasive communicators often ask questions for better reasons: They want to open rather than close doors.

For example, they ask questions that lead their executive team to reflect, consider exceptions and cautions, and change course. Their questions surface limitations and identify additional opportunities, focusing on broader considerations. These tough questions may punch holes in impossible dreams, perplex the activist, prevent irreparable damage to reputation, reaffirm values, or challenge the research or conventional wisdom.

Persuasive HR leaders have become known for the hard questions they ask—the ones that can't be answered quickly. Hard questions result in hard thinking and sometimes even harder work.

So, what's the most valuable outcome of a tough question you can pose? An executive changes their mind and direction, drops opposition to your plans, and ultimately must approve of your approach, budget, and policy recommendation.

Answer Questions Directly

Don't play dodge ball with vague generalities that confuse and do not amuse. Respond promptly to questions or requests—even if your response is simply to tell the executive that you don't have an answer yet or can't take the action immediately. Let them know when to expect your complete response.

Reframe Forced-Choice Questions to Refocus

The old "Have you stopped beating your spouse?" dilemma captures this problem well: "Yes or no?" Either way you answer, you're in trouble.

During a meeting with your executive team, an off-base question may sound like:
- "Can you or can you not get this new facility staffed by November 1?"
- "Are you confident we can get this enterprise system installed for less than $100k?"
- "Bottom line: Is Gary going to make it in this job, or should we be looking for his replacement?"
- "Which is the best approach—delay until the bugs are worked out or take advantage of the discount that ends in two weeks?"

Of course, if you can give a clear-cut, confident response to such two-pronged questions, do it. The problem with these forced-choice responses is that you frequently aren't comfortable or confident choosing either option A or option B as stated. Caveats come to mind and to your way of thinking, the "right" answer is neither choice.

Basically, you have four alternatives for clearly and correctly responding to forced-choice questions from the executive team:

- **Take your choice, … uh, their choice.** When you come to the fork in the road, take a stand if you feel confident in your opinion. State whichever choice you believe to be right—the right date, the right amount, the right employee, the best approach. The executive will be pleased that you're playing along. That is, as long as your response or opinion turns out to be correct. But if things turn out badly, you'll lose credibility.
- **Reframe the question.** That is, reframe the stated forced-choice question to fit the one you think is the right question for the situation, the most critical question, the most important question, or the most immediate question. Here's an example: "In my opinion, what's more important than full staffing by November 1 is finding the ideal engineering team. That search for engineers with X experience may take a while longer."
- **Expand the forced-choice question to offer new ideas.** The expanded option to the question "Can you or can you not get this new facility staffed by November 1?" might be this response: "I'm sure we *could* fill all the positions by November 1—with *someone*. But getting the *right* people in the best spot may take longer—up to six months. The job market now for.…"
- **Ask for time to develop new options.** Executives enjoy delays like they enjoy a root canal. So, you'll need to sell it if you choose this approach. Try something like: "Neither of the options you mentioned sounds ideal. But if I could take a few days for research, I think I can bring you a better option to achieve our goal. Can you give me a week to find that best option?"

It takes confidence to spring yourself free from a forced-choice trap set by a misguided executive. But after developing and displaying that confidence, you'll be glad you did.

Identify and Communicate a Common Purpose When Conflicts Arise

It's natural for executive leaders from different departments or divisions to have their own approaches to projects and responsibilities. But when those approaches diverge, savvy leaders continue to keep their focus on what the parties have in common (such as reaching a common revenue goal, lowering the rejection rate on widgets, developing and promoting in-house talent, or recruiting star performers from a related industry).

How do you increase the buy-in to a shared purpose? Clearly state the mission and metrics. Repeat that vision often in multiple ways and formats. That common purpose has to be communicated—measured, praised, rewarded—continually.

Summarize Succinctly

At some point, great HR leaders have to pull all the skills we've discussed in this chapter together to master one additional skill: They have to be able to synthesize what they've heard so they can communicate clearly a summary of the key conclusions and recommendations to a broad audience—either your conclusions or those the entire group has developed during the discussion.

Suggest Next Steps and Provide a Leave-Behind

Never walk away from a conversation with executives without stating next actions explicitly—as you see them. Typically, it's a great idea to provide the next steps in written form on a single page so the executives can delegate these implementation steps after deciding to move forward.

Final Thoughts

HR practitioners have a plethora of throwaway lines they hope will lead to a permanent seat around the executive conference table, including:
- "The ROI exceeded our expectations."
- "The program was rejected because it didn't seem to be a culture fit."
- "Our team will be digging into the analytics to map out the industry benchmarks."

But to stand out as a great communicator, selecting the *best* words, approaches, and processes to gain executive buy-in can make a significant difference in how others judge your competence—not to mention how willing they are to trust you with their reputation and retirement funds! (Of course, you may not be literally responsible for setting up their 401(k) options.) But your input to the executive team can either send the organization into a tailspin thanks to policy recommendations that push top talent out the door—or put people on solid footing.

So, sure, run the analytics, do the interviews, and synthesize the research. But make sure you're prepared to present what you know in a way that engages rather than enrages.

About the Author

Dianna Booher helps organizations communicate clearly and leaders expand their influence by a strong executive presence—and occasionally a published book. She's the bestselling author of 49 books, which have been published in 62 foreign-language editions. Her latest books include *Faster, Fewer, Better Emails; Communicate Like a Leader; Creating Personal Presence; What More Can I Say?;* and *Communicate With Confidence.* Clients include more than a third of the Fortune 500. National media such as *Good Morning America, USA Today, Wall Street Journal,* Bloomberg,

Forbes, BBC, FOX, CNN, and NPR have interviewed her on workplace communication. Among many other lists of leadership communication experts, Dianna's name appears on Richtopia's "Top 200 Most Influential Authors in the World" and on "Global Gurus Top 30 Communicators" (2012–2021). You can reach her at Dianna.Booher@BooherResearch.com.

Recommended Resources

Booher, D. 2011. *Creating Personal Presence. Look, Talk, Think, and Act Like a Leader*. Oakland, CA: Berrett-Koehler.

Booher, D. 2015a. *Communicate Like a Leader: Connecting Strategically to Coach, Inspire, and Get Things Done*. Oakland, CA: Berrett-Koehler.

Booher, D. 2015b. *What More Can I Say? Why Communication Fails and What to Do About It*. New York: Penguin Random House.

Cialdini, R. 2006. *Influence: The Psychology of Persuasion*, rev. ed. New York: Harper Business.

Kouzes, J., and B. Posner. *The Leadership Challenge*, 6th ed. New York: Jossey-Bass.

CHAPTER 32

Integrating DEI Principles Into TD Initiatives

Maria Morukian

Although diversity, equity, and inclusion (DEI) has been thrust into the spotlight in recent years, it is by no means a new issue. For decades, organizations have engaged in DEI efforts with varying degrees of intensity and differing levels of progress, ranging from compliance training around equal employment opportunity laws, to affirmative action policies, to managing diverse teams and addressing unconscious bias. All of these approaches have their value, yet a one-sided or solitary approach often does not yield significant results. Talent development professionals have a distinct role in ensuring DEI principles are implemented.

> **IN THIS CHAPTER:**
> - Discuss the importance of DEI for TD professionals
> - Identify best practices to integrate DEI into TD initiatives

There has been a recent shift in light of increasing cultural polarization and the titanic events of the last few years, including the COVID-19 pandemic and its adverse impact on women and racial and ethnic minorities. The murder of George Floyd and other unarmed Black people by police sparked a movement around the globe to address systemic racism. In addition, we saw laws both positively and negatively impacting the LGBTQIA+ community, and the #MeToo movement and global attention to the ongoing inequality and misogyny women face. More organizations than ever before have begun to focus on DEI in a more systematic way.

As the demand for DEI work continues to expand, so too does the demand to hold organizations accountable for making visible, sustainable progress. Talent development professionals play a critical role in this effort.

This chapter will explore the fundamental pillars of embedding DEI into TD initiatives and provide practical skills and tactics for TD professionals to weave DEI into every aspect of talent development and training.

What Is DEI?

Diversity encompasses all the dimensions of human identity that make us who we are. This includes all characteristics that shape our identity lenses—our beliefs, values, worldviews, and perceptions—which thus influence our communication, our behaviors, and ultimately our relationships with others.

Equity promotes fairness by creating a level playing field for everyone. This means providing opportunities for people to advance in their careers, receive fair compensation and credit for their work, and have equal opportunities to provide input into decisions that affect them.

Inclusion is the practice of creating an environment where everyone feels equally valued and respected for their individuality. Inclusive environments ensure that every person is able to participate fully in organizational life and has equal opportunities to leverage their talents, skills, and potential.

Why Is DEI Important for Organizational Growth and Sustainability?

Every nation in the world has diversity in terms of race, ethnicity, language, religion, and culture, to name a few. As the competition for top talent and to engage diverse populations grows, diversity has increasingly become an important topic for organizations.

Global migration has also increased in the last few decades, contributing to rising levels of ethnic and cultural diversity in countries around the world (Poushter and Fetterolf 2019). People who live in more diverse places tend to have more welcoming views on diversity and be less prejudiced (Poushter and Fetterolf 2019; Bai, Ramos, and Fiske 2020).

Nearly four out of 10 Americans identify as a racial or ethnic identity other than White (Frey 2020). In fact, by the year 2043, it is estimated that the US will be a majority minority population in terms of race and ethnicity. Women comprise half the US population and have higher levels of education than men (Hanson 2021). The population of people who identify as LGBTQIA+ has now topped 18 million, indicating a significant increase in just the last decade, which will likely continue to trend up due to changing societal norms among younger generations (Jones 2021).

Diversity Leads to Better Organizational Results

Companies with more women and people of color in management positions financially outperform their counterparts (Dixon-Fyle et al. 2020). Diverse teams make smarter decisions and are more innovative (Rock and Grant 2016). They also outperform homogeneous teams of like-minded experts because they are able to leverage the power of their unique individual knowledge, perspectives, and experiences (Page 2008).

Equity and Inclusion Are Critical for Success

Even in more diverse organizations, employee sentiments around inclusion and equity are markedly worse than diversity ratings, with less than 30 percent presenting positive opinions and 60 percent presenting negative opinions related to equality, openness, and a sense of belonging (Dixon-Fyle et al. 2020). Hiring for diversity is not enough, and in some instances can even lead to worse results if the organizational culture and structure are not equitable and inclusive. Employees who experience bias are more than three times as likely to say that they are planning to leave their current jobs within the year (Hewlett, Rashid, and Sherbin 2017). The price of employees who stay at the organization and experience bias is even greater—employees who experience bias are nearly three times as likely to be disengaged at work, which costs US companies between $450 billion and $550 billion per year (Gallup 2013).

Therefore, diversity, equity, and inclusion are not mutually exclusive. In order to build thriving organizations, these three concepts must be considered together.

Why Do Some DEI Initiatives Seem to Fail?

Organizations spend a significant amount of time, energy, and money on DEI efforts. In fact, one recent report estimated that companies spend a combined $8 billion annually in DEI training. Yet, it can be difficult to see tangible results, and in some instances DEI efforts have actually led to backlash (Dobbin and Kavel 2016).

Here are a few challenges that often hinder sustainable DEI efforts:
- Although DEI training may increase awareness of issues like implicit bias, stereotypes, and racial inequality, a generic diversity training class offered once will not likely lead to lasting behavior change if it's not part of a broader organizational strategy.

- Training individuals does not by itself address the systemic barriers and inequities that continue to perpetuate advantages for those with societal privilege and disadvantages for those without. Individuals need to experience DEI as part of the everyday fabric of their organizational life and need to feel a sense of commitment to one another and to the organization to contribute to DEI.
- Good intentions do not transform to sustainable change unless there are clearly defined DEI goals with measurable success indicators.
- DEI knowledge and skills must be reinforced across the learning landscape, systems and policies in the organization need to be DEI focused, and accountability measures must be put in place.

Integrating DEI Principles Into TD Initiatives

DEI training can't be a one-off event. It needs to be embedded into the entire training and talent development infrastructure in both content and delivery methods. This means finding ways to reinforce DEI concepts in training programs, as well as making all training programs reflective of diversity. It requires a focus on accessibility and inclusion in the way training programs are delivered. For DEI efforts to succeed, TD professionals must be role models for DEI, inviting diverse voices, continuously developing their own skills, and managing biases.

Three critical components for TD professionals to consider as an imperative to integrating DEI into their work are: walk the talk, create relevant DEI training, and embed DEI as a TD strategy (Figure 32-1).

Figure 32-1. Three Critical Components for DEI Integration

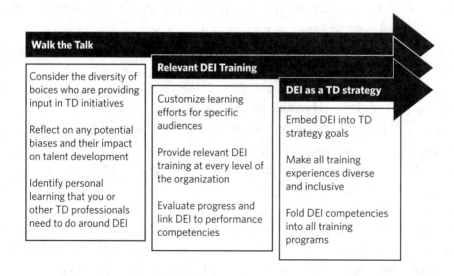

Walk the Talk

Before creating content or delivering training, start by reflecting on the amount of diversity on your own TD team and in your personal DEI experiences. Continuous self-reflection and discovery are crucial for progress in DEI work.

The US training and development industry is 83 percent White and 57 percent female. Thus, the majority of people who are responsible for building out an organization's training infrastructure and managing learning development experiences tend to fall within a narrow set of demographics.

> **WHO IS ON YOUR TD TEAM?**
> - Whose voices, perspectives, and needs are consulted when designing training?
> - Who is responsible for the design itself? Who oversees the design process and has final approval?
> - Whose voices, perspectives, and needs are absent?
> - What implications does this have on how the training content is designed and delivered?

TD professionals must be willing to do their own self-reflection and skill-building in terms of DEI. It is far easier for us to recognize blind spots and biases in others, but not ourselves. TD professionals have a responsibility to challenge their own beliefs and assumptions, examine decisions for potential biases, and continuously model inclusive behavior. DEI work is intensely challenging and requires you to be familiar with your own potential biases and blind spots.

You will make mistakes. You will be imperfect. You will unintentionally say or do something that causes friction for others. Bringing compassion for yourself and others, encouraging people to engage in thoughtful dialogue, and navigating disagreements and emotional reactions are all necessary to foster a DEI culture.

Take time to consider the following:
- The multiple dimensions of your own identity that shape the way you see the world, what you believe, and how you behave.
- Aspects of your identity that afford you automatic societal advantages and privileges (for example, race, gender, age, socioeconomic status, physical and mental ability, or sexual orientation).
- Past experiences that have shaped your personal views on DEI. For instance, have you ever been treated unfairly or excluded because of some aspect of your identity? Have you witnessed discrimination of people in your identity group? Have you witnessed discrimination of people in a different identity group? Have you ever been the sole representative of your identity in a group of people who were all alike?

- Comfort level engaging in honest conversations around DEI issues, including issues that are less familiar to you.
- Comfort level sharing your own personal stories of identity, especially if you have experienced discrimination, harassment, or bias because of an aspect of your identity.
- Willingness to make mistakes, accept feedback, and learn. We all carry good intentions but are not always aware of the impact of our actions on others. How practiced are you in managing your response when confronted by others about your potentially exclusionary or biased behavior?

Design Relevant DEI Learning

Although there are common foundational concepts and strategies for any DEI training, it is important to tailor your approach to the specific needs of the organization. Rather than treating DEI training as a one-size-fits-all experience, engage in data gathering to determine the knowledge, attitudes, and skills of different stakeholder groups in the organization, so you can effectively tailor the DEI programming to their unique needs.

DEI learning should be customized to reflect the specific competencies different individuals are expected to demonstrate to achieve the organization's DEI goals.

Review Assessment Methods

Consider the appropriate assessment methods for the kind of information you want to gather to customize the learning approach.

- **Individual interviews** with a diverse selection of stakeholders provide insights into individual perspectives and experiences related to DEI in the organization. They are a valuable tool for qualitative data gathering, and often provide rich stories from voices across the organizational landscape.
- **Focus groups** are another powerful qualitative data gathering tool that provide stories and opportunities to explore people's perceptions of DEI at greater depth. They also create a space for people to interact and exchange ideas and experiences, which can provide a thoughtful discussion and opportunity for learning as well as yield valuable data for the assessment.
- **Surveys** are valuable because they provide an opportunity for everyone in the organization to participate in the assessment process. They provide "hard" data in terms of measuring perspectives and opinions. They can also provide valuable insight into variances by diverse demographic groups.
- **Policy and documents reviews** identify the existing language, training, policies, and practices that either help or hinder organizational DEI efforts. They can identify critical

areas that must be addressed, as well as provide insights into broader organizational changes in terms of practices, policies, norms, and communications.
- **Benchmarking studies** analyze other teams or organizations that are similar in size, scope, or industry to compare their DEI efforts. This can be a powerful method for identifying best practices that are specific to your team's or organization's needs.
- **Individual skills assessments** are used to gauge the levels of exposure, knowledge, and skills of your workforce. This can be particularly useful for providing insights to senior leaders and managers, who have significant influence in setting the tone and modeling DEI behaviors. Two assessment instruments are:
  - Intercultural Development Inventory (IDI), which is a well-researched and validated instrument that assesses an individual's attitudes and competencies related to interacting with different identity groups.
  - Global Competencies Index (GCI), which was developed by the Kozai Group. This is another well-researched and validated instrument that assesses an individual's leadership competencies in terms of working effectively across cultural differences.

Provide DEI-Specific Training at Every Organizational Level

DEI-specific training should provide a shared language and behavioral expectations for all members of the workforce. How the training is designed and communicated is important for illustrating the organization's commitment to DEI.

If the training is perceived as compliance-based training, or a chore that must be endured and then forgotten, it can do more harm than good for fostering a DEI culture. The more the training content is aligned with organizational values and goals, and tailored for particular audiences, the more likely it will have its intended impact.

Thus, the most effective training for DEI:
- Is customized to align with the organizational culture
- Uses relevant scenarios and language for the audience
- Includes relevant and validated research
- Provides opportunities for honest dialogue, storytelling, and perspective taking
- Offers practical skills for making small but significant behavioral changes
- Includes individual and group action planning to encourage commitment

A comprehensive DEI training program needs to be tailored to specific audiences. For example, you may need to create distinct courses based on things like management level, job function, geographic region, or demographic group.

DEI learning should also build in complexity and give participants time to reflect and practice new skills. One recommendation is to space out DEI training for specific cohorts or participant groups over the course of several weeks or months, with shorter installments of training focusing on specific DEI knowledge and skills, and pre- and post-session application and reflection assignments to encourage accountability for behavior change. By doing so, participants have more time to become accustomed to the emotional discomfort and cognitive dissonance that often arises when discussing identity, bias, privilege, and systemic inequality.

Link DEI to Performance

TD professionals play a crucial role in providing the learning support needed for individuals to effectively model DEI and meet performance goals. Work with HR and executive leadership to develop a strategy for integrating DEI into individual performance metrics, starting with leadership.

Begin by linking leaders' performance to DEI. The organization needs to send a clear message that it is committed and ensure that those with the most power and influence in the organization are prioritizing DEI.

Then work with your team to ensure that training and development efforts adequately equip leaders and managers with the knowledge and skills they need to foster DEI and meet their performance goals.

The next step is integrating DEI competencies into performance expectations for everyone in the workforce. There may be some overlap with leadership competencies, but different job functions may require some unique skills and behavioral indicators to demonstrate their DEI commitment.

Embed DEI as a Long-Term TD Strategy

DEI is not a singular event—it is an ever-evolving journey. Goals can be achieved and milestones celebrated, but there will always be work to do to maintain success and set new goals.

TD professionals should make DEI a core part of their strategic TD goals and intentionally embed a DEI lens into the overall infrastructure, design, and delivery of all TD-related activities.

Develop Strategic DEI Goals With Measurable Outcomes

DEI efforts often lose steam or get sidelined when they are not monitored or directly related to specific, measurable performance goals. DEI needs to be a part of any TD strategy, starting with clearly outlined goals related to it from a talent development standpoint. Consider how your TD initiative's DEI goals connect with the organization's DEI vision and goals. How will your strategy contribute to the organization's efforts?

Although some goals may be more straightforward to measure, it is important to consider how to measure some of the seemingly more amorphous elements of the organizational climate and culture.

Consider which DEI outcomes can be measured in terms of learning and talent development. For example:
- High levels of participation in DEI-related events from across the organization
- Increase in self-reporting on comfort related to DEI competencies
- Increase in employees reporting satisfaction with leaders and managers' DEI competencies
- Increase in underrepresented identity groups selected to participate in leadership training programs
- Increased diversity of individuals involved in coaching or mentoring programs
- Decrease in employee complaints around discrimination, harassment, hostile work environments, bullying, or preferential treatment

It is also helpful to track broader organizational performance indicators, which may show how TD efforts contribute to broader outcomes, such as:
- Increase in underrepresented identity groups in leadership and management positions
- Increase in underrepresented identity groups in high-profile or external-facing job functions (for example, sales versus operations)
- Increase in underrepresented identity groups in career fast-track programs
- Promotions of people from underrepresented identity groups
- Lower turnover rates
- Higher employee engagement scores
- Equitable compensation and benefits packages
- Positive ratings in 360-degree assessments or employee performance evaluations on questions related to DEI

Reflect Diversity in Learning and Development Content

The learning experience needs to be accessible to and inclusive for all participants. If the materials are difficult to read or see, if the activities are not accessible for those with limited mobility, or if participants do not feel safe speaking honestly in front of others in the training session, not only will their learning be compromised but people may also become frustrated, embarrassed, or withdrawn.

This starts with content design. Consider how the content represents diversity in terms of the images and names used, as well as the authors cited, individuals quoted, and role assignments in scenarios or case studies.

What names are most commonly used in your training designs? If everyone is named Mary or Bill, it might be time to select names that are more diverse. Who is represented in your training graphics, and how? For instance, are middle-aged White people typically shown in leadership roles?

Training materials are filled with images of light-skin-toned, able-bodied, cisgender people, and males are often shown in positions of leadership or power. Moreover, many of the images that show racial diversity still feature thin or physically fit people in Western business attire smiling broadly. The subject matter experts, authors, and thought leaders that are cited or quoted tend to be overwhelmingly White, male, and Western European or North American. As a result, the stories, scenarios, and language used in training can reinforce cultural stereotypes.

Beyond graphics, consider text in terms of readability and accessibility. Is the font size appropriate? Is the reading level of the text aligned with the audience? Are there colloquialisms that would be challenging for nonnative speakers to understand?

Suggestions for reflecting diversity in content:
- Think about who is represented in the images you choose and how accurately those images reflect the population of employees, customers, or communities served.
- Be intentional about using images of people of color, people with disabilities, people of various ages, people of various sizes, and so forth.
- Illustrate culturally competent gestures, clothing, expressions, and interactions.
- Consider the clothing and hairstyles featured and whether they are representative and culturally appropriate.
- When designing scenarios or examples, make sure the roles you assign are culturally competent and equitable. Often, the default is to make the supervisor a male, and quite often the senior executive a White male. Who is the executive assistant? Who is the engineer? Who is the accountant? Who is the general counsel?
- Additionally, be intentional about using names and personas that represent diversity in terms of gender, sexual orientation, race, ethnicity, age, and national origin in your examples and scenarios.
- If you are using videos, be intentional about showcasing diverse actors, speakers, and academics. In addition to mere representation, it's important to look for video clips that are culturally appropriate and free of biases and stereotypes.
- Check for phrases or words that may be perceived as exclusionary. For example, the phrase "off the reservation" has been used in American slang to represent a person not complying with expectations. This phrase originated from the forced removal of Native Americans from their lands to describe failure to comply with new laws regulating them to the reservations.

> **PHRASING TO AVOID**
>
> A number of common English phrases have exclusive historical connotations. Avoid using them in your training materials. Let's review a few.
> - "Sold down the river" refers to enslaved people in the US who were often sold further South if they were accused of disobeying.
> - "Spirit animal" is often used to describe an animal, person, or object you strongly identify with. However, for Native people, spirit animals, also known as totems, are a deeply sacred spiritual tradition and the cultural appropriation can be harmful.
> - "One of the guys" to refer to women who engage in what are considered more masculine activities or who "fit in" with a male group is potentially harmful in that it intimates that women have to act more like males in order to be accepted.
> - "Drama queen" or "diva" are often used to describe women (and sometimes gay men) as being overly emotional or demanding, with the intention of getting attention. It perpetuates the stereotype of women being irrational and sends the message that it is not acceptable to express one's emotions.

Create Inclusive Learning Environments

Beyond its design, it is important to ensure that the learning environment fosters DEI.

Instructor Diversity

One of the first things participants will notice when they arrive for training is the person at the front of the room. Examine the diversity of the trainers, presenters, and guest speakers involved in your training programs. Be intentional about representing diversity in terms of gender, race, ethnicity, age, disability, and other relevant dimensions of identity.

When conducting DEI training, make sure that you're using diverse teams of co-facilitators who represent different identity dimensions. This can be helpful in building credibility and connection with diverse participants. Co-facilitators can also be instrumental in supporting one another if conflict or emotional reactions arise in the training environment.

Consider who is introducing the training session, participating on a panel, or serving as a guest expert speaker. Seek out diverse leaders and subject matter experts, regardless of the training topic. In fact, this might be even more important in industries or training workshops that are typically dominated by a more homogeneous population. For example, in technical training for engineering, law enforcement, or manufacturing, which are typically dominated by men, try to get guest speakers who are women and nonbinary individuals for more representation.

Inclusive Interactions

It is inevitable that you and any other instructors or speakers with whom you work will carry implicit associations and biases into the classroom. Be mindful of the messages you send to ensure every participant feels valued and included.

Greet every participant in a warm manner. Do your best to pronounce each name correctly and remember it. When possible, study the participant list in advance to have a sense of who is attending and practice their names.

Be vigilant about managing your own implicit associations and preferences in the learning environment. Give attention to all learners and avoid being overly focused on any one individual or small group of learners.

Take note of your social cues and any subtle messages you may be sending by changing your vocal inflections or giving more frequent eye contact and encouragement to some participants over others. Trainers have the power to encourage or discourage participation and engagement, and it is often in the smallest micro-messages that these moments occur.

Maximize Participation

The learning experience can be significantly influenced by who is in the room and the level of comfort participants have with one another. When possible, consider which learners to put together in the training program. For example, if the session is intended to provide an opportunity for honest conversations about challenging workplace issues, it may be more effective to separate managers from employees if there are low levels of trust or safety.

To the extent you are able, try to ensure the training session includes a diverse group of individuals. This may not be possible in open-enrollment programs, but if you are bringing together a cohort of participants for a collective learning experience, try to maximize the diversity of the group in terms of gender, racial or ethnic background (if known), age or years of experience at the organization, and so forth.

Setting group learning norms at the beginning of the program is a great way to encourage active participation and set expectations for respectful, inclusive behaviors. Regardless of the content of the training, consider taking a few minutes early in the program to post behavioral norms or guidelines.

You can reinforce an inclusive learning environment in small, subtle ways, such as requesting that breakout groups nominate a representative who has not spoken up as much. Repeat back or affirm the contributions of participants in nondominant positions.

WHEN DEI TRAINING LEAVES NO ONE BEHIND
Paul Signorelli, consultant, trainer, and author of Change the World Using Social Media

Learning sessions designed to foster increased appreciation for and commitment to diversity, equity, and inclusion may leave learners feeling wounded rather than supported. Those sessions obviously make people aware of their own deficiencies and foster guilt, embarrassment, and defensiveness without emphasizing the steps we can take to be more positive and productive in our interactions. But it is possible to have a positive and enlightening experience.

Examples from two colleagues provide reassurance that a positive training approach can nurture levels of trust, honesty, and collaboration.

The first, from a diversity session I helped arrange, started off with a brief introduction designed to define the terms we were exploring. After participants had a chance to begin looking at DEI in theoretical terms, the facilitator invited us to watch a short video. The video began with jarring, quick-cut, close-up images of the face of a Black man staring straight and unsmiling into the camera. The music in the background was dramatic and immediately invoked the fear that comes with watching a crime. The voice-over described the person in broad terms, suggesting that he was connected to our criminal justice system. It was only in the final images of the video that the camera pulled back to show that the man was in a police officer's uniform. This led to some interesting and transformative conversations about the assumptions we make and how those assumptions stand in the way of effective work and collaborative efforts. Near the end of the session, the facilitator revealed that he had an imperceptible disability that often put him at a disadvantage in terms of his own workplace and his ability to be included in those interactions.

In another situation I secured a well-respected facilitator to address transgender issues for a large public agency where security guards were being drawn into disputes about who was allowed to use which restrooms. On the day of the session, the facilitator arrived early enough to chat informally with participants as they arrived. He opened the workshop by leading people through a few scenarios, then began interacting with participants so they could describe what was most challenging for them. Bit by bit, issues were aired and dealt with positively. Near the end of the session, someone complimented him on the wonderful way he facilitated the session and helped participants openly confront and deal with the issues that had been plaguing them. That's when he revealed that he had made the transition from female to male. At least one participant called the session life changing, and many others praised the facilitator for his approach to leading them, step-by-step, to an understanding of what was causing their discomfort and what they could do to change.

That is what we all strive to produce: life-changing moments with long-term impacts that produce better experiences for everyone we meet and serve.

Integrate DEI Language and Skills Into Other Interpersonal Skills Training

Generally, DEI can and should be woven into all people-focused training to reinforce DEI principles and provide additional opportunities for skill development. Identity lenses, core values, beliefs, and personal experiences related to one's societal identity and conditioning all play a powerful role in how we understand and communicate with one another.

For example:

- **Communication.** Our identity significantly influences how we communicate with others and how we interpret their communication.
- **Managing up and influencing without authority.** By understanding the different identities our leaders and managers bring with them, we can engage in perspective taking, build trust, and influence their decisions.
- **Conflict management.** The most challenging (and destructive) form of conflict is often due to an identity problem rather than a technical one. Understanding how our brains react in times of identity-based conflict, learning about diverse conflict styles, and developing practices for dialogue are important skills for effective conflict management.
- **Feedback.** How individuals are culturally conditioned to give and receive feedback has a significant impact on workplace productivity and relationships. Knowing our own and others' perspectives, emotional triggers, and feedback communication preferences all lead to better results when giving and receiving feedback.
- **Innovation and creativity.** DEI is integral to fostering innovation and creativity. Inviting and exploring divergent perspectives and ideas and creating psychological safety so people can disagree and debate processes are pillars of innovative cultures.
- **Change management.** People have different ways of reacting to change and dealing with the emotional process of organizational transitions. Learning about and responding effectively to different individuals' needs in times of change and turmoil leads to more streamlined solutions and sustainable transformation.
- **Team building.** Teams are made up of people, all of whom bring individual identities, motivations, and needs. Fostering trust and rapport on the team requires everyone to explore their different personalities and experiences so they can build an environment where the team can thrive.
- **Customer service.** Customers bring their own unique experiences, perspectives, communication styles, and needs. To best serve them, it is important to recognize how our own identity lenses and implicit biases may affect the way we communicate with our customers.
- **Leadership and management.** Leadership, management, and supervisory skills training all play a prominent role in fostering DEI. Leadership or management training programs

for any level of leadership (from aspiring leaders to senior executive) must incorporate and reinforce knowledge and skills around DEI.

Embed DEI Into All TD Professional Roles

DEI doesn't just have to live in "people skills" training. In fact, it can play a valuable role in enhancing the skills of many different TD professionals. For example:

- **Human resources.** HR training should provide comprehensive knowledge and skills for managing biases, engaging in equitable and inclusive practices with all employees, and promoting DEI across the organization. Although this seems obvious, all too often HR professionals are not given the degree of information needed to champion DEI in their organizations.
- **Analytics and data-driven decision making.** Even when preparing and analyzing data to make decisions, implicit biases can affect results. Analytics training should include content that prepares learners to recognize and mitigate potential biases, ensure the data collected is representative of diverse populations, and present findings that consider the organization's DEI goals.
- **Project management.** Project managers need to be able to acknowledge and manage their own assumptions and implicit biases when prioritizing tasks, delegating responsibilities, and collaborating on project teams. They also need to be familiar with the organization's DEI goals and know how to align project management goals and objectives with the organization's broader DEI strategy.
- **Contracting and acquisitions.** Whether it is managing contract teams, performance monitoring and quality control, or managing challenging contractor situations, contracting and acquisitions professionals must recognize how their own biases and assumptions may influence their interactions with contractors. They also need to know how to hold contractors accountable for fostering DEI in their practices.
- **Performance management.** Performance management training requires a DEI lens. Anyone involved in the performance management process should learn how to intentionally manage their own assumptions and biases, and to foster DEI at every stage of employee performance management, from goal setting and delegating to monitoring and evaluation.

Embed DEI Into All L&D Activities

Organizations often have significant opportunities for publicizing and reinforcing DEI learning goals. By leveraging these events and resources, you further weave DEI into the organizational language and culture. For example:

- **Conferences.** If your organization leads annual events like conferences or symposiums, make DEI a regularly scheduled theme. Bring in guest speakers or host workshops that are relevant to the audience. Additionally, plan these events with DEI in mind. Make sure the speakers represent various dimensions of diversity, schedule the events in locations that are accessible, and provide materials that represent diversity and accommodate different needs.
- **Off-sites and strategic planning retreats.** Make DEI a standing agenda item. Ensure that diverse individuals are fully able to participate in the event in terms of time and location. Encourage contributions from underrepresented groups.
- **Monthly celebrations or heritage events.** Host and advertise regular events to celebrate historically underrepresented groups (for example, Black History Month, Women's History month, LGBTQIA+ Pride month, Asian Pacific Islander Heritage Month, and Hispanic/Latinx Heritage Month). You can also identify and celebrate or memorialize holidays and events that are important to underrepresented groups (such as Juneteenth, Indigenous People's Day, Ramadan, and Diwali). When planning, ask for input and participation from representatives of the identity group. Consider appropriate messaging and content to educate others and elevate the voices and experiences of those groups.
- **Learning management systems and online resources.** Many organizations offer ongoing learning for employees through a dedicated LMS or an internal library of content or resources. Review these resources to ensure they reflect your organization's DEI goals and be intentional about offering ongoing content and learning nudges to employees beyond formal training. LinkedIn Learning provides a collection of short video courses on a wealth of topics, including diversity, equity, and inclusion. In addition, Google has a free guide showing organizations how to develop whisper courses, which are easy-to-create email templates to send to managers and employees to reinforce the practice of particular skills. For example, a DEI whisper may be an email sent to managers to remind them to encourage diverse perspectives and ideas in their group and one-on-one meetings (Stillman 2017).
- **Newsletters, blogs, and podcasts.** Many organizations now host a variety of content that they share internally with the workforce and sometimes externally with the public or select stakeholders. Be intentional about reinforcing DEI in these communications—not only by spotlighting diverse individuals and groups, but also by speaking about the relevance of DEI for the organization, the industry, and the populations you serve.

Final Thoughts

As our organizations continue to evolve in terms of diversity, equity, and inclusion, the role of the TD professional will be significant. TD professionals need to be closely involved in assessment and strategy, in addition to leading efforts to ensure a comprehensive and sustainable approach to strengthening DEI through learning and development.

About the Author

Maria Morukian, president of MSM Global Consulting, has devoted her career to organizational culture change and leadership development with a specialization in diversity, equity, inclusion, and intercultural competence. She works with organizations to weave DEI principles into the organizational fabric. Maria is a TEDx speaker and *Forbes* contributor, and authored *Diversity, Equity, and Inclusion for Trainers: Fostering DEI in the Workplace* (ATD Press, 2022). She is on the faculty at American University's School of International Service, where she earned a master's degree. She also has bachelor's degrees from the University of Michigan in organizational studies and Spanish. Maria lives in Washington, DC, with her husband and two daughters. You can contact her at maria@msmglobalconsulting.com.

References

Bai, X., M.R. Ramos, and S.T. Fiske. 2020. "As Diversity Increases, People Paradoxically Perceive Social Groups as More Similar." *Proceedings of the National Academy of Sciences,* June 9.

Dixon-Fyle, S., K. Dolan, V. Hunt, and S. Prince. 2020. "Diversity Wins: How Inclusion Matters." McKinsey & Company, May 19. mckinsey.com/featured-insights/diversity-and-inclusion/diversity-wins-how-inclusion-matters.

Dobbin, F., and A. Kavel. 2016. "Why Diversity Programs Fail: And What Works Better." *Harvard Business Review,* July-August. hbr.org/2016/07/why-diversity-programs-fail.

Frey, W.H. 2020. "The Nation Is Diversifying Even Faster Than Predicted, According to New Census Data." Brookings, July 1. brookings.edu/research/new-census-data-shows-the-nation-is-diversifying-even-faster-than-predicted.

Gallup. 2013. *State of the American Workplace: Employee Engagement Insights for U.S. Business Leaders.* gallup.com/services/176708/state-american-workplace.aspx.

Hanson, M. 2021. "Education Attainment Statistics." Educationdata.org, June 20. educationdata.org/education-attainment-statistics.

Hewlett, S.A., R. Rashid, and L. Sherbin. 2017. "When Employees Think the Boss Is Unfair They're More Likely to Disengage and Leave." *Harvard Business Review*, August 1. hbr.org/2017/08/when-employees-think-the-boss-is-unfair-theyre-more-likely-to-disengage-and-leave.

Jones, J.M. 2021. "LGBT Identification Rises to 5.6% in Latest U.S. Estimate." Gallup, February 24. news.gallup.com/poll/329708/lgbt-identification-rises-latest-estimate.aspx.

Morukian, M. 2022. *Diversity, Equity, and Inclusion for Trainers: Fostering DEI in the Workplace*. Alexandria, VA: ATD Press.

Page, S.E. 2008. *The Difference: How the Power of Diversity Creates Better Groups, Firms, Schools, and Societies*. Princeton: Princeton University Press.

Poushter, J., and J. Fetterolf. 2019. "A Changing World: Global Views on Diversity, Gender Equality, Family Life and the Importance of Religion." Pew Research Center, April 22. pewresearch.org/global/2019/04/22/a-changing-world-global-views-on-diversity-gender-equality-family-life-and-the-importance-of-religion.

Rock, D., and H. Grant. 2016. "Why Diverse Teams Are Smarter." *Harvard Business Review*, November 4. hbr.org/2016/11/why-diverse-teams-are-smarter.

Stillman, J. 2017. "Google's Tiny Secret for Actually Impactful Employee Training Want People to Actually Change Their Behavior Based on Your Training? Then Make It Way Smaller." Inc., December 21. inc.com/jessica-stillman/googles-secret-for-employee-training-people-actually-use-shrink-it.html.

U.S. Bureau of Labor Statistics. 2021. "Labor Force Statistics From the Current Population Survey." BLS, last modified January 22. bls.gov/cps/cpsaat11.htm.

Recommended Resources

Livingston, R. 2021. *The Conversation: How Seeking and Speaking the Truth about Racism can Radically Transform Individuals and Organizations*. New York: Penguin Random House.

Morukian, M. 2022. *Diversity, Equity, and Inclusion for Trainers: Fostering DEI in the Workplace*. Alexandria, VA: ATD Press.

Parker, P. 2018. *The Art of Gathering: How We Meet and Why It Matters*. New York: Riverhead Books.

Winters, M.-F. 2020. *Inclusive Conversations: Fostering Equity, Empathy, and Belonging across Differences*. Oakland: Berrett-Koehler.

CHAPTER 33

Digital-Age Requirements for Talent Development Professionals

Alex Adamopoulos

As we adjust to a new virtual reality and pivot swiftly to market demands, bringing trainers and technology closer together starts with learning and applying new ways of working.

> **IN THIS CHAPTER:**
> - Apply work-based learning principles to adopt modern ways of working
> - Establish effective processes and practices for Agile and Lean ways of learning and working to align with the speed and scale of digital requirements
> - Enhance communication, collaboration, and coordination across the organization to motivate people to continuously learn

The current state of our digital world emphasizes and resurfaces some of the challenges that talent development professionals have been experiencing for years. Mainly, how do you accelerate the learning of individuals and teams so that they can respond well enough to the constant tides of change?

Companies are recognizing, in a very abrupt way, that adaptive practices of working and dynamic decision making are essential to maintain momentum and ensure products and services are delivered and sustained. Many of these changes are positive, and companies will not want to lose them or retract. For example, faster decision making, renewed organizational purpose, a focus on people, and a true manifestation of corporate responsibility have all come to the fore. Even more so, the upskilling and reskilling that is needed to close the talent gap is only growing in demand.

In these uncertain times, every organization needs to adapt a revised set of working principles, underpinned with the behaviors and capabilities to deliver them. This must be combined with an overarching ability to coordinate these principles coherently, despite disruptions to working norms. Now, more than ever, we need to ensure that we have the correct skills and capabilities to quickly deploy and further exploit technology to scale market share, revenues, and profitability.

OK, that all sounds great in business speak, but how do we make it practical and useful to understand and apply? Let's start by improving how we teach and learn so that we're not defaulting to the things we've always done. Work-based learning presents an opportunity to significantly shift the way we help others understand and apply new skills.

What Is Work-Based Learning?

It's ironic that something we understand in our daily lives gets forgotten when it comes to training in the workplace. If you want to improve your presentation skills, your boss might send you on a one-day course, or you might trawl the internet for tips. Both methods have some value, but neither will help you improve as much as testing your speech in front of a colleague, or simply presenting more frequently.

If we're trying to acquire new skills that are intended fundamentally to change the way we work, then it makes even more sense to learn through experimentation and doing.

Work-based learning presents principles and concepts and then asks learners to apply them immediately through a series of activities. The structured nature of the activities provides a supportive and secure environment where you can experiment, practice, and then evaluate how things went, before moving on to the next step. It also ensures that learning is at its most effective because it's tailored by you to your unique circumstances. Because you are working on real projects alongside your colleagues, work-based learning is designed to share the learning experience with your whole team. It has been described as a *metacompetence*—not the acquisition of knowledge, but the acquisition of learning how to learn.

Think about how we've traditionally trained others. For the most part, learning has happened in the classroom or conference room. Even with the introduction of innovation labs and all types of master classes where you get people to interact and run activities and games to help teach skills, the learning is still confined to the classroom. Now think about a framework that has been in play for some time and based on CCL research that goes back more than 40 years: the 70-20-10 framework (Lombardo and Eichinger 1996; Figure 33-1).

The 70-20-10 Framework

The 70-20-10 framework of learning focuses heavily on supporting people during their day job. It also creates the ability to provide mentoring and coaching remotely to support online training.

Figure 33-1. The 70-20-10 Framework

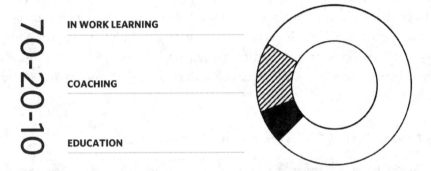

Why is this framework relevant now more than ever? The reality is that most learning happens on the job, and classroom training isn't enough. Thus, it should come as no surprise that the need to deliver education in more flexible and tailored ways (for example, remotely) to adapt to customer needs is critical to make the learning stick.

Experienced trainers know firsthand that, even in normal times, many teams are co-located. In fact, teams and trainers have been adjusting to real-world situations for years to offer support to distributed delivery, off- or near-shore, and multinational companies. And if the pandemic didn't heighten this awareness, then nothing will. By placing the emphasis on the team's work items and goals, work-based learning enables flexibility and has proven to be as effective when done remotely as it is in person.

After working closely with businesses for years, we've observed some similar patterns. We've used this knowledge to tailor the learning experience through a collection of outcome-based learning modules as well as a selection of online courses and role-based education pathways, where the knowledge is applied over time.

If you're a business leader or an HR specialist, some of the most pressing concerns in uncertain times are keeping the motivation of employees at a high level while discovering ways and tools that enable better communication, collaboration, and coordination.

Comparing Training and Work-Based Learning

The principles behind work-based learning have been around for several decades and have been analyzed by academics as well as adopted by numerous companies. As disappointment with the poor or unmeasured results of traditional training increases, work-based learning methods are gaining ground. This is crucial because we know that increasing our employees' skills is essential to our success. According to *The Global Skills Shortage*, a 2019 report from SHRM, 83 percent of respondents had trouble recruiting suitable candidates in the past 12 months, and more than a third reported a decrease in applicant quality across the board. Another 45 percent reported a decrease in quality of applicants for specific positions.

Work-based learning is a golden opportunity to develop employee skills more cost efficiently. But let's be clear—work-based learning is not e-learning designed solely to cut costs. Virtual classrooms using webinars, presentations, and digital content have similar problems to traditional training. Lowering the cost of transformation is excellent, but only because work-based learning is also more effective (Figure 33-2).

Figure 33-2. Traditional Training Failures Versus Work-Based Learning Advantages

Traditional Training Failures	Work-Based Learning Advantages
• Training is normally scripted and delivered to a group, so it will include elements not relevant to your situation. In addition, many principles may be hard to implement because of obstacles not considered by the trainer. • New information and knowledge are quickly forgotten because a single burst of information is hard to absorb and can be overwhelming. • Keeping focus and energy in a classroom is difficult. • Training can become a box-ticking exercise rather than an opportunity to improve. • Limited slots in training programs mean that knowledge is concentrated in a few employees, not the whole team. • Training professionals often lack subject expertise and credibility in a specific topic. • Objective results or business value are rarely employed to measure training effectiveness. • Training focuses on facts or tools that are quickly outdated, rather than critical thinking. • Costs are typically very high due to the need for a physical location, transport, the trainer, and any materials.	• Interactive activities require you to work within your normal team on real projects—concepts instantly applied and you adapt them as you go. • The experience delivers immediate value. You improve, even if you're not perfect at the new skill immediately. Discovering that a practice does not work for your organization is also valuable. • Knowledge retention improves dramatically because you are using the ideas immediately. • You learn at your own pace, often driven by the need of your team. This is just-in-time knowledge acquisition. • Knowledge is spread more widely among the team, not concentrated in a single individual. • Qualifications are optional, but they are the opposite to box-ticking because all assignments require working on a real project. They focus on the learning gathered from the process, not testing recall of theoretical solutions. • The cost of training is dramatically reduced.

Agile Ways of Working Are About Mindset, Not Method

When describing Lean and Agile, commentators and experts are very keen to stress that they are more of a mindset than a method (Figure 33-3).

Figure 33-3. Agile and Lean

Agile and Lean Do:	Agile and Lean Are Not:
• Offer a philosophy for the whole organization • Promote teamwork and empower people • Focus on customers • Provide a journey toward continuous improvement	• A set of tools to implement • A recipe for success • A management process

Figure 33-3 tells you something very important—if something concrete like "how to set up an Excel chart" is not taught best through a traditional training course, you can imagine how difficult it would be to teach a philosophy intended to change the essential way we develop software. Agile and Lean do not suit a one-off training session, no matter what the duration. Many organizations use coaches and mentors to help implement the practices, but this is an expensive option and mistakenly hands responsibility for success to those outside the core team.

The Agile Manifesto, which presents the original expression of Agile principles, emphasizes that "we are uncovering better ways of developing software by doing it and helping others do it." That's work-based learning in essence: You learn and discover through action. The very name Agile reveals what its proponents value: the ability to respond to change, adapt, and evolve. That's why any Agile course needs to teach principles rather than tools or methods. The reason we choose to deliver in increments, for example, is far more important than how to write a user story or how long an iteration should last.

The poet Rudyard Kipling summarized the attitude needed in a poem in which he described a child's natural curiosity:

> One million Hows,
> two million Wheres,
> and seven million Whys!

Consider the UK government, which has long been one of the main creators and consumers of training. Perhaps it's not surprising that this should make the government supremely aware of both the failings and opportunities that exist in training.

A switch to online learning is expected to save £90 million a year (more than $123 million) on training staff in the Civil Service alone, with HMRC leading the way in the number of staff taking e-learning courses. However, according to the National Audit Office (NAO), there is still plenty of room for improvement. The NAO wanted the HMRC's spending on skills to be "linked explicitly to the organization's overall business objectives." Finally, only 38 percent of staff believed that the training had improved their performance.

This is why work-based learning remains the most attractive option. Because skills are developed while solving real problems on the job, they are immediately relevant to both staff and managers trying to assess the impact of training on the business. No training can guarantee success, but work-based learning enforces evaluation of actual results and helps develop skills naturally as you work.

There are many good tools in the market to help TD professionals apply new ways of working. Value, Flow, Quality (VFQ), from Emergn, is an example of a work-based learning program in Agile and Lean principles. Comprehensive and practical, VFQ offers a critical analysis of solutions that can be implemented immediately in the workplace. Sessions cover the thinking and principles behind popular methodologies, including Scrum, Kanban, and XP. It starts with asking teams 12 questions based on VFQ principles developed to help bring immediate clarity to which areas can be most improved. These 12 questions are included in a team self-assessment that you can download on the handbook's website, ATDHandbook3.org.

Motivated Learners Are the Most Effective Collaborators

So, what does digital literacy have to do with motivating people? News stories and statistics speak to how many digital transformation programs fail or how new technology implementations don't meet the expectations of an organization. When you look closely at the reasons behind these challenges, you can see that much of the impediment to success stems from how people in the organization viewed the change, and how their uncertainty of where they fit and adapt slowed the expected outcomes.

If you couple that with a growing need for people to work and learn from the comfort of their homes, it's only logical for business leaders, HR specialists, and TD professionals to worry about motivation and productivity levels dropping. It's hard for people to stay engaged and connected to one another, and the work they do, while being dispersed. It feels more difficult to communicate, collaborate, and coordinate naturally and informally.

So, how can we do better? While remote training and learning are growing rapidly and are even more widely accepted than ever before, studies have already shown the impact the COVID-19 pandemic has had on our stress and anxiety levels not only about our wealth but also about our well-being. Thus one of the first things TD professionals can emphasize and work on is motivation toward improved ways to communicate and collaborate.

A motivated person or team will adopt knowledge quicker and be more likely to foster success within the organization. Motivation is difficult to command given that its drivers vary from person to person. As such, rather than trying to motivate certain behaviors or people, TD professionals should examine other factors and how they may help or hinder a person's ability to get the job done. This harnesses the intrinsic motivation that stems from our human desire to want to contribute to something meaningful. Given how much it can generate success for business, intrinsic motivation is something we should seek to preserve and bolster.

Key things to consider:
- Work is a highly regarded outlet for our natural desire to participate in a purpose larger than ourselves.
- Motivation and commitment to a purpose can make us do work that we would not ordinarily do because we can see the benefits for the whole.
- Ask yourself: Do people have the right working environment to learn more effectively? Do they have the right tools?
- Are schedules realistic? We are all trying to adjust to a new virtual reality over time; make sure to coordinate time commitments so that a person's ability to learn is maximized and not full of distractions.
- Give people responsibility and accountability.
- If the primary reasons for motivation struggles are personal, be sensitive when providing assistance—when restored, the individual's commitment and sense of loyalty will increase.
- Explore various topics for an individual who needs training and development.

As people struggle to adapt to the digital ecosystem with greater demands on skills and capabilities, it is critical to support them through team communication, collaboration, and coordination.

We have all been asked to be great team players if we want to succeed in our careers, but we also know that it is not always that easy to collaborate. So, what stops us from collaborating? There are four main barriers to collaboration and it's important to think hard about which barriers are most prevalent in a person's or team's situation before deciding how to tackle them. Because overcoming or lowering the barriers involves awareness and investment, you must decide what to focus on.

Overall, the command-and-control style of management is a highly efficient way of handling large groups to coordinate their activity. There is clarity about who makes decisions and how communication flows. In fact, it keeps the need to manage communication, collaboration, and coordination to a bare minimum. But while coordination by decree works in simple situations, it is not effective in complex situations.

BARRIERS TO COLLABORATION

- We frequently see managers unwilling to accept advice or solutions from those "below" them in the hierarchy (even when they have the most direct experience with the problem). Similarly, brilliant new initiatives may be dismissed because they come from "overpaid consultants" or other outsiders. We see teams hiding problems because they don't want to be seen as ineffective or risk losing their bonuses. And there's a straight-up unwillingness to speak to others because we are too focused on our own concerns to think of asking for help.
- In this situation people deliberately avoid helping their colleagues, even when asked. Although it sounds extreme, the attitude is actually not that unusual in companies where departments or teams are in competition for respect and resources. It does not have to be malicious. Imagine that you're going head-to-head with another group to see which project will get funding. You probably like those people, but right now you need to make it clear that their crazy augmented reality project is vague and risky compared with your fabulous project.
- The bigger the company, the more geographically separated the business units; the more information there is, the harder it gets. Often when we give people tools to help them find or receive information, we simply overwhelm them.
- When someone new joins your team, you need to help them learn all sorts of things. The difficulty is that much of the knowledge they require is not so easy to hand over. This is tacit knowledge—the kind of understanding that comes from doing, through years of experience and a shared history. Many people fall into the trap of grumbling "Oh, it'll be quicker to do it myself," and so never try to pass on what they know.

The opposite style would be one encouraging a great degree of autonomy within teams or functions, but that could lead to various problems as well. It could create chaos where each "self-organizing" team creates their own processes, ways of working, and practices that don't match one another, creating huge coordination errors that can be detrimental for optimizing the flow of the business and its ability to deliver value. A standard process, vocabulary, and set of tools or metrics can help avoid such coordination errors.

Figure 33-4 shows the four focus areas of learning, which are directly linked to what we are discussing in this chapter. For most trainers and learners, the emphasis is typically on the first two areas, but the requirement to maximize the learning and help people adapt quickly to the shifts before us also rests on the last two areas. Why does all this matter to the TD professional? It matters, because if the work they do with people on modern technology and digital strategy doesn't account for the nuances of behavior and mindset, then the information simply won't stick.

Figure 33-4. Four Focus Areas of Learning

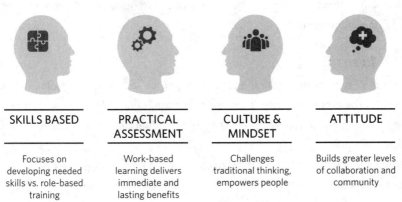

SKILLS BASED	PRACTICAL ASSESSMENT	CULTURE & MINDSET	ATTITUDE
Focuses on developing needed skills vs. role-based training	Work-based learning delivers immediate and lasting benefits	Challenges traditional thinking, empowers people	Builds greater levels of collaboration and community

Another way to view this is to consider the fixed approach that many organizations take toward learning and change versus the discovery approach, which is predicated on new ways of working and thinking. Table 33-1 compares the two and it's immediately evident why the right column is more impactful now than it's been even in the last decade. Underpinning most of the modern frameworks and methodologies for developing new products, services, and software is a mindset of discovery. There are many complexities to deal with when bringing new ideas to life, and they require a new way to manage work, lead teams, and mitigate risk.

Table 33-1. Two Approaches to Learning: Fixed and Discovery

Fixed	Discovery
• Methodology focused • Follow published standards • Optimize silos and functions • Organize around expertise • Follow a prescribed workflow • Solution centric • Resist change to standards • Do as you are told • Deliver to dates • Plan-driven and fixed	• Outcome focused • Context sensitive • Transparent and collaborative • Work in cross-functional teams • Continuously improve workflow • Customer centric • Embrace change • Challenge the status quo • Experiment, invent, and create • Discovery and growth

The way that organizations are structured and how we work often ends up looking like the first column in the table. We follow that way of working—creating standards and ensuring that we're maintaining those standards. We decide almost completely based on what needs to be done, when, and how before we even start, and completely forget to communicate why we need to do something or the outcome it is meant to create.

Today, work requires us to adapt to the change of the world around us. Old standards may no longer be suitable. We need to work together as a team with departments we may not have in the past, such as IT or procurement.

Making the Learning Last

So, how can we as TD professionals embed the right principles to help the learning last? To wrap up, I'd suggest that the emphasis is on three specific principles and three specific practices, all of which can be leveraged by adopting the VFQ body of knowledge shared earlier in this chapter.

- **Guiding Principles**
    - *Deliver value early and often.* Breaking work down to better prioritize, manage risk and return, generate real feedback, and bring value and innovation to customers faster can, in turn, allow you to create and deliver value faster.
    - *Optimize end-to-end flow.* Improve the overall flow of value by examining the entire value stream, removing the waste and improving the efficiency and effectiveness of the end-to-end working practices.
    - *Drive quality using fast feedback.* By embedding the ability to solicit faster feedback and improve products throughout every stage of their development, companies can deliver the quality products their customers want, with a focus on simplicity and usability.
- **Essential Practices**
    - *Experimentation* is at the center of understanding our context and our world, be it to discover our value, how we organize work to deliver it, or how we ensure that we are collecting the necessary feedback to make our decision.
    - *Value definition* helps us ensure that we are focusing on solving a user need, and that those needs are worth the effort required.
    - *Visualization* is needed because most of our work is now hidden and conversations are too far and few. This will help us have better conversations, collaborate more, and ensure that our work is visible to the team.

Using these principles and practices will help learners realize some of the key benefits that we teach, which are critical to any digital adoption and change program. These include:

- **Fewer dependencies.** The success of your organization is dependent on the skills and capability of your people. Accelerate their learning and adoption of modern practices and minimize your long-term dependency on external coaching and consulting. Get only the help you need and let your teams do the rest.
- **More control.** Your way of working will drive the best results and outcomes for your organization. Applying the right mix of practices and principles will help you shape the best approach for accelerating and controlling your business outcomes.

- **Better decisions.** Your culture is largely shaped by how you make decisions. Applying the most effective methods and techniques will allow your organization to better optimize for innovation and get the most valuable ideas to market faster.
- **Ability to scale.** When transforming an organization, it's important to ensure everyone gets support. You don't want to create a situation where some people get a lot of training and others get very little. But it needs to be done in a way that can scale in terms of cost and reach. Using the different delivery mechanisms can support companies of any scale and in any location. This allows you to get the right balance between in-depth learning programs, on-demand and self-study content, and the ability to develop internal coaches and trainers in different locations and roles. All to match your budget.

Final Thoughts

In the words of Peter Drucker, "Culture eats strategy for breakfast." Therefore, let's all remember that no matter how good the content and training are, the ability to help people think differently about their work is ultimately what shapes the best outcomes for the learners and the organizations they serve.

About the Author

Alex Adamopoulos's career spans more than 30 years working in technology products and services. Along with founding Emergn in 2009, Alex has had the good fortune and opportunity to serve in several leadership roles in well-known global companies, advisory boards, and thought leadership programs. Alex believes in translating values into recognizable behaviours, starting with caring for and investing in people. His work has allowed him to learn from some of the best leaders in industry and in life, with an emphasis on building high-performing teams, and developing people to help them do their best work. You can reach Alex at alex@emergn.com or learn more about his company at emergn.com.

References

Lombardo, M.M., and R.W. Eichinger. 1996. *The Career Architect Development Planner*, 1st ed. Minneapolis: Lominger.

Recommended Resources

Adamopoulos, A. 2018. "Five Mindset Shifts to Get the Most Value From Your Organization." Forbes, August 20. forbes.com/sites/forbesbostoncouncil/2018/08/20/five-mindset-shifts-to-get-the-most-value-from-your-organization.

Adamopoulos, A. 2021. "You Upgrade Your Technology, So Why Not Upskill Your IT Staff?" Forbes, June 1. forbes.com/sites/forbesbusinesscouncil/2021/06/01/you-upgrade-your-technology-so-why-not-upskill-your-it-staff.

Angelo-Eadie, S. n.d. "Why VFQ Develops a Growth Mindset." Emergn. emergn.com/articles/vfq-growth-mindset.

Seggebruch, A., M. Alter, and R. Webb. 2020. "Scaling Transformative Businesses." *The Emerging World of Work*. Emergn Podcast, Season 2, Episode 12. emergn.com/insights/podcast-scaling-transformative-businesses.

SHRM. 2019. *The Global Skills Shortage: Bridging the Talent Gap With Education, Training and Sourcing*. Alexandria, VA: Society for Human Resource Management. shrm.org/hr-today/trends-and-forecasting/research-and-surveys/documents/shrm%20skills%20gap%202019.pdf.

SECTION VI
EXPANDED ROLES OF TALENT DEVELOPMENT

LUMINARY PERSPECTIVE

Make Your Future Happen: Plan Beyond Your Current TD Role

Kimo Kippen

Talent development has been transformed significantly over the years. Advances in technology will continue to reshape how people work and live. The technologies that are driving change include artificial intelligence, robotics, and automation; they all have the potential to replace human workers in an increasing number of industries. To remain competitive, it is incumbent upon talent development professionals to upskill and reskill ourselves and our workers to ensure the best chance of success for the organizations that we support.

In addition, the number and types of roles in talent development continue to expand and evolve. The increasing demand for higher-skilled or different-skilled workers means that talent development leaders need to take a more strategic and holistic approach to talent development. The importance of workforce strategic planning to anticipate the needs of the business by having the right talent in the correct amount for the future is critical to a business's success and growth.

Businesses now more than ever need to offer training and robust, career-focused education to build a culture of lifelong learning. In fact, creating a culture of lifelong learning is a strategic decision. Why? Because it requires you to articulate your position on people and people development. I vividly remember working with a boss on a talent assessment interview for a senior leader. At the end of the session he shared his view that every interaction with a leader is an assessment opportunity. I agreed with him, but I also pushed back ever so slightly to suggest that the interaction with a senior leader was also a development opportunity for that leader. My boss responded by saying that through a good assessment process we can hire the next "Michael Jordan" into our organization. I also agreed that this was true, but then suggested another way to think about talent. I gave the example of Tiger Woods and asked, when did Tiger Woods start to play golf? Who had the most influence at an early age on his ability to play golf? The answer was simple; Tiger Woods started learning to play golf at the age of four, and his father was a key influence in his life. Further, his father was coaching and encouraging him to practice every day with feedback on how to improve his game. So, I think that the answer is somewhere in the middle—you need a good assessment process as well as targeted development efforts to build skills that drive success. I will never forget that encounter with my boss, who focused primarily on assessment.

I am excited about the future. This is probably the best time to be in talent development. I like to think of it as our "day in the sun," and at its center are the employee and the employee experience. I have always believed—and was taught in my early days as a manager—that if you take care of your employees, they will take care of the customers. This was a constant theme in my career in the hospitality industry: My managers would tell me about the importance of taking care of the employees to ensure that they were happy, secure, confident, and well-trained, and had the necessary tools to do their jobs to deliver great customer service. Great customer experiences in turn drive greater customer loyalty and happy customers, which then leads to more happy customers and business growth. Managers can bring this about by creating a culture of psychological safety, belonging, and inclusion that builds a culture of accountability and self-ownership with the knowledge that each person is responsible for their own development and career. Through coaching, mentoring, and great leadership, the TD function's ability to equip managers to become masters in the development of talent is critical.

The ability to get things done through others and drive results is also key to being successful in business. Collaboration and teamwork are the "oil" that keeps an organization vibrant and successful. Early on in my career I attended a training session in which my team was placed in a simulation called Hawks & Doves. In this exercise, participants competed to win as much money (points) as possible by buying, selling, (and stealing!) weapons in a tight timeframe. (Note that this was a long time ago, when sensitivities were different!) We fought hard to get every "point" that we could from the other teams. Unfortunately, we did not realize that if we all worked together, we could "game the system" by working faster and thus winning more! This wisdom became apparent only as we processed the exercise results. It was a formative experience for me as I reflected on my behavior and realized the need to establish trust as a first step, to be tolerant, and to strive for greater self-awareness.

One of the greatest gifts I've been given as a manager was the privilege and honor of working for and with a great leader. I once had a boss who was very tough—probably the toughest I've ever had. He continually challenged me to do better and strive for more, but he never criticized me personally. Instead, he would focus on the work and how we could do better as a department and for our guests and employees. He taught me the importance of "the long arc"—that life and work are a marathon, not a sprint, and we all run at different speeds. One year we were in a time crunch during budget time, so I asked my boss if he would come into the office over the weekend. I wanted his feedback and guidance so I could submit my budgets on time. We met on Saturday and got it done. However, at the end of our meeting, my boss told me in a friendly, good-natured tone that he would not do this again. He said that I needed to plan "my marathon" better next time to avoid dragging others into my sprints. We all need to have balance in life—to plan ahead and maintain better discipline.

Much of our work is now done in a distributed fashion, so the ability to collaborate and build teams virtually is critical to success. In the virtual environment, collaboration has become especially challenging because organic collaboration across highly distributed networks is almost impossible. The greatest lesson I gained from my Zoom-filled days is the need for disciplined time management and intentionality. Things don't just happen; you have to make them happen. You must schedule them, structure them, and deliver them. I lead many virtual meetings each week, and I have found that one of the keys to being successful in this distributed environment is to have regular, scheduled meetings with agendas (sent out in advance) that include primer questions to stimulate engagement and make the most of our time together. I have learned that you have to structure the unstructured parts of the meeting. You must build in time to promote greater listening, sharing, and collaboration. Further, it's extremely helpful to have technology platforms that allow you to work side by side, share documents synchronously, and chat in real time.

As you look at your future self—promoted and successful—think of yourself as an internal consultant. Traditionally, consultants were hired to assess the current situation and build actionable plans to drive change and performance improvement for organizations. By thinking of yourself as an internal consultant you can use this same frame of reference to add value to your department and your boss. What makes a great internal consultant? Their most important attribute is probably the ability to do outstanding work. It means looking for ways to go above and beyond the day-to-day job requirements to demonstrate how you add value to the organization.

Your career journey is a work of art that can change the trajectory of your life forever and lead to amazing opportunities and experiences. Early in my career, I had the opportunity to leave a secure job and a promising career to move across the world for a new, risky, and exciting opportunity. Although I very seriously weighed the pros and cons, in the end I asked myself whether I would regret not taking the opportunity. My answer was a resounding yes, and that was it. I moved halfway around the world for a job in a different industry in a country where I did not speak the language. It was the start of an amazing chapter of my life. All of this is to say that you have the potential to accomplish great things if you take calculated risks, work hard, and have a lifelong learning mindset. Anything is possible.

I wish you only the best in life. Lots of good health, success, joy, and, most important, lots of love. Live Aloha!

About the Author

Kimo Kippen is a native of Hawaii and resides alternately in Warsaw, Poland, and Honolulu, Hawaii. He's a thought leader, speaker, and advocate for learning and a former executive at Hilton and Marriott. He was recognized by *CLO Magazine* as CLO of the year in 2015. Kimo served as chair of the ATD Board of Directors in 2007 and has also served as chair of APIA Scholars, a board member for the Center for Talent Reporting and CTDO Next, an advisory board member at CAEL, the CLO advisor at Defense Acquisition University, and an advisory board member for Strategic Education Inc., Gnowbe, Rochester Institute of Technology, World Institute for Action Learning, and GP Strategies. He is currently program director for The Conference Board Talent and Organizational Development Executive Council, USA, and the Learning & Development Council, Europe. In addition, Kimo serves as an adjunct professor and advisor at Catholic University of America and at George Mason University. Kimo has an MS from RIT and a BS from the University of Hawai'i; he is also a graduate of the Gestalt Institute of Cleveland's Post Graduate Program.

CHAPTER 34

Building Your Organization's Learning Technology Ecosystem

JD Dillon

Technology is an essential part of every organization's talent development strategy. You may be a member of a 300-person team supporting 400,000 employees dispersed around the world. Or, you may be a mighty L&D team of one supporting a 200-person business. Right-fit technology—software and hardware—plays a critical role in helping you provide the organization with the tools and resources they need to do their best work every day.

> **IN THIS CHAPTER:**
> ♦ Apply a modern learning mindset to your digital learning strategy
> ♦ Architect a persona-based learning technology ecosystem
> ♦ Measure the value of your learning technology investment

Learning technology helps L&D overcome familiar challenges in new ways. To maximize its potential and get the most value from your investment, you must be strategic in your technology selection and application practices. Even the best tools will deliver mediocre results if they're applied incorrectly. Plus, technology is constantly changing. You must monitor and assess the impact of your technology ecosystem while keeping up with changes in the digital marketplace. Overall, building, implementing, and maintaining a right-fit learning technology ecosystem requires hard work, creativity, collaboration, and a willingness to continue developing your team's digital skills.

The Digital Learning Mindset

The process for building a high-impact learning technology ecosystem doesn't begin with technology. It starts with mindset. The entire organization, especially partners who influence and collaborate on technology-related decisions, must agree on the purpose and value of learning technology. A tool should not be implemented because it's new, innovative, or successful within another organization. Instead, every component of the learning technology ecosystem must play a clear role in providing users with the required elements of a modern learning strategy.

Successful implementation of a modern learning ecosystem requires:

- **Timely, consistent, and reliable communication.** Everyone needs the latest update if they are expected to be successful in their work. With the pace of workplace and social change, organizations must prioritize communication and knowledge sharing as the foundation of the modern learning ecosystem.
- **Training on core job knowledge and skills.** Everyone needs effective training on the basics of their roles, as well as the knowledge and skill they're expected to apply on a daily basis. This training must meet each individual where they are in their learning journey and help them quickly close knowledge and skills gaps so they can do their best work every day.
- **Access to on-demand performance support.** Everyone needs to know how to raise their hand and ask for help when required. If they're still new in their role and haven't learned how to solve a problem yet or just need help overcoming a particularly challenging situation, they need a reliable place to go for performance support.
- **Persistent, actionable coaching and feedback.** Everyone needs timely, actionable feedback as part of an ongoing coaching experience. This may come from managers, peers, trainers, or other designated coaches who participate in the day-to-day work

experience and can help performers identify their strengths and opportunities for development.
- **Ongoing practice and reinforcement.** Everyone needs the opportunity to refine their knowledge and skills, so they are ready to apply them in the moment of need. Time must be provided (within the workflow) for practice activities that allow people to learn through application in a safe, risk-free environment.
- **Opportunities to develop and apply new skills.** Everyone needs access to activities and resources that can help them prepare for the next step in their learning journey and build the knowledge and skills they need to take on future opportunities.

Every organization will apply different tools and tactics to address these core learning and development needs. Regardless of industry, audience, or strategy, a right-fit learning technology ecosystem must include the components needed to bring these activities to life.

7 Reasons to Apply Learning Technology

The marketplace is overflowing with technology options, including learning management systems (LMS), learning experience platforms (LXP), learning content management systems (LCMS), authoring tools, virtual reality (VR), augmented reality (AR), virtual classrooms, social platforms, and microlearning tools.

Every organization is unique. Therefore, the same tool may not provide everyone with the same value. Platforms are also constantly evolving. An LMS, which traditionally focuses on course management and delivery, may add LXP features, such as content curation and aggregation, thereby blurring the lines between categories and making it more difficult to find the right tool. Finally, there's the "one platform fallacy." No matter how big, fancy, or expensive an app may be, a single tool cannot do everything. Some organizations have shorter requirement lists and therefore can lean into one platform. However, other companies, especially those with large, distributed workforces across multiple functions, will benefit from a blended technology ecosystem that includes a range of purposefully selected tools.

A digital learning vision is critical for aligning your technology efforts. This is true whether you're just starting to architect your technology ecosystem or looking to maximize the value of your existing tool set. This vision should not be based on specific technology categories or features. Rather, it should establish the overall purpose of your digital ecosystem. Modern learning technology can help an organization deliver a right-fit learning experience in seven ways.

The first three ideas have been key strategic pillars behind learning technology implementations for more than 20 years: speed, scale, and consistency.

- **Speed.** Technology helps you move information more quickly from "those who know" to "those who need." Work and society change faster than traditional training tactics—such as classroom sessions and on-the-job training—can accommodate. It's simply faster to deploy an e-learning module to your audience than it is to schedule everyone to complete an instructor-led training session.
- **Scale.** Technology helps you reach more people with your available resources. A classroom trainer can only facilitate so many sessions in front of so many audiences. Digital learning can be accessed via an internet-connected device whenever and wherever the learner wants. You're no longer bound by logistical considerations, such as room size and travel schedules. One trainer can reach tens or hundreds of thousands of people via digital tools in the same amount of time required to deliver a handful of in-person sessions.
- **Consistency.** Technology helps you overcome the "this is how we really do it here" problem by ensuring every person in the audience receives the exact same content. It doesn't matter if the audience includes 100 people or 100,000 people. Technology mitigates the potentially undesirable deviations that occur whenever a person delivers a message. Everyone attends the same class, reads the same article, and watches the same video via digital means.

Our digital learning foundations, including the LMS and e-learning, were designed to address these three basic issues. However, speed, scale, and consistency are based on the digital realities of the 1990s and early 2000s. Technology has evolved exponentially over the past few decades. Mobile devices, social platforms, advanced analytics, and artificial intelligence now help us solve everyday problems. Organizations must reframe their digital learning visions to benefit from these advancements. To meet the rapidly changing needs of the modern workforce, your learning technology strategy must include four additional drivers: context, personalization, connection, and equity.

- **Context.** Technology helps you move learning closer to the flow of work so it can become a seamless part of everyone's job. What people learn is determined by their roles, but how they learn is influenced by how they work. Technology allows you to create digital experiences that fit within the day-to-day reality of the people you support. It doesn't matter if you're a clerk in a grocery store, a lift-truck driver in a warehouse, or a marketing manager working at home. Everyone can access the resources they need, when and where they're needed.
- **Personalization.** Technology helps you advance beyond the one-size-fits-none limitations of traditional e-learning content to deliver personalized, adaptive learning experiences. Every person has unique support needs based on their different backgrounds, experiences, and progression. Modern learning technology captures,

analyzes, and applies data to deliver the right resources at the right time for each person, at the scale of your organization.
- **Connection.** Technology helps you make digital learning a two-way experience. Social media and communication platforms have transformed the way we share and collaborate in our everyday lives. L&D must leverage these capabilities and provide people with greater opportunity to engage with their peers and organizations. This technology opens the door to modern learning tactics such as user-generated content, which allows the people who really know how the operation functions to contribute their insights and experiences in support of one another. This allows L&D to step out of the spotlight and focus on establishing the critical connections and channels that facilitate knowledge sharing at scale.
- **Equity.** Technology helps you provide the right learning and development experience for every person you support. However, this does not mean you should provide the same experience for everyone. An equal learning experience may not actually meet anyone's specific support needs. Instead, modern technology helps you provide an equitable workplace experience by ensuring everyone has access to the training and support they need to do their best work every day.

A right-fit learning technology ecosystem should check all seven of these boxes for the entire organization. If one of these drivers is not being met, there will likely be a gap in your digital learning strategy.

How to Build a Right-Fit Learning Technology Ecosystem

Once your organization is aligned regarding the role technology should play to support learning and development, it's time to architect your digital ecosystem. Your final design will likely include a range of tools and platforms. Some will be owned by L&D. Others will be administered by organizational partners but firmly integrated into your digital experience design. Remember—a tool doesn't have to be categorized as a learning technology to help people solve problems and improve their skills.

The following 10-step process applies to every organization, regardless of industry, use case, scale, or existing technology setup. The ultimate goal—providing an equitable learning and support experience—is the same no matter where you work or whom you support. You'll simply make different decisions along the way based on your organization's specific needs.

1. Build Your Personas

Knowledge and skill requirements are based on what a person does—their title, role, and tasks. How they learn is influenced by how they work—how they spend their time, how they manage priorities, and how they access resources. This reality is overlooked in many organizations, which results in a disconnect between their learning and working experiences.

Personas align your learning experience design with the everyday realities of the people you support. While everyone in the organization is unique, personas highlight the commonalities that influence your learning strategy. Personas are also easier to manage than job titles or roles, because an organization may have hundreds or thousands of job codes. However, when the focus shifts from what people do to how they do it, there may be only a handful of distinct employee personas. For example, grocery associates and contact center agents do very different jobs, but they also share common attributes, such as limited availability for training due to persistent operational requirements.

Consider these factors when building employee personas:
- **Function.** Does this persona work independently or directly with customers and products?
- **Foundation.** Was this persona hired based on a unique skill set or are they being taught how to do the job?
- **Scale.** Does this persona have a unique job or do many people do this kind of work?
- **Time.** Does this persona control their schedule or is their workload heavily managed?
- **Location.** Does this persona work in a specific location or are they distributed across many locations?
- **Access.** Which devices are available to help this persona access learning and support resources?
- **Motivation.** Is this persona primarily focused on building a career or meeting foundational needs?
- **Measurement.** Are this persona's performance outcomes based on subjective or objective measures?

Your learning technology ecosystem and the experiences it facilitates must align with the attributes defined within each persona. If you find that you have multiple unique personas within your workforce, you must architect a flexible ecosystem that can meet the needs of each group.

2. Clarify Your Organizational Priorities

You have to know what your organization is going to expect people to do before you can make any learning strategy or technology decisions. Job knowledge and skill requirements must align with management's short- and long-term priorities. Once you understand your organization's priorities, you can determine the types of learning experiences and resources people will need to guide their performance (Figure 34-1).

Figure 34-1. Results-Based Approach to Learning Strategy Design

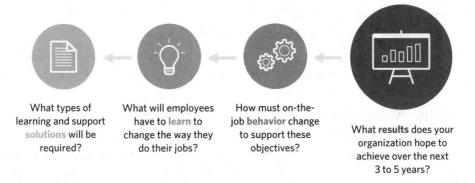

Collaborate with stakeholders across the organization, including operations, information technology (IT), human resources (HR), compliance, and safety to identify their priorities over the next three to five years. Ask the following series of questions to determine how talent development will be expected to enable performance related to these priorities:

- What measurable results do you hope to achieve over the short to long term within your function?
- How will employees be expected to change their on-the-job behaviors to help you reach these results?
- What knowledge and skills will employees need to execute these behaviors on a regular basis?
- What types of learning and support resources will employees need to improve their knowledge and skill in these areas?

These answers along with your employee personas will help you architect an ecosystem that can balance organizational objectives with individual employee needs.

3. Design Your Learning Experience

Now that you understand who you are supporting and what they will be expected to accomplish, it's time to design a right-fit learning experience. This step should answer the question, "What should the development experience feel like for a person within this organization?"

The workplace learning experience must include six key components, regardless of a person's particular role or industry:

- Training on core job knowledge and skills
- Timely, consistent, and reliable communication

- Access to on-demand performance support
- Ongoing practice and reinforcement
- Personalized coaching and feedback
- Opportunities to explore new skills and prepare for future work

Your learning experience design should include activities that bring these components to life in ways that fit within your audience's workflow and align with their knowledge and skill expectations.

The example in Figure 34-2 shows how different activities are introduced into an experience design to bring the concepts to life. Then, you'll identify the role technology should play in executing these activities based on the seven pillars of learning technology (speed, scale, consistency, context, personalization, connection, and equity). While a person may not engage directly with digital tools during every learning activity, your technology ecosystem will influence the way these solutions are made available.

Figure 34-2. Example of Learning Experience Design

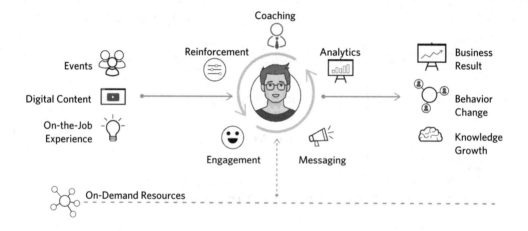

4. Architect Your Technology Ecosystem

It's time to add technology to the mix. The steps completed so far will help you determine how to plug a variety of tools into your ecosystem to execute a right-fit learning strategy. By taking a layered approach to your ecosystem architecture, you will maximize the value of your technology investments while simplifying the digital learning experience for each persona (Figure 34-3).

Figure 34-3. Persona-Based Learning Ecosystem Design

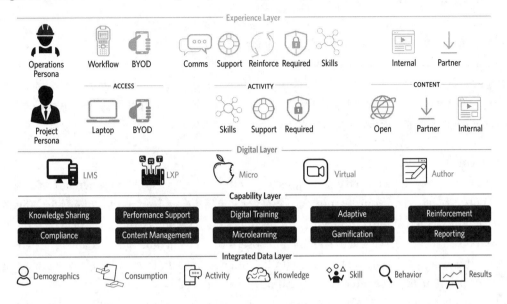

Data Layer

A modern learning technology ecosystem begins and ends with data. Data will play a foundational role throughout all phases of your learning strategy. It will help you deliver personalized, right-fit experiences to each person you support at the scale and pace of your organization. It will also help you measure the impact of your training programs. Therefore, you must begin your ecosystem architecture with data. Questions to ask include:
- What data will you need to power your learning experience design?
- What data will you need to capture within the digital learning activities?
- What data will you need to pull from outside the learning ecosystem?
- How will your technology ecosystem support the capture, storage, analysis, and application of data?

Answering these questions first will guide your technology selection and integration decisions throughout the process.

Capability Layer

What must your technology ecosystem be able to do? What capabilities and features will be required to bring your learning experience design to life across the organization? It's time to make a list. But this isn't a wish list—this layer should include digital capabilities that align directly with your persona-based learning experience design. For example, your list may include:

- Digital content authoring
- Mobile-first user experience
- Adaptive content delivery
- Social collaboration and knowledge sharing
- Dashboard reporting and data exports

Include all necessary details to make sure your feature requirements contain everything you need to execute your digital learning vision. This layer will inform the upcoming partner selection step, as well as any requests for information (RFI) or proposals (RFP).

Digital Layer

This layer connects your required capabilities to specific digital tools. The number and selection of tools will vary based on your learning vision, experience design, and requirements list. If you support a multifaceted organization with a large collection of personas, this layer may include 10 or more tools that each serve a very specific purpose. Or it may include only two or three generalist tools if you support a small business with limited personas. Rarely will this layer include a single platform that can meet all of your learning ecosystem needs.

Attaching required digital capabilities to specific technology platforms will help you define a clear purpose for each tool. You may find that your tool set includes a variety of overlapping features and functionalities. This can get very confusing for people trying to use the tools within their workflows, because they will have a difficult time deciphering where to go for what. To preemptively address this issue, make sure each tool has a clear purpose—a reason for being included within your ecosystem—and maintain this purpose during your implementation.

Your digital layer includes your current learning systems. If you are unable to match a required capability to an existing tool, you must close these gaps in your technology stack through new procurement processes. However, before you go shopping for new apps, remember that the learning ecosystem should also include tools that are not formally owned or administered by HR or L&D. For example, your intranet may be run by the corporate operations or communications team, but it may also play a central role in your learning experience design. A platform does not have to be formally categorized as a learning technology to help people improve their performance.

Experience Layer

You've identified the right data. You've aligned your capability requirements with your digital toolkit. Now, it's time to apply your technology stack and activate your learning experience design. Explain how people will use the selected tools to access training and support within the workflow. This layer must answer three important questions:

- **How will the persona access their digital tools?** Your learning software must be easily accessible on the hardware devices used within the workflow. If the persona uses a handheld device on the job, your digital experience should be available on that handheld. If they use a laptop and their personal smartphone, the experience should be designed for use on those devices.
- **In what kinds of activities will the persona engage as part of the learning experience?** Map out how your selected platforms and capabilities will bring learning and support to life. Specify the types of activities—such as virtual classroom sessions, practice simulations, or social collaboration—that will be available to a person using these tools.
- **What types of content will be made available to the persona using these digital tools?** Learning technology is only as effective as the content it delivers. While the specific topics used will change over time as knowledge and skill requirements evolve, it's important to highlight the content sources that will be accessed. For example, some audiences may leverage primarily internal, proprietary content while others access more open-source material available online.

Outline experience details for each persona within your audience, connecting the dots between your technology stack and the learning experience for each person you support.

5. Select Technology Providers

You may identify gaps in your technology stack or raise questions about your existing platforms when architecting the digital layer of your ecosystem. If you decide it's time to make some changes or additions, this process should have already armed you with the vision needed to find the right partners. The information you've put together so far will also help you more effectively execute your organization's technology procurement process.

Focusing on a laundry list of features is one of the biggest mistakes that organizations make when searching for new learning technology. When teams hunt for all-encompassing tools that can do everything they may possibly need, they'll fail to identify the right tools that can provide value-add capabilities.

Avoid submitting RFIs and RFPs that include every feature you've ever heard about (plus the kitchen sink). Instead, challenge your technology providers to demonstrate how they can bring your learning experience to life. Match their digital capabilities to your ecosystem design and determine which personas may derive value from their products and services.

In addition to functionality and the related learning experience, consider the following factors when selecting technology providers:

- **Impact.** Does their technology drive measurable results for their customers? The features may seem impressive during demonstrations, but the outcomes they help organizations achieve are much more important and will help you justify the investment.
- **References.** Go beyond case studies and speak directly with professional peers who use the same technology within their organizations. Get a real sense of what it's like to work with the provider and their tools on a daily basis.
- **Support.** Learning technology is more than a place people go to complete online training once in a while. It is a business critical application within a modern workplace ecosystem. Therefore, your providers must offer easy-to-use reference materials for do-it-yourself problems along with reliable technical support—including the option to speak with a person—when you have to escalate an issue.
- **Security.** Your technology decisions will affect the organization's entire digital infrastructure. Therefore, IT must play a major role in making sure providers adhere to required security and data management practices.
- **Education.** A technology supplier can elevate from provider to partner by helping your team continuously advance its knowledge and skills. Look for educational offerings that go beyond the basics of how to use the tools.
- **Road map.** Technology is constantly evolving, and you should look for partners that are constantly innovating and pushing the marketplace forward. Review their road map for the next 12 to 18 months to determine how your organization's digital capabilities will grow through your partnership.
- **Total cost of ownership.** Technology investment includes more than the cost of software licenses and hardware devices. Consider the total cost of ownership—including implementation, migration, training, customization, administration, maintenance, and upgrades—when making purchase decisions.

6. Establish a Governance Process

Now that you know what your ecosystem will look like moving forward, you can determine how to best administer your technology stack. Your governance process must support every stakeholder, starting with the people using the tool and including IT, compliance, management, and L&D. Make sure your guidelines address these questions:

- Who is ultimately responsible for our systems?
- Who will be the primary administrator of our systems?
- To which established standards and organizational requirements must our systems adhere?
- What are the primary risks associated with our systems?
- Who will connect with our technology partners to solve problems and request support?

- What is the process for monitoring system uptime and responding to unexpected system downtimes?
- What are the service-level agreements (SLAs) with our technology partners with regards to downtimes, troubleshooting, and other issues?
- How will system downtimes (planned and unplanned) be communicated to stakeholders?
- What is the disaster recovery process for our systems?
- How will our systems and related processes be documented?
- How will data collected from and applied within our systems be stored, and what are the related retention requirements?
- How will system upgrades be administered and communicated to stakeholders?
- What is the process and who is responsible for making timely payments related to our systems?
- How will system permissions be allocated and on what criteria will permissions be granted?
- What IT resources will be necessary to implement and maintain our technology stack?

A strong governance process will do more than just keep you out of hot water. It will maximize the value of your technology ecosystem.

7. Determine Integration Strategy

Learning technology is just one part of the organization's digital ecosystem. You must determine how your learning systems integrate with the other tools people use in their everyday work. Integration is also an important consideration within the learning ecosystem, as you will likely use more than one system to facilitate knowledge and skill development within your workforce. By moving content and data seamlessly between tools, you can create a simpler experience for your audience.

Building system integrations, such as connecting an LMS to a customer relationship management (CRM) tool, can require considerable IT resources. Even systems that include built-in integration options can require IT work to set up and maintain. Because IT resources are often limited, this can slow down or limit your ecosystem architecture. Rather than waiting for IT resources to become available, approach the concept of integration from two different perspectives (Figure 34-4):

- **Strategic integration.** Systems function in isolation but are administered with purpose to simplify the user experience across multiple tools.
- **Technical integration.** Systems connect through application program interfaces (APIs) and software development kits (SDKs) to blend data, content, and functionality.

Figure 34-4. Potential Integration Points for Learning Technology

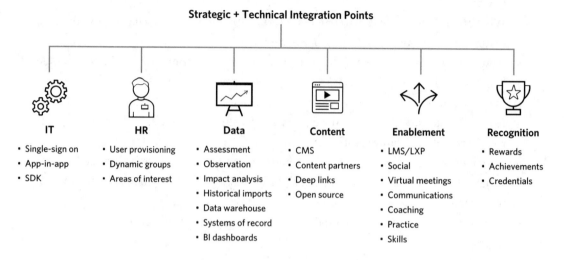

Prioritize technical integrations that can be built and maintained in a timely manner and will deliver clear value to both the user and the organization. This may include considerations such as single sign-on (SSO), user provisioning, or compliance reporting. Strategically integrate any remaining systems to make it easy for people to access the right tools at the right times. For example, place links to each tool in convenient locations and consistently use the same apps for the same reasons so people understand where to go and when.

8. Implement

Your technology implementation process will vary based on the complexity of your ecosystem. Launching an organization's first LMS is quite different from adding a new point solution to an already-established technology stack. The time and resources available to support your implementation will also heavily affect your process. That said, there are several steps you should consider including, regardless of the specific technology you're introducing:

- **Build a cross-functional team.** L&D should not launch technology in isolation. Put together a team of stakeholders—including executive sponsors, frontline management, end users, and departmental champions—who will play key roles in making the process successful.
- **Establish clear goals.** Getting a tool up and running is just the first hurdle. Determine how you will measure the effectiveness of your implementation in the short- and long-term. Set milestones throughout the implementation process to keep your team on track.

- **Apply a phased approach.** Introducing a new tool to an entire organization at once, regardless of size and scale, is a big lift. Unless the situation demands otherwise, apply a phased approach by launching to specific groups over time. This will spread the effort out over a longer period and allow you to learn and make adjustments along the way.
- **Make time for testing.** If the new tool falters early, people may lose trust and never come back, even after the bugs are worked out. Few implementations go perfectly, but you can mitigate this risk by adding time for practical field testing throughout the implementation plan.
- **Prioritize communication.** People can't take advantage of a new tool if they don't know it exists or why they should use it. Leverage your champions and stakeholders to help communicate the value of the new tool. Position the technology as the solution to an established workplace problem rather than something that's important only to L&D.
- **Continue to optimize.** Your initial implementation plan will likely look very different from the final process. Make room for adjustments. Hit your milestones while making ongoing improvements based on what you learn along the way.

9. Measure

Measurement must be an ongoing component of your learning technology strategy, with a focus applied to each tool within your ecosystem. As your organization evolves, you must determine how effectively your current tools are meeting its needs. How you measure the effectiveness of your technology will depend on how your ecosystem is constructed. You'll need to capture a range of ongoing data points, including user surveys and key performance indicators related to your technology use.

Consider these six factors as you build your measurement strategy. Evaluate these factors for each individual tool as well as the ecosystem as a whole:

- **Impact.** Does the tool play an essential role in enabling desired workplace change?
- **Engagement.** Are people using the tool with the intended frequency?
- **Sentiment.** Do people like using the tool as part of their workflow?
- **Agility.** Does the tool strengthen the overall learning ecosystem?
- **Education.** Does your technology partner help improve your team's ability to support the organization?
- **Innovation.** Does the tool push your digital learning strategy forward?

These factors must then be weighed against your technology investment—the total cost of ownership for your technology stack—to determine if you are deriving the desired value from your ecosystem. If a system costs more than the value it provides across these factors, you should consider making a change.

10. Iterate and Experiment

Architecting a learning ecosystem is a cycle, not a process. You may finish implementing a new tool, but your technology strategy will never be complete. The ecosystem must keep pace with your organization's changes as well as technological innovation. This is why it's important to build flexibility into your strategy. Focus on designing right-fit experiences for the people you support, not the tools you're currently using to execute that experience.

Dedicate time and resources in your annual plans for ongoing experimentation. Try out new tools before it's time to make wholesale changes. Engage your technology partners who demonstrate an ongoing commitment to innovation. Build your own learning technology road map based on your organization's long-term strategic plans.

Keeping Pace With Technology Innovation

Ecosystems are living, breathing biological communities. They're constantly changing and evolving to meet the needs of their inhabitants. This is why *ecosystem* is the perfect term to apply to learning technology strategy. It can be difficult to keep pace with digital innovation as you try to balance the nonstop demands of your role. The talent development marketplace is packed with thousands of tools, and this number just keeps growing. You need a plan for keeping up. Otherwise, you'll quickly fall behind, and your ecosystem may begin to falter.

Here are a few tips for maintaining your digital-learning awareness:

- **Network with digital SMEs.** Find knowledgeable and trustworthy professional peers who regularly curate and share technological insights. Connect with them on social media. Ask for advice as you explore your digital learning options.
- **Prioritize your technology skills.** Make sure digital capabilities are at the top of your professional development list for yourself and your team members. Attend online sessions and industry events that include demonstrations of the latest technological innovations.
- **Assign a digital lead.** Select a team member who has experience with or wants to learn more about digital learning. Ask them to explore new innovations and share their insights with the team as a core part of their role.
- **Experiment.** Never stop playing with new toys. Designate time and resources to try out new ideas, even if they don't seem like a perfect fit within your ecosystem architecture right now.

Final Thoughts

In the end, architecting a right-fit learning technology ecosystem is a lot like using your smartphone. You use dozens or hundreds of apps to solve problems. Some apps are integrated while others stand alone. The ones that hang around on your phone for a long time provide clear value based on their purpose. When an app isn't providing value, you delete it and find a new one. There's an overwhelming number of options available, so you lean on friends, peers, and tech experts for their recommendations.

By applying the approach outlined in this chapter, you can make digital learning simple, frictionless, and impactful—just like using your smartphone.

About the Author

JD Dillon became a learning and enablement expert over two decades working in operations and talent development with dynamic organizations, including Disney, Kaplan, and AMC. A respected author and speaker in the workplace learning community, JD continues to apply his passion for helping people around the world do their best work every day in his role as Axonify's chief learning architect. JD is also the founder of LearnGeek, a workplace learning insights and advisory group. You can find JD online at axonify.com and learngeek.co or contact him directly at jd@learngeek.co.

Recommended Resources

Dillon, JD. 2022. *The Modern Learning Ecosystem: A New L&D Mindset for the Ever-Changing Workplace.* Alexandria, VA: ATD Press.

Taylor, D. 2017. *Learning Technologies in the Workplace: How to Successfully Implement Learning Technologies in Organizations.* New York: Kogan Page.

"The Modern Learning Ecosystem Framework." LearnGeek. learngeek.co/mle-framework.

Udell, C., and G. Woodill. 2019. *Shock of the New: The Challenge and Promise of Emerging Learning Technologies.* Alexandria, VA: ATD Press.

CHAPTER 35

Equip Your Managers to Become Masters of Development

Wendy Axelrod

The ultimate goal of talent development is to achieve outstanding performance with an exceptional workforce that delivers on the company's current and long-term objectives. This is a mighty complex undertaking and the TD function is at the very heart of it. Talent development's well-crafted and creative programs for workforce development, individual development plans (IDPs), onboarding, performance management, engagement surveys, succession management, and other vital processes take us an exceptionally long way toward this ultimate goal. However, these efforts alone do not get us over the finish line. We must execute high-level performance—something that is most closely witnessed and supported by the employees' managers. We need to equip managers to become masters of development.

> **IN THIS CHAPTER:**
> - Recognize that talent development's ultimate goal requires a partnership with managers
> - Understand what masters of development actually do
> - Take actions to transform typical managers into masters of development
> - Access tools to help you transform managers

Talent Development Takes a Partnership

Today, even as demanding as their job is, the manager's most important role is developing their employees. Managers delegate assignments, provide feedback and guidance, raise confidence, help employees work through obstacles, and provide the best context for employees to thrive. According to a survey of 39,000 employers worldwide, the foreseeable future holds an increasing need for managers to have the know-how to develop their talent (ManpowerGroup 2018). Yet most managers, despite their desire to a good job of growing their workforce, struggle to fully develop their people.

You can be the one who transforms that reality. That is what this chapter is all about.

When researching for our book, *Make Talent Your Business: How Exceptional Managers Develop People While Getting Results* (Axelrod and Coyle 2011), my co-author and I found managers from scores of companies who created a development-oriented work environment. Their employees grew skills that far exceeded their current responsibilities, sought their managers' tough feedback, and looked for bigger stretch assignments. What's behind the success of these masters of development? The managers viewed the development of their people as the most important part of their job. They understood that learning is not true development until it is applied, because development occurs in the work, not separate from it. These managers implemented the simple yet profound principle of intertwining work, performance, and development on a daily basis to achieve exceptional workforce development—whether their employees were frontline workers or business leaders who managed large organizations.

Before we dive into your role of making this happen, let's take a closer look at what these great talent developers are all about.

What Developmental Managers Do

If you have met and observed managers who are exceptional at developing their team members (and I hope you have), what have you noticed that differentiates them? I've found they take a number of actions that make them true masters of development. It starts with their mindset—to always be on the ready for development opportunities big and small.

Take Josie, for example. She is a data analytics manager at a pharmaceutical support services company; her management highly prizes her for being an outstanding developmental manager. Her constant focus on development does not add to her workload; it simply reorients her way of looking at how the department's work gets done, for now and in the future. She considers the entirety of the department's work as a development trove. Josie has learned about her employees' strengths, interests, aspirations, and development needs. She works to establish a good relationship with each employee, not expecting their trust to be automatic.

Josie considers which assignments can grow which employees. She uses a distinct method of delegating new or expanded tasks, and explicitly tells the employee where the development can occur while they carry out those assignments. For example, she might say, "Lisa, please extend the market projections report you usually create by incorporating the voice of key opinion leaders. Have direct interviews with three or four of them. I know this will mean learning about how to reach out and then interview them. Let's discuss your questions and how you can get that accomplished."

Josie then uses a variety of approaches to help prepare them to use the new behaviors. And, even more important, she also regularly follows up with the employee to check in on what they are learning, what needs more practice or modifying, and what the assignment could be to cement these new skills. Research has shown that this follow-up approach makes the adoption of a new skill far more likely (Goldsmith and Morgan 2004). Along the way, Josie invites her employees' concerns, suggestions, and challenges, while also inspiring their confidence. Her employees are fully engaged, and we can see why the company views her as a talent magnet.

Here are five actions successful development managers like Josie take every day. Use this description to gain insights about how you can work with managers to extend their approaches to development.

- **Use company programs such as IDPs, performance management, and monthly one-on-ones as a launchpad.** Talent developers appreciate and use company processes that keep work accomplishments on track. Developmental managers can use these conversations to identify employees' strengths, needs, interests, and aspirations. And most important, they do not stop there. Instead, they collaborate with employees to identify growth opportunities that combine company programs with hands-on, experiential learning. For example, one employee's goal was stepping up to lead a dynamic multidiscipline project team. First, he participated in a company training program. Then, his manager provided ongoing coaching, gave him opportunities to take on partial responsibilities for the team, encouraged him in working through the challenges he encountered, lined up other people to bounce ideas off of, and continued the evolving process of increasing his team management duties to deepen his growth in this complex skill.
- **Regard the department's work as a collective of development opportunities.** Managers use a variety of methods to plan work developmentally. Some managers map out the multitude of results needed for the department's success, as well as the skills required to accomplish those outcomes. Then they look at how they can move people into assignments that offer growth opportunity. In addition, when new work arises, they delegate it to a combination of people—some for their expertise and some for their

growth. Job shadowing is yet another tactic. It is like using GPS to reach a destination—in addition to the route that is automatic and comfortable, there are many other options. You can take a straight route through the city and risk potential traffic, or you could take the longer road though the countryside. Both routes get you there; the difference is how. The main point is for the manager to move beyond thinking about who will get the job done the quickest to good standards, and instead have the long-term perspective of using work assignments developmentally for all employees.

- **Inject development into work.** These managers find ways to put learning into the crevices of each day. They modify and add to what people usually do, opening the space for people to grow skills while they are achieving expected business results. They also plan the right amount of stretch into their work so it builds skills without pushing people so far that they lose confidence. One of my favorite ways of describing this is that their employees break two ribbons at the finish line of an assignment—one ribbon for accomplishing results and another for their development. This ensures development is not an on-the-side activity, but instead is built right in. At first, the developmental managers may see this as quite risky. Over time this is one of the skills developmental managers become proficient with and, given practice, it becomes a natural way of viewing the achievement of the department's work.

- **Seize developmental moments.** When you see it, ask about it and talk about it. Talent developers recognize that developmental moments happen while employees are doing the work. They regularly ask employees to pause and reflect on what they're learning. They understand that increased self-awareness and reflection after the fact, especially when the employee can debrief with someone else, is one of the most overlooked, yet powerful learning processes. These managers also use effective methods to deliver feedback so it is well received (for example, focused on behavior rather than personality, honest in a give-and-take conversation, provide it often, and do not wait for a sit-down meeting). And it's not all about correcting performance. They also share positive feedback that spells out the added impact the employee is having, lifts confidence, and encourages risk taking to take the next steps. Making feedback a regular part of daily work is a proven differentiator of organizations with higher performance (Ledford and Schneider 2018). These managers also ask well-crafted questions that prompt broader perspective and next steps, for example, "How would you do that next time so we get customer buy-in even earlier?"

- **Create a developmental culture.** Talent developers make development an ongoing expectation and part of everyday interactions in their organization. For example, they raise curiosity about additional ways to approach a problem, ask employees to share what they are learning at staff meetings, set up work teams with a mix of people with complementary strengths and learning needs, and establish the business practice of having learning debriefs for each project. It's no surprise that they also turn mistakes into learning opportunities, normalizing them, and finding the silver lining of an action gone awry. They also periodically report to the team exactly how their increased skills have made an impact on their results. Plus, many of these managers put a fun spin on things, for example, with fact-based trivia relevant to the work of their department.

Now that we have looked at the actions these developmental managers take, let's examine how you can help transform other managers into masters of development. Figure 35-1 presents an overview of the pathway to help transform typical managers into masters of development.

Figure 35-1. Pathway to Transform Typical Managers Into Masters of Development

```
Understand the actions      →  Incorporate more direct      →  Initiate more touch
of developmental               support of managers into        points with managers
managers                       your role
        ↓
Help managers shift         →  Act as their trusted         →  Help managers grow
their mindsets about           developmental coach             their developmental
their developmental role       and consultant                  skills
        ↓
Curate ready-to-use         →  Move yourself into
tools and resources            action
```

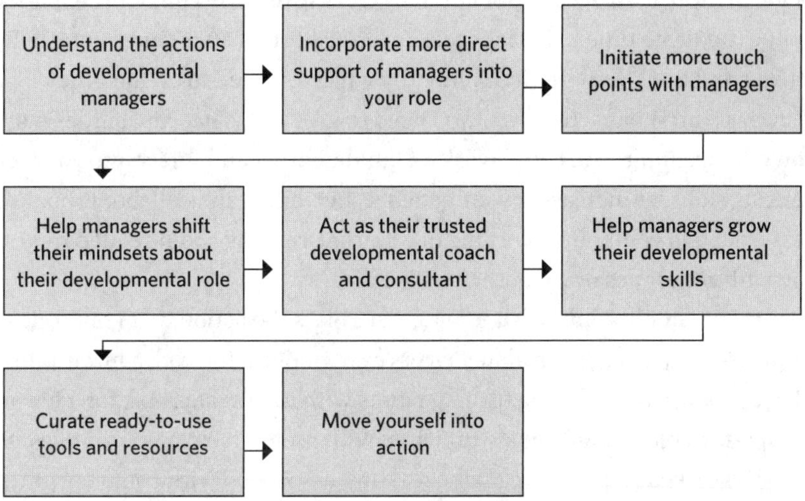

Expand Your Role to Cultivate More Developmental Managers

Whether you are a blended learning specialist, succession management professional, or L&D lead, you have a deep specialty in talent development that managers rely upon. You are in a pivotal spot to inspire and equip managers as powerful partners in the achievement of the ultimate TD objectives.

Take Nina, who works in the learning and development department at a finance company. She found herself primarily providing managers with guidance and corrective actions on the fulfillment of performance management requirements, reviewing their IDPs, and working with engagement surveys. She thought her role was more about informing and policing, and believed she needed a new job to become more long-term-looking and strategic with managers. Instead of moving to a new job, however, she worked with her mentor to plan and find ways to expand the focus of her conversations with managers. For meetings that were ordinarily geared to monitor and review managers' work, she asked for a few extra minutes so managers could discuss the future focus of development for their people. Enough managers were interested that she was able to have the opportunity to experience this new way of interacting with them. Instead of simply explaining company standards, she opened the conversation to a long-term view of the skills needed in the department and how the manager might accrue those skills. This not only changed the conversation; it changed how the managers valued her. Today, she has been promoted to a more strategic role with managers who regularly call upon her for consulting and coaching.

Like Nina, you can help leaders manage with development in mind and incorporate development into their daily routines. Here are four actions TD professionals can focus on to increase enabling managers to turn into true masters of development:

- **Incorporate more direct support of managers into your role.** This will require your discipline. Dedicate time to it each week (even as little as 30 minutes), crystallize your objectives, and track your progress. Identify what you need to do that's new or different in the near term. What actions will you need to give up? What capabilities will you need to grow? For example, you could work on building trust and safety into your relationships, influencing skills, or increasing your patience, flexibility, and collaboration. Keep this process front and center by recording in a journal, reading about related topics, and talking with colleagues or a mentor, as Nina did.
- **Initiate more touchpoints with managers.** This is the action that really opens the possibilities. No need to reach all managers every month. Instead, concentrate on those who have promise or are facing turning points with their teams. Ask for a few minutes with a focused objective and come prepared with useful questions, examples, and value that can be accrued. Use your regular check-ins, associated with company practices, and then initiate follow-up from those discussions (whether they ask for it or not). Get into a regular rhythm of touching base so they come to trust you and seek your counsel. If your job does not ordinarily allow you to have direct conversations with managers—for example, if you are an instructional designer—ask to set up an interview with a manager whose department will use the program you are designing. Do this periodically throughout the year with the same and different managers so you have opportunities for touchpoints. Let them know you are available as a thinking partner for development of their teams.
- **Help managers shift their mindsets about their developmental role and actions.** Remember the last time you tried to change the mind of a close relative or friend who was set in their ways and beliefs? Maybe you thought simply explaining your rationale would get them to adopt your point of view. It doesn't work that way. So remember that

helping managers shift their mindsets may require a bit of a campaign over time, as you provide them with the benefits, success stories, and results from other departments or other companies. Have managers envision the desired end result, employee development, rather than looking at the application of company tools as the primary development method. Then explore what gets them there—for example, actions such as delegating developmentally and job shadowing. Increase managers' understanding that they can develop their employees while simultaneously achieving the department outcomes. Be patient with them because much of the shift will occur as they begin to implement some new behaviors, take ownership for these actions, and see the proof in real time.

- **Be their trusted developmental coach and consultant.** To achieve this status, you will have to add new knowledge, actions, and ways of operating to your repertoire. Stick with it, because your support will add a welcomed dimension to the life of managers. Here is what to focus on if you want to grow yourself and the managers you support:
  - Understand the managers you are working with, their developmental capabilities, and their businesses. Individualize your approach with each one to be deemed a reliable partner from whom they seek counsel.
  - Resist temptation to do it for them; this is not about providing the definitive solution to the problems they encounter. Be courageous when they ask for off-the-shelf solutions and instead help them explore how they can combine their own interactions with employees and some resources. The outcomes from this combination will be far more impactful and long lasting.
  - Guide them to set goals for themselves as masters of development. Then help put them on the path to test out new behaviors with their employees (for example, in the way they delegate and debrief assignments); reflect on the actions they applied with their employees (for example, asking the managers, what behaviors made the difference? What do they need to overcome? What impact did they have? What do they want to do next time?); track their progress; and refine actions going forward.
  - Shift your mode from explaining to asking. Increase your use of thought-provoking questions to stimulate their thinking about the possibilities and the impact they are having. For example, "How can you approach this situation with Jacob so he feels ready to test out the newly designed engineering protocols he learned in the webinar?" Or, "What specific skills will Aisha need to influence the project team? How can she practice them?"

Check out the coaching questions tool, which provides dozens of questions you can use as you coach managers to be more developmental, located on the handbook's website, ATDHandbook3 .org. Provide learning supports for managers. It also helps to curate the many learning resources available to help managers grow their skills, which will make it easier for them to use. And encourage managers to reach out to other people who can serve as resources to support their employees, such as experienced department professionals or colleagues from other departments, rather than trying to do all of it on their own.

Help Managers Grow Skills Needed to Become Talent Developers

We don't know what we don't know. If it has not been a part of managers' repertoire to be developmental with employees, they may mistakenly believe they are already doing that, because they comply with the company's development-oriented requirements.

Here is a story from Marcos, an aspiring developmental manager in a large software development organization:

> At first, I asked each employee to complete a development plan and then we discussed their development goals. After that, a couple of them took part in a training program. When a few months had passed with virtually no progress being made, I became really worried, knowing what new products were in the pipeline. I then recognized that it was up to me to develop my own skills to develop my staff. I geared up my listening and inquiry skills, and that improved my way of interacting with employees. I also looked for opportunities to make every day a development day, like during one-on-one conversations, team meetings, and off-site meetings. I really came to rely on the learning and development lead, not just for my employees' development, but my own. Over time, when I asked my employees how things were going for them, they said with pride how much more they were able to do, and the confidence they felt to take on bigger challenges. The difference was astonishing.

Just like any great life-changing habit, this will take ongoing effort, practice, reflection, and application. Marcos's tenacity is admirable. His new capability to be developmental is a skill he treasures and it will last his entire career.

Learn to identify managers' strengths and improvement areas, so you can better support them. Here are 10 skills shared by managers who are masters of development:

- **Adopt a talent developer mindset.** Establish an outlook about the many ways to grow people on a daily basis, embedding development into multiple elements of managing people.
- **Demonstrate self-awareness.** Know your strengths and areas for improvement, be self-observant in your interactions with others, and understand your impact (which increases employees' receptivity to your coaching and feedback).

- **Build trusting relationships.** Demonstrate honesty, credibility, reliability, and caring in your relationships; ensure that the other person feels safe to speak freely with you.
- **Assess employee skills.** Understand which skills are needed to make the employee successful in their role; know what to look for to determine the level of skill the employee demonstrates.
- **Listen attentively.** Invite others to share their thoughts; take into account both the person's words and the feelings behind their words as they speak; and stay focused without mentally formulating responses before they are finished speaking.
- **Inquire productively.** Ask tailored, thought-provoking questions that encourage people to process and discover new ways of thinking and acting; use questions to open fresh perspectives and more strategic views. Once they speak, ask more to dig deeper and avoid the use of questions to make your own point.
- **Delegate developmentally.** Spell out what the employee is to learn, along with what results they are to achieve; provide sufficient detail to ensure your ideas are fully grasped by your employee; and ask questions to confirm you have a mutual understanding.
- **Make meetings learning focused.** Whether one-on-one or with the team, use meetings to help employees learn new ideas and approaches; ask questions more than you provide explanations or solve problems; regularly elicit what employees are learning from their work and what else they'd like to learn
- **Give feedback generously.** Frequently discuss timely observations about both effective and ineffective noteworthy behaviors and their impact; make it a two-way conversation with a focus on increasing an employee's self-awareness and learning, rather than giving explanations of how their behaviors should be done differently.
- **Follow through thoughtfully.** Maintain a positive attitude and forward momentum on employees' growth; during and after assignments, debrief with employees to discuss what they learned; check in periodically regarding new behaviors they are mastering and discuss next opportunities to apply those new skills; and provide appropriate resources.

Use this list for both you and the manager to assess how they are doing on their path to becoming exceptional at developing others. Have them pinpoint where they need more practice and fine-tuning. Be encouraging to managers who are in their own learning journey; it will take time, practice, and someone to discuss it with … and that person could be you.

It is not a coincidence that this list of skills may also apply to your own growth as a professional who is helping to grow developmentally focused managers. Why not highlight the ones you would like to develop further?

Curate Ready Tools and Resources

Be the go-to person who is prepared, not hesitant, when managers ask for guidance and resources. When they do ask, confidently share trusted approaches and discuss how they can gain proficiency, setting a target for their learning, testing new behaviors, getting feedback from observers, and moving on to perfect their capability in this area. It will be helpful for both you and the manager if you have ready access to potential approaches they can take.

Please heed the warning of this next point: Avoid simply handing these suggestions off to the manager! You do not want this to feel like another program or requirement, because that will undermine your value in this process. Instead use it as a springboard for your further coaching or consultation, which will make it a much richer experience and more fully cement their skills.

Here are suggestions of items you might want in your curated tools and resources. Remember, these are just as useful to you in your coaching of them as they are for their own application.

- **How to conduct a developmental conversation.** This includes the purpose and intended outcome of a developmental conversation; appropriate times the manager might conduct one; and how to prepare for that conversation, including getting employee buy-in for the conversation, a suggested outline, questions to ask, and how to wrap up the conversation and identify next steps. It guides the manager to think developmentally about work assignments and the manager's ongoing role in that complete process (that is, not dropping involvement after the assignment is given to the employee). It could also include tips on how to coach versus problem solve, handling employee concerns, and the impact of follow-up to build confidence and help ensure lasting impact.
- **Manager's guide to developing others from experiences.** This helps the manager understand and set into motion a series of actions to reap the best possible development from targeted work assignments for their employee or work teams. This could include:
  - How to assess what skills the employee intends to grow
  - How the manager and employee can creatively think about work assignments that could match the desired skill growth
  - What a manager should consider when delegating the assignments so employees understand they are about growing targeted skills as well as getting the job done
  - A set of questions managers can use to help the employee prepare to apply the new behavior, as well as specific preparatory steps that can be taken with the employee, such as role-play exercises
  - Attaining an on-the-job resource, such as a buddy, to support employees who are learning to apply new behaviors
  - Establishing a series of coaching conversations between the manager and employee to reflect on how the employee's development process is working, address challenges, and move to next steps

- **Talent developer cohorts.** This is an ongoing series of monthly meetings where managers discuss their progress and challenges in becoming talent developers. For me personally, this was one of the most gratifying tools I have used to help transform managers. At each meeting, cohort members take turns presenting what they are learning, specific approaches they have applied with employees, and where they want to get support from the group. The group coaches this manager, asking thought-provoking questions and adding wider perspective. As a bonus, the TD professional facilitating the meeting (for example, you) can add valuable content to the conversation.
- **Videos and TED Talks.** This is a prescreened set of links to videos and TED Talks on subjects relevant to managers as they learn these skills and to their employees (likely two separate lists) on topics such as influencing others, making a stellar presentation, making work developmental, and leading team meetings.
- **Peer-mentoring process.** This allows the manager to get many employees involved in a developmental process. The how-to guidance provided is important because many employees believe they know just what to do to mentor one another. However, it's important to remember that while there are many effective mentoring methods, some have the potential to be destructive (Axelrod 2019). If the manager assumes that everyone knows what's involved in mentoring, there is a high likelihood the program will fail over time. The focus needs to be on techniques that help the other person learn, not based solely on the formula that the mentor uses. It is best to get the peer-mentoring partners working from the same playbook, and TD professionals can provide the guidance on that.

These five examples provide a starting point for what you could include in your set of curated and tested talent developer resources. You and your colleagues are already experts in generating developmental resources, so go forth and create!

Final Thoughts

There is no question that the ultimate TD objectives will be achieved only in partnership with managers who are skilled talent developers. Your efforts in understanding what distinguishes talent developers, helping them adopt a new mindset, getting their buy-in to their developmental responsibilities, and coaching and setting them on a path to learn and practice those skills will be the differentiator for you and your company. While you're on that path you will also see changes as you shift and add to your work priorities, learn new skills, and establish regular interactions with managers to become an ongoing advocate and trusted coach.

Is becoming an expert in transforming managers into expert talent developers part of your future? I hope so. The rewards will be found on multiple levels: managers who have breakthroughs in their methods of developing and engaging employees, increased growth opportunities for their employees, whole departments that have a positive and dynamic way of operating, and, for you, a lasting legacy in having effected a transformation in your organization.

About the Author

Wendy Axelrod is a globally recognized author, executive coach, and talent development expert who helps organizations substantially increase their development and performance results. She is the author of *Make Talent Your Business: How Exceptional Managers Develop People While Getting Results* and *10 Steps to Successful Mentoring* and speaks at conferences including those hosted by ATD, the Conference Board, Human Resource Planning Society, and HR Summit Asia. Wendy loves directly coaching managers and mentors to become exceptional at growing the talent of others. She spurs them to move beyond simply giving solutions and directives to make others' work developmental. She guides managers and mentors to build their self-awareness, increase trust, and apply crucial developmental skills, enabling those they work with to explore new perspectives, break through obstacles, and perfect new capabilities. The result of this approach is often transformational for managers, mentors, and those they support. Reach Wendy at wendy@wendyaxelrodphd.com.

References

Axelrod, W. 2019. *10 Steps to Successful Mentoring*. Alexandria, VA: ATD Press.

Axelrod, W., and J. Coyle. 2011. *Make Talent Your Business: How Exceptional Managers Develop Talent While Getting Results*. Oakland, CA: Berrett-Koehler.

Goldsmith, M., and H. Morgan. 2004. "Leadership Is a Contact Sport: The 'Follow-up Factor' in Management Development." *Strategy+Business*, Fall. strategy-business.com/article/04307?gko=407be.

Ledford, G.E., Jr., and B. Schneider. 2018. *Performance Feedback Culture Drives Business Impact*. Institute for Corporate Productivity and the Center for Effective Organizations. ceo.usc.edu/wp-content/uploads/2019/07/Performance-Feedback-Culture-Drives-Business-Performance-i4cp-CEO-002-1.pdf.

ManpowerGroup. 2018. "Solving the Talent Shortage Build, Buy, Borrow and Bridge." 2018 Talent Shortage Survey. go.manpowergroup.com/hubfs/TalentShortage%202018%20(Global)%20Assets/PDFs/MG_TalentShortage2018_lo%206_25_18_FINAL.pdf.

Recommended Resources

Biech, E. 2021. *Skills for Career Success: Maximizing Your Potential at Work*. Oakland, CA: Berrett-Koehler.

Kaye, B., and J. Winkle Giulioni. 2019. *Help Them Grow or Watch Them Go*, 2nd ed. Oakland, CA: Berrett-Koehler.

Stainer, M.B. 2016. *The Coaching Habit: Say Less, Ask More & Change the Way You Lead Forever*. Toronto: Box of Crayons Press.

CHAPTER 36

Talent Development's Role in Strategic Workforce Planning

Barbara Goretsky

Strategic workforce planning is about having the right people, at the right time, with the right skills, at the right cost to meet business goals. As simple as that sounds on paper, many organizations either don't do it or don't do it well. As the need for new and upgraded skills in organizations increases, and the supply of people who have those skills decreases, the need to create a strategic workforce plan with talent development's involvement has become critical. This chapter explains the importance of strategic workforce planning and the role that talent development professionals play.

IN THIS CHAPTER:
- Learn why strategic workforce planning is vital to organizational success
- Name the steps to developing a strategic workforce plan
- Discover talent development's increasingly critical role in strategic workforce planning

Strategic workforce planning (SWP) is the process an organization uses to analyze the current workforce and plan future staffing needs. It refers to the process of forecasting the types and volumes of talent that will be needed to meet organizational goals and assessing those needs against both current capabilities and projected availability in the labor market. Strategic workforce planning occurs as an organization's strategy is being developed, when new strategic objectives are set, or on a regular basis as business conditions change (ATD 2020). Typically, the planning period is three to five years, which allows longer-term business needs to be properly identified and plans made to ensure that robust pipeline of talent is in place.

Operational workforce planning and *workforce planning* are terms similar to strategic workforce planning, with the main difference being the timeframe. Operational workforce planning may project talent needs for the next year, while workforce planning considers the head count needed on a daily, weekly, or monthly basis.

Hindrances to Effectively Planning Future Workforce Needs

There are varying reasons organizations don't effectively plan for their future talent needs. These reasons include:
- Not having the proper data to reasonably forecast the talent they will need
- Continual changes in the environment that affect the organization and make it difficult to forecast
- Blindly assuming that the talent will be available to hire if and when it is needed
- A disjointed, siloed approach to organizational planning

Not conducting a robust strategic workforce planning process can lead to organizations missing important strategic goals. According to *Harvard Business Review* (2016), inadequate workforce planning has prevented an overwhelming majority of organizations from meeting their business goals. A brief review of each of these reasons for often inadequate strategic workforce planning will illuminate the issues and opportunities for talent development's involvement in the process.

Data Not Available

One reason organizations don't prepare robust plans is that they don't have the proper data to reasonably forecast the talent they will need. According to the same 2016 *HBR* survey, most companies do not have sufficient information about their workforce in four areas:
- What is happening with talent acquisition and attrition and why
- How the workforce plan contributes to the success of the business plan
- How changes in the workforce will cause variance from the plan
- What roles or talent are required to meet business objectives

The talent management function is positioned very well to provide insights into this kind of information. Talent management can provide talent analytics (for example, projections on turnover, retirement, skill availability, and so forth) to help the organization craft an actionable workforce plan. If talent management has not provided this type of information in the past, it will inevitably lead to the perception that the data is not available. Talent management must continually show value by demonstrating a knowledge of the workforce as well as the business so that they are perceived as a part of the strategic workforce planning process.

Continual Changes

Coupled with the need for talent information, organizations are in a state of constant flux, which hinders effective strategic workforce planning. Jobs are changing, and the skills needed to perform these new jobs are changing too. In 2020, companies estimated that around 40 percent of workers would require reskilling that took six months or less, while other workers would require a longer period of time to reskill. The window of opportunity to reskill and upskill workers is also becoming shorter and shorter (WEF 2020). Organizations simply cannot reskill their workers fast enough to meet future needs.

This need to reskill also applies to workers who are likely to stay in their roles—for them, the percentage of core skills in their current jobs that will change in the next five years is 40 percent (WEF 2020). Add to that the rapid increase in the half-life of knowledge (that is, the length of time before knowledge gained in college courses, training programs, or work experiences becomes obsolete), and the need for reskilling becomes a strategic imperative.

Changes in technology, markets, and demographics have continually shifted organizational strategy and operations. This is not new; however, unexpected disruptions have caused problems. The loss of talent in the US workforce significantly increased during the COVID-19 pandemic. It is estimated that 3.2 million baby boomers in the US retired from their jobs during the pandemic alone (Bersin 2020a). Between October 2019 and October 2020, there were 2.2 million fewer women in the workforce due to job losses, shuttered schools, lack of childcare, and pay disparities (Matuson 2021). Non-college-educated workers also suffered worse unemployment rates than workers with a bachelor's degree or higher (Congressional Research Service 2021). This loss of talent has severely affected organizational success.

Blindly Assuming Talent Will Be Available

Without strategic workforce planning, organizations fall into a reactive mode of trying to hire and fire as business conditions change. In this cycle, the focus (and pressure) tends to be more on talent acquisition and less on talent development. As new roles emerge and new skills are needed in the organization, the pool of skilled and available workers will continue to shrink, leading to an overreliance on talent acquisition. However, recent history has demonstrated that the requisite talent needed to meet new and emerging organizational demands (like ICU nurses, data scientists, and so forth) is in short supply. No longer can organizations assume that the needed talent will be available to hire if and when it is needed.

A Disjointed Process

Another issue affecting organizations' ability to successfully plan for their future workforces is the siloed approach to the process. Many times, HR or talent management is determining the talent needs of the organization by looking at talent analytics and basing future projections on past experiences. Alternatively, business leaders are forecasting their head count needs based on where they see the business going, and not including HR or talent management in those discussions. Having a cross-functional team of business and HR or talent management leaders working collaboratively on the strategic workforce plan should lead to a better outcome. The owner of the plan could be determined by deciding who monitors the execution of the plan.

If your organization does not currently engage in this process or if the process is disjointed, you can take the lead in creating a sense of urgency with the appropriate stakeholders (such as business leaders, HR, or finance) and reviewing the benefits of creating and maintaining such a plan. As the need for talent continues to grow in organizations, all leaders must understand that future workforce planning is essential to organizational success and working together to create a strategic workforce plan will produce better results.

Traditional Steps to Developing a Strategic Workforce Plan

Strategic workforce planning is a three-phased approach: align, assess, and plan (Figure 36-1). Six detailed steps are included within that framework. You can download this tool to use as you help your organization develop its workforce plan. It is located at the handbook's website, ATDHandook3.org.

Figure 36-1. A Checklist of the Phases and Steps to Develop a Strategic Workforce Plan

Align	Assess	Plan
1. Understand the longer-term organizational strategy.	3. Assess the skills and competencies of the current workforce.	5. Develop a SWP and talent strategy that includes plans to close gaps and execute the plan.
2. Determine the critical, strategic roles for organizational success, and the future demand for those roles.	4. Compare forecasted needs to current skills and competency levels and external availability—gap analysis.	6. Monitor the plans and adjust accordingly.

Align: Step 1

Understand the longer-term organizational strategy by examining the organization's vision, mission, values, and strategic plan. Talent management professionals must be closely linked to business leaders and understand the direction the organization is taking over the planning period (that is, three to five years, depending on the industry). Additionally, talent management must demonstrate an understanding of the labor requirements for meeting such plans. Being proactive enables you to participate in the planning process and create a viable strategic workforce plan.

If you have never been a part of your organization's strategic planning process from which a strategic workforce plan can be developed, you should familiarize yourself with the strategic plan to understand the future state of your organization. If that plan is not available to you, interview business leaders about the future of their business.

Here are some typical questions asked during a needs analysis. These help ensure data collected can be used to identify training needs and conduct a strategic workforce analysis:
- What do you see happening in your business area in the next three to five years?
- What are some of the product and service shifts being contemplated?
- What do you think are the skills and competencies your business area will need to succeed in the future?
- How will technology changes affect your business?
- What other changes do you see coming?
- How can we partner with you to build the talent that you need?

Align: Step 2

The focus of this step is to identify what the critical roles and skills are for achieving the organization's strategies, and what the future demand for those roles is likely to be.

A *critical role* can be defined as a role vital to the long-term success of the organization. These are roles required by the strategic plan for success and are sometimes referred to as *strategic roles*. Of course, not all roles are considered critical to organizational success. Other potential roles include:
- *Key roles*, which are critical to delivering results related to the current business strategy
- *Core roles*, which are foundational roles that support and run the day-to-day business
- *Transactional roles*, which are not critical to business strategies, but deliver operational objectives

Once you understand what the roles are, you can begin to estimate the need in your organization. There are numerous ways to estimate future talent demands and, depending on the size and complexity of your organization, you may use one or more of them. Forecasting future demand is one method to estimate future demand; however, forecasting can be tricky because it relies heavily on making assumptions that may or may not turn out to be correct.

Strategic planning often involves examining different potential future scenarios, which enable the organization to prepare their workforce under differing circumstances. Scenario planning, for example, may be helpful in estimating future talent demands without the need to be as exacting as forecasting. There are also other approaches to estimating, which all have advantages and disadvantage. Their intent is to detail the specific skills and roles needed in the organization to achieve success.

What skills your organization needs will depend on the roles it has or will need based upon product and service changes or industry advances. Researching the labor market for these skills—especially those needed for critical roles—and understanding the competition for them is essential. If certain skills, like data science, are in high demand in your industry, yet there is a limited supply, your organization may want to develop in-house talent in those skills. Two sources for such labor market demand and availability are the Bureau of Labor Statistics and the US Census Data.

Predictive analytics and algorithms are also helping employers identify the skills required. However, even without technological assistance, research shows that some of the most needed new competencies and skills across all roles are soft or "human" skills like communication and flexibility, in addition to more technical skills like data science and cybersecurity (Shepherd and Phaup 2020).

In addition, the roles you identify as critical may not be new to the organization. Many current roles will stay, but with significant changes. As automation continues to take over some of the more mundane tasks, employees will be expected to perform new or different tasks that require new skills. A strategic workforce plan should include any new skills that the current workforce will need.

Assess: Step 3

Understanding the supply of talent by assessing the current workforce is the next step in the process. This involves looking at those individuals by roles (as defined above), starting with the critical roles. You should look at both the quantity and the quality of the current workforce in different roles:

- **Quantity.** Use talent analytics to examine the number of workers in each role; the demographics of the workers; projected turnover or retirement in these roles; the time to fill and the time to productivity in these roles; the number of high potentials; the number of certifications and licenses; and other pertinent data to help create a comprehensive view of the workforce.

- **Quality.** Use a variety of data from talent management or other processes, such as performance management, talent reviews, assessment instruments, individual development plans, assessments by leaders on the perceived gaps, employee engagement data, and other organizational processes that may yield talent gaps, such as proposal bids for work (ATD 2020). Talent development professionals can add a feedback loop from their learning programs, such as post-class skill assessments, to the strategic workforce planning process. Training courses are a rich source of data on how well learners have mastered or struggled to master a new skill.

Data analysis is where talent development professionals have a valuable role to play. As owners of much of this data, you are in a great position to know the talent of your organization far better than most other functions. Both formalized assessments such as the ones you already use (for example, Hogan, 360-degree assessments) and on-the-job measures that, in the future, may come through on-the-job data collection can help you diagnose performance and skills gaps (Shepherd and Phaup 2020).

Assess: Step 4

Compare the forecasted need (demand) to the current workforce (supply). This allows the organization to determine how big of a gap, if any, exists. Looking at gaps by roles (for example, senior software engineer or ICU nurse) can help prioritize where action is needed. A significant contribution that talent development can make here is to review high-supply roles and determine if some of the skills are transferrable to roles with lower labor supply. Again, sources for talent supply data include the US government and independent industry surveys.

Plan: Step 5

Determining how to close the identified gaps is the next step of the process. These are critical decisions that help formulate not only the strategic workforce plan but also a talent strategy. The *Six Bs*, developed by David Ulrich (2009), are six investments that can be made to upgrade the talent in an organization and close a talent gap:

- **Buy.** Getting employees from outside the organization or from another part of the organization through the talent acquisition process. One advantage to this approach is that it brings in new ideas or skills quickly when there is no time to develop the talent internally.
- **Build.** Developing employees through talent development initiatives. The advantage to this approach is that it opens up opportunities for current employees to assume new positions by having developed the requisite skills.

- **Borrow.** Partnering with others outside the organization to obtain the proper skills and knowledge. One advantage to borrowing talent is that the workers are not considered employees, so they are used only for a specified period of time. This helps keep costs down. According to Gartner, 32 percent of organizations are replacing full-time employees with contingent workers as a cost-saving measure (Baker 2020). When using the borrow strategy, a conscious decision must be made as to how your contingent workforce will be integrated into your talent strategy.
- **Bind.** Retaining high-potential and high-performing employees with incentives or other retention tools.
- **Bound.** Moving employees through the organization and into higher positions. Some best practices in this area also include programs and perks to retain talent, for example, working from home, customized benefits, and so forth.
- **Bounce.** Placing lower-performing employees in more suitable roles or removing them from the organization.

Using the *Six Bs* as guidance does not mean using only one of these strategies across all roles or business areas. Most times, you must use different approaches for different roles or business areas. Critical roles need more attention and resources than other, noncritical roles. When used for the different roles, these investment strategies form the beginning of a talent segmentation strategy, that is, different attraction, development, rewards, and retention strategies for roles based upon their criticality and unique needs.

These investment strategies also form the basis for specific goals and resourcing—without proper resourcing, these goals often languish and the organization suffers. You should work with your talent management colleagues on the different talent segmentation strategies so that everyone is aligned and focused and knows what the overall objectives and resources are.

Managers typically do not care where the talent comes from. The *buy strategy* is often used because managers need the talent quickly and claim they do not have time to build the talent. As the pool of skilled and competent talent continues to shrink, organizations will be faced with building their talent internally to meet future business needs. It is not always cost-effective to buy the talent, and in fact, it may be more cost effective to build it. However, building talent takes time, hence the need for a robust, longer-term strategic workforce plan to guide that investment. Additionally, the *build strategy* may help engage and retain employees who might otherwise leave the organization due to a lack of perceived opportunities.

Plan: Step 6

Monitor the plans and adjust accordingly. Once the strategic workforce plan and the talent segmentation strategies have been developed—including the specific goals and resource allocations—continual follow-up and analysis should be done to ensure the plans are being executed appropriately. As business conditions change or other unanticipated changes occur, the plans should be adjusted to meet the new demands. An annual, formalized review should be conducted to ensure that the plan is on track to meet its objectives. Communication among all stakeholders is a necessity to ensure goals are met or adjustments are made. The owner of the strategic workforce plan (someone who manages and oversees the plan's execution) will ensure attention is paid to the plan.

Technology Opportunities to Support Your Strategic Workforce Plan

Advances in technology are creating exceptional opportunities to help develop a strategic workforce plan. For example, some newer learning management systems have an integrated skills taxonomy database that helps assess current employees' skills, as well as hire and train strategically to close skills gaps. Jobs are changing so quickly that building competency models and formal job descriptions is getting too hard to do. Instead, these systems look at the skills that are trending in the organization by looking at employee data. They infer skills by looking at the employee's experience, performance reviews, learning patterns, and so on (Bersin 2020b). This creates a great opportunity to harvest the data and incorporate it into the strategic workforce plan.

Additionally, as more integrated talent management systems are adopted, data from all systems can be analyzed to get a complete picture of the employees. If you have such an integrated system, you can divide the talent into different talent segments (based on roles) and review the size of that group or pool, the skills the employees have and need, the turnover, the performance, the engagement levels, and so on. Having a robust system can make strategic workforce planning simpler; however, it is not a requirement to developing a solid plan.

If your organization is thinking about what technology to use, be sure to find the right tools to forecast, predict different scenarios, and track the plans. If you have a team of stakeholders developing the plan, find a solution that allows for easy collaboration. However, be careful of business planning tools that are designed more for the finance team than the HR team because they may not meet the needs of the organization's talent teams or communities.

If your organization does not have the technology to support a robust strategic workforce plan, it might be beneficial to start small, for example, with one business unit or the critical roles only, and work from there.

Talent Development's Role in Building Talent

As many organizations continue to flatten from their hierarchical, job-based constructs, the identification of the skills and competencies needed to be successful to meet business goals will become paramount. Talent development needs to pay attention to developing the skills and competencies that make a difference in organizational performance in both the short and longer term (Lawler 2017).

Talent development must be strategic and have agile practices and processes, just like the rest of the organization, so it can change quickly as the organizational strategy changes. In that light, talent development has numerous opportunities to build the talent of the organization to meet its business goals. Here are a few examples.

Internships

Working with educational institutions by providing students with internships can help prepare students for full-time jobs after graduation. Additionally, you can work with the educators to let them know which skills your organization needs. As skills gaps widen, ask if they can develop a curriculum that addresses the specific skills your organization will need. In fact, this is how the STEM (science, technology, engineering, and math) program started in the United States. The Department of Labor predicted that there would not be enough engineering graduates to fill all the available jobs, so getting more US students interested in these fields became a presidential priority. It took a partnership between the educators and the business leaders who knew what skills would be needed to make this work.

Onboarding

New employees must get up to speed quickly in their roles. Support the onboarding process by developing learning plans to help employees learn their jobs, address skill needs, and become familiar with the organization quickly. Talent development can also create communities of practice for newly hired employees to learn from one another and develop a network of colleagues. This is also a great time to pair new hires with a mentor or a peer coach to help them learn the intricacies of their position. Supporting the new hires through onboarding is a critical first step in building a relationship with them and establishing a continual learning mindset that helps them succeed and stay with the organization. Keep in mind that leading organizations consider onboarding to encompass the first six to 12 months of a new employee's tenure, when retention is a key concern!

Upskilling and Reskilling

As jobs shift and technology becomes more pervasive, employees must learn new and different skills; however, skills and competency training can be costly. Talent development can help in this regard by shifting learners' mindsets from learning as an event to embedding learning in their work. Technology can be a great tool to help in this regard. Artificial intelligence, virtual reality, and augmented reality are becoming more commonplace in the learning space and can be used in the course of the employee's work. Naturally, the more technology is used in an employee's job, the more training is needed on that technology.

Talent development can also prescribe role-based learning that employees can access through the learning technology infrastructure. The focus should first be on those in critical roles to ensure that they are prepared for changes in their roles and equipped with the right programs to learn the requisite new skills.

Career Development

Employees are seeking career mobility whereby they can learn and grow in their current organizations or move on to different opportunities elsewhere. Gartner's 2020 report on future work trends suggests that you should focus more on the requisite skills needed in the future rather than specific roles. It says you should encourage employees to develop critical skills that potentially open up multiple opportunities for their career development, rather than preparing them for a specific next role. For years, employees have asked for more transparent career paths, and for years, talent development has struggled to provide them. At the same time, organizations have flattened and structures have become more complex. As such, career paths are no longer very clear and vertical advancement may be limited. Talent development is in a unique position to support employees' career development by identifying the skills they will need and providing access to learning those skills.

Performance Management

This organizational process is undergoing significant changes as organizations try to optimize it. Performance management is used for many different purposes—from making compensation decisions like raises and promotions to identifying ways to close skills gaps. This multitude of purposes has left the process inconsistent and ineffective. Many organizations are establishing processes that focus almost exclusively on coaching and developing employees. In these approaches, frequent feedback on performance and support to develop skills and competencies replaces the focus on where performance lacks and how salary decisions are made. Talent development has a significant role in helping managers learn how to coach and develop their employees. Additionally, having formal coaching and mentoring programs can assist employees with enhancing their skills. Talent development has always had a role in fulfilling the learning and development needs that are identified in performance management processes. Even if you do not own the performance management process, you still have a very important role to play in closing skills gaps.

Management and Leadership Development Programs

Leadership positions are typically considered critical strategic roles, and as such, talent development must focus on this talent segment's learning and development. Most organizations have management and leadership curriculums in place for these critical roles, which are based on the competencies it deems critical to success. As leadership competencies continue to shift, you must refresh the competency models for these roles as well as the curriculums that develop managers and leaders. Coaching and mentoring programs also have a big role to play in developing leaders.

High-Potential Programs

Identifying and developing high potentials for critical roles has always been in talent development's portfolio of offerings. Either through looking at feeder groups or through pipeline planning, you can develop high-potential programs for those identified as having potential to move up into higher-level roles. High-potential programs have typically been focused on those who exhibit leadership capabilities; however, they can also be expanded to consider all critical roles. As talent pools shrink and the need to retain top talent takes precedence, high potentials who are lower in the organization can be identified and developed earlier—including creating development programs for new college hires to upskill them in longer-term capabilities they will need. Development programs must provide the right experiences to meet the requirements of the future roles. Coaching and mentoring programs also have a big role to play in developing high potentials.

Workforce Development

Partnering with external, local organizations (like two-year colleges or chambers of commerce) can help develop the local workforce to meet the future needs of the organization. Working together to identify and build the needed skills can help ensure a pipeline of talent from the community. Depending on the industry you are in, an apprenticeship program can help develop the talent needed by the organization and provide employment opportunities for those who may need reskilling. Aggressive outreach with community partners is another way you can reach out to potential hires. This could include having your new hires and other employees or leaders speak at public functions to encourage others to join the company. Having these same employees serve on local boards and volunteer in local organizations can also promote the organization to potential hires.

Final Thoughts

All the typical talent development processes and programs must focus on building the workforce for the future. Talent development's role in strategic workforce planning is becoming more and more critical to the success of the organization as leaders look to you to build internal talent. Understanding why it is so important, how it is done, and your role in it can help you create the proper programs and processes to ensure a properly skilled and talented workforce!

About the Author

Barbara Goretsky has spent her entire career in the talent development profession and HR. After a successful career in various organizations and industries, she began her own consulting practice specializing in talent development, team building, change management, leadership development, and executive coaching. She facilitates several programs for ATD and was a contributing author to the Talent Development Body of Knowledge.

References

Association for Talent Development. 2020. Talent Development Body of Knowledge. Alexandria, VA: ATD.

Baker, M. 2020. "9 Future of Work Trends Post–COVID-19." Gartner, April 29. gartner.com/smarterwithgartner/9-future-of-work-trends-post-covid-19.

Bersin, J. 2020a. "HR Predictions for 2021." Josh Bersin. joshbersin.com/hr-predictions-for-2021.

Bersin, J. 2020b. "The War of the Skills Clouds." Josh Bersin, January 17. joshbersin.com/2020/01/the-war-of-the-skills-clouds-skillscloud.

Congressional Research Service. 2021. *Unemployment Rates During the COVID-19 Pandemic*. CRS, August 20. crsreports.congress.gov/product/pdf/R/R46554.

Harvard Business Review. 2016. *Tackling Talent Strategically: Winning With Workforce Talent*. Boston, MA: Harvard Business Publishing.

Lawler, E. 2017. *Reinventing Talent Management: Principles and Practices for the New World of Work*. Oakland, CA: Berrett-Koehler.

Matuson, R. 2021. "How to Stop the Mass Exodus of Women Leaving the Workforce Due to COVID-19." Forbes, March 19. forbes.com/sites/robertamatuson/2021/03/01/how-to-stop-the-mass-exodus-of-women-leaving-the-workforce-due-to-covid-19/?sh=77aeb5fc1bd7.

Shepherd, E., and J. Phaup. 2020. *Talent Transformation: Develop Today's Team for Tomorrow's World of Work*. Talent Transformation Press.

Ulrich, D. 2009. "The Six 'Bs' Overview." The RBL Group, Tool 5.1. hrtransformationbook.s3.amazonaws.com/Documents/5.1%206Bs.pdf.

World Economic Forum. 2020. *The Future of Jobs Report 2020*. Cologny, Switzerland: World Economic Forum.

Recommended Resources

Gibson, A. 2021. *Agile Workforce Planning: How to Align People With Organizational Strategy for Improved Performance*. London: Kogan Page.

Lawler, E. 2017. *Reinventing Talent Management: Principles and Practices for the New World of Work*. Oakland, CA: Berrett-Koehler.

CHAPTER 37

From Ward to Steward: Enhancing Employee Ownership of Career Development

Halelly Azulay

The relationship between employee and employer used to be different in the industrial age—it was based on long-term loyalty on both sides. This was disempowering for employees, because it was rarely acceptable to have any expectations of your employment beyond a paycheck and basic benefits. But you could pretty much expect to have these until you retired and a pension to sustain you in retirement so long as you performed sufficiently well. That's no longer the case.

IN THIS CHAPTER:

- Discover why industrial-age conceptions about the employment relationship no longer apply and what to replace them with
- Identify practical ways to take ownership of your career and career development
- Recognize the value of enhancing and nurturing your personal brand and professional value proposition

---

Industrial-age employers rarely felt threatened that their employees would leave the job if they weren't happy or fulfilled, or if employees felt like their skills were stagnant. Employees were both expecting and expected to stay put, keep their heads down, and just do their job. They knew not to expect or ask for too much—just be grateful knowing that they'll get taken care of by the company. As far as their development was concerned, it was understood that training would be chosen and provided by the organization as needed. Employers would become the steward of their career growth, and employees, their wards.

Fulfilling dreams and aspirations? *Nope.* Setting the tone for your own development? *Nope.* Just do your job and leave it to the company to take care of you.

The Recession of the 1980s

The recession of the 1980s brought massive layoffs. As a result, the world of work saw huge changes marked by a mutual loss of trust, commitment, and loyalty between organizations and their people. The employee–employer relationship moved out of the industrial age, and employees started to realize that they had to shift their development mentality accordingly.

The Former Employee–Employer Relationship Is History

Over the past two decades, the steward–ward relationship has been decoupled and many employees now realize a "till death do us part" kind of a marriage to their employers is not a reality. But old habits are hard to drop, and a lot of employees still expect their company to develop them.

It's been a growing rift, and the remnants of the former mindset still hang around in today's workplace. But make no mistake—those days are over. We all need to embrace a brave new world of work, led by disruptive innovations, a new generation taking the lead in the workplace, and the future of work with its various implications.

Employees today, especially the younger generations, expect to feel like they're making a difference. As Daniel Pink (2011) wrote about in his book *Drive: The Surprising Truth About What Motivates Us*, employees expect to connect to a greater sense of purpose, to develop mastery, and to experience autonomy. And when they no longer feel like they're getting those needs met in their current organization, they go elsewhere.

According to one LinkedIn study by Josh Bersin (2018), when asked what would cause them to leave their job, those surveyed said that "their ability to learn and grow was roughly twice as important as getting a raise, and more than twice as important than the relationship with their manager!"

The new workplace sees tenures shrinking and trust diminishing. And while elsewhere in this handbook are lots of reasons for employers to heed this and ensure they develop their employees, all employees must also assume the role of stewards of their own career and development and no longer leave that responsibility solely to their employers.

> **VOLUNTEER TO DEVELOP**
>
> Michelle aspired to shift from project management into instructional design. She had recently completed her master's degree in instructional design, but it seemed her employer was so happy with her competence as a project manager that it was slow to consider any kind of changes. Taking her career development into her own hands, Michelle took action and responded to a notice we shared about board positions openings in our all-volunteer local chapter of ATD (then ASTD). While she didn't offer a perfect fit for the roles we sought to fill, her intelligence, skills, and can-do attitude were something we weren't ready to pass up. So we created a new board position especially for Michelle. (After all, when the jobs are all done on a volunteer basis, there's no budgetary constraints to prevent that!)
>
> Michelle became our chapter's first director of technology. This allowed her to gain experience as a leader and exposure to opportunities as a go-to person in a professional association—usually a hub for new jobs, new developments, and major industry challenges needing creative solutions. Michelle grew and blossomed in her new role, and as many volunteers do, shifted into other, different roles as they opened. She did all this on the side, without any negative ramifications for her performance in her day job, of course. But even there her growth and new leadership skills were shining through. Soon enough, her employer invited her to transfer into her coveted role within the instructional design team. Thanks to her leadership skills, Michelle eventually became president-elect of the chapter and was promoted to department manager.
>
> Michelle took ownership of her own development, and it yielded fruits that everyone involved enjoyed: She got the role she aspired to (and beyond) in her job while gaining amazing exposure and experience in her volunteer role. Her employer benefited from an upgraded Michelle and, without spending a dime, was able to have a person with the skill set it needed to lead the department. And the chapter benefited from Michelle's volunteer efforts to grow our capacity and serve our members even better. A win-win-win, all led by Michelle, acting as her own career's steward.

Be the Steward of Your Career

You are a startup, and your career is your product. You're the steward of your career.

As LinkedIn founder Reid Hoffman and co-author Ben Casnocha wrote in *The Start-Up of You*, "What's required now is an entrepreneurial mind-set. Whether you work for a ten-person company, a giant multinational corporation, a not-for-profit, a government agency, or any type of organization in between—if you want to seize the new opportunities and meet the challenges of today's fractured career landscape, you need to think and act like you're running a startup: your career."

There's a contract now—part of it still implicit—between employee and employer in terms of the exchange of value. Most people now see their job as much more than just an exchange of effort, time, and existing skills for money and benefits. We all come to work to grow new skills and gain new experiences that add to our personal brand and make us more marketable and more employable. And when they give their energy, time, effort, and skills to an employer but feel like the exchange is not well balanced, they look to make a change either within their job or by taking their skills and efforts elsewhere.

The sooner employers realize this, the better, because people can and need to be developed, even when there isn't a promotion around the corner or there isn't money to send them to training. As discussed in other chapters in this book, there are many ways to help people learn and grow well beyond training.

"In an era of team-centric, flattened organizations, with technology changing whom we work with and how, the [career] ladder is rotting away. The emerging model is the lattice. A career lattice is a diagonal framework that braids lateral experiences, adjacent skill acquisition, and peer networking to move employees to any of a variety of positions for which they have become qualified.... The ladder stifles the creativity and flexibility that workers need if they are to meet the challenges of a global economy" (Cleaver 2012).

Put Your Career in Permanent Beta Mode

We need to see our careers as a product in "Permanent Beta," says Andy Hargadon, head of the entrepreneurship center at the University of California–Davis (as quoted in *The Start-Up of You*; Hoffman and Casnocha 2012). "For many people '20 years of experience' is really one year of experience repeated 20 times," he continues. "If you're in permanent beta in your career, 20 years of experience actually is 20 years of experience because each year will be marked by new, enriching challenges and opportunities. Permanent beta is essentially a lifelong commitment to continuous personal growth."

Nurture Your Personal Brand and Adopt the Value-Creator Mindset

When you have a sense of ownership of your personal brand and your career, you recognize why you must tend to it and why you can't transfer the responsibility to someone else. Any job becomes a temporary station along a much bigger career path that will involve many different employers and/or free-agent independent work gigs and stints. Therefore, at each station along the way, you will have an opportunity to exchange value—to give and receive—in a way that makes the outcome a win-win.

It's very much the trader principle that says as long as there is a voluntary and fair exchange of value and both sides feel like they're getting what they bargained for, then everyone is happy. The minute that the value exchange is uneven for whatever reason, we need to reconsider the formula or renegotiate the terms.

But you're in charge of protecting both ends of the bargain: While you seek to gain opportunities, be sure that you're also delivering on your promise. Don't damage your brand and reputation and create obstacles for future opportunities like promotion, placement on a different team, garnering a rotation, or getting access to whatever you seek next. Strive to create a win-win value exchange.

WHY TRAINING AND DEVELOPMENT PROFESSIONALS NEED TO BUILD A UNIQUE BRAND
James Smith Jr., Author, Speaker, and Coach for the Dr. James Smith Jr. Consultancy

During the late 1990s I began thinking about leaving corporate and starting my own company. I had been a corporate trainer for eight years and I wanted more. I wanted a larger audience and I wanted a different audience. And I wanted to travel. I wanted to be an entrepreneur. I admired myriad trainers and speakers, but my favorite was Les Brown. I watched his videos and his PBS television specials, and listened to his cassettes. Stick a fork in me. I was Les Brown done. My impersonation began. I began to talk like him and walk like him and laugh like him. I even started finishing my sessions with his signature close, but my version was: "This is Nanci Smith's baby boy…"

At some point I realized that I had to stop. The Oscar Wilde quote "Be yourself because everyone else is taken" came to mind. I had lost myself in the Les Brown formula. I decided to go on a Les Brown diet. I had to find myself. My style. My energy. My magic. And my personal brand. I went several years without my daily doses of Les Brown and it worked. I was able to create and build my own, unique brand and style. I used my first name, Jim, and decided that my high-energy style would be called "JIMPACTing." And I set out to JIMPACT people around the world. I even called my company JIMPACT Enterprises. I quickly began to receive plenty of positive feedback and adulation. People would routinely comment on my energy. They thought it was an act, but it wasn't. It was me. As a result, I called myself Mr. Energy. This label and style fit like Spanx on a body. It was natural and perfect. I came to realize that I had been JIMPACTing people all my life—in school, during my training and consulting sessions, at home. It was who I was.

According to Marlys Hanson, MS, and Merle Hanson, PhD, in their book *Passion and Purpose: How to Identify and Leverage the Powerful Patterns That Shape Your Work/Life* (2002),

> Our passion and our purpose are already within us, waiting to be discovered, if we will just take the time to examine our lives and our work. Once we have these insights about ourselves, we must acknowledge their enduring nature. We are not made of putty, waiting to be shaped into whatever the world wants or needs. Each of us possesses a pattern that orients and directs our behavior; it also defines what will be meaningful and fulfilling in our lives. The evidence of this pattern has shown through our entire lives. We need to take the time to identify, understand and act on it.

And that's exactly what I did. And it's what I encourage training and development professionals to do. We must discover and unleash our own personal brand. What makes you unique, special, and different? Study your life patterns. Your personal brand should have three elements: your value

> **WHY TRAINING AND DEVELOPMENT PROFESSIONALS NEED TO BUILD . . .** *continued*
>
> proposition, or what you stand for; differentiation, or what makes you stand out; and your marketability, or what makes you compelling. Get clear on who you are and what you're passionate about before you build your personal brand. It's simply about getting in touch with your inner self (what's true, real, and genuine about you). You can use my James Smith, Jr. 4D Branding Model to create your own personal brand. Start with these four steps.
>
> - Discover: Begin with a little research. Obtain opinions from others to learn how they see you. Ask yourself if that's how you want to be seen. Also, determine what you're passionate about.
> - Decide: Share your research with others. Enlist their feedback and share it on social media. Practice during your sessions and meetings. Determine if it fits. Do you feel your real self coming through?
> - Design: Develop your brand look and your brand signature. People should see it and feel it in your communication, your appearance, and your attitude. You must believe in it! Leverage your look so everyone recognizes it!
> - Deliver: In essence, feature it. You are the CEO of the brand called You. Plan opportunities to inject your brand everywhere. And pay close attention to how you project your brand. How you sound. How you write. How you dress. How you communicate. Your brand should be what you stand for. How authentic you are.
>
> As you're discovering your personal brand, several culprits can hinder your brand development. Don't let low self-esteem, arrogance, poor communication skills, inconsistency, negativity, or inappropriate social media presence prevent your success. Instead, overcome these to evolve your brand. The year 2020 afforded me the opportunity to do just that. While home, like many of us, I spent a great deal of time thinking about my life—where I've been and where I was going. I didn't see COVID-19 coming and my business wasn't prepared for it.
>
> I kept the television on and paid close attention to the coverage of the George Floyd incident and the accompanying social and civil unrest. I determined that I needed to do more—that I needed to use my voice and my privilege of the platform to help with inclusion.
>
> I considered all the research that I'd completed on authenticity and thought about my future and the risks involved. And I decided to change my brand once more. I would begin using my birthname, James, add the Dr. to the front of my name, and focus on authenticity. I'd move from ally to diversity advocate as I focused on leadership, personal power, presentation skills, and DEI, with a stronger emphasis on authenticity.
>
> As talent and development professionals, you have to make a significant, meaningful difference. The world has evolved and changed and so should all of us. The change starts with you. Are you ready to make the shift? Are you ready to create, develop, and fine-tune your personal brand? The world needs people who will take a stand. Our time is now. Seize the opportunity. Create your brand. And while you're doing it, become the best possible version of you that you can.

Make Time for Learning

One way to help you deliver on your promise to yourself and your employer is to take the time to develop yourself. It's an important investment in your startup, your product, and your brand. Lots of people struggle to make time for learning, but learning-how-to-learn expert and author Michael Simmons studied top performers and found that "despite having way more responsibility than anyone else, top performers in the business world often find time to step away from their urgent work, slow down, and invest in activities that have a long-term payoff in greater knowledge, creativity, and energy. As a result, they may achieve less in a day at first, but drastically more over the course of their lives." Simmons calls this *compound time* "because, like compound interest, a small investment now yields surprisingly large returns over time" (Simmons 2017).

According to Simmons, "many widely admired business leaders like Elon Musk, Oprah Winfrey, Bill Gates, Warren Buffett and Mark Zuckerberg, ... despite being extremely busy, set aside at least an hour a day (or five hours a week) over their entire career for activities that could be classified as deliberate practice or learning." Simmons calls this phenomenon the five-hour rule. He says that the five-hour rule typically comprised three types of self-development activities: reading, reflection, and experimentation (Simmons 2021).

Moreover, writes Simmons, "Those who work really hard throughout their career but don't take time out of their schedule to constantly learn will be the new 'at-risk' group. They risk remaining stuck on the bottom rung of global competition, and they risk losing their jobs to automation, just as blue-collar workers did between 2000 and 2010 when robots replaced 85 percent of manufacturing jobs."

Engage in Career and Development Conversations With Your Employer if Possible

Employees should engage with their employer in conversations about what interests them. I certainly teach managers and leaders to regularly have development and career development conversations with their employees, so that they're not missing opportunities and have employees that end up doing it on their own and moving on.

Talent development professionals can play an important supporting role in this effort by guiding managers in their organization to help them realize their role in ensuring that their employees accept ownership of their own careers. To embrace this advisory role, leverage the examples in this chapter. In addition, you can identify and share additional success stories of employees in your organization who exemplified this career steward mentality and how this approach supported their growth and satisfaction as well as the organization's goals. It might also be helpful to create job aids or other support mechanisms to give managers the knowledge, tools, and reinforcement they need to adopt this philosophy and practice.

It's an important option for employees. If you're able to have a transparent and trusting relationship with your supervisor—where you can be open about your career goals and aspirations, what you're looking to learn, and what career moves interest you for the future—then your employer can become a partner in keeping you engaged and happy in your job, and facilitating those opportunities for you.

But, you are not dependent on your employer doing it for you, because ultimately you can and must take charge of your own development.

Personal Development Takes Many Forms, Both Inside and Outside Your Job

When you see yourself as the steward of your career—your startup—it frees you to work on developing yourself anytime and anyplace instead of feeling tied down to your employer's sanction. Engage in development in a goal-directed way, whether it is within or outside of the employment relationship. In my book *Employee Development on a Shoestring*, I suggest 11 different methods for development outside the classroom that people can do when on a tight budget. One of those suggested methods is volunteering, just like Michelle. Volunteering is an activity that anyone can do. You can shape it to your own schedule, needs, interests, passions, and constraints. It's infinitely scalable and yields many types of rewards (Azulay 2012).

You could also develop yourself by acquiring a mentor, becoming a mentor, or seeking coaching—even with a peer. You can serve on special teams, look for job rotation opportunities, and observe or shadow people in roles or places that interest you. These and other nontraining development methods don't require an official program within your organization.

Totally Transferable Skill Ideas

Most professionals develop a variety of skills in every job they hold. Some skills are technical and job-specific, like operating certain machinery or programming certain proprietary software. But many skills are completely transferable to new jobs, new organizations, and even new industries.

Here are five important, transferable skills that you could build now, while still in your current role, to help you on your path to your dream job. Use these ideas to develop your competencies with little budget and limited employer involvement.

Leadership

There is always a need for employees at all levels who can demonstrate the capacity and willingness to lead others in projects, on teams, or in bona fide leadership roles. In episode 143 of

The TalentGrow Show podcast, I described three specific ways to develop your leadership skills inexpensively: volunteering, mentoring, and serving on special teams.

Communication

Another skill that is essential and transferable is communication—both written and oral. There isn't a job in the world that doesn't involve communicating clearly and effectively, and any employer will benefit from new employees who bring with them the ability to communicate well. What can you do in your current job that can help you become a more competent, effective, and confident communicator?

One activity is leading a lunchtime learning session for your colleagues on a topic of your choice. This allows you to speak to your peers in a low-pressure environment because you can present on a topic you have great familiarity with or one you want to learn more about. It can be a short presentation that allows just enough "outside the comfort zone" development without reaching the "panic zone" that might be brought on by a full-day workshop or speaking in front of large or public audiences.

Another idea is to engage in digital storytelling. Become a roving reporter and digitally capture (audio or video recording) hot stories from the front lines, from customers, or from star performers about difficult challenges, workarounds, or new ideas. Then share these stories with the rest of the organization. Leverage this method to develop your interpersonal skills, your interviewing skills, and your public speaking skills.

Finally, develop your written communication skills by taking on a volunteer role that allows you to practice, such as writing a newsletter or crafting website copy for your favorite charity or professional association's local chapter. Remember, volunteering is a great way to practice on someone else's turf while building skills that you put to good use back on the job.

Networking and Relationship Building

Hone your ability to connect with others both within and outside your current organization and build trusting relationships. This practice will allow you to continue to expand your access to information, new ideas, opportunities, and support. You will bring your network with you to every new role, expanding the circle of available supports, resources, and inputs that enhance innovation in your new organization.

It's important to be in the business of building and maintaining bridges in every job, not just not burning bridges when you leave. Become an active bridge maintenance person: Ensure that you connect with current co-workers in a way that you can keep up even when you're no longer in the same workplace. The most obvious form would be ensuring you are linked on LinkedIn, which people tend to keep up to date. In addition, be sure that your own LinkedIn account is not tied to your current work email, but rather to a permanent email address that will stay with you as you shift employment.

You can also set up small, doable daily or weekly networking habits that have you checking up on your contacts. For example:
- Like, comment on, or share their business-related social media updates and posts.
- Introduce your contacts to others in your network whom they should know (just ensure that you make them double-opt-in introductions).
- Share articles that might be of interest. Include a personal note about why you sent it and ask how they're doing or wish them well.
- Send a simple note of appreciation (bonus points for handwritten, snail mail notes, but emails and even text messages will do fine).

Flexibility

In our VUCA (volatile, uncertain, complex, and ambiguous) world, being able to respond in a more flexible and nimble way to unexpected information or changes in plans is a crucial skill. Assuming that a class on flexibility is either not an option or not the best way to develop this skill, you can develop it outside the classroom and on a shoestring budget in at least three ways (Azulay 2012):
- **Self-directed learning.** Read at least three books on change and flexibility and write a summary of the key lessons you can apply from each book.
- **Special teams.** Join an action-learning taskforce where you take on a more observant role during problem-solving and project-planning meetings to understand multiple views and perspectives for each problem. List three alternative explanations to each idea that you think of before articulating your opinion in meetings.
- **Job rotation assignment.** Complete a job rotation assignment in a department or location that is under a lot of stress and pressure to gain a new perspective on organizational issues. Keep a journal of challenges and insights and how you could handle those aspects in the future.

Creativity

An IBM study of CEOs found these leaders thought that "more than rigor, management discipline, integrity or even vision—successfully navigating an increasingly complex world will require creativity" (IBM 2012). Let's go deeper into this idea:

- In episode 7 of my podcast, whole-brain-thinking expert Ann Hermann-Nehdi suggested a way to build the habit of cultivating your creativity. She said to "carve out time in [your] schedules every single week, devoted to [your] own learning development ... make stretching outside your comfort zone a daily habit ... [and] start with something small, even just 20 minutes a day."
- Use Google Image searches as a creativity-building exercise, suggested Annalie Killian in an interview with Center for Creativity's Michelle James for the Creativity in Business Telesummit. In the interview, Killian described a practice she called algorithmic brainstorming: When contemplating a new goal, topic, or question you're grappling with, do a Google Image search on that word or question and see what comes up. Looking at the images generated by Google's algorithm encourages your brain to use both hemispheres as it thinks about the idea: both the linear, logical, linguistic left brain and the metaphoric, imagery-based right brain. It enhances your ability to think creatively about the subject at hand and generate fresh insights. You could also try this kind of search in Flickr's Creative Commons gallery, which brings even richer images than Google. This is especially true if you apply a trick I learned from author and podcaster Tim Ferriss: Click the "interesting" button on your search results in Flickr.

Continue to Pursue Your Development

As long as you're delivering on your performance expectations, you can pursue your own development in a way that doesn't detract from your current job. And if your current employer is unsupportive, you can always do it on the side, like Michelle did.

Additionally, consider taking an active creator role to develop your skills and your brand. According to career and personal-branding expert and author Dorie Clark (2016), "One of the most underused forms of professional development is creating. Many people think of professional development as a more passive form of skills building. But creating content and sharing your insights is a valuable form of professional development on two fronts. First, the act of writing (or giving speeches or making podcasts or creating videos) forces you to crystallize your knowledge into a form that's comprehensible and engaging to others. That sharpens your own understanding and prompts you to think more deeply about the issues."

Second, as Clark (2015) describes in her book *Stand Out*, "One key element of developing yourself as a professional is cultivating your personal brand. When you share your knowledge publicly, your expertise can be recognized—and you'll reap the benefits in the form of new client inquiries, respect from your peers, and opportunities you likely can't yet imagine. Developing an expert reputation doesn't happen overnight, but a steady creation drip of, say, one blog post per week can pay enormous professional dividends within a year or two."

For example, Hassan Osman has successfully built his side hustle brand by publishing blogs, books, and online courses while effectively serving as a global director at a Fortune 100 company. When I interviewed Osman in episode 29 of my podcast, he said his motives were continuous learning and job security: "You just pick up so many skills, from public relations to networking with other likeminded people to learning a little bit more about marketing and how you write so that you grasp the attention of whoever is reading. And so, by building that additional skill set, you can learn so much more, where if you, God forbid, lose your job or get to move on to something that is more exciting for you, you're way more prepared than someone who is starting from scratch."

Jessica Kriegel became a sought-after speaker and author while successfully serving as a high-level leader in a Fortune 100 corporation. In her case, her research and book were aligned with her work and supported by the company. "I'm working on the side project, which is this book that I've written, but there's also a lot of synchronicity with the work I do at [my job] and it's helping [my employer] also be at the forefront of research in generational stereotyping," explains Kriegel in episode 53 of *The TalentGrow Show*. "I've had the opportunity to have enough of an impact within our organization internally that I think they really see the value and have supported the work that I'm doing and the book that I've written, so it's been wonderful, because it's really been embraced."

Eric Barker's *WSJ* bestselling book, *Barking Up the Wrong Tree: The Surprising Science Behind Why Everything You Know About Success Is (Mostly) Wrong*, is based on his popular articles and newsletters curating the science of happiness and high performance, which garner hundreds of thousands of subscribers. Yet he's still working a full-time job at a video game development company. It's not easy, he says, but it's rewarding: "Yeah, it was a big challenge to do that at the same time as a full-time job," Eric recalls in episode 54 of my podcast. "I remember there were a few years there where I would wake up at six, I'd work on the blog until nine, I'd be at work by 10, I'd work until seven or eight. Hours at the video game industry are a little bit different than your standard workforce. They come in a little bit later and they work a lot later. At the end of the day, I'd come home and read until I went to sleep, so that I would have something to write about the next day."

Final Thoughts

The days of putting the responsibility of your development in your employer's hands are over. We are moving into a world where many will partake in the new gig economy, where artificial intelligence will render some of our jobs historical relics, and where jobs will be more like tours of duty and short project-based partnerships, as Hoffman and his co-authors described in *The Alliance*. Be prepared for your future.

You will find tools to help you start to take ownership of your career development on the handbook website at ATDHandbook3.org. All employees must become stewards of their own careers, owners of their own startup, and cultivators of their product and its brand.

About the Author

Halelly Azulay is a consultant, facilitator, leadership development strategist, author, and speaker at international conferences and corporate meetings. In 2006, she founded TalentGrow, a consulting company focused on developing leaders and teams, especially for enterprises experiencing explosive growth or expansion that want a more proactive, strategic approach to leadership development. An expert in leadership, communication skills, emotional intelligence, and authentic networking with more than 20 years of experience, Halelly develops leaders that people want to follow. She is the author of two books, *Employee Development on a Shoestring* and *Strength to Strength: How Working From Your Strengths Can Help You Lead a More Fulfilling Life*. She offers actionable leadership insights and advice on her blog and her leadership podcast, *The TalentGrow Show*. Learn more about Halelly at TalentGrow.com or reach her at halelly@talentgrow.com.

References

Azulay, H. 2011. "Dancing at the Edge of Comfort: How to Develop Employees Without Demotivating Them." The TalentGrow Blog, September 8. talentgrow.com/blog/dancing-at-the-edge-of-comfort-how-to-develop-employees-with.html.

Azulay, H. 2012. *Employee Development on a Shoestring*. Alexandria, VA: ASTD Press.

Azulay, H. 2014a. "Digital Storytelling for All!" The TalentGrow Blog, April 4. talentgrow.com/blog/digital-storytelling-for-all.

Azulay, H. 2014b. "How to Leverage Lunchtime for Learning." The TalentGrow Blog, August 4. talentgrow.com/blog/lunchtime-learning.

Azulay, H. 2015. "Ep 07: Think Like a CEO to Accelerate Performance and Results: Mindhacks for Leaders From Thinking Expert Ann Herrmann-Nehdi." *The TalentGrow Show* podcast, June. talentgrow.com/podcast/episode7.

Azulay, H. 2016. "29: How to Lead Virtual Teams, Write Better Emails, and Grow Your Career by Being a Great Corporate Leader While Writing Books and Blogs on the Side With Hassan Osman." *The TalentGrow Show* podcast, May. talentgrow.com/podcast/episode29.

Azulay, H. 2017a. "53: How to Ditch Generational Stereotypes and Optimize Leadership With Jessica Kriegel." *The TalentGrow Show* podcast, May. talentgrow.com/podcast/episode53.

Azulay, H. 2017b. "54: Science-Based Advice on Achieving Career Success and Happiness With Eric Barker." *The TalentGrow Show* podcast, May. talentgrow.com/podcast/episode54.

Azulay, H. 2017c. "Career Advice: Be in the Business of Building and Maintaining Bridges." The TalentGrow Blog, August 15. talentgrow.com/blog/career-advice-building-maintaining-bridges.

Azulay, H. 2018. "109: [Solo] Why and How to Make Only Double Opt-In Introductions." *The TalentGrow Show* podcast, October. talentgrow.com/podcast/episode109.

Azulay, H. 2019. "143: [Solo] How to Build Leadership Skills Outside the Classroom and on a Shoestring Budget." *The TalentGrow Show* podcast, June. talentgrow.com/podcast/episode143.

Bersin, J. 2018. "New Research Shows 'Heavy Learners' More Confident, Successful, and Happy at Work." LinkedIn Pulse, November 9. linkedin.com/pulse/want-happy-work-spend-time-learning-josh-bersin.

Clark, D. 2015. *Stand Out: How to Find Your Breakthrough Idea and Build a Following Around It*. New York: Portfolio/Penguin.

Clark, D. 2016. "Plan Your Professional Development for the Year." *Harvard Business Review*, January 7. hbr.org/2016/01/plan-your-professional-development-for-the-year.

Cleaver, J. 2012. *The Career Lattice: Combat Brain Drain, Improve Company Culture, and Attract Top Talent*. New York: McGraw-Hill.

Ferriss, T. n.d. The Blog of Author Tim Ferriss. tim.blog.

Flickr Creative Commons. n.d. flickr.com/creativecommons.

Hoffman, R., and B. Casnocha. 2012. *The Start-up of You: Adapt to the Future, Invest in Yourself, and Transform Your Career*. New York: Crown Business.

Hoffman, R., B. Casnocha, and C. Yeh. 2014. *The Alliance: Managing Talent in the Networked Age*. Boston: Harvard Business Review Press.

IBM. 2012. "IBM CEO Study: Command & Control Meets Collaboration." Press Release, May 22. newsroom.ibm.com/2012-05-22-IBM-CEO-Study-Command-Control-Meets-Collaboration,1.

James, M. n.d. "Creativity in Business: Discovery Dialogues." The Center for Creative Emergence.

Pink, D. 2011. *Drive: The Surprising Truth About What Motivates Us*. New York: Riverhead Books.

Simmons, M. 2017. "Why Successful People Spend 10 Hours A Week On 'Compound Time.'" Accelerated Intelligence, August 10. medium.com/the-mission/why-successful-people-spend-10-hours-a-week-on-compound-time-79d64d8132a8.

Simmons, M. 2021. "5-Hour Rule: If You're Not Spending 5 Hours Per Week Learning, You're Being Irresponsible." Accelerated Intelligence, March 24. medium.com/accelerated-intelligence/5-hour-rule-if-youre-not-spending-5-hours-per-week-learning-you-re-being-irresponsible-7815c7ce4a3e.

Recommended Resources

Azulay, H. *The TalentGrow Show* podcast. talentgrow.com/podcast-index

Azulay, H. 2012. *Employee Development on a Shoestring*. Alexandria, VA: ASTD Press.

Biech, E. 2021. *Skills for Career Success: Maximizing Your Potential at Work*. Oakland, CA: Berrett-Koehler Publishers.

Clark, D. 2015. *Stand Out: How to Find Your Breakthrough Idea and Build a Following Around It*. New York: Portfolio/Penguin.

Hoffman, R., and B. Casnocha. 2012. *The Start-up of You: Adapt to the Future, Invest in Yourself, and Transform Your Career*. New York: Crown Business.

Kaye, B., and J. Winkle Giulioni. 2019. *Help Them Grow or Watch Them Go: Career conversations Employees Want,* 2nd ed. Oakland, CA: Berrett-Koehler Publishers.

CHAPTER 38

Implement a Mentoring Program That Works

Jenn Labin and Laura Francis

Learning from others remains a prime way for people to gain knowledge and insights. It's in our nature to want to talk to one another, examine how someone else accomplished a task or goal, and try to put those revelations to work for ourselves as we seek to improve our own skills or expand our own career opportunities. And therein lies the power of mentoring.

> **IN THIS CHAPTER:**
> - Identify three important success factors for mentoring programs
> - Leverage organizational initiatives to identify program purpose
> - Determine the best population to participate as mentees and mentors
> - Describe metrics that can be used to evaluate mentoring program success

Mentoring relationships are about creating human connections where we can share with one another, learn from one another, and develop in ways that we could not do alone. Providing this type of personal and professional development experience to our employees is a critical factor in creating talented, engaged, and productive workforces.

Most talent development practitioners focus on the structural aspects of mentoring programs, such as matching processes or whether relationships are one-to-one or in groups. However, three often overlooked factors have a large impact on the sustainability and scalability of your mentoring program. To implement a mentoring program that works for your organization, be sure to:
- Define the *purpose* of the mentoring program.
- Recruit mentee and mentor *participants*.
- Identify the *metrics* for success

Purpose: What Is Driving Mentoring at Your Organization?

The first step to take is to determine why you are starting a mentoring program to begin with. Is it something your executive team has told you to do? And if so, do you know why? Did you conduct an employee survey to see what people want from your company and found out they wanted mentoring? Is there a development initiative that would benefit from mentoring to support its goals?

Defining the purpose of mentoring at your organization gives you a focal point against which you can design, launch, and measure your mentoring program.

From increasing employee engagement and addressing diversity and inclusion to improving employee turnover rates and building a pipeline of leaders, the purpose of your mentoring program (and the outcomes you hope to achieve as a result) will take shape based on the unique needs of your company.

To help clarify the purpose of mentoring at your organization, consider the following questions:
- What leaders, departments, or functions are requesting mentoring programs? If requests are from specific departments, consider using skills-coaching programs.
- Does your organization experience high employee turnover between six and 12 months of tenure? If so, consider implementing an onboarding mentoring program.
- Does your organization have enough skilled leaders to fill upcoming leadership positions successfully? If not, consider incorporating high-potential mentoring programs or succession planning programs.
- Does your organization need to provide support and development for underrepresented groups? If so, consider starting DEI mentoring programs, such as women's networks, BIPOC resource groups, or veterans' mentoring programs.

Need some ideas to help get your creative juices flowing? ATD's 2017 research report *Mentoring Matters: Developing Talent With Formal Mentoring Programs* found that the top five reasons a company has a mentoring program are to:

- Develop current and future leaders (59 percent)
- Professional development (49 percent)
- New employee onboarding (35 percent)
- Knowledge management and knowledge transfer (23 percent)
- Organization development (14 percent)

Once you have a clear purpose in mind for your mentoring program, it is time to identify your mentoring program participants.

Participants: Who Will Engage With Your Mentoring Program?

Identifying your participants is a critical factor for designing a mentoring program. Define the pool too narrowly, and you may overlook potential mentees and mentors who could benefit from the program. Define it too broadly, and you run the risk of diluting the program's purpose and confusing people as to the overall reason you implemented mentoring in the first place.

The good news is that identifying your participants should flow easily from the work you already did when defining the purpose of the mentoring program. For example, if the reason you want to have a mentoring program is to help retain and engage new hires, then you know that your mentees will be new hires. If you are designing a program to improve skills in the sales function, then your mentees will be anyone in a sales-related role.

From there, you can identify the cohort you think will be best suited for mentoring. Some mentoring programs have clear mentor cohorts—senior executives for succession planning, for example. Typically, mentors are asked to meet certain eligibility guidelines designed to ensure credible and experienced learning relationships. A common example is requiring several years of tenure at the company before mentors can participate in a high-potential mentoring program. On the other hand, you should avoid implementing too many eligibility requirements and ultimately restricting the potential mentor pool beyond usability. For example, requiring years of tenure at the company likely won't be relevant for a DEI-type program. Be sure that any eligibility guidelines, such as tenure or job level, are important for the mentoring relationships to succeed.

Use these questions as a starting point for identifying mentees and mentors in your program:

- What audience are you trying to influence—such as high-potentials, new managers, women in leadership?
- Are there others who could take part as mentees, but fall outside the scope of that initial audience?

- Who is in the best position to help as mentors?
- Is it possible for an employee to qualify as a mentee in the program, while also being a mentor to someone else?
- Will mentees be required to participate (for programs such as onboarding), will specific employees be invited to participate (for select programs such as high potential), or will the program be available for any qualifying employees?
- Will mentors be invited to participate or nominated by others, or will the program be available to anyone interested in that role?
- How will you market and recruit new mentees and mentors into the program?
- Will participant roles remain static or can roles change as the program progresses. For example, can mentees become mentors?

To help get you started, Table 38-1 lists some sample mentee and mentor programs based on program purpose.

Table 38-1. Examples of Mentor and Mentee Programs

Program Purpose	Mentees	Mentors
Onboarding	New employees; matched first week	Employees with 1 to 3 years' tenure
High-potential development	Emerging and rising leaders	Department and function leaders
Succession planning	Next-gen executives	Current executives
New manager development	Employees new to management	Employees with 3 to 5 years' experience managing others
Women in leadership	Members of the women's employee resource group	Senior leaders (any gender)
Black or BIPOC employee network	Members of the Black or BIPOC employee resource group	Senior leaders who have shared identity; allies
Sales enablement	Employees aspiring to or currently in a sales enablement role	Successful employees in sales enablement roles
Cross-functional development	Open to all employees across the organization	Any employees; recommend 2+ years' tenure
Breaking down silos	Employees from across different departments	Cross-functional leaders

Recruiting Mentees and Mentors

While some employees will eagerly join the mentoring program, you may need to spend some time and effort recruiting mentees and mentors. Messaging can play a key role here. Craft your message in such a way that it speaks to each specific audience. Think about the questions potential mentees and mentors might need answered before they commit to the mentoring program.

For example, you may need to let mentees and mentors know the benefits of mentoring and what's in it for them. According to ATD's *Mentoring Matters*, the most frequently reported benefits for mentees participating in a mentoring relationship are:
- Professional development (36 percent)
- Better understanding of organizational culture (30 percent)
- Develop new or different perspectives or awareness of other perspectives (27 percent)
- Personal development (24 percent)
- Increased network (23 percent)

Beyond the top reported benefits seen in the study, mentoring programs have also proven effective in helping mentees:
- Improve self-awareness and career development skills.
- Explore potential in development areas yet untapped.
- Increase company, market, or business knowledge.
- Expand their leadership abilities.
- Increase their technical skills.
- Enhance opportunities for career advancement.

While the benefits to mentees might be intuitive and easy to identify, most practitioners miss the opportunity to identify the benefits mentorships bring to mentors. Clearly linking mentoring program participation with career benefits is a great tool for recruiting mentors—particularly if you expect to have fewer mentors than mentees. The *Mentoring Matters* report listed these top benefits for mentors:
- Develop new or different perspectives or awareness of other perspectives (59 percent)
- Develop leadership skills (49 percent)
- Gain insight into the organization or broader organizational perspective (38 percent)
- Increase professional development (31 percent)
- Increase communication skills (26 percent)

Additionally, many mentors reported the following value received from participating in mentoring programs:
- Share their expertise with another in the company.
- Prove themselves as valuable leaders.
- Expand their professional network.
- Invest in the future of the company.
- Enhance experience in their areas of expertise.
- Cement their role as subject matter experts.

Once your message is prepared, determine how to share it. Participation in mentoring programs increases significantly when individuals receive personal invitations or are nominated. One highly effective way to reach mentors is a cascading recruitment model. In this approach, mentors are invited into the program by someone in a senior leadership role, which adds credibility and a personal touch.

Having a person in a senior leadership role take an active part in the recruitment strategy adds a layer of tacit permission to spend time mentoring and shows that the leadership team is supportive of the program. In addition, most people feel more favorable about a program or product when someone they know and trust recommends it. Having that personal invitation as part of the recruitment strategy can help increase sign-up numbers.

A cascading recruitment process to sign up mentors could look like this:
- Senior leaders sign up to be mentors in the program.
- Those leaders then identify additional potential mentors within the one or two job levels immediately below their own.
- The leaders personally invite the identified mentors to participate in the program.

Engaging in a recruitment strategy like this can help build a grassroots advocacy effort that organically grows and thrives.

The cascading recruitment process can be repeated at various employee levels and adjusted for different audiences as your needs dictate. For example:
- **Middle managers.** Ask middle managers who are mentors to identify peers who would be good mentors. Then have the active mentors invite their identified peers to join the mentoring program.
- **Emerging leaders.** Ask emerging leaders who are mentors to identify potential mentors who are directly above or below them in your organizational hierarchy. Then ask those active mentors to invite the people they have identified to join the program.

Cascading recruitment strategies can also be used to increase your mentee pool:
- **Senior leaders.** Have senior leaders invite up-and-coming employees to be mentees in the program.
- **Peers.** Ask individuals at all levels of the organization who are already active members of the mentoring program to identify and invite peers they think would find value in the program.
- **Immediate supervisors and managers.** Ask supervisors and managers to identify any of their direct reports who would benefit from mentoring, and then have those leaders invite the employees to take part.

Mentoring is a personal learning and development process, so it should not come as a surprise that a personal invitation approach to join the program works well. By showing that you have given some thought to them as future mentees and mentors, you can build goodwill with a growing audience who may later become advocates and recruiters for you in years to come.

Getting Executive Sponsorship and Buy-In

In addition to identifying and recruiting mentees and mentors for your program, another critical aspect of your program's success is identifying those who can act as sponsors and champions for your mentoring program. These are the people who can help secure funding for your program, give your mentoring program credibility and staying power within the organization, and help socialize it to other areas of the business and within the executive ranks. Gaining executive sponsorship and buy-in means that your program receives the funding and support it needs from leadership in the short term and is scalable and sustainable in the longer term.

To get buy-in from executive sponsors, an important first step is making the business case for mentoring. Many executives understand the power of working with a mentor as an individual, but may need to be convinced about the impact of launching a structured mentoring program for the company. In *Mentoring Matters*, ATD's researchers found that the top benefits organizations received from mentoring programs were:

- Higher employee engagement and retention (reported by 50 percent of companies)
- Supporting growth of high-potential employees (reported by 46 percent of companies)
- Stimulating creation of intra-organizational relationships and collaboration (reported by 37 percent of companies)
- Knowledge management and transfer (reported by 37 percent of companies)

Sharing information with executives shows how mentoring affects the organization and business objectives. When trying to gain buy-in from executives and leadership, remember to:

- Inform them of the latest research indicating the impact of mentoring on the area most valued by the organization.
- Present a short vision statement for your mentoring program that is compelling and integrated into the core business practices of the enterprise.
- Ask for their feedback and input on your preliminary thinking, as well as for further discussions to explore the business impact of mentoring in more depth.
- Engage them around their experiences and views of mentoring; you may find that you have an ally already or that they already have assumptions about mentoring.
- Provide preliminary ROI information or other business drivers you are aware of that demonstrate how mentoring is a win for them and the organization.
- Get their input on your business case: Where it is strong, where do they think it needs work, what business drivers are you missing?
- Help them recall their own personal examples of positive developmental relationships that may or may not have been identified as mentoring partnerships.

Once you have secured executive buy-in, get creative about how to leverage their support. Participants in mentoring programs appreciate knowing that senior leaders both endorse and are participating in mentoring relationships. Brief testimonials or comments from leaders add credibility to the program and give permission for people to invest time in mentoring.

Metrics: What Results Do You Need to See?

As with any employee development initiative, your mentoring program needs to track results. The data and metrics you track should be tied to the purpose of your program and the goals and objectives you set for it in the beginning.

For example, a high-potential development mentoring program may have a goal tied to it that seeks to increase the number of diverse, skilled, promotion-ready leaders for key positions by 15 percent. Therefore, you would need to track the participants in the program and their career progression to measure if your mentees are achieving the promotion rates you've set.

In an onboarding mentoring program, success metrics are more likely to involve reducing new-hire turnover. Therefore, evaluating the retention rates of new employees between the three-month and 12-month timeframe is a relevant and measurable goal for your mentoring program. In that case, measuring success would include identifying the retention rate for new hires prior to the launch of the mentoring program, as well as tracking mentees and evaluating how many stay with your company over a set period of time. Comparing these metrics will illustrate a clear picture of the mentoring program's strategic impact.

Understanding the overall strategic metrics that indicate success for your mentoring program is important—however, using a single point of data presents a risk. Referring to our onboarding retention metrics example above, consider this possible scenario:

> The company onboarding mentoring program has been making a significant impact on retention since its launch two years ago. Retention for new employees with less than 12 months of tenure has skyrocketed and almost reached the stated retention goal. However, halfway through year three, those retention numbers start to plummet. Without any other data to refer to, the program sponsor decides the mentoring program is no longer working and dismantles it. Unfortunately, the sponsor missed a key change to the hiring process that influenced the retention numbers from outside the mentoring program.

So, how do you avoid the single data point risk? Make sure to consistently review data from multiple points to tell a success narrative. Track and report data about participation in the program, goals set and accomplished, and participant comments on their relationships.

In the onboarding example, the program might have been saved if program participants were given frequent pulse surveys to assess obstacles, expectations, challenges, and progress. This would have identified the hiring process change so it could be reported as a challenge. And, whether the change was addressed or not, the sponsor would have factored in its impact when deciding whether to suspend the mentoring program.

With all of that in mind, consider tracking the following metrics for your mentoring program:
- Number of applicants to the program
- Number of mentees and mentors accepted
- Number of relationships matched
- Goals set, progress made, goals accomplished
- Participant satisfaction rates
- Employee retention rates
- Employee promotion rates
- Participants recommending the program to peers

Final Thoughts

The most successful mentoring programs have intentionally defined a strategic purpose, engaged mentees and mentors to participate in the program, and identified metrics to track the success of the program. Each of these three factors can have a tremendous influence on the ultimate results of mentoring in your organization.

Clearly defining a purpose is an essential, but often overlooked, step of designing a mentoring program that works. Whether the drivers for your organization are to retain talent, improve engagement, increase skill and productivity, or build support and communities, a clear mentoring program purpose is key to success.

Of course, most talent development practitioners know they need to recruit mentees and mentors into their mentoring programs. However, it is important to be clear about who is eligible to participate in different roles, as well as how they will be recruited. Another key to success is finding leaders across the organization who will sponsor and champion the mentoring program, which adds credibility and momentum.

As with any employee development initiative, your mentoring program needs to track results. The data and metrics you track should be concretely tied to the purpose of your program and the goals and objectives you set for the program in the beginning. Mentoring programs also benefit from measuring these factors at different points in time, and from different perspectives, to build a comprehensive narrative of success.

Building an effective, sustainable, and scalable mentoring program takes more than just a good matching process. Design a mentoring program that works for your organization. You will find a template for the three-step process to guide you through the design of your mentoring program on the handbook website at ATDHandbook3.org. The ultimate success of mentoring programs that work is built from being intentional and clear with program purpose, participants, and metrics.

About the Authors

Jenn Labin, chief diversity officer at MentorcliQ, has more than 15 years of experience in talent development, training, and design. She helps clients to launch world-class mentoring programs for career development, skills coaching, and diversity, equity, and inclusion enabled by MentorcliQ's award-winning mentoring software. Jenn is the author of *Mentoring Programs That Work*, which describes a unique approach to building scalable and sustainable mentoring programs. Jenn's work has been featured in previous editions of the *ATD Handbook*, *TD*, *Chief Learning Officer*, and HR.com. She is a regular presenter at the ATD International Conference, ATD chapters, and MentorCom.

Laura Francis is the chief knowledge officer for MentorcliQ. She has more than 20 years of experience focused on mentoring, writing, thought leadership, and strategic innovation. The proud mom of a child with disabilities, she enjoys writing about the connections she sees in her personal and professional life. Her articles can be found on the ATD website, *TD*, *Training Journal*, *Chief Learning Officer*, *Training Industry*, and on MentorcliQ's website.

References

ATD (Association for Talent Development). 2017. *Mentoring Matters: Developing Talent With Formal Mentoring Programs*. Alexandria, VA: ATD Press.

Recommended Resources

Emelo, R. 2015. *Modern Mentoring*. Alexandria, VA: ATD Press.
Francis, L. 2019. "3 Reasons Why Mentoring Programs Fail." ATD blog, November 15. td.org/insights/3-reasons-why-mentoring-programs-fail-and-what-you-can-do-about-it.
Labin, J. 2017. *Mentoring Programs That Work*. Alexandria, VA: ATD Press.
Moss, S. 2016. "All About Mentoring." *TD,* October 5. td.org/magazines/td-magazine/all-about-mentoring.

CHAPTER 39

Consulting on the Inside: Roles, Competencies, and Challenges

B. Kim Barnes and Beverly Scott

At the time the second edition of *Consulting on the Inside* was published, the world of the internal consultant hadn't changed very much since the 1970s. Suddenly, in early 2020, almost everything about most organizations changed—including the life of the internal consultant. Many of the aspects of the role are still true, but the daily practices have changed in both predictable and less predictable ways. This chapter addresses applications to the post-pandemic organization.

> **IN THIS CHAPTER:**
> ♦ Review the differences between external and internal consultants
> ♦ Learn the requirements, advantages, and challenges of an internal consultant
> ♦ Review a process for internal consulting
> ♦ Consider ways in which the role of the internal consultant has changed
> ♦ Identify opportunities to continue developing the role of internal consultants in the changing world of work

The term *consultant* may raise images of highly paid business consultants from large (or small) firms brought in by senior management to address problems that the organization cannot solve. These external consultants bring the advantages of outsider status and expertise drawn from a wider base of experience—the basis for their perceived value to executives. An internal consultant, on the other hand, has different requirements, advantages, and challenges that need specific roles, unique competencies, and other determinants for success.

There are similarities between the two roles as well as differences. Competent internal and external consultants both have:

- Knowledge of human systems as well as organizational and individual behavior
- An understanding of the process of change
- A desire to be successful and recognized for the value they bring to their clients
- A commitment to learning
- Passion about their work
- The ability to influence and lead
- Skills to analyze needs and design initiatives
- Credibility or authority

It's also useful to consider the differences because each role has its strengths and one may be more appropriate for specific situations than the other. For a comparison of internal and external consulting roles, review Table 39-1.

Table 39-1. Comparison of Internal and External Consulting Roles

Internal Consultants	External Consultants
Are accepted as a member of the group and congruent with the internal culture	See culture and organization with outsider perspective
Have credibility as insiders	Have credibility as outsiders
Know organization and business intimately	Bring broader experience from other organizations
Build long-term relationships and establish rapport more easily	Confront, give feedback, and take risks with senior management more easily
Coordinate and integrate projects into ongoing activities	Focus their involvement on a project with an end point
Have opportunities to influence, gain access, and sit at the table as insiders	Use broader experience to offer credibility, power, and influence
Can leverage and use informal and formal organizational structures	Can avoid or ignore the organizational structure and move around the organization to achieve results
Lead from position and character (trust)	Lead from competence, reputation, and expertise
Know which cultural norms should not be violated	Can acceptably challenge or violate the informal rules of the culture

Internal Consultants	External Consultants
Know the history, traditions, and "where the bodies are buried"	Are seen as objective and not part of the problem
Can take an advocacy role	Bring more objectivity and neutrality
May be expected to be broad generalists	Often seen as specialists with narrow expertise
Have a lot more skin in the game	Can always move on to other clients

Advantages of Internal Consultants

The internal consultant offers unique benefits as an insider with deep knowledge of sensitive issues, cultural norms, and organizational history. External consultants are often engaged for their unique and specialized skills and knowledge, but the internal practitioner has the benefit of intimate, detailed, hands-on knowledge of the organization's business, strategy, and culture. You can download a tool from this handbook's website, ATDHandbook3.org, that provides guidance for you about when to use each.

Internal consultants understand organizational politics, webs of relationships, and details of past history to a degree that few externals can match. Internals can also use inside jargon and language. Their deep, sometimes personal relationships with clients and colleagues build trust and credibility over time. Consequently, internals have an enhanced ability to assess situations and use the right approach with a shorter ramp-up time on new projects.

A second advantage is that internal consultants are active participants in the life of the organization. They are aware of business challenges, customer issues, and management decisions and actions. External consultants often enter the system for a short time to implement a specific solution and then leave. The internal consultant remains in the organization long after the project is completed and can thus follow progress, identify challenges or barriers to the solution, and follow up quickly with members of the organization to support the effort or ensure that actions are carried out or adjusted as necessary. Insider knowledge allows internals to recognize potential links to allied initiatives in other parts of the organization, involve other staff, or expand an initiative to include other issues.

Third, internal practitioners are a ready resource for senior leaders, internal change partners, and employees. They collaborate across the organization, build a commitment for change initiatives, and can give spontaneous coaching or advice. Immediate action may head off a potential problem, defuse a budding conflict, encourage a project leader, or provide needed support in developing new behaviors.

Issues and Challenges of Internal Consultants

Internal consultants' intimate knowledge of the organization and the business makes them valuable business partners. However, this also challenges their role of neutrality and objectivity; they may be seen as too familiar, not capable of providing an objective outsider's worldview. Sometimes they must stand at the edge, operate at the margins, and maintain distance. This delicate balance of having organizational knowledge, yet keeping a marginal position defines the paradox that confronts the internal consultant. Belonging to the organization and finding acceptance helps internal consultants be congruent with their clients, yet they must be cautious and avoid collusion (such as failing to tell senior managers the truth).

Many internal consultants are placed in a middle tier of the reporting hierarchy within the human resource function. Many organizations do not appreciate the value of a strong, skilled internal consulting function. Practitioners may find this status and reporting relationship to be a barrier to establishing competence and credibility, especially with a senior executive. In addition, when senior leaders bring in external consultants to lead change initiatives, the success of these efforts often depend on follow-up work by internal practitioners. Developing a professional relationship with external experts and a seat at the table for major initiatives can be difficult. Internal consultants must show that they are more than a pair of hands to implement projects driven by an external firm. Several conditions will lead to success in such partnerships, while others can undermine them (Scott and Hascall 2002, 2006):

- Internal–external partnership conditions for success.
  - Both parties are flexible and practice open communication with each other.
  - They have a sense of being in it together and share accountability.
  - The organization acknowledges the opportunity to leverage cost, efficiencies, knowledge, and credibility.
  - The external partner recognizes and values the knowledge and skills of the internal partner.
  - The internal partner is open to learning from the external partner and is not competitive.
  - They both appreciate the value of pairing insider knowledge with outsider perspective and credibility.
  - They both respect the organization's culture.
- Internal–external partnership conditions that undermine success.
  - Internal consultants do not have the organizational influence to lead major change initiatives.
  - Senior management does not understand the value of the internal consultant's organizational ties and thus fails to support the partnership.
  - External consultants ignore or go around the internal function, promoting themselves to senior management.

- Internal consultants are left out of the contracting process and thus feel resentful, threatened, or marginalized, resulting in a lack of commitment.
- External consultants are seen as arrogant, exclusive, and judgmental; in turn, internals are perceived as ineffective or incompetent.

Successful internal consultants have access to the hierarchy. However, many internal consultants face pressure from senior-level clients to break confidences, take on unrealistic projects, or make inappropriate changes. Internal consultants may also experience resistance and a lack of cooperation from their human resource peers. While the internal consultants are advocating and facilitating change, their peers in human resources, in contrast, are more focused on protecting and stabilizing the organization. These challenges and paradoxes create conflict and stress for internal consultants who aren't prepared for these challenges (Foss et al. 2005; Scott 2000).

Developing collegial relationships within the organization may present difficulties, due to the confidential nature of much of the work that internal consultants undertake. For example, friendly colleagues may expect them to share inside information. Internal consultants often have to find their best confidants, mentors, and coaches—people with whom they can discuss their concerns and issues to learn and gain new perspectives—outside the organization.

A key part of the internal consultant's role in many organizations is educational—letting others know what they can expect and gain from developing a strong working relationship with them. This is a marketing challenge and may require the internal consultant to help clients and colleagues unlearn certain expectations (for example, that the consultant will fulfill an order as requested) and learn new ones (for example, that the client will be expected to provide their time, energy, and wholehearted support). Initial meetings with new clients offer opportunities to negotiate an effective working relationship and establish realistic expectations of one another. The internal consultant should be alert to other opportunities to promote a broader understanding in the organization of their value proposition and how to best access and take advantage of it.

The role of a consultant, whether internal or external, is dependent on their ability to influence clients, colleagues, team members, and others in the organization. A strong set of influencing skills and a sophisticated ability to apply them in the service of important organizational or client goals are essential to success. The consultant may be called upon to lead important change efforts and take an active role in moving the organization toward achieving key strategic goals. Perhaps the most important challenge any internal consultant faces is that of adding real value by influencing others to take actions they might not otherwise take. However, this may not win them recognition—in fact, if they are successful, as Lao Tzu once wrote, the people will likely say, "We did it ourselves."

Opportunities for Internal Consultants

Despite the challenges, internal consultants have a unique opportunity to exploit their position and have a long-term, significant influence on the organization. Internal consultants' holistic knowledge of the organization enables them to take a systems view, ensuring that organizational structures and processes support the change targets. When they partner with external consultants, they can be multipliers by disseminating and reinforcing expertise and cutting-edge concepts, integrating them into the culture of the organization through their day-to-day work. Using inside knowledge of the business and organization, they can be catalysts for needed change, ensure organizational alignment with the business strategy, prepare employees with skills to cope with forthcoming changes in a tumultuous business environment, and provide candid perspectives as confidential sounding boards for senior executives.

Internal Consulting Roles

The internal consultant, like the external consultant, uses expertise, influence, and personal skills to facilitate a client-requested change without the formal authority to implement recommended actions. The change usually solves a problem, improves performance, increases organizational effectiveness, or helps people and organizations learn.

Being a successful internal consultant requires both process skills and business or organizational expertise. Internal consultants are expected to bring more than their presence, process, and observation skills. They also bring technical competence and content knowledge. Consultants may balance the process or technical roles or emphasize one over the other. Let's review some of the roles an internal consultant might choose (Lipsey and Scott 2008):

- Classic consulting roles:
    - **Doctor.** The consultant's role is to make a diagnosis and recommend a solution. The client is dependent on the consultant to offer a prescription.
    - **Expert.** The client determines what the problem is, what kind of assistance is needed, and whom to go to for help. Then the consultant is asked to deliver the solution.
    - **Pair of hands.** The consultant serves as an extra pair of hands, applying specialized knowledge to achieve the goals defined by the client (Block 1981).
- Traditional organization development roles:
    - **Change agent.** This is the classic OD consultant role in which the consultant serves as a catalyst for change as an outsider to the prevailing culture and external to the subsystem initiating the change effort (French and Bell 1999).
    - **Process consultant.** The consultant provides observation and insights, often at a larger system level, which helps sharpen the client's understanding of the problem (Schein 1988).

- **Collaborative consultant.** This is similar to the change agent and the process consultant, but with the key assumption that the client's issues can be addressed best by joining the consultant's specialized knowledge with the client's deep understanding of the organization. The client must be actively involved in the data gathering, analysis, goal setting, and action plans, as well as sharing responsibility for success or failure (Block 1981).
- Newer consulting roles:
    - **Performance consultant.** The demand for increasing organizational and employee performance has contributed to a role that transcends the traditional description of a skills trainer. This role combines the whole-system focus of organization development with the understanding and techniques of skills training. The performance consultant partners with the client to identify and address the performance needs within the organization and provides specialized services that change or improve performance outcomes.
    - **Trusted advisor.** The rapid pace of change and the complexity of the environment place organizational leaders in unforeseen and unknowable challenges and dilemmas, such as competitive global markets and rapidly changing technology; thus, they must chart a radically new strategic direction for their organizations. Amid this turmoil, they must focus internally on maintaining cultural alignment while still meeting the needs of customers, employees, and other stakeholders.

The role the internal consultant plays in the change initiative reflects four considerations: the characteristics of the consultant, the characteristics of the client, the client–consultant relationship, and the organizational situation. While internal consultants may occupy many or even all these roles in the course of a single week, each one is particularly well suited to certain situations and it is the consultant's job to choose based on these considerations (Scott 2000). Each consideration can be explored by using these questions:

- Characteristics of the consultant
    - What are my interpersonal strengths?
    - What is my consulting competency?
    - What is my technical expertise?
    - How well do I grasp core business processes?
    - How is my expertise relevant to the client?
- Characteristics of the client
    - Who are the sponsor, primary client, and secondary clients?
    - What support is there for the initiative at different levels in the organization?
    - Is the client committed to being involved and participating in the project?
    - What is the client's readiness for change?

- The client–consultant relationship:
    - Does the consultant understand the client's definition of success?
    - Is there a commitment to help the client learn skills and insights?
    - Have expectations been explored and clarified?
    - Has the client's trust been established?
- The organizational situation
    - Are the organization's vision and strategy clear and understood?
    - What are the key strategic needs of the organization?
    - What are the effects of the current market and competition on the organization?
    - What is the focus of attention?
    - What resources are available to support the project?
    - Are other strategic initiatives being driven in the organization? How might they affect the current initiative?
    - What cultural norms and mindsets will influence the project?
    - What are the organizational expectations of internal consultants?
    - What organization needs are not being met?
    - Is the expertise of the consultant relevant to the organization's needs?

Competencies for Internal Consultants

We have discussed the advantages, challenges, and roles of internal consultants. However, the competencies required to deliver the desired results are perhaps even more critical. Competency includes the knowledge, skills, and attitudes (KSAs) needed to be successful. Organizational consulting, whether from outside or inside, requires a sophisticated set of competencies. Many of these are the same for both groups, but internal consultants have a more complex role as insiders with an outside view. Internal consultants report that their success requires consulting competencies that are different from those of external consultants. Table 39-2 shows behavioral descriptions of eight important competencies for the internal consultant. The categories of internal consulting competencies and some of the descriptive behaviors were developed from the results of interviews with internal consultants. While the descriptive phrase might occasionally resemble that of external practitioners, internal practitioners demonstrate the competencies differently because the context of the internal practitioner is different. A self-assessment can be found on the handbook website at ATDHandbook3.org.

Table 39-2. Critical Competencies for Internal Consultants: Behavioral Descriptions

Competency	Behavioral Description
Collaborates with others	• Ensures that interpersonal relationships with clients, peers, and others in the organization are collaborative, healthy, and team-based • Seeks balanced, win-win partnerships • Emphasizes follow-up and good customer service • Is humble, caring, compassionate, and capable of celebrating client's success
Establishes credibility	• Establishes credibility and respect by doing good work, delivering value, and achieving results • Holds high ethical standards and maintains integrity through professionalism, ethics, and contracting • Provides a realistic picture to the client of what is achievable in the time available through clear expectations for the role of client and consultant partners, the degree of difficulty of change, and the approach used
Takes initiative	• Is assertive in taking a stand, delivering tough messages, and pushing for decisions and outcomes • Demonstrates entrepreneurial spirit • Acts to achieve results tied to the organization's goals • Understands, respects, and effectively uses power in the organization to assist clients in achieving their goals
Maintains detachment	• Remains detached from the organization to maintain independence, objectivity, and neutrality • Is not only sufficiently aligned with the client organization to find acceptance, but also able to keep an external mindset to provide a more balanced perspective • Avoids getting trapped into taking sides or carrying messages
Markets the value of area of expertise	• Helps clients and the organization understand the value of the work the consultant delivers to them and the organization • Works toward clarity of roles with other staff units (for example, HR consultants, quality improvement, finance, or IT) • Offers a clear statement of products and services that is distinct from those offered by others in the organization • Clarifies products and services as distinct from external consultants and, at times, manages contracts with external consultants
Demonstrates organizational savvy	• Understands and knows how to succeed in the organization • Builds a relationship with senior leadership and develops an extensive network of contacts at all levels • Leverages insider knowledge to address organizational issues • Uses appropriate judgment, recognizing cross-functional interdependencies, political issues, and the importance of cultural fit • Recognizes the importance of systems thinking
Acts resourcefully	• Uses imagination, creativity, and forward thinking • Is resourceful, flexible, and innovative in using methods and resources • Is not wedded to a specific approach • Takes advantage of windows of opportunity and usually functions with a just-in-time approach to client needs
Understands the business	• Knows what makes the business run and the key strategies • Thinks strategically and leverages support for critical strategic issues • Supports managers in aligning the organization with the strategy

Keys to Success for Internal Consultants

The most critical key to success for an internal practitioner is gaining the trust and credibility of both leadership and employees. Trust and credibility are based on both competency and personal integrity. The credibility of internal consultants, more than any other staff function, is influenced by the integrity, self-awareness, and self-management of individual practitioners. This strong foundation relies on developing authentic partnerships with clients and making careful judgments regarding the client's resistance, readiness to take the risk of change, need for support, ability to lead the organization through transition, and openness to tough feedback. To achieve the successful outcomes internal consultants envision with their clients, they must also build strong relationships with their managers, other levels of management, and peers and colleagues in HR or other staff functions. Building strong relationships requires internal consultants to educate and prepare others to understand and appreciate the role of consultant; take the initiative to understand the others' perspectives; and be strong, clear, self-aware, and self-managing. Misunderstanding of behavior or agreements can quickly destroy many years of effort by the internal practitioner (Foss et al. 2005).

More than the external consultant, many of whom specialized in a limited area of practice, the internal consultant must be a generalist, familiar with and competent in a broad range of approaches and solutions. The internal practitioner must master a wide range of potential initiatives. However, this also represents a potential pitfall. Internals cannot be successful trying to do everything, so they must be selective in offering their services to maximize the benefits of their efforts. By making conscious choices and aligning with organizational strategy and priorities, the internal consultant will add more value to better meet the needs of the organization.

The Process of Internal Consulting

Though similar, the consulting process for internal consultants is different from that practiced by external consultants. It is usually messy and organic; the steps are seldom linear, often overlap, and may require cycling back to repeat or expand an earlier phase (Figure 39-1). The consulting process does not begin with entry as it does for external consultants. It begins with the initial contact with the client and is heavily influenced by the consultant's reputation in the organization. That reputation is as valuable as a popular product brand name, and many internal consultants use it successfully to market themselves within the organization. Internal consultants can help to position their reputation by setting the stage at the time of hiring and negotiating their charter with their managers and most senior potential clients. The ability to manage relationships and the dynamics of living inside the organization is a requirement for successful movement through the consulting process.

Figure 39-1. The Process of Internal Consulting

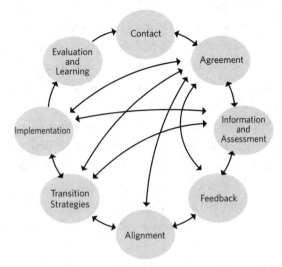

Scott and Barnes (2011)

There are eight phases in the internal consulting process (Scott and Barnes 2011):
- **Contact.** Seek an understanding of the client's organization or business need. Lay the foundation of the consultant–client relationship.
- **Agreement.** Confirm consultant and client roles and expectations, and the actions each will take. Define the need to be addressed and the goal or outcome to be achieved.
- **Information and assessment.** Gather information about the issue, business, performance, and organization. Assess or analyze the data and information collected. Gain an independent view and interpretation of the issues.
- **Feedback.** Provide the client with the information or data; seek acceptance or ownership of the data. Offer a consultant's analysis or interpretation.
- **Alignment.** Seek alignment with the client on the desired outcomes or future state and the approach to be used to achieve it.
- **Change targets and transition strategies.** Clarify which components of the system need to be changed and identify the necessary support and resources. Develop a transition strategy to navigate from the current state to the desired future.
- **Implementation.** Complete the project by providing guidance, coaching, facilitation, and leadership to implement the planned change.
- **Evaluation and learning.** Evaluate the success of the project with the client system by supporting the client's reflection and identification of learned skills, knowledge, and self-awareness. Explore enhanced knowledge, skills, and self-awareness.

Challenges and Opportunities for Consultants in the Post-Pandemic World

The year 2020 forced organizations and practitioners to accelerate changes that were, for the most part, already under way. Remote and hybrid work teams became the norm for most information and technical employees. Most formal learning processes and team meetings now take place via webinar or video. A great deal of informal and formal communication has also migrated to communication platforms and apps.

These changes offer challenges and opportunities to internal consultants who need to help their clients learn to navigate and manage continuing changes in structure and culture. For example:

- Building an aligned community with people who are geographically dispersed or who seldom meet face-to-face
- Creating a sense of fairness and equal opportunity within hybrid teams, where those who are remote can feel isolated from and less important or visible than co-located team members
- Communicating in ways that are memorable and engaging with team members and colleagues at a distance
- Inventing and practicing revised approaches to problem solving, decision making, and other important processes that can work in a variety of formats
- Devising ways to use flexible structures that can change according to individual and organizational needs

Internal consultants also experience their own challenges in this hybrid environment, such as:

- Supporting and facilitating the required changes as organizations and teams become structurally more flexible—moving from remote to hybrid to in-person and back again
- Finding ways to replace the watercooler conversations that keep them informed about below-the-surface issues and interests
- Designing remote meetings and experiential learning sessions that are interesting and engaging
- Developing new approaches that involve remote or hybrid groups in ideation, strategic thinking, and decision making
- Facilitating virtual meetings that build trust and enable the team to address sensitive interpersonal and team issues

There are also new opportunities to explore. Organizations have learned that employees can be trusted to work at home and that they need direction based on outcomes rather than supervision of the process. Technology makes it possible to collaborate across boundaries. Internal consultants can encourage and support these new ways of working and coach leaders to make the changes needed to be successful in this shifting environment.

Many consultants have also found it easier to develop informal relationships with clients given the looser organizational boundaries and more informal settings. For example, meeting someone's dog or toddler on camera can offer a way of becoming more real to one another and lead to deeper conversations about things that matter in the organization.

Because organizations and teams have become more flexible, even shape shifting, internal consultants will be an especially valuable asset to leaders whose roles have changed in significant ways. Internal consultants' work will address the same issues as before, although perhaps in new forms. Stress, conflict, and change continue to create difficulties for leaders who may find it more difficult to know and understand the individual members of their teams when they mostly see and hear them on a screen. Achieving high-quality results remains a continuing challenge, so learning new skills and developing their own and their team members' careers are as important as ever. By educating, supporting, coaching, and challenging their clients, internal consultants have new opportunities to contribute to the reinvention and growth of their organizations.

TD PROFESSIONALS USE INTERNAL CONSULTING SKILLS TO CREATE A PURPOSE-DRIVEN ORGANIZATION
Kimberli Jeter, Founder, River Wolf Group

Although an organization's internal consulting focus may have changed, the COVID-19 pandemic also generated an opportunity for every organization to be introspective and create a purpose that benefits society and the environment. Purpose defines an organization's reason for being and its impact on the world. TD professionals can play an active role to support their organization's purpose using internal consulting skills.

As an internal consultant you need to stay on top of the data, research, and trends related to purpose and stakeholder value to help future-proof the business. Investors, employees, customers, and community stakeholders are looking for organizations to focus on purpose and create value for society. The world needs businesses to take a leading role in tackling systemic issues and complex problems. More stakeholders at every level are choosing purpose-driven businesses over their profit-focused competitors.

Businesses are embracing this challenge, and research shows that purpose-driven businesses:
- Grow three times faster and achieve higher workforce and customer satisfaction.
- Attract and retain talent more effectively.
- Achieve higher employee engagement and productivity scores.
- Spark loyalty by consumers, who are four times more likely to purchase from the brand, six times more likely to protect the brand in a challenging moment, and four and a half times more likely to recommend the brand.

> **TD PROFESSIONALS USE INTERNAL CONSULTING SKILLS TO CREATE ...** *continued*
>
> As a TD professional, you live and work in a purpose zone. Because people and purpose are at the heart of every action you take, the emerging trends in corporate purpose and the shift from shareholder to stakeholder capitalism are no surprise to you. What might surprise you, however, is the vital role you play in the company's purpose journey.
>
> TD professionals understand how aligning individual and organizational purpose can inspire employees, increase productivity and employee engagement, strengthen employee retention, positively influence the customer experience, and ultimately add value to the bottom line.
>
> The C-suite needs you. As a talent leader, you are uniquely poised to support your leaders as they explore the value of social purpose. You know that purpose and people are intrinsically linked. When you apply the tools and strategies shared in this book, you will be able to create a world-class TD organization and serve as a strategic advisor to the C-suite. You can weave purpose throughout the employee experience and leverage the relationships, systems, technologies, tools, and processes to amplify your company's purpose and elevate its impact on society.
>
> In addition, CEOs need your strategic guidance to help them deliver on the company's purpose promise. According to the *2020 Porter Novelli Executive Purpose Study*:
> - 91 percent of executives believe businesses must benefit all stakeholders.
> - 85 percent believe being purpose-driven drives profit.
>
> Sharing research and data such as this can reassure leaders that you have the skills, tools, and organizational means to effectively activate and amplify your organization's purpose. You can help your organization identify, champion, and live its purpose. And with purpose, the organization can leave a lasting, positive corporate legacy.

For internal consultants and leaders, we have a great opportunity and significant challenge to take what we have learned during this difficult period and bring the best of it forward into whatever the new normal becomes. We will probably be more relaxed about where team members are located, even though we aren't face-to-face, especially if our trust in one another has stayed the same or even increased. We will likely offer more online learning experiences that people can attend from anywhere in the world. And we can make our meetings both more efficient and more inclusive.

Having lost the opportunity for so long, we've also come to appreciate the value of meeting one another in person and know how and when that's important. We may also have a better understanding and empathy for team members who are parents or caregivers and work to help them have a more balanced life. Internal consultants will want to reflect on what they've learned about themselves during this period of enforced isolation from their usual colleagues. What new options for working and relating to clients and colleagues have opened up for you? What did you find that you could live and work without? COVID-19 provided a natural experiment to test new ways of working—let's make the most of the opportunity.

Final Thoughts

Internal consultants offer unique benefits with their deep and intimate knowledge of the organization. They are a ready resource to management and staff. Insider knowledge makes them valuable partners to external consultants; however, being internal challenges their neutral and objective role and requires them to manage a delicate balance of having deep organizational knowledge with maintaining a position at the boundary.

Successful internal consultants cultivate trust and credibility as business partners to senior managers, supported by demonstrated competence. Competence includes their professional expertise as well as the unique capabilities required of internal consultants. Knowledge of themselves, their clients, and the organization allows them to choose appropriate roles. Professionals who are committed to successful outcomes for the organization, willing to step out of the limelight, and remain humble and generous of spirit can find rewards and make a significant contribution to the organization to which they belong.

The whitewater we are all navigating now creates new opportunities for internal consultants to contribute to their clients and help shape the nature of their organizations. It's a time of uncertainty and constant change—conditions under which creative thinkers and intelligent risk-takers can thrive. Those who are drawn to the field of internal organizational consulting have an exciting and fulfilling ride ahead.

About the Authors

Beverly Scott served as a consultant to organizations for more than 35 years. She served for 15 years as the director of organization and management development for McKesson Corporation in San Francisco. She is the co-author of the second edition of *Consulting on the Inside: An Internal Consultant's Guide to Living and Working Inside Organizations*. She has served on the faculty of organization psychology at John F. Kennedy University, and as chair of the OD Network board of trustees. Bev also published the historical novel *Sarah's Secret: A Western Tale of Betrayal and Forgiveness*, based on the uncovered family secrets in the lives of her grandparents. You can reach Bev at bev@bevscott.com or on her website, bevscott.com.

B. Kim Barnes, CEO of Barnes & Conti Associates, has more than 40 years of experience in leadership and OD, working globally with organizations in many industries. A frequent speaker at professional conferences, Kim is the developer or co-developer of popular Barnes & Conti programs, including Exercising Influence, Managing Innovation, and Consulting on the Inside. Her books include *Exercising Influence: A Guide to Making Things Happen at Work, at Home, and In Your Community*; *Consulting on the Inside: An Internal Consultant's Guide to Living and Working Inside Organizations* (with Beverly Scott); and *Building Better Ideas: How Constructive Debate Inspires Courage, Collaboration, and Breakthrough Solutions*. She also writes mystery novels with an internal consultant as the protagonist. You can reach Kim at bkbarnes@barnesconti.com or on her website, barnesconti.com.

References

Block, P. 1981. *Flawless Consulting: A Guide to Getting Your Expertise Used*. San Diego: Pfeiffer.

Foss, A., D. Lipsky, A. Orr, B. Scott, T. Seamon, J. Smendzuik-O'Brien, A. Tavis, D. Wissman, and C. Woods. 2005. "Practicing Internal OD." In *Practicing Organization Development: A Guide for Consultants*, edited by W.J. Rothwell and R. Sullivan. San Francisco: John Wiley & Sons.

French, W.L., and C.H. Bell, Jr. 1999. *Organization Development: Behavioral Science Interventions for Organization Development*. Upper Saddle River, NJ: Prentice-Hall.

Lipsey, J., and B. Scott. 2008. "Consulting Skills Toolkit: Roles." OD Network, odnetwork.org/resources/toolkit/consultingskills.php.

Porter Novelli. 2020. *The 2020 Porter Novelli Executive Purpose Study*. Porter Novelli, September. porternovelli.com/wp-content/uploads/2020/09/PN_Executive_Reasearch_Report_9.8.2020.pdf.

Schein, E.H. 1988. *Process Consultation: Its Role in Organization Development*, 2nd ed. Upper Saddle River, NJ: Prentice-Hall.

Scott, B. 2000. *Consulting on the Inside*. Alexandria, VA: ASTD Press.

Scott, B., and B.K. Barnes. 2011. *Consulting on the Inside*, 2nd ed. Alexandria, VA: ATD Press.

Scott, B., and J. Hascall. 2002. "Inside or Outside: The Partnerships of Internal and External Consultants." In *International Conference Readings Book*, edited by N. Delener and C. Ghao. Rome: Global Business and Technology Association.

Scott, B., and J. Hascall. 2006. "Inside or Outside: The Partnerships of Internal and External Consultants." In *The 2006 Pfeiffer Annual, Consulting*, edited by E. Biech. San Francisco: John Wiley & Sons.

Recommended Resources

Barnes, B.K. 2015. *Exercising Influence: A Guide to Making Things Happen at Work, at Home, and in Your Community*. Hoboken, NJ: John Wiley & Sons.

Bellman, G.M. 2001. *Getting Things Done When You Are Not in Charge*. San Francisco: Berrett-Koehler Publishers.

Biech, E. 2018. *ATD's Foundations of Talent Development*. Alexandria, VA: ATD Press.

CHAPTER 40

Becoming a Successful Consultant: From Startup to Market Leadership

Andrew Sobel

Consulting can be one of the most challenging yet highly rewarding professions. Being your own boss, doing meaningful work, choosing exciting projects, and working with organizations and people you respect is satisfying. But there are hard realities too. Success requires that you sell and market your services, that you have a strong network and know how to build relationships, and that you have robust intellectual capital that others value and that draws clients.

IN THIS CHAPTER:

- Identify the six competencies to become a successful solo consultant
- Recognize how strong relationships and intellectual capital lead to accelerating growth
- Identify what it takes to achieve market leadership

I once had a client who had clearly experienced too many internal meetings and too much corporate hierarchy. One day he said to me, wistfully, "You're lucky. You don't have a demanding boss telling you what to do. You get to travel to interesting places and give speeches. You write books. You're always working on some new and different project."

I smiled politely, knowing full well that my client didn't realize how much careful planning, hard work, and commitment has to go into building an independent consulting practice. And on some days, truth be told, I was a far worse boss than his.

To my client, however, it looked easy. It is a challenging journey, and there are some land mines you must watch out for on your road to independence. But you can achieve great success—and hard-to-achieve personal satisfaction—if you follow some basic strategies that have helped many go from startup to market leadership.

So how do you develop and sustain a successful, independent consulting practice? During my own 40-year career as a management consultant, I have built or helped to build four significant consulting businesses. The first two were for a large global consulting firm, where I worked for the first 15 years of my career and served as a senior vice president and country CEO. Then, in 1995 I founded my own global firm, Andrew Sobel Advisors, which has grown steadily in revenue to exceed seven figures today. The fourth is a successful online learning business based on my books, research, and client practice, which has attracted clients from around the world.

Based on these experiences, I have developed a practical approach to help consultants develop, grow, and sustain a consulting business—and ultimately, achieve market leadership in your chosen niche. I call it the practice growth model. It comprises three concepts:

- The six competencies for success
- Accelerating to breakthrough growth
- Achieving market leadership

The 6 Competencies for Success

You must master six major competencies to become a successful solo consultant who is able to sustain and grow a practice over many years. Let's look at each in more detail.

Robust Intellectual Capital

Intellectual capital (IC) comprises the set of frameworks, ideas, strategies, points of view, and analytical approaches that you have developed to help solve your clients' important challenges. These constitute your thought leadership, and they underpin and inform your client work.

Intellectual capital becomes intellectual property (IP) when it is embodied or expressed in a product, such as a how-to framework, assessment, video, or tool. Generally speaking, you can copyright or trademark IP, whereas IC is too general for legal protection.

In a world crowded with lookalike competitors and clients who are overwhelmed with choices, robust IC is essential for setting you apart from the masses. Two keys to developing strong intellectual capital are consistency and freshness.

For the topics you want to be known for, you must create a flywheel effect by writing and speaking regularly. Over time, your recognition will grow. Not least, when clients search for your topic, your name will be near the top of the search results. Freshness means having a new or different perspective on the issues you write about. If you are simply parroting what everyone else is saying about leadership or teamwork, you won't stand out.

Strong Client Relationships

Consultants must not only be able to form enduring relationships with a core group of clients; they also have to earn repeat and referral business from them.

How do you know you have a strong client relationship? Here are six signs:
- **Trust.** Your client has confidence in you, enabling you to work informally and without frequent check ins.
- **Value.** Your client perceives strong value-add from your relationship.
- **Respect.** Your client listens to what you have to say and respects you as a professional and as a person—and vice-versa.
- **Transparency.** Your client communicates frequently and openly and is willing to share their plans with you.
- **Loyalty.** In your area of expertise, your client will always call you first to discuss their need.
- **Reference-ability.** If asked, your client would provide an enthusiastic review of your work. In the best relationships, your clients will actively promote you to their colleagues and peers.

A good consultant needs many different skills, and, frankly, some are the same as what you need in any professional job. I tend to focus on what sets you apart from the crowd around you, not just the table stakes. For example, your analytical skills may get you in the door, but being able to synthesize and engage in big picture thinking will make you truly stand out in your clients' eyes.

There is a critical mindset shift that enables you to develop trusted advisor relationships with clients—the move from expert for hire to client advisor (Figure 40-1).

Figure 40-1. The Expert Versus Advisor Mindset

The Expert Mindset	The Advisor Mindset
"Tells"—talks about expertise	"Asks"—poses thought-provoking questions
Is an expert for hire	Has independence and will push back or say no
Builds professional credibility	Builds deep personal trust
Analyzes	Analyzes and synthesizes—sees the big picture
Is a specialist	Is a deep generalist with both expert depth and business breadth
Is reactive	Is a proactive agenda setter
Has a transition focus	Combines short-term drive with a long-term focus
Accepts narrow client focus	Reframes to define the totality of the problem and the solution

In short, entry-level capabilities include deep expertise in an area important to your clients, analytical skills, being seen as credible to prospective clients, rapport building, and other more general qualities like intelligence and communications skills. But in the client marketplace, these don't truly set you apart from other "experts."

Those who stand out bring something else. They have well-developed questioning skills, deep listening, big picture thinking (synthesis), the ability to go beyond professional credibility and build deep personal trust, a deep generalist knowledge set that adds breadth (business acumen) to their expert depth, and a mindset of independence (enabling them to disagree and push back).

I once worked with a client who was facing a demotion and pay cut from his firm because of a gradual decline his consulting practice had seen over several years. When I first met him, he said: "Andrew, my clients know what I do and when they need me they'll call me." I knew right away that this reactive, expert mindset was holding him back because he was simply waiting for clients to call.

To be a consultant you need deep expertise. But to build great client relationships you need to shed the expert mindset and develop a client advisor mindset. This mindset shift affects every aspect of your day-to-day behavior. When you have an expert mindset, for example, you tend to set a high bar before you see a client—you think you need a great idea and most likely a PowerPoint deck to boot. When you have the advisor mindset, in contrast, you lower your threshold. You know that you can go have a cup of coffee with a client, ask some thoughtful questions, make some observations about practices that are helping your other clients, and have a great conversation.

A Network of Valuable Contacts

This competency expands on the previous one. My research has found that in their careers, most professionals have around 20 to 25 key relationships that really make a difference. And not all of these relationships are with clients. In fact, it turns out you need to think broadly about your relationship capital and consciously develop relationships in several major categories:

- Clients and prospective clients
- Catalysts who can introduce you to others and make deals happen
- Collaborators, which could include law firms, banks, and accounting firms
- Counselors, who advise and mentor you
- Companions, your friends and family who nurture your emotional and spiritual side

If you work in a firm, then your colleagues would be an additional, important category. I call these 20 to 25 individuals the "critical few," and they merit a substantial amount of your time investment in relationship building.

In addition, there are also "the many"—the hundreds of other contacts in your database whom you should stay in touch with using a cost- and time-effective approach.

Try writing down a list of your 20 most important professional relationships. How easy was it to make your list? Are there people on it whom you have been ignoring and need to re-engage with? Do you understand the priorities and needs for each individual? How could you help them achieve one of their goals?

A Compelling Value Proposition

A *value proposition* describes how you add value to your clients. Some consultants mistake their methodology for a value proposition, saying things like "I coach executives" or "I re-engineer supply chain processes." However, I have always described my value proposition—how I tangibly help my clients—as follows: "I help organizations and individuals develop their clients for life." Or a longer version would be, "I can help your company grow revenues by developing the individual and institutional capabilities needed to consistently expand existing client relationships and acquire new clients."

In conversation, it's often effective to follow up your value proposition statement with a short client example. For example: "I help clients dramatically strengthen their leadership capabilities to support their strategic goals. Let me share an example of that."

How you frame what you do for clients can make all the difference. One consultant I coached was marketing her workshop facilitation services to HR managers who constantly tried to bargain about fees due to their limited budgets. After we redefined her value proposition toward helping clients make faster, better decisions, she was able to attract business unit executives as clients and charge higher fees.

Effective Marketing and Sales: A Client Attraction Strategy

There is a big difference between calling on a prospective client to pitch your services and getting a call from someone who says, "I need to speak with you!" Do you want to knock on doors? Or do you want to wake up and open your email to see the subject line: "Keynote Speech Request"?

You should communicate a well-articulated value proposition to your chosen target clients through carefully selected channels. There are several dozen ways to do this, such as through publishing, speaking, newsletters, direct mailings, whitepapers, client referrals, your website, blogging, videos, and client forums that meet regularly.

Once you are in front of a prospective client, you then have to build a trusting relationship. To go from a general conversation to a sold project you must achieve five objectives:
- Build rapport.
- Establish your credibility.
- Understand their issues.
- Go deep and add value to a specific challenge.
- Bridge toward a proposal and sale.

Remember, your goal is to build a *relationship* and create an eager *buyer*, not sell your solution. A key strategy during business development is showing rather than telling. *Telling* is when you say you're the best, provide statistics about your practice, and describe your methodologies. *Showing* is when you share short client examples, best practices, potential ideas, and references with your prospect.

Self-Management and Development

The previous five capabilities require a foundation that consists of what I call your "deep generalist" capabilities. A deep generalist is a professional with great depth of knowledge in their core expertise, as well as a breadth of knowledge about the business world and the markets and industries their clients operate in. Deep generalists can squarely place their services within the context of their clients' business goals, and, because of their breadth, they are able to make creative knowledge connections that others do not. They also connect with senior executives more effectively than narrow specialists. To become a deep generalist you must engage in continual personal development, maintaining a burning curiosity as you read widely and hone your intellect. Because you are basically selling your know-how as a consultant, it follows that regular investment in your personal development and skills is essential.

Accelerating to Breakthrough Growth

Each of these six factors is important. Two of them, however—intellectual capital and relationships—are especially critical and explain a great deal of an individual consultant's success.

To create a simplified view of what it takes to grow a practice, let's apply Occam's Razor to our list. Occam's Razor was postulated by the 14th century English theologian William of Ockham, who wrote that "entities must not be multiplied beyond necessity." In other words, "the simplest explanation is usually the best one."

So, if we combine the two super factors intellectual capital and relationships into a two-by-two square, we get the Practice Growth Matrix (Figure 40-2). Let's look briefly at the four quadrants.

Figure 40-2. The Practice Growth Matrix

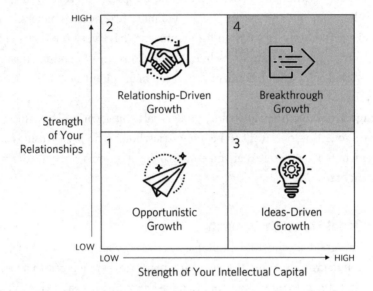

Quadrant 1. Opportunistic Growth

At this stage you are bringing your work experience, education, and historic relationships to the table as you launch and establish your practice.

The challenge: If you don't develop a network of buyers, deepen your relationships, and start to build your intellectual capital, you'll be living hand-to-mouth forever—your growth will be based on opportunistic factors rather than a systematic approach.

Quadrant 2. Relationship-Driven Growth

Often, during the first few years of a new consulting practice, you rely on just a couple major clients for your work. They don't care if you haven't written a bunch of articles, published a book, or developed a three-factor model for remote learning—they know you and trust you and appreciate your knowledge of their organization, your skill, and your judgment. (That's how I got started when I left my old consulting firm 25 years ago!)

The challenge: It's wonderful to have a core group of just a couple relationship clients, but it is also risky to be reliant on so few. If you're just starting out, remember that acquiring one or two clients is a great start but does not constitute a sustainable practice!

Quadrant 3. Ideas-Driven Growth

By developing compelling thought leadership around a topic, you create your attraction strategy. This draws clients to you and makes you appealing to prospective buyers. A powerful idea that you can package into a ready solution for clients can drive very rapid growth—just look at the early days of strategy consulting firms like Boston Consulting Group, whose growth-share matrix and time-based competition concepts attracted many clients, or Bain & Company's work on customer loyalty.

The challenge: Even with great ideas and intellectual capital, you still have to acquire, manage, and retain clients. You also don't want to be a one-trick pony who is so strongly identified with just one management tool or service that you end up being a hit-and-run consultant with a purely transactional client base.

Quadrant 4: Breakthrough Growth

When you combine great intellectual capital with strong client relationships, you can drive breakthrough revenue growth. Your IC gives you a platform to reach out to a broader network with your marketing efforts (a published book, a newsletter, forums, speaking engagements, and so on) as well as the right to charge high fees. In addition, your powerful, core relationships provide a steady revenue stream, a low cost of sales, a referral business, and a testing ground for newer services that a longstanding client will willingly buy from you. In this quadrant, you are also often perceived as a trusted advisor by your clients.

You can approach the breakthrough growth quadrant from either angle—from a position of having deep, core client relationships or by leading with strong intellectual capital—or through an equal blend of both. I actually started out with a relationship-based model and then shifted to an intellectual capital model when I wrote my first two books, *Clients for Life* and *Making Rain*. At that point the pendulum swung back as I built a new set of core relationship clients who had been drawn to my books.

CERTIFICATION IS A HOT TOPIC FOR CONSULTANTS
Sharon Wingron, CPTD, Leadership Consultant for DevelopPEOPLE

As our workplace evolves, and the gig economy heats up, many TD professionals are leaving their nine-to-five jobs to become consultants. New consultants often wonder whether certification in specific instruments is valuable and, if so, how to decide which tools to add to their skill set repertoire.

What Kinds of Tools Are Available?

Most tools used by consultants fall into four broad categories:
- Self-assessments involve individuals answering questions about their own preferences, behavior, approach, or style.
- Team assessments focus on how well a team works together or aligns to key concepts within a model of team effectiveness.
- Rater-based assessments build on self-assessments by incorporating the observations, ratings, and feedback of others regarding an individual's behavior. These are often used for leadership development.
- Organizational assessments are different from surveys because they provide data on how an organization is performing relative to an established framework, such as creativity or employee passion.

You will also find designations available in learning programs, conceptual models, and talent development approaches. Consultants have learned that having a credential in a tool enhances their credibility; selling their program as a certification can also be a nice income generator!

What Are the Benefits of Earning a Designation?

Assessments and other credentials add tools to your toolbox, and credibility to your LinkedIn profile. The more tools you know and are skilled in applying, the more you will be able to recommend the right solution for your clients. As you deepen your knowledge, you will be able to integrate those concepts into your client organizations, creating a more cohesive culture and providing a better ROI.

How Can I Put These Tools to Use?

Tools, such as assessments and learning methodologies, can be used in a variety of ways. One of the most popular is as pre-work for individual, team, management, and leadership development programs. They provide data to base your initiative on, including areas of focus for development. If you choose to administer the tool pre- and post-program, you will have data to articulate progress and form the basis for an ROI analysis.

CERTIFICATION IS A HOT TOPIC FOR CONSULTANTS *continued*

How Do I Decide Which Tool to Pursue?

Answering several questions will help you determine which tools to pursue. Consider this checklist as a starting point:
- What type of work do I specialize in?
- How will this tool fit into my areas of focus and other offerings?
- What is the reputation of the company?
- What is the research behind the tool?
- Is the tool valid and reliable?
- What materials and support come with the certification?
- What type of training and support is provided post-certification?
- What rights will I have for marketing my certification?
- Do I have a market already developed for using this tool?
- Do I have a client or project willing and able to pay for my certification?
- How frequently will I have an opportunity to use the tool?

Answering these questions provides direction for selecting a tool that will be useful for your clients and add an appropriate dimension for your offerings.

Achieving Market Leadership

Solo practices can develop through four phases:

- **Startup.** You are just finding your first clients and trying to get established as a solo practitioner.
- **Sustainability.** Here, you bridge the gap between starting with a few projects for one client and having a sustainable practice based on multiple clients and a variety of projects. This can happen in the first year or it might take a couple years.
- **Market penetration.** At this stage you further expand your practice and build a long-term network of past, present, and prospective clients. You have achieved strong capability in most, if not all, six competencies described earlier.
- **Market leadership.** If you make it to this stage—and not everyone does—you become an acknowledged thought leader and a leading practitioner in your chosen market niche. Often, this does not occur until later in your career, simply because it takes time to build up a body of work and cultivate the lifelong network of relationships that support a position of market leadership. However, by focusing on and investing in the development of your core competencies, you can reach market leadership more rapidly—it can happen in years, not decades. Well-chosen investments in yourself will always have a significant payoff.

We can take these four stages of practice development and overlay them on the practice growth matrix (Figure 40-3) to show how much you need to develop your relationships and IC to progress toward market leadership.

Figure 40-3. Phases of a Solo Practice

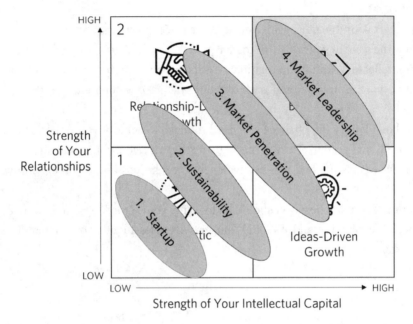

Do You Have the Right Mindset?

There is one final thing that is essential if you want to work as an independent professional—I call it the mindset of independent wealth. Some years ago, I was interviewing a CEO of a $20 billion telecommunications company for one of my books. I'll never forget what he said to me: "You know, Andrew, I wish all of my advisors were independently wealthy. That way, I'd know that they are putting my agenda first, being truly objective about my issues, and always telling me the straight story without regard to financial outcomes."

You may not be independently wealthy, but you can cultivate a similar mindset regardless of your economic condition. This requires three things:

- You need to treat your clients like a peer (not look up to them or down at them).
- You must never have the clock running—you have to be completely in the moment when you're with a client.
- You need to exude enthusiasm and passion for your work (we all love enthusiasm—it's contagious).

If you exemplify these behaviors, you'll have an attractive aura that draws clients closer. After all, aren't these the very same qualities that would attract you to someone else in your professional life? If you embody the mindset of independent wealth, you'll have a centered quality that will serve you well in every aspect of your professional practice.

Final Thoughts

I suggest you start your journey by answering these basic questions:
- What is the state of your practice today?
- What intellectual capital and relational assets do you have that you can build on?
- What are your aspirations and goals for your practice development over the next three years?

You can then identify the changes you need to make to achieve your goals. Does your value proposition need sharpening? Do you need to further develop your thought leadership? Are you reaching out to existing and prospective clients regularly? Should you expand your service offerings?

To better understand where you should be focusing your efforts right now, download the Six Competencies Assessment at andrewsobel.com/growth-assessment or on the handbook website, ATDHandbook3.org.

About the Author

Andrew Sobel is the leading authority on the strategies and skills required to earn lifelong client loyalty and build trusted business relationships. He is the most widely published author in the world on this topic, with nine acclaimed books that have been translated into 21 languages. His books, which focus on earning clients for life as a trusted advisor, include *It Starts With Clients* and the international bestsellers *Clients for Life* and *Power Questions*. As founder and CEO of the international consulting firm Andrew Sobel Advisors, he has advised many of the world's leading companies on their client development and growth strategies. For more information and to contact him, visit andrewsobel.com.

Recommended Resources

Sobel, A. n.d. "Andrew Sobel's Learning Academy." learning.andrewsobel.com.

Sobel, A. n.d. "Knowledge Archive." andrewsobel.com/articles.

Sobel, A. 2009. *All for One: 10 Strategies for Building Trusted Client Partnerships*. Hoboken, NJ: John Wiley and Sons.

Sobel, A. 2020. *It Starts With Clients: Your 100-Day Plan to Build Lifelong Relationships and Revenue*. Hoboken, NJ: John Wiley and Sons.

Sobel, A., and J. Panas. 2012. *Power Questions: Build Relationships, Win New Business, and Influence Others*. Hoboken, NJ: John Wiley and Sons.

CHAPTER 41

Building Teams and Understanding Virtual Teamwork

Tammy Bjelland

Teamwork in the digital age requires intentional planning and changes to ensure the outcomes desired. Virtual teamwork requires that you clarify the characteristics of teams whose members may not be colocated, embrace the value of documentation, and be aware of challenges that virtual teamwork incurs.

> **IN THIS CHAPTER:**
> - Describe four critical characteristics of effective teams in an increasingly digital workplace
> - Identify solutions to common challenges in teams

It feels great to be part of a productive team, and, of course, the opposite is also true. While it may seem logical to chase that good feeling by focusing on team-building activities, sometimes more action is necessary. While team-building activities have their place, it's important to first establish the foundations of team success with documentation, especially when teams are dispersed across distance, time, and function.

That great feeling of being part of a high-functioning team doesn't happen by accident—it happens because the team has established a solid structure and clear expectations that allow people to thrive. You need to understand the characteristics of effective teams in an increasingly digital workplace, enable effective teamwork by building a culture of documentation, and identify solutions to common challenges. These concepts are relevant for both new and seasoned teams, as well as for teams you are part of and teams you are supporting.

However, note that overhauling an entire team's way of being may not be realistic or feasible. If your role doesn't have the authority to fully change your team's ways, you can instead make an immediate impact through tiny actions you can implement within a day or a week to make an immediate impact. Get your whole team involved by asking them to commit to their own tiny actions—the collective impact of these small shifts will be more than if you were to attempt sweeping changes on your own without commitment from everyone.

Modern Teams

Modern teams are flexible, mobile, and nonpermanent. Gone are the days when you were on a single team for a long period of time—the current reality of work is that we are on many teams, with multiple purposes, and for different lengths of time. You may be on a function-based learning team, but also collaborate closely with a human resources team for certain projects or initiatives. As a talent development professional, not only are you on your own team, but you're also likely to support other teams by providing learning experiences and programs aimed at improving collaboration skills and team dynamics. The mutable nature of modern teams means that collaboration is more complex, and with added complexity comes increased potential for challenges.

Heavy dependence on technology to allow collaboration at a distance, combined with the probability of a workforce that is 25 to 30 percent remote multiple days a week, means that you are almost guaranteed to work on a virtual team at some point in your career (Lister 2020). If you use technology to collaborate with someone who does not work in the same office as you, you are part of a virtual team. Not only that, but you will also likely experience virtual distance, which is "a measurable social and emotional disconnect (conscious or unconscious) that arises when we increasingly rely on digitally mediated communication technology" (Lojeski and Reilly 2020).

One of the best ways to prepare for working on a virtual team is to act like you already do. By following virtual team best practices even if your team is hybrid (some members virtual and some in the office), you'll build a team that is prepared to succeed no matter the team makeup or external circumstances that threaten the continuity of its activities.

Teams can be defined by the duration of their existence, their function, and even by the geographical location or distance among team members. Defining a team in these terms helps to set expectations about purpose, people, processes, and performance (Table 41-1).

Table 41-1. Types of Teams

Duration	Temporary	Teams that work for a short, defined period
	Project-based	Teams that work on a defined project
	Long-term	Teams that work together for an extended, sometimes undefined, period
	Permanent	Standing teams or teams that work together indefinitely
Function	Departmental (or functional)	Teams of people from the same department who meet on a regular basis
	Cross-functional	Teams made up of people from different functions or departments to achieve a goal or solve a problem
Location	Multiregion	Team members come from more than one region or multiple time zones
	Global	Team members come from more than one country
	Virtual	Team members use technology to work together digitally
	Hybrid	Team members are both virtual and in person

Characteristics of Effective Teams

Members of effective teams have a sense of belonging and connectedness to one another and to the team's purpose. Effective team members take four actions to ensure a successful partnership:
- Create a foundation of trust.
- Commit to team documentation to ensure equal access to shared knowledge.
- Ensure clarity for accomplishing tasks.
- Practice balanced team communication.

In virtual or hybrid teams, establishing these characteristics is more difficult than in traditional, office-based teams. This is because teams tend to default to the methods they are used to relying on, such as in-person communication and other behaviors, to connect, build trust, and stay informed.

When office-based practices take precedence, teams risk alienating and isolating not just remote team members, but also other team members who are not able to participate in these practices on a regular basis. Make it a habit to ask yourself, and your team, whether the team's behaviors and processes make it possible for everyone, regardless of location, to thrive.

Create a Foundation of Trust

Trust is the foundation of success in any interpersonal relationship. One way to look at trust in teams is to consider two dimensions: task-based trust and relationship-based trust. Task-based trust is how you can delegate responsibilities within in a team and believe that each person will follow through. Relationship-based trust refers to whether you're comfortable sharing that a crisis in your personal life has had an impact on your well-being, because you know you won't be penalized for your disclosure (Table 41-2). Modern teams need indicators of both dimensions; however, the exact mix of indicators will depend on factors like individual working preferences and culture (Meyer 2014).

Table 41-2. Example of Virtual-Friendly Processes and Rituals

Task-based trust	• Tasks and action items are assigned using a project management tool; task owners are responsible for updating the task watchers on progress • Share daily priorities and blocks via an internal chat channel
Relationship-based trust	• Team members share energy levels with one another using a simple stoplight activity (green = high energy, focused; yellow = neutral; red = low energy, unfocused) • Every two weeks, randomly assign partners to meet up for a casual conversation • Devote a channel to nonwork topics, using random, team-member-generated prompts to drive discussion and sharing

Office-based work cultures often prioritize face-to-face interactions because they believe that is the only way to develop trust. However, this mentality keeps teams from developing more inclusive practices that allow remote or part-time members to develop trust on an ongoing basis. It's important for teams to intentionally design ongoing processes and rituals that allow all team members, regardless of location, to participate.

Earlier in this chapter I mentioned "tiny actions" that you can take to build your team, no matter what your team-member role. This chapter presents several tiny-action ideas you can take, starting with this check-in activity.

> **TINY ACTION**
>
> During a live session, use this check-in and anonymous voting features to identify any gaps you need to work on. For each of the seven statements, indicate your level of agreement on a 1-5 scale, with 1 representing "disagree" and 5 "agree."
> - We trust one another.
> - Everyone is in the loop when it comes to discussions and decisions.
> - Our teammates are connected to one another.
> - We feel connected to our work.
> - We have autonomy over our work and schedule.
> - Team members have the same experience regardless of where they are located.
> - I know what is expected of me.

Commit to Team Documentation

Effective teams document everything, and that documentation is consistent, accessible, and useful. Having thorough documentation prevents miscommunication, misalignment, and unproductive conflict. Documentation of decisions, work history, processes, and tasks enables teams to work without having to rely on getting information from other people.

When we minimize our reliance on others, we can:
- Decrease interruptions.
- Make quicker progress on projects.
- Onboard new people more quickly.
- Reduce information silos.
- Create more consistent outcomes.
- Save time by not repeating discussions.

This also levels the playing field for all team members because they can access and use information as needed, instead of having to depend on being able to contact someone else. Everyone has the knowledge they need to perform and their performance stays visible to others.

Additionally, it is not enough just to share expectations and assume team members will interpret those expectations in the way they were intended. As a team member or leader, you need to confirm clear and accurate understanding by asking team members to state what they heard. Provide ample opportunity for feedback and clarifying questions.

The Right Amount of Documentation

There is also such a thing as too much information. If there are too many places we need to update, too much reading to do, too many meeting minutes, and too many meetings, people will just stop paying attention. Your team needs to determine the right balance of documentation so members can quickly access the information they need.

One option is to adopt a single source of truth (SSoT) approach to documentation. SSoT is a concept from information systems design, which we can reframe to represent a single place that houses all the information you need to know about a certain topic. This is helpful because, when implemented correctly, it reduces or eliminates the chance that duplicate information will exist in multiple places. It also eliminates information silos.

The SSoT is where you go when you have questions about how to perform a process, want context, or need to ask a question. Adopting an SSoT framework can help alleviate the feeling of documentation overload. However, remember that an effective SSoT relies on people setting and following clear expectations and guidelines for its use and updates.

What documents does a team need? Effective teams use team agreements, user manuals, communication charters, performance expectations, agendas, meeting notes, and so on. Team documents should be clear, accurate, and complete. They should have single-person ownership and provide links when possible. For a complete list of essential team documents, visit the handbook website at ATDHandbook3.org.

> **TINY ACTION**
>
> Choose an essential team document and make a plan for creating or updating one for your team.

Practice Accountability

Of course, the idea of documentation is one thing—the practice of documentation is another. One reason that teams fail to document effectively is because documentation takes work, both upfront and ongoing. Team members need to be committed to documentation and accountability for reading the documentation that is developed.

Help your team practice a habit of responding to questions by also referencing where to find the answer, when possible. Or, simply point them to the SSoT to find the answer. If it has not yet been documented, use the process you developed as a team to answer the question and then include that in a findable location.

Find ways to keep team members accountable for updating and reading documentation. For example, you could:

- Add fun to a meeting or a channel with a quiz on your team's documentation practices.
- Have an information location challenge where team members race to find answers to questions.
- Add contributing to and reading documentation to individual deliverables and tasks.
- Add documentation KPIs to performance goals.

> **TINY ACTION**
>
> If someone asks you a question and the answer is documented, share that documentation in your response. Creating a habit of answering with documentation trains others to remember there are readily available answers to many questions if they know where to look.

While it may seem as if a focus on documentation would make it hard for teams to adapt quickly, the opposite is actually true, because constraints are valuable for creativity and innovation (Acar et al. 2019). When the essential components of teamwork are well documented, members are free to channel their time and energy into developing valuable connections and fostering creativity and innovation. Framing documentation this way can generate buy-in from team members to commit to more consistent practices.

Ensure Clarity for Accomplishing Tasks

Whether you are standing up a new team or developing one you already have, aligning on key definitions and expectations is crucial to getting work done. The primary elements that need to be explicitly defined are purpose, people, process, and performance.

Purpose

The first step to building an effective team is to identify its purpose. Looking backward is helpful in designing effective learning experiences as well as building effective teams—think of the desired outcomes of the team's activities and how you determined success. These are examples of team purpose:

- Improve data collection and analysis across a function.
- Deliver client services.
- Create a marketing campaign.

In addition to driving the team's focus, clearly articulating their purpose will help team members understand how their efforts contribute to the goal. When they can see how their work directly influences a greater purpose, team members are more likely to be engaged and satisfied in their work (Pink 2011).

People

Once the purpose of the team is clearly defined, you can accurately identify the people who need to be on the team to accomplish the goal. The people on the team should have the right mix of skills and other attributes that will enable them to complete the goal.

Processes

The processes of a team determine how the work gets done. Defining workflows and rituals gives clarity to team members on how they should be completing their tasks.

Performance

Team performance refers to how successful the team is in achieving its purpose. Defining standards for performance lets team members and other stakeholders know when they have achieved their goal or missed the mark. This allows them to stop, assess, and possibly change course.

Virtual teams sometimes struggle with articulating what performance looks like because they can't rely on the visual cues they would see in the office. When this happens, it is a signal that the team is measuring input rather than performance. Virtual teams and in-office teams alike benefit from evaluating performance based on output instead of input.

> **TINY ACTION**
>
> Use the scale below to inventory team members' expectations for the four main elements of a team: purpose, people, processes, and performance. How does your team rate for each category?
> - 1: Expectations are not existent.
> - 2: Expectations are vague.
> - 3: Expectations are clear.
> - 4: Expectations are explicit.

Practice Balanced Team Communication

You send a message to a team member requesting some information. Time goes by—minutes, then hours. It's now the next day. You wonder: Did they see the message? Should I follow up? When?

Has this ever happened to you? Or, have you been in the other person's shoes?

You receive a message requesting some information. You're in a meeting and then you've blocked off time for deep work because you have to finish a deliverable by the end of the day. These are all high-priority tasks.

Miscommunication, inconsistency, and mismatched expectations when it comes to response times all wreak havoc on team dynamics. Setting clear expectations for all communication can help prevent these problems from occurring.

Teams use an average of three communication channels to communicate (Mazareanu 2020), although with the current, rapid adoption pace of tools, it's likely you're using many more platforms to communicate with your team. (I once worked with a team that used more than 100 tools to perform their work.) These channels all need to be updated and checked regularly. Too often, multiple communication platforms are used the same way, which creates a heavy burden on the receiver of all those messages because they then have to filter through multiple inputs before they can determine how to respond.

Instead of using multiple communication tools that do the same thing, create a practice of matching the message type to the correct communication channel. Start by categorizing types of messages or communication and the urgency of response they typically require. Use Table 41-3 as a guide for your team.

Table 41-3. Communication Team Guide

Priority Level	Expected Response Time	Communication Channel	Example Communication
Urgent	Immediately	Phone	Issues relating to customers' ability to access their accounts
High	Within 1 business day	Email	Communication related to sales
Normal	Within 2 business days	Slack	Project updates
Low	Response not required	Email	Informing team members of schedule changes

Make sure these definitions are documented in a communication charter, which is another essential team agreement. The communication charter should also describe in detail what the expectations and uses are for each communication channel. See the example communications charter for Zoom meetings in Table 41-4.

Table 41-4. A Sample Communication Charter for Zoom Meetings

Using Zoom	Expectations
Internal meetings	• Encourage cameras on, but cameras can be turned off if it's a recurring meeting, there are bandwidth issues, or in other circumstances. • Mute yourself if you are not talking. • Use the reactions menu to indicate when you would like to talk. • Do not take meetings if you are driving.
External meetings	• Cameras should be on. • Mute yourself if you are not talking. • Use the reactions menu to indicate when you would like to talk. • Do not take meetings in a location that is not suitable for cameras to be on.

Additionally, avoid ambiguity by setting expectations. For example, set standards for how team members should:
- **Acknowledge receipt.** How and when should the receiver indicate that they have received the message and will respond according to the expectations outlined in the communication charter?
- **Close the loop.** How should the receiver and sender signal that the issue is resolved?
- **Follow up.** How and when should the sender follow up if they have not received a response?

You can, for example, set the expectation that everyone needs to acknowledge receipt of a message within four hours. The receiver then knows that while they have to acknowledge receipt, they can continue to focus on their priorities. And neither team member has to spend extra mental energy to figure out what to do in the situation. This may seem like a small gain, but small gains add up over a day and the overall impact on the team is substantial.

> **TINY ACTION**
>
> When you send a message to someone, include your expectations for when they should respond, as well as when to expect a follow-up from you if they do not respond as expected.

Dysfunctional Teams

A dysfunctional team is one that is experiencing conflicts or situations that have a negative impact on the team's goals or team member engagement and satisfaction. Every team will experience conflict of some kind—this does not inherently mean that the team is dysfunctional. However, it is appropriate to classify a team as dysfunctional if it fails to function and fails to meet its purpose. When conflicts are ignored or left unresolved, they become systemic, which contributes to long-term problems.

Team issues can usually be traced to problems with the purpose (the work does not align with the purpose), people (interpersonal conflict), process (workflows are not accurately defined), and performance (the team did not meet its objectives).

There are several symptoms of dysfunctional teams, and each can be addressed as discussed here.

Burnout

Burnout looks like:
- People working more hours than they should
- Exhaustion

- Increased and prolonged feelings of stress
- Tension among co-workers
- Complaining of uneven or unfair distribution of work
- Team members feeling like they must be always on
- Working on the weekends or after hours
- Responding to every message immediately
- Spending too much time in back-to-back meetings

What causes it: Burnout occurs from overworking and failing to set and maintain boundaries.

How to address it: Teams can address burnout by establishing a boundaries agreement. Overworking can be prevented by assessing the workload and communication expectations for each team member and reallocating resources when necessary. The boundaries agreement serves multiple purposes—it is an opportunity for the team to have an open dialogue about what boundaries look like and how they should respond when their boundaries are stretched.

Spending too much time in unnecessary meetings can breed frustration and wasted time. Improve your team's balance of synchronous and asynchronous communication to reduce meeting time, interruptions, and the need to respond immediately to all requests. Virtual teams are especially prone to burnout because remote employees tend to work longer hours and may find it more difficult to maintain healthy boundaries between their work and personal lives (DeFilippis et al. 2020).

Isolation

Isolation looks like:
- Team members are withdrawn and disconnected.
- Team members don't seem engaged or like they care about their work.
- Team members feel like they are out of the loop.

What causes it: There are two types of isolation: social isolation and information isolation. Social isolation occurs when one or more people are disconnected from a group. Information isolation is when people are disconnected or lack access to information.

Both types of isolation can be caused by distance bias, which is the tendency to assign greater value to people and events that are close to us in space or time (Lieberman et al. 2015). In virtual teams, distance bias can result in unequal distribution of recognition and opportunities, as well as people being excluded from discussions, decision making, and access to information. Social isolation can also be caused by not allocating resources to permit team members to develop meaningful connections.

How to address it: As a cognitive bias, distance bias is likely to happen more unconsciously than consciously—but just because a bias is not intentional does not mean that the impact is any less harmful. All team members should be aware of distance bias and recency bias and how they influence team dynamics. Recognizing these natural biases allows teams to build processes and systems that prevent them from affecting team dynamics.

To combat social isolation, reserve some synchronous meeting time for developing meaningful connections. If your schedule is already meeting-heavy, convert meetings that focus on information sharing or updating to asynchronous formats.

Micromanagement

Micromanagement looks like:
- Managers expecting nonstop updates from team members
- Team members focusing more on pleasing the boss than doing their work
- Managers taking credit for everyone's successes
- Team members being afraid to speak out

What causes it: Managers that don't trust their employees to do their work become micromanagers. This is magnified in virtual teams, because micromanagers rely on visual cues of work input (like arrival and departure times or people being at their desks) and don't believe their employees are working if they can't see them.

How to address it: Curing micromanagement involves a three-pronged approach:
- Dive into wider cultural issues that foster micromanagement. Take time to create a culture canvas to align the values of your team and how those values are reflected in team behaviors. During the team's conversation on values, discuss any gaps that are uncovered and how to address them. Use the check-in activity described earlier to take the pulse of your team on an ongoing basis.
- Document expectations and feedback. Setting clear expectations for work products can alleviate the need to micromanage.
- Dedicate resources to developing effective management and leadership skills. Preference for micromanagement is a product of both environmental and individual factors. Some managers, even in organizations with high levels of trust and solid documentation practices, still resort to micromanaging because it's what they know. Provide those managers with training to help them develop the attitudes they need to trust and foster trust in their team.

Low Performance

Low performance looks like:
- Missing deadlines
- Making mistakes
- Low productivity

What causes it: Low performance can be a product of other symptoms of dysfunctional teams, like burnout or isolation. It can also be caused by an issue involving one of the team foundations. For example:
- The team no longer understands or feels connected to the mission (purpose).
- The team does not have the right people (or the right number of people) to do the work (people).
- The processes may not be working as intended (process).
- The metrics for success may be out of date (performance).

How to address it: Revisit the team charter and performance expectations to see if there is a discrepancy in the team's purpose, people, processes, or performance. If those expectations still align with the goals, refer to the solutions suggested in the sections on isolation or burnout.

Final Thoughts

Building effective teams in the digital age requires the intentional design and modification of the structures that enable the outcomes you want. These desired outcomes include measurable outcomes like productivity and performance as well as less tangible ones like diversity of thought and that good feeling of being part of a great team. By defining the characteristics of effective teams in a virtual context, committing to a culture of documentation, and recognizing the signs and solutions for common challenges, you'll be prepared to support your team's success in any circumstance.

About the Author

Tammy Bjelland is the founder and CEO of Workplaceless, a training company that improves remote and hybrid team effectiveness by developing the capabilities that workers, managers, and executives need to succeed in distributed environments. With her background in higher education, publishing, EdTech, e-learning, and corporate training, Tammy is committed to driving and supporting the future of work by developing people. She holds a BA and an MA from the University of Virginia and is a Certified Professional in Talent Development and Certified Master Trainer from the Association for Talent Development. She lives in Winchester, Virginia.

References

Acar, O., M. Tarakci, and D. van Knippenberg. 2019. "Why Constraints Are Good for Innovation." Harvard Business Review, November 22. hbr.org/2019/11/why-constraints-are-good-for-innovation.

DeFilippis, E., S. Impink, M. Singell, J. Polzer, and R. Sadun. 2020. "Collaborating During Coronavirus: The Impact of COVID-19 on the Nature of Work." National Bureau of Economic Research, July. nber.org/papers/w27612

Lieberman, M.D., D. Rock, H.G. Halvorson, and C. Cox. 2015. "Breaking Bias Updated: The Seeds Model." *NeuroLeadershipJOURNAL* 6, November. scn.ucla.edu/pdf/Lieberman(2015)Neuroleadership.pdf

Lister, K. 2020. "Work-At-Home After Covid-19—Our Forecast." *Global Workplace Analytics*. globalworkplaceanalytics.com/work-at-home-after-covid-19-our-forecast.

Lojeski, K., and R. Reilly. 2020. *The Power of Virtual Distance: A Guide to Productivity and Happiness in the Age of Remote Work*. Hoboken, NJ: Wiley.

Mazareanu, E. 2020. "Average Number of Employee Communication Tools Worldwide by Region 2019." Statista, January 13. statista.com/statistics/1085376/average-organizational-communication-tools-worldwide-region.

Meyer, E. 2014. *The Culture Map: Breaking Through the Invisible Boundaries of Global Business*. New York: Public Affairs.

Pink, D.. 2011. *Drive: The Surprising Truth About What Motivates Us*. New York: Riverhead Books.

Recommended Resources

Bjelland, T. 2021. "Async vs Sync: Balancing Remote Team Communication." Workplaceless, April 13. workplaceless.com/blog/async-vs-sync-communication.

Lencioni, P. 2016. *The Ideal Team Player: How to Recognize and Cultivate the Three Essential Virtues*. Hoboken, NJ: Jossey-Bass.

Scheuer, K. 2021. "Async Wins: What Teams Gain by Going Async." Workplaceless, June 1. workplaceless.com/blog/what-teams-gain-by-going-async.

Scheuer, K.D. 2020. "Remote Team Building Activities: Create Trust While Distributed." Workplaceless, March 2. workplaceless.com/blog/remote-team-building-activities.

Workplaceless. 2020. "6 Expert Steps to Improving Your Remote Team's Communication." Workplaceless, July 22. workplaceless.com/blog/improving-remote-team-communication.

CHAPTER 42

The Trifecta: Project Management, L&D, and Talent Development

Lou Russell

The importance of effective project management can't be overstated. It allows everyone in the organization to focus on the work that matters, ensures strategic alignment, maximizes resources, controls cost, and encourages teamwork. A solid project management approach is critical for talent development and learning and development.

> **IN THIS CHAPTER:**
> - Identify how to use project management to ensure that talent development is being implemented effectively
> - Leverage a project management charter and project schedule to define, plan, manage, and review talent projects
> - Establish the rationale for consistent practices to create synergy among talent development, learning and development, and project management

As TD and L&D projects continue to get larger and more complex, our need to incorporate a solid project management approach grows larger too. You are likely serving multiple customers with conflicting needs, changing business requirements, and other uncertainties. And, your projects may seem more complex due to constant multitasking.

When creating L&D workshops in the past, you may have been able to wing it. However, we are now not only being asked to develop course materials about things we know little about, but we're also tasked with delivering that content in a week or less. L&D experts must become experts at negotiating requirements, working with multiple clients, and building workshops with face-to-face, online, and hybrid options. The realistic project management processes shared in this chapter will help you grow and pivot in your ability to deliver learning.

Dare to Properly Manage Resources is a mnemonic for simplifying the project management process in four critical steps or phases:

- Define
- Plan
- Manage
- Review

We call this the Dare project management approach.

The Synergy of Project Management, Talent Development, and L&D

Talent development and L&D professionals must be able to constantly juggle multiple projects. However, without a specific, repeatable, and realistic process, it is not possible to for us be effective if those projects change. The COVID-19 pandemic changed everything. Now, as we go back to our workplaces or experience a hybrid work model, we must evaluate our work's purpose and processes, how teamwork may change, and how project management (PM) could help improve our workplaces.

Talent development focuses on the building of knowledge, skills, and attitudes to help an organization's employees achieve success in their field. When done well, it allows organizations to succeed and grow. Fostering employee learning, development, and engagement, talent development helps employees drive organizational performance, productivity, and results. It is an important tool for unleashing human potential, so much so that the heart of talent development is people. Talent development offers a set of practical capabilities for driving organizational results and creates effective processes, systems, and frameworks that advance employee development, define succession planning, and create other employee opportunities.

If talent development is going to be effective, it must be intentional, planned, and executed well. To be most successful, the TD function should:

- Get leadership involved.
- Align to the organization's mission.
- Identify talent needs accurately.
- Ask for employee feedback.

In some organizations learning and development is a subset of the talent development function that focuses on solving problems using learning strategies. The goal of L&D is to identify, design, and implement strategies to solve specific learning needs. Once called "training," this can include coursework, curriculum, workshops, case studies, and other learning processes. Talent development tends to be focused on the future, as a continuous process to develop professionals for their next position of responsibility. L&D is often a partner in this process.

If L&D is going to be successful, its role must be well defined. It is responsible for developing and implementing an organization's learning strategy and should:

- Develop and implement learning strategies and programs that meet the business needs.
- Evaluate organizational and individual employee development needs.
- Ensure that the L&D function is aligned to the organization's business goals.
- Optimize learning processes to drive ROI.
- Manage and procure L&D technology (virtual, hybrid, and face-to-face).
- Implement consistent and shared organizational training methods.

Every organization defines the boundaries of talent development and L&D differently, so you may see some crossover of responsibilities between the two. However, both have responsibilities that require a general process to ensure efficiency, accuracy, quality, and consistency of purpose. That's where project management comes in.

Defining Project Management

A project management process is required whether talent development is building a culture of learning or implementing an employee engagement survey, or L&D is designing team-building events to engage remote employees or evaluating its digital delivery systems. Effective project management generally follows the four steps or phases in the Dare project management approach: define, plan, manage, and review.

Before you begin any project management process, be sure that everyone is on the same page by defining terms such as *project, process, task, project sponsor, project manager,* and *stakeholders*. It's especially important to clarify what *task, project,* and *process* represent, because many mistakenly believe they are interchangeable:

- Task—a single unit of work able to be completed in one sitting
- Project—a group of tasks that work together to complete a project
- Process—a series of steps that repeat

In addition, you and your team should clarify who is filling three important project management roles:
- Project sponsor—the business champion and steward of the project
- Project manager—the person who owns the planning, organization, and managing responsibilities that keep the project moving; note that this person does not own the project and cannot control it
- Stakeholders—everyone else involved, most of whom are working on smaller projects within the overarching project; stakeholders must receive something from and provide something to the project

Several common mistakes can cause challenges as you build your project:
- If you are allowing individuals to juggle multiple roles during a project, they may become conflicted and overworked, creating poor results.
- Having more than one project sponsor or project manager creates churn.
- A project manager should not try to own the project—collaboration is critical on a project team.
- One project manager is better than many.
- A project manager must be able to differentiate between *doing* the project and *managing* the project.
- Allowing people to create a schedule without data results in a plan that hasn't taken critical information into account, such as who is involved, what the risks are, and what the objective is.

Consider this definition stage to be the pre-project phase. Once you're all clear on terms, continue with the Dare method to follow the four phases:
- **Define the project.** Create a project charter that includes scope, project objectives, risks and constraints, communication, and governance.
- **Plan the project.** Identify tasks, order of tasks, and methodologies; build the project schedule with due dates and costs.
- **Manage the project.** Implement, revise, adapt, track, and influence stakeholders.
- **Review the project.** End, transition, and evaluate the project.

Remember that all projects and tasks have a beginning and an end, which means that your project will have a beginning and an end. What do you do that has a beginning and an end? Your response might include creating a one-day workshop, designing a compensation plan, or conducting a needs analysis. Therefore, each of these is a project. On the other hand, managing a learning strategy and supervising employees do not have concrete beginnings and ends. They are ongoing and not defined as projects. Both are processes.

Project management is a process with a beginning and an end. It consists of planning, organizing, and managing work:
- **Planning** is anticipating and trying to predict how to set up tasks in the best order for a project. But keep in mind, the project will never go the way you hoped. Ever.
- **Organizing** is coordinating all the moving tasks, people, dates, budgets, and quality needs once the project begins and until it reaches its final goals.
- **Managing** is adapting to the reality of the project and being resilient to address any surprises that occur.

As we dive into the four steps of project management, review Table 42-1 to see the overall flow of the process.

Table 42-1. The Process Flow of Project Management

Dare to	Properly	Manage	Resources
Define	*Plan*	*Manage*	*Review*
Establish the project scope	Finalize learning objectives	Control the work in progress	Implement the learning event
Set the initial business objective	Create the schedule	Provide feedback	Hold project reviews as needed
List risks and constraints	Assign resources	Negotiate for resources	Complete the project for the customer
Evaluate alternatives	Create the budget	Resolve differences	Release resources
Choose a course of action			

Define the Project

The define phase answers the question "Why are we spending money on this project instead of something else?" which establishes the business purpose. The project sponsor plays a critical role at this point by helping the project manager prepare for the work.

The project charter is an important outcome of this phase because it determines why the organization is doing this project instead of spending money and time on something else. Many project managers and teams build a project charter quickly to get approval from the project sponsor before they move on to the plan phase. The charter is a draft that includes the project boundaries. If you fall into the trap of trying to control or manage a project, you'll have a difficult time, so it's best to encourage communication and collaboration.

The define phase should take about 45 minutes and include items listed in Table 42-2, which should then be included in the project charter. Note that there can be only one business objective.

Table 42-2. Define Phase Questions

Business objective (only one)	Is the project going to increase revenue or avoid cost?
Learning objectives	What outcomes (goals) exist for the project?
Quick 'n' dirty risk assessment	How might size, structure, or technology be risk factors that mess everything up?
Constraints	What is most critical to the project sponsor: time, cost, or quality?
Risk factors	What is the likelihood or impact of the risk? Can you prevent or react to it?
Scope diagram	What does the graphic show about how stakeholders interact and what communication is required?

The project charter helps organize the big picture view of a new project. Developing the project charter creates the project's baseline. You can download a project charter template on the handbook website at ATDHandbook3.org.

Plan the Project

The plan phase answers the question "How are we going to complete this project?" The project manager plays a critical role at this point, working out the logistics for a comprehensive list of tasks assigned to specific people with due dates.

The deliverable created in this phase is the project schedule, which ensures everyone can remember what to do and when. During this phase you'll also determine milestones, schedule task dependencies, adjust for resource dependencies, and create a budget. Ideally the project schedule will include only one date and name for each task within the project. Note that the project plan may change frequently.

Manage the Project

This phase answers the question, "How can I adapt to the surprises and glitches that happen to my project?" As you begin to implement the project, resiliency and flexibility will be your most valuable traits as you manage all the changes, update the project charter, and schedule everyone with tasks. This is a good time to remember that "you can't control a project, but you can adapt."

During the manage phase you control work in progress, provide status and feedback, leverage governance, and resolve conflicts. The final deliverable is a finished or cancelled project—thus, your customer is responsible for defining the project's end.

Review the Project

The review phase answers the question "What can we learn from this project that will help us next time?" The deliverable in this phase is a project that has completed a final project review and transitioned closed. In this last phase you will close the project, transition by turning over deliverables, hold a project review, and celebrate accomplishments. It's the project manager's responsibility to determine when the project has ended.

> ## STRONG BEGINNINGS: THINKING AHEAD TO REDUCE RISKS AND AVOID PROJECT MELTDOWNS
> *Crystal Richards, Principal and Owner, MindsparQ*
>
> Projects fail all the time—no matter the size of the organization or the project. Unfortunately, the causes are frequently overlooked (or ignored!). Some common reasons for project failure include missed deadlines, communication breakdowns, disengaged stakeholders, project team members who are pulled away to work on other projects, and project burnout. There can be even more challenges, but you get the picture!
>
> In 2018 Build-a-Bear Workshop ran a one-day national marketing campaign that turned into a very public project failure. "Pay-Your-Age Day" meant that children on summer break would be able to spend less than the usual $20+ to build a teddy bear. And the promotion quickly went viral. On the day of the event, customers began waiting in line hours before stores even opened—stores were quickly overrun and employees overwhelmed. The influx was so massive that Build-a-Bear Workshop shut down the event by midday. The company then had to deal with the negative publicity as angry customers turned to social media to share their ire.
>
> Why was this project such a failure? The main contributing factor was lack of risk management. No one had considered key questions dealing with inventory levels or the ability to meet demand. If they had, the company could have put plans in place to anticipate customer demand.
>
> Risk management is a key strategy to address such questions, but unfortunately many project managers do a lackluster job when it comes to identifying and managing risks.
>
> Let's review some useful tips to help you avoid project management pitfalls.
>
> ### Begin With the End in Mind
> A mindset of "I don't like thinking about the worst" can bring disaster on your project. While optimism is great, failure to do a thorough risk assessment and develop a plan of action will certainly lead to trouble. The key to avoiding this situation is to look at the big picture and consider as many possibilities for failure as you can.
>
> I like to use a crystal ball exercise to help look at the big picture. (It's basically a premortem, but that sounds a bit morbid and clinical to me.) Here's how it works:
> - Imagine the project's failure in detail.
> - Generate the reasons for the failure.
> - Consolidate the list of reasons.
> - Develop action plans (and back-up action plans).
> - Revisit the plan.

> **STRONG BEGINNINGS: THINKING AHEAD TO REDUCE RISKS . . .** *continued*
>
> This exercise can help you think creatively, rather than getting stuck in the weeds. Once you identify all the risks, you can develop a plan to deal with them before they happen.
>
> **Include Stakeholders in the Risk Management Conversation**
> Conversations around risk management should involve everyone—from the stakeholders to the support staff. Lack of stakeholder engagement can create problems on many fronts and potentially lead to a total derailment of your project.
>
> **Keep Your Eye on the Prize**
> Just because you've spent time up front identifying risks and making a plan for how to deal with them doesn't mean your job is done once you start implementing the project. Be ready to take action should new or unexpected issues pop up. It's called risk management for a reason!
>
> Dealing with project setbacks can be one of the most disheartening experiences of your professional life, forcing you to deal with fear, frustration, and feelings of failure. However, identifying potential issues that can derail your project and having a solid plan for dealing with them when they arise can alleviate those negative experiences. Remember, it's all about planning and prevention!

Suggestions for Success

Throughout the four Dare phases, prepare to make changes to your plan. Over the years, we've worked with other project management experts who have documented their own processes and shared the tools and techniques they have developed for effective project management. Let's review some of their advice to prepare you for whatever comes along.

Document the Scope

One of the most useful things you can do is spend some time on a project scope diagram like the one in Figure 42-1. We like to start by placing a star or circle in the middle to represent the project. Then we place sticky notes representing stakeholder roles around the outside of the star. The flow of information is documented with arrows going into or out of the center.

While the project manager is not shown in the graphic, you can think of that person as being "in the star" role. They sit in the middle, keeping track of the stakeholders and guiding the information flow. There are other rules as well:

- The project sponsor is always on the top. Like all work, it's good practice to communicate frequently with the leader.
- Each arrow (in and out of the center) represents work that someone must do.

- Each arrow must touch the middle on one end or the other and should never be double-headed, because that will create confusion.
- A dotted line connecting critical stakeholders is a useful visual cue.

Figure 42-1. Sample Project Scope Diagram

Document the Project Objectives

You will have one (and only one) business objective. For example, the project may require choosing between increasing revenue or avoiding cost based on the goal. Unlike the business objective, project objectives can have many variations. Project objectives clarify the promise you made to deliver the project. Objectives are measurable and attainable. Remember, everything you establish will always be in draft until the project is over.

Communicate With Stakeholders

During the project it is critical to communicate with each stakeholder as much as possible. Great project managers build confidence by sending regular, predictable status reports.

Identify all Support Materials

Eventually, your project will be completed, and you will move on to another one. As you are building the project, be mindful of the artifacts you may need. In L&D, that may include things like facilitator guides, logistic guides, supply lists, cutover plans, marketing plans, and other support related to your development options.

Customize for Your Preferred ISD Process

There are many variations for building out the tasks and task dependencies required to complete a project. This will also include methods like ADDIE, SAM, Agile, or design thinking. Use your preferred process as a reminder of the steps to take while you create your project plan.

Remember the Keys for Scheduling

There are three key concepts for building the project schedule:
- **Tasks and duration.** What work needs to be done, in what order, and for how long?
- **People.** Who can do the work? (List names, not roles.)
- **Time and dates.** When must the work be completed?

If you are using a methodology like ADDIE, you'll need to take its five steps into consideration as you schedule the work. How much time should your ADDIE process take? In 1986, IT genius Capers Jones built a guide for the time to complete phases of ADDIE. Use his estimates for your planning purposes (Table 42-3).

Table 42-3. Capers Jones's ADDIE Guide

Stage	Time Requirement
Analysis (needs assessment and requirements)	30%
Design (blueprint)	30%
Develop (build)	15%
Implement (pilot, finish, transition)	15%
Evaluate (measure performance change)	10%

In addition, consider the following:
- Analysis and design take the most time, but when they're done well the next steps are easier.
- Expertise is critical to duration. But it always takes longer than you think.
- Always sketch out a schedule before you start.

Manage Change

Managing change is not the same as controlling change. Project managers who are determined to control the schedule will crash and burn. Instead, they need to expect change to occur. Sharing a simple project governance plan can be used to differentiate roles and define how changes will be addressed.

Learn With a Post-Project Review

After a project is completely delivered, it's not unusual for people to run away as fast as they can. If you reflect just a little before you jump into another project, you will become a more effective project manager and stakeholder in the future.

Here are some questions to ask after a project is completed and before you start another one:
- How close was the project to the scheduled completion date and what drove the issues?
- How accurate was scheduling and could you improve it?
- How close to the budget was the final project cost? What happened?
- How would you improve the budgeting process?
- Did the project output meet customers' specifications, and how was that measured?
- Was additional work required? Why?
- What did you learn about communication?
- How did staffing affect project success?
- How did the constraints influence the project and what was the cause?
- What techniques will you use on your next projects?
- How could you improve collaboration among stakeholders?
- If you could do the project again, what would you do differently?

Final Thoughts

To be able to deliver the quality content required for our customers requires synergy between the talent development staff, learning and development staff, and project management staff. Typically, talent development has a broad scope. People in talent development work at a higher and broader level, such as talent acquisition, onboarding and engagement, performance management, succession planning, and workforce planning. Depending on your organization, L&D could be involved with some or all of these.

In many organizations, L&D focuses on building learning artifacts (courses, activities) that may reside in only the development and performance management parts of talent development. There could be a disconnect and confusion if talent development and L&D are not collaborating to clearly identify the scope of each other's work. In some instances, this could cause confusing overlap or gaps. Therefore, it's important to be clear about responsibilities in each area before starting a project.

Talent development is often more of an ongoing process. Its role doesn't end—it is a critical element of a strong learning organization. On the other hand, L&D usually builds learning projects for specific outcomes with an end date. To summarize, TD processes don't have an end date, but L&D projects usually do. Be diligent in your work and make sure the two functions work and complement each other. Remember, the staff running each must be clear about the boundaries of their work and able to react to changes in the business quickly, efficiently, and expertly.

Project management can be used as a stable and repeatable process that keeps both talent development and L&D delivering value to customers. In any case, it is critically important to follow the define, plan, manage, and review process to ensure the results desired.

Whether talent development or L&D, both ensure that a systematic process exists to build employees' skills and knowledge, resulting in better performance and a more productive workforce to support the organization. Project management can be an extremely valuable tool to talent development and L&D, enhancing organizational success to maximize profits for its owners and stakeholders while maintaining corporate social responsibility.

About the Author

Lou Russell, practice director at Moser Consulting, is an executive consultant, speaker, and author whose passion is to create growth in companies by guiding the growth of their people. In her speaking, training, and writing, Lou draws on 40 years of experience helping organizations achieve their full potential. She inspires improvement in leadership, project management, and individual learning. Lou is the author of seven popular and practical books: *IT Leadership Alchemy, The Accelerated Learning Fieldbook, Training Triage, Leadership Training, Project Management for Trainers, 10 Steps to Successful Project Management*, and *Managing Projects*. As a sought-after international speaker, Lou blends her humorous stories with on-the-ground experience to speak to the real problems of the people in the room.

References

Seely, T. 2018. "Build-a-Bear CEO Apologizes for 'Pay Your Age' Sale Fail." *USA Today*, July 13. usatoday.com/story/life/allthemoms/2018/07/13/build-bear-ceo-apologies-failed-pay-your-age-sale/782550002.

Recommended Resources

Devaux, S.A. 2015. *Managing Projects as Investments: Earned Value to Business Value*. Boca Raton, FL: CRC Press.
Russell, L. 2012. *Managing Projects: A Practical Guide for Learning Professionals*. San Francisco: Pfeiffer.
Russell, L. 2016. *Project Management for Trainers*, 2nd ed. Alexandria, VA: ATD Press.

SECTION VII
ALIGNING THE LEARNING FUNCTION TO THE ORGANIZATION

LUMINARY PERSPECTIVE

Be the Leader People Want and Organizations Need

Ken Blanchard

A while back, I sent out a Facebook post with a photo of a woman carrying a briefcase and jumping a hurdle, with the headline: **Hire smart people, train them properly, then get out of their way.**

That post received thousands more views than my usual posts. Something about that simple message really resonated with people. Why? I think it's because people know that at its best, leadership is a side-by-side partnership that involves mutual trust and respect among people working together to achieve common goals. Leaders and their team members influence one another—they both play a role in figuring out how to get things done. In other words, leadership is about *we*, not *me*. As a talent development professional, you are an important part of the *we* in your organization. You must be the kind of leader your organization needs. You must model the kind of leader others want.

So, let's focus in on three steps you can take to become the kind of leader people want and organizations need.

Hire Smart People

What should you look for when you have a position to fill in your department or company? First and foremost, you want someone who resonates with your organization's values. Of course, the person needs to possess either the required skills for the position or the potential to develop those skills. You're also looking for someone with the ability to think, plan, and communicate effectively. And it wouldn't hurt if they showed initiative, creativity, confidence, and a desire to learn and grow. In short, you're looking for a winner.

Our company's careers webpage states:

> We are always looking for committed, talented people who:
> - Share our company's values
> - Possess a strong work ethic
> - Are able to work well both independently and on a team
> - Enjoy being part of a fun, dynamic, and productive culture
> - Embrace learning and are willing to try new, innovative approaches
> - Are flexible and adaptable to change
> - Are committed to exceeding our clients' expectations

Now let me pose this question: How often do you go out and hire losers? Sadly, too many organizations still use the normal distribution curve model, where managers are expected to rate only a few people high, a few people low, and the rest as average performers. That's nonsense. Do you go around saying, "We lost some of our worst losers last year, so let's hire some new ones to fill the low spots"? Of course not! You hire either winners or potential winners—people who can perform at the highest level.

Train Them Properly

After the initial onboarding period, even if a new hire has the technical skills to do a job, it's essential that they receive continuing training and support. Too often leaders hire someone, give them some rudimentary training, and expect them to immediately become a winner. But great leaders don't leave people to sink or swim. They support them through the three stages of an effective performance management system:

- **Performance planning**—setting clear goals
- **Day-to-day coaching**—providing feedback through praising, redirecting, and conducting regular one-on-one meetings
- **Performance review**—getting an A

Performance Planning

As soon as a new hire is brought up to speed and shows an understanding of the organization's vision and direction, it's time for goal setting. All good performance starts with clear goals. Effective goal setting happens when leaders and individuals work together to agree on goals and objectives—what needs to be done, when, and how. It's the leader's job to ensure each team member understands what they are being asked to do (areas of accountability) and what a good job looks like (expected performance standards). After clear goals are established between the manager and team member, those goals should be written down and kept close at hand so they can be read in a minute or less and used as a reference to compare actual behavior to targeted behavior.

Goal setting is a powerful motivational tool in a leader's toolkit. It provides purpose, challenge, and meaning. Goals energize people. They are the guideposts along the road that make the organizational vision come alive.

Day-to-Day Coaching

Once goals are agreed upon, effective leaders turn the traditional hierarchical pyramid upside-down so they can serve their people. When this happens, who is at the top of the organization? The frontline, customer-facing people. And who is at the bottom? The "top" management. As a result, who works for whom? You, the leader, work for your people. This change makes a major difference—the difference between who is responsible and who is responsive. When you turn the organizational pyramid upside-down, rather than your people being responsible to you, they become responsible (able to respond) to your customers. Your job as the leader is to be responsive to your people—to help them accomplish goals, solve problems, and live according to the organizational vision.

Day-to-day coaching is rarely given the attention it deserves as a significant aspect of managing people's performance. Providing feedback—praising progress and redirecting inappropriate behavior—is important and needs to happen on an ongoing basis.

Praising

Someone once asked me, "If you had to give up every lesson you've ever taught over the years except one, which one would it be?" I answered that it would have to be the concept that the key to developing people is to catch them doing something right and give them praise.

An effective praising focuses on reinforcing behavior that moves people closer to their goals. It's a good idea to not only praise goal achievement, but also praise progress toward a goal. When you catch someone doing something right or approximately right, follow these steps:
- Praise the person as soon as you see or hear about what they did.
- Let the person know what they did right—be specific.
- Tell them how good you feel about what they did and how it contributes.
- Encourage them to do more of the same and make it clear you support their future success.

Redirection

When people are still learning and are clear on a goal, but their performance isn't quite up to standard, a redirection is effective. When a learner makes a mistake, follow these steps to help them get back on track:

- Redirect the person as soon as possible after the error.
- As the leader, be sure you have made the person's goal clear. If not, be accountable and immediately clarify the goal.
- Confirm the facts and review their misstep together. Be specific about what went wrong.
- Let the individual know how you feel about the error and its impact on results.
- Tell them you think well of them, know they are better than their mistake, and will continue to support them as they move toward goal achievement.

Remember, the ultimate aim of redirection is to build people up so they continue to learn, improve their skills, and achieve their goals.

One-on-One Meetings

My wife, Margie Blanchard, and our colleague Garry Demarest developed a one-on-one process that requires managers to hold 15-to-30-minute meetings at least once every two weeks with each of their direct reports. The manager is responsible for scheduling the meeting, but the direct report sets the agenda. This is when people can talk to their managers about anything on their hearts and minds—it's their meeting. The purpose of one-on-ones is for managers and direct reports to get to know each other as human beings.

In the old days, most businesspeople had a traditional military attitude of, "Don't get close to your direct reports. You can't make hard decisions if you have an emotional attachment to your people." Yet rival organizations will come after your best people—so knowing and caring for them is a competitive edge.

Too often, talented people report that an executive recruiter knows and cares more about their hopes and dreams than their manager does. Don't let this be said about you. One-on-one meetings create genuine relationships and job satisfaction. They are almost like an insurance policy for effective leadership.

Performance Review

I don't really believe in traditional annual performance reviews. I think of a performance review as an ongoing process that happens throughout the year. If you've been providing feedback on a consistent basis and having regular one-on-one meetings all year, there are no surprises at performance review time. Your team members have stayed focused on their goals and know what a good job looks like because their manager has connected with them through day-to-day coaching and one-on-one meetings to ensure they get an A. Now that's the kind of performance review I'd like to see more often!

Life Is All About Getting A's

You may or may not know that I spent 10 years as a college professor. I was always in trouble with the faculty. What drove them crazy more than anything was how, at the beginning of every course, I gave my students a copy of their final exam.

When the faculty first found out about it, they came to me and said, "What are you doing? You can't give students the final exam ahead of time!"

"I won't only give them the final exam ahead of time," I replied. "What do you think I'll do throughout the semester? I'll teach them the answers so that when they get to the final exam, they'll get A's. Because life is all about getting A's."

I tell you this little story because I think it's a great metaphor for an effective performance management system. Here's why:

- Giving out the final exam at the beginning of the year is like setting clear goals during performance planning: it lets people know exactly what's expected of them.
- Teaching people the answers is what day-to-day coaching is all about. Check in with each person on a regular basis. If you see or hear about someone doing something right, don't wait a year to congratulate them during their performance review—give them a praising on the spot. If they do something wrong, don't save your feedback for their review—redirect them right away to give them a chance to get back on track toward their goal.
- Finally, when people get the final exam again at the end of the year—in the form of a performance review—they will get an A: a great evaluation!

Get Out of Their Way

Once you have collaborated with your people on goals and given them the direction and support they need to master their job, you have to let them run with the ball. You knew they had brains when you hired them—it's time to let them use them! A well-trained person doesn't need micromanaging; they need autonomy to grow and thrive.

Even though it's appropriate to provide a hands-on, directing leadership style when someone is learning a new task or skill, the goal is always to move to a hands-off delegating style. This means trusting your team to act independently and turning over responsibility to them for day-to-day decision making and problem solving. In other words, it means getting out of their way!

But don't disappear completely. The highest achievers still need a leader who praises them, celebrates their wins, and provides new challenges to keep them engaged. So, continue having regular one-on-one meetings, no matter how long someone has been with you or how well they do their job.

I'll close with a quote from Margie Blanchard—my wonderful wife for 60 years. Someone once asked her, "What do you think leadership is all about?"

"Leadership is not about love—it *is* love," Margie responded. "It is loving your mission, it's loving your people, it's loving your customers, and it's loving yourself enough to get out of the way so that other people can be magnificent."

I couldn't have said it better myself. God bless.

About the Author

Ken Blanchard, one of the world's most influential leadership experts, is co-author of more than 65 books, including *The One Minute Manager*, with combined sales of more than 23 million copies in 47 languages. Co-founder of the Ken Blanchard Companies, a leadership training and consulting firm in San Diego, California, Ken has received numerous honors for his contributions to the fields of management, leadership, and speaking, including the Thought Leadership Award from ISA, the Association of Learning Providers. When he's not writing or speaking, Ken teaches in the Master of Science in Executive Leadership program at the University of San Diego. Born in New Jersey and raised in New York, Ken received an MA from Colgate University and a BA and PhD from Cornell University.

Recommended Resources

Blanchard, K., and S. Johnson. 2003. *The One Minute Manager*. New York: HarperCollins.

Blanchard, K., and S. Johnson. 2015. *The New One Minute Manager*. New York: HarperCollins.

Blanchard, K., and R. Conley. 2022. *Simple Truths of Leadership: 52 Ways to Be a Servant Leader and Build Trust* Oakland: Berrett-Koehler.

Blanchard, K., and R. Broadwell. 2018. *Servant Leadership in Action: How You Can Achieve Great Relationships and Results*. Oakland: Berrett-Koehler.

Blanchard, K. 2018. *Leading at a Higher Level: Blanchard on Leadership and Creating High Performing Organizations*. Upper Saddle River, NJ: FT Press.

Blanchard, K., P. Zigarmi, and D. Zigarmi. 2013. *Leadership and the One Minute Manager*. New York: Harper Collins.

CHAPTER 43

Learning and Development's Role in Achieving Corporate Vision

Jack Zenger and Joe Folkman

The late Jack Welch once said, "If you want to change an organization, change the training." Several things stand out about this statement. First, that it was the CEO of a large organization who said it—not the HR VP or the head of learning and development. Second, that among the many levers a CEO can pull to shape a company's culture, Welch selected people development. Third, he personally acted on his conviction. Welch frequently attended leadership development sessions at Crotonville, the firm's residential education center. He also initiated a series of development processes including Work Out (an organization development process designed to take out unnecessary work) and Six Sigma (which emphasizes improving quality).

IN THIS CHAPTER:

♦ Discuss how L&D can be a powerful lever to assist organizations in achieving their vision

♦ Explain how L&D can create behavior change for leaders at all levels in the organization

♦ Use evidence-based methods to enhance organizational progress

♦ Understand the importance for L&D to hold itself accountable

♦ Demonstrate ultimate success that results when L&D provides sustainment tools for its initiatives

As noted by Jack Welch, L&D is critical to ensure that an organization achieves its vision. Welch knew that many forces shape an organization's ability to achieve its vision, including:
- Mergers, acquisitions, and divestitures
- Product development and innovation
- Supply chain management
- Financial engineering
- Marketing and sales innovations

Yet, Welch noted training. The fundamental thesis of this chapter is not that we believe L&D to be the only powerful lever that enables an organization to achieve its vision. However, the combination of the magnitude of people development activities, along with the effectiveness of the methods they use, will make a big difference. Learning and development leaders play a major role in making this come together efficiently.

6 Key Components for People Development

What drives an organization's success in people development, which in turn enables the organization to fulfill its vision? We submit that six key components combine to have the optimum outcome.

1. Learning and Development Tailored Specifically for the Organization

One organization is not well served to merely transplant the development processes from some other firm into its own. Tailoring is required. Yes, specific elements may be migrated, but the overall system will be unique. As Oscar Wilde observed, "Be yourself; everyone else is already taken." If the organization aspires to a distinctive vision, it follows that the learning and development processes will ideally be distinctive to align with the unique vision.

This demands that the L&D function be crystal clear about the organization's intended vision and that this vision be articulated and repeatedly emphasized in all it does. The vision is its North Star, becoming the answer to the question, "Why do we exist?" It is the starting point.

However, tailoring does not end with aligning L&D activities with the unique mission of the organization. Beyond that, it considers the specific objectives, encompassing the unique work processes that define and describe the way the organization goes about attaining results. Each organization has its unique history, and there are big differences between startup organizations and those with long histories.

2. Development Linked With Business Outcomes

People development is undertaken for a fundamental reason. You desire a change in how people think and act: *This behavior change is the output and intervening variable.* Conducting a development program focused on improving problem solving does not result in a sudden burst of efficiency, productivity, and profitability for the organization. Those outcomes are the result of new behavior exhibited by an intentionally developed group of people. The accomplishment of a new vision is an outcome of the magnitude and breadth of the behavior change. Therefore, achieving the corporate vision is beholden to the success of achieving defined behavior change from a number of individuals in the organization.

For example, we know that the healthiest organizations are highly flexible and resilient. The COVID-19 pandemic showcased a fascinating microcosm of resilience. One industry that was dramatically affected by the pandemic was the restaurant industry. Chances are that in any city, you could find restaurants that could see no way forward other than closing their doors, laying off employees, and waiting for the pandemic to subside. Then there were those that did not define their business as serving food to patrons who came into their restaurant to be waited on by staff who both took their order and brought them their food. Those restaurants pivoted immediately to serving customers the same food but as takeout. People could phone in their orders or place them via website or app and then come by and safely pick up their food to take home and consume. These restaurants maintained their client base, kept their kitchen staff busy, and generated revenue to pay the rent and be ready to change back when the appropriate time came.

3. Sponsorship by Senior Executives

Through decades of experience in the learning and development arena, we have observed a wide spectrum of connections between senior executives and the development of people in the organization. On one hand, we've seen organizations where the senior executives would come in and welcome the group as they began their journey together. This may expand to the senior executive spending an evening with the group, and often speaking to and answering questions from participants.

We have also seen organizations where one or more senior executives would became deeply engrossed in defining the development they sought for their leaders and key individual contributors. They were active participants in the process, conveying the message that every leader, regardless of position, could become more effective, and everyone was expected to get better every year.

If an organization concludes that they wish to rapidly, consistently, and fully attain their corporate vision, this intense level of leadership support is an extremely valuable element in making it happen.

4. Powerful Development Methods

If the mechanism by which the learning and development function helps the organization achieve its vision is behavior change, then the amount and quality of behavior change is a direct function of the development methods that are employed.

Like many disciplines, there is a tendency for the latest business guru's book to be the shiny object that attracts attention. Many have accused the learning and development function of being especially prone to chasing the latest fads. The countervailing force to this tendency is the sentiment that we must follow the lead of the medical world and insist on evidence-based methods.

In 1975 David Eddy was in the midst of his residency program in cardiovascular surgery. One morning he remarked to his wife that he believed only 15 percent of what physicians did in treating patients had any basis in scientific fact. So, he dropped out and returned to Stanford to get a degree in engineering mathematics. He decided to apply what he had learned to the practice of medicine. After publishing how physicians made decisions on the use of mammograms for breast cancer, he met with great resistance. Eddy then tried another arena: how ophthalmologists treated ocular hypertension, a medical condition that had been well defined for more than 75 years. After studying and finding that the majority of published studies showed patients becoming worse after treatment, he noted, "I then realized that medical decision making was not built on a bedrock of evidence or formal analysis, but was standing on Jell-O."

Eddy concluded that when patients go to their primary care physician with a very common problem like lower back pain, the physician would deliver the right treatment for the patient about half the time. And, if those patients went to several physicians, they would receive extremely different treatments. Clearly, they cannot all be the optimum treatment.

Worse yet, give surgeons a written description of a surgical problem, and half of the group would recommend surgery, while the other half would not. Survey them again two years later, and as many as 40 percent of the same group would disagree with their previous opinions and change their recommendations. Research studies back up all these findings, according to Eddy.

What if we applied this same thinking to the learning and development practices used by corporations? After all, hundreds of billions of dollars are being collectively spent on these endeavors. It would make perfect sense to want to ensure that the methods we are using are supported with good evidence that they produce the desired results. Occasional studies are published regarding various development techniques, but they seldom involve a rigorous research design. That doesn't have to be the case.

Several development methods are well-established and have been analyzed enough to ensure their efficacy. Our favorites include:
- **360-degree or multirater feedback.** Hundreds of published articles exist, some of them describing the rigorous analysis of this method. Unfortunately, there are wide variations in how this is implemented. Results parallel the thoroughness of the implementation.
- **Personal development plans.** Research emanating from the positive psychology movement has fostered the emphasis on building strengths rather than the traditional focus on fixing weaknesses. The existence of an individual development plan that includes

clear and actionable steps has consistently been found to improve results. While there is little disagreement that this method is highly effective, when talking with groups of leaders we often find that the majority do not have a personal development plan they are actively working to improve.
- **Behavior modeling to build skills.** Grounded in the extensive research on social learning theory and pioneered by Stanford's Albert Bandura, this is a well-proven methodology for developing skills.
- **Coaching as a catalyst for development.** A growing body of research confirms the catalytic effect of coaching when combined with other development methods. In and of itself, coaching has positive impact. It is personalized and ongoing, two of the requirements for behavior change to occur.
- **Simulations.** This learning method combines the benefits of experiential learning and is particularly powerful for helping participants gain greater insight into the impact of decisions on the interconnections that occur in every business organization.
- **Linking current job to development.** When the objective is to develop leaders who are capable of leading within an organization, logic argues to use an existing organizational structure as the context in which to develop the leader. A leader's current organization and their position within it become the ideal classroom for development. An artificial situation need not be created for an optimum classroom and laboratory to exist.
- **Involve senior executives in development.** If one of the goals of learning and development is to assist the organization in attaining its vision, then get the organization's senior leaders actively involved in planning and creating the development, along with assisting in its delivery. Better results are consistently obtained when executives are deeply embedded in the process.

5. Line Management Responsibility

Who is responsible for the learning and development activity ensuring that the firm's strategic vision is accomplished? It is easy and understandable if others look to the L&D leaders or the HR function in general for accountability for success. However, this is a big mistake. To demonstrate how line management needs to feel responsible for learning and development efforts, we studied high-potential (HiPo) employee development (Zenger and Folkman 2017). Having a large pool of leaders ready to take over important leadership positions is essential for every organization to succeed, but having the wrong leaders in the HiPo group is a significant problem.

A HiPo employee is a person who has been identified as possessing the ability and the potential to not merely be promoted, but to ultimately ascend to the most senior levels of the organization. This is a distinction usually reserved for the top 4 percent of an organization's employees. The assumptions are that this person not only possesses technical knowledge and intellectual capacity, but also has leadership capability. Placing someone in this group also assumes that the individual is somewhat aware of the rewards and personal costs of ascending to a senior-level position, has or wants to develop the interpersonal skills required of senior leaders, and has the motivation to reach these higher levels. In sum, these are the best and brightest, most capable, and highly motivated people in the organization. They are deserving of further investment in their development to help ensure their preparation for positions of responsibility and power.

Through analysis of HiPo programs at three large, highly respected corporations from widely different industries, we collected data for 1,964 individuals who had been selected by their organizations as HiPo candidates. Using a 360-degree assessment to measure the leadership effectiveness of each candidate, we obtained evaluations from managers, peers, direct reports, and others. On average, each leader received feedback from 13 different assessors. We know that the 360-degree leadership assessment is a valid predictor of a leader's effectiveness because it is highly correlated with organizational outcomes such as employee engagement, employee turnover, customer satisfaction, and productivity. This held true in all three of the organizations we studied.

We found that the HiPo employees were indeed rated overall as more effective leaders than others in the firms—but only moderately better. Concerns arose when we began analyzing data from the three large organizations and found that more than 40 percent of the individuals in HiPo programs clearly did not appear to belong there, falling below the 50th percentile of the leaders we assessed in their firms. In fact, for our three subject organizations, our assessments found that 33 to 52 percent of HiPo leader candidates were below average. In addition, 12 percent of these individuals had overall leadership effectiveness scores that put them in the bottom quartile. That is a long distance from the top 5 percent to which they supposedly belonged (Figure 43-1).

Figure 43-1. Percent of HiPo Leaders at Leadership Quartiles

We believe that several groups of people fall in the accountability lineup ahead of HR and L&D in this situation:
- We believe senior line managers, all the way up to and through the C-suite, should be setting the example of having a clearly defined development objective. No matter who you are or what your position, you should be working on getting better at something. Many organizations hold leaders accountable for the development of their direct reports and then fail to hold leaders accountable for their own development.
- We would argue that leadership is a widely shared process that happens at the group and organization level. As noted earlier, all leaders should have one or more people above them in the hierarchy who both know and care about their development. This is the most sure-fire guarantee that the development initiatives will support the organization's vision. Given that learning and development is ultimately geared toward making behavioral change, it is easy to understand why the involvement of each participant's immediate manager would make a difference. Changed behavior is much more apt to happen if each participant's immediate manager both knows and cares about what is happening.
- We also see strong arguments for putting far greater emphasis on the individual leaders for their own development. Learning happens best when the individual is given the information and tools to assume more responsibility for their development. For example, it has long been observed that one of the most difficult transitions for a leader to make is the jump from being a capable individual contributor, responsible for their own performance, to a manager responsible for the performance of a group. This has been described as moving from stage 2 in a career cycle to stage 3. Think of stage 1 as a novice—a person learning the ropes in a given discipline and taking guidance and direction from a manager. Stage 2 is the professional, individual contributor who is increasingly knowledgeable and self-directing. Stage 3 is the manager or leader with oversight over a group. Who should be responsible for the development of someone who selected to be a stage 3 leader? The transition involves both a new mindset and new skills. The necessary development requires both horizontal and vertical development.

Emphasize the Development of Strengths

In our earliest research on leadership effectiveness, we analyzed a database of 22,000 leaders' results from a multirater feedback assessment, commonly referred to as 360-degree feedback. Each manager had been assessed by approximately 13 raters consisting of subordinates, peers, their manager, and their own rating. On occasion, they would include customers or vendors with whom they worked. We identified the leaders who in the aggregate received the highest scores and then noted which behaviors were most powerful in identifying who would score the highest in contrast to those who scored the lowest.

A number of insights emanated from that analysis, but one that stood out to us was that the most effective leaders were not good at everything a leader does. Instead, the most effective were those who were extremely good at a handful of leadership behaviors. Contemporaneous with our analysis, there was a strong movement in the psychological world, spearheaded by Martin Seligman, that came to be known as positive psychology. Seligman's work, along with others, supported what we had found. Leaders who were perceived to be at the 90th percentile on five leadership competencies produced superior results on virtually every measure of business outcomes, including employee engagement, customer satisfaction, productivity, innovation, revenue generation, and employee retention. Our database now includes 1.5 million 360-degree-feedback assessments, describing the behavior of more than 130,000 leaders worldwide. While the statistical results have shifted somewhat as the database expands, the fundamental conclusions have remained the same.

L&D can help the organization attain its vision by helping people shift their focus away from automatically wanting to work on their weaknesses to having the majority focus on developing their strengths. However, if a leader is performing badly on some behavior that is important to their current position, it needs to be fixed. Leaders at the 10th percentile or below on a competency that was important in their current position invariably fell to the bottom quartile of all leaders. Really poor performance was a millstone about their neck—for the 27 percent of leaders with this "fatal flaw," we recommend they fix that before moving on to developing strengths.

Use Multipath Development

Another insight that came from our analysis of 360-degree-feedback data expanded our view of how leaders could best change their behavior and improve their overall effectiveness. The fundamental concept underlying multipath development is analogous to cross-training in athletics. Most people are aware that great tennis players run, lift weights, swim, and engage in other activities that help them become better tennis players. The same applies to golfers, bicycle racers, and football players. While some cross-training endeavors are obvious, others are not as understandable. One of our favorites was the football coach who had his linemen take ballet lessons. He found it greatly improved their footwork, but the image this conjures up always brings a smile to our faces.

Our research has found that there is a group of behaviors that goes hand in hand with every differentiating leadership competency. Some are obvious, while others are less so. Table 43-1 provides a few examples of competencies and behaviors with a strong statistical connection.

Table 43-1. Leadership Competencies and Companion Behaviors

Differentiating Competency	Companion Behavior
Integrity	Assertiveness
Technical expertise	Relationship building
Problem solving	Decisiveness
Practices self-development	Listens, respects others, open to other's ideas
Develops others	Practices self-development
Collaboration and teamwork	Establishes stretch goals

The power of this research is for those individuals who want to excel at a leadership competency but find that they have done all the seemingly obvious, logical things to get better. "If I want to increase my technical expertise, then I know I need to read more books, search out more articles, attend seminars, and get involved in technical gatherings in my industry. But I've already done those things! Now what?" Our statistical analysis shows that there are, for whatever reason, many things closely linked to the competency you wish to improve. We have research that supports the conclusion that improving companion behaviors will move the needle on the differentiating competency.

6. Emphasis on Sustainment and Follow-Through

A frequent criticism of the learning and development function is that it will hold an excellent, engaging learning event, and participants are enthused about the information and ideas they have acquired, but then nothing follows. People revert to their previous behavior because nothing is done to reinforce or sustain what was learned. The organizers of the learning event hoped that participants would apply what they learned in a constantly escalating way. Instead, it was out of sight and out of mind.

If the true function of L&D is to help the organization achieve its vision, then participants need to understand that the development event is intended to provide the information and motivation to do something different in the future. The participant gains some new information, personal insight, and motivation to experiment with new behavior. It is especially helpful if they understand that the value of the learning event is entirely dependent on what happens afterward.

One helpful outcome of any learning event is for the participant to leave with an understanding of the specific behaviors and actions they should implement in the future. Their plan ideally defines a new pattern of behavior that enables them to develop new habits. One way to increase the likelihood of a habit being formed is to help the participant to analyze the forces in their life, along with any beliefs and assumptions that may block their successful adoption of new and elevated behavior. Ask questions like these to help participants think about what could get in the way of their plan:

- Is this really of great importance to me and my future?
- How confident am I that I can successfully do this?
- What beliefs do I hold that are counter to my new behavior?
- Why have I not done this in the past?

Final Thoughts

This chapter focused on how the learning and development function aids the organization in reaching its vision. Let's summarize by starting at the finish line and working backward to see how we can best organize this journey. Here is the chain as we see it:

- Achieving a vision requires that the vision be clearly spelled out.
- Progress toward that vision can be measured with various business metrics, such as market position, customer satisfaction, employee engagement, productivity, product excellence, and profitability.
- Business metrics are the product of effective leadership and improved business results come from elevating leadership behavior.
- Learning and development staff guide the organization to combine the necessary elements for developing effective leadership behavior.

Everything hinges on behavior change. This can be accomplished. The behavior must be closely linked to the desired vision for the organization. Emphasizing learning and development is not the only solution, but it is one for which we have solid research.

By the way, David Eddy believes that the practice of medicine has improved since 1975, when he and others took up the crusade for evidence-based medicine. He believes it has moved from 15 percent to 25 percent. We hope learning and development makes at least the same progress.

About the Authors

Jack H. Zenger, PhD, is the co-founder and chief executive officer of Zenger Folkman, a firm focused on elevating the effectiveness of leaders. His career has combined entrepreneurial, corporate, and academic activities. Jack taught at the University of Southern California and the Stanford Graduate School of Business. He has received ATD's Lifetime Achievement in Workplace Learning and Performance Award and has been inducted into the HRD Hall of Fame. He has a doctorate in business administration from the University of Southern California, an MBA from UCLA, and a bachelor's degree from Brigham Young University. The author or co-author of 250 articles on leadership, productivity, and teams, as well as 14 books on leadership, teams, and productivity, Jack currently writes blog posts and articles for *Forbes, Harvard Business Review*, and LinkedIn.

Joe R. Folkman, PhD, co-founder and president of Zenger-Folkman, is a respected authority on assessment and change. As one of the nation's renowned psychometricians, Joe has developed unique measurement tools that use a database composed of more than a million assessments on more than 125,000 leaders. Joe's research has been published in the *Harvard Business Review* and the *Wall Street Journal*. He regularly posts on *Harvard Business Review, Forbes*, and LinkedIn. Joe holds a doctorate in social and organizational psychology and a master's in organizational behavior from Brigham Young University. He is the author or co-author of nine books, including *Speed: How Leaders Accelerate Successful Execution* and *New Extraordinary Leader*. Joe and his family reside in Orem, Utah.

References
Eddy, D.M. 2011. "The Origins of Evidence-Based Medicine—A Personal Perspective." *American Medical Association Journal of Ethics* 13(1): 55–60.

Zenger, J., and J. Folkman. 2017. "Companies Are Bad at Identifying High-Potential Employees." *Harvard Business Review,* February 20. hbr.org/2017/02/companies-are-bad-at-identifying-high-potential-employees.

Recommended Resources
Biech, E. 2018. *ATD's Foundations of Talent Development: Launching, Leveraging, and Leading Your Organization's TD Effort*. Alexandria, VA: ATD Press.

Zenger, J.H., and J.R. Folkman. 2020. *The New Extraordinary Leader: Turning Good Managers into Great Leaders* New York: McGraw-Hill.

CHAPTER 44

Structuring TD to Meet the Dynamic Needs of the Organization

William J. Rothwell, Angela Stopper, and Aileen G. Zaballero

As you think about structuring your talent development team to include the critical components for organizational success, consider two aspects: How do you ensure your team's priorities directly meet the organization's dynamic needs? How do you align your activities to meet your organization's overall business goals and objectives?

The answer is—strategically. Managing and developing people is not only an operational necessity but also a strategic imperative. When talent development is structured as a critical function that is necessary to meet strategic objectives, everyone wins. By doing this, your team will have a seat at the table where critical business decisions are made.

IN THIS CHAPTER:

♦ Describe ATD's Talent Development Capability Model and Talent Development Framework and use them to customize a talent development structure

♦ Review a model that offers different TD portfolio products

♦ Complete actionable steps to customize a dynamic TD framework

♦ Build an action plan that engages C-suite leadership to support the creation of a TD function for organizational impact

---

Let's begin with an overview of ATD's Talent Development Capability Model and Talent Development Framework, which can support you in the creation of a customized TD structure. We'll also examine the You-Me-We Learning Model, which presents an alternative view of the CCL's 70-20-10 framework. This chapter will also help you identify steps to ensure your structure and functional activities support the needs of the workforce and the goals of the business.

ATD's Talent Development Capability Model

Based on a study conducted in 2018–2019, ATD launched an interactive Talent Development Capability Model that recognizes the changing dynamics of the TD field. "The model is personalizable, updatable, and future-oriented, reflecting the field of talent development now and also five years in the future" (ATD 2021). It responds to the trends affecting talent development, such as digital transformation, data analytics, information availability, and partnerships between talent development and business. The model is subdivided into three domains of practice:

- **Building Personal Capability:** The knowledge and interpersonal skills (soft skills) needed to build effective organizational or team culture, trust, and engagement.
- **Developing Professional Capability:** The knowledge and skills needed to be effective in creating the processes, systems, and framework that foster learning.
- **Impacting Organizational Capability:** The knowledge, skills, and abilities to ensure talent development is aligned with business goals for organizational success.

The Talent Development Capability Model is customizable and interactive, so TD professionals can explore and build a framework for themselves based on their individual roles, responsibilities, and how their organization is structured. This model is an excellent tool to start with when building a dynamic TD function that meets the needs of your organization (Figure 44-1).

ATD's Talent Development Framework

After you consider how your team can aid in building, developing, and impacting capability (personal, professional, and organization), select the components that must be part of your TD strategy. This is what the Talent Development Framework was designed for.

In 2014–2015, ATD and Rothwell & Associates partnered to study how organizations around the world were structuring and aligning talent development. What they found was that many talent development thought leaders said that describing talent development was complex (Rothwell, Stopper, and Zaballero 2015a). Based on their research, ATD and Rothwell & Associates developed a Talent Development Framework containing 39 different components that influence the success of the TD department. The framework is designed so that you can determine and define the primary and secondary components required to develop a TD strategy that enables the organization to successfully reach its stated operational, business, and strategic goals. This exercise is important because it will help you determine what and how many resources to devote to each component of the strategy. The customizable framework can also be used to help organizations rearrange, remove, and add functions to fit their changing needs (Figure 44-2).

Figure 44-1. The Talent Development Capability Model

Figure 44-2. Talent Development Framework

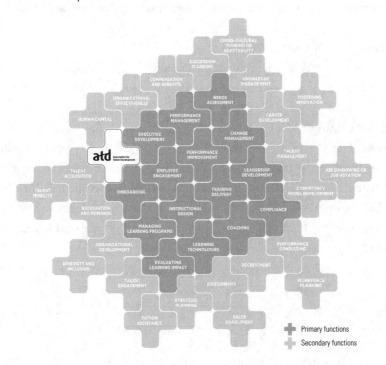

How ATD's Capability Model and TD Framework Support Each Other

ATD's Talent Development Capability Model helps professionals understand the knowledge and skills necessary for success and identify development opportunities for an individual's professional learning journey. The model also provides direction for individuals and teams to assess their knowledge and skills in the profession against 23 capabilities organized into three domains of practice. You can connect with ATD's interactive Talent Development Capability Model on the ATD website.

Similarly, the Talent Development Framework helps guide organizations to prioritize their talent development components. It focuses on the specific functions necessary for a group or department to be successful, aligning what they do to the needs of their organization. The framework is best suited to determine which components should be prioritized in an organization's talent development function or structure. You will find an interactive version of ATD's TD Framework Puzzle on the handbook website at ATDHandbook3.org.

Once organizations prioritize the components within their talent development function or structure, they can then look to the related capabilities in the Capability Model to ensure their employees and teams have the knowledge and skills necessary to be most effective.

As you think about how these two models can help you structure a customized framework to meet the dynamic needs of your organization, it's essential to consider which components align with the business goals and what capabilities you and your team need to be successful.

The You-Me-We Learning Model

Now that we've covered the Talent Development Capability Model and TD Framework, we'd like to introduce one more model you can use to structure your TD function to meet your organization's business needs.

The You-Me-We Learning Model, developed by Angela L.M. Stopper, provides a way for learners to see themselves in the learning model (Figure 44-3). Current learning models tend to focus on the "products," such as how many formal learning program hours make up a program portfolio or how many hours of informal learning are pushed out to clients. You-Me-We turns those questions (and the discussions that we have about them) upside-down and asks the learner how our programs support their learning needs. How can we support and enable you to be the very best that you can be?

Figure 44-3. You-Me-We Learning Model

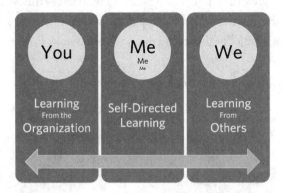

The model is designed from the learner's perspective, so "me" is found at its center. *Me Learning* represents the strategies the TD function incorporates into its portfolio that empower your learners to find and use self-directed learning. It asks "What can I, me, the learner, do to own my development?" and "How can you, the TD function, support my individual journey?"

To the left of *Me Learning* is *You Learning*. In the view of a learner, *You Learning* is anything that they expect you, the organization, to provide. In other words, what formal course and learning opportunities does the organization provide to support their learning journey?

The third piece of the model is *We Learning*. As the old saying goes, no person is an island, and no learning journey can be complete without the help of a personal learning network. That is what We Learning encompasses.

As you look at your learning strategy through the You-Me-We Learning Model, you are forced to think about what the TD function is doing to build and sustain safe spaces within your organization for the formation and use of those personal learning networks.

5 Steps to Developing a TD Structure

Together, the Talent Development Capability Model, Talent Development Framework, and You-Me-We Learning Model create a foundation for ensuring your TD structure meets the dynamic needs of your organization. Now let's look at a five-step process that will guide you through the use of these tools:

- Prioritize
- Re-vision
- Launch
- Communicate/celebrate
- Evaluate/recalibrate

Figure 44-4 represents an interactive approach you can use when developing and structuring your customized TD framework. This cyclical process emphasizes the need to continuously assess and adjust to ensure your organization's evolving needs are met. Worksheets to guide you through the first four steps are available for download on the handbook website at ATDHandbook3.org.

Figure 44-4. Steps to Developing a Talent Development Structure

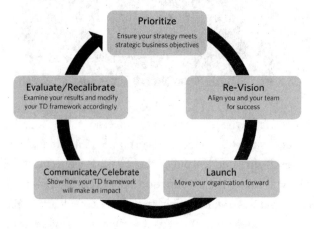

Step 1. Prioritize

First, you must prioritize the proper talent development components to ensure your strategy meets your organization's strategic business objectives. Follow these prompts as you navigate this step:

- **Identify and list your organization's business priorities.** Name the strategic business objectives. Then, working with the leadership team, determine what the organization needs to be successful, and root your TD function in support of achieving those objectives and goals.
- **Name your primary components.** Create a table and, in partnership with your leadership, department, or unit, review the TD Framework's 39 components to identify which are mission critical. These are your primary components and will have the biggest positive impact on one of the business priorities you listed in the first prompt. (Note that you can list multiple components for each priority.) Use the interactive TD Framework Puzzle to highlight your primary components in red.
- **Name your secondary components.** Create a second table and work with your leadership, department, or unit to review the remaining components and identify which are important. These are your secondary components and will have a moderate, positive

impact on one of the business priorities listed from the first prompt. (Note that you can list multiple components for each priority.) Update your puzzle, highlighting the secondary components in orange.
- **Remove (for now) nice-to-have components.** Now it's time to take stock of the components that remain. Work with your leadership, department, or unit to discuss each one, asking, "Are you willing to remove this component from your framework (for now)?" If you say no, the component may belong in your framework. However, before you make it a primary or secondary piece, provide your rationale for keeping it in your framework. For example, if it doesn't directly align to a current business objective or goal, why should you focus on it? Is your answer strong and forward thinking, or are you rooting future-focused decisions in the past ("We've always done it this way")? Validate your reason: Is there someone else within your sphere who could take this over for you? Do others agree that no one else can take it over? Do others think this component is mission critical? Important? Is your reasoning strong? Do others agree? If, after this analysis, you are still unwilling to remove the component from your framework, highlight it with red or orange (depending on if you wish to call it a primary or secondary component). Anything that remains is now a nice-to-have component and can be removed from your framework (for now).
- **Revisit the framework as your organization's business priorities, goals, or resources change.**

Step 2. Re-Vision

Next, determine what you need to do to re-vision a robust, organization-wide talent development framework as well as the structure that will align you and your team for success. Using the tools and models we've discussed, ensure you have a mix of You Learning, Me Learning, and We Learning in the products, services, and opportunities available within your components to build the capabilities needed to meet the dynamic business needs of the organization.
- **You Learning.** Remember, when a learner looks to you, the organization, for a learning experience, that's You Learning. It's important to create learning journeys for your employees as opposed to one-and-done programs that aren't integrated into the business strategy. Engage your top leaders to talk about the importance and impact of development and market your offerings like you are the top learning and development company in the world!
- **Me Learning.** Anything in your Me Learning strategy should focus on creating content that people search for and can find right when they need it or are ready for it. They own their learning journey, and know where to go and whom to ask for help. A good Me

Learning portfolio allows learners to feel in control, supported, and ready to seek out learning opportunities throughout the day, as part of their job, right in their workflow.
- **We Learning.** As you build your We Learning portfolio, focus on developing vehicles you can distribute to engage your clients as they build and use a personal learning network. Think, "How is my team creating and enabling safe-space opportunities for people in the organization to gather and learn from one another?" and then build a portfolio that does that.

Step 3. Launch

When you get to the launch step, we like to point to a quote from Arthur Ashe: "Start where you are, use what you have, do what you can." Launching a new strategy can feel overwhelming, and this quote helps us center and focus. Remember, you won't get to the perfect TD structure overnight; it is a marathon, not a sprint. Here are some important things to remember:
- List your programs and products.
- Define what's existing and what's new.
- Determine the input needed to make each item happen, the impact it will have, and the budget you will need.
- Assign accountability and timelines.

Think *actionable* (what do we need to do?) and *measurable* (how will we know it's being done [numbers] and by when [timelines]?) for every strategic step you wish to take. Remember that in business, what gets measured is what gets done, and what is rewarded is what gets repeated.

Step 4. Communicate and Celebrate

This takes us directly into our next step—sharing the TD framework with the whole organization and acknowledging your outcomes.

It's not sufficient to simply hold one town hall meeting to announce the launch of your TD strategy. One-shot communication efforts are here today and gone tomorrow. People listen, nod politely, and promptly forget what they heard. In fact, this is why many change efforts fail—people forget what the change goals are, who is involved, what results are desired, why those results are necessary, and what that means (and why that is important) to managers and their teams.

A communication strategy is comprehensive in scope. Each step in a change plan should include a corresponding step focused on the communications needed to ensure people understand the "what," "why," and "how." Work to ensure that each communication step you outline describes:
- Who is (or should be) the target for communication? Who are the stakeholders?
- What is the objective, or gist, of the message?
- What three takeaways should your reader remember after receiving the communication?

- When should the message be delivered?
- Where should the message be delivered?
- Why is the message important, and what change goals will it support?
- How should the message be delivered, and how can redundancy be built in so that there is more than one way to reach a targeted audience?

In addition to planning the communication strategy, decision makers should hold celebrations. It is not good enough to launch a change effort and manage it effectively. People also need to celebrate their successes. Celebrations help dramatize what has been achieved in the change effort, who was involved, and why that matters. They also engage and motivate people so they feel good about themselves, the change, and the value of talent development. This step is the reward that ensures that what you want to happen will continue to happen.

Step 5. Evaluate and Recalibrate

Measuring the impact of your program and products allows you to modify your TD framework to ensure it remains relevant for years to come. As the business goals change, your TD strategy should also change.

Evaluation has long been emphasized by TD professionals. In fact, it has been a preoccupation of many in the field. Perhaps the best-known model of evaluation is Donald Kirkpatrick's Four Levels of Evaluation. For Kirkpatrick, evaluation rests on four important questions:

- **Level 1: Reaction.** How much did participants like the learning experience?
- **Level 2: Learning.** How much did participants learn from the experience?
- **Level 3: Behavior.** How much did participants change their on-the-job behavior due to the learning experience?
- **Level 4: Results.** What measurable results—productivity gains—were realized from the learning experience?

Jack and Patti Phillips expanded on the idea of the four levels of evaluation by adding impact, which includes calculating the return on investment. ROI examines the benefits provided by talent development minus the costs of analyzing, designing, developing, delivering, and evaluating TD experiences. In other words, ROI measures the financial impact of the TD function.

You may also want to examine the strategic business impact of change efforts such as TD experiences. This looks at how well the TD experiences contributed to meeting the organization's strategic goals as measured by the Balanced Scorecard strategic goals and key performance indicators (KPIs) of each division, department, work group or team, or individual.

Use a timeframe to examine Kirkpatrick's four levels, ROI, and the business impact and create an evaluation grid. This makes it possible for you to forecast each level before the TD experiences, during the experiences, after the experiences, and into the future. The grid is shown in Figure 44-5.

Figure 44-5. Rothwell's Grid Model of Evaluation

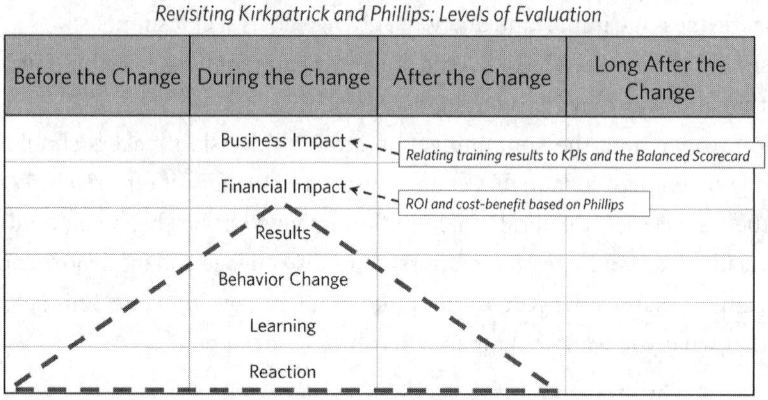

Revisiting Kirkpatrick and Phillips: Levels of Evaluation

	Before the Change	During the Change	After the Change	Long After the Change
Business Impact				Relating training results to KPIs and the Balanced Scorecard
Financial Impact				ROI and cost-benefit based on Phillips
Results				
Behavior Change				
Learning				
Reaction				

The TD Framework is a strategic model and should therefore be evaluated strategically. Indeed, evaluating long-term and strategic issues is not the same as evaluating one-shot, short-term, tactically focused change (Jones and Rothwell 2017). How much does the TD effort contribute to meeting organizational needs and achieving organizational goals? To what extent does the organization have the right people in the right places at the right times to achieve the right results? These are the questions that the TD framework seeks to address, and it is a useful issue to bear in mind as the framework's relative success is evaluated.

Thus the results of evaluation can help you periodically recalibrate your TD framework, ensuring it remains dynamic—linked to business needs and aligned to the strategic goals of your organization now and in the future

Final Thoughts

Building a TD strategy and team to meet the dynamic business needs of your organization is not only good business, but also a necessary task in remaining relevant to your organization. Budgets will continue to get smaller, organizations will continue to get flatter, and resources will continue to get more scarce. By aligning your TD strategy with the larger organizational goals, you will show your value as a strong member of the organization's leadership team and earn your seat by helping make strategic business decisions.

About the Authors

William J. Rothwell, PhD, SPHR, SHRM-SCP, CPTD Fellow, is president of Rothwell & Associates and a professor in charge of workforce education and development on the University Park campus of Pennsylvania State University. As a professor, he heads a top-ranked program in learning and performance; as a consultant, he travels the world presenting on his 104 published books. In 2012, he was honored with ATD's Distinguished Contribution to Workplace Learning and Performance Award, and in 2013 he was honored by the ATD Certification Institute by being appointed a Certified Professional in Talent Development Fellow. Visit his website at rothwellandassociates.com.

Angela L.M. Stopper, PhD, is the chief learning officer and director of people and organization development at the University of California, Berkeley. She is responsible for the team that creates and delivers campuswide learning initiatives supporting supervisory, management, functional, technical, and nontechnical learning efforts for the campus's 9,000 staff and faculty administrators. Angela is also a member of the teaching faculty with Penn State World Campus, where she has developed and is teaching a course for the online master of professional studies degree in organization development and change.

Aileen G. Zaballero, PhD, CPTD, is a senior partner at Rothwell & Associates and a Certified Professional in Talent Development since 2009. She helped develop a competency model and career map for the advanced commercial building workforce and redesigned a performance management system for a senior living community. Aileen recently co-authored the book *Increasing Learning & Development's Impact Through Accreditation* (Palgrave 2020).

References

ATD. 2021. "About the Model." The Talent Development Capability Model. td.org/capability-model-cert/about.

Galagan, P., M. Hirt, and C. Vital. 2019. *Capabilities for Talent Development: Shaping the Future of the Profession.* Alexandria, VA: ATD Press.

Jones, M.C., and W.J. Rothwell, eds. 2017. *Evaluating Organization Development: How to Ensure and Sustain the Successful Transformation.* Boca Raton, FL: CRC Press.

Kirkpatrick, J.D., and W.K. Kirkpatrick. 2016. *Kirkpatrick's Four Levels of Training Evaluation.* Alexandria, VA: ATD Press.

Phillips, P.P., and J.J. Phillips. 2006. *Return on investment (ROI) Basics.* Alexandria, VA: ATD Press.

Phillips, P.P., and J.J. Phillips. 2009. *Return on Investment: Handbook of Improving Performance in the Workplace*. New York: Routledge.

Rothwell, W., A. Stopper, and A. Zaballero. 2015a. *Building a Talent Development Structure Without Borders*. Alexandria, VA: ATD Press.

Rothwell, W., A. Stopper, and A. Zaballero. 2015b. "Measuring and Addressing Talent Gaps Globally." *TD at Work*. Alexandria, VA: ATD Press.

Recommended Resources

Rothwell, W. 2009. *The Manager's Guide to Maximizing Employee Potential: Quick and Easy Strategies to Develop Talent Every Day*. New York: AMACOM.

Rothwell, W. 2012. "Advance Organizer." In *Talent Management: A Step-By-Action-Oriented Guide Based on Best Practice*, edited by W. Rothwell, M. Jones, M. Kirby, and F. Loomis. Amherst, MA: HRD Press.

Rothwell, W. 2012. "Talent Management and Talent Development: What They Are, and Why You Should Care." In *The Encyclopedia of Human Resource Management*, vol. 2, edited by W. Rothwell, J. Lindholm, K.K. Yarrish, and A. Zabellero. San Francisco: Pfeiffer.

CHAPTER 45

The Five Fundamentals of Learning Leadership

Jim Kouzes and Barry Posner

Leadership is everyone's business. Talent development professionals are leaders, as are their internal and external clients. Ask yourself:
- How am I doing today, right now, as a leader?
- What kind of leader do I aspire to be?
- How can I grow and develop into an exemplary leader?
- How can I help my internal and external clients develop their leadership skills?

Understanding and practicing the five fundamentals of leadership helps you fulfill your role as a TD professional who fosters a climate conducive to developing your organization's leaders.

IN THIS CHAPTER:

♦ Define the five fundamentals of learning leadership

♦ Evaluate a set of beliefs with self-reflective questions and practice

♦ Explore an evidence-based framework for fostering a climate that is conducive to the growth and development of exemplary leaders

---

This chapter is adapted from *Learning Leadership: The Five Fundamentals of Becoming an Exemplary Leader*, by James M. Kouzes and Barry Z. Posner. Hoboken, NJ: John Wiley & Sons. 2016. Copyright © 2016 James M. Kouzes and Barry Z. Posner. All rights reserved.

We've been researching, writing, and speaking about exemplary leadership for more than 40 years, and throughout that time people have asked us one question more often than any other—"Are leaders born or made?" As a talent developer, maybe you've been asked this as well. Maybe you've even wondered the same thing.

Our answer to that question has always been the same: "We have never met a leader who was not born." We've also never met an accountant, artist, athlete, engineer, lawyer, physician, scientist, teacher, writer, or zoologist who was not born.

You might be thinking, "Well that's not fair. That's a trick question. Everyone is born." And that's precisely our point. Every one of us is born, and every one of us has the necessary material to become a leader.

And just for the record, no one has ever asked us, "Are managers born or made?"

We believe that asking if leaders are born or made is not a very productive question. It's the old "nature versus nurture" argument, which doesn't get at the more important questions we must ask and answer: The more useful question is, "Can you, and those you work with, become better leaders than you are today?" The answer to that question is a resounding, "Yes."

So, let's get something straight right from the start. Leadership is not some mystical quality that only a few people have and everyone else doesn't. Leadership is not preordained. Neither is it the private reserve of a special class of charismatic men and women. Leadership is not a gene. It is not a trait. There is just no hard evidence to suggest that leadership is imprinted in the DNA of some people and not others. Leadership is simply a set of skills and abilities that are learnable by anyone.

Leadership Potential Is Pervasive

We've collected assessment data from millions of people around the world. We can tell you without a doubt that there are leaders in every profession, in every type of organization, at every level, in every religion, and in every country, from young to old, male and female. There is leadership potential everywhere we look. Still, the question often arises as to whether or not everyone is capable of exercising leadership.

To check our assertion that everyone is capable of exercising leadership, we took a deep dive into data from our Leadership Practices Inventory (LPI; Kouzes and Posner 2017a). The LPI is a 360-degree assessment that determines how often individuals are currently engaging in the Five Practices of Exemplary Leadership—behaviors and actions that are associated with people being at their personal best as leaders (Kouzes and Posner 2017b). The LPI comprises 30 leadership behaviors, and each one is assessed on a 10-point frequency scale from 1, indicating that this individual "almost never" engages in that specific behavior, to 10, indicating that they "almost always" engage in the behavior described. The LPI provides a 360-degree look—from the leader's self-perspective, as well as the vantage point of their managers, colleagues, direct reports, and others—at the extent to which the actions identified as essential leadership behaviors are being used.

In our more than 35 years of collecting data on leadership behaviors, practically no one who completed the LPI has scored a "zero" across all five leadership practices. To do so would mean that the individual (or their manager, colleagues, and/or direct reports) reported they "almost never" engaged in any of the 30 leadership behaviors. Out of more than 3.52 million respondents, there have been a total of 581 people who reported a "zero" score—that's 0.0165 percent.

Do the math, and you will find that in an organization with 100 employees, the probability of finding an individual with "zero" leadership behaviors is zero. If you make that a 1,000-person organization, the probability is still zero. Even in a 10,000-person enterprise, the probability increases only to fewer than two people. And, if you included only respondents who were not in management positions in your calculations, the percentage of zeros (I almost never engaged in any of these 30 leadership behaviors) is even more unlikely (0.0074 percent). The percentage of peers who assess one of their colleagues to never engage in any of these 30 leadership behaviors is even more remote (0.0054 percent).

The empirical findings and mathematical results support the assertion that everyone is capable of engaging in leadership behaviors. In fact, almost everyone is exhibiting *some* (or more than "almost never") leadership behaviors already. The chances of finding someone in your most immediate group who cannot exercise leadership is zero. At the same time, however, it would be an exaggeration to claim that because 99.9835 percent of people are already demonstrating some leadership behaviors, everyone will become an exemplary leader. It takes years of practice and dedication to get to that point, and not every person in a family, company, community, or nation will want to make the commitment or devote the energy and effort necessary to become exemplary.

The point is that leadership isn't something some people have and other people don't. It's much more broadly distributed than traditionally accepted views suggest. We are certain that no matter your current level of skill and ability, you can learn to more frequently exercise leadership than you do now. And, as is true in mastering any set of skills and abilities, it always helps to have a few principles that can help you organize your learning journey. To that end, we offer the Five Fundamentals of Learning Leadership to guide you on the path to becoming the best leader you can be (Kouzes and Posner 2016):

- Believe you can.
- Aspire to excel.
- Challenge yourself.
- Engage support.
- Practice deliberately.

Let's briefly examine each fundamental and then review some questions to ask yourself to aid in creating a culture that fosters the development of more and better leaders. At the end, we also provide an activity to nudge you down the path to exemplary leadership.

Fundamental 1. Believe You Can

Believing that you can lead is essential to developing your leadership skills and abilities. Even if some people think that you're not able to learn leadership, *you* must believe that you can. That's where it all starts—with your own belief in yourself.

You have to believe that what you do counts. You have to believe that you can have a positive impact on others. You have to believe that your words can inspire and your actions can move others. Believing that you can lead is essential to developing your leadership skills and abilities. If you don't, it's unlikely that you will make any effort at all, let alone a sustained effort to become a better leader over time. No one can put leadership into you. You have to bring it out of yourself.

Let's look deeper into this concept by reviewing a case example about a state government administrator, whom we'll call Jane Blake. Note that while Jane is a pseudonym, this story is true and the quotes come directly from correspondence with her (Kouzes and Posner 2016).

> Jane Blake shifted her entire self-concept once she started believing that she could be a leader. She told us that she'd been working in state government for about 20 years, that she had two bachelor's degrees, and that she never aspired to appear more than what she was—"a mother, grandmother, and coal miner's daughter." Still, Jane continued her university studies. She was currently enrolled in a master's degree program in leadership where, she reported, she sometimes struggled with the coursework and felt intimidated by classmates who were military leaders, company supervisors, and government managers. However, Jane had an aha moment when reading about leadership in one of our books—It "opened my eyes that maybe someone like me does have the possibility of being a leader," she explained. That moment transformed how she saw herself and what she believed she could become.

As Jane learned from her own experience, it wasn't something "out there" that held her back. It was a limiting narrative she was telling herself that, once she realized it, she could change. Jane's story demonstrates how, when you fundamentally believe you are capable of growing, you can open yourself to the possibilities of doing more than you originally assumed.

Stanford Professor Carol Dweck (2006) refers to this as a *growth mindset*. "The growth mindset," she says, "is based on the belief that your basic qualities are things you can cultivate through your efforts." Individuals with a growth mindset believe people can learn to be better leaders—that they are made and not born. Dweck (2016) compares this with a *fixed mindset*—"believing that your qualities are carved in stone." Those with a fixed mindset think leaders are born, and that no amount of training or experience is going to make them any better than they naturally are.

Evidence of this was also found in a study by Tae Kyung Kouzes on the relationship between growth and fixed mindsets and leadership behavior. "An examination of the influence of fixed and growth mindset on managers' assessment of how frequently they engaged in the five leadership practices showed that those with a growth mindset engaged in all five leadership practices more often than did managers with a fixed mindset" (Kouzes and Posner 2019). Mindset matters, and holding beliefs that you can learn how to lead enables you to perform more frequently as an exemplary leader.

> **QUESTIONS TO ASK YOURSELF: BELIEVE YOU CAN**
>
> - To what extent do I believe people's talents are innate gifts?
> - To what extent do I believe that I learn to lead?
> - To what extent do I believe that others can change their behavior?
> - To what extent do I identify myself as a leader?
> - How secure do I feel in my leadership abilities?

Fundamental 2. Aspire to Excel

Becky Schaar, a technical program manager at Google, told us that reflecting on her personal-best leadership experience revealed how important it was to understand "what you deeply believe, because people won't follow you, or even pay much attention to you, if you don't have strong beliefs." Olivia Lai, associate product strategist at Moody's Analytics (Hong Kong), said that "becoming a leader is a process of internal self-discovery. In order for me to become a leader and become an even better leader, it's important that I first define my values and principles. If I don't know what my own values are and determine expectations for myself, how can I set expectations for others?"

Through their processes of self-discovery, Schaar and Lai and so many other leaders around the globe have realized a fundamental lesson about leadership: To become an exemplary leader you have to discover what is important to you. To become the very best leader you can be, you need to be clear about the core values and beliefs that guide your decisions and actions as well as the vision you and others look forward to achieving. The same is true for learning leadership. You have to be clear about your motivations for wanting to be a leader. *Why* do you want to become a leader? Exactly what kind of a leader do you want to be?

This isn't mere theory or conjecture. We know from our research that those who are clearest about their personal values, for example, feel the strongest likelihood of achieving their life ambitions, are most willing to work long and hard, are most committed to their organizations, and feel less stress from work (Posner 2010). Clear personal values enable you to be more fully involved, focused, motivated, creative, and committed to your work. You feel empowered, willing to take initiative, and ready to move forward.

Keep this in mind, however. Your motivation needs to be intrinsic and not instrumental. Research has found that top-performing leaders don't focus on making money, getting a promotion, or being famous. They want to lead because they care deeply about the mission and people they are serving (Kolditz 2014). Having a clear sense of mission and purpose also helps you continue your learning journey when times are particularly challenging. Exemplary leaders and their constituents are in service of a larger purpose—a purpose beyond the self. Your success as a leader is inextricably linked to how successful you can make others. What is your purpose as a TD professional?

> **QUESTIONS TO ASK YOURSELF: ASPIRE TO EXCEL**
>
> - Why do I want to become a leader? Are my motivations mostly intrinsic or extrinsic?
> - To what extent do I have a clear ideal image of the kind of leader I want to be?
> - To what extent does my organization have a clear image of the kinds of leaders who are best for the organization?
> - How are these ideal images communicated, assessed, and reinforced?

Fundamental 3. Challenge Yourself

Challenge is the defining context for leadership. It's also the crucible for learning. To develop as a leader and do your best, you have to step outside your comfort zone. You have to seek new experiences, test yourself, make some mistakes, and keep climbing back up that learning curve. Just ask Ginni Rometty, IBM's chair and CEO. At the 2015 *Fortune* Most Powerful Women Summit, she offered this advice: "Think of when you ever learned the most in your life? What experience? I guarantee you'll tell me it was a time you felt at risk" (Sellers 2015).

Becoming a better leader not only requires you to challenge the organizational status quo; it also requires you to challenge your internal status quo. You have to challenge *yourself*. You have to venture beyond the boundaries of your current experience and explore new territory. Those are the places where opportunities exist to improve, innovate, experiment, and grow. Growth is always at the edges, just outside the boundaries of where you are right now.

In fact, we find that the more that people report they're actively searching outside the boundaries of their organizations for innovative ways to improve what is going on, the more effective and engaged they feel in their workplaces. And this action, along with seeking out challenging opportunities to test their skills and abilities, are seen by their managers and colleagues as directly correlated with how favorably they evaluate that individual's effectiveness (Kouzes and Posner 2017a).

Studies on the state of leadership and executive development reinforce these findings. In one survey, executives reported that they believed the most effective methods for leadership development were action-learning projects and stretch assignments (Hagemann et al. 2014). In another study, participation on cross-functional teams, working on a team to solve a specific customer issue, or being part of a global project team were the kinds of experiences that were most effective in developing their leadership capabilities (Davis 2015).

The only way you can learn new skills and abilities is to do things that you've never done before. If you do only what you already know how to do, then you will never develop new competencies or the confidence that comes with increased competence.

To get better at leading, you also have to get gritty (Duckworth 2016). Everyone stumbles in the process of developing, so don't let missteps sidetrack or dissuade you. Bounce forward from the setbacks. Persist and strengthen your resilience.

> **QUESTIONS TO ASK YOURSELF: CHALLENGE YOURSELF**
>
> - What challenging opportunities to learn and develop are available to me—or can I seek—as part of my development?
> - How curious am I about the latest developments in learning and leadership?
> - How is curiosity promoted and rewarded in my organization?
> - How are failures handled?
> - How persistent am I in the pursuit of goals that I am passionate about?

Fundamental 4. Engage Support

You can't learn to become the best leader all by yourself. The top performers in every endeavor, including leaders, seek out the support, advice, and counsel of others. This has a lot to do with why they turn out to be the most successful.

We have argued that to become the best at leading, or anything else, you have to challenge yourself, take on stretch assignments, step outside your comfort zone, experiment with new ways of doing things, make mistakes, and learn from failure. That's all well and good; however, you're not likely to do these things if there's no one there to teach you, coach you on how to improve, cheer you on and cheer you up, catch you when you fall, and comfort you when you hit a wall.

Learning to lead requires getting help from others. Social support is a necessary condition for growth and development, particularly when that learning is challenging. "The single most important thing you can do to help ensure your future success," according to Gallup's study of more than 27 million employees worldwide, is to find someone who has an interest in your development (Busteed 2015).

To learn to become an effective leader, you need to get connected. You need good advice and counsel, and you need people who can open doors for you. Identify who those people are, how you can reach out to them, and determine what you can do to improve the quality of your relationships with them. You're going to have to take the initiative to create and sustain relationships. Find people who are role models; observe how they do what they do.

You need those connections to be strong and personal, not simply transactional (Dutton 2014). Connections open doors and can give you an opportunity to observe exemplary leadership up close and in action. You're often going to have to take the initiative to create and sustain these relationships.

As you advance in your career, the *quality* of your connections becomes more and more significant. Researchers have shown that "high-quality connections contribute to individual flourishing and to team and organizational effectiveness" (Dutton 2014). People who have high-quality connections are healthier, have higher cognitive functioning, are broader thinkers, are more resilient, are more committed to the organization, and know better whom to trust and not trust. They also exhibit more learning behaviors. With high-quality relationships, people are more open, which means they more readily and fully understand themselves and the viewpoints of others. Greater quality in your connections also results in more attentiveness to what's going on around you and how to approach different activities. The quality of your relationships significantly influences the quality of your ability to learn.

You will also have to rely on the people around you to let you know the impact your actions and behaviors have on them. Their feedback is the only way you can learn how you are doing. Getting open and honest feedback happens only when there is a foundation of mutual trust. You have to go first in creating a climate in which people trust one other enough to provide valid and useful information that will help you grow.

And don't worry about other people thinking less of you if you seek advice. In fact, just the opposite is true. "Contrary to conventional wisdom and lay beliefs," report researchers, "we find that asking for advice increases perceptions of competence" (Brooks et al. 2015). As long as the task is difficult, you make the request personally, and you ask for advice from someone who's competent in the area, your request for advice will strengthen the perception that you know what you are doing. Reaching out to others for advice on tough challenges on which you need help not only builds your competence; it also increases the sense in others that they can have confidence in your leadership. Look around. As a TD professional, whom could you ask for support?

> **QUESTIONS TO ASK YOURSELF: ENGAGE SUPPORT**
> - Do I have a leadership coach?
> - Do I have a personal board of directors—a group of individuals I can turn to for mentoring, coaching, advice, and counsel?
> - How visible and accessible to me are role models of exemplary leadership?
> - How competent are leaders at coaching others in the organization?

Fundamental 5. Practice Deliberately

In a conversation about the importance of practice in developing leadership skills, Don Schalk, a university administrator with four decades of experience as a senior corporate executive, told us a story about his collegiate baseball experience. Don related how, every year on the first day of training, his coach, Dick Rockwell, would tell players that "practice begins at 3 and ends at 5. If that's all you do, we won't win, and you won't play." Don's story is a reminder that becoming the best demands more than just doing the minimum required. You've got to put in extra effort.

You can't get any better at leadership, or anything else, without practice. Raw talent alone is not sufficient to achieve greatness. It takes practice; however, researchers who have studied top performance across a wide variety of domains—such as surgery, acting, chess, writing, computer programming, ballet, music, aviation, and firefighting—say that you can't do just any kind of practice. "To people who have never reached a national or international level of competition, it may appear that excellence is simply the result of practicing daily for years or even decades," they report. "However, living in a cave does not make you a geologist. Not all practice makes perfect. You need a particular kind of practice—*deliberate practice*—to develop expertise" (Ericsson et al. 2007).

So, what does it mean to practice *deliberately*? To begin with, you will not be engaged in just any activity. Instead, you are engaged in an activity that's designed specifically to improve performance. Second, practice is not a one-time event. Engaging in a designed learning experience just once or twice won't cut it. You have to practice over and over and over again until it's automatic. You also need to be immersed in it. Focused attention on the specific content or methods you are learning is critical.

Another important characteristic of deliberate practice is the availability of feedback. Without knowing how you are doing, it's difficult to gauge whether or not you're getting close to your goal and whether you're executing properly. While there may come a time when you're accomplished enough to assess your own performance, you generally need a coach, mentor, or some other third party to help you analyze how you did.

Finally, there's just no getting around the fact that practice takes time. Time is such a precious commodity that you may think you don't have enough of it to go around, let alone add more activities to your agenda. You are likely familiar with the notion that it takes "10,000 hours of practice" if you want to become an expert (Gladwell 2008), but the truth is there is no specific number. You have to put in the time, but don't make a big deal about the exact number of hours required. Most important, it is about how you use your time to maximize your potential and master your craft.

Devoting time to one's development has benefits that go beyond skill improvement. In a study with LinkedIn, Josh Bersin (2018) concluded that "if you want to really enjoy your job, *spend more time learning*." Study researchers found, for example, that heavy learners (those who spent more than five hours per week learning) versus light learners (less than an hour per week) were 74 percent "more likely to know where they want to go in their career" and 48 percent "more likely to have found purpose in their work" (Bersin 2018).

> **QUESTIONS TO ASK YOURSELF: PRACTICE DELIBERATELY**
> - How many hours per week do I devote to learning?
> - How open am I to soliciting feedback and suggestions from others?
> - Is devoting time to learning leadership encouraged and supported in my organization?
> - Are there easy-to-access "practice fields" in my organization?
> - How is daily learning supported and rewarded?

Final Thoughts

To become the best leader you can be, you have to *believe in yourself*. You have the power and capacity to be exemplary, and you need to truly believe that deep down. Do not let anyone tell you anything different. You also have to *aspire to excel*. You need a set of values and a vision greater than you are, and you need to think long term. You have to *challenge yourself* to go beyond your current levels of performance and experiment with new and different ways of doing things. Your growth opportunities start at the edges of your current capacity. You have to *engage support* to learn and grow. Learning leadership is not something you do all by yourself. You need other people to help you become your best. Finally, you have to *practice deliberately*. Bringing out the best in yourself takes practice, and practice takes time. You have to make learning a daily habit.

Being an exemplary leader requires a lifelong commitment to learning. No matter how many summits you've ascended, you have to take a step every day to improve—one reflection at a time, one question at a time, one lesson at a time. You have to commit to the habits of learning something new every day and the habit of assessing your progress every day. Need a reminder? The tool on the handbook website (ATDHandbook3.org) shares five questions you should ask yourself every morning and evening.

This perspective echoes what Jim Whittaker shared with us. Jim was one of the founders of the outdoor equipment company REI and the first American to summit Mt. Everest. Among his many other outdoor adventures, he twice captained a sailboat in the 2,400-mile Victoria-to-Maui International Yacht Race and made the 20,000-mile voyage from Washington State to Australia four times. Upon reflecting on his adventures, Jim said that you have to make "the most of every moment, about stretching your own boundaries, about being willing to learn constantly, and about putting yourself in situations where learning is possible" (Whittaker 2013).

The instrument of leadership is the self, and mastery of the art of leadership comes from mastery of the self. *Leadership development is self-development*, and self-development is not simply about stuffing in a whole bunch of new information or trying out the latest technique. It's also about maximizing the potential you already have. Seeing yourself as a leader and exercising leadership more often will fundamentally change who you are. You're no longer an individual contributor. When you think of yourself as a leader, it changes how you:

- Present yourself day in and day out—you are expected to be a role model for the values that you and the organization espouse.
- See the future—you are expected to be able to imagine exciting future possibilities and communicate them to others.
- Respond to challenges—you are expected to be comfortable with uncertainty, champion experimentation, and learn from experiences.
- Relate to others—you are expected to build relationships, foster collaboration, strengthen those around you, and forge trust.
- Show others that you appreciate them—you are expected to sincerely recognize contributions and celebrate team successes.

Being true to these expectations and leading with your best self means that you need to be clear and comfortable with the kind of leader you want to become. Start the journey to become the best leader you can be by envisioning how you want to be seen as a leader by others. Kick-start that conversation with yourself by imaging the following scenario:

It's 10 years from today, and you are attending a ceremony in which you're being named "Leader of the Year." One after another, colleagues and co-workers, members of your family, and good friends take the stage and talk about your leadership and how you have made a positive difference in their lives.

To help think about what you want people to say about you that day and how you would hope to be remembered, record your responses to this L.I.F.E. paradigm:

- **Lessons.** What vital lessons do you hope others will say you have passed on? (For example, she taught me how to face adversity with grace and determination. He taught me the importance of giving back to those who've given to you.)
- **Ideals.** What ideals—values, principles, and ethical standards—do you hope people will say you stand for? (For example, she stands for freedom and justice. He believes in always telling the truth, even when it isn't what people want to hear.)
- **Feelings.** What feelings do you hope people will say they have or had when being with you or when thinking about you? (For example, she always made me feel like I was capable of doing the impossible. He made me feel important.)
- **Evidence.** What is the evidence that you made a difference; what lasting expressions or contributions—tangible and intangible—will people say that you leave to them and to others yet to come? (For example, she is really the one who turned this organization around. His dedication to others' lives was clear through the homes he helped us build and design.)

The next step is to ask yourself: How am I doing right now in teaching these lessons, living up to these ideals, creating these feelings, and providing the evidence that I am contributing as a leader? Then ask yourself: What can I do to do better?

We are confident that you will become an even better leader than you are today. And when you use those skills to make extraordinary things happen, you will bring a lot more hope to those you lead. Your neighborhood, organization, and world need this to be true.

About the Authors

James M. Kouzes and **Barry Z. Posner** are co-authors of the award-winning, bestselling book *The Leadership Challenge*, which has sold more than 2.8 million copies worldwide. They have been researching and writing about leadership and leadership development for more than 35 years and have authored more than a dozen other books on the topic. Jim is a fellow at the Doerr Institute for New Leaders at Rice University and was previously the Dean's Executive Fellow of Leadership at Santa Clara University's Leavey School of Business. Barry holds the Michael J. Accolti, S.J. Chair at Santa Clara University and is a professor of leadership with the Leavey School of Business, and chair of the department of management and entrepreneurship. He previously served 12 years as dean of the school.

References

Bersin, J. 2018. "New Research Shows 'Heavy Learners' More Confident, Successful, and Happy at Work," LinkedIn, November 9. linkedin.com/pulse/want-happy-work-spend-time-learning-josh-bersin.

Brooks, A.W., F. Gino, and M.D. Schweitzer. 2015. "Smart People Ask for (My) Help: Seeking Advice Books Perceptions of Competence." *Management Science* 61(6): 1431. dx.doi.org/10.1287/mnsc.2014.2054.

Brown, L.M., and B.Z. Posner. 2001. "Exploring the Relationship Between Learning and Leadership." *Leadership & Organization Development Journal,* May, 274–280.

Busteed, B. 2015. "The Two Most Important Questions for Graduates." Gallup, June 12. gallup.com/opinion/gallup/183599/two-important-questions-graduates.aspx.

Davis, S. 2015. "The State of Global Leadership Development." *Training,* July/August. trainingmag.com/sites/default/files//030_trg0715AMA3.pdf.

Duckworth, A. 2016. *Grit: The Power of Passion and Perseverance.* New York: Scribner.

Dutton, J.E. 2014. "Build High Quality Connections." In *How to Be a Positive Leader: Small Actions, Big Impact,* edited by J.E. Dutton and G. Spreitzer San Francisco: Berrett-Koehler.

Dweck, C.S. 2006. *Mindset: The New Psychology of Success.* New York: Random House.

Dweck, C. 2016. "What Having a "Growth Mindset" Actually Means." *Harvard Business Review,* January. hbr.org/2016/01/what-having-a-growth-mindset-actually-means.

Ericsson, K.A., M.J. Prietula, and E.T. Cokely. 2007. "The Making of an Expert." *Harvard Business Review,* July-August.

Gladwell, M. 2008. *Outliers: The Story of Success.* New York: Little, Brown.

Hagemann, B., J. Mattone, and J. Maketa. 2014. *EDA Trends in Executive Development 2014: A Benchmark Report.* Oklahoma City, OK: EDA; San Antonio, TX: Pearson TalentLens.

Kolditz, T. 2014. "Why You Lead Determines How Well You Lead." *Harvard Business Review,* July 22. hbr.org/2014/07/why-you-lead-determines-how-well-you-lead.

Kouzes, J.M., and B.Z. Posner. 2016. *Learning Leadership: The Five Fundamentals of Becoming an Exemplary Leader.* San Francisco: The Leadership Challenge—A Wiley Brand.

Kouzes, J.M., and B.Z. Posner. 2017a. *LPI: Leadership Practices Inventory,* 5th ed. Hoboken, NJ: The Leadership Challenge–A Wiley Brand. leadershipchallenge.com/LeadershipChallenge/media/SiteFiles/resources/sample-reports/tlc-lpi-360-english-v5.pdf.

Kouzes, J.M., and B.Z. Posner. 2017b. *The Leadership Challenge: How to Make Extraordinary Things Happen in Organizations,* 6th ed. San Francisco: Wiley.

Kouzes, T.K., and B.Z. Posner. 2019. "Influence of Managers' Mindset on Leadership Behavior." *Leadership & Organization Development Journal* 53(8): 829–844. doi.org/10.1108/LODJ-03-3019-0142.

Posner, B.Z. 1990. "Individual Characteristics and Shared Values: It Makes No Nevermind." Paper presented at the Academy of Management, Western Division, Salt Lake City.

Posner, B.Z. 2010. "Another Look at the Impact of Personal and Organizational Values Congruency." *Journal of Business Ethics* 97(4): 535–541.

Posner, B.Z., J.M. Kouzes, and W.H. Schmidt. 1985. "Shared Values Make a Difference: An Empirical Test of Corporate Culture." *Human Resource Management* 24(3): 293–310.

Posner, B.Z., and W.H. Schmidt. 1992a. "Demographic Characteristics and Shared Values." *International Journal of Value-Based Management* 5(1): 77–87.

Posner, B.Z., and W.H. Schmidt. 1992b. "Values Congruence and Differences Between the Interplay of Personal and Organizational Value Systems." *Journal of Business Ethics* 12:171–177.

Posner, B.Z., and R.I. Westwood. 1995. "A Cross-Cultural Investigation of the Shared Values Relationship." *International Journal of Value-Based Management* 11(4): 1–10.

Sellers, P. 2015. "What Happens When the World's Most Powerful Women Get Together." *Fortune*, November 1.

Whittaker, J. 2013. *A Life on the Edge: Memoirs of Everest and Beyond*, anniv. ed. Seattle, WA: The Mountaineers.

Recommended Resources

Coyle, D. 2009. *The Talent Code: Greatness Isn't Born. It's Grown. Here's How*. New York: Bantam Books.

Kouzes, J.M., and B.Z. Posner. 2010. *A Coach's Guide to Exemplary Leadership*. With E. Biech. San Francisco: Pfeiffer.

Kouzes, J.M., and B.Z. Posner. 2017. *The Leadership Challenge: How to Make Extraordinary Things Happen in Organizations*, 6th ed. San Francisco: Wiley.

Newport, C. 2012. *So Good They Can't Ignore You: Why Skills Trump Passion in the Quest for Work You Love*. New York: Grand Central Publishing, 33.

CHAPTER 46

Building Your Business Acumen

Kevin Cope

Whatever your background, schooling, or experience, there is nothing about business that is beyond your grasp. As a talent development professional, make a commitment to building your business acumen through ongoing study and action. By doing so, you will not only build your own career but also help your organization in the process.

> **IN THIS CHAPTER:**
> - Clarify why business acumen is important
> - Determine how to take action for building your business acumen to enhance your career and improve your organization
> - Identify seven steps an individual can take to build business understanding

Ralph Waldo Emerson said, "What lies behind us and what lies before us are tiny matters compared to what lies within us." When I first got out of college, I began my career in banking. I remember my enthusiasm and desire to excel in my first job and set the organization on fire with the sheer brilliance of my performance.

Well, as it turned out, I created more smoke than fire. I quickly began to realize how little I had actually learned in school. I struggled even to keep up a stumbling pace with my associates, who had already spent a few years in the real world.

I remember how discouraging it felt to be dressed for success and feel like a failure—sitting in a meeting with managers and senior executives, totally in over my head, trying to follow important concepts of the financial discussion. I was usually at a loss to make any intelligent comments, much less any meaningful contribution. I regularly found myself hoping that no one would call on me for anything important in case I actually had to say something and reveal that I had only a faint clue as to what they were talking about.

This embarrassment of ignorance compelled me to make a commitment to competence early in my career.

There is no more empowering feeling in business than to be in the company of experienced leaders and to be able to follow the flow of their discussion and make intelligent contributions to it. To sit in important meetings with colleagues, peers, and managers and be able to share your own insightful comments and recommendations.

Business leaders often describe this as having business acumen. I would suggest that business acumen is more about understanding how your company makes money than making good decisions that improve company performance. There are two important parts to this definition; one is knowing how a company makes money, including your company. The other is making good decisions.

A Seat at the Table

A Fortune 500 CEO says, "When I walk into a meeting, I want to see people surrounding me who are smarter than I am."

Many people express a desire to have a seat at the table. Why? Because that is where decisions are made and the course is set for the team or company going forward. It is where you can have a bigger impact on your organization. But people get a seat at the table only if they can contribute to the conversation that is going on at the table. And much of that discussion has to do with how the company is performing financially and what decisions need to be made to improve performance. To secure your seat at the table, you must know the business generally, your business specifically, and how to make and act on sound decisions.

Your application of business acumen requires a focus on the chief concerns and goals of your boss or the CEO. You'll need to have a current understanding of market trends, competitor analysis, partner relationships, strategic choices, financial markets, consumer trends, technology, and more. You'll also need to effectively communicate strategic goals if you want to contribute to your company's growth, and to your own.

As you grow in your influence at the decision table, you'll need to stretch yourself and move outside your comfort zone. It can be challenging to find the time and energy to do so, but the rewards will be worth it. Your knowledge, contributions, and the impact on your company and career will be obvious.

I challenge you to move forward with a commitment to take action.

In pursuing your worthy personal or business objectives, you must never omit the hard work of preparation. An admiring audience member said to the virtuoso concert pianist, "I'd give my life to play like that." The predictable response: "I have."

7 Steps for Building Business Acumen

Let's review seven practical ideas to encourage and support your ongoing development and application of sound business acumen.

Commit 15 Minutes Each Day for Business News

Set aside time for regular study and research, and to read business news. Your days are already crowded with professional and personal activities, but you can likely find opportunities to carve out the time to advance your career and your business. For example, how much time do you spend watching television? Can you use your lunchtime more productively?

Find a business news site you like and scan the key articles. Look for trends affecting your industry, business, and the economy in general. Look up phrases, business terms, or financial metrics you do not understand.

Many news sites allow you to track articles related to companies you are interested in. By tracking your company, competitors, key suppliers, and key customers, you can stay current on what is happening in your industry. In addition, making good business decisions isn't only a matter of knowing your company; it often requires an understanding of the overall industry. You might learn important information about a key customer that would allow you to anticipate their needs and become a better business partner. And you might be amazed by the number of ideas you glean from other organizations inside or outside your industry that could be applied to your company as well.

Stay Current on Your Company's Direction, Strategy, and Objectives

Devote time to learning how your company is organized and operates: its organization and internal structure, who the key officers are, your primary products and services, and your present and future goals. Understand the important priorities, values, and strategies of your CEO, division head, and direct supervisor.

Do you know how your company is doing financially or what its financial goals are? Go deeper than your company's big picture and, if possible, explore the financials of each division or department.

You can learn this by reading annual reports, emails, and other communications from your boss and company officers; company press releases; all materials on the company website; information about your company on the SEC website; quarterly Form 10-Q filings and annual 10-K filings; and other resources about your company, such as interviews of your senior leadership in all media. Ask your supervisor how to access more internal operating data if it isn't publicly available.

Also, if you work for a publicly traded company, listen to your CEO's quarterly conference calls with Wall Street analysts. This quarterly call provides a current report on the company's operations and financial performance, and your CEO's priorities and future plans.

Talk With Key Company Managers

Build relationships with your key company leaders and managers, starting with your boss or supervisor. In addition, talk regularly with peers or teammates in different departments who have specific expertise. Meet people for lunch; set brief appointments in their office. Ask questions that reveal your own research. Share helpful insights in return. Let your reasons be known—you want to become more knowledgeable in order to make more effective contributions.

When you talk with your boss or supervisor, discuss the big picture of your organization and how your work team or department, and you personally, can have a more significant impact. Learn about the key measures and dashboard metrics that your boss and division or company senior management are focused on. Discuss how to better achieve these targets so you know how your team, and your job function, fits in.

Consider asking someone in finance to meet with you to explain your company's financial statements. You will likely be amazed at how willing they are to help and how few people take advantage of this opportunity. Set up a regular meeting to coincide with when the financials are released so you can stay current on what is happening in the business and better understand the nuances of the statements.

As Harold S. Geneen, once CEO of ITT and father of the international conglomerate, once said, "When you have mastered numbers, you will in fact no longer be reading numbers, any more than you read words when reading books. You will be reading meanings."

ALIGNING T&D WITH ORGANIZATIONAL STRATEGY
Dean Griess, Managing Director, Learning Delivery and Design, Charles Schwab HR Talent Solutions

Working within a company that has various business entities like we have at Schwab can create a challenge for any learning professional. We look at our interactions as if we were hired as consultants or experts. Although we are an internal resource, our focus is to create remarkable experiences in the classroom and commit to delivering excellence with our learning products (such as designed content).

Because we set the bar so high, it is imperative that our customers feel that commitment to excellence in our interactions.

We strive to get to know our partners and to understand their unique challenges. We follow several key steps that have afforded us the capability to work closely with our partners while operating as a center of excellence within the firm. These steps are:

- Cultivate the relationships; be the learning consultant or expert they need.
- Ensure performance success measures are clearly defined.
- Create a plan (by initiative or annually), yet remain adaptable.
- Commit to communicate early and often.
- Adapt learning to the business or culture.
- Provide a review of the results, especially key success measures.

Each of these steps plays a vital role in our success as a learning expert for our partners. We have been forced to think not just outside the box, but beyond the box itself.

For example, we wanted to provide an overview of the impact our leadership development classes have had on the firm. This became quite challenging because the objectives and content were both varied. In partnership with our program managers, we centered our approach on acknowledging that the overarching success of our firm is defined by our guiding principles. With this in mind, we created a post-session survey for all learners to respond to a series of questions that align with these guiding principles and leverage the Brinkerhoff measurement strategy. Even though more than 50 percent of the learners surveyed hadn't been in a session for at least three months, we had a very high response rate that showed a combined alignment of more than 90 percent applicable improvement to the guiding principles following the class they attended. This level of creativity in measuring impact allowed us to improve our partnership by telling a compelling story for the combined classes, instead of just sharing a handful of individual stories.

Build Relationships

Be proactive; contribute and follow through. Whenever an assignment or opportunity for action results from your study, discussions, or meetings, follow through and do it. Report back in a timely way to the appropriate parties so others will realize what you have done.

When realistic or appropriate, put your comments and questions into succinct, meaningful, and timely emails or memos addressed to appropriate personnel. However, don't overwhelm people with a flood of ideas or recommendations. Be targeted in your approach.

Draw up a brief written action list. Link your actions to results that move the needle in areas important to your boss and senior management and that support the key measures they have identified. Note in writing how your learning and performance initiatives affect the business. Give a copy to your boss or supervisor and discuss.

Attend Industry Meetings and Make Outside Contacts

If your company provides any occasion for you to attend industry or major customer conferences or meetings, take the opportunity. Read the literature available. Network with those you meet there. Grow your own database of contacts and keep in touch with them over time, as possible. Gain your own direct sources of helpful industry, economic, or business information. Stay in communication with those you meet.

Use a Buddy for Accountability and Mentoring

Use the buddy system. Ask a co-worker—maybe a fellow TD professional or senior manager—to work with and mentor you. At the very least, identify someone to whom you can make a commitment regarding your business acumen action plan and ask them to hold you accountable. Perhaps that person would want to further their own knowledge, and you can help and support each other. Being a mentor to someone else will help you both.

Above all, accept an assignment from and be accountable to yourself to continue to develop your business acumen.

Influence Management

To influence senior management, you have to follow all the above recommendations to prepare yourself to present an idea or opportunity. Then, when asking a leader to consider seriously your views or recommendations, follow these four important suggestions—principles that have worked for thousands of employees across many industries and types of companies:

- **Listen to understand.** Listen first. Your sole purpose in listening? To understand where the individual or management team is coming from to get what's important to them. In every meeting, listen carefully for opportunities to ask insightful questions to learn even more. If you deeply understand their point of view, their needs and priorities, it will first influence you. Then you'll better be able to influence them.
- **Present their case and needs to them.** Once you have deeply listened, in classic consultative form, make a "my understanding of your needs and objectives" summary

before making your own proposals. Once managers know that you really do understand their perspective, they will be more open to listening to your analysis and proposals. You'll have built greater trust.
- **Speak their language.** Once you've established mutual understanding, connect your analysis and recommendations to their strategic goals, concerns, needs, and mindset. Link your message to what's important to them, in financial language they understand. Demonstrate the impact of your proposal or analysis on drivers that are important to them. Remember that every department or function has somewhat differing priorities.
- **Use ROI analysis.** As a TD professional, I don't have to tell you how important ROI analysis is. Ultimately, every business decision boils down to determining how best to use capital for maximum return on investment. Make a convincing case for a favorable ROI through your recommendation.

Final Thoughts

Your ultimate ability to become a more valuable and valued employee is primarily up to you. Your contribution to the success of your department, division, or company at large will add to your own career success. Helping others along the way will add dimensions of experience, knowledge, and insights that will benefit both them and you.

As you become better known for your insightful business acumen, you will become more visible as a contributor and a more valued member of your company team. Wherever you go in your future professional career, your ability to understand the keys that drive business and exercise the acumen associated with them will lead to sustained profitable success.

I encourage your continued commitment and hard work. You can begin by turning to the online tools on the handbook website at ATDHandbook3.org, and use the worksheet to consider what you need to do. Persevere. I'm confident it will pay off. The ultimate key? To engage. My very best wishes for your success, and my encouragement once more to stay with it!

About the Author

Kevin Cope is the founder and CEO of Acumen Learning, the leader in finance and business acumen training. Kevin's number 1 *Wall Street Journal* and *New York Times* bestseller, *Seeing the Big Picture: Business Acumen to Build Your Credibility, Career, and Company*, has helped business leaders the world over develop this critical skill. Kevin's work includes engagements with some of the most respected and profitable businesses in the world, including 30 Fortune 50 companies. He's been recognized as a top-rated speaker at national conventions, including those held by SHRM and ATD; interviewed by top radio and podcast programs; and featured in top publications, including *Chief Executive*, *Fast Company*, and *Industry Week*. Kevin and his wife, Karen, reside in Utah and love relaxing and spending time in Cabo with their six children and seven grandchildren. You can learn more at acumenlearning.com.

Recommended Resources

Christensen, C.M. 2012. *How Will You Measure Your Life?* New York: HarperCollins.

Collins, J. 2011. *Good to Great: Why Some Companies Make the Leap… and Others Don't.* New York: HarperCollins.

Cope, K. 2012. *Seeing the Big Picture: Business Acumen to Build Your Credibility, Career, and Company.* Austin, TX: Greenleaf Book Group Press.

Covey, S.M.R. 2006. *The Speed of Trust.* New York: Free Press.

Tracy, J.A. 2009. *How to Read a Financial Report.* Hoboken, NJ: John Wiley and Sons.

CHAPTER 47

Supporting Your Organization's Onboarding Efforts

Norma Dávila and Wanda Piña-Ramírez

An employee's experience with onboarding creates an indelible first impression of the company's business, politics, unwritten rules, culture, and values. If this experience is positive, it reinforces the employee's decision about joining and staying in the company. In contrast, if the experience is not positive, it may trigger a decision to start a new job search while staying in the company as a disengaged employee.

> **IN THIS CHAPTER:**
> - Understand the importance of employee onboarding
> - Describe the three main phases of employee onboarding
> - Apply useful tools to support your organization's onboarding efforts

Learning and development is the source of knowledge about how people learn, acquire skills, and master their competencies, with the goal of influencing individuals and groups to do their work better. Therefore, even though many debate where onboarding should reside in the organization, whether it should be in human resources or L&D, we propose that L&D should be the owner of this important business process. It is up to L&D, as onboarding's owner, to make sure that employees have the best possible onboarding experience.

Vedran Ismaili (2020) shared this data about onboarding in an infographic:

- 88 percent of employees say their employer did not provide a productive onboarding program.
- 69 percent of employees are more likely to stay with a company after a great onboarding experience.
- 76 percent of organizations are underutilizing employee onboarding practices.
- A third of all employee attrition happens during the first 90 days.
- 54 percent higher employee engagement is found among employees who went through a structured employee onboarding program.
- A structured onboarding program improves productivity by more than 70 percent.
- 35 percent of companies spend zero dollars onboarding their employees.
- 70 percent of the employee onboarding experience is dependent on their manager and their skills in onboarding a new hire.
- 69 percent of managers describe onboarding as time consuming.
- A 97 percent increase in productivity was seen among employees who were assigned an onboarding buddy.

Thus, we can conclude that a positive onboarding experience has a considerable impact on employee engagement, retention, and productivity.

In addition, the average cost per hire may be approximately $4,000 for lower-level employees, while average costs per hire for executives can easily be 10 times as high (Peterson 2020). Regardless of these numbers, the costs of hiring during the COVID-19 pandemic doubled, in some cases, because of the additional challenges involved in finding the right talent at the right moment. Therefore, dedicating time and resources to designing effective onboarding programs is always in the organization's best interests.

Other benefits of onboarding include:

- Greater capacity to attract top talent
- Creates a pipeline for succession planning
- Increased understanding of brand and value proposition
- A focus from management and HR on the business instead of on transactions

Why, then, are so many organizations still overlooking this significant component of employee experience that clearly makes business sense? What can L&D do to ensure that organizations have solid onboarding programs? Who can take care of this important business component in organizations that do not have formal HR or L&D functions, units, or departments?

The answer to these questions depends on the size, type, and business model of the organization. Ultimately, in the absence of L&D and HR functions, whether internal or outsourced, the organization's management has the responsibility to design and implement an effective onboarding program.

In this chapter, we will discuss how L&D can add value by taking an active role and ownership in creating and deploying effective onboarding programs. We also share examples based on our consulting experiences as well as our review of the latest trends in onboarding.

Let's begin with some definitions to establish a common ground for our discussion. In *Effective Onboarding* (2018), we defined *onboarding* as:

> The process through which companies engage new employees or new-to-role employees in the company's culture and with their role. This process is designed to ease the movement of employees through the organizational threshold to become productive contributors and team members in the least possible time. Onboarding's influence on employee performance is companywide. Therefore, it is directly connected to business outcomes and warrants a sizeable investment in resources.

Many organizations still mistakenly refer to new employee orientations as onboarding. We compare the main characteristics of both in Table 47-1.

Table 47-1. Characteristics of Employee Orientation and Employee Onboarding

Employee Orientation	Employee Onboarding
Delivered after an employee's first day of work or before they assume a new role	Starts before the employee's first day of work or first day at new role
Provides a general business overview (including the history, products, competitors, rules, benefits, financials, policies, and vision)	Facilitates familiarity and comfort with the company's culture to reduce time to productivity
One to three days in duration	Six months to a year in duration
Similar content for new and new-to-role employees from all organizational levels as well as for nonexempt or exempt employees, managers, supervisors, and executives	Content for new and new-to-role employees is customized by role, organizational level, and previous experience, as well as for whether the employee is exempt or nonexempt
Single event	Process that includes employee orientation and role-specific onboarding
Easy to deliver virtually or in person	Best to combine virtual and in-person delivery

Onboarding is a process, and, as such, it includes three phases (Figure 47-1).

Figure 47-1. Three Phases of the Onboarding Process

Pre-Onboarding ➔ General Onboarding ➔ Role-Specific Onboarding

Let's look at each phase in more detail (Dávila and Piña-Ramírez 2018):
- **Pre-onboarding.** Comprises all the activities that take place before the new employee or new-to-role employee receives the employment offer. The organization's recruitment and selection activities are part of this component.
- **General onboarding.** Introduces the employee to the company's culture (how things are done) by establishing commonalities among all employees regardless of position. This establishes the ground rules to engage newcomers with the workplace.
- **Role-specific onboarding.** Entails a uniquely tailored process for each position in the company because it seeks assimilation of the new or new-to-role employee into the nuances of the department's or unit's culture. Activities are highly individualized for each position and require a transfer of knowledge from the learning and development function to the manager or immediate supervisor.

Thus, onboarding is the final stage of the recruitment process and the first step of the employee experience. When designing your organization's onboarding program, make sure that you include the following must-have components:
- Content and duration
- Communication, presentations, and exercises
- Introductory videos
- Company vision, mission, and history
- Policies and procedures
- Industry-specific details
- Structure and business model
- Employee handbook
- Organizational charts
- Who's who in the organization
- Updated job descriptions
- Mandatory and optional training sessions
- The onboarding timeline and milestones
- The building's floor plan
- An onboarding checklist
- Role-specific elements

These elements must be placed in the appropriate onboarding phase prior to delivery. Note that when onboarding is delivered 100 percent virtually, all elements will reside in the system and will need to be tailored for each employee.

Onboarding should create an atmosphere of openness and trust to ask questions and address the cultural nuances that are typical of units and departments by having separate sessions for all participating groups, whether they are in person or virtual. Keep in mind that when employees assume a new role they'll need to be brought up to date on the latest changes in the organization. They should also participate in the entire onboarding process because assuming a new role requires completing many transactions that resemble those completed by new hires.

The multidimensionality of the onboarding process demands the involvement and participation of several players and stakeholders whose contributions require seamless coordination. Whether the organization is currently operating under in-person, virtual, or hybrid models, the employee's supervisor or manager, company management, HR, and L&D are usually involved. They may be present in person or through different media options, such as videoconferencing tools, prerecorded videos, or other company communication channels.

In the end, onboarding must foster the employee's sense of connection and engagement with the organization, regardless of whether it is delivered fully in person, virtually, or both.

Onboarding in Our Post-Pandemic World

The COVID-19 pandemic forced many organizations to accelerate their use of alternative ways to conduct business under different circumstances. What once were considered temporary arrangements to maintain business continuity during emergencies, such as natural disasters and political upheaval, became "permanent until further notice" for many. Working remotely moved from being a wish for those who wanted more flexibility and control over their time to a reality loaded with uncertainty during the rush to implementation. Yet, working remotely became the only way for many organizations and their employees to remain in business.

While many organizations reduced their workforces during the pandemic, others found opportunities to grow and diversify their products and services. They also found ways to source, recruit, onboard, train, and retain those new employees. Often, L&D led the conversion of in-person processes into virtual processes almost overnight. Onboarding was not the exception.

A successful onboarding program must be carefully orchestrated so that all its components, namely, pre-onboarding, general onboarding, and role-specific onboarding, are delivered on time and the program serves its purpose, especially during times of uncertainty. What happens when those components and players are dispersed geographically, perhaps even around the world? These new circumstances call for L&D to design every detail even more thoroughly and put additional contingency plans in place. L&D must proactively minimize the likelihood of interruptions, errors, and other costly mistakes, which could have a negative impact on those crucial first impressions and even prompt the new or new-to-role employee to question the decision to join the organization, accept the new position, or stay in the organization.

We acknowledge that many organizations are rethinking how they will do business, including to what extent they will remain working remotely and how they will bring in employees to perform functions that did not exist earlier. However, we also believe that remote working will remain a major component of how organizations do business. Therefore, L&D has to be ready to embrace this reality, just like it embraced the sudden shift from in-person to virtual operations.

The good news is that L&D now has experience with virtual technologies, which are more commonly available than they were earlier. Thus, designing and delivering virtual and hybrid programs has become a regular component of how to do business. Inclusivity, respect, and personalized attention will make a difference in the experience, whether the program is delivered in person, virtually, or both.

Regardless of how easy or available virtual technologies may be, we still believe that using them demands more than uploading a presentation and hoping audiences will obtain some benefit from it. This is why expertise in how people learn and how organizations operate is absolutely essential for organizations to move forward at this juncture. L&D cannot overlook the possibility of having some new and new-to-role employees participating in onboarding programs who are working remotely for the first time and will need additional assistance as they handle multiple issues related to how and where they will work. Let's review an example:

> Rodrigo is a recent hire. Until now, he had always worked as an accountant in an in-person environment as part of an organization with offices in several states. He accepted this offer because it had better benefits and the opportunity to work remotely, which would save his usual commuting time. Rodrigo was the typical employee who would get up from his desk several times during the day to get coffee, share stories in the hallways, and chitchat with his co-workers.
>
> His first encounter with his new reality was the link to access his onboarding program. He was using the company computer he had received a few days earlier and had set it up with telephone technical support. When Rodrigo opened the employee platform, he found all the forms and documents that he had to sign, along with the information he had to read and acknowledge having read, such as the employee handbook. On the platform he could register attendance, request leave, and access payroll information, as well as review his performance goals and required trainings. After much navigation, he finally located a welcome letter and video from the company president.
>
> Rodrigo started his process without being prepared for the information overload he was about to receive. And worse, no one was available to answer questions or chitchat.

Rodrigo's organization, and perhaps your own, could have anticipated and addressed some of these issues by answering the questions outlined in the tool 9 Questions to Determine Suitability for Remote Work. This tool is available for download on the handbook website, ATDHandbook3.org.

In the tool, we posit that employees are best suited for remote work if they:
- Work in an organization that has a written remote-work policy
- Have results measured by product instead of by time
- Are less dependent on others to do their work
- Require lower levels of direction and guidance to do their work
- Need minimal equipment to do their work, such as desk, chair, filing cabinets, computer, printer, access to high-speed internet, and perhaps an extra monitor, laptop, or dedicated cell phone
- Can access technical support from either specialized staff or informal experts
- Have low levels of interaction with other areas of the organization
- Can find ways to connect with others meaningfully, whether in person or virtually
- Are politically savvy to enhance their visibility to their managers and supervisors even when they are working remotely

We recommend using this tool to gain a solid perspective on which employees are best suited for remote work and identify the specific needs of those who are not so they can be addressed. Differentiate responses by employee when appropriate.

After working with organizations of all sizes and structures, we are even more convinced of the importance and value of in-person contact during the onboarding processes. Because working remotely is here to stay, so will onboarding remotely. However, we recommend you follow a hybrid model for onboarding, which combines in-person and virtual experiences for new and new-to-role employees. This allows organizations to maximize the benefits of both to create positive first impressions and, thus, reduce time to productivity. At the very least, someone from the organization should meet with the new and new-to-role employees—whether in person or virtually (remembering to turn on the camera)—once before or during the onboarding process, even if the new and new-to-role employee will work remotely.

All employees have unique learning needs, so you'll want to adapt your program's design and delivery to the type of content and employee learning needs. The ATD website features many resources you can use to design and evaluate programs focused on individual learning needs.

In our pandemic and post-pandemic world, the need for consistent and reliable communication is critical. Therefore, communications about onboarding, such as those discussing buddies and mentors, schedules and road maps, expectations and milestones, contact lists and mandatory training sessions, must be delivered consistently and on time to all necessary parties through the most appropriate channels. Regardless of the delivery method, the messenger of choice for general information is company management, whereas the new or new-to-role employee's direct supervisor is preferred for delivering more specific information.

Table 47-2 lists who should deliver what content during each onboarding phase.

Table 47-2. Onboarding Communications: Channel, Content, and Phase

Who	What	Onboarding Phase
Top management	• The organization's overview, vision, mission, values, history, products, services, business model • General cultural norms	General orientation or general onboarding
Human resources	• Organizational structure • Company policies • Benefits • Onboarding program phases and facilitators • General directory	General orientation or general onboarding
Manager or supervisor	• Specifics of position • Role clarification for the buddy, mentor, coach, and others • Performance expectations • Performance management • Specific contact lists • Department or unit norms • Career mapping	Role-specific onboarding
Learning and development	• Buddy or mentor • Mandatory trainings	Role-specific onboarding

The Onboarding Communications Status Tool can help you to track the progress of your onboarding communications. It allows you to add information about the status of each component of the onboarding phase within your organization. Select the communications and messengers that your organization will use during the onboarding process. Write "completed," "in progress," or "not started" under the status column or use colors such as yellow, green, or red for additional visual effects. Be sure to update the status column regularly. The Onboarding Communications Status Tool is available for download on the handbook website at ATDHandbook3.org.

Onboarding's Three Phases

Let's dive into the three phases of onboarding: pre-onboarding, general onboarding, and role-specific onboarding.

Pre-Onboarding

Pre-onboarding signals the start of customization for the general onboarding phase, as well as for planning role-specific onboarding based on the person's role and employee profile.

New employees will need to complete documentation to begin to work; doing so before their first day will begin to instill a sense of belonging while saving worthwhile time for other activities. This is also a good time to make the appropriate introductions, in person or virtually, to promote relationships.

In today's technological world, many companies are sending links and granting access to systems, usually accompanied by a tutorial, before employees formally start to work. Acknowledging that onboarding is an emotional experience and a learning journey, as well as that so much of the employee's performance is contingent upon the onboarding program's design and delivery, we recommend tailoring the introduction to what employees will find in those systems.

Based on our list of must-have elements, pre-onboarding should include content and duration, introductory videos, information about the organization's structure and business model, the employee handbook, the onboarding timeline and milestones, and an onboarding checklist.

Use the pre-onboarding worksheet on the handbook website (ATDHandbook3.org) to help you describe each element in your organization's pre-onboarding plan.

General Onboarding

New and new-to-role employees at all levels would benefit from receiving general onboarding as a starting point to connect with the workplace, their roles, and with one another. We recommend tailoring the organization's onboarding program to meet the specific needs of contractors and gig workers, with a general orientation at a minimum.

These must-have elements should be included in general onboarding:
- Content and duration
- Communication, presentations, and exercises
- Introductory videos
- The company's vision, mission, and history
- Policies and procedures
- Industry-specific details
- Organizational charts
- Who's who in the organization
- Mandatory and optional training programs
- The building's floor plan

The general onboarding worksheet on the handbook website at ATDHandbook3.org will help you keep track of each element in this phase.

When necessary, you should redesign the presentations about the organization's history and how it has changed over time to emphasize the lessons learned to build a better organization for the future. In addition, consider interspersing unstructured time for participants to interact and share stories and experiences. Employees will benefit from receiving information about the topics in the general overview; however, they also will have specific needs and expectations. Be sure to address these separately either in customized sessions by role or organizational level or during role-specific onboarding. Choose facilitators, speakers, and presenters wisely to ensure look and feel, fit, and credibility. If possible, schedule required trainings for everyone during the same week and before they join their teams. Regardless of the current trends toward self-onboarding, we recommend that all new and new-to-role employees come together to go beyond organizational charts and connect names, faces, roles, and departments.

General onboarding must emphasize that employee safety is always a priority. Some organizations are redesigning how they meet, use individual and collective spaces, get together informally, clean work areas, and maximize available hands-free technology. New policies, procedures, and protocols keep safety top of mind. For those employees working remotely, safety practices at home must also be part of the onboarding process.

Let's meet Beatriz:

> Beatriz was eager to start to work from home. The company delivered her equipment, and she was proud to set it up by herself. She even converted a section of her dining room into a new workstation.
>
> However, while completing her new employee documentation, she decided to get some water. On her way to the kitchen, she tripped on the computer cable she had laid across the floor and fell, fracturing her wrist. This was her first week.

Beatriz's example highlights the importance of clearly defining safety practices in the workplace, wherever that workplace may be. A simple oversight, such as not having the right lighting or not properly securing cords and cables, can cause an avoidable occupational accident.

Discussions about cybersecurity are also gaining strength in the hybrid workplace. Make sure that employees know your organization's dos and don'ts to protect system and information integrity. Create a glossary of frequently used technical terms for those who are less familiar with technology.

After general onboarding ends, it is time to transition each new and new-to-role employee to the most important phase of the process—role-specific onboarding.

Role-Specific Onboarding

L&D should partner with managers and supervisors to design role-specific onboarding for each new and new-to-role employee. Managers and supervisors will ultimately be directly responsible for the role-specific onboarding of their direct reports, with the support and monitoring of L&D. Depending on the manager's experience as a manager and managing remote workers, L&D's role in the process and level of involvement will vary.

You should include the following must-have elements in role-specific onboarding:
- Content and duration
- Updated job descriptions
- Training sessions
- Performance goals, expectations, and reviews
- Role-specific systems
- Career development
- Information about the supervisor's working style, availability, and communications preferences
- Information about employee's working style, availability, and communications preferences
- The department's size, reporting structure, products and services, internal and external clients, current projects, common acronyms and jargon, core processes, main contribution to the business, culture, business plans, and goals
- Mentors and buddies

You can use the role-specific worksheet on the handbook website at ATDHandbook3.org to help you describe each element of your organization's role-specific onboarding.

The formal training program included as part of role-specific onboarding should address topics related to specific details about working remotely or in a hybrid model so that employees gain the necessary skills and increase their confidence if and when they need them. Consider providing resources—such as coaches, subject matter experts, and short instructional videos—to support employees and managers in this transition, always keeping in mind employee wellness.

Let's look at how L&D can use technology to create virtual and hybrid onboarding programs based on an organization's context and circumstances.

Technology in Onboarding

Employee onboarding is reaping the benefits of new technologies introduced by organizations. Whether in pre-onboarding, general onboarding, or role-specific onboarding, these tools enhance employee experience and expedite the completion of otherwise routine tasks, thus allowing everyone to focus on what matters.

New and new-to-role employees must have the technological tools that they need available and ready to use before an onboarding program starts, whether it is completely virtual or hybrid. Organizations must clarify what equipment and tools they will provide (for example, cell phone, computer, monitors, camera, ergonomic desk, access to applications, and secure virtual networks), as well as how and when employees can expect to receive them and be ready to use them. Organizations must also define what they expect the employee to secure, such as a high-speed internet connection, and whether they will install all equipment on-site or provide direct telephone support for the new or new-to-role employee to do it themselves. Some video tutorials may be useful to delve into specific online resources after the new or new-to-role employee has become familiar with the new equipment and tools.

Establishing virtual and hybrid onboarding programs demands proficiency in the use of technology from all key players, including the use of collaboration applications as well as desktop, laptop, and mobile devices. Even though L&D owns and leads the new employee orientation and general onboarding components, company management and new and new-to-role employees must also have a basic level of familiarity with this technology so they can focus on the experience. Otherwise, technical details like freezing transmissions, uncooperative cameras, and slow connectivity on either the organization or the employee's side may derail what would otherwise have been a seamless introduction to the organization and its culture.

Let's meet Petra:

Petra just accepted a position at Balsamic Kitchen Supplies, which has 150 employees distributed across two brick-and-mortar stores and an administrative office. She is the new customer service manager. Her in-person onboarding experience in the administrative office went smoothly; however, Petra lives in a different city from where the administrative offices are located.

Petra always carries her laptop computer so she can work remotely. The first time she tried to log in to complete a section of her general onboarding, she could not access the page. She used her company cell phone to open a ticket with information systems, but she did not receive a response until more than 48 hours later. In the meantime, she could not complete her onboarding or do any work. The positive impact that the in-person onboarding experience had on Petra was gone.

L&D would be wise to secure the services of a technology expert, ideally throughout the program's virtual deployment but at least during the critical program features that have the greatest potential to become showstoppers, as in Petra's case.

L&D must find the best possible combination of components, such as live streaming, instructional videos, general communication videos, and quick reference guides, to make onboarding lively and engaging. Short videos by co-workers introducing themselves and welcoming the new and new-to-role employee add a personal dimension to the process.

The aphorism "everything in moderation, even moderation" holds true, especially for onboarding programs to address participant needs. Avoid information overload by programming multiple short sessions (lasting one to two hours) and distributing them across several days for the new employee orientation and general onboarding components of the program. Mandatory training sessions can also be redesigned as shorter sessions distributed across several days. In the meantime, buddies, mentors, and managers can answer questions through the organization's internal communications tools. The previous points about technology and scheduling also apply for role-specific onboarding, even though it is a more individualized experience between the employee and manager.

L&D needs to monitor the progress of onboarding programs and be prepared to show its impact. Let's look at how this can be accomplished.

Impact of Onboarding Programs

Organizations need to gauge the impact of their onboarding programs to demonstrate why they are a good investment. Because onboarding programs are strategically connected to employee and business performance, documenting metrics, measurement, and evaluation needs to become part of the organization's day-to-day operations.

The meaning of *metrics*, *measurement*, and *evaluation* must be clear before we can address these issues correctly. *Metrics* are standards of performance and progress that can be quantified, while *measurement* is the process of assigning value to metrics and *evaluation* refers to making judgments about what was measured (Dávila and Piña-Ramírez 2018).

The task of assessing the impact of onboarding programs can seem daunting at first, especially when an organization's culture is gradually moving along the data-driven decision-making continuum. The increasing availability of big data and algorithms is stretching the possibilities for thorough analyses.

Table 47-3 outlines some of the metrics organizations track and who owns them. Use it to see which metrics are available for you to use.

Remember to speak the language of your audience. You will want to track, analyze, and convert all measures to business and financial terms because that is the language of the organization's decision makers. Use the checklist to document availability of common onboarding metrics on the handbook website (ATDHandbook3.org).

Table 47-3. Common Metrics by Owner

Owner	Metric
Human resources	• Recruitment costs • Interview costs • Personality-testing costs • HR staff time • Compliance with legal issues • Retention rates • Turnover rates • Exit interviews (guiding questions and data analysis)
Learning and development	• Skill- and competency-testing costs • Welcome packet • Learning and development staff time • New employee orientation materials • Computer room use for online training sessions (in-house or rented) • Facilitator preparation, design, and materials • New and new-to-role employee satisfaction surveys • Participant evaluation forms (digital and printed)
Communications	• All internal and external communications • Communications staff time
Information systems	• Costs of internal or outsourced technical support for virtual interviews and meetings, online learning, and electronic communications
Different departments	• Facilitator time

Final Thoughts

The COVID-19 pandemic and resulting changes have demonstrated the importance of being ready for all types of onboarding, whether in person, virtual, or hybrid. This chapter has outlined the basics of an employee onboarding program; you must be ready, at a moment's notice, to add and delete different elements to keep it consistent, relevant, and current. You also have what you need to re-onboard employees who were onboarded virtually and then move back into working in the in-person environment.

Onboarding programs demand time and resources to guarantee their ability to sustain and benefit the organization. Make sure to:
- Monitor, communicate, anticipate, and remove obstacles.
- Provide ongoing learning opportunities to support career paths and preferences.
- Reinforce what happened during onboarding.
- Remember the learning curves.
- Seek best practices.
- Revise, revise, and revise your design.
- Foster the human side of onboarding even when relying on technology.
- Own it.

About the Authors

Wanda Piña-Ramírez is an action-driven and strategic management and executive consultant with a proven track record of contributing to the bottom line in companies spanning from multinational corporations to small businesses located in Puerto Rico, the United States, the Caribbean, and Latin America. She addresses those topics that no one wants to address, such as business metrics, labor law, sexual harassment, and domestic violence. Reach Wanda at pixiepinaramirez@aol.com.

Norma Dávila guides her career management clients through targeted introspection and self-assessments to identify strengths and interests as well as build self-confidence before embarking on career changes. She focuses her practice on entry-level and mid career professionals across the entire employee life cycle. Norma communicates complex ideas in easy-to-understand and relatable terms to all audiences. You can reach her at normadavila47@gmail.com.

Together, Wanda and Norma complement their areas of expertise as business partners in the Human Factor Consulting Group (thehumanfactorpr.com) and are co-authors of *Cutting Through the Noise: The Right Employee Engagement Strategies for You*, *Passing the Torch: A Guide to the Succession Planning Process*, and *Effective Onboarding*.

References

Anderson, B. 2020. "8 Steps to Creating a Virtual Employee Onboarding Program." LinkedIn Talent blog, November 3. business.linkedin.com/talent-solutions/blog/onboarding/2020/steps-to-creating-virtual-onboarding-program.

Bannan, K.J. 2020. "6 Things About Virtual Onboarding That Worry New Hires." SHRM Talent Acquisition, June 4. shrm.org/resourcesandtools/hr-topics/talent-acquisition/pages/6-things-about-virtual-onboarding-that-worry-new-hires.aspx.

Costa, A. 2020. "Back to the Workplace: 5 Things to Consider When Reboarding Returning Employees." eLearning Industry, November 10. elearningindustry.com/what-consider-when-reboarding-returning-employees-back-to-workplace.

Dávila, N., and W. Piña-Ramírez. 2018. *Effective Onboarding*. Alexandria, VA: ATD Press.

Deal, J. 2020. "Virtual Onboarding: How to Welcome New Hires While Fully Remote." The Enterprisers Project, April 13. enterprisersproject.com/article/2020/4/virtual-onboarding-best-practices.

Gallup. 2017. "State of American Workplace Report." Gallup. gallup.com/workplace/238085/state-american-workplace-report-2017.aspx.

Graves, J., A. Tapia, and K.H.C. Huang. n.d. "Onboarding During a Pandemic." Korn Ferry. kornferry.com/insights/articles/onboarding-executive-talent-acquisition-coronavirus.

Gurchiek, K. 2020. "Tips for Employee Orientation During COVID-19." SHRM Talent Acquisition, April 27. shrm.org/resourcesandtools/hr-topics/talent-acquisition/pages/tips-for-employee-orientation-during-covid19.aspx.

Hirsch, A.S. 2017. "Don't Underestimate the Importance of Good Onboarding." SHRM Talent Acquisition, August 10. shrm.org/resourcesandtools/hr-topics/talent-acquisition/pages/dont-underestimate-the-importance-of-effective-onboarding.aspx.

Ismaili, V. 2020. "10 Mind-Blowing Employee Onboarding Statistics." Typelane, January 29. typelane.com/10-mind-blowing-employee-onboarding-statistics.

Klinghoffer, D., C. Young, and D. Haspas. 2019. "Every New Employee Needs an Onboarding Buddy." *Harvard Business Review*, June 6. hbr.org/2019/06/every-new-employee-needs-an-onboarding-buddy.

Lifeworks. 2021. "How the Pandemic Changed the Onboarding Process—and How You Can Retain Top Talent in the New Normal." Lifeworks. us.morneaushepell.com/resources/how-pandemic-changed-onboarding-process-and-how-you-can-retain-top-talent-new-normal.

Maurer, R. 2020. "Virtual Onboarding of Remote Workers More Important Than Ever." SHRM Talent Acquisition, April 20. shrm.org/ResourcesAndTools/hr-topics/talent-acquisition/Pages/Virtual-Onboarding-Remote-Workers.aspx.

Miller, B. 2020. "What Is Reboarding?" HR Daily Advisor, June 23. hrdailyadvisor.blr.com/2020/06/23/what-is-reboarding.

Navarra, K. 2020. "Onboarding New Employees in the COVID-19 Era Takes Planning, Effort." SHRM Talent Acquisition, December 8. shrm.org/resourcesandtools/hr-topics/talent-acquisition/pages/onboarding-new-employees-in-the-covid-19-era-takes-extra-planning-effort.aspx.

O'Donnell, R. 2020. "Reimagining New Hire Onboarding Post-COVID-19." Workest, September 4. zenefits.com/workest/reimagining-new-hire-onboarding-post-covid-19.

Peterson, A. 2020. "The Hidden Costs of Onboarding a New Employee." Glassdoor for Employers, February 26. glassdoor.com/employers/blog/hidden-costs-employee-onboarding-reduce.

Pollack, S. 2020. "Virtual Onboarding Checklist for Remote Employees." Workest, March 26. zenefits.com/workest/virtual-onboarding-checklist-for-remote-employees.

Profico, R. 2020. "How to Onboard New Employees When You're All Working From Home." Fast Company, March 21. fastcompany.com/90480127/how-to-onboard-new-employees-when-youre-all-working-from-home.

PwC. n.d. "Future of Work: What Boards Should Be Thinking About." PwC. pwc.com/us/en/services/governance-insights-center/library/covid-19-returning-workplace-boards.html.

Society for Human Resources Management (SHRM). 2020a. "How to Establish a Virtual Onboarding Program." shrm.org/resourcesandtools/tools-and-samples/how-to-guides/pages/how-to-establish-a-virtual-onboarding-program.aspx.

Society for Human Resources Management (SHRM). 2020b. "Virtual Onboarding." shrm.org/resourcesandtools/tools-and-samples/exreq/pages/details.aspx?erid=1616.

University of Pennsylvania. n.d. "COVID-19 Toolkit Reboarding PDF." med.upenn.edu/uphscovid19education/assets/user-content/documents/leading/covid19-toolkit-reboarding.pdf.

Wallace Welch & Willingham. 2020. "5 Tips for Onboarding Employees Remotely During the Coronavirus Pandemic." HR Inshights. w3ins.com/wp-content/uploads/2020/04/5-Tips-for-Onboarding-Employees-Remotely-During-the-Coronavirus-Pandemic.pdf.

Wuench, J. 2021. "Remote Onboarding Is Taxing for New Hires: Here's What Organizations Can Do Better." Forbes Women, April 2. forbes.com/sites/juliawuench/2021/04/02/remote-onboarding-is-taxing-for-new-hires-heres-what-organizations-can-do-better.

Recommended Resources

Dávila, N., and W. Piña-Ramírez. 2018. *Effective Onboarding*. Alexandria, VA: ATD Press.

Sims, D.M. 2011. *Creative Onboarding Programs: Tools for Energizing Your Orientation Programs*. New York: McGraw Hill.

Stein, M.A., and L. Christiansen. 2010. *Successful Onboarding: A Strategy to Unlock Hidden Value Within Your Organization*. New York: McGraw Hill.

Watkins, M.D. 2013. *The First 90 Days: Proven Strategies for Getting Up to Speed Faster and Smarter*. Boston: Harvard Business Review.

CHAPTER 48

Determining Talent Development's Organizational Impact

David Vance

We all agree that talent development initiatives can make a significant contribution to achieving an organization's goals and meeting its critical needs. There is much less agreement, however, on how to determine the impact of talent development. In other words, how much of a difference did the initiatives make and what is the organization getting for its investment in talent development?

> **IN THIS CHAPTER:**
> - Define effective approaches to determine talent development's organizational impact
> - Provide examples for each approach

There is no consensus within the profession on how best to answer the questions of how to show the impact of talent development on an organization. In fact, this is one of the most contentious issues in our field, and there are strongly held beliefs on all sides; this is also what makes it so interesting.

There are four approaches to determine organizational impact. I've listed them here in the sequence I recommend:
1. Show alignment.
2. Show results.
3. Show impact.
4. Show return on investment (ROI).

All practitioners, even the beginner, should be familiar with all four approaches. This chapter covers the first two (showing alignment and results), while the last two (impact and ROI) are covered in two tools on the handbook's website at ATDHandbook3.org.

The first approach, show alignment, is an excellent planning tool and introduces the concept of planned impact. It answers questions like "Are the talent initiatives aligned to the organization's goals?" and "What is the planned impact on each goal?"

The second approach, show results, does not seek to isolate the impact of the talent development initiative and consequently does not involve any calculations. While this is a plus for many, the drawback is that it will not provide a quantitative measure of impact. Instead, it simply attempts to answer the question, "Did the initiative produce results or meet the goal owner's expectations?"

The third and fourth approaches require more work because they seek to provide definitive answers with regard to the isolated impact and value. However, the case for impact will be much stronger if you employ all four approaches rather than choosing just one.

Show Alignment

This is the natural starting point for any discussion about determining impact and showing value. It is also a key tenet of what it means to run learning like a business. If TD initiatives are not aligned to organizational goals or needs, senior leaders may not perceive any value whatsoever, even if there is measurable value. Or leaders might grudgingly admit to seeing some value in an unaligned initiative, but say it should not have been undertaken or that the funds would have been better spent elsewhere.

So, what do I mean by alignment? Alignment is the proactive process of meeting with senior leaders to understand their most important goals or needs, and then jointly agreeing on TD initiatives to help achieve those goals or meet those needs. The key here is "proactive," meaning that alignment is completed before the initiative is begun. This process can take place at the enterprise level or business unit level and involve all the goals or needs or focus just on one.

Let's start by examining the alignment process at the enterprise level.

Proactive Alignment to Enterprise Goals

Ideally, enterprise alignment begins when the chief talent officer (CTO) or chief learning officer (CLO) meets with the CEO several months before the start of the fiscal year. The meeting's purpose is to:

- Outline the key goals and needs for the coming year.
- Understand the priority of those goals.
- Learn the names of the goal owners.

The discussion should provide the CTO or CLO with a good sense of the challenges facing the organization and might even begin with a reflection on how the organization did in the current year. Because this is a discussion with the CEO, they'll likely be outlining strategic goals and needs. Table 48-1 shows an example of the output of this discussion.

Table 48-1. CEO Prioritized Goals

Priority	Goal	Goal Owner
1	Increase sales by 10%	SVP of Sales Kronenburg
2	Decrease injuries by 5%	COO Tipton
3	Improve quality by 5 points	COO Tipton
4	Improve employee engagement by 3 points	SVP of HR Goh
5	Improve leadership by 4 points	SVP of Strategy Floyd

The CTO or CLO should leave the meeting knowing the goals, their relative importance, and the names and positions of the owners of those goals. For example, in Table 48-1, revenue is the number 1 priority and Kronenburg, SVP of Sales, is the goal owner.

The next step is to talk with each goal owner and learn more about the goal, its challenges, what has been tried before, what has worked, and what hasn't, as well as how the goal owner is planning to achieve the goal this coming year. The discussion can then turn to whether any talent initiatives might help achieve the goal. If it appears there may be, both leaders can direct their staff to explore options and report back with a recommendation.

In the next meeting, staff make their recommendation for talent initiatives. For example, the CTO may recommend consultative selling skills and product features training to help SVP Kronenburg's team meet its goal. They would then discuss target audiences, completion dates, and other particulars. If Kronenburg agrees that these initiatives will help achieve the goal, then we can say they are aligned because the initiatives were developed and approved in direct response to a need to increase revenue by 10 percent, which is a key CEO goal.

Ideally, these discussions will go one step further and the CTO and goal owner will agree on the planned or likely impact of the talent initiatives. For example, the two initiatives to help achieve the sales goal, taken together, might contribute about 20 percent to the goal, resulting in a 2 percent increase in sales due just to these two initiatives. (In equation form: 10 percent goal x 20 percent planned contribution from the initiatives = 2 percent increase in sales due just to the initiatives.) If it seems too daunting to discuss planned percent contribution, the alternative is to agree on a high, medium, or low impact. Either way, discussing planned impact is important for two reasons:

- The higher the planned impact, the more effort and resources will be required from both the goals owner's organization and the talent department.
- The higher the planned impact, the earlier in the fiscal year the initiatives will have to be completed so they have time to influence the results.

Consequently, budget, staffing, and timing all depend on the planned impact, which is why it is important to reach agreement with the goal owner.

The CTO will repeat this process with each goal owner before the new fiscal year begins. In each case, a decision is made about whether talent initiatives have a role in achieving the organizational goal. When it seems likely that a talent development initiative will help achieve the goal, then all parties should agree on the particulars, including planned impact. As a result of this alignment process, we can generate a table like Table 48-2 showing the alignment of talent initiatives to the organizational goals, including the planned impacts.

Note that in Table 48-2, the goal owners were comfortable using quantitative impacts (percent contribution) for the first three goals, but only qualitative impact (use of an adjective like *high*) for the other two. Once the strategic alignment table is complete, it should be shared with the CEO and a high-level governing body for talent to review and approve.

This very powerful table can go a long way to show the potential impact of learning because it shows that:

- The CTO or CLO knows the top goals of the organization in the CEO's priority order
- The goal owners have been consulted and agreement has been reached on the role of talent initiatives in achieving their goals, including the planned impact
- The goal owners and talent leaders are committed to delivering this planned impact

Even if planned impact is not determined, the table is still a huge step forward for many organizations. Most CEOs will be impressed by the amount of planning that goes into it. Further, they are likely to believe that if the goal owners (many of whom are their direct reports) have agreed to the initiatives and are willing to be jointly responsible for their success, then they will have impact. Thus, the table becomes a very effective instrument for showing the planned impact of talent initiatives.

Table 48-2. Strategic Alignment of Talent Initiatives to Goals

Priority	Goal	Planned Talent Initiatives	Planned Contribution From Talent Initiatives	Planned Impact From Talent Initiatives	Goal Owner
1	Increase sales by 10%	• Consultative selling skills • Product features training	20%	2% higher sales	SVP Kronenburg
2	Decrease injuries by 5%	• Safety training for the plant • Safety training for the office	70%	3.5% reduction in injuries	COO Tipton
3	Improve quality by 5 points	• Six Sigma	20%	1 point increase in quality	COO Tipton
4	Improve employee engagement by 3 points	• IDPs for all employees	Medium	Medium	SVP Goh
5	Improve leadership by 4 points	• Leadership training for VPs • Leadership training for department heads • Leadership training for managers • Leadership training for supervisors	High	High	SVP Floyd

Proactive Alignment to Business Unit Goals

This process can be used at the business unit level as well as for those who are supporting a particular unit instead of the enterprise. Simply substitute the business unit head for the CEO, and the business unit talent leader for the enterprise CTO or CLO, and then follow the steps outlined above. Your discussions will focus on how talent can help the unit leader achieve their goals.

Reactive Alignment for Individual Initiatives

The strategic alignment process described thus far has focused on ideal situations in which a good portion of the year's talent initiatives can be planned in advance (proactively) with senior leaders. Unfortunately, the real world does not always meet this ideal, as the talent development team often receives one-off requests that weren't addressed in these initial planning meetings. In this case, the goal should be to make the best of the situation, bringing as much focus as possible to the alignment and planning of particulars, especially planned impact.

The talent leader should ask the person requesting help how it will help achieve an enterprise or business unit goal. In other words, will the talent initiative be aligned to an important goal? If not, perhaps it should not be done or should be undertaken only after better aligned and higher-priority initiatives have been completed. If the initiative appears to be aligned and able to contribute to achieving a goal or meeting a critical need, then the discussion should turn to the particulars of the recommended initiative, including planned impact (either quantitative or qualitative).

Show Results

The strategic alignment approach is an excellent way to set yourself up for success in determining the impact of a talent initiative. The next three approaches focus on how to determine impact once an initiative has been concluded. (They may also be used to gauge impact while the initiative is under way, but for the purposes of this chapter, we will limit our discussion to their use after completion.)

The first and most obvious of these is to *show the results* of the talent initiative. This can be accomplished several ways, including employing a compelling chain of evidence, showing a comparison of the results with and without the initiative, and determining whether goal owner expectations were met. We begin with the compelling chain of evidence.

Compelling Chain of Evidence

This approach is very appealing intuitively. Because the talent initiative was designed to help achieve an organizational goal or help meet a critical need, the question is, "Did it?" Of course, we have to allow sufficient time for the initiative to show results. In some cases, like safety training, this may be immediate. In others, like initiatives to improve leadership or employee engagement, it may take several months or even quarters before results appear.

Assuming sufficient time has passed for the results to be visible, we are now ready to assess whether the desired results were achieved and whether it is likely that the talent initiatives contributed to them. For example, if the goal was to increase sales, did sales increase? If the answer is yes, can we show a compelling chain of evidence that the talent initiatives likely contributed to that increase?

Answering the first question is usually easy; determining the answer to the second part is harder.

Let's say that sales did increase. We have the answer to the first question—yes. Now you need to find a compelling chain of evidence for impact from the training program. One approach would be to look at Levels 1 to 3 of Kirkpatrick's Four Levels of Evaluation, plus participant completion:

- The right people (target audience) completed the training.
- The participants liked the training, found it helpful, and would recommend it to others (Level 1 participant reaction).
- The participants took a knowledge test covering what had been taught and passed it (Level 2 learning).
- The participants demonstrated their new behaviors or used their new skills on the job to improve their performance (Level 3 application).

Let's return to the sales example. Suppose the agreed-upon sales representatives completed the required training on consultative selling skills and product features. The post-event survey showed they liked the training and would recommend it. The knowledge test showed they mastered the new skills, and in-class role plays demonstrated they had mastered the new behaviors. Let's also assume that supervisors in the field observed the reps after training and confirmed their successful application of the new behaviors and knowledge. Wouldn't a reasonable person conclude that the sales training had indeed been impactful? I believe most would.

The case for impact could be strengthened further if SVP Kronenburg and the talent program manager had agreed on target values for these measures ahead of time. These targets should represent the values that both parties believe will be required to have the intended impact. For example, they could agree that for training to increase sales, 100 reps need to complete the training by March 1 with an average test score of 90 percent, and then the reps need to apply at least 80 percent of their newly acquired skills and knowledge successfully on the job. If these targets are met, that strengthens the case for training impact.

The case could be further strengthened if they identified leading indicators in the sales process (like prospect identification and request for quotes) and if the initiative had been designed to achieve them. If targets were set for these leading indicators and if they were achieved, the case for training impact is strengthened even more.

This approach is used by many to demonstrate the impact of training programs, but the concept of collecting a compelling chain of evidence can be applied to other types of talent initiatives as well. For many, this approach is all that is required to convincingly show impact.

Comparison of Actual Results to Baseline

Another popular way to show results is to compare a baseline without the talent initiative to the actual results with the initiative. This will work if the initiative is the only thing (or at least the only significant factor) that has changed. The baseline is often represented by historical results, like last year's results. The expectation is that this year's results would be just like last year's unless we did something different; thus last year serves as a baseline and any improvement this year over the baseline would reflect, at least in part, the results of the talent initiative. This effect is often shown graphically (Figure 48-1).

Figure 48-1. Graphical Depiction of Results

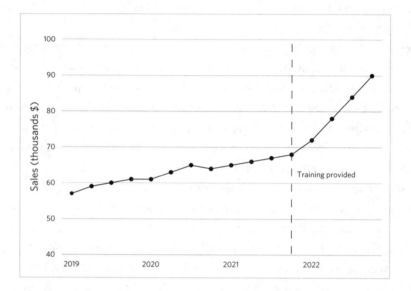

For example, suppose the sales training initiatives were deployed and completed in the first quarter of 2022. If nothing else of significance had changed since 2021, most people would probably agree that sales training positively impacted sales in 2022.

Of course, we cannot say for sure with this method. While the improved sales are certainly correlated with training, we have not proven that sales training was the cause—correlation does not mean causation. Still, many would be convinced that the training must have played a role in the sales increase.

While last year's results are often used as the baseline, the goal owner could also establish a baseline for the plan year without the talent initiatives. This happens when historical results are not available or other factors are changing as well. For example, suppose two new products are being introduced and a competitor is going out of business. In this case, sales would be expected to increase regardless of any new talent initiatives, so the goal owner establishes a baseline of a 20 percent increase in sales without the new initiatives. If the year's sales increase by more than 20 percent, then the goal owner might conclude that the sales training was at least partly responsible for exceeding the baseline. The obvious drawback to this method is that the baseline might have been set too low or too high, giving the training initiative undue credit or lack thereof.

Survey Question on Goal Owner Expectations

A final way to show results is to ask the goal owner. This approach will be most meaningful if the goal owner and CTO or CLO have agreed up front on expectations for the initiative. The question may take several forms and can be easily incorporated into a survey instrument. For example, questions for a learning program might ask:

- The results from the learning program met my expectations.
- The impact from the learning program met my expectations.

Then participants would answer using 5- or 7-point Likert scale, with responses ranging from strongly disagree to strongly agree.

This question may be added to the post-event Level 1 goal owner survey, which may also include additional Likert questions not related to impact, such as:

- L&D was easy to work with.
- The program was delivered on time and on budget.
- I would recommend L&D to my colleagues.

Results can be aggregated for all goal owners, which should allow the CTO or CLO to make a statement like, "90 percent of goal owners indicated that the learning program met their expectations for results."

Final Thoughts

Alignment is an excellent starting point in the quest to show impact; it ensures the planned initiatives are the right ones to undertake and provides estimates of planned impact. Once the initiative is completed, we need to show results using a compelling chain of evidence or comparisons to a baseline. This, however, does not quantify the results. For that, we need to take the third and fourth approaches, isolating the impact of learning and ensuring that the impact was worth it by determining the ROI.

The approaches of showing alignment and some level of results are good methods to use if your resources are limited. Showing impact is typically the most difficult and time consuming, so start with alignment and results. Plus, if the program is not aligned to critical goals or needs, you probably should not be doing it, regardless of impact and ROI. In other words, high ROI does not trump alignment.

I recommend using all four approaches, beginning with alignment and then proceeding through results to impact and ROI. This will provide the most convincing business case and mitigate the risk that your audience might not be convinced by any one of them taken alone. As a reminder you can learn more about the other two approaches—show impact and show ROI—on the handbook's website at ATDHandbook3.org.

Determining impact using these approaches will not only answer questions about value for just-completed initiatives, but will also help make a convincing business case for future investments. Furthermore, it will uncover opportunities for continuous improvement and strengthen your strategic partnership with goal owners and senior leaders.

About the Author
David Vance is the executive director of the Center for Talent Reporting, which is a nonprofit, membership-based organization dedicated to the creation and implementation of standards for human capital measurement, reporting, and management. He is the former president of Caterpillar University, which he founded in 2001. Prior to this position, Dave was chief economist and head of the business intelligence group at Caterpillar. He teaches in the PhD programs at Bellevue University and the University of Southern Mississippi, as well as the executive education program at George Mason University. Dave also serves on the Metrics Working Group for the International Organization for Standardization. He is the author of *The Business of Learning*, now in its second edition, and co-author, with Peggy Parskey, of *Measurement Demystified* and *Measurement Demystified Field Guide*.

Recommended Resources
Kirkpatrick, D., and J. Kirkpatrick. 2006. *Evaluating Training Programs: The Four Levels*. San Francisco: Berrett-Koehler.

Parskey, P., and D. Vance. 2021. *Measurement Demystified Field Guide*. Alexandria, VA: ATD Press.

Phillips, J.J., and P.P. Phillips. 2016. *Handbook of Training Evaluation and Measurement Methods*, 4th ed. New York: Butterworth-Heinemann.

Vance, D. 2017. *The Business of Learning: How to Manage Corporate Training to Improve Your Bottom Line*, 2nd ed. Windsor, CO: Poudre River Press.

Vance, D., and P. Parskey. 2020. *Measurement Demystified: Creating Your L&D Measurement, Analytics and Reporting Strategy*. Alexandria, VA: ATD Press.

CHAPTER 49

Best Practices for a Talent Development Department of One

Emily Wood

Being a training department of one has advantages and disadvantages. You need to know a little bit about everything and a lot about many other things. You are the leader and the follower, the decision maker and the doer, the creator and the analyzer. You do it all.

> **IN THIS CHAPTER:**
> ♦ Explore what it's like to be a department of one and how to market yourself to the organization
> ♦ Demonstrate to senior management the wide-ranging skills that you possess and value you provide to the organization
> ♦ Determine ways to prioritize your workload, manage your time effectively, and build your skills

Welcome to your job as a talent development department of one! The position requirements include:
- Master's degree in instructional design or educational technology
- 10+ years of progressive management experience, graphic design experience, DEI experience, and organizational change management
- Ability to plan strategically and implement effectively
- Five years of UX design experience and LMS administration experience as well as xAPI coding experience
- CPTD, PMP, and Agile certifications
- Expert-level knowledge of all Adobe Creative Cloud programs, Adobe Captivate, and the Articulate 360 suite
- Expertise in any new trends and tools that arise while you're in the position

That's quite the set of job requirements, isn't it? Somehow, talent development jobs are making the members of our industry the modern Renaissance person. I recently heard a discussion in which available department of one talent development jobs were described as the equivalent of full-stack engineers.

A Day in Your Life

What's a typical day like for a talent department professional in a department of one? As you might expect, there is no *typical*. In the last week, my days have consisted of many, many meetings. I met with co-workers and management to discuss strategic planning, project check-ins, budgets, travel planning, and inventory levels. I met with SMEs about starting a new project, working on the reviews on storyboards, getting feedback on alphas, and looking at evaluation data. And I met with end users to get beta program feedback, review assessments and evaluations from existing courses, reset passwords, and answer tech support questions about interactions that won't load or devices that aren't behaving as expected.

If you let them, meetings will eventually eat up all your work time and you'll never actually be able to get any work done. It's a good idea to set boundaries around your time by booking meetings with yourself to ensure you have the blocks of development time that best suit your circadian rhythm. For example, I am most effective at working in the evenings, so I block out late afternoons several days a week and use that for my focused work time. Make a habit of figuring out when you can do deep instructional design and development work and schedule yourself to optimize that time.

Onboarding to the Job

When coming into any new position, onboarding is a critical time for building commitment with the organization and setting the tone for the future. According to *TD* magazine, 33 percent of new hires quit within their first 90 days, 44 percent of new hires say onboarding lacked personalization, and 55 percent said no one followed up on the satisfaction of orientation (ATD Staff 2021).

During onboarding with a new company, it's hard to avoid rewriting the content as you're experiencing it. Instead, use the time to conduct your own needs assessment. Just like you would when developing a new training program, spend the first few weeks getting to learn more about the people who work there, the culture of the organization, and the reason your position was created. Keep notes on what your experience is like as the new learner as well as in your talent development role; then think about how these are interrelated and what you can do to support and build out your organization.

Learn About the Learners

Who are the learners for whom you're delivering the training? What is a typical day like for them? When will they be taking their training? How do they feel about training?

You can gather this information a few ways. One option is to do an organizational needs assessment, which provides a baseline to understand which needs aren't specifically related to a specific topic or training development. You can find an organizational needs assessment checklist on the handbook website at ATDHandbook3.org.

Learn About Your Authority

Interestingly, training departments are found in a variety of different locations within an organization, especially as a department of one. You could be housed under anything from operations, human resources, or marketing to sales, safety, customer service, or somewhere else. It's important to set clear expectations with your supervisor or the sponsor of your projects to establish your role and level of authority.

Once you establish whether there is a need for a training program, you'll need a procedure for determining whether you create a program or buy it from another vendor. This is called your make or buy decision. Surprisingly, purchasing a program can sometimes meet organizational needs better than building a customized performance support initiative. Buying a program allows you to focus your time on targeting content that is specific to your audience. As part of the needs assessment, consider comparing the cost and requirements of off-the-shelf products to those you would develop internally. Do you have the authority to purchase services and content? Know what authority you have.

Learn About the Needs

You can learn about the organization's needs by meeting with subject matter experts (SMEs) to identify training goals for specific departments. Then work with department supervisors to identify the high achievers you can interview to learn what makes them successful. You may even shadow them in their job to identify what they're doing differently from other employees. Talk to them about future initiatives to learn their thoughts about training goals and how they think new initiatives can be successfully introduced to other employees.

> ### MY SOLO JOURNEY TO LESSONS LEARNED
> *Jeff Irwin, Talent Development Coordinator, Brandt Holdings Company, Retail Agriculture Division*
>
> I started in the farm equipment business, working on the front line as a parts sales rep for 10 years and then as a parts department manager for another 10 years. In 2000, I became a John Deere parts instructor at a junior college. It was a partnership program that involved John Deere, the sponsoring John Deere dealership, the college, and the student. I taught the students for nine weeks in the classroom and then they would go out into the field to apply what they'd learned. I loved teaching and seeing these students grow and become productive employees. Some are now managers.
>
> This led to my passion for learning and development. I eventually took on a parts and service role for a large John Deere dealer group with several locations, which would still allow me to teach and coach and coordinate training events. I was later asked to lead and start training and development for the retail agriculture division of our company in a solo role. We have 32 locations in five states, and I was humbled by the responsibility of affecting so many people as we continue to grow.
>
> I was eager but had no idea about how to approach or start. My marching orders from our VP, a retired Marine, were to build and organize a training and development platform. "We are way behind and need it up and running fast!"
>
> Our LMS was being used only as a payroll portal and an internal employee review program built by our business systems person. All product training came from John Deere's online university.
>
> I began listing our different training activities to assess what we were currently doing internally and externally. We had some great programs, but they rarely built on each other and there was little follow through. We had taken a flavor of the month approach that wasn't based on any overall learning or business strategy. I also made a master list of things I wanted to do and timelines to complete them within. A learning strategy was on this list, but I had no idea how to build a strategy, get buy-in from leadership, or communicate to the rest of the organization.
>
> I needed help! So, I decided to join a professional development organization and found a local ATD chapter. I also attended the lunch & learn workshops to find resources for starting a talent development program. I learned that training was out and learning was in. I also completed my DTM (Distinguished Toastmaster) goal.
>
> One of my counterparts from another dealer organization connected me with their HR person, who shared the systems they were using. I had initially intended to build my own system, but then I learned about all the HR systems available. This now became my new focus—to find a software system that would serve us. Still no strategy to guide us, but I was on a mission.

MY SOLO JOURNEY TO LESSONS LEARNED continued

I noticed that Deere used SAP SuccessFactors, so I called the company and spoke with an implementation and consulting partner. I had no idea what I was getting into. After looking at four different companies, I narrowed it down to SAP SuccessFactors because what had started as just an LMS and development module had become a complete HR suite. Their presentation was irresistible, and we added succession, onboarding, recruitment, and compensation as well.

Implementation time arrived. It was June and I had a team of three to get the system configured, tested, and launched by year end. We were excited to get started but had no idea of the project's scope or amount of work it required. We faced several challenges, but the worst was losing our LMS consultant twice, with the last time happening right before we went live. I was desperate to find an LMS consultant. I reached out to the author of an SAP LMS book I'd read to see if we could contract with her. She was helpful, and we ended up contracting with another firm while still working with the original one. It was not the best situation, but we finally signed off on production.

We were planning to hold an April 2020 live roll-out training with our location managers and then COVID hit, forcing us to recalibrate for a digital rollout. I started the presentation based on the book *Help Them Grow or Watch Them Go* to explain why we were expanding talent development. We rolled out the modules that were configured in phase 1 and developed learning aids and a presentation over Zoom. We held six one-hour sessions with one-way communication, which meant we couldn't do any hands-on exercises or give valuable feedback. I'd never created process guides or job aids before, and while the ones I made were somewhat well received, they still weren't strategic. We also had lots of issues with our onboarding module and found out it was configured wrong, so we had to spend several thousand dollars to get it corrected.

The next major task I was given was to create a competency model for each job role, which would be the foundation of our development platform. Thankfully, I was able to work with a former Deere trainer to structure the models into three levels: learning, skilled, and mastery. This worked with the software and we were able to test it and solicit input from the field. I also created career paths for different positions so anyone could identify a future position on their development plan, see what was expected for that position and role, and then work on those skills. By year end these were finished and tested for launch.

In January, we rolled out phase 2 modules focused on performance and development. Then we launched. I broke the presentation into two phases, starting with the importance of career conversations with managers as coaches but empowering our employees to take ownership of their careers and development. We started with a career worksheet assessment.

We launched the current role assessment using competency models in February. These initiatives outlined the importance of having career conversations and taking ownership of development. We also made it possible for employees to discover what they'd need for development. Where were the gaps? The goal was conversation and not confrontation.

> **MY SOLO JOURNEY TO LESSONS LEARNED** continued
>
> As I expected, this has been the most difficult phase and took longer than I hoped for everyone to complete. Some managers were not comfortable or lacked the skills to work through this process. I now know that we need to help our managers become coaches and understand that their role is to help develop people.
>
> Currently I am working on learning paths and curating content to support the competencies. Our next steps are creating effective development plans and accountability. Our system has built-in accountability that helps drive this process.
>
> I recently read an ATD article on starting a talent development program and ordered the book it was based on, *Starting a Talent Development Program*, by Elaine Biech. I wish I'd been exposed to the material from the beginning, because it provided the detailed steps and resources I needed. I reached out to the author on LinkedIn and she sent me additional ATD books to help me create the strategic plan that I should have done at the beginning. I still have much to learn about becoming a talent development trusted advisor, but I have more confidence moving forward now that I can reference my ATD books and have Elaine as a resource.
>
> I've learned more than I ever imagined in my role as a talent development department of one. Here are just a few things:
> - Assess and take inventory of learning and development initiatives that are already taking place, then curate and organize to minimize scrap training.
> - Develop a strategic plan that aligns with business strategy before doing anything else, including choosing an LMS or HR system.
> - Spend time on the strategy and engaging with senior leaders, managers, and front line. This takes more time, but it is time well spent in terms of relationship building and buy-in.
> - Never assume everyone understands the process. Take time to make sure before moving on.
> - Meet people where they are but don't lower your standards and expectations. Help them get there.
> - Help managers become comfortable being uncomfortable and improve their ability to coach and develop their teams.
> - Help people understand why developing competencies is the only way to improve performance.
> - Help everyone see the big picture and value of becoming a learning organization to do rather than just learn.
> - Follow the advice in ATD's talent development books rather than reinventing the wheel.

Defining your Role

Having a good working relationship with your SMEs is one of the most important things you can do. They are typically the people who can either keep you from the content and learning information you need or share more information than you ever knew you didn't need to know. Given the option, more is better. Try inviting them out for lunch or getting to know them as individuals before starting a conversation about training. The better the foundation of your relationship, the easier your long-term development will be.

When you're meeting with the SMEs and building your foundations, take time to establish who you are in the relationship. The SME is the person of authority on a particular topic. You, as the training and development person, bring the expertise in adult learning. You are responsible for designing the learning experience; establishing which knowledge, skills, and attitudes need to be addressed; and providing the best practice methodologies for teaching and assessing them. You combine the content from the SME with the information you gather in the needs assessment and build a comprehensive solution.

Where Do You Fit?

You're a department of one, so management may not think to include you in meetings, not because they don't care about your input, but because the department is a single person and possibly new to the organization. You need to make sure you are visible and contributing to the organization.

If you're not already familiar with it, spend some time listening to how senior management talks about company goals and strategy. What is their one-year and five-year vision? What are the gaps between where they are now and where they want to be? How can your role help change behaviors and address those gaps?

Find out how to get invited to executive planning meetings. As the person solely responsible for all aspects of training, you need to know about upcoming initiatives and partner with change management to help the organization meet its goals. Strategize about the right mix of marketing, instructor led, e-learning, and performance support opportunities.

Establish regular touchpoints with senior management. Consider scheduling weekly or monthly updates on the initiatives your work is supporting and your status. See if you can integrate your project management tool with the business insights dashboards that the executives already use. You want to be top of mind when management is thinking about how to solve a problem. You are the person who can help assess if it's a training issue or not—if it does need training, you can handle it; if it doesn't, you can find the department that can provide the solution. You are more than an order taker. You are a solutions expert.

Choosing Your Projects

"Here's a PowerPoint deck with the voice-over in the notes. It's two hours when I teach it, so it'll take about 45 minutes online, right? Can you just make that an e-learning program for me this week?"

We've all been in this situation. SMEs are the best advocates for their content. They know *everything*, and they want to share their knowledge. Generally, they're well intentioned, but they're not learning theory experts. There are a few things we want to do to set the expectation with the SME, or any other stakeholder, to make the most of our time.

Consider what is being done about the behavior now and what information you can get about it. If this is completely new, you can start by finding out what the employees have been doing to this point and why that's no longer acceptable. Typically, the reason for the change is new legislation, a new company initiative, or a response to an incident. Collect whatever information you can related to the change from the current behavior and then determine how that change will affect the employees. In this case, you'll want to be covering the full scope of your department of one needs. You'll want to implement change management philosophies to explain the change to learners. You'll want to develop formal training to explain the process. You'll want to set up team support programs, supervisory checklists, and other social pressure initiatives to support the new behavior. Finally, you'll want to create job aids and on-the-job support to help solidify the new behavior. Remember that it takes the average person 60 days to learn a new behavior and only four to forget it. With that, you'll want to build a spaced learning plan with lots of triggers to help the learners be successful with their new behavior.

Leveraging Project Management Tools

Think of yourself as the limited resource in the talent development process. Anything that you're doing related to your work should be a value add. Leveraging project management tools that other members of your organization have access to will allow them to see what you're working on and your expected timelines, without interrupting you doing your work. Because instructional design and authoring tool coding require a headspace that many people can't easily transition in and out of, project management tools allow you to block out your schedule to give you protected time to make your content.

Think about yourself as the service industry for the content provider. Allowing the content providers to see your backlog of work and prioritization will build trust and set strong expectations for timelines. There are several project management philosophies specifically targeted to training development that are worth considering, such as works by Lou Russell or the Project Management Institute.

Obtaining Resources to Support Training

Chances are that if you're a department of one, you're working on a limited budget. Fortunately, there are a number of ways to be resourceful and build quality content with very low cost.

Development Tools

Quite a bit of your planning and development can be done with software already in use with your organization. Microsoft Office Suite programs cover many of your immediate needs. Word and PowerPoint can be leveraged for creating storyboards. Outlook or Excel can be used for basic project management. The more advanced version of Office includes Visio or Access, which you can use for curriculum planning. Open-source software is a great solution if paid programs aren't available, and there are several MS Office competitors. For photo or illustration software, Gimp and Inkscape can meet your needs.

Many people prefer paid software for their authoring tools. If you purchase content from other developers or work with outside contractors, it can be useful to have a more mainstream title. They all offer free trial periods so you can get familiarized with their features. One open-source tool for this is H5P.

Learning Management Systems

You might consider choosing the level of complication that you can manually maintain. This could be a set number of learners or a set number of training programs that have to happen in a particular timeframe before you need the support of an official learning management system. The benefits of a learning management system include maintaining the individual training records for each member of the staff, allowing learners to see a calendar of future training sessions, allowing learners to sign up for training, and making it possible for learners to take that program if it's an online, on-demand session.

Multimedia

Presentations are far more engaging when they include photos and videos than just a screen full of text. If the course won't be sold, you can use Creative Commons media to meet this need. Many authoring tools also offer access to a multimedia library. Just pay attention to copyright law and licensing agreements of external content if you're going to sell the course or use it externally.

For audio, you can consider using adding voice-overs using text-to-speech technology, recording your own voice, or recording your co-workers, all of which can be free.

Advocating for Your Development

Especially as a department of one, the most important person for you to take care of is you. At the start of the chapter I listed "Expertise in any new trends" as the last bullet in my job description. While tongue-in-cheek, there is definitely an expectation that the talent development professional will be able to speak competently about the latest research in learning theory, change management, and training return on investment. Consider taking the Talent Development Capability Model assessment on the ATD website to create a personal learning plan. This can help you determine your strengths and interests as well as identify gaps or areas for learning.

The capabilities are divided into three domains:

- **Personal,** which embodies the foundational or enabling abilities all working professionals should possess to be effective in the business world. These interpersonal skills, often called soft skills, are needed to build effective organizational or team culture, trust, and engagement.
- **Professional,** which embodies the knowledge and skills talent development professionals should possess to be effective in their roles of creating the processes, systems, and frameworks that foster learning, maximize individual performance, and develop the capacity and potential of employees.
- **Organizational,** which embodies the knowledge, skills, and abilities needed by professionals to ensure talent development is a primary mechanism driving organizational performance, productivity, and operational results.

Whatever you choose to use as your goal for professional development, plan some time for yourself to build your skills. This can be anything from following different authoring tool blogs and learning about the latest features and writing those into storyboards, to attending instructor-led classes with staff to see how different members of your organization teach the courses you're writing and experience how the learners respond to it. Be as data-driven as possible in making your decisions and try to mix up the ways in which you extend your knowledge.

Benefits of Being a Department of One

There are drawbacks to being a department of one: having limited opportunity to problem solve with co-workers, being the only one who can fix things that go wrong, and ultimately being responsible for everything from the planning, development, communication, and implementation to evaluation. However, there are many benefits to being a department of one as well. You have complete information about every piece of content that is being developed for your organization. When a new initiative is proposed, you can own everything from the planning timeline, all the parts of the deliverables, the program's change management and marketing plans, and the dissemination. You'll be able to review all the results from the learners and make decisions about what is built or purchased.

THRIVING AS A DEPARTMENT OF ONE
By Maria Chilcote and Melissa Smith, The Training Clinic

The first step in thriving as a learning and development "department of one" is to adjust your perspective. Being a department of one, believe it or not, is a gift!

OK. Before you skip this sidebar, please indulge us a moment and read on.

Being a training department of one gives you an advantage. Because you don't have staff, you are forced to go outside your department and rely on your relationships with others in the organization to help you achieve your goals.

Develop Partnerships

Developing relationships with others in the organization has many desirable results. For starters, it's easier to gain access to management and support for your initiatives. Your partners also become advisors and so share in decision making, which contributes to the success of planned initiatives. Having partnerships within your organization promotes your brand, helps clarify expectations, and reduces the feelings of powerlessness and stress that can come with running solo.

What's Important to Them

Spend time with managers or key stakeholders in an informal setting and ask questions to learn their perspective on what is important to them. Learning what they see as valuable and how it affects their processes will foster a collaborative relationship. Move from the "trainer fix it" role to a consultant who is genuinely interested and curious about their performance challenges and needs.

Toot Your Own Horn!

If you are feeling underappreciated, perhaps it is because others are not aware of how the training function contributes to the organization's objectives. When the training function publicizes its results and accomplishments, its efforts are seen and more appreciated by others! Our article "So No One Told You You're a Marketeer of Training?" and our webinar of the same name provide key tactics to publicize training department accomplishments while building key relationships within the organization.

Sort Training From Nontraining Issues

When analyzing a training request, you may have to work with HR and the manager to discover the "training issue." You might discover the need is actually a performance issue, which means that job aids are a more appropriate nontraining solution. Sometimes the task at hand is discovering why people don't perform and what to do to solve that issue. And remember, the solution isn't always training!

THRIVING AS A DEPARTMENT OF ONE *continued*

Start by assessing the key training and development roles needed in your organization to support performance goals. This will help determine your priorities when operating solo: What can you reasonably take on and what critical roles do you need to outsource within your organization?

By the way, looking at what you are doing—and not doing—can reveal an implicit function mission. Based on the major activities your department is doing, what would you say is your purpose in the organization? That's your function mission statement! If you find you're not doing what is needed to support performance goals, it's time to review the organization's vision and mission statements. Make sure that everything you do is linked to those statements. But that's a topic for another article!

Recruit and Train Supporters

Developing partnerships with others may mean recruiting (or begging, exchanging favors, you know the drill) and training folks on adult learning and facilitation skills. Fortunately for them, these two skill sets will make them better supervisors, managers, and employees. Now that is the true gift you are bestowing upon them!

Facilitating and partnering with subject matter experts (SMEs) helps provide effective education, which facilitates getting knowledge from the SME when fielding questions from trainees. Build the SME's confidence in your desire to collaborate by asking them what they think makes that thing easy for other colleagues. Help improve the training content by identifying SMEs who can be coached to create job aids. Finally, recognizing their contribution and expertise in your initiatives allows them to be the "brains" behind your content and fosters a relationship of collaboration between you and the SME.

The Gift of Being a Training Department of One

You see, my friends, your lack of staff forces you to reach out and train others sooner than you would have otherwise. In essence, you are out there developing employees and allowing the organization to enjoy the benefits of this new skill set much quicker than someone with a staff.

Next time you are about to shout your familiar cry of "I'm only ONE person!" remember that you really are ahead of the development game and you're reaping the benefits much sooner than someone with a full staff. Think about it!

Maintaining Your Motivation

As the only person doing your job at an organization, there may be times when it's hard to maintain your drive and positivity. There will be difficult projects that overrun in time, where the scope creep is so far that it can't be called "creep" anymore, and you're being pressured by co-workers and clients about "just getting it done." When this happens and it feels like it's coming in from all fronts, there are a few things you can do to maintain your motivation.

- **Apply for awards.** Submit your work for professional recognition. Get feedback from experts about what you're doing; you'll be validated by the process or you'll have an opportunity to improve.
- **Join professional organizations.** Many organizations offer professional development and networking opportunities where you can mentor, be mentored, learn about new trends, and have a good time with people who share similar experiences. Join your local ATD chapter to keep abreast of the latest content and for essential networking. To multiply your benefits, be sure your membership includes ATD National.
- **Attend conferences.** Sometimes you'll get stuck in a rut. Attending a conference and seeing what cutting-edge training development is out there will send you back to your organization with lots of new ideas about what you can apply to the learning practice and how to improve behavior change and processes.
- **Build a recognition program.** Reward the employees or clients taking your training programs. The more people go through your programs, upskill, and grow in their careers the more you will feel inspired to continue building learning paths for others. Encouraging others will make happier employees, a more enjoyable work environment, and, ultimately, more motivation for you.

Final Thoughts

It's not going to be easy. Having a strong sense of how long each part of the development process will take you to complete and the likelihood of emergency projects to break your flow will help you manage projects better. Consider using a project timeline, where you can see a breakdown of time for each step of development based on the size of the project to use for future estimates. The more projects you develop, the more accurate numbers you'll have. When in doubt, underpromise and overdeliver, or estimate longer timelines and beat your goals.

Ultimately, being a talent development department of one is an exciting opportunity that allows you to experience the breadth of everything that can be encompassed within learning and development. You can get into organizational development, facilitation, e-learning development, change management, talent development, and so much more.

About the Author

Emily Wood, MS, CPTD, PMP, has worked for nonprofit, government, and corporate clients as an in-house employee, and now as part of her own L&D consulting company, Serenity Learning. She has implemented software training, soft skills training, and compliance projects as instructor led, virtual instructor led, and asynchronous e-learning. She presents at the ATD International Conference & Exposition, TechKnowledge, and DevLearn. Emily's first book, *E-Learning Department of One*, is about creating quality technology-assisted learning products when faced with limited resources, help, and time.

References

ATD Staff. 2021. "There's Room for Improvement With Onboarding." *TD,* June. td.org/magazines/td-magazine/theres-room-for-improvement-with-onboarding.

Recommended Resources

Biech, E. 2016. *The Art and Science of Training*. Alexandria, VA: ATD Press.
Biech, E. 2018. *ATD's Foundations of Talent Development*. Alexandria, VA: ATD Press.
Biech, E. 2018. *Starting a Talent Development Program*. Alexandria, VA: ATD Press.
Hall, MJ, and L. Patel. 2020. *Leading the Learning Function: Tools and Techniques for Organizational Impact*. Alexandria, VA: ATD Press.
Wood, E. 2018. *e-Learning Department of One*. Alexandria, VA: ATD Press.

SECTION VIII
TALENT DEVELOPMENT'S ROLE FOR FUTURE SUCCESS

LUMINARY PERSPECTIVE

The Future Is Closer Than You Think

John Coné

The future is much closer than we think. We speak of the past, present, and future in the same way we talk about the Earth, horizon, and sky or the sea, shoreline, and shore. The horizon and the shoreline are imaginary dividing lines. The present is a lot like that. It is a line we imagine between the past and the future.

In the section that follows you will find outstanding thinking about a future that is so close. It is a future in which talent development professionals will leverage artificial intelligence, virtual and augmented reality, machine learning, and analytics. One in which mass personalization, bots, and geofencing will all be part of our repertoire. A future in which the role of talent development expands to concerns about organization development, performance management, inclusion, equity, employee experience, culture, and brand.

Learning Will Be the Job

I think that these essential aspects of the future are driven by a single monumental shift: Learning will be the work. Learning will be the job. We have long thought of lifelong development as an increasingly necessary support for job success. This is different. Learning will be the preeminent requirement of the job itself.

It is easy to apply this notion to researchers or to those who work to discover a new therapy or invent a new machine or algorithm. But it will soon apply to most of those we support. As AI takes on more repetitive and straightforward tasks, jobs are being deconstructed and reformed into new and often temporary constructs where learning may be the only lasting responsibility.

Organizations have declared that their future success demands they be agile and innovative. If that is true, then everyone in the organization should, as a part of their job, learn new things and do things they have never done.

Creating a culture of learning is not going to be about initiatives or programs. It will not even be about embedding learning in the flow of work. It is going to be about enabling *learning as work*. It is incumbent on all of us to begin the process (if we have not already) of looking at each job and understanding which part of it will be learning. Upskilling and reskilling will not be a process of retraining employees from one set of capabilities to another; rather, it will be the nature of every job. In fact, in just a few years reskilling will likely be the top responsibility of many jobs.

Everyone Will Own Their Development

We are already in an era when learners control their own development. Technology enabled us to create more tools, make them more widely available, and make them more time and cost effective. We found we could make talent development more flexible, personal, and immediate. This is the dominant mode of talent development in corporations today. As learning becomes a requirement of the job, people will exercise their control to take ownership of their development. Organizations will still place requirements on their employees, but talent development will cede control of the process. In doing so, we will help learners optimize what they control. Talent development's role will be to create immediate connectivity and a massive, ubiquitous availability of resources to support universal authorship and make development resources searchable, editable, sampleable, linkable, feedable, and taggable.

Modular Talent Will Require Modular Talent Development

Universities are already rethinking the value of degrees, and companies are reconsidering their curriculums. The future is a place where jobs will be constructed in the moment of need and expire when the purpose they serve has been met. Sometimes those jobs will expire in hours or days. Sometimes they will last months or even years, although they will shift and change constantly. (Eventually, no job will last for long.) We and the AI that supports us will identify combinations of capabilities needed for a task or project and temporarily assemble those capabilities by rapid identification of the person or group of people who possess them. Job titles will give way to capability collections. We have long argued that breaking down information into smaller and smaller bits makes it easier for the learner to consume. In the future, microlearning will be a requirement of development as possible combinations of capabilities become too complex and requirements of learners too varied to anticipate.

Modular talent means that workplace considerations will give way to a focus on the workforce. Place and time will become increasingly irrelevant. The workforce will be unlimited, and the workplace will be always and everywhere. Development resources, therefore, will also need to be always and everywhere.

Democratization of Development Will Be Essential

If traditional jobs do not exist, neither will traditional roles. Individuals will have multiple specializations and credentials that will be constantly changing. What we think of as leadership and management responsibilities will move from person to person. Roles and teams will be in constant flux. This requires everyone to have equal access to all development opportunities. One of the most critical aspects of inclusion will be a fully democratized development landscape. Our commitment to diversity will require us to make sure that every source of human potential is maximized.

In this future, procession will replace succession. We will not be looking for replacements for existing jobs but for people who can do jobs that will soon be vastly different or do not yet exist. We will focus on developing people for multiple potential opportunities, rather than movement or promotion into a specific role. Agility plans will replace career paths. The responsibility of the talent development function will be to ensure that everyone has the environment, tools, and opportunity to do the next job or any job.

Discovery Will Supersede Authoring

Imagine an Olympic swimming pool filled with LEGOs—about 100 million of them. With about 4,000 different types of LEGOs in 51 different colors, that adds up to about 3 googolplexes of possibilities. That is the future open landscape of learning assets. The role of the talent development function will be to leverage that incredible resource. Our responsibility will be discovering where the best tools and information reside and where and how development is naturally occurring so the good can be maximized, the bad mitigated, and the superfluous reduced. Talent development will constantly reconsider and reimagine what is best for use in that moment, enable its use, and then discard it. That will require us to understand what the organization knows and is capable of, where knowledge and capability reside, how to access them, and where they are likely to be needed next.

Soon the line between staffing and development will be blurred because finding and developing the right talent will become two inseparable aspects of the same thing. Linking to the business will not be so much about connecting curriculums and programs to organizational strategies and goals as it will be about connecting instances of development to immediate needs (which are derived from those strategies and goals). The primary focus of knowledge management will be tracking what we know and what we need to know in real time. And a critical responsibility of talent development will be to help the organization follow the swiftly changing boundary between what needs to be known and what needs to be accessed.

Let's go back to the LEGO metaphor. In the short term, we may be able to get great value by mining those LEGOs ourselves. In doing so, we will develop the search expertise we will need, because very soon, we will have no hope of being able to find everything that anyone might need. Instead, we will have to help people to do a better job of looking for themselves.

Trust Will Be a Key Deliverable

Where discovery dominates, curation becomes an exceedingly small part of the job, because we keep so little. We are always in search of the new and the next. The greatest service then is guiding the organization and the individuals in it to find and use the best developmental resource most efficiently. To do that, the TD function will be the most trusted source for guidance and coaching of self-development. The future of talent development is helping the organization and each person in it understand where they want to go and how to get there as quickly and safely as possible.

The TD function will serve as the guarantor of quality and utility, acting as the underwriters of development resources for the organization. Clearly, we cannot be everywhere, so we will create and set in motion processes that review and codify development options. We will create guides for self-service, even portals that prioritize the sources and solutions we trust. We will make clear the better or safer options—those we certify as proven (by our analysis) to meet organizational and individual goals, those we endorse as effective though not as directly aligned with the organization's priorities, and those we accept as containing good information, even if they're not yet proven effective. In other words, we will make it easy and natural for people to use the methods and sources that are true and trustworthy.

Experience Will Dominate

In a world where learning is work, learners will have little patience or time for learning that is not experiential. Experiential development is the ultimate personalized learning. It is inherently social and mobile. For most people, it is virtual. There is no gap between theory and practice and most of the time assessment will be immediate and practical. Whether the experience is individual, group-based, or broadly collective, the TD function will excel at providing it. Our skill set will evolve from managing programs and curriculums to managing experiences.

Our discovery capability will enable the TD function to identify, capture, and promulgate meaningful and successful development experiences. We will layer iteration and reflection on the experiences we find to exponentially increase their impact. We will strategically plan and curate real world experiences and even design and manage some of them. Our simulations and games will enable people to safely fail, to test hypotheses, and to see the now unseeable things that are part of our lives. And in the process, those being developed will provide a real service to customers, companies, and communities.

The TD Function Will Own the "of" of Culture

In our near future, purpose and culture will be what defines an organization and what holds it together. As people move in and out of teams, even in and out of the organization itself, shared purpose and culture will be what binds them. As people gain more and more control over their work choices, they will create their own employee experience through the decisions they make. Organizations will focus on enabling those very personal employee experiences. Even more than today, culture will be critical.

There is a lot of debate about who owns culture. Is it the CEO? All leaders and managers? Everyone? When we begin to describe the culture we want, the uncertainty diminishes because we inevitably speak in behavioral terms. We want a culture of something behavioral—and developing those behaviors is the work of talent development.

The culture of learning we seek is not the holy grail of culture. Organizations strive for a culture of belonging, agility, innovation, customer focus, collaboration, service, and more. To achieve such aspirations will be even harder in the constant flux of work teams, a hybrid workforce, gig partners, and rapidly changing alliances.

The work of talent development will be to enable every "of." Because culture is about what we do, we will help people develop the capabilities that serve customers, make organizations agile, increase innovation, and encourage the things that welcome and treasure people of all backgrounds and persuasions. We will help leaders understand the levers of culture and fully engage in shaping it.

The TD Function Will Be the Model

With all this flux, how can we still talk about talent development as a function? Or think about our jobs within the function? One possibility is that the work of talent development will be distributed very differently than today, that ownership for this critical organizational capability will shift and change. But it seems more likely that talent development will take its place among a critical few organizational functions. Just like sales, finance, customer service, and so on, the teams and jobs within it will constantly shift. The capabilities needed and the people doing the work will be in constant flux and evolution.

I think talent development will go first. Because we live and work in the future, talent development will be the first part of the organization to operate in these new ways. We will constantly be reskilling. Our agility as a function will result from our ability to create and combine new capabilities. We will master discovering where development is happening and the capability to quickly find the tools we need to develop ourselves.

I think we will have to first learn and then share how to succeed in this near future. We are best prepared to do it. After all, our work is in the future and always has been.

We can start now. That you are reading this book suggests you already have. So, continue. For yourself, be the future. Take ownership of your own development and start reskilling yourself. Learn everything you can about new developments in our field. Network, especially with people outside your comfort zone (and outside talent development). Model continuous learning. Experiment. Flex. Embrace the digital.

For those you serve, start letting go of yesterday's approaches and habits. Do not rely on the tried and true. Listen to what people are asking for and even wishing for and try to help them find it. Get out and discover how people are learning in the organization and find ways to optimize and spread it. Give up control. And start democratizing the products and services you provide so that everyone has equal access, regardless of their location.

This is the future I see us heading for. It is closer than we think, and we need to move in its direction with every decision we make. For now, there will still be classrooms and facilitators. We will add incredible value through programs targeted at groups. We will enhance careers with curriculums. But even as we do, we will be building the future. Technology and world events pull us inexorably toward it. And what we can imagine, we can begin.

About the Author

John Coné is a former CLO who consults and writes on issues of talent development and organizational learning. He has advised dozens of companies, universities, and the US government, and has served on the boards of both for profit and nonprofit education organizations. He chairs the Chief Learning & Talent Officer Board for i4cp and is the catalyst for ATD's CTDO Next group. He serves as a jurist for the CLO Learning Elite Awards. He is a past ATD Board chair, a jurist for the BEST Awards, and an advisor to multiple ATD initiatives. In 2005 he received the Gordon M. Bliss Award for lifetime achievement. He is a futurist, a painter, a bicycle mechanic, and a sock aficionado.

Recommended Resources

Diamandis, P.H., and S. Kotler. 2020. *The Future is Faster Than You Think*. New York: Simon and Schuster.

Elkeles, T., ed. 2020. *Forward Focused Learning*. Alexandria, VA: ATD Press.

Gutsche, J. 2020. *Create the Future + the Innovation Handbook: Tactics for Disruptive Thinking*. New York: Fast Company Press.

Jesuthan, R., J. Boudreau. 2018. *Reinventing Jobs: A 4-Step Approach for Applying Automation to Work*. Boston: Harvard Business Review Press.

Jesuthan, R., J. Boudreau, and D. Creelman. 2015. *Lead the Work: Navigating a World Beyond Employment*. Hoboken, NJ: John Wiley and Sons.

McCauley, C., and M. McCall, eds. 2014. *Using Experience to Develop Leadership Talent*. San Francisco: Josey Bass.

Oakes, K. 2021. *Culture Renovation: 18 Leadership Action to Build an Unshakeable Company*. New York: McGraw Hill.

CHAPTER 50

6 Essentials for a Thriving Learning Culture

Holly Burkett

Employees must learn continuously. The rise of automation and robotics, increased globalization, and a multigenerational and diverse workforce require 21st-century employees to learn faster, work smarter, and be more agile. According to Peter Senge, "The organizations that truly excel in the future will be the organizations that discover how to tap into people's commitment and capacity to learn at all levels in an organization."

> **IN THIS CHAPTER:**
> - Explore the essential elements of a thriving learning culture
> - Discover insights, examples, and suggested actions for enhancing your own learning culture
> - Consider recommendations for long-term success

What do a multinational technology and research company and a US manufacturer and distributor of automotive oil products have in common? Both have adapted quickly to the new realities of the workplace, where new ways of working and new demands for work have accelerated the need for continuous learning. And both have earned awards for exemplary and innovative learning solutions geared to support high performance in an age of disruption.

For example, the talent development team at IBM designed a dashboard that provides "Fitbit-like" nudges to managers for leadership behaviors they can apply immediately. The nudges encourage managers to consider questions like, "Who hasn't been taking vacation and is in danger of burning out?" or "Who's due for a coaching session?" Results to date show increased retention rates and high approval rates by participating teams (Castellan 2020). At Valvoline, the learning team developed an enterprise video portal, where managers produce high-quality videos with their cell phones to show technicians the surest routes around pesky assignments (Harris 2020).

Automation, robotics, increased globalization, and a diverse workforce make it clear that employees need solutions like these to learn faster and be more agile to survive and thrive in the world of 21st-century work. Organizations that emphasize continuous learning are better able to:
- Attract and retain top talent.
- Develop leaders at all levels, which is essential in succession planning.
- Foster employee engagement.
- Accelerate change readiness.
- Enhance employee well-being.

In addition, organizations with strong learning cultures have been shown to consistently outperform their peers in terms of revenue growth, profitability, market share, product quality, and customer satisfaction (ATD 2016). In short, a learning culture is the best way for organizations to reset and refresh for the next normal.

What Is a Learning Culture?

A learning culture isn't about training; it's about learning. In a learning culture, employees across all levels are encouraged to continuously seek, share, and apply new knowledge and skills for the benefit of themselves, the company, and the clients and communities they serve (ATD 2016).

A learning culture focuses on *organizational* learning and performance for the purpose of growing collective learning and performance capabilities. The focus is less about isolated training events and more about building meaningful learning *experiences*. Here, continuous learning opportunities are systemically built into the flow of work with short, frequent, pull versus push bursts of information that are readily accessible and available to all employees at the time and place of need.

LEARNING IN THE FLOW OF WORK

Wipro, an India-based global IT, consulting, and business process services company, provides user-friendly learning platforms and simple, useful tools with gamified content to promote daily learning and enable employees to work on real-world business challenges. For example, Wipro uses a social-learning platform called TopGear to offer structured paths for employees to acquire in-demand skills at their own pace. Once skills are acquired, employees can further hone their abilities by working on real business problems that are crowdsourced on the platform. Learning platforms like TopGear can enhance productivity by reducing the ramp-up time for employees to become ready to handle business challenges (Castellan 2020).

Providing learning opportunities that sync with job performance recognizes that:
- Learning is always occurring—both formally and informally.
- Performance and productivity gains most often occur in informal moments.
- Employees prefer to learn at work, at their own pace, and at the point of need (Figure 50-1).

Figure 50-1. How Employees Prefer to Learn

68% of employees prefer to learn on the job

58% of employees prefer to learn at their own pace

49% of employees prefer to learn at the point of need

LinkedIn (2018)

6 Essentials for a Thriving Learning Culture

Now that we've explored the what and why of a learning culture, how can you build one that ensures your organization can successfully future-proof its workforce and thrive in an increasingly chaotic and uncertain world? Focusing on the six essentials outlined in Figure 50-2 can help pave the way.

Figure 50-2. Six Essentials for a Thriving Learning Culture

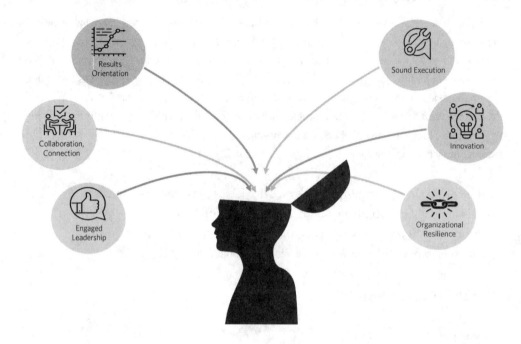

Engaged Leadership

The sustained success of a learning culture depends on the support of the leaders who own the business need, have the authority to put learning on the agenda, and make decisions about how learning resources will be allocated (Dearborn 2015). Executive decisions about learning investments tend to be based upon the value they place on learning and the business's perceived value of the learning function.

Make Learning a Core Value

Leaders set the tone for a learning culture by the values and behaviors they model, reward, and reinforce. Meaningful values, as a management practice, were a core differentiator of companies that maintained a healthy culture during the COVID-19 pandemic (Hancock, Schaninger, and Weddle 2021). Organizational values are important to learning cultures—90 percent of mature learning organizations have corporate values that specifically address learning and development (ATD 2016). For instance, Garry Ridge, WD40 CEO and one of the "World's Top Ten CEOs," says, "My job is to create a company of learners" (Taylor 2016).

The drive to support learning as a core value comes from a growth mindset, which asserts that basic abilities can be developed through practice, input from others, and continuous learning. With this perspective, individuals are more likely to embrace challenges, persist in the face of setbacks, view effort as the path to mastery, learn from criticism, and find inspiration from others' success (Dweck 2007). Inspired by Carol Dweck's research on a growth mindset, Satya Nadella made lifelong learning a priority at Microsoft when he took over the helm in 2014—it's even highlighted on the badges of more than 131,000 employees worldwide. The company's focus has shifted from "know it all to learn it all," and Nadella reinforces this cultural value by putting out a video every month on what he's learned (Vander Ark 2018).

Activate Buy-In

While many executives may buy-in to values that support learning and a growth mindset, a persistent challenge is getting executives to put those values into action. Findings from LinkedIn's *2020 Workplace Learning Report* suggest that only 27 percent of L&D professionals view their CEOs as active champions of learning (LinkedIn Learning 2020).

Based on these findings, LinkedIn's L&D team decided to host a LinkedIn Learning Challenge, a week-long, company-wide competition where each executive's organization competed to be the team who learned the most. This executive championship proved a powerful way of driving learner engagement and inspiring employees to spend more time learning.

> When it comes to activating executives, I approach them the same way I approach anyone else. I regularly ask them what they are learning and share with them what I'm learning. By bringing this into our everyday conversations, it generates even more sharing, which has a multiplying effect. That energy is what inspires people to learn and helps create a culture of continuous learning.
> —Kevin Delaney, VP of Learning and Development, LinkedIn

In another example of creating buy-in at the top, Rose Sheldon, head of enterprise L&D at Allstate, reportedly spent a year doing road-show meetings with senior leaders to help transform a culture of tenure and longevity to one where investments in a continuous learning culture were seen as opportunity versus sunk costs (Sheldon 2021).

Reimagine Leadership Development

While most CEOs clearly recognize that developing leaders is vital to their organization's ability to survive and thrive, many lack confidence in their leadership development processes and believe that learning professionals are not doing enough to build talent and leadership bench strength (Korn Ferry Institute 2015). In addition, reimagining a hybrid workplace has placed new demands on leaders as they move toward a post-pandemic future. To that end, thriving learning cultures continually enhance and reinvent their leadership development efforts so they remain relevant to changing business needs and evolving skill demands.

For instance, when Thor Flosason joined Kellogg as senior director of learning and development, he sought to evolve the traditional "classroom heavy, resource heavy, and events-driven" learning culture he inherited (Linkedin n.d.). To shift Kellogg's learning culture from its one-size-fits-all approach, Flosason used a multiprong method to secure support. Key tactics included getting leaders to advocate for learning, creating an internal marketing campaign called #IGotThis, and kicking off a friendly competition that included prizes and recognition.

Consider these examples of how other organizations have reimagined leadership development:
- Verizon, Cisco, ServiceNow, and DBS Singapore have all embedded empathy in employee interactions and relaxed their expectations for employees. For instance, managers are being trained to identify situations where employees can benefit from time off to recharge and re-energize themselves (Bersin 2020).
- Microsoft wanted to promote the value of a growth mindset, so the talent team created conversation guides for managers to explore what a growth mindset might look with their teams. Leaders were encouraged to share success stories, and various incentives—games, quizzes, and a mobile empathy museum—were used to reinforce desired behaviors.

In general, TD professionals can reimagine leadership development practices by:
- Expecting leaders to examine their own mindsets, assumptions, and biases
- Ensuring the proper blend of formal learning, learning from others, and experiential learning
- Designing powerful learning journeys rather than traditional learning events
- Integrating social networking tools so leaders can share knowledge
- Matching specific skills and scenarios to real-world challenges for each leadership level (frontline, midlevel, senior level)
- Putting a stronger emphasis on programs that foster creativity, innovation, intellectual curiosity, inclusion, and empathy
- Enabling leaders to share what they know as leader-teachers, coaches, or mentors

Distribute Leadership

As Steve Jobs once said, "It doesn't make sense to hire smart people and tell them what to do; we hire smart people so they can tell us what to do." To prime the pump with middle and frontline managers, thriving learning cultures focus on *collective leadership* versus *hero leadership*. This creates a pool of talented people who can assume any leadership role when the need arises.

For example, at Valvoline Instant Oil Change (VIOC), 100 percent of the company's service center and area managers have been promoted from within its ranks, where they started in hourly positions. Jamie Hinely, director of global learning solutions, builds collective leadership skills through a carefully structured blend of instructor-led and virtual training, including a popular customer-facing initiative and a new inward-facing initiative designed to build relationships within crews at Valvoline locations. Technicians are also given a wide array of e-learning courses, hands-on training, practice and certification checklists, check-in meetings with trainers, and reading and comprehension exercises (Harris 2020).

Coaching is another effective way to build collective leadership capability. Telus, a Canadian telecommunications company and 10-time ATD BEST Award winner, restructured its corporate coaching program to involve all employees in providing coaching and feedback, not just leaders. Since implementation, the employee ratings for executives and directors have gone up and the program has achieved a 92 percent satisfaction rating from employees (Castellan 2020).

Many TD professionals—like those at the University of Texas MD Anderson Cancer Center—use group coaching to revamp leadership development. Here, a skilled professional coach is brought together with a small group to maximize members' combined experience and provide a safe space for the group to work on goals and deepen learning. Leaders who use a coaching style of leadership are also more likely to develop emerging leaders who can fill a leadership pipeline (Cavanaugh, Deveau, and Holladay 2021).

Rethink Performance Management
High-functioning performance management processes strengthen the links between strategic business objectives and day-to-day job behaviors (McCormick 2016). Many companies, from global giants to small startups, have slowly moved away from traditional performance management to give their processes a complete makeover. This includes building metrics into performance reviews that measure whether supervisors are developing and coaching employees.

Valvoline, for example, eliminated performance ratings for hourly store team members, following a pattern launched for office employees the prior year. The new process focuses on quarterly guided career discussions and features individual manager-employee discussions about triumphs and challenges regarding customer service and internal relationships. In addition, managers have increased discretion over merit pay, rather than basing compensation decisions solely on individual performance (Harris 2020).

At AB InBev and Atlassian, the performance management process has become more continuous. Both companies created new financial and operating metrics, along with employee rewards and recognitions for supporting COVID-related changes, innovation, and team collaboration. Leaner and more agile processes have put more focus on employee centricity (Bersin 2020).

Amplify Management Support

Managers can make or break a learning culture. While learning cultures start at the top with leadership, they are driven most by middle managers (ATD 2016). In fact, an employee's experience of company culture will be largely dependent on their manager. Consider the following:

- Managers account for at least 70 percent of employee engagement scores—they can actually negate the positives of executive support.
- Employees look to their managers for learning recommendations 22 percent more often than their official learning systems, and 73 percent more often than their organization's L&D team (Palmer 2020).
- More than 50 percent of employees say that they would spend more time learning if their manager directed them (LinkedIn Learning 2020).

Because employees frequently complain that managers do not allow enough time for learning, Allstate supplements managers' performance measures to include "time to learn" (Sheldon 2021).

TD professionals can help managers prioritize time for learning and provide strategies for helping them manage time wisely by encouraging them to:

- Make a to-learn list.
- Set aside dedicated learning time on their calendar that employees can see.
- Join an online workplace learning channel.
- Share skill-building efforts during check-ins with their teams.
- Make development part of their daily work.

Figure 50-3 presents some other common ways to enhance management support for continuous learning. Of course, the best approach is to continue cultivating relationships across all organizational levels and show how learning helps solve real performance issues.

Figure 50-3. Enhance Management Support

Help managers set performance goals and co-create development plans with employees

Provide tools and peer networks to prepare managers for new roles, including coaching

Help managers improve team collaboration, inclusion, and recognition practices

Help managers provide development opportunities and challenging work

Invite managers to serve on advisory groups to guide strategies and reinforce continuous learning on the job

Collaboration and Connection

Thriving learning cultures share knowledge across boundaries to build collaboration, connection, and shared purpose. High levels of connection create greater employee engagement, tighter strategic alignment, better decision making, higher rates of innovation, and greater agility and adaptability (Stallard 2021). From a business perspective, jobs simply require more collaboration than they did in the past. Leadership is becoming more horizontal, structures are getting flatter, and organizations need solid networks to enable fast and free information flow (Morgan 2015).

However, the prolonged stress of COVID-19 and its accompanying loss of normal emotional and social support systems have led employees to feel more disconnected, more isolated, and more lonely. Remote workers are especially vulnerable. The impact of disconnection and its associated emotions upon engagement and performance is significant and includes:

- Reduced cognitive performance (brain fog)
- Impaired self-control
- Narrowed perspectives
- Increased lethargy
- Emotional distance from work (Stallard 2021)

To combat these issues, there are a few practices you could consider. Let's look at each more closely.

Be Intentional About Inclusion

Organizations that prioritize inclusion strategies are eight times more likely to achieve better business outcomes (Bourke 2018). With the hybrid workforce here to stay, more planning is needed to foster inclusion among the remote, dispersed workforce population (Hancock, Schaninger, and Weddle 2021). TD professionals can help by encouraging managers to put processes in place to help remote workers feel included. For example:

- Making sure everyone in the conference room is on their own individual video screen
- Updating messaging app channels to reflect office conversations
- Reaching out by phone, email, or periodic pulse surveys to see how remote workers are doing and what performance support is needed
- Establishing weekly Fri-YAY meetings for informal Slack time and socialization

Showing efforts for inclusion and respect reduces workplace stress and conflict, improves teamwork, and increases productivity and knowledge-sharing (Stallard 2021). In general, TD professionals can enable inclusion by helping leaders address and overcome unconscious biases and showing managers how to create open, safe discussion forums where respect and positive recognition of differences are cultivated. Keep in mind, however, that true collaboration and inclusion must be tied into overall talent management processes, as well as the social fabric of an organization and the commitment of its leaders to be trustworthy, inclusive, and equitable (Kelly and Schaefer 2015).

Teach Collaboration

Many organizations expect employees to work well together without properly teaching them how or defining what collaboration looks like in terms of daily practice and behavior. TD professionals play a critical role in terms of building collaborative capabilities and creating mechanisms for employees to connect and share information (Burkett 2017). Some places to start include:
- Identifying what a collaborative environment looks like
- Leveraging technologies that break down silos and enable knowledge sharing
- Teaching leaders and teams new processes for working together, resolving conflicts, providing constructive feedback, and making decisions
- Creating mechanisms for employees to recognize the collaborative efforts of their co-workers
- Ensuring that talent management processes recognize and reward collaboration, inclusion, and diversity

Remember, true collaboration is more than just an activity in which team members are working on a project together. It represents the way that individuals collectively explore ideas, address biases, learn from others, and include multiple perspectives to generate solutions. Collaboration is founded upon a climate of trust and safety (Delizonna 2017). In a truly collaborative environment everyone has a voice, and as a result they feel more included, are more able to contribute, and are more likely to engage with the group or organization (Stallard 2015).

Build Peer Networks and Communities

Another way thriving learning cultures enable collaboration and connection is through peer-learning networks that drive high performance, engagement, and innovation. Here, learning is managed with an eye toward social learning experiences that enable employees to work with others to solve problems, stretch their comfort zones, and steer their own career path (Biech 2018).

Consider the example of UL, a safety consulting and certification company. Its global leadership program builds a global network of leaders through conversation and facilitation. During program sessions, cohorts work together on important company issues and present their recommendations to senior leadership. The program is designed to provide a powerful, collaborative experience as a learning tool with a focus on how learners can succeed working across cultures and time zones (Graber 2016).

Results Orientation

In mature learning cultures, it's less about the output of training programs and more about outcomes that show how learning is adding business value. With today's data revolution, high-performing learning cultures are increasingly relying on advanced measures and analytic tools to communicate their value and apply a data-driven lens to strategic decisions about attracting, retaining, and growing talent. While cheaper, faster technologies are more available and more affordable for collecting and analyzing talent data, many TD functions still operate in a reactive, ad hoc mode when fielding requests for data. This often hampers their ability to connect talent initiatives to higher-level business results like revenue, profit, and customer satisfaction (Robinson et al. 2015). To show business value, the basics still apply.

Focus on Alignment

One of the most common reasons learning cultures fail to add value is that they are not effectively aligned or integrated with all phases of talent acquisition, talent management, and talent development processes (Oaks and Galagan 2011).

To align talent strategies, Valvoline integrates its entire gamut of talent-related functions, including acquisition, succession planning, and performance management. Beginning with a blended learning plan for the company's 5,000 new hires each year, Valvoline's promote-from-within strategy is touted and just-in-time learning resources are provided. The result is a turnover rate that is half the industry average and a core employee population primed for success (Harris 2020).

Link Learning and Performance

Many learning cultures fail to gain traction because TD professionals become more focused on the training than the performance that results from the training. A thriving learning culture is distinguished by its focus on driving better outcomes and stronger business results (Oaks and Galagan 2011).

For example, thriving learning cultures are nearly three times more likely to measure either or both employee behavior change and business impact and to use results to identify improvement opportunities. Consider the case of the award-winning learning function of OhioHealth. This not-for-profit system of hospitals and healthcare providers located in Columbus, Ohio, launched a Return on Learning (ROL) initiative in 2016 to begin demonstrating its business value in more cost-efficient terms. A key component of the initiative was the adoption of the ROI Methodology as a disciplined, evidence-based process for helping associates summarize and report on the impact of their L&D programs to key stakeholders. Goals also included growing the number of evaluation experts. Since the ROL implementation, the learning team has successfully grown its evaluation capabilities, expanded its access and credibility (both inside and outside the organization), and effectively demonstrated how learning has contributed to business outcomes like employee engagement, process improvement, and quality improvement. In addition, the learning team was recognized in 2018 and 2020 for its Excellence in Learning by Brandon Hall Group (Nguyen et al. 2021).

Develop a Reskilling and Upskilling Agenda

More than 87 percent of executives report skills gaps in their organization and more than 25 percent of organizations increased their spending on reskilling in response to COVID-19. Yet as the shelf life of skills shrinks, many business leaders worry that talent developers are too focused on training for today's skills, at the expense of preventing tomorrow's skills gaps.

> L&D's upskilling and reskilling programs should always be tied to key business priorities. We have two: attracting and retaining the best talent and building the capabilities needed to support the strategy. To help us do that effectively, we have started to embed learning leads into our strategy teams so we can identify the skills we'll need several years out and create a plan on how to close them.
> —Simon Brown, Chief Learning Officer, Novartis

Here's how some TD professionals are developing a broader skill set in their employees to prepare for future role disruption:

- IBM created a custom mobile app called YL Boost, which contains learning pathways for acquiring popular roles and skills. Employees can use the app to track their progress toward qualifying for those roles, and the app also sends nudges to complete daily and weekly goals.
- Amazon developed Career Choice, which is an innovative reskilling and outskilling program serving 40,000 employees in 14 countries and eight languages. Employees are eligible for the program after a year. The company prepays for textbooks and fees, but funds training or education only for in-demand skills—as validated by education partners who provide the training and business partners who make hiring decisions. Trainees may also choose to leverage their new skills in positions outside Amazon (Sheldon 2021).

Finally, don't neglect your own need to continually reskill and upskill so you can be a more effective business partner. For example, people analytics has been consistently cited as one of the biggest capability gaps among TD and HR practitioners (Bersin 2015). While developing talent analytic skills and capability to use supporting technologies may take time (up to several years) and continuing investment, it's important for TD professionals to embrace measurement for what it is and what it can do to revolutionize the value of learning (Canlas 2015). Keep in mind, however, that the real value isn't so much in the metrics themselves, but rather how they are presented to stakeholders and used to inform strategic decisions.

Sound Execution

Execution is where the rubber meets the road. Even when learning and business strategies are well aligned, executing them can be difficult. In many organizations, translating learning strategy into execution is an exercise characterized by stalled initiatives, politically charged turf battles, opportunities that have fallen by the wayside, and important work that remains undone. In addition, many organizations struggle to disinvest from initiatives that continually drain resources and fall substantially short of their intended impact (Sull et al. 2015). Knowing when to hold and when to fold is a big factor in effective execution.

While there are a host of approaches for closing the gap between strategy and execution, proven best practices include:

- Consistency of purpose
- Disciplined use of data-driven approaches (including change management, risk management, instructional design, measurement and evaluation, project management, design thinking, Six Sigma, Agile, HPT)
- Role clarity and accountability
- Defined success indicators
- Timely and accessible performance support
- Structured governance processes
- Regular reflection and review

Conducting after-action or lessons-learned reviews is perhaps the easiest way to support a learning culture. However, a common problem with lessons-learned reviews is that the insights they generate remain within a particular silo of an organization. Sharing is essential so that different parts of the organization can gain insights from the challenges and lessons learned in other areas.

Thriving learning cultures that use consistent, systemic practices—like regular reflection and review—outperform those with no systems. Finally, making exceptional execution part of your daily TD work will build your credibility for doing what you say and saying what you do, and will help brand your learning function as a pocket of excellence.

Organizational Resilience

Resiliency is the process of not only bouncing back from adversity, setbacks, uncertainty, or stress, but also bouncing forward to grow *and* thrive during challenging experiences. Organizations with high resiliency levels are more agile, innovative, engaging, and productive as well as more responsive to customers (Nauck et al. 2021). Resilient leaders are not only more effective in responding and recovering from business disruptions; they are better able to create the kind of positive disruption that drives innovation and growth. Individuals and teams with high resiliency levels are more positive and satisfied with their jobs, as well as more open to organizational change.

Resiliency not only makes good business sense; it pays off. For example, a 2014 study published by PwC found that practices promoting a resilient workplace returned $2.30 for every dollar spent—with the return coming in the form of higher productivity, lower absenteeism, lower healthcare costs, and decreased turnover (meQuilibrium 2017).

Let's look at a few ways organizations can build resilience.

Build Change Capability

Change is at the center of every learning and performance improvement strategy, talent development efforts are designed to drive organizational change, and today's learning leader plays a vital role as change agent. Thriving learning cultures continuously improve the way that change capabilities are grown, recognized, and rewarded (Burkett 2015). They adapt development approaches to fit the capabilities required of specific change roles and responsibilities, including:
- Change sponsors (those who lead change strategy)
- Change managers (those who manage the change plan)
- Change agents (those who build commitment and advocate for change efforts)

They also recognize that growing change capability is about more than stand-alone leadership development programs. For example, developing a network of change-ready teams across the entire organization not only helps nurture change responsiveness and innovation; it also accelerates business performance. To build enterprise-wide change capability, an organization needs to:
- Routinely assess the talent pool for change capability needs and gaps.
- Continuously improve leadership development to grow strategic change capability.
- Use disciplined, planned change processes for initiating and implementing change.
- Provide real-time performance support immediately after changes are introduced and during the change management process.
- Help leaders anticipate and manage the risks of change implementation, including the risk of change fatigue.

- Regularly monitor and measure the impact of change initiatives.
- Promote personal energy, rest, and recovery as strategic imperatives.

Monitor Burnout and Change Fatigue

"A resilient workforce is created when high-activity or high-intensity times are navigated by managing personal energy and balanced with periods of recovery" (CCL 2020). In today's organizations, individuals and teams experience daily brain drain and stress as they constantly grapple with issues like Zoom fatigue, change fatigue, information overload, the accelerated pace of work, health and safety concerns, and lingering uncertainties about the future of their work and workplace (Alexander et al. 2021). The overall impact of chronic workplace stress is so problematic that burnout has been officially recognized as a disease by the World Health Organization (Borysenko 2019). Burnout is characterized by:
- Reduced professional efficacy
- Increased mental distance from one's job
- Feelings of energy depletion or exhaustion

Change fatigue can contribute to burnout when people feel pressured to make too many transitions at once or when change initiatives have been poorly thought through, rolled out too fast, or put in place without adequate preparation. TD professionals should recognize the impact that being burnt-out, fatigued, and hyper-connected has upon an employee's ability to learn, perform and stay engaged. After all, the message of a perfectly aligned, designed, and delivered learning initiative will be lost if employees are too exhausted to hear it (Burkett 2017).

Make Time for Well-Being

To foster the kind of employee-centric work environment that reduces burnout and increases well-being, TD professionals must partner with business and HR leaders to replace the "more is more" culture with one focused on resilience. Employees across roles and levels must be encouraged—even expected—to rest, recharge, and recover as a matter of personal effectiveness and well-being and to maintain and sustain peak performance (Nauck et al. 2021). LinkedIn, Cisco, and SAP have all established weekly mental health days for global teams to recharge. Investments in employee health and well-being pay off with a direct impact on such business outcomes as greater productivity, stronger staff morale and motivation, and greater retention and loyalty (Economist Intelligence Unit 2021).

Take, for example, Autodesk's commitment to well-being. The global software company with 11,000 employees operating in 38 countries and 105 cities has many employees based in China. As COVID-19 began to spread, Autodesk leaders realized that they were on the brink of a potential crisis that would require global coordination for a wide range of situations, people, and geographies. To meet the challenge, the HR team refocused its training initiatives to cover employee resilience, physical and emotional well-being, and social connections. They also provided resources for managers focused on how to lead under stress, how to share authentically, how to take care of yourself and others, how to create inclusive work practices, and how to create a culture of belonging. As one of the world's leading users of Slack, Autodesk's culture of sharing helps employees communicate with peers around personal, professional, and family issues and topics. The company also relies heavily on Zoom, Mural, Slack, and Autodesk technology for remote working (Bersin 2020).

According to the Center for Creative Leadership, there are several things you can do to help your organization shift away from the old "work-harder" belief:

- **Educate people about resiliency.** Teach specific practices and habits that focus on resilient skill sets and mindsets. Connect resiliency to overall health and well-being and to improved job performance.
- **Show how to set boundaries with email.** Adopt a daily out-of-office email reply for after-work hours to let teams know that emails won't be answered during this time.
- **Emphasize the role of gratitude.** A key aspect of resilience is cultivating gratitude practices. Encourage leaders, teams, and individuals to routinely express gratitude.
- **Provide resiliency-building opportunities at work.** Financial incentives or reimbursements for fitness classes can encourage employees to replenish their energy levels.
- **Consider contemplative practices.** Many large organizations have launched mindfulness programs to help people learn how to rest and recover properly.

Keep in mind that improving resiliency at an individual level is necessary but not enough to create a resilient organization. Research shows that it takes a wide range of cultural levers to influence and embed resilient capabilities at the organizational level (Lucy and Shepard 2017).

Foster Learning Agility

In a *New York Times* interview, Laszlo Bock, former SVP of people operations at Google, said: "For every job, the No. 1 thing we look for is general cognitive ability, and it's not I.Q. It's learning ability. It's the ability to process on the fly" (Zoe 2019).

In unpredictable business environments buffeted by constant change, organizations need employees who have resilience and agile learning abilities to move forward. Learning agility is the ability and willingness to learn, unlearn, and relearn. It consists of nine dimensions, with flexibility and speed being the two main drivers. *Flexibility* refers to the ability to give up old habits or behaviors for new behaviors that better meet the needs of the future. *Speed* has more to do with how quickly an individual can read a situation and change their behaviors to adapt and respond with a plan of action.

Learning agility has been shown to be an excellent predictor of leadership success. While it may not always come naturally, learning agility can be honed and developed. TD professionals can help grow learning agility by:
- Immersing employees in parts of the job or company that they haven't experienced before
- Providing job shadowing, job rotation, and temporary assignments
- Teaching problem-solving approaches
- Using validated learning agility assessments in recruitment, selection, and talent development

Innovation

What sets thriving learning cultures apart is their commitment to continual innovation and their ability to renew or reinvent themselves and their organizations as new conditions and demands emerge (Burkett 2017). In fact, research suggests that companies with strong learning cultures are a staggering 92 percent more likely to be innovators in product development and sustainable value and growth (Bersin 2015). Yet many learning functions lack strategies or systems that foster innovation and many others are not up to speed with innovative technologies. Talent development professionals cannot expect to help drive innovation within the business if their own practices are stagnant and out of touch.

Figure 50-4 shows how to move the dial and get out of "business as usual" approaches. Let's look closer at one of the suggestions outlined in the figure.

Figure 50-4. Embrace the Art of Innovation

- Create systems that support innovation
- Reward innovation with engaging work
- Link innovation to compensation
- Hire for innovation and creativity
- Leverage technology for knowledge sharing
- Foster innovative values and mindsets
- Make innovation a core competency
- Approach innovation as a learnable skill

Adapted from Burkett (2017)

Leverage Technology

Talent developers are depending more on digital learning solutions than ever before—not only to deliver content but also to measure learning success. While technology has the potential to strengthen a learning culture, many organizations report concerns about limitations with their technology infrastructure, including reduced investments and difficult access.

For example, the team of progressive learning leaders at DuPont Sustainable Solutions rose to the challenge of leveraging technology during the COVID-19 pandemic. The company's L&D team partnered with Arist, a global leader in text messaging learning, to develop safety courses delivered through text messages. The approach, which was designed to get adaptable coursework to global employees quickly, continues to be an important delivery alternative for internal and external compliance training. It allows the team to "break down complex subjects—which tend to show low engagement levels with traditional learning methods—into short bursts of simple and engaging learning." It also makes it easier to track learner data for compliance purposes (Arist 2021).

In addition, when technology becomes well integrated with a learning culture, organizations see a positive business impact (Figure 50-5).

Figure 50-5. The Business Impact of Well-Integrated Technology

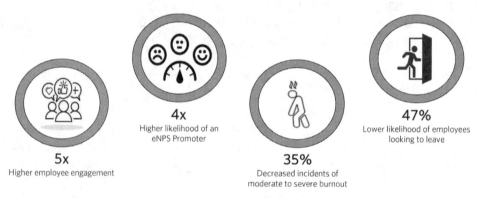

O.C. Tanner Institute (2021)

Tips for leveraging technology:
- Develop and follow a change management plan for any new technology. Without such plans in place, adoption of the latest technology drops by 51 percent and the overall employee experience decreases by 32 percent.
- Don't assume employees will easily adopt new technology. Even those who trend toward very open acceptance may resist if it disrupts their flow of work.
- Use nudge versus nag reminders to help learners overcome obstacles and apply new knowledge (O.C. Tanner Institute 2021).

Make It Safe to Fail

Findings from Google's two-year study on team performance revealed that the highest-performing teams have one thing in common: psychological safety, which is the belief that you won't be punished when you make a mistake. Thriving learning cultures create space for people to learn from failures and successes—they encourage individuals, teams, and the whole organization to embrace experimentation, risk, and surprise.

Paul Santagata, head of industry at Google, periodically asks his team members how safe they feel and what could enhance their feeling of safety. In addition, his team routinely takes surveys on psychological safety and other team dynamics; for example, the survey might ask, "How confident are you that you won't receive retaliation or criticism if you admit an error or make a mistake?" (Delizonna 2017).

Meet the Needs of the Modern Learner

Easily accessible and user-driven learning opportunities that meet the needs of the modern learner are hallmarks of innovative learning cultures (Hart 2019). Modern learners expect learning to be:

- **On-demand** (as needed) and **continuous**, rather than just an intermittent activity
- **In short bursts** (minutes) rather than long periods (hours or days)
- **Easily accessible** on **mobile devices** (smartphones and tablets) and able to pull learning modules at the time and place of need as opposed to only reacting to required push courses
- **Social**, with tools, technologies, and resources (including coaches, mentors, wikis, smartphones, and tablets) for creating and sharing learning content
- **Personalized** to allow individuals to organize and manage their own continuous self-improvement and self-development rather than adhere to a one-size-fits-all experience
- Largely **experiential** to involve learning by doing rather than just theorizing

Final Thoughts

As the future rushes toward us at dizzying speed, mature learning cultures are more important than ever before. As Bill Schaninger of McKinsey says, "This is an unbelievable opportunity to remake culture. It's rare in a leader's lifetime to have such a clean drop for reshaping how you run the place."

The need for transformation is here; the time for action is now. In a call to action, thought leader and multiple-award-winning learning advocate Kimo Kippen of Aloha Learning Advisors urged chief learning officers to seize existing opportunities for transformation: "Now is learning and development's time in the sun."

Keep in mind, however, that a learning culture doesn't change overnight; rather, it evolves over time. Building a thriving learning culture—one that is fully embedded in an organization's

DNA—is a development process that may take several years to achieve. As shown in Figure 50-6, this evolution follows the common stages of maturity, where processes gradually transform from being more ad hoc and undisciplined to being more consistent, disciplined, and value-added. This maturity model will be a helpful road map to your future.

Figure 50-6. A Maturity Model for Learning Cultures

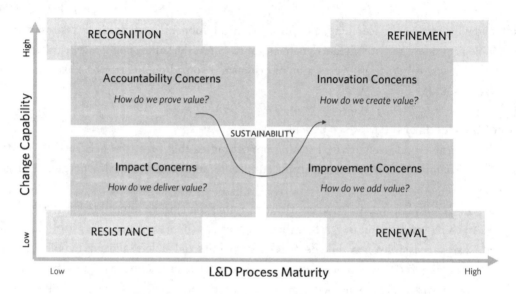

Organizational change capability and L&D maturity are both drivers of sustainability.

Adapted from Burkett (2017)

Thriving is not about doing one of the six essentials really well; it's about integrating all six essentials to create a sustainable learning culture that stands the test of time (Burkett 2017). You will find two tools—a reminder of the six essentials and a self-assessment to rate your learning culture—on the handbook website (ATDHandbook3.org). Use these tools to help create a thriving learning culture in your organization.

While the effort might seem daunting, the key is to focus on manageable, achievable actions that keep you moving. After all, culture is shaped by daily behaviors, interactions, and practices. Use the tips, self-assessment tool, and examples from this chapter to prepare the soil and plant the seeds for learning transformation to take root in your organization. Seize your day in the sun and make it happen!

About the Author

Holly Burkett, PhD, SPHR, SCC, is an accomplished talent builder, change leader, and workplace learning professional with more than 20 years' experience as a trusted business advisor for diverse global organizations. She is passionate about developing resilient leadership capabilities that enable high engagement and performance. Formerly with Apple, Holly's clients include the State Bar of California, the National Park Service, Chevron, and the National Security Agency. As a Prosci certified change practitioner, a Marshall Goldsmith Stakeholder Centered Coach, and a select member of the Forbes Coaches Council, Holly is a sought-after speaker, coach, and facilitator. Her publications include the award-winning book *Learning for the Long Run* and contributions to *ATD's Foundations of Talent Development*, *ATD's Action Guide to Talent Development*, and the Talent Development Body of Knowledge. Her doctorate is in human capital development. Holly can be reached at holly@hollyburkett.com.

References

Alexander, A., A. DeSmet, M. Langstaff, and D. Revid. 2021. "What Employees are Saying about the Future of Work." McKinsey & Company, April 1. mckinsey.com/business-functions/people-and-organizational-performance/our-insights/what-employees-are-saying-about-the-future-of-remote-work.

Arist. 2021. "Case Study: DuPont Sustainable Solutions." Arist, February 17. arist.co/dupont-sustainable-solutions.

Association for Talent Development (ATD). 2016. *Building a Culture of Learning: The Foundation of a Successful Organization.* Alexandria, VA: ATD Press.

Bersin, J. 2015. "Becoming Irresistible: A New Model for Employee Engagement." *Deloitte Review* 16 (January 27). deloitte.com/us/en/insights/deloitte-review/issue-16/employee-engagement-strategies.html.

Bersin, J. 2020. "The Big Reset Playbook: What's Working Now." Josh Bersin, August 26. joshbersin.com/2020/08/the-big-reset-playbook-whats-working-now.

Biech, E. 2018. *ATD's Foundations of Talent Development: Launching, Leveraging, and Leading Your Organization's TD Effort.* Alexandria, VA: ATD Press.

Borysenko, K. 2019. "Burnout Is Now an Officially Diagnosable Condition: Here's What You Need to Know About It." *Forbes*, May 29. forbes.com/sites/karlynborysenko/2019/05/29/burnout-is-now-an-officially-diagnosable-condition-heres-what-you-need-to-know-about-it/#2d9692a42b99.

Bourke, J. 2018. "The Diversity and Inclusion Revolution: Eight Powerful Truths." Deloitte Review, January 22. deloitte.com/us/en/insights/deloitte-review/issue-22/diversity-and-inclusion-at-work-eight-powerful-truths.html.

Burkett, H. 2015. "Talent Managers as Change Agents." In *Talent Management Handbook*, edited by T. Bickham. Alexandria, VA: ATD Press.

Burkett, H. 2017. *Learning for the Long Run: 7 Practices for Sustaining a Resilient Learning Organization*. Alexandria, VA: ATD Press.

Burkett, H. 2018. "Valuing a Learning Culture." In *ATD's Action Guide for Talent Development* by E. Biech. Alexandria, VA: ATD Press.

Canlas, L. 2015. "How We Built Talent Analytics at LinkedIn." LinkedIn Pulse, November 5. linkedin.com/pulse/how-we-built-talent-analytics-linkedin-lorenzo-canlas.

Castellan, S. 2020. "Small Actions Nurture Company-Wide Learning Cultures." *TD*, July 20. td.org/magazines/td-magazine/small-actions-nurture-company-wide-learning-cultures.

Cavanaugh, K., M. Deveau, and C. Holladay. 2021. "Reframing Leadership Through Coaching." *TD*, April 30. Alexandria, VA: ATD Press.

Center for Creative Leadership (CCL). 2020. *Unlearning Your Organizational Culture: A Playbook for Leading in an Unpredictable, Virtual World*. Greensboro, NC: CCL

Dearborn, J. 2015. "Why Your Company Needs a Learning Culture." *Chief Learning Officer*, June 3. clomedia.com/2015/06/03/why-your-company-needs-a-learning-culture.

Delizonna, L. 2017. "High-Performing Teams Need Psychological Safety. Here's How to Create It." Harvard Business Review, August 24. hbr.org/2017/08/high-performing-teams-need-psychological-safety-heres-how-to-create-it.

Dweck, C. 2007. *Mindset: The New Psychology of Success*. New York: Ballantine Books.

Economist Intelligence Unit (EIR). 2021. "The Employer Imperative." Infographic. impact.economist.com/projects/healthy-workforce/infographic.

Graber, J. 2016. "UL's Unique Look at Development." *Chief Learning Officer*, April 8. clomedia.com/2016/04/08/uls-unique-look-at-development.

Hancock, B., B. Schaninger, and B. Weddle. 2021. "Culture in the Hybrid Workplace." McKinsey & Company, June 11. mckinsey.com/business-functions/organization/our-insights/culture-in-the-hybrid-workplace.

Hart, J. 2019. "Modern Workplace Learning 2019: A Framework for Continuous Improvement, Learning and Development."

Harris, P. 2020. "Cranking on All Cylinders." *TD*, July 20. td.org/magazines/td-magazine/cranking-on-all-cylinders.

Kelly, K., and A. Schaefer. 2015. *Creating a Collaborative Organizational Culture*. Chapel Hill, NC: UNC Executive Development.

LinkedIn Learning. n.d. "Kellogg's Customer Story." LinkedIn Learning Solutions. learning.linkedin.com/elearning-case-studies/kelloggs.

Linkedin Learning. 2018. "2018 Workplace Learning Report." LinkedIn. learning.linkedin.com/content/dam/me/learning/en-us/pdfs/linkedin-learning-workplace-learning-report-2018.pdf.

LinkedIn Learning. 2020. "2020 Workplace Learning Report." LinkedIn. learning.linkedin.com/content/dam/me/learning/resources/pdfs/LinkedIn-Learning-2020-Workplace-Learning-Report.pdf.

Lucy, D., and C. Shepard. 2017. *Organizational Resilience: Building Change Readiness.* UK: Roffey Park Institute. roffeypark.com/wp-content/uploads2/Organisational-Resilience-Developing-Change-Readiness-Reduced-Size.pdf.

Lutin, L. 2020. "Superlearning: Reskilling, Upskilling and Outskilling for a Future-Proof Workforce." Deloitte Insights, June 29. deloitte.com/us/en/insights/focus/technology-and-the-future-of-work/reskilling-the-workforce.html.

McCormick, H. 2016. *7 Steps to Creating a Lasting Learning Culture.* Chapel Hill: UNC Executive Development.

meQuilibrium. 2017. "3 Critical Ways Resilience Impacts Your Bottom Line." Human Resource Executive. hrexecutive.com/critical-ways-resilience-impacts-bottom-line.

Morgan, J. 2015. *The Future of Work: Attract New Talent, Build Better Leaders, and Create a Competitive Organization.* Hoboken, NJ: John Wiley and Sons.

Nauck, F., L. Pancaldi, T. Poppensieker, and O. White. 2021. "The Resilience Imperative: Succeeding in Uncertain Times." McKinsey & Company, May 17. mckinsey.com/business-functions/risk-and-resilience/our-insights/the-resilience-imperative-succeeding-in-uncertain-times.

Nguyen, N., P.P. Phillips, J.J. Phillips, and H. Burkett. 2021. "ROI and Best Practices in the Age of Disruption." ISPI Annual Virtual Conference, April 29.

Oaks, K., and P. Galagan. 2011. *The Executive Guide to Integrated Talent Management.* Alexandria, VA: ATD Press.

O.C. Tanner Institute. 2021. *2021 Global Culture Report.* Salt Lake City, UT: O.C. Tanner Institute. octanner.com/content/dam/oc-tanner/images/v2/culture-report/2021/GCR-2021-sm.pdf.

Palmer, K. 2020. "Overcoming Obstacles: Managers Are Perfectly Positioned to Help Workers Learn." Degreed blog, June 29. blog.degreed.com/managers-are-positioned-to-help-workers-learn.

Robinson, D.G., J.C. Robinson, J.J. Phillips, P.P. Phillips, and D. Handshaw. 2015. *Performance Consulting: A Strategic Process to Improve, Measure, and Sustain Organizational Results,* 3rd ed. San Francisco: Berrett-Koehler.

Salopek, J. 2015. "Training at the Crossroads of Tradition and Technology." *TD* 69(11).

Senge, P.M. 2006. *The Fifth Discipline: The Art and Practice of the Learning Organization*. New York: Broadway Business.

Sheldon, R. 2021. "A Conversation With Allstate's Rose Sheldon." CLO Breakfast Club June 2021: Resilience & Transformation Through Crisis and Recovery, June 29. app.socio.events/ MTA1NzU/Overview/139342.

Skibola, N. 2011. "Leadership Lessons From WD-40's CEO, Garry Ridge." *Forbes*, June 27. forbes.com/sites/csr/2011/06/27/leadership-lessons-from-wd-40s-ceo-garry-ridge/?sh= 3b3dd3f91fae.

Stallard, M. 2015. *Connection Culture: The Competitive Advantage of Shared Identity, Empathy, and Understanding at Work*. Alexandria, VA: ATD Press.

Stallard, M. 2021. "What NASA Can Teach Us About Post-Pandemic Workplace Re-Entry." Michael Lee Stallard, June 5. michaelleestallard.com/preparing-re-entry-physical-workplace-lessons-nasa.

Sull, D., R. Homkes, and C. Sull. 2015. "Why Strategy Execution Unravels—and What to Do About It." *Harvard Business Review*, March. hbr.org/2015/03/why-strategy-execution-unravelsand-what-to-do-about-it.

Taylor, B. 2016. "How WD-40 Created a Learning-Obsessed Company Culture." *Harvard Business Review*, September 16. hbr.org/2016/09/how-wd-40-created-a-learning-obsessed-company-culture.

Vander Ark, T. 2018. "Hit Refresh: How A Growth Mindset Culture Tripled Microsoft's Value." *Forbes*, April 18. forbes.com/sites/tomvanderark/2018/04/18/hit-refresh-how-a-growth-mindset-culture-tripled-microsofts-value/?sh=3f5630da52ad.

Zoe, E. 2019. "Learning Agility: What Is It and How Do You Nurture It?" eFront Learning, March. efrontlearning.com/blog/2019/03/learning-agility-what-is-how-nurture-it.html.

Recommended Resources

Burkett, H. 2017. *Learning for the Long Run: 7 Practices for Sustaining a Resilient Learning Organization*. Alexandria, VA: ATD Press.

Marquardt, M.J. 2011. *Building the Learning Organization*, 3rd ed. Boston: Nicholas Bealy.

Quinn, C. 2014. *Revolutionize Learning & Development*. Alexandria, VA: ATD Press.

Schawbel, D. 2018. *How Great Leaders Create Connection in the Age of Isolation*. New York: DeCapo Press.

CHAPTER 51

Sustaining Diversity, Equity, and Inclusion

Tonya Wilson

Diversity, equity, and inclusion (DEI) are important to every aspect of talent development. The nature of talent development is to ensure the availability and efficacy of talent to support the needs of the organization. By refreshing our definitions of *diversity*, *equity*, and *inclusion*, we can ensure we are aligned as we begin to understand the strategies, insights, tools, and techniques associated with sustaining DEI. The definitions in this chapter, which are also located in the glossary, were developed by the Tuskegee University DEI initiative.

> **IN THIS CHAPTER:**
> - Define the sustainability of diversity, equity, and inclusion (DEI)
> - Discuss key elements associated with assessing sustainability
> - Explore the importance of a diversity climate
> - Determine ways to connect DEI to business strategy

Diversity, equity, and inclusion seems to be illusive for many leaders. Companies spend about $8 billion annually on diversity and inclusion training (Kirkland and Bohnet 2017). And, according to recent research by Traliant and WBR Insights, 79 percent of companies plan to allocate more budget and resources in 2022 (VB Staff 2021). Despite the significant investment in diversity and related training, however, many companies still struggle with institutionalizing DEI. The good news is that some companies, like Target, Google, and Apple, are making great strides in their DEI strategies. This chapter presents strategies, insights, tools, and techniques associated with sustaining diversity, equity, and inclusion.

Sustaining an Organizational DEI Culture

If you reflect on the science classes you took in grade school, you may recall the study of biomes and ecosystems. One of the key lessons beyond species and classifications was the fact that every element within the system had value. In addition, certain types of disruptions, neglect, or lack in those systems would result in an imbalance and a loss that influenced the entire community within the system. This is why we carefully monitor the health and viability of life within these systems (Figure 51-1).

Figure 51-1. The DEI Ecosystem

Sustainability is about how we monitor the life and environments of systems. As we apply sustainability to DEI, we also look at the life and viability of our organizations. When we look at the DEI ecosystem within an organization, we look at how we treat our people, manage our organizations, and influence our communities. This view aligns with the perspective of the triple bottom line—commonly known as people, planet, and profit—which was first put forward in 1994 by author and sustainability pioneer John Elkington. It defines *sustainable practices* as:

- At a minimum, do not harm people or the planet and at best create value for the stakeholders.
- Focus on improving environmental, social, and governance (ESG) performance in the areas where the company or brand has a material environmental or social impact (operations, value chain, or customers).

Like any other sustainability effort, DEI is a long-term journey with significant benefits. Most leaders would agree that DEI is important to the viability of an organization. It is also the right thing to do for the people who are part of the organization, for the profitability of the organization, and for the customers that it serves. Without a strong commitment and action toward diverse, inclusive, and equitable environments, however, we may find ourselves with lower levels of profitability, higher levels of turnover, lower levels of engagement and commitment, smaller margins, less innovation, weaker brands, or increased healthcare costs. This is supported by several studies conducted by McKinsey, Boston Consulting Group, and other well-known consulting and research firms (Hunt et al. 2020; Lorenzo et al. 2021).

Therefore, it is imperative that we look at DEI as a significant part of the overall business strategy that can contribute to growth, profitability, and innovation, thereby affecting competitive advantage and market differentiation. While DEI activities are important, sustainability is linked substantially to program outcomes. An outcome-based DEI strategy that is strongly linked to the business and people strategies for the organization will have long-term positive results. Sustainable DEI must be linked to business outcomes and profitability. Research by McKinsey also indicates that boards with diverse representation in gender and ethnicity are 21 to 33 percent more likely to outperform in profitability. As evidence of the importance of board representation, NASDAQ filed with the US Security and Exchange Commission (SEC) in 2020 to adopt new listing rules related to board of director diversity for publicly held companies (Gonzalez-Sussman and Berenblat 2020).

Business leaders need to understand qualitative and quantitative data that indicate what is working and what is not. These are critical questions that will inform how resources should be allocated as the strategies for DEI continue to be executed. Most leaders will want to put their time and money in places where they will see a return on their investment. Sustaining DEI requires a look at the original business case to determine how the organization has progressed.

Organizations need to ask hard questions about success in DEI, such as:
- What did we accomplish over the past [x amount of time]?
- What progress have we made against our goals and objectives?
- What does the data (qualitative and quantitative) say about our progress from the view of key stakeholders, especially those in diverse populations (including interviews and focus groups)?
- Are we having crucial conversations?
- Does our representation of diverse populations look different in management, leadership, and partnership than it did before we initiated our plan?
- Does our succession plan allow us to tap into a diverse talent pipeline?
- Have we seen changes in our EEOC actions or employee relations cases related to bias or unfair treatment?
- What is our net promoter score with diverse groups?
- Are our leaders and managers actively engaged in promoting a positive diversity climate?
- Are we resourcing our diversity strategy, initiatives, and leaders for continued success?

TARGET'S PRIORITY ON GOALS IS MAKING A DIFFERENCE

Target has been intent on building a culture of diversity, equity, and inclusion that aligns with its strategic imperatives. The company's diversity and inclusion goals focus on three primary areas: working to have a team that's more representative of customers; helping all team members have an inclusive experience; and investing in suppliers, products, and marketing that help Target meet the needs of all customers.

Target measures many dimensions of difference across their goals. One example is their supplier diversity goal, which measures the amount spent with companies that are owned by women, people of color, LGBTQ+ individuals, veterans, and people with disabilities.

In addition, Target's diversity and inclusion strategy has been in place for more than 15 years, and the company sets measurable goals every three years. Each business unit leader tracks, reports on, and is held accountable for diversity and inclusion goals for their team.

In September 2020, in addition to issuing a workplace diversity report, Target also announced systemic changes to increase the representation of Black team members across the company by 20 percent over the next three years (Shumway and Estrada 2021). To accomplish this goal, they are focusing on:
- Leveraging store, supply chain, and headquarter experiences to provide broader leadership pathways for Black team members
- Developing programs to hire and retain Black team members in career areas with low levels of representation, including technology, data sciences, merchandising, and marketing

> **TARGET'S PRIORITY ON GOALS IS MAKING A DIFFERENCE** *continued*
>
> - Creating a network of mentors and sponsors to help Black team members accelerate and advance their careers
> - Ensuring benefits and partnerships drive wellness and safety for Black team members
> - Conducting anti-racist training sessions for leaders and team members that educate, build inclusion acumen, and foster a sense of belonging (Target Bullseye View News 2020)
>
> Through 2020, Target has increased the representation and advancement of women of color and people of color, increased sales in product categories that help make the company relevant for all customers, and is on track to meet its spending goal with diverse suppliers.

Diversity Climate and the DEI Ecosystem

The climate of the ecosystem is particularly important in sustainability. And likewise, the diversity climate is particularly important to the organization. The Centre for Global Inclusion (GDEIB) defines diversity climate as:

> A measure of perceptions of the degree to which employees belonging to equity-seeking groups are valued, socially included, and treated fairly by colleagues; and the degree to which the organization and its top leadership strive for the numerical representation, social inclusion, and elimination of discrimination toward equity-seeking groups.

GDEIB also supports a diversity climate assessment that is maintained by researchers at the University of Guelph. You can access the Workplace Diversity and Inclusion Climate Scale for free on the university's website (see this chapter's list of additional resources).

If we as leaders, managers, and talent development professionals treat DEI as an accessory that is optional or a check the box for compliance, it will be reflected in the overall organizational climate. If leaders want to see outcomes that positively affect their people, organizations, and communities, then they must show authentic commitment and sponsorship to DEI initiatives.

Monitoring the amount of time and resources that continue to be dedicated to DEI will be an indicator of how well the organization will sustain these programs and culture as you go forward. Leadership is often tempted to reduce the amount of resources dedicated to change initiatives within organizations once key milestones and goals are met. According to the *Wall Street Journal*, turnover for diversity leaders is high (Cutter and Weber 2020). Often leaders are not given the authority commensurate with the role nor do they have the proper resources to support the initiatives. There is also the challenge of role clarity, because many diversity leaders have extrarole expectations or are also charged with leading other aspects of the human resource or business functions. Unfortunately, some chief diversity officers or diversity leaders are not selected with specific competencies in mind and are not always given the opportunity to build the skills or competencies they need to drive results in this important business area.

When DEI resources are reduced, it's almost guaranteed that these initiatives will not be fully institutionalized or ingrained in the company culture. So, make sure to include DEI as an agenda topic for all strategy meetings, business reviews, and organizational design and planning meetings. In addition, when reviewing processes and developing procedures organizations, should consider the impact all initiatives will have on their diverse populations.

Because a key objective of DEI is to influence the way of thinking and doing work daily, DEI should also be a part of any discussions around organizational changes. For example, when going through business transformation, digital transformation, mergers, acquisitions, organization redesigns, or other significant changes, it is important to watch the talent pool implications. Technological advancement (such as AI or machine learning) may challenge the dispersion of diverse populations at various levels, so it's important to include plans for reskilling to ensure that great talent is retained. This is not only for keeping representation of diverse team members, but also to ensure inclusion in decision making and the fairness of treatment regarding access to resources.

DEI and Compliance

Compliance may be the first thing many think about, but sustaining DEI goes beyond the realm of compliance. DEI is not about establishing a quota system. It is important to realize that DEI is a part of how companies establish a culture of inclusion where people are treated fairly, which results in high performance, greater innovation, and a competitive advantage. Such a view recognizes DEI as an integral part of the corporate DNA. This gives us a view of what is being gained instead of a fear of what might be lost. However, if compliance is in jeopardy, then it's likely that there is a fundamental problem with the strategy or operations related to integration of DEI into the organization systems.

So, what is required of compliance in the US? SHRM's "HR Q&As" state that:

> Under Executive Order 11246, federal contractors and subcontractors with 50 or more employees who have entered into at least one contract of $50,000 or more with the federal government must prepare and maintain a written program, which must be developed within 120 days from the commencement of the contract and must be updated annually. The program should cover recruitment, hiring and promotion of women and minorities. Any depository of government funds in any amount or any financial institution that is an issuing and paying agent for U.S. savings bonds and savings notes in any amount must develop and maintain written affirmative action programs as well.

Affirmative action programs define an employer's standard for proactively recruiting, hiring, and promoting women, minorities, disabled individuals, and veterans. Affirmative action is deemed a moral and social obligation to amend historical wrongs and eliminate the present effects of past discrimination for companies. Although an affirmative action program is intended to eradicate the effects of past discrimination in employment, it is also meant to be inclusive without regard to race, gender, disabilities, or veteran status. Historically, the support for affirmative action was instituted to achieve goals such as bridging true inequalities in employment and pay, increasing access to education, promoting diversity, and redressing apparent past wrongs, harms, or hindrances. EO 11246 also requires a statistical look at the population data from where talent is sought after to help the organization's population mirror that of the business community.

Diversity initiatives measure acceptance of minorities by embracing cultural differences within the workplace. They are twofold in that they both value and manage diversity. The value of diversity is achieved through awareness, education, and positive recognition of the qualities, experiences, and work styles that make individuals unique within the workplace. The management of diversity frames the experience and establishes the business case for diversity that is closely aligned with an employer's organizational goals. The combination of required or voluntary affirmative action programs and diversity initiatives is important to create opportunities for cultural inclusion, respect for differences, acceptance, and respect for all workers.

DEI Is Good Business

Diversity, equity, and inclusion is good business. The organization's business strategy is critical to its viability, which means it would be exceedingly difficult to sustain DEI within an organization if it was not aligned with the strategy. Foundational to every business strategy are the company's mission, vision, and values. The organization's values are critical to its longevity because they guide the decision-making process, and a close examination will provide clues regarding how the organization values those who are different. Periodic organizational values checkups are warranted for organizations that are intent on sustaining DEI. If individual behaviors do not demonstrate value for employees, there should be consequences. For example, if a very successful sales leader sexually harasses a team member, there could a financial impact if the company loses key customers and there could also be legal consequences for the organization.

Organizations that value teamwork, respect, diverse perspectives, collaboration, innovation, people-first, trust, integrity, and fairness have set an expectation that DEI is part of the behavioral expectations. Oftentimes a strategy for growth or disruptive innovation is at the core of an organization's future plans. The business objectives derived from the strategy should be developed with a lens to diversity, equity, and inclusion. As those objectives are aligned, they serve to inform the people or talent strategy, which also must be viewed with a lens to DEI. The ability to develop capability and enhanced capacity to support the strategy may involve building, buying, or borrowing talent with the skills and competencies needed for the work (Figure 51-2).

Figure 51-2. Alignment of Business Strategy and Talent Strategy With an Integrated View of DEI

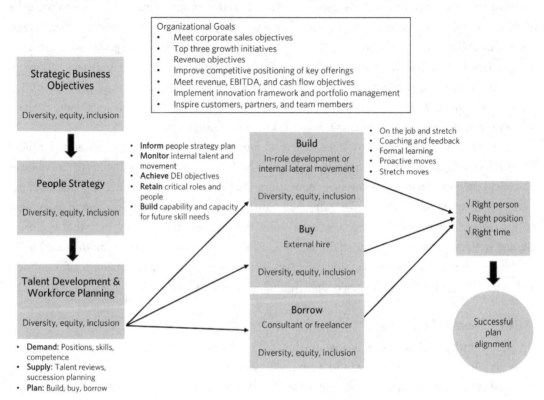

The business case for DEI is compelling. Studies show substantial increases in financial performance for companies with higher levels of diversity and inclusion in their employee population (Lorenzo et al. 2021; Hunt et al. 2020). Increases in EBITDA and revenue for such companies range from 9 to 21 percent (Figure 51-3). This type of performance has the potential to enhance the competitive advantage of these companies because they may outperform their competitors. Additionally, outcomes such as increased engagement, higher levels of retention, learning nimbleness, and a stronger employee value proposition bring great benefit to the organization.

And yet, diversity may not remain a priority in the business strategy if business leaders do not fully understand the return on investment for DEI. Leaders can assess DEI outcomes and ask questions such as "What is the value and benefit to our company?" "How did DEI help achieve our goals?" "How did it help our customers by providing competitive products?" "How did it help our employees perform better and be more engaged?" (Figure 51-4).

Figure 51-3. Financial Performance and DEI

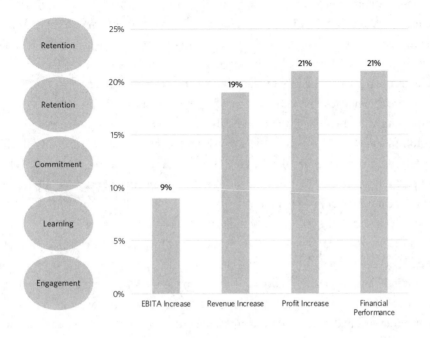

Figure 51-4. DEI Outcomes

Sustaining Diversity, Equity, and Inclusion | 781

Outcome-based strategies have greater long-term positive effects than strategies solely based on DEI. These outcomes not only influence the life of the organization; they also have revenue consequences. Jack and Patti Phillips (2014), founders of the ROI Institute, have reviewed the ROI of DEI in numerous case studies, including those discussed in their Measuring ROI series.

For example, the ROI Institute has explored such questions as:
- What is the business need that is satisfied by DEI in our organization?
- What are the metrics that allow us to understand the impact?
- Is the data accurate, reliable, and accessible as we consider the outcomes?

The Phillips's view of business needs analysis and diversity scorecards is insightful to calculate the return on investment for DEI. Their ROI case study focuses on outcomes. When looking at the DEI ecosystem, we consider outcomes from the perspective of each member of the system, because they are our primary stakeholders.

Data analytics and DEI sustainability are critical. Data is necessary for decision making and resource allocation. It helps to continue to root out any bias that influences decisions that may be inequitable. For example, Target discovered that disaggregating its data and conducting a deeper analysis helped it clarify its areas of focus, make more specific commitments, and hold itself accountable for progress. The data also made it clear that there was much more work to be done. Its prior actions had not resulted in equitable outcomes for its Black team members, and it needed to do more to increase representation and advancement opportunities and reduce turnover (Target Bullseye View News 2020).

Ensure that your analysis includes continued representative items for diverse populations. Qualitative and quantitative data collection may come from various sources, such as:
- Engagement surveys
- Employee satisfaction or opinion surveys
- Leadership assessment surveys
- Change readiness surveys
- Pulse surveys
- Talent acquisition data
- New team member onboarding interviews
- Focus groups
- External data from social sites
- Employee relations cases
- Legal case reviews
- LMS completion data
- Performance management aggregated data
- Affirmative action reports
- Leadership

- Storyboards
- Net promoter score data
- Customer satisfaction or voice data
- Supplier satisfaction data
- Supplier utilization data
- Compensation analyses
- Exit interviews

Because most organizations do not have unlimited resources, use data to support how you prioritize the DEI initiatives or goals that will have the most impact. The data may point to many areas of opportunity, so resist the temptation to take on too many objectives. In some instances, the less is more approach makes it more likely that success and change are achieved. For example, setting three to four goals in the areas of supplier diversity, community engagement, leader/employee awareness, and succession could be aggressive but doable. Sustaining DEI has unique considerations based on individual business needs and the ability to resource initiatives. A charter for these outcome-based initiatives could set the organization up for success, resulting in buy-in and delivering real results.

An effective practice to motivate employees is to tie metrics to rewards. Using metrics focused on actions to incentivize certain behaviors will require significant coordination with the total rewards and finance. These actions are more likely to occur if the CEO demonstrates the priority to the employee population. Sustainable DEI measures will address the questions in the DEI Key Questions chart (Table 51-1).

Table 51-1. DEI Key Questions

DEI Key Question	Dimension Alignment
Is it fair or just?	**Justice (Organizational)** • Distributive. Is the outcome fair? • Procedural. Is the process by which decisions are made fair? • Interactional. Is there respect and an explanation when processes and procedures are implemented?
Is it honest?	**Integrity:** Is reliable, accurate, and transparent information available and are workplace behaviors aligned with values?
Is it safe (environmentally)?	**Environmental safety:** Are physical conditions safe, healthy, accessible, and conducive to the performance of the work?
Is it safe (psychologically)?	**Psychological safety:** Is the work climate conducive to the individual or team expressing themselves without fear of negative consequences or retaliation?
Is it real?	**Authenticity:** Can you be true to your own personality, values, and spirit, regardless of the pressure you're under to act otherwise?

Table 51-1. DEI Key Questions (cont.)

DEI Key Question	Dimension Alignment
Is it beneficial?	**Positive outcome:** What level of performance or achievement occurred because of the activity?
Is it sustainable?	**Wellness (physical and mental):** Are actions being taken to accomplish an objective that can consistently promote physical, mental, emotional, and social well-being over a period of time? It is important to note that lack of sustainability in DEI for employees may require additional use of EAP to manage stress and trauma.

Beyond the Business Case

There are other considerations that affect employee perceptions and opinions. The employee's perceptions of cultural beliefs and behaviors are linked to the way individuals and leaders live their organizational values. Sustainability of DEI requires intentional pulsing of these dimensions to help focus on resources and attention to areas that will make a difference in the DEI journey.

The DEI key questions outlined in Table 51-1 can provide guidance into the development of processes and policies. When used with the Talent Wheel (Figure 51-5) we can gain insight into biases that may exist in our strategy and infrastructure. The Talent Wheel is an important visual reflecting the way that we think about the development and management of our people resources. If we were to apply the DEI Key Questions to each element of the Talent Wheel, we would be better informed about where we need to place our efforts and resources.

Figure 51-5. The Talent Wheel

Surveys can be the best way to assess how well your organization is performing against objectives and demonstrating evidence of successful DEI integration. They may include engagement surveys, change surveys, leadership assessment surveys, and other types of pulse surveys that help determine the employee's perception about specific behaviors. It is important to ensure the items included in the surveys are appropriate for the topic and have been validated. A sample of validated questions is listed in Table 51-2. A more complete list of questions for securing employee perceptions around diversity, inclusion, and justice can be found on the handbook website at ATDHandbook3.org.

Table 51-2. Survey Validation Questions

Survey Type	Sample Validation Questions
Engagement survey	Example items: • I can be myself around here. • I feel valued as an employee of my company. • I am treated with respect and dignity at work.
Leadership survey	Example items: • My manager/team leader acts with the intent of ensuring employees feel included at work. • My manager/team leader treats all employees fairly and consistently leverages the diverse perspectives of employees to drive business results.
Procedural justice	To what extent: • Have you been able to express your views and feelings during those procedures? • Have those procedures been free of bias?
Distributive justice	To what extent: • Does your (outcome) reflect the effort you have put into your work? • Is your (outcome) justified, given your performance?
Interpersonal justice	To what extent: • Have they treated you with respect? • Have they refrained from improper remarks or comments?
Informational justice	To what extent • Have they been candid in their communications with you? • Have they communicated details in a timely manner?

As we learn more about what is working and what is not, we can assess the risk in relation to the reward. It is incumbent upon every organization to set a standard of accountability. A critical question that is often asked is "Who is responsible for DEI?" The answer is everyone. If DEI is to be sustained, there must be a sense of personal and collective responsibility. If DEI is treated as another critical business imperative, each functional and operating leader will have a designated accountability for DEI.

Sustainment requires organizations to continually monitor their environments. This may include doing risk assessments to determine opportunities to improve in areas that still have a high-risk level. You will find a risk assessment example on the handbook website at ATDHandbook3.org.

DEI Maturity

Every organization's journey to DEI will be different. There is no one-size-fits-all approach that works for DEI. The maturity of each organization is influenced by factors such as its culture, ability to commit, vision, resourcing, leadership, and tolerance for change. Managers in diversity-mature organizations define diversity for clarity and understand the difference between inclusion, equity, and diversity. These organizations design their infrastructure, policies, environments, systems, and processes to meet these requirements, and refuse to let preferences, conveniences, political views, and traditions intervene.

In moderately diversity-mature organizations, leaders have connected diversity management adeptness with achieving mission and vision. However, in highly diversity-mature companies, leaders also live their values. They know that they must have a compelling business motive for managing diversity, which they develop and articulate by identifying strategic diversity mix while ensuring that the practices associated with their organizational infrastructure are equitable. They understand that DEI must be addressed successfully if they are to remain viable (Thomas and Woodruff 1999).

As you consider the importance of diversity in your DEI ecosystem, remember that DEI is a major change management initiative designed to bring behavioral and mindset change. Application of these fundamental change management principles will support your change environment:

- Charter the initiatives and ensure that there is senior-level support and resourcing.
- Form a strong cross-functional team that can develop a viable plan and excellence in execution.
- Ensure the vision is clear from the strategy and people understand how change will affect them.
- Engage others in cross-functional activities that support the strategic goals.
- Perform stakeholder analysis to understand resistance and support.
- Monitor and manage communications with great intentionality and consistency.
- Assess and update policies, procedures, systems, and tools.
- Evaluate progress.

Final Thoughts

DEI at its best is fully integrated into every aspect of organizational life. No single activity or aspect of DEI programming will result in sustainability. It is the interdependence of functional entities with revenue-generating units and external consumers that require healthy symbiotic relationships. Commitments to being the voice at the table that speaks for those people who are not in the room are necessary for sustainability. This requires culture change and humility.

Cultivating a culture that embraces courage, truth, and forgiveness is also important to sustaining DEI. This can be accomplished by developing a strategic road map that includes checkpoints for behavior change. Cultivating this type of culture involves going deeper and having several things in place:

- Values that are aligned with the organization's DEI commitment
- Accountability for incongruent or unfair behaviors, policies, procedures, and practices
- Safe spaces or platforms for ongoing conversations (without judgment or retaliation)
- Training for self-advocacy, basic onboarding, and a code of conduct
- Ongoing opportunities to learn about and experience cultural differences
- No tolerance for invalidation of the ideas, thoughts, and presentations of others
- A practice of "do no harm" in talent development and management
- Encouragement and reward of allyship

Biodiversity in ecosystems is essential to the overall health of the system. The same is true of DEI. Without DEI, our organizations will be unbalanced, lack innovation, have unaddressed bias that affects practices, and be generally unhealthy. Unhealthy organisms have difficulty fulfilling their purpose, mission, and vision. On the other hand, DEI practices are good for our employees, the organization, suppliers, customers, and the community.

About the Author

Tonya Wilson, MAIOP, CPM, is president and founder of AFC Consulting Group. She is a business leader, an entrepreneur, and a consultant with expertise in organizational effectiveness, change management, and diversity. She connects people to strategy and creates capacity through change enablement. Her business background in operations, contracts, and supply chain brings a unique perspective to her clients. Tonya's passion results in the design, development, and delivery of DEI learning modules and presentations. She has worked in manufacturing, aerospace, telecom, government markets, and healthcare, and been in leadership at McKesson, Change Healthcare, Meggitt, and AT&T. Tonya works with leaders to drive alignment between business and people strategies, leads supplier diversity initiatives, provides leadership for ERGs, and coaches leaders on diversity issues, change management, strategic action planning, organizational design, and organizational health assessments. Her mission statement is "setting you up to win." Reach Tonya at linkedin.com/in/tonya-j-wilson-maiop-cpm-b4663898 or learn more on her website at afcconsultinggroup.com.

References

Cutter, C., and L. Weber. 2020. "Demand for Chief Diversity Officers Is High. So Is Turnover." *Wall Street Journal*, July 13. wsj.com/articles/demand-for-chief-diversity-officers-is-high-so-is-turnover-11594638000.

Elkington, J. 2017. "The 6 Ways Business Leaders Talk About Sustainability." *Harvard Business Review*, October 17. hbr.org/2017/10/the-6-ways-business-leaders-talk-about-sustainability.

Eswaran, V. 2019. "The Business Case for Diversity in the Workplace Is Now Overwhelming." World Economic Forum, April 29. weforum.org/agenda/2019/04/business-case-for-diversity-in-the-workplace.

Gonzalez-Sussman, E., and R. Berenblat. 2020. "Nasdaq Proposes New Listing Rules Related to Board Diversity." *The Harvard Law School Forum on Corporate Governance*, December 13. corpgov.law.harvard.edu/2020/12/13/nasdaq-proposes-new-listing-rules-related-to-board-diversity.

Hunt, V., S. Prince, S. Dixon-Fyle, and K. Dolan. 2020. *Diversity Wins: How Inclusion Matters*. McKinsey and Company. mckinsey.com/~/media/mckinsey/featured%20insights/diversity%20and%20inclusion/diversity%20wins%20how%20inclusion%20matters/diversity-wins-how-inclusion-matters-vf.ashx.

Kirkland, R., and I. Bohnet. 2017. "Focusing on What Works for Workplace Diversity." McKinsey & Company, April 7. mckinsey.com/featured-insights/gender-equality/focusing-on-what-works-for-workplace-diversity.

Lorenzo, R., N. Voigt, M. Tsusaka, M. Krentz, and K. Abouzahr. 2021. "How Diverse Leadership Teams Boost Innovation." BCG, January 23. bcg.com/en-us/publications/2018/how-diverse-leadership-teams-boost-innovation.

Menzies, F. 2018. "Meaningful Metrics for Diversity and Inclusion." Include-Empower.Com. culturepluscosulting.com/2018/10/16/meaning-metrics-for-diversity-and-inclusion.

Phillips, J.J., and P.P. Phillips. 2014. *Measuring ROI in Employee Relations and Compliance*. Alexandria, VA: SHRM Press.

SHRM. 2021. *Managing Federal Contractor Affirmative Action Programs*. SHRM, February 1. shrm.org/resourcesandtools/tools-and samples/toolkits/pages/managingaffirmativeactionprograms.aspx.

Shumway, E., and S Estrada. 2021. "Diversity as a 'business imperative': A Q&A with Target's D&I Chief." HR Dive, April 14. hrdive.com/news/diversity-as-a-business-imperative-a-qa-with-targets-di-chief/598389.

Target Bullseye View News. 2020. "Target's Taking Bold Steps to Increase Black Representation Across the Company." A Bullseye View, September 10. corporate.target.com/article/2020/09/workforce-diversity-report.

Thomas, R.R., and M.I. Woodruff. 1999. *Building a House for Diversity: How a Fable About a Giraffe and Elephant Offers New Strategies for Today's Workforce.* New York: AMACOM.

VB Staff. 2021. "Report: 79% of Companies Say They Will Raise DEI Budget in 2022." Venture Beat, October 15. venturebeat.com/2021/10/15/report-79-of-companies-say-they-will-raise-dei-budget-in-2022.

Whelan, T., and C. Fink. 2016. "The Comprehensive Business Case for Sustainability." *Harvard Business Review*, October 21. hbr.org/2016/10/the-comprehensive-business-case-for-sustainability.

Recommended Resources

Phillips, P.P. 2021. "Measuring the Success of Diversity, Equity, and Inclusion Programs." HRDQ-U, April 9. hrdqu.com/diversity-events/measuring-the-success-of-diversity-equity-and-inclusion-programs.

Sakr, N., and L.S. Hing. n.d. "Workplace Diversity and Inclusion Climate Scale." Department of Psychology, University of Guelph. uoguelph.ca/psychology/page/workplace-diversity-and-inclusion-climate-scale.

"The Centre for Global Inclusion." centreforglobalinclusion.org/gdib.

CHAPTER 52

How L&D Can Partner With Executives

Andy Trainor

Learning and development needs have changed dramatically over the years. No longer can the L&D function simply provide training for associates. No longer can we be order takers, doing only what an organization requests. And no longer can we sit back and wait for direction.

Organizations face a competitive global market, environmental issues, rapidly evolving technology, and constant change. High-level executives want L&D to provide informed guidance, make recommendations that support the organization's strategy, and lead workforce development to ensure the right talent is available to meet organizational need. Executives want L&D to be knowledgeable and skilled, understand what's most important for success, and create a lasting relationship built on trust and confidence.

> **IN THIS CHAPTER:**
> - Learn how to communicate clearly with your top-level executives
> - Ensure the L&D department's learning strategy aligns with the organization
> - Identify metrics that get executives' attention
> - Determine how to help your leaders prepare for the future

Executives need L&D associates to be trusted advisors and partners who understand business complexities and can advise on the skills and knowledge the workforce requires to overcome them. At Walmart, we ensure L&D is a great partner to our executives by building just that—a partnership. L&D can't be order takers in today's ecosystem. However, this was standard practice for some organizations not long ago, when executives would deliver marching orders and L&D would scramble to execute without pushback, conversation, or even a strategic plan of its own. At Walmart, efficacy and autonomy go hand in hand. We take a consultancy approach—executives identify a need to fill or a problem to solve, and our L&D department has the freedom to build its own solution. This creates a shared vision where all key stakeholders have a seat at the table and a voice in the discussion. And critically, this vision must be future focused—if we know where the business is but not where it's going, we run the risk of delivering too little too late. The reality is that staying even with the business actually means falling behind; to deliver what the business needs, when needed, we have to stay two steps ahead.

L&D teams can become trusted advisors to and partners with executive leadership by focusing their energy in several areas. A learning department must be able to communicate with top executives. Know what's important and how to present your solutions. Your department must ensure that the learning strategy supports the direction your organization is heading. Understanding which metrics are important to your leadership team will be key to measuring L&D's success too. Finally, and perhaps most important of all, determine how you can prepare your leaders for the future.

For their organizations, L&D must invest time and energy putting in the work; that is, doing the research, planning, and risk assessment months in advance of any initiative. That's when the executive team is making decisions. Let's examine how you can do this.

Communicate Clearly With Executive Leadership

Executives focus less on the minutiae of a given department and more on leading the organization as a whole. They authorize business models, offer insights and strategies that contribute to key decisions, endorse succession plans and talent structures that create a competitive edge, and have a broader focus that reaches beyond the specific area they lead. Therefore, communication with executives must focus on what's important at the executive level—the broader picture that encompasses the entire organization. For example, even though I'm primarily responsible for learning in our 5,000 stores across the US, I also consider how my decisions affect my counterparts in other departments and business segments.

I see myself as a Walmart leader more than the VP of learning. My conversations are less about learning techniques and more about how developing the company's talent will drive revenue, improve market share, or make a positive impact beyond our walls. That means that when others in L&D share data or key information, I immediately reframe the message for the organizational perspective. How will the communication affect Walmart as a whole?

As a trusted advisor to executives, your message should be easy to understand and act upon. Your communication should be strategic, concise, and well thought out. Executive leadership is your customer; know what they need and why. Communicate in their language. Understand their challenges. Focus on goals, build in metrics, anticipate their needs, and seize opportunities to solve their problems.

Learning and development isn't a simple, salable business segment. And sometimes, it's less than palatable for executives without a background in learning. This makes it critical for us to focus on tangible business outcomes, avoid jargon, and speak in a language that executives can understand. As fascinating as some might find a 40-minute presentation on the application of adult learning theory, making that kind of presentation to execs is a surefire way to hamstring your initiative. When it comes to getting buy-in, *sounding* right is as important as *being* right. When we couch our tactics in simple, relatable terms; demonstrate not just our learning expertise but our broader business acumen; and avoid overwhelming executives with raw, out-of-context data, we deliver communication that drives wins for the organization.

Executive communication was key, for example when pitching our Community Academy (CA) initiative. For context, CA is an initiative dedicated to opening our Walmart Academies to the public and providing free, foundational courses on everything from the basics of personal finance, to interview skills, to college admissions prep. What makes the program unique is that it offers no direct benefit to our business. Its benefits are wholly community and associate based. With that in mind, our executive conversation around CA had less to do with dollars and cents and more to do with culture. We'd already built a trusting relationship with the decision makers using all the tactics I've mentioned, and now—rather than discussing KPIs and business outcomes as usual—we focused on what we cared about and why. In the end, CA was greenlit less because of tangible outcomes and more because it was aligned to our goal of helping people.

Ensure the L&D Strategy Aligns With the Organization

Strategic alignment ensures that all actions taken within an organization are designed to accomplish the same goals. An effective L&D leader focuses on keeping things that the team does (or wants to do) aligned with the organization's strategy.

One of the most basic contributions L&D can make is to ensure the strategy created for learning embraces and supports that of the organization. What L&D goals and objectives will support the organization's strategic priorities? What development do associates require so that the business strategy can be executed successfully? This means that L&D must understand the organization as well as the industry. Who are the competitors? What changes are required for success in the future? How can L&D demonstrate that it will enhance business value?

Once the strategy is developed, L&D leaders must make sure everyone in the department understands the L&D strategy and how it ties to the organization's strategy. This may require translating the strategy and communicating in the associates' language. In addition, L&D must help all associates understand their roles and how they fit in the organization. This is particularly challenging at Walmart because we must reach 1.5 million US associates. To ensure our strategy is communicated to all associates, we work closely with our communications teams to target high-traffic channels with simple, easy-to-digest messaging framed around a go-do format. One of the most critical aspects of Walmart's strategy is a focus on serving customers, and when it comes to our training, rather than dictating subject matter as an L&D group, we look to our customers' needs, leveraging data to understand where training can fill gaps in their experience.

Walmart is a massive but strategically nimble organization. Based on market trends, new technology, or the evolving needs of associates and customers, our business strategies can and do evolve. These changes often affect L&D strategies, and if we're not aligned with senior leadership, we can't course-correct to reflect executive-level changes. This creates inefficiencies, which are then compounded by the size of our organization. I like to make a "measure twice, cut once" analogy for our company because our sheer size makes high-level alignment critical.

It starts with staying connected to the business. Our L&D associates get out into the field as much as possible to get hands-on experience with operations because adult learning theory in a vacuum is just that—theory. We need our people plugged into an associate's day-to-day experience so we can adapt our training to their needs. Once we have that daily pipeline of practical information, we use it to inform our strategy. We've found that as long as we're grounded in the reality of the business, we often view our work through the same lens as the senior executives do.

We also take steps at Walmart to achieve strategic alignment between the learning department and the organization. For example, the executive steering committees and cross-functional workgroup are major factors in maintaining alignment. The former brings every key decision maker into the room, prevents the formation of work silos, and allows information to flow freely between different departments. The latter layers on expertise. We like to partner learning expertise, business expertise, and financial acumen to create diversity of thought that drives business outcomes.

Identify Metrics That Get Your Executives' Attention

Executives want to see results from every function within the company, and that includes the L&D department. The L&D function adds value to the organization, but it needs to know which metrics matter at the executive level as well as how to present the data. For example, can you show that L&D adds value by increasing customer satisfaction? Decreasing costs, rework, or time to market? Increasing retention and reducing attrition? Enhancing learning agility? Increasing customer satisfaction?

It is difficult to provide an ROI on training because everyone in an organization is working to improve the same metrics. At Walmart, we make sure we engage business partners who may have a stake in the final ROI. This includes our tech teams, the operators who run our stores, and anyone else with a vested interest in a given initiative. When possible, we demonstrate the learning potential to our business partners by having them take part in the training. This helps them experience and understand what the initiative is about and helps them buy in to the plan. A critical role for an L&D trusted advisor is to get buy-in from partners throughout the organization. You'll need to prove the ROI of training initiatives if you want to claim your value as a trusted advisor and getting buy-in from others in the organization is critical.

But the ROI and metrics aren't only organizationally focused. L&D also adds value for associates, and metrics can demonstrate this. Metrics can show how L&D increases job satisfaction by making the work more meaningful. In addition, development can also increase morale, commitment, engagement, and confidence. At Walmart, our associates make all the difference, and we believe that investing in them makes an impact not only on business metrics but also on their opportunities to enjoy a great career.

L&D can be more effective when focusing on metrics. And remember that when it comes to metrics, context is king. It's one thing to take your seat at the table armed with data; it's another thing entirely to be able to frame that data in terms of practical impact. We like to take a *what* and *why* approach to presenting metrics. We open with the *what*: These are the numbers. We follow it with the *why*: Here's why they matter. An additional layer of context can mean the difference between a path forward for future initiatives and a hard stop.

Metrics are a great measuring stick for celebrating wins, and we use metrics to increase support for L&D efforts. When we link a given initiative to a dollar value outcome for the business, we're speaking the language of the career operators in the C-suite. Rather than pitching them on what our training *might* do for the business, we're informing them of what our training has done. Metrics are the difference between supposition and fact, maybe and definitely, a green light versus a red light for future work.

Help Executives Prepare for the Future

An incredible number of pressures are placed on organizations today thanks to rapid technological changes; new, tougher competition; a demographically changing workforce; increased globalization; higher customer expectations; greater associate expectations; and a constantly increasing rate of change. Every one of these pressures requires the attention of the learning department. You can help prepare your organization for the future in many ways. Start by determining what is most important.

New challenges create a need for new knowledge and skills. The role of the L&D department is to stay ahead of these challenges and, acting as a trusted advisor, provide recommendations to the senior leadership team and keep them informed of what's happening in other organizations and industries. It's important to help senior leadership embrace the speed of change and understand the kind of development associates will need to support the future of the organization.

At Walmart, we often say that we're moving faster than ever before, but the truth is, we're still accelerating. Like all businesses, retail is evolving, and our customers' needs are drastically different today than they were even five years ago. This means our associates' work is changing. It's important that every organization provide associates with learning experiences that prepare them for the future. And to deliver these learning experiences in a timely fashion, we have to stay two steps ahead with our strategy. Ultimately, we want our associates to have skills that will be useful to them professionally and personally. In addition, we want to ensure that we provide training that they want, when they want it, and how they want it. Achieving both—what our associates need and what the organization needs—has always been a Walmart goal.

We also need to recognize the importance of technology for a successful future. We see it as a means of breaking down barriers between associates and the information they need. At Walmart, we partner with our tech teams using a four-in-the-box model to pursue convenience, efficiency, and consumer-grade technology. For example, our IT and L&D teams worked together to create our Academy App, a platform that puts microlearning based on our existing training programs directly into the hands of associates.

Additionally, technology is a key enabler for our pull approach to learning content. In traditional L&D, associates are pushed content based on any number of factors, including role, performance, and compliance needs. While pushing some content is necessary, however, it's also important to do the reverse. Tools like the Academy App help us take on a marketing mentality with our associates—rather than exclusively pushing prescribed training, we can also leverage AI and machine learning to market recommendations. This increases engagement with learning content and helps create an environment where associates are more empowered.

We also look for ways to use technology for critical learning, such as using VR as a means of replicating challenges and situations that would be otherwise difficult to capture in training. Our Moments of Care VR module is focused on customer relations and gives associates real-time, reactive practice dealing with a distressed customer. This allows associates to practice their responses in a simulated environment with all the nuance but none of the consequences of the real thing.

L&D must be preemptive. When it comes to future-proofing the business, there's no substitute for proactivity. Being late on a key piece of technology or an evolving best practice can mire an L&D team and create a ripple for associates. L&D is constantly on the lookout for the next wave of innovations, and we're not afraid to look outside the company. We maintain a strong network of other learning professionals, and we're always interacting with consultants and other experts to maintain our forward focus.

L&D must help executives prepare for the future. They need to strip away the marketing façade and deliver the raw facts of what we know, what we think will happen, and how we propose to react. It's also important to frame up worst-case scenarios. No matter how much planning, projection, or data analytics we do, we'll never be crystal clear on the future. That makes it important to identify risk. It's easy to focus on outcomes that can benefit the company, but while we want to highlight them for the organization's leaders, if our projections aren't balanced, we risk an awful lot.

Additionally, the importance of a future-focused strategy is worth repeating. If we're not ahead, we're behind. To deliver for our executives, we have to know where the business is going.

Final Thoughts

As a trusted advisor to your leadership, you must be at the forefront of talent development, offering an innovative and bold yet effective and practical approach to addressing the developmental needs of all associates. Your job is to help guide your organization's future.

I've addressed four responsibilities to enhance the learning department's value to the organization: communicating clearly with executives, aligning learning strategies to the organization, choosing appropriate metrics, and helping leaders prepare for the future. Of course, there are many other things you need to do, but this is a place to start. These steps will help you gain a reputation as a trusted advisor who is accountable to your C-level executives.

Let me add one last thought from a personal perspective. When it comes to driving executive buy-in on a given learning initiative, the conversation is won or lost months in advance based on the work you put in or the work you don't. Make sure it's the former.

About the Author

Andy Trainor is the vice president of Walmart US Learning. In this role, he and his team focus on the strategy, innovation, content development, and delivery of training for the entire Walmart US Field, including all training for the 1.5 million associates in supply chain and stores. Andy spearheaded the implementation of more than 200 academy locations across the US, including determining locations, managing construction, staffing trainers, and creating content to support a renewed focus on associate development. Today these locations facilitate the core and area-specific courses for new role leaders as well as offering classes to the community. Previously, Andy spent four years as the senior director for China implementation for international business processes and was responsible for sharing and implementing Walmart global best practices within the China business. He also led the international logistics engineering team, where he was responsible for establishing, developing, and working with the logistics engineers in 28 countries to improve productivity and processes within the logistics and transportation businesses. Andy has also worked on the US grocery industrial engineering team designing mechanized grocery distribution centers, developing process improvement projects, and managing a team of field industrial engineers. Andy has 21 years' experience with Walmart. He holds a bachelor's degree in industrial engineering from the University of Memphis and a master's degree in business from Webster's University.

References

Biech, E. 2018. *ATD's Foundations of Talent Development*. Alexandria, VA: ATD Press.

CHAPTER 53

Organizational Design Practices That Can Make or Break Your Organization

David C. Forman

The third decade of the 21st century is off to a difficult and perilous start. Enormous strains have been placed on society, organizations, and individuals by the COVID-19 pandemic, a struggling economy, assaults on democratic institutions, rising global tensions, the spreading of intentional disinformation, and the continuing quest for social justice. As painful as these experiences have been, the worst action would be to pretend they did not occur, were an aberration, or were just simply bad luck. Let's examine what we can do.

> **IN THIS CHAPTER:**
> - Describe the reasons for the emergence of organizational design and its role in improving organizational performance
> - Describe six organizational design practices and discuss how they can lead to greater organizational success
> - Challenge yourself to identify at least two organizational design ideas and practices that you will try to implement in your organization

The world during the COVID-19 pandemic can be characterized by three interacting factors:
- Change is occurring at an unrelenting pace. Stability has vanished as we are buffeted by a growing legion of factors and forces, many of which are not controllable.
- The world is a smaller place—we are not just interconnected but interdependent. Just consider the impact of supply chains that extend around the globe. We need a bigger lens because something that happens in a remote part of the world can now affect us in a flash.
- The future is hazy at best, given all the disruptions that can occur at any time. While we cannot predict what's going to happen, it is increasingly incumbent on leaders to anticipate and prepare for possible futures now, or else be caught flat-footed again and again.

> The greatest danger in times of turbulence is not the turbulence.
> It is to act with yesterday's logic. —Peter Drucker

So, what do we do? How do organizations adapt and respond to these conditions in this increasingly unsettled world? Thankfully, respected leaders and researchers have given these challenges some thought. In *Talent Wins*, Ram Charan and his colleagues (2015) share three pieces of advice for how to succeed in an economy that has "decimated predictability."
- Put your best people in positions that contribute significant value.
- Free people from bureaucratic structures designed for a different age.
- Provide opportunities for people to continue to learn and expand their skills.

When Satya Nadella, the CEO of Microsoft, discussed the pandemic and its lessons for his company, he observed that the last six to nine months of 2020 had constituted the world's largest experiment for remote work ever conducted (Whittinghill 2020). His primary insight: "Going forward, we are thinking about productivity in an organization as being defined by the combination of three things—collaboration, learning and well-being."

In *Humanocracy*, Gary Hamel and Michele Zanini (2020) underscore the challenge to create rejuvenated organizations that are as amazing as the people inside them. The culprits, they believe, are the bureaucratic barriers that are equivalent to a tax on productivity. They argue that organizations need to be more innovative, adaptable, inspiring, and resilient. A truly resilient organization overcomes barriers and is characterized by:
- Rushing out to meet the future
- Changing before it had to
- Continually redefining customer experiences

- Capturing more than a fair share of opportunities
- Never experiencing an unanticipated earnings shock
- Growing faster than rivals
- Having an advantage in attracting talent

These are great ideas and aspirations, but again, how do we get there? Choices will have to be made and prioritized, but this journey can begin by improving the capacity of our organizations to deal with difficult and unforeseen threats and by applying lessons from the discipline of organizational design.

The Purpose and Value of Organizational Design

Organizational design (OD) has been around for decades and is generally defined as building organizational capabilities to improve strategy, structure, processes, and outcomes. As the name implies, its emphasis has been on the organization and its collective talent, although it is often contrasted with more familiar human resource practices that focus on individual talent. Its focus on hiring and retaining the best and brightest people was advocated for in McKinsey's groundbreaking book, *The War for Talent* (Michaels, Handfield-Jones, and Axelrod 2001). While there were some early dissenters (Malcolm Gladwell, for example), most people believed the approach made sense: Bring in a bunch of really smart people, surround them with traditional talent management practices, and the organization will prosper.

This approach seemed to work, but then warning signs emerged. Organizations began to see seismic failures revolving around very smart but dysfunctional people. In addition, there were numerous examples of how IQ and intelligence were not nearly as important to high performance as we thought (for example, Google's Project Aristotle). There is also now a growing recognition that "the way we have always worked isn't working" in a world of constant change, interconnectedness, and hazy futures. Problems include declining productivity, once-successful management models becoming barriers, waning innovation, and organizations failing to change as fast as the world around them (Hamel and Zanini 2020).

Dave Ulrich predicted this future in his book *Victory Through Organization—Why the War for Talent Is Failing Your Company* (2017). His view—backed by research—was that by improving the workplace, the workforce can flourish. He argued for building organizational capabilities to improve innovation, enhance collaboration, reduce bureaucratic barriers, and open participation for all. By focusing on these organizational capabilities and strengthening how people worked together, Ulrich said, the return would be four times greater than just developing individual talent. This is an incredibly significant finding that heralds the increased meaning and value of OD to organizational success.

> Even the brightest flower will wither in a barren garden. —Unknown

Michael Arena (2018) reinforced these findings when he said it is not enough to bring in the best people, but to bring out the best in all people. He believed in creating organizations where the genius is not what happens inside people's heads, but between or among them as they work together. It is about providing opportunities for any person to do extraordinary things.

6 OD Practices for Turbulent Times

This new emergence of OD coincides with the realization that improving the workplace is the surest and most viable path to achieving organizational success. The OD Practices Model depicts specific areas that, when accomplished together, can have the most enduring impact and chart the truest course through turbulent times (Figure 53-1):

- **Results-based accountability.** It is impossible to be a high-performance organization without getting results. Leaders at all levels need to be accountable to themselves and their colleagues for producing results and outcomes for employees, stakeholders, and citizens alike.
- **Strategic alignment and focus.** Given the pace of change, it is easy to get out of alignment and do things that don't benefit the organization. Huge amounts of talent and energy can be wasted.
- **Culture and values.** What does the organization stand for? What value does it bring to employees, customers, and citizens? Culture is the most effective governance system because it determines how people act and perform better than any set of rules and regulations.
- **High-performance-workplace practices.** What are the secrets of high-performing organizations? There are none. The keys to unleashing talent are evident but not well practiced.
- **Flexible, agile, and resilient structures.** Gary Hamel once said that "communities outperform bureaucracies every day of the week." In this ever-changing world, strength and advantage are gained by creating more access, transparency, and opportunity for all, not just a select few.
- **Learning mindset.** Learning has now become a survival skill—we all need to be learners and embrace the challenge to keep adapting and growing, regardless of our previous experiences and role within the organization. As Will Rogers once said, "Even if you are on the right track, you'll get run over by standing still."

Figure 53-1. OD Practices Model

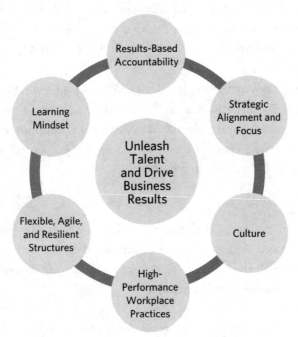

Let's look closer at each area in the model.

Results-Based Accountability

It is fitting that this discussion of the OD Practices Model starts at the end. Traditionally, HR and L&D professionals have shied away from impact and results because they are, as the thinking goes, difficult to measure and control. Instead, L&D and HR often measure what is easy to measure, and this is precisely why they have not been more influential in affecting organizational performance. HR and L&D analytics primarily track activity and efficiency, not effectiveness and impact. Business leaders care about effectiveness and results, and so must we.

There are at least five ways in which organizational practices can drive business results. These business outcomes are described more completely in *Fearless Talent Choices* (Forman 2020).

Optimizing Talent

Jim Collins introduced the notion that people are not your most valuable asset; the right people are. This has been extended to the 6 *R*s: Are the right people in the right job with the right skills—for the right cost—in the right place at the right time? Another way to operationalize this lever is to ask: Are our best people working on the most important projects? This parameter should be true wherever talent is expected to perform, whether on athletic teams, dramatic productions, orchestras, or even business endeavors. There needs to be an extraordinarily strong fit between what is required for success and the talent deployed. If not, individuals and organizations will suffer.

A business impact. The cost of losing a valued employee is 1.5 times the fully burdened yearly salary of that individual. For an individual earning $100,000 fully burdened, this equates to a cost of $150,000 to the organization for lost productivity, extended timeframes, and more out-of-pocket expenses. If the employee who leaves is a high performer (not just a capable employee), then the cost skyrockets by a factor of five to $750,000.

Cost Savings

It is important to streamline processes so that waste, inefficiencies, old practices, and extra costs are identified and eliminated. Because cost savings hit the bottom line quickly, they are spotlighted by executives and are usually the easiest business impact to identify. Among possible examples:
- Reduced participant travel and expenses
- Smaller footprint (location costs)
- Fewer recurring costs (such as room rental and instructor fees)
- Changing delivery platforms
- Fewer people
- Restructured benefit programs

A business impact. For global organizations, a huge cost savings can be realized by replacing expert global staff from headquarters (expatriates) with qualified local talent. A fully burdened expatriate compensation package can cost 20 times more than capable local talent.

Productivity Improvements

Productivity pertains to doing the same or better work, faster. It is an efficiency measure that can be influenced by automation, intelligent technology, smarter and more committed employees, informed practices, and better methods. A key workforce factor is how quickly employees can become proficient, especially in such a rapidly changing world. One surprising example is to have an open talent marketplace and hire more internally. Why is this the case? Because internal hires get up to speed faster and more efficiently than external hires. They become "ready" 33 to 50 percent faster than their external colleagues.

A business impact. The most meaningful leading indicator of productivity improvement is engagement. Since Gallup's pioneering work decades ago, findings have been remarkably consistent: Productivity varies by level of engagement. On a four-point engagement scale in which being engaged is level 3, productivity increases or decreases by at least 20 percent per level. When this finding is monetized over the entire workforce, the impact of poor engagement can be in the millions of dollars.

Better Outcomes

This outcome pertains to improving business performance in such areas as revenues, profits, innovative new products, product quality, brand credibility, supply-chain effectiveness, quality of new customers, and faster time to market. These outcomes are hugely important to all stakeholders and business leaders, and one of any leader's first activities should be to list the business outcomes that are most meaningful to that organization. These outcomes should be closely related to the strategic alignment assessment, which also focuses on the critical priorities of the organization.

A business impact. While not all organizations get involved in mergers or acquisitions (M&As), they are an example of the huge impact that talent and organizational practices can have on business results. In 2018, more than $4 trillion in M&A activity was reported. Interestingly, many (70 percent) of these transactions fail to achieve their intended objectives, and a primary reason is poor human factor integration. Fully 30 percent of M&A failures can be ascribed to this purpose, which translates to a $1 trillion loss for businesses.

Leveraging Communities, Resources, and One Another

One of the great frustrations of leaders is that organizations rarely learn from past mistakes and are less than the sum of their very capable parts. They yearn for a company where the genius happens among people and social capital becomes a vital competitive advantage.

A business impact. When connections and collaboration occur, the power of professional networks and connections become apparent. People with robust and extensive professional networks are 25 percent more productive than people who do not have these connections. This makes sense. If you do not know the answer to a simple question, you Google it. If you need more nuance, thoughtfulness, and wisdom, you talk to people you trust. The network boost of 25 percent is a huge multiplier that few people embrace. As the great Satchel Paige once said, "Ain't none of us as smart as all of us."

These results need to be firmly in mind because the ultimate outcome of OD practices is to improve organizational performance. Now, we can turn to other parts of the OD Model to see how to unleash talent to achieve organizational success.

Strategic Alignment and Focus

It is easy for organizations to think they are working on mission-critical projects and initiatives. But often they are not. When a car is out of alignment, it wanders all over the road. When an organization is misaligned, tremendous amounts of resources, talent, and energy are wasted. It is not just about "doing things right"; it is more about doing the right things in times of instability and limited resources. Use "line of sight" tools and techniques to ensure a close linkage to strategy and competitive positioning and to remove barriers that affect performance. Focus on the consequential few priorities, as opposed to the inconsequential many. Be able to answer the question, "What will we stop doing to achieve better alignment?" Instead of just having a "to do" list, also have a "to stop doing" list.

One significant barrier is the amount of time spent in meetings and monitoring mobile devices. Doshi and McGregor (2015) estimate we devote two days a week to these activities. This equates to 40 percent of our available time being wasted or poorly used. Some organizations are adopting practices that, for example, limit meetings to 30 minutes, restrict the number of participants in meetings, ban meetings on certain days, schedule meetings only in afternoons, turn off email servers at 7 p.m., and prohibit email during vacations and holidays. See the handbook website ATDHandbook3.org for two tools you can use to check for strategic alignment.

Culture and Values

Every organization has a culture and set of values that influence how decisions are made and people behave. The real question, however, is whether the default culture is the desired culture. There is often a sizeable gap between the two—especially when comparing the answers from business leaders and employees.

Cultures can be intentionally changed with diligence and perseverance. It takes the hard work of everyone, not just leaders. In the past, many believed that culture was determined by CEOs and managing directors, so why bother trying to change it? However, in today's more open, transparent, and horizontal organizations, culture becomes everyone's business. Among the key players that affect culture are leaders, customers, employees, stakeholders, supply chain partners, and citizens.

Culture also needs to work for both the organization and the individual. Favoring one side over the other will not endure. And culture needs to strike a balance between the soft stuff and the hard stuff—between soul and rigor—because both are key contributors to organizational success.

Each organization responds to pressures and contexts differently, and each has its own traditions and legacy, so cultural values will and should be different. Visit ATDHandbook3.org to see an example of an embracing culture's values and ways to assess and develop them.

High-Performance-Workplace Practices

What do we know about high-performing workplaces? In turns out, quite a lot. More than 30 years of research has provided remarkably consistent findings about the characteristics of workplaces that lead to productive, engaged, and energized employees. While it is always useful to add more to this body of knowledge, there is much that can be done right now. Consider what we know:

- People have three primary intrinsic motivators: autonomy, mastery, and purpose (Pink 2009).
- The top three reasons people leave companies are a poor relationship with their direct manager, little opportunity to grow and develop, and lack of meaningful work (Forman 2015).
- The Gallup 12 questions that define engagement have remained relevant and meaningful 20 years after their first unveiling.
- Doshi and McGregor (2015) have identified three characteristics of high-performing cultures: play, purpose, and potential.
- Bersin (2014) characterizes the "simply irresistible organization" as one with irresistible work, great management, a fantastic environment, growth opportunities, and trust in leadership.
- The Human Capital Institute (2017) highlights the importance of purpose, growth opportunities, flexibility, personal balance, and collegial networks in improving engagement and performance.
- Zak (2017) has identified eight management behaviors that generate trust and lead to high performance: recognize excellence, provide challenging assignments, enable people to have discretion in how they do work, encourage job crafting, share information broadly, intentionally build relationships, facilitate whole-person growth, and show vulnerability.
- The World Economic Forum (2019) highlighted the top four reasons people join and stay with organizations: good relationships with colleagues, effective work-life balance, good relationships with superiors, and ample learning and development opportunities.

It is important to observe that these studies, unlike popular coverages of best places to work, do not focus on perks such as having a dry cleaner at work or the highest pay package. They all address intrinsic motivators that enable people to work more productively. If these qualities are genuinely embedded in the workplace, the data suggests that the impacts on people will be significant. Context matters, so one organization's short list will be different from another's, but the data is clear that these qualities are the ones that count (Figure 53-2; Forman 2020):

- **Purpose.** People want to belong to an organization that provides meaning to others. They seek significance, a higher purpose, and value beyond a paycheck. Chip Conley (2007) refers to this as moving from "a job to a career to a calling." The organization should have multiple bottom lines.

- **Growth opportunities.** Skills and experiences are the new currency valued in the marketplace. People want to sharpen their skills and become better candidates for their next job, either within the organization or elsewhere. Continue to provide opportunities for people to grow and gain new experiences.
- **Flexibility and choice.** Provide choices, options, and flexibility for people to make their own decisions. Open opportunities for all to participate and contribute, such as crowdsourcing innovation, bureaucracy-busting suggestions, or providing opportunities for anyone to participate in community work projects.
- **Collaborative networks.** People want to collaborate with colleagues, build a sense of community, and grow their professional network. This becomes a huge source of learning, growth, and next steps, and enables the organization to learn from its successes and mistakes. The value people bring to the organization is directly related to the breadth and depth of their professional networks.
- **Meaningful touchpoints and recognition.** It is extremely difficult to keep connected and reward performance in a fast-changing world. But simple formal and informal steps can have a major influence on performance. Have frequent huddles—not meetings—to keep teams informed and working together. You get what you reward.
- **Personal balance.** This has been a time of incredible tension and stress. Energy, attention, and will are all exhaustible resources. We must find ways to rebound, rejuvenate, and replenish to ensure we are making the best use of our time, talent, and energy. For example, try to limit meetings to 30 minutes, take a 20-minute morning walk outside, don't schedule appointments before 10 a.m., monitor your own time, and only check e-mail twice a day. (For more examples, refer to Forman 2020.)
- **Serendipity.** Who says that work must be boring and dull? Think about ways to incorporate fun, quirkiness, and unconventional approaches. Some examples include new product idea bake-off, company garden, employee film festival, and roast-the-leaders lunches.

Each of these qualities, reinforced and nurtured by a culture that values reciprocity, trust, and transparency, leads to what Gary Hamel (2012) has called an "opt-in organization—one in which people want to come to work and are proud to be associated with." Companies that achieve this opt-in status are, on average, 40 percent more productive than their counterparts who did not (Mankins and Garton 2017).

Figure 53-2. High-Performance Workplace Model

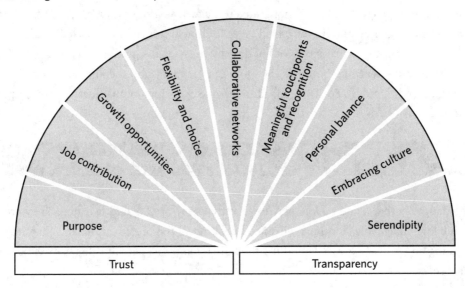

Flexible, Agile, and Resilient Structures

There has been a dramatic shift in organizational structures because the times demand it. Previously, most organizations were designed to enhance control, compliance, predictability, and efficiency. Top-down, command-and-control organizations of the 19th and 20th centuries were well suited to these goals and extremely successful. But the world is different now, and these vertical bureaucracies have been too slow and cumbersome—what was once a strength is now a weakness.

Instead, cross-disciplinary and self-governing teams are on the rise. These teams are business and customer focused, enable contribution by all, are built for experimentation, are open and transparent, and change as fast as the world around them. They are resilient and always looking for challenges, and rush out to meet the future. Today more than 80 percent of the work is done in medium to large organizations and emanates from teams, and yet they are largely ignored (Buckingham and Goodall 2019). Individuals may win trophies, but teams win championships.

A key aspect of high-performing teams is psychological safety (Edmondson 2018). Each team member must be respected, listened to, free to challenge conflicting views, and participate equally. Make psychological safety an important part of cultural values going forward to benefit from the agility and responsiveness of fast-moving teams.

Learning Mindset

Learning is now a survival skill. It is not a nice to have; it is a requirement given the continual uncertainty and changing conditions we all face. Technical information has a diminishing half-life and what we learn in university is out of date by the time we graduate. The only remedy for this condition is that learning becomes the most critical meta skill. Leading organizations have clearly recognized this shift. For IBM, the number-one criterion for an effective hire is a propensity to learn.

> The future belongs to the learners, not the knowers. —Eric Hoffer

The danger is that some people may believe that they are beyond learning. They are likely successful, knowledgeable, and in an advanced position in the organization, and they may think that learning and schooling was something they did a long time ago. But this view is now a sure path to obsolescence and obscurity.

Instead of technical skills and specific experiences, the emphasis needs to be on meta skills that endure and guide future learning. Each organization's list of meta skills will vary, but this example is from *Fearless Talent Choices* (Forman 2020):

- Gritty learning mindset
- Learning velocity
- Curiosity
- Anticipating change
- Resilience
- Influencing others
- Systems thinking

While several of these meta skills seem like personal traits (for example, curiosity, resilience, and influencing others), there are ways to improve them even if you are not naturally good at asking questions or persuading other people. Visit the handbook website at ATDHandbook3.org for a tool you can use to assess these seven learning meta skills.

Final Thoughts

Organizational design is experiencing a renaissance. There is growing recognition that the smartest and most direct path to high performance is to enhance the workplace so the workforce can flourish. The six OD practices discussed in this chapter are all extremely important. If one or two are less than effective, the organization and its talent will suffer, and results will be less than desired. But when these six practices are working together, there is a synergy that is extremely powerful. There are no guarantees in this turbulent and volatile world, but the wisdom and experience in these OD practices are a great foundation to build upon.

> Maximizing human potential is now the primary purpose of all organizations. —Clifton and Harter (2019)

About the Author

David C. Forman has spent the last four decades focused on improving the knowledge, skills, and performance of people. As a learning scientist, business leader, chief learning officer, author, and adjunct professor at the Pepperdine Graziadio School of Business, David has been recognized all over the world for his actions, courses, and writings. He has worked closely with such business clients as Apple, IBM, FedEx, Ford, American Express, SAP, Prudential, Deloitte, PwC, DuPont, and Allstate Insurance. In the nonprofit arena, David has worked with The Ford Foundation, Children's Television Workshop, Cedars Sinai Hospitals, Johns Hopkins University, AID, and many governmental agencies. David's latest book, *Fearless Talent Choices*, is a global bestseller. You can reach him at dforman1@cox.net and learn more about what he does at fearlesshr.com.

References

Arena, M. 2018. *Adaptive Space*. New York: McGraw Hill.

Bersin, J. 2014. "The Five Elements of a 'Simply Irresistible' Organization." *Forbes*, April 4. forbes.com/sites/joshbersin/2014/04/04/the-five-elements-of-a-simply-irresistible-organization.

Boch, L. 2015. *Work Rules*. New York: Twelve.

Boudreau, J. 2010. *Retooling HR*. Boston: Harvard Business Press.

Buckingham, M., and A. Goodall. 2019. *Nine Lies About Work*. Boston: Harvard Business School Press.

Charan, R., D. Barton, and D. Carey. 2015. *Talent Wins*. Boston: Harvard Business Review Press.

Clifton, J., and J. Harter. 2019. *It's the Manager*. New York: Gallup Press.

Collins, J. 2001. *Good to Great*. New York: Harper Business.

Conley, C. 2007. *Peak: How Great Companies Get Their Mojo from Maslow*. San Francisco: Jossey-Bass.

Dignan, A. 2019. *Brave New Work*. New York: Portfolio.

Doshi, N., and L. McGregor. 2015. *Primed to Perform*. New York: HarperCollins.

Edmondson, A. 2018. *The Fearless Organization*. New York: Wiley.

Forman, D. 2015. *Fearless HR*. San Diego: Sage Learning System Press.

Forman, D. 2020. *Fearless Talent Choices*. San Diego: Sage Learning System Press.

Hamel, G. 2012. *The Future of Management*. San Francisco: Jossey Bass.

Hamel, G., and M. Zanini. 2020. *Humanocracy*. Boston: Harvard Business Review Press.

Hoffman, R., B. Casnocha, and C. Yeh. 2014. *The Alliance*. Boston: Harvard Business Review Press.

Mankins, M., and Garton, 2017. *Time, Talent, Energy: Overcome Organizational Drag and Unleash Your Team's Productive Power*. Boston: Harvard Business Review Press.

Michaels, E., H. Handfield Jones, and B. Axelrod. 2001. *The War for Talent*. Boston: Harvard Business School Press.

Pink, D. 2009. *Drive*. New York: Riverhead Books.

Schwartz, T. 2010. *The Way We Are Working Isn't Working*. New York: Free Press.

Ulrich, D., M. Ulrich, D. Kryscynski, and W. Brockbank. 2017. *Victory Through Organization*. New York: McGraw Hill Education.

Whittinghill, J. 2020. "In First Person: Satya Nadella." *People + Strategy*, Fall. shrm.org/executive/resources/people-strategy-journal/fall2020/Pages/in-first-person.aspx.

Zak, P. 2017. *The Trust Factor*. New York: AMACOM.

CHAPTER 54

Agility for the Future Workforce

Christie Ward

What comes to mind when you think of agility? Have you ever seen a baby put all their toes in their mouth? What a surprise when they discover those wiggly things are attached. This takes amazing physical agility, one of the gifts of the very young. While most of us are born with short-lived physical agility, we all need to develop neural and emotional agility as we mature.

> **IN THIS CHAPTER:**
> - Identify the critical characteristics of an agile organization
> - Illustrate how global agile organizations operationalize these critical characteristics
> - Plan your next steps to create an agile organization using insights from your global colleagues

Have you witnessed emotional agility? You may have. For example, have you seen an elite athlete finish in second place and then compliment the winning competitor? That's emotional agility. The runner-up, though enormously disappointed, turns their attention in a gesture of genuine sportsmanship to congratulate the winner. The quality of emotional agility is learned, not inborn. Much like the agility we need in business, emotional agility is intentional.

As we head into the next 10 years and look at what kind of agility our organizations will need, we can see that this ability to adapt and pivot easily and with minimal effort will determine our success or failure. Our organizations need to be quick and nimble, responding to the dynamic environments created by markets, politics, pandemics, and leaders. Having the right people in place is no longer optional. It is essential. Having the right structures in place is also critical; the hierarchical structures of the past are not going to work. This is a time for collaborative structures and teams that can make decisions quickly without checking in or getting approval.

None of our businesses will survive without being agile—regardless of their size, scope, or industry. It doesn't matter if you are a one-person consultancy, a small- to medium-sized family business, or a multinational corporation. We are living in a world filled with volatility, uncertainty, complexity, and ambiguity.

When a business or an organization can right itself by adjusting and adapting quickly to chaotic environmental changes, it creates organizational agility. This type of resourcefulness is not a natural trait. It must be learned, practiced, and refined. For organizational agility to work, we can't rely on hierarchal systems, rigid structures, or the way we've always done things. To be an agile enterprise, we must know the context for any change, be clear on our overall purpose in business, and know what we do well. Because continuous improvement is a trait of organizational agility, knowing is not enough. We must be open to feedback and adapt along the way.

Creating enterprise agility means moving strategy, structure, people, processes, and technology toward a new way of doing business that is built around high-performing and self-directing teams. And this needs to be based on a stable foundation created by the organization's culture. However, culture seems to be the toughest element to transform when a company wants to become more agile.

Culture emerges when an organization's purpose and mission are embodied by its people through their behaviors. Trading in caution for a culture willing to experiment and make mistakes, for example, is a hallmark of an agile culture. Listening to a variety of perspectives and voices rather than focusing on only leaders' voices is another attribute of an agile culture. Culture grounds people so they know where they belong and where they can look to boost their expertise. Serving as the roots of an agile enterprise, culture is the stabilizer—it's what grounds the tree, whose branches are the various processes and technologies that channel their products and services (Jurisic et al. 2020).

This chapter highlights several organizations that were forced to pivot quickly and demonstrate exceptional agility in the face of economic disruption and global crises. Chaos and change are no longer rare occurrences—they are part of the day-to-day business landscape. Let's look at what it takes to be agile and what others are doing to meet these unprecedented challenges.

Agility, Culture, and Leadership

McDonald's was able to endure the economic crisis of 2020–2021 because of its agility, explained CEO Chris Kempczinski in an interview with McKinsey and Company. At the beginning of the COVID-19 pandemic, Kempczinski simplified the business by focusing on the process McDonald's had perfected: great drive-thru service featuring their core menu items. He first expanded the offering through order-ahead service and curbside delivery. Then, in cooperation with a third-party company, Uber Eats, he drastically increased the number of restaurants offering delivery services. McDonald's is currently experimenting with self-delivery. Throughout the COVID-19 pandemic, Kempczinski has continuously adapted to the needs of his customers, taking the company from virtual shutdown back to profit through agile leadership.

Overlaid with a customer focus, Kempczinski stated, there is no such thing as overcommunicating with staff. According to a survey given at the end of 2020, 90 percent of McDonald's employees responded "yes" when asked if they had felt supported that year (Kelly 2021).

"Putting people first" stands at the heart of CHG Healthcare's core values and is the starting point for its other core values: growth, continuous improvement, integrity and ethics, and quality and professionalism. As a healthcare staffing business with 2,900 employees, CHG maintains a strong internal culture across its seven divisions. The company's core values are the foundation of its people-centric culture, and the behaviors that define its values begin with the employee-selection process. CHG makes decisions with the best interests of its people in mind and expects its employees to do the same, so new hires discuss scenarios representing each value. This in-depth exploration during the onboarding process tests their understanding and decision making to anchor CHG's core values into their everyday behaviors.

Eleonore Ruffy, vice president of the RNnetwork division, reports that CHG's Putting People First approach builds strong loyalty among its employees, providers, and clients alike. With a turnover rate averaging around 20 percent annually, leadership deftly redeployed and reskilled support teams into other roles, retaining key talent when COVID-19 and economic uncertainties in 2020 and 2021 affected specialty-sector placements. When reskilling existing team members (including CHG trainers) proved challenging, leaders and line-level managers stepped up into training functional roles in addition to their normal responsibilities. With CHG's core values central to its culture and an all-hands-on-deck attitude, teams were motivated to manage the ever-changing market conditions.

Technology is crucial to this organization's competitive strategy, but even as CHG launched upgrades at breakneck speed, the organization never lost sight of its people. By upskilling line-level leaders to handle tech rollouts and training, CHG could keep pace with the increased demand for new product enhancements.

Workplace flexibility requires an infrastructure that keeps CHG's culture strong, while supporting new demands. When the new hybrid workforce created challenges for communication, hiring, onboarding, retention, and ongoing training and development, the company adapted by creating new communication channels, developing and delivering diverse topics via multiple training modes, and adopting new ways to recognize its people. Moreover, upskilling leaders to use Zoom and Microsoft Teams meeting platforms, along with traditional face-to-face channels, required different ways of applying emotional intelligence to ensure full inclusion, participation, and understanding of team members (Ruffy 2021).

QUESTIONS TO CONSIDER

With competition for qualified talent increasing, culture may be what attracts new talent and retains seasoned talent. Today, when people can live anywhere and work remotely, culture isn't about the office ambiance. Rather it looks at how colleagues will exchange ideas both virtually and in person. Things to think about include:
- Will face-to-face meetings become an unnecessary, outdated ritual?
- How does your organization's culture foster collaboration?
- How will employees interact with their managers?
- How do teams strengthen their engagement?

In addition, time boundaries have been upended and as the world gets smaller our colleagues may be in different time zones. Do you have constraints or restrictions that limit whom you can talk to and when? How does that affect work-life balance, or is that now a passé term? Does your organization require 24/7 availability? If so, are your employees comfortable with that?

Leaders are not the only voice that should determine direction and strategy, and leadership can make or break an organization's agility. Agile teams falter when leaders focus on maintaining their power. This can be particularly difficult for top-down leaders whose influence routinely stands unchallenged. They may need to remind teams about their purpose and focus them on a vision from time to time. In other words, leaders need to inspire, then leave teams to set their own pace, make decisions, and accomplish their goals. There's no room for autocrats or dictators—this is equally true for those supervising teams. For leaders, getting the right people on the team rises above all other concerns. Allocation of resources, talent management, and consistent modeling of organizational values should occupy their time. Most decisions should be left to the teams, not the leader. Team members may ask leaders for their insights, but leaders don't call all the shots. When they participate as learners with their teams, leaders embed learning in their organization's culture. Agile leaders are company culture role models and their actions set the pace and embed the values written on their corporate walls.

An agile mindset increases your employees' depth and breadth and builds your organization's vertical and horizontal bench strength. When Bruno Rouffaer interviewed Skelia's founder and CEO, Patrik Vandewalle, and its chief HR officer, Olivia Vandesande, he saw how the company was using agility to work cross-culturally, even in times of disruption (Vandesande and Vandewalle 2021). Using this approach, Skelia grows its people internally, launching qualified candidates into leadership roles. For example, its first employee was recruited in 2008 and is now serving as a managing director.

Skelia is an international outsourcing enterprise that builds cross-border IT and engineering organizations, including affiliates in Eastern Europe. Creating more than 150 cross-border teams with customers in 14 countries across Europe and the United States, Skelia has earned its reputation as an organization builder. Unlike traditional outsourcing companies, Skelia gives its customers the unique opportunity to transfer their Skelia team into a fully customer-owned legal entity.

"We don't sell individuals; we sell teams and organizations," Vandewalle explained. Team transfer opens up exciting strategic scenarios for companies that want to launch their Eastern European affiliates in a risk-free way.

Skelia's employees are guided by regulated work from home and remote work policies, which allow them to work easily from any location using laptops. They collaborate with secured communication tools, following business processes adapted for virtual, multisite operations.

"We are a hyper-agile organization able to cope effectively with constant change and disruptions," Vandewalle said.

Cultural matching of people, companies, and jobs remains Skelia's most important long-term success factor. If things go wrong, it's more often due to culture than technology. Software developers working within the same technology area may require very different profiles when selected for teams with a large international bank versus a Silicon Valley startup. When choosing candidates, Skelia includes interviews with their prospective organizations—giving them a voice in the match and creating a transparent culture.

By applying several complementary techniques, Skelia has systematically posted remarkable team stability with less than 10 percent employee turnover. This was achieved despite the disruptive COVID-19 pandemic, the diversity of its customers, and an overheated IT staffing market.

According to Vandesande, Skelia has always listened to its people and a core value is taking care of employees' families. Once COIVD-19 vaccines were available, Skelia offices set up vaccination sites. The company also assisted with special needs and even sent socks to people working from home. Skelia's personal approach to making work fun with employee activities, games, and parties extends to their family members.

"We look at people as whole human beings, and part of the Skelia family," explained Vandesande. "Employees remember these kinds of gestures and realize how much we care when we take care of them."

Team stability is paramount. When connection is lost with employees, stability falters. Thus, preserving team stability promotes agility. Because the company's HR and operations leaders are close to their people, personal and professional issues surface quickly and concerns can be anticipated in dialogue and resolved without delay.

Upskilling and Reskilling

According to the World Economic Forum, almost half of the global workforce already needs to either expand or replace its current skills (WEF 2018). The time to acquire future-critical skills and talent is short. Agile organizations are acting in haste with these workforce initiatives:

- Upskilling and reskilling
- Hiring or downsizing
- Right-sizing (a mix of internal employees and external contractors)

How do you measure the effectiveness of upskilling and reskilling? You need a business case for further training. Without it your organization can't leverage the insights and metrics that measuring provides.

Upskilling works side by side with effective change management. When a company introduces a new technology or system, employees must understand why they are being asked to use it. They want to know "What's in it for me?" (WIIFM). As employees acquire new skills that create greater value, they expect an upgrade in their compensation plans to reflect this increased value. When companies launch new technology, their employees need training to use it. Unfortunately, this doesn't always happen.

Amit Nagpal, a training industry veteran at Pursuitica Learning Solutions, can attest to the success of the Elevate program, which was launched in spring 2020 by India's Tata Consultancy Services (TCS), a global leader in the IT sector (Nagpal 2021).

The program was envisioned by Janardhan Santhanam, TCS global head of talent development, and its aim is to develop the next generation of leaders from the more than 450,000 employees at TCS. Elevate is structured as a democratic process based on the premise that top talent exists everywhere. It is designed to recognize talent by offering a transparent process tying together personal growth, rewards, and business outcomes. It features:

- An employee skill taxonomy validating existing skills
- A democratic learning plan formulated with evaluation exercises focused on current and future requirements
- A focus on frontline and midlevel emerging leaders across all units
- A push to enhance workforce resilience by realigning and investing in hot skills
- Udemy and LinkedIn Learning partnerships to guide TCS with curated training content

In an interview with *Economic Times India HR World* (Rahman 2021), Santhanam said that "learners should have absolutely zero friction in the process of learning."

Like Skelia's founders, Santhanam emphasizes the rise in internationally dispersed cross-cultural teams. Employees today must possess a comfort level to quickly and easily learn and unlearn an array of technical skills and be driven by a curiosity mindset. Upskilling and reskilling require both nimbleness and nuance applied along the entire path of an employee's career. To advance in their careers in the decades ahead, people can no longer rely solely on their required competencies; they will also need to commit to a lifelong pursuit of personal development.

In his article "Let's Stop Talking About Soft Skills: They're Power Skills," Josh Bersin (2020) redefined soft skills. According to him, hard skills (which are commonly thought of as technical or mechanical) are actually soft because they change all the time, are constantly becoming obsolete, and are relatively easy to learn. Soft skills (like communication, leadership, and management), on the other hand, are hard because they are difficult to build, critical, and take extreme effort to obtain. Bersin's point was that our workforce requires more "soft" skills—like adaptability, communication, and collaboration—that are actually overly complex and take years to learn. L&D professionals must help employees build these skills, and the process is much more difficult than teaching an employee how to use a new software program.

So, how do you upskill your employees with the soft skills they need to be agile while advancing the hard skills they need to remain technically competent? Management styles must change with the changes in the workforce. Agility requires a manager's focus to encourage peer-to-peer coaching and decision making at the team level, along with experimentation and calculated risk taking.

Employees must acquire skills like a willingness to adapt, time management, the ability to work on teams, and effective communication. A culture of lifelong learning is now imperative, because these power skills take longer to acquire. Empathy, for example, may take years to cultivate and is difficult to teach in a traditional classroom. Yet empathy is highly prized in leaders, managers, and supervisors and may be the quality that keeps your valued talent engaged and productive. Upskilling takes on a whole new level of importance when we want to modify our employees' behavioral skills. The nuance of being an effective negotiator, for example, makes that skill sound easy; however, it is complex and difficult to master. It is even more difficult to upskill someone to become a great negotiator. The job of a manager as we move forward will involve guiding their team to acquire these power skills and may even include serving in a training function.

We've examined upskilling, but what pushes people to reskill and pivot in an entirely different direction? How quickly can they become productive? Rachel Carlson, CEO of Guild Education, cautioned that "we're witnessing the tale of two labor markets. Food service, beauty, and hospitality are fueling unemployment rates not seen since the Great Depression.... At the very same time, employers are grappling with the seemingly endemic skills gaps in healthcare, supply chain, and skilled trade fields" (Guild Education 2020).

Whether the cause is a crisis or cost-saving technology, the poorest in society are often hit hardest. Perhaps we need to realign our thinking. Instead of focusing on technology designed to increase profitability or efficiency, we can shift our focus to technology that promises better jobs. We simply must include more people in the dialogue as we explore new and better ways to work. While we can support every employee, those at the lower end of the pay scale need it the most.

To meet this skills gap, Guild Education announced Next Chapter, a collaboration with Walmart, TTEC, Gainsight, Paschall Truck Lines, and Utility Technologies. The Next Chapter platform "helps bridge that gap and works with employers who are stepping up to help workers navigate the labor market riptide," explained Carlson.

The core of the Next Chapter platform is a collaboration between employees adversely affected by the crisis and employers in healthcare, the supply chain, and tech that are hiring. Unlike traditional outplacement services designed to place workers in jobs similar to the ones they left, Next Chapter helps workers make the leap to higher wage roles with access to education and training resources so they can transition into new careers or industries. With any disruption often comes opportunity, and the silver lining for these displaced workers is the chance to find more rewarding and lucrative work in in-demand fields.

"Rapid reskilling and access to education will be more important than ever as we emerge from this crisis," said Drew Holler, Walmart's senior vice president of associate experience and HR operations. "Next Chapter will play a crucial role in matching Americans who are suddenly out of work with future-proof skills so they can transition to in-demand jobs" (Guild Education 2020).

Partnering with Guild Education, Walmart's Live Better U invests in their employees' futures. Instead of tuition reimbursement, it is a way for new employees to enroll in learning at Walmart from the start; the cost is $1 per day. Dedicated coaches help navigate the myriad opportunities, and Guild partners with the nation's top universities and learning providers to offer classes, certificates, and programs focused on serving working adults.

According to Holler, Walmart also created virtual internships and teaming opportunities to provide opportunities for associates to learn and grow from peers and leaders (OneWalmart n.d.).

Creating Job Equality and Opportunity

Can business and civic leaders broaden their perspective by including other points of view? With inspired partnerships among companies, government, and workers, we can create job equality and opportunity.

In Singapore, the SkillsFuture program is a national economic partnership between the government, industry, unions, and educational and training institutions to foster a culture that supports and celebrates lifelong learning (Skillsfuture n.d.). In 2012, WEF ranked Singapore's economy as the most open in the world, the third-least corrupt, and the most pro-business. It remains a leading economy to this day (Skillsfuture n.d.).

As reported in the *Job Skills 2020* report from WEF, the top skills and skill groups that employers see as rising in prominence in the lead-up to 2025 include critical thinking and analysis as well as problem solving and skills in self-management (such as active learning, resilience, stress tolerance, and flexibility; Table 54-1). To address concerns about productivity and well-being, about a third of all employers are expected to take steps to create a sense of community, connection, and belonging through digital tools and to tackle challenges to well-being posed by the shift to remote work (World Economic Forum 2020).

Table 54-1. Top 15 Skills for 2025

1. Analytical thinking and innovation	9. Resilience, stress tolerance, and flexibility
2. Active learning and learning strategies	10. Reasoning, problem solving, and ideation
3. Complex problem solving	11. Emotional intelligence
4. Critical thinking and analysis	12. Troubleshooting and user experience
5. Creativity, originality, and initiative	13. Service orientation
6. Leadership and social influence	14. Systems analysis and evaluation
7. Technology use, monitoring, and control	15. Persuasion and negotiation
8. Technology design and programming	

World Economic Forum (2020)

Neuro-Link founder André Vermeulen suggests that these coveted skills can broadly be categorized as brain power skills or emotional intelligence (EI) skills. Future workers will need neuro-agility to easily learn, think, and draw conclusions fast and flexibly to execute their skills with precision and efficiency.

Final Thoughts

Being agile with learning, thinking, emotions, leadership, and performing in teams can be achieved when people optimize the drivers that influence the ease and speed with which they learn, think, and process information. Our understanding of why some people learn, think, and process information faster and are more flexible than others leads to innovative solutions that serve to identify and unleash a person's unique learning potential (Vermeulen 2021).

Using a fresh, neuroscience approach to develop talent enhances candidate selection and career advancement decisions. It informs instructional design and learning objectives that improve performance and lower the risk of human errors.

Agile organizations thrive when they cultivate great teams, and psychological safety is key to this. Much has been written about psychological safety, which Wikipedia defines as "a shared belief that the team is safe for interpersonal risk taking." Google's Project Aristotle research team found psychological safety to be the quality that separated great teams from all the rest. With agile teams, the conventional tactic of pairing the best and the brightest may not be the best approach. Instead, fostering curiosity and social cohesion through shared exploration and vulnerability among team members of diverse backgrounds can lead to exceptional productivity and innovative breakthroughs (Duhigg 2016).

The shift to agility in the workplace was accelerated by the events of 2020, but the rationale to convert our enterprises to agile models has been present for some time. The impacts of artificial intelligence, augmented reality, and virtual reality have accelerated processes and enabled more productivity. However, our mastery of behavioral skills and emotional intelligence is falling woefully behind. We talk about critical thinking and communication yet continue to focus on the latest tech gadget. Many organizations are stuck in hierarchical models rather than filled with autonomous teams free to make decisions. Collaboration is touted as a value and may even be included in the mission statement, yet we remain in silos.

For agility to become the norm, many old models will need to change. I am encouraged by the strides the companies mentioned in this chapter are making. None would tell you it is perfect, but they are moving in the right direction. Learn from them and focus on one or two things you can do to move your culture toward agility. Encourage individual effort. Build strong teams. Make sure people feel safe when they share their ideas, make decisions, and take risks. Strive to instill psychological safety. Become cognitively and emotionally agile yourself and share your enthusiasm with others. If you lead, maximize your own strengths first, then help others do the same. The agile enterprise will always rise to the top. Don't get left behind.

About the Author

Christie Ward, CSP, is principal of the Impact Institute, a consulting firm that helps clients with interpersonal communication skills, team skills, leadership skills, and presentation skills. Christie has advanced in her leadership roles with ATD, beginning with a position on the board of ATD's Rocky Mountain Chapter, then a spot on the National Advisors to Chapters in 2008, and culminating with her selection to the ATD National Board of Directors in 2011–2012. She has spoken at ATD's International Conference & Exposition and given keynotes in Brazil and throughout Southeast Asia. Christie chaired the ATD 2016 Program Advisory Committee and keynoted a 2019 ATD Core 4 Conference. In 2021, Colorado Personalized Education for Professionals awarded Christie the Martha Illige award for improving the care of patients through her work with healthcare professionals. Learn more about Christie and the Impact Institute at christieward.com.

References

Bersin, J. 2020. "Let's Stop Talking about Soft Skills: They're Power Skills." Josh Bersin, November 19. joshbersin.com/2019/10/lets-stop-talking-about-soft-skills-theyre-power-skills.

Duhigg, C. 2016. "What Google Learned From Its Quest to Build the Perfect Team." *New York Times Magazine,* February 25. nytimes.com/2016/02/28/magazine/what-google-learned-from-its-quest-to-build-the-perfect-team.html.

"Economy of Singapore." Wikipedia. Last updated May 21, 2021. en.wikipedia.org/wiki/Economy_of_Singapore.

Guild Education. 2020. "Employers Team Up to Connect Laid Off Workers in the U.S. to New Skills, Higher Wage Careers." Press release, May 8. guildeducation.com/press/employers-team-up-to-connect-laid-off-workers-in-the-u-s-to-new-skills-higher-wage-careers.

Jurisic, N., M. Lurie, P. Risch, and O. Salo. 2020. "Doing vs Being: Practical Lessons on Building an Agile Culture." McKinsey and Company, August 4. mckinsey.com/business-functions/organization/our-insights/doing-vs-being-practical-lessons-on-building-an-agile-culture.

Kelly, G. 2021. "Keeping McDonald's 'Relevant': An Interview With CEO Chris Kempczinski." McKinsey and Company, March 19. mckinsey.com/industries/retail/our-insights/keeping-mcdonalds-relevant-an-interview-with-ceo-chris-kempczinski.

Nagpal, A. 2021. Written interview with A. Nagpal. May 24, 2021.

OneWalmart. n.d. "Live Better: Higher Learning, Lower Tuition." Walmart. one.walmart.com/content/usone/en_us/company/news/popular-content/education-articles/unlock-the-future--introducing-live-better-u.html.

Rahman, A. 2021. "Evolving Mentality of Learners Ensures Smooth Learning Process for Everyone: Industry Leaders." *Economic Times HR World*, February 3.

Ruffy, E. 2021. Written Interview With E. Ruffy. May 30, 2021.

Skillsfuture. n.d. "About Skillsfuture." Government of Singapore. skillsfuture.gov.sg/About SkillsFuture.

Vandesande, O., and P. Vandewalle. 2021. Written Interview with O. Vandesande and P. Vandewalle. May 2021.

Vermeulen, A. 2021. Written Interview with A. Vermeulen. May 2021.

World Economic Forum. 2018. *The Future of Jobs Report 2018*. WEF, September 17. weforum.org/reports/the-future-of-jobs-report-2018.

World Economic Forum. 2019. *Towards a Reskilling Revolution Industry-Led Action for the Future of Work*. WEF, January. weforum.org/docs/WEF_Towards_a_Reskilling_Revolution.pdf.

World Economic Forum. 2020. *The Future of Jobs Report 2020*. WEF, October 20. weforum.org/reports/the-future-of-jobs-report-2020.

Recommended Resources

Clark, T.R. 2020. *The 4 Stages of Psychological Safety: Defining the Path to Inclusion and Innovation*. San Francisco: Berrett-Koehler.

Edmondson, A. 2018. *The Fearless Organization: Creating Psychological Safety in the Workplace for Learning, Innovation, and Growth*. Hoboken, NJ: John Wiley & Sons.

Vermeulen, A. 2014. *Tick Tock This Makes Your Brain Rock: A Brain Fitness Guide for 21st Century People*. Scotts Valley, CA: CreateSpace Independent Publishing Platform.

CHAPTER 55

Developing a Change-Ready Organization

Jennifer Stanford

Change is inevitable. Technology continues to evolve and change at a more rapid pace than most organizations can adapt. In addition, the events of 2020 challenged how we connect, innovate, and perform. Organizations that do not have the capacity to change will become irrelevant. And that means that organizations must ensure their employees have the capacity to change as they develop others for the future.

IN THIS CHAPTER:
- Determine organizational and workforce readiness for future changes
- Set strategic direction and communicate change to employees
- Build a learning and competency framework that reflects the needs of your workforce

The organizations that thrived in 2020 were already primed for change because it was a well-known expectation managed by the organization through transition and growth. However, despite the importance of managing change, more than 75 percent of organizational change efforts fail (Ewenstein, Smith, and Sologar 2015). Misaligned expectations and underestimation of the complexity of change are two of the top reasons for that failure.

To prepare for change and develop the workforce for the future, organizations need to be clear about their strategic goals. When an organization's leaders set a clear strategy and communicate it properly, the rest of the organization can develop plans that align with that future. An evolving learning and development model that allows for point-of-need skill building can help provide the necessary skills for times of change. Organizations should review lessons learned from 2020 and note when (and why) they fell short on attaining organizational goals and objectives as well as maintaining culture, values, and engagement.

Is Your Organization Change Ready?

One of the factors that hurt organizations—some to the point of extinction—during the chaos of the COVID-19 pandemic was a lack of readiness for change. Before it can truly change and evolve for the future, an organization must be ready and resilient. However, many change initiatives are launched without regard for the readiness factor. Before launching a change effort, consider these key readiness questions:

- How do you determine if now is a good time for change?
- Are you changing just to change?
- Do you have a history of successful or failed change efforts?
- Are you forced into change due to circumstances out of your control (hello, pandemic)?

It is important to measure change readiness on a regular basis (at least annually) through a pulse survey or an annual engagement survey. In addition to planting direct questions around change, it is important to review past change efforts as a predictor of future success as well as seeing what employees think about the organization's ability to handle change. Yes, reviewing the organization's history can reveal quite a bit, but perhaps not as much as simply asking key individuals their thoughts on the organization's ability to achieve a successful change initiative. Now that we have all experienced a global crisis and are forming a new normal, take a minute to step back and ask employees how the organization performed during the COVID-19 pandemic. You can find a change readiness predictor on the handbook website at ATDHandbook3.org.

You also need to understand what is going on in your organization. Many innovative ideas fall short because timing or other factors are not considered. This can be avoided by taking stock of the current level of support for the initiative from both clients and employees before embarking on a change effort. The first step should be producing a preliminary plan to ensure you have adequate resources (including budget, people, and tools), otherwise you may discover too late that there isn't anyone to execute the initiative.

There are two primary ways to form a talent pool that can execute in the future: Grow skills organically or acquire new talent that has the required skills. Conduct a make-versus-buy analysis to determine whether you have the in-house talent to drive the change or if external talent will be required.

Additionally, take time to get to know the organization, its culture, and the personalities the culture fosters. For example, are there competing stressors? Do some organizational personalities deal better with change than others? If you were to evaluate your employees, would you define them as strategic and logical, relationship and team oriented, organized and process driven, or risk takers with action-oriented focus?

Understanding the organization's dynamics can lead to great readiness insight. Groups that are more action oriented and willing to take risks are typically more comfortable with change, and are not only ready for change but need it to feel engaged at work. Conversely, groups that are very process driven and appreciate their daily routine are typically the least comfortable with change. While this doesn't mean that a process-driven organization comfortable with the status quo can't have a successful change effort, it does mean that you have to focus change-related communications to appeal to this population and help them find a new normal in the change. In other words, translate everything you know about your organization into what you think employees need to be ready for change. How can you help them be more successful? What skills do they need? How does the culture support what is needed? How can talent development ensure that everyone is change ready?

Why the "Why" Is Important

Does your organization know where it wants to go in the future or how it wants to evolve? Change is rapid, and technology and consumer behaviors have already disrupted several industries. Understanding systems thinking and the relationship between a change effort and other organizational initiatives requires a definitive *why*. Many efforts fail because the *why* behind them is too weak. So, how strong is your *why*?

Creating a strategic imperative is one of the first steps in change management. Organizations have to continually conduct environmental scans, which monitor internal and external factors to detect opportunities or threats to their current or future plans. Successful leaders keep a watchful eye on their internal and external environments to determine the timing and the fashion of change.

For example, one organization created a think tank of cross-functional employees to conduct environmental scans and drive innovative and necessary change. The group met monthly to discuss potential change initiatives and determine which ideas to share with the board for consideration.

In preparing to present its ideas, the group wrote business cases in which noticeably clear why statements were defended. This first message for change generated excitement because it was a well-known process created by organizational peers who were focused on the future and aligned behind strategic objectives. Ideas developed through this approach also had more sticking power—they weren't weighed down by the typical top-down directive because they came from an invested employee base.

A study by Towers Watson research found that 68 percent of senior managers believed their organization successfully communicated why major organizational decisions were being made. Below the senior management level, the message dwindles. Only 53 percent of middle managers and 40 percent of first-line supervisors said their management did a good job of explaining the reasons behind the major decisions. Leaders can't wait for the message to be heard—they need to ask the right questions and be proactive in clarifying the why. A communications strategy and plan should accompany every change event.

Employees want to know that their leaders are truly on board with what is going on. However, leaders often provide conflicting responses when asked why a change is occurring. It is difficult to have confidence in a change effort if you can't be confident that every senior leader is in agreement. So, how can you help leaders be better prepared for the workplace of the future? One way is to ensure consistent messaging starting at the top of the organization by interviewing senior leaders. They need to be ready to share with the rest of the organization how the proposed change links to a strategic goal or desired outcome. Interviewing organizational leaders can help you determine whether conflicting views exist. If they do, you can facilitate a meeting of the minds to get them on the same page. If this action is overlooked, the change effort will be doomed from the start.

Employees want to know their leaders are truly on board with what is going on. If you are the change leader, it is your responsibility to ensure you clearly understand the why behind the change and that you can endorse it. You also need to understand the expectations of the change for the organization, the leaders, and the employees. Encourage senior leaders and the change management team to communicate those expectations as often as necessary.

How we relay the change to each person is critical to their level of acceptance. This is also the largest challenge area for misaligned expectations. Managers play a key role in translating the why from executives to their staff. To increase the chances that an employee will participate in a change experience, managers need to make sure their direct reports can see themselves in the change—not only how they benefit but also their role in the initiative. However, this is not possible if the managers don't understand the message themselves. Make sure that managers—and thus their reports—know what key responsibilities they're fulfilling to ensure the future workplace is achieved. What skills will they need to bolster to thrive in their future role?

Communicate Your Message Effectively

Once frontline managers receive the message, we need to make sure they can deliver it in a way that ensures everyone hears it. However, thanks to the complexities of the human brain, this isn't as easy as it may seem. The frontal lobe—which is responsible for planning, reasoning, problem solving, morality, personality, and social skills—employs four perspectives that influence our thoughts and behaviors:

- **Logical** thinks first in terms of big picture, strategy, and facts to support decisions.
- **Relationship** thinks first in terms of people, teams, and relationships.
- **Organized** thinks first in terms of process, policies, and routines.
- **Action** thinks first in terms of challenges, risks, and getting to the goal.

Employees who understand these four perspectives make better connections with those around them. Different personalities deal with and accept change differently. Up to 50 percent of employees will naturally be concerned and even stressed over change. Getting in front of the change and communicating strategies in a way that appeals to everyone will help build trust. Statistically, if there are more than 12 people in a group, all four ways of thinking will be represented. Thus, to ensure the changes and communications are meaningful to all, you need to address the change in terms that each perspective can appreciate.

We typically default to our primary thought perspective when communicating. I once supported a client whose primary way of thinking was relationship. She was wonderful at explaining how changes were going to affect the people and teams and feelings around the office. However, her changes were receiving poor feedback and even criticism. After looking closer at the situation, we found that the problem wasn't the change itself, but the connection her staff was making to it. The majority of her staff was very logical and organized—concerned about the data and the processes, not people's feelings about change. Once my client changed her messaging to ensure it catered to each perspective, buy-in increased exponentially. People understood the change in her language, and her message became meaningful to the entire organization, not just the 25 percent who responded to the relationship perspective.

Determine Understanding With Powerful Questions

As this chapter has established, change can be accomplished only when participants understand the reasons and are connected to the change. One way to determine a person's understanding of future strategies and emotional reaction to change is by asking powerful questions. Here are a few examples of powerful questions (they are also available as a handout on the handbook website at ATDHandbook3.org):

- What is the purpose of the current change effort?
- Describe your level of confidence that leadership can successfully implement this change.
- Where do you see your role after the change is complete?
- Do you trust that this change is for the better of the organization? How?
- How has this change affected you personally?
- How has this change affected you professionally?
- What do you think leadership needs to know about this change?

Powerful questions elicit substantive responses, which helps avoid survey fatigue. Work with the communications leader to determine what timing, frequency, mode, and feedback pool will provide maximum effectiveness. You could ask these questions on a monthly basis to a separate set of roles in each department. For example, ask all people managers in the first month of the change initiative, then ask all engineers in month two. Be sure to share your intent and plan for the information you gather with the respondents.

Build a Competency Framework

Be sure that competencies and skills are present for staff in the right capacity at the right time. A competency framework and learning and development model will help you build the core foundation to manage change. The framework needs to demonstrate resiliency and model cultural values while providing skill-building opportunities. This is the key to ensure that employees can execute the strategies.

Planning ahead for future competencies is no easy feat. It requires understanding the organization's future strategic objectives, as well as the anticipated changes and disruptive technologies in your market space.

Artificial intelligence (AI) and machine learning are examples of technological disruptions that have shaped the future workplace. Using AI, computers and computer programs are becoming smart enough to imitate human behaviors. Machine learning, which is a subset of AI, uses the science of designing and applying algorithms to learn things from past cases. If there is data on past behaviors around organizational change, then you may be able to predict if it will happen again. AI and machine learning will have powerful places in the workplace of the future, not only the technological implications but also how they measure behaviors around change. Francesco Rulli is an AI and machine learning authority and CEO of Querlo with whom we discussed the role of AI in HR during the pandemic. You can find it listed in the additional resources at the end of this chapter. Consider what future disrupters or enhancements will occur in your industry. Knowing which areas are consistent and core to your business and what will change or sunset is important when considering the workplace of the future.

LEADERSHIP CONSIDERATIONS TO PREPARE A GENERATIONALLY DIVERSE TEAM
By Jill Mellott, COO, Emergent Performance Solutions

Five generations currently coexist in the workforce. Generational differences and age diversity can add immense value to workplace dynamics and overall productivity when planning for the workplace of the future. Successfully manage this diversity by viewing the differences as a blend of backgrounds and experiences, not a shift from one demographic to another. The COVID-19 pandemic caused many teams to become virtual teams for an extended period, and the trend is likely to continue even after the pandemic has ended. In going virtual, relationships either flourished or suffered, depending on the willingness and abilities of team members to leverage available collaborative technology, communicate together, and adapt to working in a remote environment. Let's look closer at three areas where understanding individual preferences is critical to build a productive workplace for the future.

- **Technology.** It's easy to assume that an employee who is newer to the workforce is younger and more technologically savvy than a co-worker who has spent more time in the workforce. This may or may not be true. Make sure you remove any predetermined assumptions and ask team members directly about their technological abilities. If people have different skill levels, encourage your team to work together to ensure everyone is competent in the required technology. Set a baseline technology knowledge level everyone must meet, and then make sure the team is open to teaching or being taught regardless of their tenure or experience. This presents a great opportunity for anyone above the baseline to share their knowledge with others and for anyone who needs improvement to be willing to learn from other team members.
- **Communication.** We also have preconceived notions about how someone may communicate. For example, according to the *Harvard Business Review*, "Most of the evidence for generational differences in preferences and values suggests that differences between these groups are quite small. In fact, there is a considerable variety of preferences and values within any of these groups." Learn about your team and communicate in the way they prefer to communicate, not how you think they prefer.
- **Virtual versus in person.** Some employees value connecting and engaging remotely, while others may be more comfortable engaging with teams in person. Strong teams adapt in-person practices into the virtual world. For example, to strengthen your virtual team you could schedule virtual, collaborative coffee breaks or lunch & learns. Encourage the use of virtual breakout rooms to enhance cross-functional communication. Schedule and hold team meetings and one-on-ones with employees. This helps ensure you have a pulse on your team engagement and morale.

Most important, ask each member of your team what they prefer—don't make assumptions. Then adapt to meet as many needs as possible.

When developing a competency model, consider these factors:

- **Overall competencies.** These are required for everyone in the organization to maintain the desired culture, values, and behaviors. Overall competencies may be enhanced over time but should remain relatively stable in a thriving culture.
- **Functional core competencies.** These are required to run the organization (such as core skills in human resources, finance, and IT). Core knowledge, skills, and abilities will have a core foundation that is sustained during times of change.
- **Focused specialty competencies.** These are the competencies that support the points of need. What emerging technologies will be developed to support your customer base? What enterprise tools will be adopted to improve internal efficiencies? What new markets will be added to the corporate portfolio? Merger and acquisition strategies and plans may require additional specialty focus.

Once you've developed competency frameworks and models and they have been accepted, it is important to review them every few years to ensure they remain relevant for the future your organization is moving toward. If you evaluate and change competencies too frequently, your organization may find itself in a constant state of change (that is, chaos), but if you wait too long or never review the competencies, the organization will be at risk of becoming irrelevant.

After the competencies and understanding of tasks are cemented, determine what training programs the organization will need to gain the knowledge, skills, and attitudes (KSAs) to achieve the competencies. Point-of-need training should be available when employees take on new roles, technologies, processes, or customers. When training is linked to routine times (compliance) or rolled out to all employees it creates learning events that may not have a lasting impact, especially if employees don't have the opportunity to execute the KSAs on the job. We cannot train people on competencies that won't be required until five years from now.

Training should happen before the change occurs, especially for emotional intelligence and communication. There are times, however, that training around core competencies and values needs to happen more frequently. If your organization goes through a lot of change or is in a cycle of increased new hires or acquisitions, quarterly training will be beneficial, even if it's just a shorter, more pointed training program.

Final Thoughts

The COVID-19 pandemic caused many leaders to re-evaluate the future of their organizations. As you think of the desired future state and the workplace and workforce that will form and execute it, take the time to ensure clarity around what, why, how, and who. Ask: Is our organization and workforce ready for change? Why do we need to change for the future? What competencies are needed to reach that future state? Who is communicating changes? How can we build the required skills to prepare our employees for the future?

About the Author
Jennifer Stanford is the CEO of Emergent Performance Solutions and author of the *TD at Work* "Breaking the Cycle of Failed Change Management." She is a sought-after trust coach and organizational change expert with 25 years of experience in high-level consulting. She is also a Vistage Worldwide speaker. She leads facilitators, coaches, and consultants whose purpose is to create high-performance environments and relationships that thrive where people live, work, play, and pray. Her company supports a wide range of clients across the Department of Defense, federal agencies, midtier industry, and nonprofits. She lives with her husband and dogs in Hamilton, Virginia. Learn more about her company at emergentps.com.

References
Ewenstein, B., W. Smith, and A. Sologar. 2015. "Changing Change Management." McKinsey and Company, July 1. mckinsey.com/featured-insights/leadership/changing-change-management#.

King, E., L. Finkelstein, C. Thomas, and A. Corrington. 2019. "Generational Differences at Work Are Small. Thinking They're Big Affects Our Behavior." *Harvard Business Review*, August 1. hbr.org/2019/08/generational-differences-at-work-are-small-thinking-theyre-big-affects-our-behavior.

Personality Resources. Performance Management Applications. personalityresources.com.

Recommended Resources
Brower, T. 2021. "The Future of Work and the New Workplace: How to Make Work Better." Forbes, February 7. forbes.com/sites/tracybrower/2021/02/07/the-future-of-work-and-the-new-workplace-how-to-make-work-better/?sh=cde539e450ab.

Maruti Techlabs. "Artificial Intelligence and Machine Learning Made Simple." marutitech.com/artificial-intelligence-and-machine-learning.

Snook, A. 2019. "How to Effectively Manage Different Generations in the Workplace." I-sight, July 2. i-sight.com/resources/how-to-effectively-manage-different-generations-in-the-workplace.

Sondey, S. 2020. "Re-Engaging and Re-Energizing Employees Through Effective Communication in the Post-COVID Era: A Conversation With Jennifer Stanford." Querlo, June 12. blog.querlo.com/artificial-intelligence-interviews/re-engaging-and-re-energizing-employees-through-effective-communication-in-the-post-covid-era-a-conversation-with-jennifer-stanford.

CHAPTER 56

Emerging Technology and the Future of Learning

Karl Kapp and Jessica Briskin

The futurist William Gibson said, "The future is already here; it's just not very evenly distributed yet." This statement has particular relevance for learning and development professionals because our task is to make learning as efficient and effective as possible. However, continually changing and evolving technologies mean that we need to constantly evaluate and, possibly, change how we are delivering instruction.

If they're applied properly, we can use emerging technologies to push boundaries and facilitate learning in ways and places that were never possible. If they're misapplied, on the other hand, we risk wasting time, money, and goodwill chasing the "next big thing."

IN THIS CHAPTER:

- Describe why it's important for L&D professionals to keep abreast of the latest technology trends
- List new technologies that will influence the design and delivery of instruction within the next 10 years
- Apply a methodology for determining if an emerging technology is right for your organization's learning initiatives

Decades ago, field technicians had to know as much as possible about servicing any device they might encounter in the field, which meant hours of training and lugging around massive technical handbooks to help solve problems. As mobile devices became more ubiquitous, mobile learning became possible. The advent of mobile learning, as well as widely available Wi-Fi and microlearning practices, allows field technicians to have massive amounts of training, troubleshooting tips, and content available at their fingertips. They can simply pull up an appropriate troubleshooting video and be walked, step by step, through a piece of equipment they may never have seen before. In the not-so-distant past, allowing technicians to pull up a short video and troubleshoot problems was unheard of—new technology has made it commonplace. This is just one example of how technology has changed learning and development for good.

These technologies can be effective, but they must be adopted carefully. Successful L&D organizations, both large and small, integrate emerging learning technologies into a solid, well-designed program. They do not adopt technologies just because they are new; instead, they adopt emerging technologies because they lead to improved learning outcomes and enhanced performance for the organization.

While it is important for L&D professionals to stay up to date with emerging technologies, they also need to keep a healthy dose of skepticism or risk being seduced by the latest technology. Intelligent and careful use of learning technologies leads to success; haphazard use of and randomly adopting the newest technology leads to confusion and cost overruns.

RISSCI Factors

As we discuss emerging technologies, it's good to have a list of criteria you can use to determine if the technology is worth adopting. Whether you are part of a large, medium, or small organization, the RISSCI (pronounced *risky*) method of technology assessment is useful for deciding if a new technology makes sense for your learning initiatives.

The RISSCI methodology looks at six dimensions of new technology—reach, insight, safety, scalability, compatibility, and innovation—and compares them with existing methods of delivering the instruction. If the factors in the RISSCI method outweigh existing approaches, the new technology should be considered for adoption. Let's look closer at each dimension.

Reach

Does the technology allow the training to reach areas, people, or levels of sophistication that were not possible previously? The use of mobile technologies to deliver content to technicians in the field is a good example of reach. Mobile technology made it possible for training to reach areas where it could not previously.

Insight
Does the technology provide insights into learner performance or behavior that are not available using existing methods? For example, learners can play physical card games and report results, but determining which cards were used, how much time a player spent looking at a card, and what cards were sorted and unsorted by the learner are all difficult to track. However, suppose the card game is digitized. In that case, the system can track every learner's action and use those actions to provide information about the learning process and learner's decisions while interacting with the digitized cards.

Safety
Does the technology allow skills to be practiced in a safer manner than currently available methods? An example here would be using virtual reality to allow a worker to explore the inside of a chlorine tank in the safety of a computer-generated environment without any real danger.

Scalability
Does the technology allow training to scale or to be constantly available? For example, does it use a chatbot to answer basic questions about troubleshooting a piece of equipment? The chatbot can respond at any time and never gets frustrated about answering questions.

Compatibility
Is the technology compatible with your current systems, the organization's culture, and the desired learning goals? An example would be replacing a sales representative's desktop computer with a tablet or laptop. These people are busy and lead hectic lives, and lugging around a large computer is cumbersome. A tablet is lightweight, can process a great deal of information, and fits into the representative's workflow.

Innovation
Does the emerging technology truly provide a new and unique way of solving an organizational problem? This is the dimension that helps prevent chasing a "shiny new object." If the technology is not solving a problem more effectively or efficiently than previous methods, it might not make sense to adopt it. For example, it could use virtual reality to simply mimic the inside of a classroom. The technology has so much potential, but if that's all you're doing with it, there are likely better ways to mimic the existing physical classroom.

> **EMERGING TECHNOLOGY FOR SMALL AND MEDIUM-SIZED COMPANIES**
>
> It used to be that without a large information technology department, organizations didn't have access to the latest technologies. However, with the advent of cloud computing, increased Wi-Fi access, and a focus on easy-to-use, no-coding-necessary applications, small and medium-sized training departments now have the same access to leading-edge technologies as large companies.
>
> Additionally, in some cases, the available technologies can be used across multiple platforms. You don't always need to program one solution for a virtual reality and one for a virtual world; often, modern software will do both.
>
> For example, several virtual reality software platforms that cost less than $100 a month are easy to program and run through laptops, smartphones, and VR goggles. This gives small and medium-sized L&D departments a tool to create virtual worlds and virtual reality environments for low cost and with low levels of difficulty. Once the scenario or environment is created, it can be deployed either in a VR situation, as a virtual world, or even on a mobile device.
>
> But VR technology is not the only technology available to smaller L&D departments. Many of the technologies mentioned in this chapter, such as chatbots, augmented reality, whiteboards, and digital cards, are easily obtainable and programmable. This means that with some imagination, a focus on specific learning outcomes, and minimal development effort, emerging technologies can be put to use by any organization of any size.
>
> In fact, the careful deployment and implementation of emerging technologies can act as a force multiplier for smaller organizations. Emerging technologies can help accomplish tasks and training initiatives that would not be possible otherwise. As a resource-strapped L&D department, it's in your best interest to carefully examine emerging technologies by applying the RISSCI factors to determine if they provide the right solution for your organization's L&D needs.

Overview of Emerging Technologies

It is impossible to review all emerging technologies that might influence the learning and development field in the next 10 to 20 years. In fact, we have already seen sudden, successful applications of technology that we didn't even initially consider using as learning tools.

The technologies outlined in this chapter were chosen based on their potential for wide-scale impact on learning and development. In addition, many of these technologies are already being used on the fringes of the industry, and we predict they will emerge as valuable tools for our field.

Augmented Reality (AR)

AR is when a computer superimposes images, sound, or items onto the real world. A person holds up a smartphone, puts on glasses, or looks through a car's windshield and can see items that are not really there but appear to be because of the technology. This causes the reality the person is experiencing to become enhanced, made better, or provide more information. A well-known example is the augmented reality game *Pokémon Go*. The game uses a smartphone to superimpose an image of a Pokémon onto an actual physical space, like a shopping mall or park.

Augmented reality is already used in factories to help shop-floor workers properly assemble parts and access refresher information when needed quickly. Many factories use glasses that provide AR elements, such as directions for picking materials, information about what materials to pick to fill an order, or the correct internal running temperature of a piece of equipment. Because the glasses are hands free, the workers won't need to carry items with them and can use both hands on a task while still receiving instructions and information.

In addition, AR can provide location-based information to your smartphone or other device. This could allow you to learn about landmarks or items in your physical environment, such as a statue or building, simply by looking at them through the phone.

Augmented reality provides information that is easily and consistently available and is helping improve employee performance because it gives employees the information they need when they need it. AR's performance support focus uses instructions and heads-up displays to assist the employee by providing step-by-step instructions for how to perform their job.

Virtual Reality (VR)

Virtual reality (VR) is when a learner is immersed completely in a world or scene simulated by a computer and feels like they're interacting with it in a real or physical way thanks to special wearable electronic equipment—for example, using goggles with a screen or gloves fitted with sensors that give physical feedback to the wearer.

When a learner "goes into" VR, they put on a headset and are no longer in touch with reality. The only thing they can see is the computer-generated virtual environment displayed on the screen in front of them. Thus, it is a purely virtual experience without any intent to integrate with the real world.

The military uses VR to help war fighters practice their craft and hone their skills in a safe environment. Additionally, they can network the VR environment to allow multiple trainees to interact at the same time. This allows them to practice group maneuvers and gain experience working together under pressure, without putting them in actual danger.

VR environments have also been used to teach bank tellers how to remain calm in a robbery situation or to teach inclusion and diversity topics by immersing the learner in an environment that safely exposes their unconscious biases.

An ideal VR learning experience should create engaging interactions that help the learner assimilate new information, ideas, and concepts, resulting in new transferable skills. VR can be used to teach all types of activities, such as how to run meetings, assemble items, empathize with others, or conduct a sales call. IT tends to have a training or learning focus because users are immersed in a safe but realistic environment.

Mixed Reality (MR)

Mixed reality represents the convergence of different realities—the continuum from the real setting to a completely artificial environment (VR). One example of how this might work is mixing VR and AR. Imagine being fully immersed in a VR environment when, all of a sudden, the goggles' built-in cameras show your reality through a heads-up display (a form of AR) presenting data about a particular object. This is mixed reality—blending VR, AR, and the physical world.

Another example of MR would be an instructor giving learners a piece of equipment to examine and investigate. If the equipment had codes that a smartphone could read and display more information about, that's a form of AR. So, the learner could touch and see the actual piece of equipment and then use AR to learn more about it. The classroom might also have VR goggles learners could don to see how the equipment is used in the actual manufacturing setting. This is an example of mixing several types of realities.

Extended Reality (XR)

Labeling these categories of reality is cumbersome and constantly changes—this is where our final term, extended reality (XR), comes into play. XR was created to be an all-encompassing term developers could use to address all experiences, regardless of reality. The *X* represents any term placed in front of the word *reality*. As technology continues to evolve, more terms will inevitably arise to describe various forms of computer-enhanced environments.

Deep Fakes

In a deep fake video, a person's likeness, mannerisms, and voice are manipulated to make it appear they are saying something or doing something they never did. Recent technological advances and specialized techniques have made deep fakes highly realistic, complex, and more challenging to distinguish from the actual video.

While fake news and false statement attributions have been around since the dawn of time, the ability and technology necessary to create a convincing, realistic fake video are increasingly available to the masses. Over the next few years, it is predicted that the concept of deep fake videos will be perfected.

Simultaneously, another related development that's occurring is the creation of "artificial humans." Many companies are actively working to combine artificial intelligence with photo-realistic images. Their goal is to create a computer that mimics human-like interactions in a highly realistic fashion by combining natural speech, natural eye movement, realistic gestures, and a natural appearance.

For an L&D professional, this means being able to orchestrate a cast of thousands. You will be able to create the perfect cast by entering a description, facial expressions, gender, race, and so on. Type actions and scenes into the program, and the artificial humans will play out the scene in much the same way actual humans will. When you need to update clothes, hairstyles, and other elements that age quickly in a video, you'll simply type in a few commands, upload a few clothing styles, and have a brand-new, refreshed video.

Don't have an entire video, just pictures of a person in multiple poses and locations? No problem. Type in what you need and the location, screen capture the image, and import it into your e-learning module.

Suppose you need your organization's CEO to make an impactful statement about diversity and inclusion or a critical safety initiative. No problem—just record a few moments of her talking and then let the deep fake technology finish her speech. You never have to do more than one take. If it's wrong, you can fix it in post-production. This will dramatically reduce production costs and decrease the time it will take to create training videos.

As magical and ideal as this may sound, deep fakes also come with a caution. You need to recognize the powerful control that could be used inappropriately to, for example, make your CEO deliver messages without their knowledge or consent.

Virtual Worlds

Virtual worlds are three-dimensional environments in which you can interact with others and create objects as part of that interaction. Virtual worlds are most familiar in their use in multiplayer online video games, but a range of enterprises are beginning to adopt them for day-to-day applications. Examples of virtual worlds include multiuser virtual environments (for example, *World of Warcraft*) and virtual learning environments (like *Second Life* and *Active Worlds*; Girvan 2018). Most virtual worlds are populated by avatars representing players and virtual representations of virtual world characters. They can mimic environments learners are familiar with or include completely different inhabitants and rules of nature (such as people who can fly).

For an L&D professional, the virtual world can supplement traditional face-to-face training and replace uninspiring two-dimensional presentations. Constructing a virtual world that includes AR/VR technology is becoming more popular because it creates a fully immersive training experience that enables facilitators to see a participant's authentic, natural reactions to scenarios. Learners can be tested and observed on a range of soft skills, including empathy, communication, collaboration, innovation, and continuous improvement. For example, in a leadership training program, managers can privately and without risk practice giving performance evaluations, delivering bad news, and dealing with difficult employees. They can experiment in the virtual world with different leadership approaches to see how they can lead more effectively in the real world. Learners experience the what, how, and why of the initiatives, making learning exciting and compelling (Greene 2018).

Chatbots

A chatbot is a computer program designed to simulate conversations with humans through websites, mobile apps, wearable devices, or home appliances (Lee 2019). Chatbots are powerful tools for performance support because when employees ask the bot questions it returns possible answers. In L&D, chatbots have been rising in popularity.

Learners can use chatbots for just-in-time training support thanks to their ability to find information across multiple sources. Chatbots can be used as performance support by anticipating questions, proactively pushing out performance support material, and further refining and personalizing the information for individual users. The ability to provide consistent answers is helpful, because they are available 24/7. Additionally, chatbots can be used to scale personalized coaching and mentoring sessions, and they help learners feel less judged when they ask questions and seek clarifications (Lee 2019).

Chatbots can create individualized learning experiences and support performance. Most important, chatbots are not just delivering learning content; they also provide information about how people learn and what they need to learn. They record data (and conversations) from their interactions, which can be analyzed to see what people are learning and when. This allows learning to become a continuous process rather than an episodic event for L&D.

It is important to remember, however, that chatbots cannot replace humans; they can only work alongside humans to enhance the overall workplace learning experience. Humans converse in a way that chatbots cannot; we incorporate emotional intelligence in our decision-making process, understand context, and make connections or draw inferences.

Artificial Intelligence

Artificial intelligence (AI) refers to machines performing tasks that require or use a human-like intelligence or that humans would otherwise perform. This behavior is built on algorithms, which are a set of rules or processes that an AI-powered machine uses to guide its performance of a task (Belhassen and Hogle 2020). It's also possible to set up AI to recommend content that similar learners (or those in the same job role or who are enrolled in the same courses) have also completed or to find and explore content libraries.

AI can gauge an individual's ability and progression, tailoring course content based on the results assessments and shortening the learning process by suggesting only the specific modules the employee needs to improve the skills they need for their job. Furthermore, AI can predict whether a learner will correctly answer their assessment questions based on their behaviors, cognition, and engagement. For an L&D professional creating digital content, AI can generate narration from the text (that is, text-to-speech). For example, authoring tools like Storyline can autogenerate narration in various "voices," which can reduce the cost and logistics of recording narration.

It is predicted that the combination of AI within VR will create realistic, dynamic characters that speak in more natural ways. This would help make scenarios more real; for example, generating environments and characters that appear and move more naturally increases the realism of immersive games and simulations. Learning games that incorporate machine learning (which is discussed in the next section) and adaptive learning could adjust as players learn and advance, including dynamic character development, changes in the content, and challenges based on their performance and feedback. These games could offer a unique, targeted experience to each learner (Belhassen and Hogle 2020).

For AI to be utilized fully, organizations need to harness vast amounts of data, which is typically done through the organization's learning management system (LMS). L&D departments can use this data to gain insights into the learner journey and create training programs that drive value and promote adaptive learning. Breakthroughs like this are changing L&D. AI is transforming how learning content is delivered, leading to greater alignment with business values.

Machine Learning

Machine learning (ML) provides data to a computer, which uses that information to analyze future data. ML is a type of artificial intelligence that automates data processing using algorithms without necessitating new programs (Gold, Nichol, and Harrison 2020). It is often used in web searches, email spam filters, marketing personalization, product recommendations, and chatbots.

In L&D specifically, ML can be used to solve challenges in analytics and reporting, feedback and assessment, and personalization (Walsh 2019):

- **Enhance analytics and reporting.** Companies can use this information to develop reports on the effectiveness and return on investment of learning within an organization. This helps learners, trainers, and the organization better understand how learning functions in the organization to help identify trends and take protective action (for example, by supporting learners at risk of not completing a course). Organizations can also use this data to improve employee retention by identifying development needs and proactively supporting employees (Walsh 2019).
- **Provide dynamic and effective assessment strategies.** For example, ML helps create more intuitive, intelligent tests and quizzes. Some systems can even automatically

formulate appropriate test questions in reaction to learner activity. L&D can use this information to determine skills gaps.
- **Provide personalization and recommend learning resources.** ML can support adaptive learning, which is the personalization of learning experiences through computer-based technology. ML interprets vast amounts of data to match appropriate content for learners' needs based on their past learning experiences and assessments (Gold, Nichol, and Harrison 2020). This allows for more targeted planning and development using learning behaviors, performance indicators, and emerging patterns to personalize online training.

Adaptive Learning

Adaptive learning technologies are computer-based e-learning systems that alter the sequence, difficulty, or nature of the material in response to a learner's performance or responses. In addition, many adaptive learning technology systems capture data—such as the length of time hovering over an answer or the time it takes to automatically respond—and use it to adjust the content shared with the learner. This is also known as *personalized learning*.

One mistake made with early e-learning programs was that we didn't take advantage of the computer's ability to deliver different content to different people based on their inputs. We simply took what was done in the classroom and modified it for online learning. Fortunately, designers and vendors are starting to realize that they can save time and accelerate learning by first diagnosing what a person knows when they log in to an e-learning course and then only delivering content based on what the learner doesn't know.

Adaptive learning can be done simply by providing different levels of content, but it will eventually progress to an adaptive learning presentation through the learning process. This will require a detailed breakdown of content and learning outcomes into enabling objectives from the design perspective.

Digitization of Analog

There is a growing movement toward taking traditional face-to-face activities commonly found in workshops or classroom settings and converting them into a digital version. While the trend accelerated during the COVID-19 pandemic, it was already under way before the pandemic began.

Many activities have become digitized. You will find links to each of these digital tools on the handbook website, ATDHandbook3.org. These activities and examples of their associated tools include:
- Digitizing the physical act of placing sticky notes on a whiteboard in a conference room (Miro, Padlet, and Stormboard).
- Digitization of raising your hand and interacting in a classroom with audience response tools (Kahoot and Poll Everywhere).

- Digitization of traditional card games for sorting competencies, conducting role plays, or including other learning activities. The goal of digital card games is to give the learners the feeling of sitting around a virtual card table—they still draw, discard, and sort cards like they would in a physical game (Enterprise Game Stack).

Digitization of the traditional tools used in the face-to-face classroom experience will only continue to grow and diversify. This will allow digital experiences to become closer and closer to actual physical experiences. It also means that live and virtual learning experiences can be designed to mimic more traditional in-person experiences. It is possible to brainstorm sessions with a virtual whiteboard, conduct a role-playing game with virtual cards, or even run a business simulation using a virtual board game.

Final Thoughts

What can you do as an L&D professional? We've included a tool to help you measure the viability of implementing an emerging technology by using the RISSCI methodology. This assessment—which is available on the handbook website, ATDHandbook3.org—can help you to determine if the technology is appropriate for your L&D organization.

There has been a shift in how technology is influencing the way L&D professionals design learning and training. With new advances in augmented reality, virtual reality, mixed reality, extended reality, deep fakes, virtual worlds, chatbots, artificial intelligence, machine learning, adaptive learning, and digitization of analog, technology is transforming the training industry at an accelerated pace.

Organizations that embrace these technologies will see dramatic results. With advances in technology, an extensive number of options, and not-unlimited budgets, L&D departments must determine what technology is best for their needs. Technology has the power to redefine work, performance standards, and leadership responsibilities over the next decade. Leveraging the right emerging technology will not only improve employee performance and affect skill development but also save time and money.

About the Authors

Karl Kapp, EdD, is a professor of instructional technology at Bloomsburg University, in Bloomsburg, Pennsylvania, where he teaches instructional game design, gamification classes, and online learning design. He keeps busy with both academic and more corporate pursuits. Karl is a senior researcher on a grant sponsored by the National Institutes of Health that involves applying microlearning and gamification to help childcare workers identify child abuse. He is co-founder of

Enterprise Game Stack, a company that created a digital card game tool for instructional designers. Karl keeps busy writing and researching; he has authored or co-authored eight books, including *The Gamification of Learning and Instruction* and *Microlearning: Short and Sweet*. His current passion project is creating a series on YouTube called "The Unauthorized, Unofficial History of Learning Games." He is also a LinkedIn Learning author and has created several courses on the platform. You can reach Karl at karlkapp@gmail.com.

Jessica Briskin, PhD, is an assistant professor and a graduate coordinator in the department of instructional technology at Bloomsburg University, in Bloomsburg, Pennsylvania. She teaches e-learning and multimedia development courses, authoring tools, visual design for learning, and online learning. Her research focuses on design frameworks, online collaboration methods, and mobile and multimedia development regarding translating learning spaces into online spaces. Jessica has experience in corporate and educational industries, designing and developing e-learning and m-learning courses, instructor-led training, videos, infographics, and performance support tools. Her doctorate in learning, design, and technology is from the Pennsylvania State University.

References

Belhassen, D., and P.S. Hogle. 2020. *AI in eLearning 2020: Demystifying Artificial Intelligence and Its Impact on Digital Learning.* Neovation Learning Solutions. assets-global.website-files.com/5fb5104a3035525f5b6e6afd/607f02b6a4c5a2a9470f4e51_AI%202020_v1.1.pdf.

Girvan, C. 2018. "What Is a Virtual World? Definition and Classification." *Education Tech Research Dev* 66:1087–1100. https://doi.org/10.1007/s11423-018-9577-y.

Greene, E. 2018. "Reimagining the World of Corporate Learning in a Virtual Environment." *Training Industry Magazine*, Training Toolbox 2018. nxtbook.com/nxtbooks/trainingindustry/tiq_20180708/index.php?startid=24#/p/24.

Gold, J., L. Nichol, and P.A. Harrison. 2020. "L&D Must Be a Participant Not a Bystander in Machine Learning." People Management, September 10. peoplemanagement.co.uk/voices/comment/ld-must-be-participants-not-bystanders-in-machine-learning#gref.

Kapp, K.M., and T. O'Driscoll. 2010. *Learning in 3D: Adding a New Dimension to Enterprise Learning and Collaboration.* San Francisco: Pfeiffer.

Lee, S. 2019. "The Role of Chatbots in Workplace Learning." *Training Industry*, January/February. trainingindustry.com/magazine/jan-feb-2019/the-role-of-chatbots-in-workplace-learning.

Quote Investigator. 2012. "The Future Has Arrived—It's Just Not Evenly Distributed Yet. William Gibson? Anonymous? Apocryphal." Quote Investigator, January 24. quoteinvestigator.com/2012/01/24/future-has-arrived.

Walsh, N. 2019. "Are HR and L&D Missing a Trick? Machine Learning for Corporate Learning and Performance." Learnovate. learnovatecentre.org/13241-2.

CHAPTER 57

Talent Development's Role in Aligning People Analytics With Strategy

Larry Wolff

According to Gartner HR, "People analytics is the collection and application of talent data to improve critical talent and business outcomes. People analytics leaders enable HR leaders to develop data-driven insights to inform talent decisions, improve workforce processes, and promote positive employee experience." Today, people analytics apply artificial intelligence, machine learning, and data visualization techniques to large databases of talent information. The result is better informed decisions throughout the workforce life cycle.

IN THIS CHAPTER:
- Understand the importance of linking people analytics and strategy
- Review keys to implementation and adoption
- Recognize talent development's role in measuring business impact

The term *business outcomes* is critical to Gartner's definition of people analytics. The impact on business outcomes is what separates a great talent development team from a good one, and that is what we will explore here.

Strategic Business Outcomes

Having spent much of my career in digital transformation and strategy management (the marriage of strategy and execution), I have seen countless businesses that dream up a strategy that they have no coherent way to execute or ability to measure. I also see many transformation efforts fail because of a technophobic culture and fear of change. These are challenges that talent development must consider, plan for, and overcome to successfully embed people analytics in the organization.

The purpose of strategy is to protect and extend our differentiators. You do this by developing:
- Customer-focused objectives
- Related process improvement objectives
- Organizational objectives that address people, tools, systems, and data

Talent development translates those strategic objectives into measurable goals and action plans. Then, they carefully manage the execution and measure the results.

Alignment with the company strategy and understanding how to measure the impact of people analytics are key challenges for talent development. Here are some important tips on how to embed people analytics in the company strategy so that talent development can have a much greater impact on the business than ever before.

Enhancing Strategy With People Analytics

When talent development studies the company's strategic objectives, it can contemplate how people analytics will help achieve those objectives. This next part is key. You collaborate with business leaders, managers, and staff across the organization to help them consider decisions and internal processes based on the insights the TD function gains from people analytics. The business managers can then update their goals in the company strategy to reflect these process improvements.

Many talent development teams still only consider the impact of people analytics on hiring and talent development. But few can objectively measure the strategic business impact. It is talent development's role to not only apply people analytics, but also measure how the results influence the customer experience, employee experience, and top and bottom lines. You achieve that by collaborating with leaders, managers, and staff across the business.

Strategic Impact of People Analytics

People analytics are commonly used to improve hiring, guide and track training, and improve retention. They help you identify top talent and understand career pathing, anticipate skills gaps and talent shortages so you can be more strategic in your talent acquisition decisions, and understand why employees leave so you can drive down the cost of attrition. These all affect the company's financial results. Much of that impact can be felt outside HR and within business operating units. It is up to the talent development team to bring it to light and influence change across the organization.

Here is an entertaining story to demonstrate how my TD team helped a large insurance company through people analytics a few years ago. The company was shifting into a digital transformation and needed data science and other related skills to execute that strategy. So, I was asking about the business strategy so we could align specific services. When we reviewed our online people analytics platform, we discovered that the company's geographic recruiting area simply didn't have the people it needed. It turned out that a few small insurtech startups were scooping up these people. In that moment, the insurance company changed its strategy. It decided to acquire one of the insurtech companies rather than spending a year or more trying to recruit talent that may not exist. This small element of people analytics had a dramatic impact on the company's business outcomes because it allowed it to accelerate its digital transformation.

Impact of People Analytics Beyond HR

Talent development needs to look beyond hiring, training, and retention. You need to focus on how people analytics may change business processes, improve the customer experience, and give your business a sustainable competitive advantage.

If the manufacturing team suffers from poor quality due to high turnover, talent development can use people analytics to understand the root causes of that turnover, which may lead to improvements in training and changes in business processes. The team can also drive better hiring decisions, which will reduce turnover and improve quality. Thus, it is not just about the people analytics you deliver, but also the process improvements they enable.

While the data may pertain to hiring, training, and retention, talent development needs to demonstrate how the application of people analytics and the improvements it drives will have a measurable impact on the customer, employee, and business outcomes. These improvements should be embedded in the company's strategic plan, not by talent development but by the business leaders that apply the people analytics.

Talent development is the facilitator of the analytics, and the business leaders are accountable for the results. That is a very important point.

Keys to Implementation and Adoption

Several steps are required to implement or adopt a people analytics effort. Use the strategy map in Figure 57-1 to guide you. Note that while strategic objectives are defined from the top down, they are then refined from the bottom up. Talent development contributes to the organizational perspective at the foundation of the company strategy by introducing people analytics. Collaborating with business leaders, you then define process improvements that are informed by people analytics. Those improvements enable you to make the changes your customer requires, resulting in improved financial outcomes. You can download this template from the handbook website, ATDHandbook3.org.

Figure 57-1. Aligning People Analytics With Company Strategy

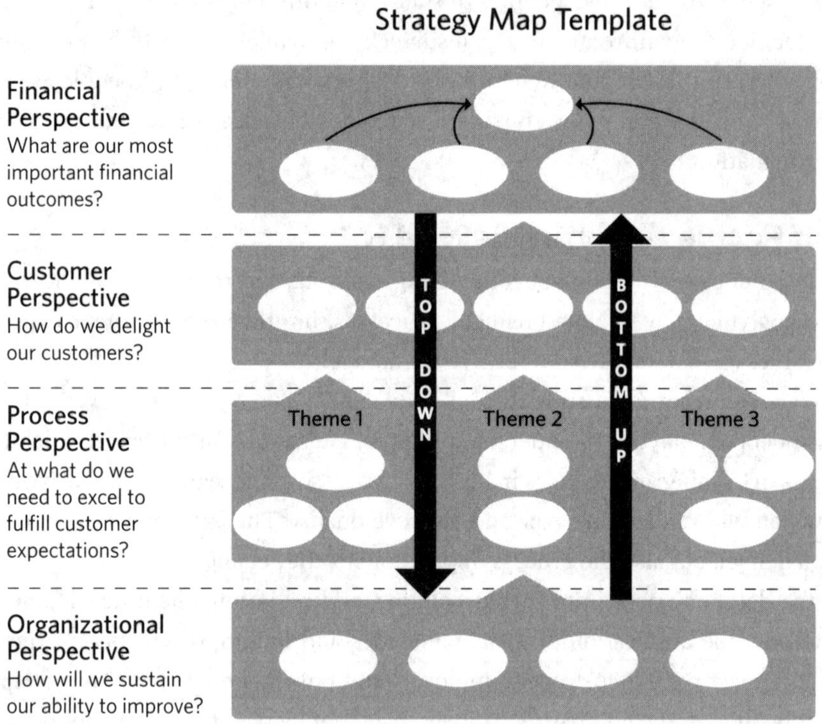

Strategy Map Template

Financial Perspective
What are our most important financial outcomes?

Customer Perspective
How do we delight our customers?

Process Perspective
At what do we need to excel to fulfill customer expectations?

Organizational Perspective
How will we sustain our ability to improve?

Theme 1 Theme 2 Theme 3

TOP DOWN / BOTTOM UP

Define People Analytics in the Context of Your Business

The first step of mastering people analytics is aligning with the company strategy. The strategy should begin with customer-facing objectives, followed by specific internal processes that you need to start, change, or stop to deliver on the customer objectives. Talent development then looks at the organization and examines the structure, skills, tools, and culture. This is where you need to have a strong voice in shaping the strategy.

The organization layer builds the very foundation of the strategy. Any flaw in the organizational components will diminish your ability to execute the internal processes that your customers need.

When talent development translates the objectives (customer, process, and organization) into measurable goals, you must consider people analytics. This is one of the most important and impactful roles of talent development.

You can refine the process improvements in the company strategy to exploit people analytics. Can the company develop the needed skills or does it need to hire or outsource them? And how will that affect the timing of process improvements? How will you retain key talent to reduce turnover and improve the customer experience? What do people analytics tell you about training requirements and how they will affect the company's financial results? In general, how do analytics drive changes to company processes and, more important, can you influence business leaders to make those changes?

Can you imagine ways in which people analytics may improve your customer experience and employee engagement? The TD function can brainstorm these ideas with leaders in HR and across the company. You will be amazed by the creative ways in which people view their business functions once they see what is possible with people analytics.

All these questions should translate into how people analytics will enable the company to improve the customer experience and business outcomes.

Master People Analytics Across the Organization

People analytics are only as good as the people who use them. If nobody embraces people analytics, then you'll gain no value. Engaged users translate to great value. People tend to dislike change—and forget about change that uses technology. Throw in some heavy analytics and you'll really scare some people.

So, how does talent development get people across the business excited to adopt people analytics? You need to embrace all available change management resources, including contracting outside expertise to coach your team through the rollout. You also need to recognize people's apprehension. Some of your colleagues may be afraid of technology. Others may not trust the numbers. Yet others may resist changes to their organizations and processes.

Once again, linking the initiative to the company's strategic plan is an important first step. When executive leadership underscores the importance of people analytics, management and staff will pay attention. It is also important to educate the entire company slowly and carefully. Take the mystery away. Show how people analytics will not only help you delight your customers by providing what they need, but also make people's jobs better and more rewarding.

Employees want to understand their role in the big picture. They want to know how their work influences the overall strategy. Help people personalize the experience, relate to the role of people analytics, and understand how it will improve their ability to contribute to the big picture.

Finally, train, train, and train. Teach the company how to interpret analytics. Help them understand where the data comes from and, in simple terms, how it is crunched. Build their confidence in what the analytics tell them and let them know it is OK to occasionally challenge the data.

Change the Culture of the Organization

Talent development, through people analytics, should change the culture of the company in two important ways:
- By building a data-driven culture, the company shifts from gut reactions or emotional responses to well-informed decision making. People also become more inclined to challenge one another to prove their assumptions. And they develop better ways to measure results.
- By building a certain level of technical proficiency, the company can leverage technology more and more to create a differentiated customer experience. This is critical in today's digital age.

Talent development must take the lead on cultural change. You can explain the benefits, coach people through the changes, share success stories, and demonstrate the business benefits derived from the adoption of people analytics.

Engage Marketing and Corporate Communications

Talent development has a job: developing talent. It is not marketing, and it is not internal communication. You will need your colleagues in other departments to help you manage the change that people analytics introduce. Use these resources to communicate frequently and tailor the messaging to the audience.

Here are some tips on communicating the changes driven by people analytics:
- The board may want brief progress updates.
- Executive leadership wants to know about risks, adoption rates, and adherence to budget.

- People managers likely need the most communication because they will probably be the top users of the analytics.
- Staff need to know that talent development is not playing big brother but, rather, is using data to improve their jobs, engagement, and development.

Utilize change managers, if you have them, across the organization. And work closely with marketing, corporate communications, and influential end users to reinforce that change is here and is wonderful.

Use Performance Objectives

A key to the adoption of people analytics will be to measure staff at all levels on how they use the analytics and the results they deliver. If talent development believes they can reduce the time a requisition is open by 20 percent, put that in the performance goals for your recruiters and recruitment managers. If you determined that you could reduce undesired attrition by 15 percent through targeted training, build that into the training team's objectives. Understand how people analytics will improve internal processes in various parts of the company and measure how that will influence the customer experience and financial results. Measure individuals across the company on the metrics that are stated in the strategic plan.

Of course, performance management is outside the scope of talent development. Just as you need to partner with managers and staff across the company's operating units, you also need to coordinate across HR to help implement performance objectives and the policies and processes that reinforce the adoption of people analytics.

Identify Tools

Talent development needs to seriously consider the goals of the company and use them to define the requirements for people analytics software. Do you invest in Tableau or is Lattice a better fit? Do you like the SplashBI reports or can you do more with Sisense? You know the answers only when you understand the company's strategic goals and can match software features to those goals.

Do not be distracted by a pretty user interface and colorful dashboards. Understand precisely what you want to achieve and have the vendors demonstrate how their products will satisfy your needs. Work with the IT department to ensure compatibility with existing systems, verify security, and support the installation.

Justify the Investment

Once talent development understands the goals and how a software package will help, the team should shift its focus to documenting the return on investment. Accounting can help break down capital costs versus operating expenses and amortization. That is the easy part.

The real fun, and I do find this to be fun, is evaluating how your people analytics will influence the employee experience, employee engagement, and, ultimately, the customer experience. This can then be translated into cost savings and revenue-growth opportunities.

Cost savings may come in the form of reduced recruitment costs, reduced cost of attrition, or increased productivity of a better trained staff. Savings will also come from the process changes across the business that are informed by people analytics. Revenue opportunities may include reduced product development time, faster speed to market, or more creative ways to serve your customers. People analytics can directly or indirectly affect all of these.

Meet with organizational leaders, department heads, and staff. Let them drive the ROI analysis. They must own the results and be held accountable for delivering the desired business outcomes that are enabled through people analytics.

Own Implementation

Talent development will own the implementation of people analytics but will engage the help of others. Marketing and corporate communications play a role in the change management process, which begins long before implementation of any software tools. IT will surely play a role in software installation and security. And your operating units need to be involved in the application of the analytics.

Remember that every change initiative, transformation, system implementation, or other disruption will have its peaks and valleys. Talent development needs to manage expectations at all levels of the company. The implementation project will take on a personality with emotional highs and lows, just like in any other change.

Recognize and reward achievements. Watch for the first person to alter a business decision based on the new analytics and send them to a nice dinner. Reinforce positive behavior and nip negativity in the bud. Word will get around and people will adapt.

If the implementation feels like it is going off the rails, acknowledge it and discuss the actions required to recover. And let everyone know when the project turns the corner and is back on track.

These peaks and valleys are a recognizable phenomenon in any significant initiative. Anticipate them, communicate, and let the company know that everything will be OK.

Make It Actionable

Talent development should have already embedded people analytics in the company's strategic plan and worked with managers and staff to identify the process improvements that are anticipated as a result of what you learn from the analytics. During implementation and as you develop the analytic reports and dashboards, you need to remind your business colleagues about the objectives in the strategic plan.

It is easy to lose sight of your goals when you are in the thick of an implementation. Check in periodically with your colleagues. Verify that the business outcomes you anticipated are still likely to materialize. Make sure the analytics are delivering the expected insight. And make changes, as needed, to keep the implementation on track with the strategic goals.

Measuring Business Impact

Remember that the whole point of people analytics is to drive better business outcomes, and it is the responsibility of talent development to make sure that happens. So how do you measure the impact before, during, and after implementation?

Before you implement any people analytics solutions, talent development will examine the company's strategic plan to identify where it could improve the customer experience, employee experience, and the top and bottom lines. You'll then collaborate with business managers to establish metrics and introduce improved processes that enable the company to achieve the desired results.

During implementation, talent development will check in with managers that are using people analytics and ensure that they are maintaining their focus on the critical strategic outcomes. A gentle reminder of why everyone is doing this work often goes a long way.

The most important measurements come after implementation and are ongoing. The company won't always see the results of people analytics immediately because it takes time for talent decisions, process improvements, and cultural changes to settle in. It is, therefore, crucial that talent development continue to track the metrics you established during the initial strategic planning stage.

The expectation is that the investment in people analytics will be far outpaced by the return. Are the financial impacts always directly related to the work that talent development did? Not necessarily. But did that work enable others to introduce better business processes, hiring practices, training, and other improvements? Absolutely. Would those changes have happened without people analytics? Probably not.

So, talent development needs to work with business leaders to establish metrics and track the results on an ongoing basis. This will also inform you when it is time to add, change, or delete analytics as the business matures in its application of, and reliance on, people analytics.

Final Thoughts

The role of talent development in people analytics goes far beyond just the implementation and decisions that follow within HR. Success depends on definitive strategic alignment, careful implementation, and ongoing tracking of business outcomes. You will find an implementation road map on the handbook website at ATDHandbook3.org.

A successful people analytics deployment puts talent development in a leadership role in the company. The analytics that we align with the company strategy will drive critical decisions, improve internal processes across the company, and, ultimately, improve the customer experience—which gives the company a competitive advantage in the markets they serve.

About the Author

Larry Wolff is the founder and CEO of Wolff Strategy Partners, a boutique consulting firm specializing in enterprise strategy management and digital transformation. Larry has served as CEO, COO, CIO, CTO, chief digital officer, and management consultant for public, private, international, and emerging growth companies. He devoted more than 12 years of his career to higher education and corporate training and has worked closely with human resources organizations for more than 20 years to innovate and deliver breakthrough results. His specialties include corporate and IT strategic planning, technology-led business transformation, business and IT turnarounds, merger integration, and large-scale project rescues. His methodologies have spanned industries and scaled to companies of all sizes. You can learn more at WolffStrategy.com and reach Larry via email at LWolff@WolffStrategy.com.

References

Gartner HR. n.d. "Definition of People Analytics." Gartner Glossary. gartner.com/en/human-resources/glossary/people-analytics.

Guenole, N., J. Ferrar, and S. Feinzig. 2017. *The Power of People: Learn How Successful Organizations Use Workforce Analytics to Improve Business Performance*. Upper Saddle River, NJ: Pearson FT Press.

Van Vulpen, E. 2019. *The Basic Principles of People Analytics*. Rotterdam: AIHR.

Wolff, L. 2014. "The Paradox of Business Intelligence: How to Prevent BI from Crippling Your Business." Wolff Strategy Partners, March 5. wolffstrategy.com/strategic-planning-facilitator/paradox-business-intelligence-prevent-bi-crippling-business.

Recommended Resources

Becker, B., M. Huselid, and D. Ulrich. 2001. *The HR Scorecard*. Boston: Harvard Business School Press.

Duarte, N. 2019. *DataStory: Explain Data and Inspire Action Through Story*. Oakton, VA: Ideapress Publishing.

Edwards, M.R., and K. Edwards. 2016. *Predictive HR Analytics: Mastering the HR Metric*. New York: Kogan Page.

Waters, S.D., V.N. Streets, L. McFarlane, and R. Johnson-Murray. 2018. *The Practical Guide to HR Analytics: Using Data to Inform, Transform, and Empower HR Decisions*. Alexandria, VA: Society for Human Resource Management.

Wolff, L. 2021. *The Authentic C-Suite Guide to Digital Transformation*. Scottsdale, AZ: Wolf Strategy Partners. wolffstrategy.com/the-authentic-c-suite-guide-to-digital-transformation.

APPENDIX A

Glossary

A

Accelerated Learning (AL) is the practice of using a multimodal, multisensory approach to instruction to make learning more efficient. It's accomplished by honoring the different learning preferences of each participant and using experiential learning exercises (such as role plays, mnemonics, props, and music).

Accessibility most often refers to ensuring that employees with disabilities have comparable access to information or services as those without disabilities.

Accomplishments refer to the specific outputs a performer is asked to achieve.

Active Training is an approach that ensures participants are involved in the learning process. It is based on cooperative learning, in which participants learn from one another in pairs or small groups, such as in group discussions, games, simulations, and role plays.

Adaptive Learning is defined as an approach that works to tailor the learning experience to the specific needs of the individual, often using technology that makes it scalable across a larger number of learners.

ADDIE is an instructional systems development model composed of five phases: analysis, design, development, implementation, and evaluation:
- **Analysis** is the process of gathering data to identify specific needs—the who, what, where, when, and why of the design process.
- **Design** is the phase in which objectives are determined and planning occurs.
- **Development** is the phase in which training materials and content are selected and developed based on learning objectives.
- **Implementation** occurs when the course is delivered, whether in person or virtually.
- **Evaluation** is the ongoing process of developing and improving instructional materials based on feedback received during and following the ADDIE process.

Adult Learning Theory is the collective theories and principles of how adults learn and acquire knowledge. Popularized by Malcolm Knowles, adult learning theory provides the foundation for L&D professionals to meet learning needs in the workplace.

Affective Learning is one mode of knowledge acquisition based on Benjamin Bloom's taxonomy, which identifies three learning domains: cognitive, affective, and psychomotor. *Affective* refers to the learner's outlook, attitude, or mindset.

Affinity Diagrams (also referred to as **affinity maps**) are used to organize a large number of ideas (often generated by brainstorming) into logical groups based on the natural relationships among the ideas. Each idea group is defined and labeled. The tool is effective when a group of people need to make a decision. (See also *Interrelationship Digraph*.)

After Action Review (AAR) was first developed by the US Army to encourage individuals to learn for themselves after an activity, project, or task by evaluating and analyzing what happened, why, and how to improve performance.

Alt Text is a text description added to visual media that describes the media for someone who can't see it.

Alternate Reality Game is a story-like game that manifests in the real world, spread over time and space, using varied media.

Americans With Disabilities Act (ADA) is legislation passed by the US Congress in 1990 that prohibits discrimination in employment, public services, transportation, public accommodations, and telecommunications services against persons with disabilities. An individual is considered to have a disability if they have a physical or mental impairment that substantially limits one or more major life activities, has a record of such an impairment, or is regarded as having such an impairment. The ADA prohibits discrimination in all employment practices, including job application procedures, hiring, firing, advancement, compensation, training, and other terms, conditions, and privileges of employment.

Analysis is a systematic examination and evaluation of data or information that uncovers interrelationships by breaking them into their component parts. Common analyses in training and development include:

- **Audience Analysis** is conducted to gather data about a target population, demographics, and other relevant information prior to job analysis, training, or other solutions.
- **Gap Analysis** describes the difference between desired results and actual (current) results.
- **Job Analysis** identifies all duties and job responsibilities, as well as and the respective tasks done on a daily, weekly, monthly, or yearly basis that make up a single job function or role.
- **Root Cause Analysis** identifies the true cause(s) of the gap between desired and actual knowledge, skills, or performance.
- **SWOT Analysis** is a process that identifies an organization's internal strengths and weaknesses, as well as its potential external opportunities and threats. The analytical framework provides input for planning.
- **Task Analysis** is the process of examining a single task within a job, breaking it down into the actual steps of performance.
- **Training Needs Analysis** is the process of collecting and synthesizing data to identify how training can help an organization reach its goals.

Analytics is the discovery and communication of meaningful patterns in data; for example, talent management analytics refers to the use of HR and talent data to improve business performance.

Andragogy (from the Greek meaning "adult learning") is the method and practice of teaching adults. It was advanced by Malcolm Knowles, whose theory outlines five key principles of adult learning: self-concept, prior experience, readiness to learn, orientation to learning, and motivation to learn.

Appreciative Inquiry (AI) is an approach to large-scale organizational change that involves the analysis of positive and successful (rather than negative or failing) operations. The AI 4-D cycle (discovery, dream, design, destiny) includes identifying areas for improvement, analyzing previous successes, searching for solutions, and developing an action plan.

APTD (Associate Professional in Talent Development) is a professional credential offered by the ATD Certification Institute for TD professionals with at least three years of experience.

Artificial Intelligence is typically defined as the ability of a machine to simulate human cognitive processes, such as perceiving, reasoning, learning, interacting with the environment, problem solving, and creativity.

Assessment Center is a process that organizations use to determine candidates' suitability for a job or during a performance appraisal. It may include a variety of activities such as simulations, problem analysis, interviews, role plays, written reports, or group exercises.

Assessment-Based Certificates are awarded to program participants who meet the performance, proficiency, or passing standard for the assessment by a non-degree granting program that provides instruction, training, and evaluation on specific knowledge, skills, or competencies associated with intended learning outcomes.

Assistive Technology refers to devices used by individuals with disabilities to perform functions that might otherwise be difficult or impossible.

Asynchronous Training or Learning is learning in which the trainer and the learner do not participate simultaneously in time or location; for example, on-demand e-learning.

ATD HPI Model is a results-based, systematic process used to identify performance problems, analyze root causes, select and design solutions, manage solutions in the workplace, measure results, and continually improve performance in an organization.

Audio Editing is the process of cutting out unwanted content from an audio recording. Traditionally performed by literally cutting tape, it is now performed using audio editing software where "umms" and "ahhs" and other elements can be cut from the audio. Audio editing also includes adding music, sound effects, and processing the audio elements with tools such as the graphic equalizer and compressor.

Audio is one-way delivery of live or recorded sound.

Augmented Reality (AR) overlays digital information onto real-world environments through a mobile or head-mounted device. This information may include navigation directions, location information, or a wide range of other location-based details. AR is of particular value for talent development as a means of performance support, because targeted information can be displayed in context without requiring users to stop their work.

Authoring Tools are software programs that allow a content expert to interact with a computer in everyday language to develop courseware.

Avatar is a graphical representation of the computer user or the user's alter ego or character.

B

Baby Boomer refers to the generation born from 1946 to 1963 in the US who are typically characterized as competitive and loyal to their employers.

Behavioral Objectives are goals that specify a new observable skill or knowledge that a learner should be able to demonstrate after training or a learning event.

Behaviorism is a learning theory focused on observable and measurable behavior. It is usually associated with psychologist B.F. Skinner, who predicted that animal and human behavior occurs through conditioning, which is the reinforcement of desired responses.

Benchmarking is a measure of quality by comparing business process metrics to standard measurements or the best industry measures. The purposes of benchmarking are to compare and analyze to similar items to learn how other organizations achieve performance levels and to use this information to make improvements.

Best Practices are techniques that are believed to constitute a paradigm of excellence in a particular field.

Blended Learning is the practice of using several media in one curriculum. It refers to the combination of formal and informal learning events, such as classroom instruction, online resources, and on-the-job coaching.

Blog is an extension of a personal website consisting of journal-like entries posted on the internet for public viewing. Posts usually contain links to other websites, along with the blogger's thoughts, comments, and personality.

Bloom's Digital Taxonomy is an update to Bloom's Revised Taxonomy that attempts to account for the new behaviors and actions emerging as technology advances and becomes more ubiquitous.

Bloom's Taxonomy, developed by Benjamin Bloom, is a hierarchical model used to classify learning into three outcomes or domains—cognitive (knowledge), psychomotor (skills), and affective (attitude)—referred to as KSAs. The domain categories use verbs to define behavior in a hierarchical relationship that becomes progressively more complex and difficult to achieve. The taxonomy is useful for writing learning objectives.

Brainstorming is a group process used to generate multiple ideas through spontaneous and unrestrained participation.

Branching is a form of interactive learning that uses a process to create options, which allows learners to make their own decisions.

Breakout Rooms are private meeting sub-rooms where participants have discussions and collaborate on tasks. In a virtual classroom, the facilitator creates a breakout room as a whiteboard or chat; in an instructor-led in-person classroom, the facilitator identifies additional space, often located in a separate room.

Browser is a software program for finding and viewing information on the internet. Firefox and Google Chrome are two common browsers.

Burden of Evidence is the degree to which an evaluation must be able to isolate the effects of the program being evaluated, and to provide compelling proof on a solution's impact.

Business Acumen is the understanding of how a company makes money in order to make prompt and wise decisions that are likely to lead to a good outcome.

Business Awareness is the understanding of key factors influencing a business, such as its current situation, influences from its industry or market, and factors affecting growth. Having business awareness is essential to strategic involvement with top management.

Business Case is a presentation of the rationale and justification for initiating a project or task.

Business Intelligence (BI) Tools is an umbrella term that includes applications, infrastructure, tools, and best practices enabling access and analysis of information to optimize decisions and performance.

Business Partnership is the cooperative effort between the training department and other business and support units in the company.

Buzz Group is a small, intense discussion group that usually involves two to three people briefly responding to a specific question during a learning event.

C

Capability is the integration of knowledge, skills, and personal qualities that demonstrate individuals have the potential to learn and respond effectively and appropriately to varied, familiar, and unfamiliar circumstances.

Career Advisor is a professional responsible for helping individuals grow and develop in preparation for new job options. This person is also called a *career coach*.

Career Development is a planned process of interaction between an organization and an individual that allows the employee to grow within the organization.

Case Study is a learning method in which a real or fictitious situation is presented for analysis and problem solving.

Cause-and-Effect Analysis is a technique that helps identify all likely causes of a problem. It uses the fishbone or Ishikawa diagram to visualize the data.

Certificate is a document that identifies knowledge or skills acquired using attendance and program completion as the requirements; competencies are not tested.

Certification is a process for increasing technical competencies through studies, testing, and practical application while also working toward a recognized designation.

Chain of Evidence refers to the data, information, and testimonies at each of the four evaluation levels that, when presented in sequence, act to demonstrate value obtained from a business partnership initiative.

Chat Room is a synchronous feature used in virtual training events that allows participants and facilitators to send text or auditory messages in real time to interact. They are similar to break-out rooms in face-to-face training sessions.

Chatbot is a computer program designed to simulate conversations with humans usually in the format of an online chat.

Chief Talent Development Officer represents the talent development function at the executive level of an organization. Known in some organizations as *chief learning officer*, this role reports directly to the CEO.

Cloud-Based refers to applications, services, or resources users can access on demand via the internet from a cloud computing provider's servers.

Coaches are qualified professionals who partner with individuals or teams to maximize their potential through a process that involves establishing goals, using strengths, pursuing development, and achieving results.

Coaching is a widely used term with multiple definitions. The International Coach Federation defines coaching as "a professional partnership between a qualified coach and an individual or team that supports the achievement of extraordinary results, based on goals set by the individual or team. Through the process of coaching, individuals focus on the skills and actions needed to successfully produce their personally relevant results." It is not counseling, mentoring, training, or giving advice. Coaching may also be used on the job, when a more experienced person, often a supervisor, provides constructive advice and feedback to develop or improve an employee's performance.

Cognition is the mental process of acquiring knowledge and understanding through the five senses, thought, and experience. The word dates back to the 15th century, meaning thinking and awareness.

Cognitive Dissonance Theory states that when contradicting beliefs occur, the human mind invents new thoughts or beliefs or modifies existing beliefs to seek consistency and minimize the amount of conflict between beliefs.

Cognitive Load refers to the amount of effort needed to process new information in the working memory, which has a very limited capacity. TD professionals need to design content so that it does not overload this capacity.

Cognitivism is a learning theory that attempts to answer how and why people learn by attributing the process to inner mental activity (thinking, problem solving, language, concept formation, and information processing) and how information is processed, stored, and retrieved.

Collaborative Learning is an instructional approach in which two or more learners work together to discover, learn, solve problems, and share information either in person or online. It may be used by facilitators to encourage engagement and involvement.

Commentary is a media term used to describe narration in audio or video. In video, commentary provides additional information that has not been conveyed by picture.

Community of Practice (CoP) is a group of people who have a common interest in an area of competence and share the experiences of their practice.

Competencies include the knowledge, skills, and behaviors necessary to successfully perform current key work functions in a job, industry, or occupation.

Competency Modeling is a corporate initiative designed to align the skills and knowledge of employees with the organization's strategic goals.

Computer-Based Training (CBT) is any course of learning that encompasses the use of computers in both instruction and management of the teaching and learning process. There is no single definition because many other terms are included under the CBT umbrella, including computer-aided instruction, computer-managed instruction, and computer-based instruction.

Concurrent Validity is the extent to which an instrument agrees with the results of other instruments administered at approximately the same time to measure the same characteristics.

Conditional Logic is an interactive design technique that provides the ability to create if/then statements.

Conditions of Learning refers to Robert Gagné's theory of nine events of instruction that ensure learning occurs.

Consultant is a person who uses expertise, influence, and personal skills to facilitate a client-requested change or improvement. Consultants may be employees of organizations (internal) or under contract with organizations (external) to solve problems or help individuals, groups, or organizations move from a current state to a desired state.

Content Management System (CMS) is a computer software system that supports the creation, organization, and modification of digital documents and other content by multiple users for an organization's web content or digital assets.

Control Group is a group of participants in an experiment that is equal in all ways to the experimental group except that they have not received the experimental treatment, benefit, or training. This group represents a reference point for comparison (for example, a group that has undergone training versus a group that has not). Types of control groups include:
- **One-Way Analysis of Variance.** This model compares several groups of observations, all of which are independent but possibly with a different mean for each group. A test of great importance is whether all the means are equal. All observations arise from one of several groups (or have been exposed to one of several treatments in an experiment). This method classifies data one way—according to the group or treatment.
- **Two-Way Analysis of Variance.** This model studies the effects of two factors separately (their main effects) and together (their interaction effect).

Core Role is a foundational role that supports and runs the day-to-day business.

Correlation is a measure of the relationship between two or more variables; if one changes, the other is likely to make a corresponding change. If such a change moves the variables in the same direction, it is a positive correlation; if the change moves the variables in opposite directions, it is a negative correlation.

Cost-Benefit Analysis is a type of return-on-investment analysis used to prove that an initiative either paid for itself or generated more financial benefit than costs.

Counseling is the professional assistance or guidance provided to individuals to evaluate and resolve personal, social, or psychological difficulties and to learn more productive behavior patterns.

CPTD (Certified Professional in Talent Development) is a professional credential offered by the ATD Certification Institute for TD professionals with at least five years of experience.

Credentials are qualifications, achievements, personal qualities, or aspects of a person's background typically used to indicate that they are suitable for a role, job, or responsibility.

Criterion Validity is the extent to which an assessment can predict or agree with external constructs, determined by looking at the correlation between the instrument and the criterion measure.

Critical Behaviors are the few key behaviors that employees must consistently perform on the job to bring about targeted outcomes.

Critical Key Role is a function essential to the current business strategy.

Critical Strategic Role is a function vital to the long-term success of the business.

Crowdsourcing is the practice of obtaining needed services, ideas, or content by soliciting contributions from a large group of people, and especially from an online community, rather than from traditional employees or suppliers.

CSS stands for *cascading style sheets*, a standard for separating out how information looks from what it says, supporting flexible content delivery.

Current Capability Assessment is a measure of an organization's talent and how current skills match the needs of the organization now and in the future.

D

Data Collection is the act of gathering of all facts, figures, statistics, and other information for analyses and assessments; examples of data-collection methods or tools include questionnaires, interviews, and observations.

Decorative Graphic is a visual that is added for aesthetic or humorous effect.

Deep Fake is a video where a person's likeness, mannerisms, and voice are manipulated to make it appear as if they are saying something or doing something they never did.

Delivery is any method of transferring content to learners, including instructor-led training, web-based training, CD-ROM, and books.

Design is the second phase in ADDIE, in which objectives are determined and planning occurs.

Development is the acquisition of knowledge, a skill, or an attitude that prepares people for new directions or responsibilities. It may also refer to the third phase in ADDIE, in which training materials and content are selected and developed based on learning objectives.

Discovery Learning is a specific learning process in which participants encounter a problem in an activity, respond to the problem, identify useful knowledge or skills gained, debrief what was learned, and plan for transferring what they learned. This process is also known as *experiential learning* or *experiential learning activity*.

Distance Learning is an educational delivery in which the instructor and students are separated by time, location, or both. Distance learning can be synchronous or asynchronous.

Diversity refers to the presence of differences that may include race, gender, religion, sexual orientation, ethnicity, nationality, socioeconomic status, language, [dis]ability, age, religious commitment, or political perspective, and may also include learning preferences, personality, and communications preferences.

Double-Loop Learning is changing underlying values and assumptions as decision making progresses. It is also referred to as *reframing* or *changing the context*.

Drivers are processes and systems that reinforce, monitor, encourage, and reward performance of critical behaviors on the job.

Dyads consist of two learners working together as a team to conduct discussions, role plays, or other experiential activities in a training session.

E

Editable Assets can be altered and manipulated by anyone (especially learners) to be improved, repurposed, updated, or changed. The best editable assets include notices that let the editor know if their changes compromise veracity.

Effect Size is a way of quantifying the difference between two groups using standard deviation. For example, if one group (the treatment group) has had an experimental treatment and the other (the control group) has not, the effect size is a measure of the difference between the two groups.

E-Learning is a term covering a wide set of applications and processes, including web-based learning, computer-based learning, virtual classrooms, and digital collaboration.

Electronic Performance Support System (EPSS) is software that provides just-in-time, on-demand information, guidance, examples, and step-by-step dialog boxes to improve job performance without the need for coaching by others.

Embodied Interaction occurs during human-computer interaction in physical and social spaces emphasizing practical engagement over abstract reasoning and situated meaning over generalization.

Embodied Space is the location where human experience and consciousness takes on material and spatial form.

Emotional Intelligence is the ability to accurately identify and understand one's own emotional reactions and those of others. This eighth intelligence, based on Gardner's multiple intelligences theory, was popularized by Daniel Goleman in his book *Emotional Intelligence*.

Employee Onboarding is a process designed to facilitate a new or new-to-role employee's integration into the organization and acquire the necessary skills for success.

Employee Orientation is often a one-day event to introduce new employees to the organization, allow them to complete paperwork, and initiate building relationships.

Enabling Objectives are goals that define the skills and knowledge learners must achieve during a learning event. They are also called supporting objectives because they support terminal objectives by breaking the terminal objectives into manageable chunks. (See also *Terminal Objective*.)

Engagement is a heightened emotional and intellectual connection that employees have for their jobs, organizations, managers, or co-workers that, in turn, influences whether they apply additional discretionary effort to their work.

Environment is the setting or condition in which an activity occurs. It is a factor that affects human performance and can include tools, equipment, furniture, hardware and software, and physical conditions, such as light, temperature, and ventilation.

Equity refers to promoting justice, impartiality, and fairness within the procedures, processes, and distribution of resources by institutions or systems. Tackling equity issues where there is diminished access requires an understanding of the root causes of outcome disparities within our society.

Evaluation is a multilevel, systematic method for gathering data about the effectiveness of training programs. Measurement results are used to improve the offering, determine whether the learning objectives have been achieved, and assess the value of the training to the organization.

Evidence-Based Training is a process of making decisions regarding the design, development, and delivery of training on data rather than opinion or tradition.

Experience-Centered Instruction is a philosophy of adult learning that focuses on the learners' experience during instruction and the production of fresh insights.

Experiential Learning Activity (ELA) is a specific learning process that emphasizes experience and reflection using an inductive learning process that takes learners through five stages: experiencing, publishing, processing, generalizing, and applying. Learners participate in an activity, review the activity, identify useful knowledge or skills that were gained, debrief what was learned, and transfer what was learned to the workplace. This is sometimes called *discovery* or *experiential learning*.

Experiential Learning is a specific learning process in which learners participate in an activity, review the activity, identify useful knowledge or skills that were gained, debrief what was learned, and transfer what was learned to the workplace. It is also known as *discovery learning*.

Explanatory Graphic is a visual that illustrates qualitative or quantitative relationships among lesson content elements.

Explicit Knowledge, sometimes referred to as know-what, is typically captured in information systems. It is found in databases, memos, notes, documents, and so forth, and is fairly easy to identify, store, and retrieve.

Extant Data are archival or existing records, reports, and data that may be available inside or outside an organization. Examples include job descriptions, competency models, benchmarking reports, annual reports, financial statements, strategic plans, grievances, turnover rates, and accident statistics.

Extended Reality (XR) is an all-encompassing term used by developers to address all experiences, regardless of reality.

Extraneous Cognitive Load refers to irrelevant mental work imposed on working memory that impedes learning.

F

Facilitating usually refers to taking less of a delivery role, being learner-centered, and acting as a catalyst for learning. When a trainer uses facilitative methods, learners assume responsibility for their own learning.

Feedable Assets are a continuous and scalable stream that operates across multiple connected applications. The stream can be data, text, audio, video, or any combination.

Five Moments of Learning Need is a learning theory from researchers Bob Mosher and Conrad Gottfredson that describes five occasions that drive a person to seek learning.

Fixed Mindset is one's implicit belief that they and others are unable to change their talents, abilities, and intelligence.

Flipped Classroom is a form of blended learning in which new content is learned independently online by watching video lectures or reading, followed by more personalized guidance and interaction with the trainer instead of lecturing.

Force Field Analysis, developed by Kurt Lewin, is a tool to identify the driving forces and the resisting forces that create an equilibrium that resists change; individuals can influence change by strengthening the driving forces or weakening the resisting forces.

Forecasting Models are used to isolate the effects of training. With this approach, the output variable is predicted with the assumption that no training is conducted. The actual performance of the variable after the training is then compared with the forecasted value, which results in an estimate of the training impact.

Formal Learning is a planned learning program that derives from activities within a structured setting and includes instructor-led classroom, instructor-led online training, certification programs, workshops, and college courses. There is a curriculum, agenda, and objectives that occur within a pre-established timeframe.

Formative Evaluation occurs throughout the design of any talent development solution. Its purpose is to improve the draft initiative and increase the likelihood that it will achieve its objectives. For example, in performance improvement the assessment measures the progress throughout the HPI model, such as a client's expectations and whether the root cause has been identified. TD professionals should conduct a formative evaluation while an initiative is being developed and use this information to immediately revise the training to make it more effective. Formative evaluation ensures the effort is understandable, accurate, current, and functional; it could include pilot tests, beta tests, technical reviews with SMEs, production reviews, and stakeholder reviews.

Freemium is a version of a fee-based tool that does not have a charge for a limited time.

Front-End Analysis is a term credited to Joe Harless that refers to performance analysis. It includes carrying out a business analysis, identifying performance gaps, completing a task analysis, performing a cause analysis, and usually identifying a key performer or exemplar.

G

Gagné's Nine Events of Instruction were developed by Robert Gagné, a pioneer in the field of instructional design. The nine events are meant to help ensure that learning occurs—from gaining attention and informing learners of the objective to assessing performance and enhancing retention and transfer.

Gamification is the application of typical elements of game playing (point scoring, competition, rules of play) to the design of development initiatives. It is used as either the optimal learning approach or as a technique to encourage engagement.

Gantt Chart, when used in project management, is a bar chart used to provide a graphical representation of a schedule so project tasks and milestones can be planned, coordinated, and tracked.

Gap Analysis describes the difference between desired results and actual (current) results.

Gardner, Howard, developed the Multiple Intelligence Theory, which states there's no single way in which everyone thinks and learns. Gardner devised a list of intelligences, which define how people process information: linguistic/verbal, logical/mathematical, spatial/visual, bodily/kinesthetic, musical, interpersonal, intrapersonal, naturalistic, existential, and emotional.

Generation X refers to those born from 1964 to 1979 in the US, who are typically characterized as independent free agents accustomed to taking care of themselves and making lifestyle choices that contribute to their happiness and health.

Generation Y, also called *millennials*, are the members of the generation born after 1980 in the US, who are characterized as outspoken and empowered. They are socially conscious, interested in self-care, and have high expectations of organizations.

Gilbert's Behavior Engineering Model, created by psychologist Thomas F. Gilbert, identifies six factors that can either hinder or facilitate workplace performance: information, resources, incentives or consequences, knowledge and skills, capacity, and motivation.

Goals are the end states or conditions toward which human effort is directed.

Governance is the oversight of process, such as strategy or content life cycle, including policy and management.

Growth Mindset is a concept developed by Carol Dweck in which people believe they are in control of their abilities and can learn, improve, and develop them.

H

Hard Data are objective, quantitative measures commonly stated in terms of frequency, percentage, proportion, or time.

Harless's Front-End Analysis Model is a diagnostic model designed by Joe Harless to identify the cause of a performance problem. It is based on the belief that the cause should drive the solution.

Heads-Up Display (HUD) is any transparent display that presents data without requiring users to look away from their usual viewpoints.

Herrmann Brain Dominance Instrument is a method of personality testing developed by W.E. (Ned) Herrmann that classifies learners in terms of preferences for thinking in four modes based on brain function: left brain, cerebral; left brain, limbic; right brain, limbic; right brain, cerebral.

Horizontal Development uses a broad topic and typically produces a large number of results over a wide range. (See also *Vertical Development*.)

HR/OD (Human Resources/Organization Development) Professional may serve in various roles aimed at optimizing talent and organizational processes or systems toward the achievement of business goals.

HTML5 is the fifth revision of the markup language for the World Wide Web, standardizing a variety of advanced features supporting animation and interactivity across web applications' responsive design.

Human Capital describes the collective knowledge, skills, competencies, and values of the people in an organization.

Human Performance Improvement (HPI) is a results-based, systematic process used to identify performance problems, analyze root causes, select and design actions, manage solutions in the workplace, measure results, and continually improve performance. It is based on open systems theory, or the view that any organization is a system that absorbs environmental inputs, uses them in transformational processes, and produces outputs.

Human Resource Development (HRD) is the term coined by Leonard Nadler to describe the organized learning experiences of training, education, and development offered by employers to improve employee performance or personal growth. It is also a former name for the field and profession sometimes called *training* or *training and development*.

I

Icebreakers are activities conducted at the beginning of training programs that introduce participants to one another, may introduce content, and help participants ease into the program.

Implementation is the fourth phase in the ADDIE model, in which a course is delivered in person or virtually.

Inclusion is an outcome to ensure those that are diverse feel welcomed. Inclusion outcomes are met when you, your institution, your organization, and your programs are truly inviting to all, providing a sense of belonging. The degree to which diverse individuals can participate fully in the decision-making processes, have the power commensurate with their roles, and have access to development opportunities within an organization or group are ways to measure inclusion.

Independent Consultant in the talent development profession helps teams and organizational leaders assess employee learning and performance gaps and recommends or creates solutions to address those gaps.

Independent Variable is what influences the dependent element or variable during an experiment; for example, age, seniority, gender, or level of education (independent variable) may influence a person's performance (dependent variable).

Individual Development Plan (IDP) is a plan for personal improvement in a current job or for job advancement. Content may be tied to performance data; however, a development discussion is usually held at a different time from a performance appraisal discussion.

Infographic is a chart, diagram, or other visual image used to represent data or information.

Informal Learning is what occurs outside a structured program, plan, or class. This type of learning occurs naturally through observations, trial and error, and talking and collaborating with others. It is usually spontaneous, and could include coaching, mentoring, stretch assignments, or rotational assignments. It can also include reading books and blog posts, watching online video platforms such as YouTube, listening to podcasts, searching the internet, and retrieving other digital content.

Innovative Design refers to using a new, unique, or unexpected approach in one's learning design process.

Instant Feedback is a feature that allows participants to communicate with facilitators at any time throughout a virtual classroom by selecting from a menu of feedback options such as raise hand, agree, or stepped away; may also be referred to as a *raise hand feature, emoticons,* or *status changes.*

Instruction is imparted knowledge as well as the practice of instructing—it is used to fill a learning need. In the workplace, instruction covers many types of content and can be delivered in many formal and informal ways.

Instructional Designer is a person who applies systematic methodologies rooted in adult learning principles and instructional theories and models to design and develop content, experiences, and other solutions that support the acquisition of new knowledge or skills. An instructional designer also creates mechanisms to assess the learning and evaluate its impact on the individual and the organization.

Instructional System is the combination of inputs (such as subject matter and resources) and outputs (such as curriculum and materials) transformed by the process to build a training course.

Instructional Systems Design (ISD), also known as instructional systems development, is the practice of creating learning experiences. It is a systems approach to analyzing, designing, developing, implementing, and evaluating any instructional experience based on the belief that training is most effective when it gives learners a clear statement of what they must be able to do as a result of training and how their performance will be evaluated.

Instructor-Led Training (ILT) modalities are synchronous (or same-time), same-location learning experiences facilitated by an instructor.

Instructor-Led, Online Training modalities are synchronous or asynchronous varied-location learning experiences led by an instructor.

Integrated Talent Management (ITM) is a series of HR processes that are integrated for competitive advantage. For example, ITM builds an organization's culture, engagement, capability, and capacity by integrating talent acquisition, employee development, retention, and deployment. ITM ensures that these processes are aligned to organizational goals and strategy. It is sometimes described as putting the right people with the right skills in the right jobs at the right time.

Interrelationship Digraph is a follow-on tool to affinity diagrams that chart cause-and-effect relationships among groups of ideas. (See also *Affinity Diagrams*.)

Interval Variable is a measurement where the difference is meaningful enough to make it possible to rank measured items and quantify and compare the size of the differences between them.

Intranet is a computer network that's accessible only to authorized users; for example, to employees of an organization.

Intrapreneurship was defined in 1978 by Gifford and Elizabeth Pinchot and refers to employees who work internally but are expected to act using entrepreneurial attributes.

J

JavaScript is a popular programming language.

Job Aid is a tool that provides guidance about when and how to carry out tasks and steps. Job aids reduce the amount of recall needed and minimize error. They may take the form of checklists, video demonstrations, or audio instruction.

Job Analysis identifies all duties and job responsibilities, as well as the respective tasks done on a daily, weekly, monthly, or yearly basis that make up a single job function or role.

Just-in-Time Training is instruction delivered when it's needed, where it's needed, and usually on the job.

K

Kirkpatrick, Donald, was a pioneer of training evaluation who first postulated his evaluation model in the 1950s. The model has four levels of evaluation: reaction, learning, behavior, and results. (See also *Evaluation*.)

Knowledge Exchanges, also known as *knowledge exchange networks*, enable different groups in an organization to share documents and information, create lists of links in simple webpages, and discuss issues of mutual interest.

Knowledge implies understanding that is a product of an individual's experience and education. It encompasses the norms by which people evaluate new inputs from their surroundings.

Knowledge Management (KM) is a systematic approach to achieving organizational goals by creating, capturing, curating, sharing, and managing the organization's knowledge to ensure the right information and knowledge flow to the right people at the right time.

Knowledge Mapping is a process for identifying and connecting the location, ownership, value, and use of knowledge and expertise in an organization. Examples of knowledge maps include network charts, yellow pages of experts, or a matrix relating knowledge to key processes.

Knowledge Repository is the storage location of information and data in a knowledge management system.

Knowles, Malcolm, is considered the father of adult learning theory. He defined six assumptions about adult learning and published *The Adult Learner: A Neglected Species* in 1973.

KSA is an abbreviation standing for two different things, depending on who is using it:
- Knowledge (cognitive), skills (psychomotor), and attitude (affective) are the three objective domains of learning as defined by Benjamin Bloom's taxonomy in the 1950s. Bloom's classification of learning objectives is used in education and training to determine the goals of the educational process.
- Knowledge, skills, and abilities are the KSAs used by the US Federal Government and some private hiring agencies to distinguish qualified candidates.

L

Leadership Development is any activity that increases an individual's leadership ability or an organization's leadership capability, including activities such as learning events, mentoring, coaching, self-study, job rotation, and special assignments to develop the knowledge and skills required to lead.

Leading Indicators are short-term observations and measurements suggesting that critical behaviors are on track to create a positive impact on desired results.

Learner Persona is a descriptive story of a subgroup within your target learner group that relays the key differences in demographics, learning needs, life at work, performance gaps, and most likely moments of learning need.

Learning Asset is a general term for a range of strategies that help people learn. It might be content to read, an online search, a class (face-to-face or online), a discussion, a video, or even a motivational poster. It can be as small as a 30-second audio recording or as large as a three-month class. In traditional training, a learning asset most often takes the form of a class, an e-learning course, or a blended learning program.

Learning Cluster is a set of learning assets intended to address a specific performance gap across multiple contexts or learning touchpoints.

Learning Content Management System (LCMS) is software technology that provides a multi-user environment where developers, authors, instructional designers, and subject matter experts may create, store, reuse, manage, and deliver digital e-learning content from a central object repository. An LCMS focuses on the development, management, and publication of content that is typically delivered via a learning management system (LMS).

Learning Experience is any interaction, program, activity, game, or other event in which knowledge, skills, or attitudes have been gained or changed.

Learning Information Systems are complementary networks of hardware and software used to create, deliver, and administer learning. LMSs and LCMSs are examples of such tools.

Learning is the process of gaining knowledge, understanding, or skill by study, instruction, or experience.

Learning Management System (LMS) is software technology for delivering online courses or training to learners while performing learning management functions, such as creating course catalogs, keeping track of learners' progress and performance across all types of training, and generating reports. An LMS is not used to create course content; that work is performed using an LCMS.

Learning Modality is how information is received through the five senses: hearing, seeing, smelling, tasting, and touching.

Learning Objectives are clear, observable, measurable goal statements of behavior that a learner must demonstrate for training to be considered a success.

Learning Objects are self-contained chunks of instructional material used in an LCMS. They typically include three components: a performance goal, the necessary content to reach that goal, and some form of evaluation to measure whether or not the goal was achieved.

Learning Touchpoints are the points of contact between modern learners and how they get the knowledge they need in the way that they need it to succeed in their work. These can be tagged as having characteristics that are social (involve people), formal (have a beginning and end), and immediate (available 24/7 or when at work).

Learning Transfer refers to how individuals transfer learning from one context to another, especially their ability to use what they learned on the job.

Level 1: Reaction is the first level of Kirkpatrick's Four Levels of Evaluation. It measures participants' reaction to and satisfaction with a training program.

Level 2: Learning is the second level of Kirkpatrick's Four Levels of Evaluation. It measures the participant's acquisition of cognitive knowledge or behavioral skills.

Level 3: Behavior is the third level of Kirkpatrick's Four Levels of Evaluation. It measures the degree to which training participants are able to transfer what they've learned to workplace behaviors.

Level 4: Results is the fourth level of Kirkpatrick's Four Levels of Evaluation. It measures the effect of the learning on organizational performance.

Likert Scale is a linear scale used in data collection to rate statements and attitudes; respondents are given a defined scale, such as 1 to 5 or 1 to 10.

Linkable Assets can be connected to other development assets, tools, or documents, and can even be combined with other assets to create new ones. Linkable assets prompt shares, citations, and backlinks because of the value that users find in them.

M

Machine Learning (ML) incorporates algorithms that are composed of many technologies (including deep learning, neural networks, and natural language processing) that operate guided by lessons from existing information.

Mager, Robert, defined behavioral learning objectives with three elements: what the worker must do (performance), the conditions under which the work must be done, and the standard or criterion that is considered acceptable performance.

Maslow's Hierarchy of Needs is a motivation theory that Abraham Maslow introduced in his 1954 book *Motivation and Personality*. Maslow contended that people have complex needs, which they strive to fulfill and which change and evolve over time. He categorized these needs as physiological, safety/security, social/belongingness, esteem, and self-actualization. He contends that basic needs must be satisfied before a person can focus on growth.

Mean is the average of a set of numbers.

Measures of Central Tendency are three statistical averages:
- **Mean** (the average of a set of numbers)
- **Median** (the middle of a distribution where half the numbers are above the median and half are below)
- **Mode** (the most frequently occurring value in a group of numbers)

Media is a term traditionally used to describe the radio, television, and print industries; however, in a broader context it includes anything that facilitates transmission of a message such as the web, instructional workbooks, and radio or television.

Median is the middle of a distribution arranged by magnitude; half the numbers are above the median, and half are below it.

Mentor is a key individual in an organization who shares knowledge and experience with others to guide and advise them as they move forward in their careers.

Mentoring is a development opportunity that encompasses receiving valuable information, guidance, and feedback from an experienced individual to gain understanding of organizational culture and unwritten norms.

Meta-Analytic Research is a statistical procedure for combining data from multiple studies. When the effect size is consistent from one study to the next, meta-analysis can be used to identify a common effect.

Milestones are the indicators of an event within a process, usually placed at the end of a phase to mark its completion. They are used to ensure that a deliverable or project can be completed on time.

Millennials (See *Generation Y*.)

Mind Mapping is a creative, converging technique that organizes thoughts and ideas in branching subcategories around one central topic.

Mindset is an established set of attitudes, beliefs, and thoughts that predetermine how individuals interpret and react to situations, events, and comments.

Mixed Reality (MR) refers to the convergence of different realities; it represents the continuum from a "real" setting to a completely artificial environment known as *virtual reality* (VR).

Mobile Learning is learning that takes place via wireless devices, such as smartphones, tablets, or laptop computers.

Motivation Theory is based on the idea that when people have the right environment to work in, they will be inspired to grow and become connected to that environment. This theory is important to coaching.

Multimedia is a computer application that uses combinations of text, graphics, audio, animation, and full-motion video. Interactive multimedia enables users to control various aspects of training, such as content sequence.

Multiple Intelligence Theory, popularized by Howard Gardner in *Frames of Mind* (1985), describes how intelligences reflect how people prefer to process information. Gardner believed that most people are comfortable in three to four of these intelligences and avoid the others. For example, if learners are not comfortable working with others, doing group case studies may interfere with their ability to process new material.

Multi-Rater Feedback, also known as 360-degree feedback evaluation, is information gathered from superiors, direct reports, peers, and internal and external customers to assess how a person performs in a number of behavioral areas.

Multisensory Learning engages the learner and increases retention by using different senses. When the brain receives information visually, it stores that content differently than if the information was heard or gained using the other senses. If more senses are involved in learning, more of the brain is involved in storing the information.

Myers-Briggs Type Indicator (MBTI) is an instrument that helps determine personality type based on preferences for extraversion or introversion, intuiting or sensing, thinking or feeling, and judging or perceiving. It's often used in career development and team building.

N

Needs Analysis is a systemic process of collecting and synthesizing data and information to determine the difference between the current condition and the desired future condition.

Neuroscience is any of the sciences, such as neurochemistry and experimental psychology, that deal with the structure or function of the nervous system and brain.

New-to-Role Employee is someone who has already been working in the organization and is now assuming different responsibilities resulting from promotion, demotion, lateral move, or special assignment.

Nominal Data is a number or variable used for labeling or to classify a system, such as the digits in a phone number or numbers on a sports jersey.

Normal Distribution refers to a specific way in which observations tend to gather around a certain value instead of being spread evenly across a range of values. The normal distribution is generally most applicable to continuous data. Graphically, the normal distribution is best described by a bell-shaped curve.

O

Objective is a target or purpose that, when combined with other objectives, leads to a goal.

Objective-Centered describes a theory of instruction that concentrates on observable and measurable outcomes. It is based on behaviorism, the primary tenet of which is that psychology should concern itself with the observable behavior of people and animals, not the unobservable events that take place in their minds.

Observation occurs when participants are directed to view or witness an event and be prepared to share their reflections, reactions, data, or insights. Observation is also a methodology for data collection.

Onboarding (General) is a component of the onboarding process focused on the information and cultural elements that are common across the organization as well as the skills and competencies everyone must demonstrate. (See also *Employee Onboarding*.)

Open Space Technology is an approach for facilitating meetings, conferences, symposia, and so forth that is focused on a specific purpose or task—but starting without any formal agenda beyond the overall purpose or theme. Open space meetings ensure that all issues and ideas people are willing to raise are discussed.

Open Systems continuously interact with their environment. In organizations, an open system is said to allow people to learn from and influence one another because of their interconnectedness and interdependence within the system.

Open Systems Theory, also known as living or general systems theory, is the concept that open systems are strongly affected by and continuously interacting with their environments. Organizations are viewed as open systems.

Open-Source Software is made freely available and grants all rights to use, study, change, or share to users.

Ordinal Data is a number or variable that allows for ranking order of importance from highest to lowest.

Organization Development (OD) is the process of developing an organization so that it's more effective in achieving its business goals. OD uses planned initiatives to develop the systems, structures, and process in the organization to improve effectiveness.

Organizational Culture is the unspoken pattern of values that guide the behavior, attitudes, and practices of the people in an organization.

Outlier is a data point that's an unusually large or unusually small value compared with others in the data set. An outlier might be the result of an error in measurement, in which case it distorts interpretation of the data, which has undue influence on many summary statistics.

Outsourcing Training is when an organization uses external services or products to meet its learning requirements.

P

Pedagogy is the art or practice of teaching that usually refers to children. Pedagogy focuses on the skills teachers use to impart knowledge and emphasizes the teacher's role. It is contrasted with andragogy, the teaching of adults, which focuses on the learner, who is assumed to be self-directed and motivated to learn. (See also *Andragogy*.)

Performance describes the execution and accomplishment of some activity; it is not an adjective that describes the action itself.

Performance Gap Analysis is a process that measures, describes, and compares what employees currently accomplish and what is required in the future.

Performance Support provides just enough information to complete a task when and where a performer needs it. The support is embedded within the natural workflow and is organized for use within a specific context, such as the location or role that requires completion.

Personal Learning Network (PLN) is an informal group of people seeking or sharing knowledge in a subject area. Members, who may be inside or outside a work group or organization, enjoy a mutually beneficial relationship.

Phillips, Jack, and Patricia Phillips developed a model for measuring the return on investment or ROI of training programs.

Plugin is a software component that adds specific abilities to a larger software application; for example, plugins are commonly used in web browsers to play video, scan for viruses, and display new file types.

Podcast is a series of audio digital-media files distributed over the internet using syndication feeds for playback on portable media players and computers. The term *podcast*, like broadcast, can refer either to the series of content or the method by which it is syndicated; the latter is also called *podcasting*. The term derives from the words *iPod* and *broadcast*.

Poll is a virtual classroom feature that allows the facilitator to post questions to participants and show poll results in real time or after all responses have been received.

Producer is a technical expert who assists a facilitator during a live online session; they may specialize in technology-only assistance or co-facilitate sessions.

Professional Development Plan (PDP) is a working document or blueprint for career goals and the strategies for achieving them.

Program Evaluation is an assessment of the effect of a training program on knowledge acquisition. (See also *Evaluation*.)

Program Evaluation Review Technique (PERT) Chart is a diagramming technique that enables project managers to estimate a range of task durations by estimating the optimistic, pessimistic, and most likely durations for each task.

Project Life Cycle is everything that happens from the beginning of a project to the end.

Project Management is the planning, organizing, directing, and controlling of resources for a finite period to complete specific goals and objectives.

Project Scope is the part of project planning that determines and documents a complete list of specific objectives, goals, deliverables, processes, and tasks that will be achieved for project completion.

Prototype represents a way to present the final product; it provides partial functionality of the end results. It also enables testing.

Psychological Safety is a condition in which human beings feel included, safe to learn, safe to contribute, and safe to challenge the status quo without fear of being embarrassed, marginalized, or punished.

Pull Learning allows learners to select what they want, is self-directed, and may be called *informal learning*.

Push Learning is directed by others, requires learners to accept knowledge and skills as presented, and may be called *formal learning*.

Q

Qualitative Analysis is the examination of non-measurable data, such as individuals' opinions, behaviors, and attributes or an organization's image, customer support, or reputation.

Qualitative Data is information that characterizes, but does not quantifiably measure, attributes or properties.

R

Random Assignment is the use of chance in the process of assigning participants to different groups or treatments in a study, ensuring that every participant has the same assignment opportunity.

Random Sampling is a method of selecting options (data points, people, documents) from a statistical population, ensuring that every choice has a definite probability of being chosen.

Random Selection is the process of how study participants are chosen from a population for inclusion in a study.

Randomization is a method that uses chance methods (such as flipping a coin or random number tables) to assign subjects to experimental groups. It helps diffuse covariates across experimental and control groups.

Rapid Instructional Design (RID) is a flexible approach to the conventional ISD model that uses a collection of strategies to quickly produce instructional packages. RID strategies include incorporating existing material, using templates, and using subject matter experts efficiently.

Reliability is the ability of the same measurement to produce consistent results over time.

Required Drivers are processes and systems that reinforce, monitor, encourage, and reward performance of critical behaviors on the job.

Reskilling involves developing individuals to gain new knowledge or skills that enable them to perform new jobs or enter new professions.

Result is the measure of objectives or goals an organization, department, improvement plan, or employee establishes.

Results-Based Approach is driven by a business need and ensures that the performance need justifies the business need.

Return on Expectations (ROE) is the measure of what a successful training initiative delivers to key business stakeholders demonstrating the degree to which their expectations have been satisfied.

Return on Investment (ROI) is a ratio of the benefit or profit received from a given investment to the cost of the investment itself; for example, it can be used to compare the monetary benefits of training programs with program costs. ROI is usually displayed as a percentage or cost-benefit ratio.

RISSCI Methodology is a process for taking a systematic look at emerging technologies and determining if they are appropriate for your organization. RISSCI (pronounced "risky") looks at six dimensions of a new technology. The dimensions are Reach, Insight, Safety, Scalability, Compatibility, and Innovation.

Role Play is an activity in which participants act out positions, attitudes, or behaviors in a controlled environment to practice skills or apply skills and knowledge. Observers may provide feedback to those in a role play.

Role-Specific Onboarding is the longest and most important phase of the onboarding process, where the new or new-to-role employee learns the specifics of the position and becomes acclimated to the unit's subculture.

Root Cause Analysis is used to determine why a performance gap exists and identify the contributing factors.

Rummler-Brache's Nine Box Model is a matrix approach to performance management based on three levels of performance (organization, process, and performer) and three dimensions of performance (goals, design, and management).

S

Sampleable Assets are designed and organized so that useful and valid samples can easily be drawn from them.

Schein's Career Anchors Theory is a concept developed by Edgar Schein to identify employees' self-concept about their talents and abilities, basic values, and motives and needs related to their career.

Scope Creep is when work or deliverables are added to a project that were neither part of the project requirements nor added through a formal change process.

SCORM (Shareable Content Object Reference Model) defines a way of constructing learning management systems and courses so they can be shared with other compliant systems.

Searchable Assets are organized in a structure that is machine-readable and works easily with natural language query.

Self-Directed Learning (SDL) is when the learner determines the pace and timing of content delivery. It occurs through a variety of media (print products or electronically).

Seven Transformation Story Beats are the most important moments when seeing learner growth through the lens of story.

Significant means probably true (not caused by chance) in statistics.

Simulation is a self-contained immersive environment the learner interacts with to learn or practice skills or knowledge. It can range from simple live exercises to complex computer software. A branching story is a common type.

Single-Loop Learning refers to a type of knowledge acquisition in which people learn and use new skills for necessary but incremental change.

Six Sigma Methodology is a disciplined, data-driven approach for improving business processes; the goal is to improve output quality by identifying and eliminating causes for defects. The name originated from statistical modeling in a manufacturing process where 99.99966 percent of products are free from defects, or a maximum of 3.4 defects per million opportunities.

Skill is a proficiency, facility, or dexterity that is acquired or developed through training or experience.

Smile Sheet is a common name for the form used in Level 1 evaluation of instructors and training classes.

Social Learning refers to learning that occurs through interacting with and observing others. It is often informal and unconscious, and often happens as an organic result of living and moving in the world.

Social Media are electronic communication tools used to extend social interactions and learning across organizations and geography.

Soft Data are qualitative measures that are intangible, anecdotal, personal, and subjective; for example, opinions, attitudes, assumptions, feelings, values, and desires. They're not always measurable, but they often help explain the measurable hard data.

Stakeholders may be a single person, group, or the organization that has interest in a project and who can influence its success.

Standard Deviation is a measure or indicator to quantify the amount of variation or dispersion (how spread out) of a group of data values.

Storyboard is a graphic organizer developed by Walt Disney Studios in the early 1930s to help visualize a movie's storyline. Storyboards allow TD professionals to move learning steps around before doing a large amount of development, which provides an opportunity to experiment with changes early in the process.

Strategic Planning is the process an organization uses to identify its direction for the future. No single process exists, but it usually includes envisioning the future, defining goals and objectives, aligning structure and resources, and implementing the plan.

Strategic Workforce Planning is the process an organization uses to analyze the current workforce and plan for future staffing needs.

Structured Mentoring is a time-limited process focused on a protégé's acquisition of a particular skill set based on specific behavioral objectives.

Subject Matter Expert (SME) is a person who has extensive knowledge and skills in a particular subject area.

Succession Planning is the systematic process of identifying, evaluating, and developing personnel who have the potential to assume leadership or mission-critical positions upon the resignation, termination, transfer, promotion, or death of an incumbent.

Summative Evaluation occurs after a TD solution has been delivered. It focuses on the results or impact of the solution to provide evidence about the program's value. It may include measuring participants' reactions, the effect on business goals, the initiative's costs, and stakeholders' expectations. A summative evaluation measures the outcome and could include standardized tests, participant reaction forms, stakeholder satisfaction surveys, and final return on investment.

Survey is a data collection tool that may consist of questions or rating statements and appear in an online or paper format; may also be called a *questionnaire, feedback form,* or *opinion poll*.

Synchronous Training occurs when the facilitator and the learner participate in the training at the same time. It is most often used when discussing virtual training, which can be synchronous or asynchronous.

Systems Thinking is based upon the belief that the component parts of a system can be best understood by examining relationships with one another and with other systems, rather than in isolation. The holistic view is important to change initiatives because small changes to any part of a system affect the whole system based on the level of interconnectedness.

T

Tacit Knowledge was originally defined by educator Michael Polanyi and is sometimes referred to as *know-how*. It is primarily experience based and intuitive, residing in the memory and mind alone, which makes it hard to define and communicate. It is the most valuable source of knowledge because it is based solely on successful experience and performance, is not broadly disseminated, and usually isn't shared or understood by many. Many knowledge management experts view tacit knowledge as the most likely to lead to breakthroughs in the organization. Gamble and Blackwell link the lack of focus on tacit knowledge directly to the reduced capability for innovation and sustained competitiveness. Knowledge stakeholders (holders of tacit knowledge) know about the organization's cultural beliefs, values, attitudes, mental models, skills, capabilities, and expertise.

Taggable Assets are simple pieces of data that make it easy to locate related items that have the same tag. Metadata tagging assigns tags to all related assets.

Talent Development (TD) refers to the efforts that foster learning and employee development to drive organizational performance, productivity, and results.

Talent Development Capability Model is a framework to guide the TD profession in what practitioners need to know and do to develop themselves, others, and their organizations. The capability model features three domains of practice:
- Building Personal Capability
- Developing Professional Capability
- Impacting Organizational Capability

Talent Development Framework is a model that TD professionals can use in selecting the components necessary to include in an organization's TD structure in order to meet strategic business objectives.

Talent Development Reporting Principles (TDRp) establishes internal reporting standards for planning and collecting human capital data and defining and reporting critical outcomes, effectiveness, and efficiency measures needed to deliver results and contribute to organizational success. TDRp is an industry-led, grassroots initiative.

Talent Segmentation Strategy identifies critical roles in the organization where gaps are present and defines strategic objectives for filling the gaps for those specific roles.

Task Analysis is the process of examining a single task within a job and breaking it down into the actual steps of performance.

Terminal Objective is the final behavioral outcome of a specific instructional event. It's also called a *performance objective* because it defines the ultimate, specific, and measurable KSA learners demonstrate as a result of participating in a learning event. The terminal objective may be broken down into enabling objectives.

Theory X is a theory of human motivation developed by Douglas McGregor in the 1960s. The theory assumes that employees are inherently lazy, dislike work, and will avoid it if they can. Belief in Theory X leads to a management philosophy of close supervision and tight control of employees.

Theory Y is a theory of human motivation developed by Douglas McGregor. In contrast to Theory X, Theory Y assumes that most employees are self-motivated, enjoy working, and will work to achieve goals to which they are committed. Belief in Theory Y leads to a management philosophy of trust that employees will take responsibility for their work and do not need constant supervision.

360-Degree Feedback Evaluation is based on opinions and recommendations from superiors, direct reports, peers, and internal and external customers on how a person performs in any number of behavioral areas.

Traditional Mentoring is the career development practice of using an experienced person or group to share wisdom and expertise with a protégé over a specific period of time. There are three common types of traditional mentoring: one-on-one, group, and virtual.

Traditionalists refer to the generation born before 1946 in the US who are typically characterized as loyal, dependable, responsible, altruistic, and hard working.

Trainer (or Facilitator) is a TD professional who helps individuals improve performance by facilitating learning in a traditional or virtual classroom, one on one, or on the job in an organization.

Training Needs Assessment is a systemic process of collecting and synthesizing data and information to determine the difference between the current performance and the desired future performance and decide if training is the solution.

Training Objective is a statement of what a TD professional hopes to accomplish during a training event.

Training Transfer Evaluation is a process to measure the success of the learner's ability to transfer and implement learning on the job.

Transactional Role is a role not critical to business strategies.

Trend Lines are used to project the values of specific output variables if training had not been undertaken. The projection is compared to the actual data after training, and the difference represents the estimate of the impact of training. Under certain conditions, this strategy can accurately isolate the training impact.

Triple-Loop Learning is a model (along with single- and double-loop learning) that helps TD professionals understand the dynamics of learning that is frequently defined as "learning how to learn." Learners reflect beyond what they learned to how they learned, how they think about what they learned, and how others feel about what was learned. This causes them to transform by willingly altering their beliefs and values about themselves and about the world.

Tuckman Group Development Model is a model that depicts five stages of team maturation: forming, storming, norming, performing, and adjourning.

U

Upskilling is training designed to augment existing skills with new or significantly enhanced knowledge. This enables individuals to continue to succeed in the same profession or field of work. Upskilling does not refer to normal, ongoing development.

V

Validity means the evaluation instrument measures what it is intended to measure.

Variable is any element, feature, or factor that is subject to change.

Variance is a measure of the spread between numbers in a data set—specifically, how far each number is from the mean.

Vertical Development is elevating one's ability to make meaning of one's world in more cognitively and emotionally sophisticated ways. The outcome of vertical stage development is the ability to think in more complex, systemic, strategic, and interdependent ways. (See also *Horizontal Development*.)

Video Editing is the process of assembling video footage in a video editing software program, cutting out redundant elements of the footage and trimming them so they run together naturally. Music, sound effects, and special effects are combined during the edit process to create a final video file.

Video is the one-way delivery of live or recorded full-motion pictures.

Video Script is written text of a video that includes all spoken word content plus a description of each shot along with camera moves, positions, and angles. Factual scripts such as those used in industrial video tend to follow a two-column format. In the left column the shot is described visually, and any monologue, dialogue, or commentary is included in the right column. Any audio such as music is also noted in the right column.

Virtual Classroom is an online learning space where learners and facilitators interact.

Virtual Reality (VR) is computer-generated simulation that uses a head-mounted display to give learners the ability to explore a fully rendered digital environment and manipulate objects with handheld controls and voice commands. This powerful tool allows learners to perform skills in a realistic, engaging simulation of a real-life environment. It's especially valuable for training learners in dangerous or hard-to-replicate situations, such as emergencies or heavy equipment simulations.

Virtual World is a three-dimensional environment where you can interact with others and create objects as part of that interaction.

W

Web 2.0 is the use of internet technology and web design to enhance information sharing and, most notably, collaboration among users. These concepts have led to the development and evolution of online communities and hosted services such as social networking sites, wikis, and blogs.

Web Portal is a website that collects information from diverse sources—early portals included AOL, MSN, and Yahoo.

Web-Based Training (WBT), more often called *virtual learning,* is the delivery of educational content via a web browser over the internet, a private intranet, or an extranet.

WIIFM is an acronym that stands for "what's in it for me." It is used by TD professionals to remember to help learners recognize the value of the training to them personally.

Wiki is a collection of web pages in one location that anyone with access can contribute to or modify. It's useful for collaboration and data compilation.

Wireframe is a simple black-and-white layout that outlines the specific size and placement of page elements, site features, conversion areas, and navigation. It is devoid of color, font choices, logos, or any other design element that take away from purely focusing on the structure.

Work Breakdown Structure (WBS) is a deliverable-oriented decomposition of a project's or department's tasks. It is used in project management and systems engineering.

Workforce Planning is the systematic process for identifying the gaps between the talent capability of today and the talent needs in the future. It is often completed in conjunction with a strategic plan—analyzing current talent, identifying skill gaps, developing an action plan, implementing the plan, and monitoring and evaluating progress.

X

xAPI is the Experience Application Programming Interface, an e-learning software specification to record learning experiences an individual has on and offline. It's also known as *Tin Can API* or the *experience API*.

Y

You-Me-We Learning Model is a learner-focused framework that TD professionals can use to provide a diverse portfolio of products and offerings that will meet the learning and development needs of their client learners.
- **Me Learning** is learning that your organization's workforce seeks out and makes time for on their own, as part of their workflow.
- **We Learning** is learning that your organization's workforce seeks to learn from others in their personal learning network.
- **You Learning** is learning that your organization's workforce looks to you to provide for them.

APPENDIX B

List of Tools

Contributors to *ATD's Handbook for Training and Talent Development* provided tools to help you implement the concepts you learned in each chapter throughout the book. The tools are available for download at ATDHandbook3.org. As long as you maintain the copyright information and the "used with permission" designation on the tool, you will be able to use it in your daily work. These tools were available at the time of publishing. More may be added.

Chapter 2. Critical Adult Learning Basics in Action
Becky Pike Pluth
- Tool 2-1. 55 Ways to Add Variety to Your Training
- Tool 2-2. Checklist for Facilitating Activities

Chapter 3. A Learning Science Strategy: Deepening the Impact of Talent Development
Jonathan Halls
- Tool 3-1. Learning Science Mindset: Trainer and Instructional Designer Self-Assessment
- Tool 3-2. Learning Science Mindset: Talent Executives Self-Assessment

Chapter 4. The Business Case for Learning
Preethi Anand
- Tool 4-1. A Framework to Prepare a Business Case

Chapter 5. The Talent Development Capability Model
Morgean Hirt
- Tool 5-1. Links to Talent Development Capability Model Tools

Chapter 6. Give Your Career a Boost With Certification
Rich Douglas
- Tool 6-1. Credential Consideration Tool

Chapter 7. Thriving in Your Career: Powerful Plans for Lifelong Learning
Catherine Lombardozzi
- Tool 7-1. TD Capability Framework Sources
- Tool 7-2. Self-Directed Learning Project Planning Worksheet

Chapter 8. The Irreplaceable Growth Mindset
Ryan Gottfredson
- Tool 8-1. Resources for Developing a Growth Mindset

Chapter 9. An Oath of Ethics for Learning and Development Professionals
Travis Waugh
- Tool 9-1. The Ethical Learning and Development Job Aid

Chapter 10. What's EQ Got to Do With a TD Career?
Jean Greaves
- Tool 10-1. EQ Strategies for TD Professionals

Section III. Luminary Perspective: Train to Add Value and Make a Difference
Bob Pike
- Tool S3-1. Learning Preferences Continuum

Chapter 12. Using Evidence to Assess Performance Gaps
Ingrid Guerra-López
- Tool 12-1. Identifying Objectives and Activities for the Alignment Process
- Tool 12-2. Deployment Tips to Maximize Data Collection
- Tool 12-3. Data Collection and Analysis Planning Matrix

Chapter 13. Design Thinking for TD Professionals
Sharon Boller
- Tool 13-1. Step 1: Strategy Blueprint
- Tool 13-2. Step 2: Empathy Map
- Tool 13-3. Step 3: Learner Personas
- Tool 13-4. Step 4: Learning Journey Map
- Tool 13-5. Step 5: Create Learner Stories
- Tool 13-6. Step 6: Testing Tool

Chapter 14. Innovative Design: Uncovering the Art of the Possible
Brian Washburn
- Tool 14-1. Guide for Developing an Innovative Learning Design

Chapter 15. We Need It Personalized, Accurate, and NOW!
Lisa MD Owens and Crystal Kadakia
- Tool 15-1. Upgrade Tool
- Tool 15-2. Learn Learner-to-Learner Differences Tool
- Tool 15-3. Surround Learners With Meaningful Assets Tool
- Tool 15-4. Change On-the-Job Behavior Tool
- Tool 15-5. Track Transformation of Everyone's Results Tool

Chapter 17. 21st-Century Media Skills: Put Learning Where the Work Is
Mhairi Campbell
- Tool 17-1. Top 10 Tips to Improve Your Video

Chapter 18. Using Story Structure to Influence
Nancy Duarte and Jeff Davenport
- Tool 18-1. The Seven Transformation Story Beats
- Tool 18-2. Three Opportunities to Use Story

Chapter 19. Implementing the Four Levels of Evaluation
Jim Kirkpatrick and Wendy Kayser Kirkpatrick
- Tool 19-1. Kirkpatrick Blended Evaluation Plan

Chapter 20. Impact and ROI: Results Executives Love
Jack J. Phillips and Patricia Pulliam Phillips
- Tool 20-1. The Alignment Conversation Toolkit
- Tool 20-2. Project Selection Worksheet
- Tool 20-3. ROI Methodology Application Guide

Chapter 22. Keys to Designing and Delivering Blended Learning
Jennifer Hofmann
- Tool 22-1. Blended Learning Scoring Tool

Chapter 23. The Many Aspects of Accessibility
Maureen Orey
- Tool 23-1. Learning Environments and Access to Learning Matrix

Chapter 24. Learning Transfer: The Missing Link
Emma Weber
- Tool 24-1. Action Planning Tool

Chapter 25. Critical Tools to Support the Fundamentals of E-Learning
Diane Elkins
- Tool 25-1. Common Game Elements
- Tool 25-2. Authoring Tool Feature Analysis
- Tool 25-3. Authoring Tool Links

Chapter 26. Designing and Delivering Virtual Training
Cynthia Clay and Cindy Huggett
- Tool 26-1. Sample Virtual Class Outline
- Tool 26-2. Virtual Facilitator Strengths Checklist

Chapter 27. Essential Skills for TD Professionals
Wendy Gates Corbett
- Tool 27-1. Checklist of Essential Skills for TD Professionals

Chapter 28. Initiating a Talent Development Effort
David Macon
- Tool 28-1. 90-Day Planning Template

- Tool 28-2. A Tool to Define Make or Buy Decisions
- Tool 28-3. Developing Learning-Solution Objectives Template

Chapter 29. Working Effectively With SMEs
Greg Owen-Boger and Dale Ludwig
- Tool 29-1. Criteria for Selecting Instructional SMEs
- Tool 29-2. Frame a Training Session

Chapter 30. Perfecting Your Facilitation Skills: The Facilitative Trainer
Michael Wilkinson
- Tool 30-1. Engagement Strategies for Facilitators

Chapter 31. Communicating With Executive Leadership to Gain Buy-In
Dianna Booher
- Tool 31-1. Checklist of Tough-Question Prompts and Discussion Starters for Your Next Executive Briefing, Proposal, or Conversation

Chapter 32. Integrating DEI Principles Into TD Initiatives
Maria Morukian
- Tool 32-1. Checklist for Creating Diverse, Equitable and Inclusive Learning Experiences

Chapter 33. Digital Age Requirements for Talent Development Professionals
Alex Adamopoulos
- Tool 33-1. Self-Assessment for Agile Teams

Chapter 35. Equip Your Managers to Become Masters of Development
Wendy Axelrod
- Tool 35-1. Coaching Questions for Managers

Chapter 36. Talent Development's Role in Strategic Workforce Planning
Barbara Goretsky
- Tool 36-1. A Checklist of Phases and Steps to Develop a Strategic Workforce Plan

Chapter 37. From Ward to Steward: Enhancing Employee Ownership of Career Development
Halelly Azulay
- Tool 37-1. A Plan to Take Ownership of Your Career Development

Chapter 38. Implement a Mentoring Program That Works
Jenn Labin and Laura Francis
- Tool 38-1. Design a Mentoring Program That Works

Chapter 39. Consulting on the Inside: Roles, Competencies, and Challenges
B. Kim Barnes and Beverly Scott
- Tool 39-1. Know When to Use Internal or External Consultants
- Tool 39-2. Internal Consulting Competencies Self-Assessment

Chapter 40. Becoming a Successful Consultant: From Startup to Market Leadership
Andrew Sobel
- Tool 40-1. Become a Successful Consultant: Six Competencies Self-Assessment

Chapter 41. Building Teams and Understanding Virtual Teamwork
Tammy Bjelland
- Tool 41-1. Essential Documents for Virtual Teamwork

Chapter 42. The Trifecta: Project Management, L&D, and Talent Development
Lou Russell
- Tool 42-1. Project Charter Template

Chapter 44. Structuring TD to Meet the Dynamic Needs of the Organization
William J. Rothwell, Angela Stopper, and Aileen G. Zaballero
- Tool 44-1. ATD's TD Framework Puzzle
- Tool 44-2. Step 1: Building Your Talent Development Framework Template
- Tool 44-3. Step 2: Populating Your Talent Development Framework Template
- Tool 44-4. Step 3: Launching Your Talent Development Framework Template
- Tool 44-5. Step 4: Communication Strategy Template

Chapter 45. The Five Fundamentals of Learning Leadership
Jim Kouzes and Barry Posner
- Tool 45-1. Five Questions to Ask Yourself

Chapter 46. Building Your Business Acumen
Kevin Cope
- Tool 46-1. 7 Steps to Build Your Business Acumen

Chapter 47. Supporting Your Organization's Onboarding Efforts
Norma Dávila and Wanda Piña-Ramírez
- Tool 47-1. 9 Questions to Determine Suitability for Remote Work
- Tool 47-2. Onboarding Communications Status
- Tool 47-3. Pre-Onboarding Planner
- Tool 47-4. General Onboarding Worksheet
- Tool 47-5. Role-Specific Worksheet
- Tool 47-6. Checklist to Document Availability of Common Onboarding Metrics

Chapter 48. Determining Talent Development's Organizational Impact
David Vance
- Tool 48-1. Impact
- Tool 48-2. ROI

Chapter 49. Best Practices for a Talent Development Department of One
Emily Wood
- Tool 49-1. Organizational Needs Assessment Checklist

Chapter 50. 6 Essentials for a Thriving Learning Culture
Holly Burkett
- Tool 50-1. Six Essentials for a Thriving Learning Culture
- Tool 50-2. Self-Assessment to Rate Your Learning Culture

Chapter 51. Sustaining Diversity, Equity, and Inclusion
Tonya Wilson
- Tool 51-1. Validated DEI Survey Questions
- Tool 51-2. DEI Risk Assessment Options
- Tool 51-3. DEI Definitions

Chapter 53. Organizational Design Practices That Can Make or Break Your Organization
David C. Forman
- Tool 53-1. OD Practice Tool for Strategic Alignment
- Tool 53-2. Sample Competitive Differentiation Matrix
- Tool 53-3. Assessing Characteristics of an Embracing Culture
- Tool 53-4. Fearless Learning Skills Assessment and Plan

Chapter 54. Agility for the Future Workforce
Christie Ward
- Tool 54-1. Becoming an Agile Enterprise Infographic

Chapter 55. Developing a Change-Ready Organization
Jennifer Stanford
- Tool 55-1. Change Readiness Predictor
- Tool 55-2. Ask Powerful Questions

Chapter 56. Emerging Technology and the Future of Learning
Karl Kapp and Jessica Briskin
- Tool 56-1. Digital Tools Resource List
- Tool 56-2. RISSCI Implementation Viability Assessment Tool

Chapter 57. Talent Development's Role in Aligning People Analytics With Strategy
Larry Wolff
- Tool 57-1. Strategy Map Template
- Tool 57-2. Implementation Road Map to Align People Analytics With Company Strategy

Index

A

accessibility, 138–139, 240, 341–348, 371
accountability, 291, 356–357, 418–419, 622–623, 657, 803–805
accountability buddies, 694
Ackoff, Russell, 188
acquisition professionals, 493
action idea list, 41, 44
action-learning taskforce, 570
ACTION stages, TLA model, 357–358
action thought perspective, 829
adaptive learning, 844
ADDIE model, 173–176
Adobe After Effects, 380
Adobe Captivate, 368, 369, 373, 378
Adobe Illustrator, 380
Adobe Photoshop, 380
Adobe Premiere Pro, 380
adult learning, 23, 35–47
advertising industry, 220
advocacy, in department of one, 723–724
affirmative action programs, 778–779

agility
  ICS team, 324
  in learning cultures, 764–765
  organizational, 802, 813–822
  project management, 137–138
  TD function, 413–414, 745–746
  work-based learning, 501–502
agreement phase, of consulting, 597
agricultural and mechanical (A&M) education, 17
alignment, 191–192, 551–552, 597, 716. *See also* strategic alignment
alt text, 347
ambiguity appreciator mindset, 81
Americans With Disabilities Act (ADA), 343
analysis planning, 195–196
analytics training, 493
animation, 261, 374
application activities, 114
applications (apps), 269
apprenticeships, 15–16
APTD certification, 97

aptitude, attitude vs., 79–80
Arena, Michael, 802
art, design inspiration from, 220
Articulate Rise 360 program, 367, 368
Articulate Storyline 360 program, 368, 372, 373, 378
Articulate Studio 360 suite, 376
artificial humans, 840–841
artificial intelligence (AI), 314, 831, 842–843
Asia Pacific Institute for Learning and Performance, 109–110
assessment, 6–7, 188–190, 216, 379, 485, 541, 552–553, 843–844
asset management tools, 383
Association for Talent Development (ATD), 97, 109
asynchronous online training, 242, 244, 246–249, 345, 494
attitude, 79–80, 289, 407–408
Audacity, 380
audience, 134–135, 189, 259, 261, 387–388, 395
audio descriptions, of videos, 347
audio equipment, 263–264
audio recordings, 267, 374, 380
auditory access, 347
augmented reality (AR), 253, 398, 837–838
authoring tools (e-learning), 364–377
authority, 727
author role, 47
Autodesk, 763–764
automation, 19, 27

B

bachelor's degree, 101
balanced communication, 624–626
Barker, Eric, 572
BAR model, 165
baseline, results compared to, 721–722
Behavior (Level 3), Kirkpatrick, 286

behavioral psychology, 19
behavior modeling, 655
believing in yourself, 678–679
bencmarking studies, 485
benefit-cost ratio (BCR), 300, 301
benefit maximization, 133
Bersin, Josh, 819
bias, 481
Biech, Elaine, 730
bind talent strategy, 554
black box thinking, 308
blended learning, 253, 327–339
blogs, 494
Bloom, Benjamin, 20
Bloom's taxonomy, 19, 245
boards of directors, diverse, 775
borrow talent strategy, 431, 554
bottom liner mindset, 81
bounce talent strategy, 554
bound talent strategy, 554
brain, 36–37, 145–147, 220–221, 272–275
brainstorming, 208, 218
branching scenarios, 378
BranchTrack, 378
breakout rooms, 268
Breakthrough Growth, 610
breakthrough moments, 3–11
breathing techniques, 154
Brown, Simon, 760
budget, 260, 430
Build-a-Bear-Workshop, 637
Building Personal Capabilities domain, 86–87, 664
build talent strategy, 430–431, 553, 554
burnout, 626–627, 763
business acumen, building, 595, 689–695
business case
    for DEI efforts, 779–784
    for improving EQ, 149–150

for L&D function, 65–74
for TD efforts, 429–430
business-centered thinking, 201
business impact, 671, 803–805, 855
business needs, 71, 229–236
business news, 691
business objectives, 663, 692
business outcomes, 652–653, 848–850
business unit goals, 719
buy-in, 469–476, 583–584, 753
buy talent strategy, 431, 553, 554

C

calibration, 671–672
camera angles, 262–263
camera shots, 261–262
Canva, 380
capabilities, 72, 219–221, 523–524
Capability Model. *See* Talent Development Capability Model
Captivate workshop, 279–280
career development, 87, 103, 110, 557, 561–573
career lattice, 564
career planning, 315, 511–514
Carey, Lou and James, 176–178
Carlson, Rachel, 819–820
cascading recruitment process, 582
causal analysis, 189
celebrations, 494, 671
Centre for Global Inclusion, 777
CEO. *See* executives
certificates, 99, 104–105
certification, 97, 99, 105, 114, 611–612
chain of evidence, 296, 720–721
challenging yourself, 680–681
change, 228, 353, 404–405, 549, 762–763, 827–830
change agents, 403–408, 592

change chaser mindset, 82
change fatigue, 763
change management, 89, 492, 640–641, 825–833
change readiness, 406, 826–827
"chapters" of careers, 315
Charan, Ram, 800
chatbots, 359–360, 842
CHG Healthcare, 815–816
Christiansen Institute, 330
chunking, 249
CIO model, 165
CIPD New Profession Map, 110
clarity, 266, 623–624
Clark, Dorie, 571–572
classroom training, 329–330, 389
client attraction strategy, 607–608
client–consultant relationship, 593–594, 605–606
Clifton, J., 811
Closers, in CORE model, 40–42
close-up shots, 262
cloud-based authoring tools, 376
coaching, 88, 252, 253, 315, 449–452, 516–517, 539, 647–648, 655
Coach M chatbot, 360
coach role, 47
co-facilitation, with SMEs, 444–445
cognitive challenges, 316, 347
cognitive load theory (CLT), 56
cognitive neuropsychology, 36–37
cognitive neuroscience, 36–37
cohort-based training, 364
collaboration, 29, 86, 416–417, 439–453, 502–506, 512–513, 593, 595, 757–759, 808
collective leadership, 754–755
command-and-control style, 503
commitment, 104, 205, 289
common purpose, 475

communication
 about career and development, 542, 567–568
 about change, 828, 829, 852–853
 about TD structure, 670–671
 about technology implementation, 528
 in breakthrough moments, 3–4
 in Capability Model, 86
 in digital learning mindset, 516
 for effective teams, 624–626
 with executives, 469–476, 731, 792–793
 generational differences in, 831
 identity and, 492
 in onboarding, 703–704
 in ROI Methodology Process Model, 308
 with stakeholders, 639
communication channels, 337–338, 625
communication guides, 625
communication skills, transferability of, 569
communications training, 138
communities, 758–759, 805
Community Academy initiative, 793
compatibility, in RISSCI methodology, 837
competencies, 24, 111, 594–595, 604–608, 831–832
completeness, of data, 193
complex personalization, 229–230
compliance, 86, 778–779
compound time, 567
concept matrix, for accessibility, 348
conferences, 494, 737
confidence, 289
conflict management, 9–10, 475, 492
connection(s), 55–56, 220, 519, 682, 757–759
conscious connector mindset, 81
consistency, 248, 264, 518
constructivism, 23
consultation, 88, 596–597. *See also* internal consultants; solo consultant practice

contact phase, of consulting process, 597
context, 346–347, 518, 851
continuous learning, 112, 113. *See also* lifelong learning
contracting professionals, 493
control, 506
CORE model of training, 40–45
core values, 752–753, 802, 806
corporate universities, 22
corporate vision, achieving, 651–660
cortisol, 274, 275
cost savings, 133–134, 328, 804, 854
courage, leading with, 419–420
Covey, Stephen, 407–408
COVID-19 pandemic, xiii, xiv, 314, 316, 332, 598–600, 653, 701–704, 800, 802–803, 832–833
CPR rule, 164
CPTD certification, 97
creativity, 492, 570–571
credentials, 91, 95–105
credibility, 307–308, 595, 596
critical behaviors, 290
critical roles, 551–552
cross-functional teams, 528, 681, 809
crowdsourcing, 233
cultural awareness, 86. *See also* organizational culture
customer outcomes, 288, 849–850
customer service, 492
cyber threats, 316

D

Dare approach, 632, 634–637
data, 89, 193, 194, 471, 548–549
data analysis, 89, 188–190, 195–196, 307–308, 316, 782–783, 843
data collection, 194–196, 306
data layer, of technology ecosystem, 523

day-to-day coaching, 647–648
decision making, 86, 258, 275, 276, 278, 281–282, 507, 690–691
deductive analysis, 195
deep fake videos, 840–841
deep generalist capabilities, 608
define phase, in Dare approach, 635–636
degrees, as credentials, 100–101, 105
DEI Key Questions chart, 783–784
DEI maturity, of organization, 786
DEI-specific learning, 484–486
Delaney, Kevin, 753
delegation, 541, 649–650
deliberate practice, 58, 683–684
delivery of training
    for blended learning, 335
    in Capability Model, 87
    coaching SMEs on, 449–452
    from facilitative trainers, 458–459
    learner preferences for, 233–236
    and learning transfer, 353
    modality selection, 239–254
    as orderly conversation, 441–442
    story-minded, 272
    in videos, 260
    virtual, 390–395
democratization, of development, 743
dependencies, 506
Descript, 380
descriptive statistics, 195
design thinking, 71–72, 199–209, 345–346
detachment, for consultants, 595
detail, in graphics, 264
Developing Professional Capabilities domain, 87–88, 664
development
    to achieve corporate vision, 653–655
    at agile organizations, 820–821
    democratization of, 743

discussing, with employer, 567–568
experiential, 744–745
growth vs., 98
ownership of, 563, 608, 723–724, 733, 742
as a way of work, 10–11
developmental managers, 533–544
developmental planning of work, 535–536
development goals, 108, 110–111
development outcomes, business and, 652–653
Dick, Walter, 176–178
digital capabilities, 530
digital layer, of technology ecosystem, 524
digital lead, 530
digital learning mindset, 516–517
digitization, 844–845
direct costs of L&D, 134
direction, company, 692
discovery, 505, 743–744
dissolve transitions, 265
diversity, xvii, 480, 481, 483–484, 487–489
diversity, equity, and inclusion (DEI) efforts, 479–495
    business case for, 779–784
    compliance view of, 778–779
    defined, 480
    environments that foster, 489–491
    in interpersonal skills training, 491–492
    in L&D activities, 493–494
    in long-term strategy, 486–493
    organizational benefits of, 480–482
    performance monitoring, 776, 784–786
    relevant DEI-specific learning, 484–486
    and roles of TD professionals, 493
    sustainability of, 773–787
    in TD initiatives, 482–483
diversity climate, 777–778
doctorates, 101–103
doctor role, of consultant, 592

documentation, 621–623, 638–639
document reviews, 484–485
drama beats, of story, 276–278
Drucker, Peter, 800
dry runs, of presentations, 451
Dump and Clump strategy, 463
Dupont Sustainable Solutions, 766
Dweck, Carol, 678–679
dysfunctional teams, 626–629

E

ease of use, in user experience, 202
Eddy, David, 654, 660
editing videos, 265–266
educational psychology, 19–20
effective teams, 619–626
Eisner, Elliot, 320
e-learning, 25–26, 242, 247–249, 314
e-learning tools, 363–383
    asset and file management, 383
    authoring, 364–377
    hosting and tracking, 383
    interaction, 377–379
    media, 379–380
    project management, 382
    prototyping, 382
    for quality assurance/reviews, 382–383
    storyboarding, 381–382
elevator speech, 464–466
emerging technologies, 835–845
emotional agility, 814
emotional component, of adult learning, 37–38
emotional intelligence (EQ), 86, 143–156
empathy, 315, 449
empathy mapping, 207
employee–employer relationship, 561–563
employee orientation, 217–218, 699
employee outcomes, people analytics and, 849–850

employee ownership of career development, 561–573, 742
Energizers, in CORE model, 44–45
energy level, facilitative trainers', 459
engaged leadership, 752–756
engagement, in Kirkpatrick model, 288. *See also* learner engagement
Engstrom, Craig, 98, 104
enjoyment, 202, 684
enterprise goals, 717–718
entrepreneurial mindset, 563–564
entry requirements, professional, 97
environmental analysis, 190
envisioner mindset, 80
equipment, video, 259, 263–264
equity, 136–138, 480, 481, 519. *See also* diversity, equity, and inclusion (DEI) efforts
ethical behavior, 86, 131–141
evaluation, 305–306, 338, 353, 597, 671–672, 709
evidence collection, 193–194
excellence, aspiring to, 679–680
exclusionary phrases, 488–489
executives. *See also* senior leaders
    buy-in from, 469–476, 583–584, 753
    communication with, 469–476
    expectations of, 68–71
    impact and ROI results for, 303–304
    involving, in development, 655
    partnerships with, 791–797
    sponsorship by, 583–584, 653
expectations, 68–71, 191, 386–387, 626, 723
experience layer, technology ecosystem, 524–525
experiential learning and development, 744–745, 767
experimentation, 506, 530
expertise, 324–325
expert role, for consultant, 592

extended reality (XR), 840
external consultants, 588–591. *See also* solo consultant practice
extreme close-up shot, 262
eye contact, 450
eye-level angle, 262

F

facilitation, 87, 245, 444–445, 450–451
facilitative trainers, 455–466
facilitator guides, 447–448
facilitator role, 47
factory schools, 17
fade transitions, 265
failure, 481–482, 767
fashion industry, 220
feasibility, 305
feedback, 111, 153, 155, 243, 451–452, 492, 506, 516–517, 541, 597, 682, 683
field technicians, 836
field trips, 44
file management tools, 383
financial assistance, for credentialing, 105
financial goals, of company, 692
financial impact, 69–70
financial performance, 780, 781
first-time leaders, 8–9
Five Fundamentals of Learning Leadership, 676–686
Five Moments of Learning Need, 226–227, 332
five-step process for developing TD structure, 667–672
fixed approach to learning, 505
fixed mindset, 122–128, 678–679
flexibility, 328, 570, 764, 802, 808, 809
"flipping the classroom," 329–330
focused specialty competencies, 832
focus groups, 484

following through, 306, 541, 659–660
forced-choice questions, 474–475
formal learning touchpoint, 231, 232
4D Branding Model, 566
four corners (activity), 44
Four Levels of Training Evaluation. *See* Kirkpatrick Model
framing learning conversations, 445–447
free authoring tools, 365–366
functional competencies, 832
future readiness, 89, 795–797

G

Gagné, Robert Mills, 22
gallery walk (activity), 44
game playing, 219
gamification, 249, 379
general learners, 40, 162–163
general onboarding, 700, 705–706
generationally-diverse teams, 830–831
get one, give one (activity), 41
Global Competencies Index (GCI), 485
global mindset, 414–415
goal owner expectations, 723
goals, 108, 110–111, 275–277, 486–487, 528, 646–647, 717–719
Golden Rule, 135
Goodman, Frederick, 322–325
Google, 9–10, 767
Google Docs, 381
Google Slides, 381
Gottfredson, Conrad, 332
governance, 526–527
graphics, 264, 380
gratitude practices, 764
group learning, in breakthrough moments, 9, 10
growth, 98, 808
growth mindset, 119–128, 678–679, 752–753

Guetzkow, Harold, 321
guilds, 16
gun mics, 264

H

handheld recording devices, 264
hands-on experience, 243
Hanson, Merle, 565
Hargadon, Andy, 564
Harter, J., 811
health-related workplace disruptions, 316
Heider, Fritz, 272–273
heritage events, 494
Hermann-Nehdi, Ann, 571
hero
    introduction of, 275–277
    learner as, 276–280
high-angle shot, 262
high-five review, 41
high-performance-workplace practices, 802, 806–809
high-potential programs, 558, 655–656
hiring, 645–646
Hoffer, Eric, 810
Hoitt, Rob, 100, 103
Holler, Drew, 820
home-based work. *See* remote working
horizontal development, 125, 127–128
hormonal response to storytelling, 274–275
hosting tools, for e-learning, 383
HR Certification Institute (HRCI), 110
human-centered design, 200–201, 322–323.
    See also design thinking
human lineup (activity), 45
human performance improvement (HPI), 21
human performance systems, 188–190
human resource development (HRD), 25
human resources training, 493
human scramble (activity), 45

hybrid programs and environments, 268, 314, 598–599

I

icebreakers, 165
Ideas-Driven Growth, 610
IEEI format, 459–461
illustrations, 374
immediate learning touchpoint, 231, 232
immediate supervisors, 582
impact. *See also* organizational impact
    business, 671, 803–805, 855
    discussing, with management, 695
    for facilitative trainers, 459–461
    learning science on, 58–60
    of people analytics, 849–850
    positive, of program, 305–308
    and ROI determination, 302
    of technology providers, 526
Impacting Organizational Capability domain, 88–89, 664
implementation
    aligning, 192
    of Behavior (Level 3), 289–290
    in consulting process, 597
    of Learning (Level 2), 289
    of learning technology ecosystem, 528–529
    of people analytics, 850–855
    of Reaction (Level 1), 288
    of Results (Level 4), 293–294
inclusion, 86, 136–138, 342, 345–346, 480, 481, 490, 757–758. *See also* diversity, equity, and inclusion (DEI) efforts
independent wealth mindset, 613–614
indirect costs of L&D, 134
individual assessment, of DEI efforts, 485
individual interviews, 484
individual learning, in breakthrough moments, 9, 10

individual use of Capability Model, 90–91
inductive analysis, 195
industries, inspiration from other, 220–221
industry meetings, 694
inferential statistics, 195
influence, 281–282, 415–416, 492, 690–691, 694–695
informal learning, 27
information phase, of consulting process, 597
informative learners, 40, 162
initiation, of TD effort, 423–437
initiative, for consultants, 595
innovation, 492, 530, 765–767, 837
innovative design, 211–221
in-person learning, 345, 389
inquirer mindset, 80
inquiry skills, 541
insight, 243, 837
inspiration, 220–221, 457–458
installed authoring tools, 375
instructional design, 61, 87, 345–348, 351–355
instructional design models, 168
instructional design theories, 168
instructional goals, 333
instructional systems design (ISD), 18, 26, 167–183, 640
instructional systems development model, 168–169
instructor-led training
   as delivery modality, 242–244
   online, 242, 244, 246–247
   participant-centered method for, 38–40
instructors, 414, 489
intangible benefits, 308
integration of learning, 246
integration strategy, technology, 527–528
integrity, 417
intellectual capital, 604–605
intelligence quotient (IQ), 145
intentional practice, 57–58
interaction tools, 377–379
Interactive Communications and Simulations (ICS) group, 322–325
interactive design, 372–374, 386–389
interactive exercises, 248, 387–388
Intercultural Development Inventory (IDI), 485
interleaving instruction, 57
internal consultants, 513, 539, 587–601, 735
International Board of Standards for Training, Performance, and Instruction (ibstpi), 110
International Coaching Federation (ICF), 100
internships, 556
interpersonal skills training, 491–492
Interservice Procedures for Instructional Systems Development (IPISD) model, 170–173
interviews, 484
interview-style videos, 260–261
Ismaili, Vedran, 698
isolation, on teams, 627–628
iterations, 219, 530

J

job aids, 220
job equality, 820–821
Job Instructor Training (JIT) program, 18
job rotation assignment, 570
journaling, 41

K

Kempczinski, Chris, 815
Kemp model, 178–180
key concepts, sharing, 41
key message, of presentation, 472–473
key roles, 551
key takeaways, for executives, 470–471
Killian, Annalie, 571

kinetic graphics, 264
Kipling, Rudyard, 501
Kirkpatrick, Donald, 286, 297
Kirkpatrick Foundational Principles, 294–296
Kirkpatrick Model (Four Levels of Training Evaluation), 19, 285–297, 671
knowledge, in Kirkpatrick model, 289
knowledge-based objectives, 336
knowledge management, 87, 516, 743–744
Knowles, Malcolm, 24
Kriegel, Jessica, 572

L

labs, 244
lapel mics, 264
Launch step, in TD structure development, 670
launch strategy, 427–428
layered architecture, for technology ecosystem, 522–525
L&D Oath of Ethics, 131–141
leaders, 92, 582, 685–686, 694–695. *See also* executives
leadership
   of agile organizations, 815–818
   in Capability Model, 86
   design thinking for, 71–72
   and diversity climate, 777–778
   leading by example, 139–140
   leading with courage, 419–420
   in learning culture, 752–756
   modeling, 645–650
leadership development
   in Capability Model, 87
   DEI topics in, 492–493
   equity and inclusion in, 137
   Five Fundamentals model, 676–686
   in learning cultures, 753–754
   for line managers, 655–659
   as self-development, 685
   in strategic workforce planning, 558
leadership potential, 676–678
Leadership Practices Inventory, 676–677
leadership skills, transferabilty of, 568–569
leadership transitions, 4–6
leading indicators, Kirkpatrick model, 292–293
Lean principles, 501
Learn, in LCD model, 229
learner assessments, 216
learner-centered mindset, 58
learner characteristics, 241, 314–315
learner data, collecting, 433
learner engagement, 387–388, 390–396, 449–450, 458, 459, 461–463
learner personas, 207, 230, 519–520, 523, 525
learner roles, in story-minded programs, 276–280
learning. *See also* lifelong learning
   as core value, 752–753
   curators of, 314–315
   custodians of, 72–73
   defining, 53–54
   for developmental managers, 536
   focus areas of, 505
   growth mindset and, 120–121
   as job, 741–742
   in Kirkpatrick models, 286
   making time for, 567
   nine elements of, 227
   push training vs., 332
   removing barriers to, 138–139
   steps in, 54–58
   work-based, 497–507
learning activity preferences, 163
learning agility, 764–765
Learning and Development Capability Framework, 109–110

Learning and Development (L&D) function
   and corporate vision, 651–660
   DEI in activities of, 493–494
   drivers of evolution for, 225
   learning science applications for, 60
   Oath of Ethics for, 131–141
   onboarding as responsibility of, 698
   project management by, 632–633
   strategic plans for, 406–407
   tailoring, to organization, 652
learning and development model for change management, 831–832
Learning and Performance Institute Capability Map, 109
Learning Cluster Design model, 228–229
learning conversation, 441–443, 445–450
learning culture, 424–425, 749–768
learning data, in ROI Model, 306
learning data strategy, 359–360
learning ecosystem mindset, 59
learning environments, 344–345, 489–491
learning experience design (LXD), 202–208, 319–325, 521–522
learning journey, 204–205, 207–208, 276–281
learning management systems (LMS), 376, 494, 733
learning materials, curating, 113
learning mindset, 802, 810
learning objectives, 331, 346, 353
learning organizations, 26
learning plans, designing, 108, 112–114
learning preferences, 39–40, 161–163, 751
learning programs, impact from, 305–308
learning purpose preferences, 161–162
learning resources, 113–114, 732–733
learning science, 51–62, 87
learning skill, 108, 115–116
learning solutions, 434–436
learning strategy success factors, 71–73
learning structure, preferences in, 162–163
learning team capabilities, 72
learning technology ecosystem, 515–531
   benefits of developing, 517–519
   building a right-fit, 519–530
   and digital learning mindset, 516–517
   governance process for, 526–527
   implementation process for, 528–529
   integration strategy for, 527–528
   iteration and experimentation with, 530
   keeping pace with innovation in, 530
   layered architecture for, 522–525
   learner personas for, 519–520
   learning experience design for, 521–522
   measurement strategy for, 529
   organizational priorities for, 520–521
   technology providers for, 525–526
learning touchpoints, 230–232
learning transfer, 250, 351–361, 506–507
learning transfer strategy, 359–360
Learn stage, of learning journey, 205
leave-behind documents, 476
Lectora, 368, 369
lectures, 244
legacy of leader, 685–686
legality mindset on accessibility, 343–344
lessons-learned reviews, 761
L.I.F.E. paradigm, 686
lifelong learning, 86, 107–117, 511, 684
line managers, 655–659
listening, 274–275, 473, 541, 694
live events, in blended learning, 336–337
location-defined teams, 619
location scouting, for videos, 264–265
logical thought perspective, 829
long-term memory, 54
long-term strategy, 425–426, 486–493
low-angle shot, 262
low-performing teams, 628–629

M

machine learning, 314, 831, 843–844
Mager, Robert F., 21
Make Me Feel Good About Me (MMFG-AM), 37–38
management development programs, 492–493, 558
manage phase, in Dare approach, 636
managers, 91–92, 533–544, 582, 655–659, 692, 756
marketing, 220, 607–608, 852–853
Market leadership phase, 612–613
Market penetration phase, 612–613
master's degree, 101
mastery, 55, 57–58, 109, 116–117, 331–332, 335–336
matching activity, 45
maturity models, 768, 786
McDonald's, 815
McKeachie, Wilbert, 320–322
meaningful improvements, 132–134
meaning making, 122
measurement, defined, 709
measurement strategy, technology, 529
Medhat, Aya, 99, 103–104
media options, authoring tool, 374–375
media skills, 257–269, 733
media tools, e-learning, 379–380
medium shot, 262
medium-sized companies, 837
meetings, 494, 541, 648–650, 694, 806
Me Learning, 667, 669–670
memory, 55–57, 273–275
mentees, benefits for, 581
mentor, role of, 47
mentoring programs, 577–586
    potential participants in, 579–584
    purpose of, 578–579
    tracking results of, 584–585

mentors, 276–280, 581
mentorship programs, 252–253, 694
metacompetence, 498, 810
metrics, 430, 709–710, 794–795
microlearning, 249
micromanagement, 628
microphones, 263–264
Microsoft PowerPoint, 374–376, 378, 381
Microsoft Word, 381
microteaching, 267–268
middle managers, 582
mid shot, 262
mindfulness programs, 764
mindset. *See also specific mindsets*
    about career, 563–564
    about development, 538–540
    on accessibility, 342–344
    assessing your current, 124
    of change agents, 407–408
    of facilitative trainers, 457–459
    functions of, 121–122
    learning science on, 58–60
    of TD professionals, 79–82
mirror race (activity), 45
mixed reality (MR), 840
mnemonics, 45
mobile devices, 248, 249, 767, 806
mobile learning (m-learning), 248, 249
modeling leadership, 645–650
modernizing learning assets, 234
modern learners, 223–236
    characteristics of, 224–226
    delivery preferences of, 233–236
    Five Moments of Learning Need for, 226–227
    LCD model, 228–229
    meeting needs of, 767
    needs of businesses and, 229–236

nine elements of learning for, 227
personalized training for, 229–231
up-to-date content for, 231–233
modern teams, 618–619
modular talent development, 742–743
Moments of Care module, 796
monetary value, 307
monitoring, of performance, 554–555, 784–786, 854
monologues, in presentations, 473
mood, 155
Morrison, Ross, and Kemp (MRK) model, 178–180
Mosher, Bob, 332
motivating stories, 280
motivation, 115, 280–282, 502–506, 679–680, 736–737
motivators, on empathy maps, 207
multipath development, 658–659
Multi-Store Model of Memory, 53–54
museum exhibits, 219
music, in videos, 266

N

Nadella, Satya, 800
narrowing in on solutions, 218
needs assessments and analysis, 187–196, 229–236, 333–334, 727–728
network finder and minder mindset, 82
networks and networking, 530, 569–570, 606–607, 758–759, 808
neural pathway, for emotional intelligence, 145–147
neuroscience, 36–37, 220–221
new leaders, assessment for, 6–7
newsletters, 494
New World Kirkpatrick Model, 287–293
Next Chapter platform, 820
next steps recommendations, 476

9 Questions to Determine Suitability for Remote Work, 703
nine elements of learning, 227
nine events of instruction, 23
90/20/8(4) rule, 164
90-day plan, 426–427
Notice stage, of learning journey, 204
nudges, for learners, 315

O

oath of ethics, 131–141
obstacles, sizing up, 275–277
occupations, professions vs., 96–98
off-site meetings, 494
OhioHealth, 759–760
onboarding, 556, 584–585, 697–711, 726–730
Onboarding Communications Status Tool, 704
on-demand learning, 767
one-on-one coaching and training, 252, 648–650
one-person TD department, 725–737
one platform fallacy, 517
one-time purchase agreements, for authoring tools, 366
one word whip (activity), 42
online learning resources, DEI in, 494
on-the-job training and learning, 14, 291
openers (opening activities), 42–43, 165, 387
operable web content, 342–343
Opportunistic Growth, 609
opportunities assessment, 187–196
optimization, technology, 528
opt-in organizations, 808
orderly conversations, 441–443
organizational capability, 88–89, 664, 734
organizational culture. *See also* learning culture
at agile organizations, 814–818
attracting talent with, 816

organizational culture (*continued*)
   in Capability Model, 88
   DEI as part of, 774–777
   developmental, 536–537
   future of TD function and, 745
   of learning, 424–425, 749–768
   of lifelong learning, 511
   and organizational design, 802, 806
   people analytics to change, 852
organizational design (OD), 799–811
organizational development, 20, 88
organizational environment, consultants', 594
organizational growth, DEI for, 480–482
organizational health and performance data, 433
organizational impact, 715–724
   demonstrating results, 720–723
   isolating, 723–724
   of onboarding programs, 709–710
   reporting, 795
   and return on investment, 301–308
   and ROI, 723–724
   strategic alignment for, 716–720
   of technology, 766
organizational needs assessment, 727
organizational performance, 101, 481
organizational priorities, 429, 520–521, 668, 717–718
organizational resilience, 762–765, 800–802, 809
organizational strategy, 429, 551, 692. *See also* strategic alignment
organizations
   benefits of mentoring for, 583
   Capability Model for use by, 92
   learning science applications for, 61
organized thought perspective, 829
organizing, in project management, 635
orientation, employee, 217–218, 699

Osman, Hassan, 572
outcome, realizing, 275, 276, 278–279
outside contacts, 694
overall competencies, 832
ownership
   of career development, 561–573, 742
   of learning transfer, 352, 356
   of organizational culture, 745
   of people analytics implementation, 854
   total cost of, 526
O WOW format, for elevator speech, 465
oxytocin, 274

P

pace
   of change, 404–405
   of learning, 9, 10, 248
pain points, 207
pair of hands role, for consultant, 592
Pareto Optimality (Pareto Efficiency), 303
participant-centered method, 38–40
participative learners, 40, 163
partnerships
   in Capability Model, 88
   between consultants, 590–591
   with developmental managers, 534
   with executives, 791–797
   Kirkpatrick Principle on, 295
   learning strategies for, 73
   in TD department of one, 735
passive attitude, 408
pausing, in presentations, 450
payback period (PP), 301
Pay-Your-Age-Day promotion, 637
peer-learning networks, 758–759
peer-mentoring, 543, 582
people analytics, 847–856
people development, 652–660
perceivable web content, 342

performance
  improving, 89, 805
  in learning cultures, 759–760
  team, 623, 628–629
performance consultants, 593
performance management, 493, 535, 557, 649, 755
performance needs, 331–332
performance objectives, 234, 235, 334, 486, 853
performance planning, 646–647
performance reviews, 648–649
performance support, 241, 242, 250–251, 516, 756
"permanent beta mode" for career, 564
Perry-Knights, Shermaine, 102, 104
persona-based ecosystem design, 523
personal balance, 808
personal branding, 564–566
personal capabilities, 86–87, 664, 734
personal development, 102–103, 568, 654–655
personality, 144–145
personalized learning, 9, 10, 229–231, 518–519, 767, 844
personalized support, 242, 251–253
personal learning plan, 734
personal presence, 471–472
personal responsibility, 288, 418
personas, learner, 207, 230, 519–520, 523, 525
perspective taking, 323
phased approach to implementation, 528
Philips, Jack J., 300
photos, 374
PHR certification, 100
physical access, 347–348
Piaget's model of development, 21
piece to camera (PTC) videos, 260
pilot testing, 208, 218–219
Pinocchio (film), 277

planned impact, 717–719
planning phase
  in Dare approach, 636
  in project management, 635
  in strategic workforce planning, 553–555
  of video making, 261–263
planning skill, 115
PMP certification, 100
podcasts, 267, 494
point-of-need training, 832
policy reviews, 484–485
polish, in presentations, 471–472
polls, 42, 393–394
pop-ups, 42
positive training approach, 491
post-project reviews, 641
POUR approach to accessibility, 341–342
practical learners, 40, 162
practice
  deliberate, 58, 683–684
  to develop EQ, 152
  digital learning mindset about, 517
  in ILPC method, 39
  in learning science, 56–57
  with shifting mindsets, 126
Practice Growth Matrix, 609–610
practice growth model, 604–610, 612–613
praise, 647
pre-active attitude, 408
pre-onboarding, 700, 705
presence, in presentations, 471–472
presentations, 215–217, 472–473
prior experience or knowledge, 39, 396
priorities, organizational, 429, 520–521, 668, 717–718
Prioritize step, in developing TD structure, 668–669
private practice, credentialing for, 103
proactive attitude, 408

proactive goal alignment, 717–719
problem definition, 218
process, defined, 633
process consultants, 592
procuring assets, for TD efforts, 432–433
productivity improvements, 804–805
profession, of talent development, 96–98
professional capabilities, 87–88, 664, 734
professional doctorate, 102–103
professional excellence, 108–110
professional gatherings, 114
professional learner mindset, 59–60
professional organizations, 97, 737
program alignment, in ROI Model, 305
program costs, in ROI Model, 308
program effects, in ROI Model, 307
program interest, in Kirkpatrick model, 288
programmed instruction, 21
programming code, for e-learning, 365
program value, 37
Progress Review Forms, 359
project, defined, 633
project charters, 635–636
project management, 86, 137–138, 382, 493, 631–642, 732
project manager, defined, 634
project objectives, 434–435, 639
Project Outreach, 320–322
project schedule, 636, 640
project selection, in TD department of one, 731–732
project sponsor, defined, 634
proposed L&D Oath of Ethics, 131–141
prototyping, 208, 323–324, 382
psychological safety, 767, 809, 822
published output, of authoring tools, 371
pull approach to learning, 332, 796
pulse checker mindset, 81
purpose, 424–425, 623, 807

purpose-driven organizations, 599–600
push training, 332

Q

qualitative data, 193, 195, 553
quality assurance, 382–383
quantitative data, 193–195, 552
question features, of authoring tools, 370
questions
 asking, 393, 474, 829–830
 from executive leadership, 474–475
quizzing, 370, 379

R

rapid prototyping, 323–324
Raptivity, 379
rarely-used skills, 250
reach, in RISSCI methodology, 836
Reaction (Level 1), in Kirkpatrick models, 286
reaction data, in ROI Model, 306
reactive alignment, 719–720
reactive attitude, 408
recognition, 735, 737, 808
recruitment, for mentoring programs, 580–582
redirection, 648
references, of technology providers, 526
reflection, 114, 205, 355–356, 483–484, 536
reflective learners, 40, 163
reframing forced-choice questions, 474–475
reinforcement, 517
relationship-based trust, 620
relationship building, 541, 569–570, 693–694
Relationship-Driven Growth, 609–610
relationship management skills, 148–149, 155
relationship thought perspective, 829
relevance, 193, 288, 484–486
reliability, data, 193
remembering step, in learning, 55–57

remote working, 314, 405, 701–703, 757, 831
repetition, 205
required drivers, Kirkpatrick model, 290–291
research mindset, 58–59
resilience, 420–421, 653, 681, 762–765, 800–802, 809
reskilling, 29–30, 70–71, 112, 511, 556–557, 760–761, 818–820
resolution beats, of story, 276, 278–279
resource consumption, 132–134
resourcefulness, 115, 595
resource management, 302–303
responsibility, personal, 288, 418
results
    aligning, 191–192
    baseline comparison of, 721–722
    demonstrating, 720–723
    in Kirkpatrick models, 286
    Kirkpatrick Principle on, 294
    presenting early, 434–436
    tracking, 584–585
results-based accountability, 802–805
results-driven training, 161–165, 521
results optimization, in ROI Model, 307, 308
results orientation, in culture, 759–761
results planning, in ROI Model, 305
retention, of blended learning, 328
retrieval practice, 57
return on expectations (ROE), 294–295
return on investment (ROI), 299–309
    benefit-cost ratio vs., 301
    in business case, 430
    communicating, 470, 695, 795
    defined, 300–301
    for DEI efforts, 782
    ensuring delivery of, 305–308
    and organizational impact, 723–724
    organizational importance of, 301–304
    for people analytics, 853–854

    question answered by, 303
    target, 301
    for TD function, 671
reusing materials, 232
review features, of e-learning tools, 382–383
review phase, in Dare approach, 636–637
Re-vision step, in TD structure development, 669–670
Revisiters, in CORE model, 43–44
right-fit learning technology ecosystems, 519–530
risk management, 637–638
RISSCI methodology, 836–837
road maps, technology provider, 526
robotics, 314
robust web content, 343
ROI Institute, 304, 782
ROI Methodology Process Model, 305–308
role(s) of TD professionals, xiv
    in adult learning, 46–47
    as catalysts for learning, 72–73
    and corporate vision, 651–660
    DEI skills and, 493
    and developmental managers, 537–540
    as internal consultants, 591–594
    planning beyond current, 511–514
    in story-minded programs, 276–280
    in strategic workforce planning, 555–558
    in TD department of one, 730–733, 736
role-specific onboarding, 700, 706
roll-out plans, 234
Ruffy, Eleonore, 815–816

S

safety
    psychological, 767, 809, 822
    in RISSCI methodology, 837
sales skills, of consultants, 607–608
Sander, Dawn, 415–416

Santhanam, Janardhan, 818–819
savviness, of consultants, 595
scaffolding, 356
scalability, 507, 518, 837
schedules and scheduling, 390, 567, 636, 640, 726
schemata, 54
scholarly doctorates, 102
science, defined, 52–53
scope of project, documenting, 638–639
SCORM standard, 371
screen capture videos, 261, 378
screen simulations, 375
script writing, for videos, 266
security, of technology providers, 526
self-awareness skills, 147–148, 153, 540
self-development, 685
self-directed learning, 115–116, 570
self-efficacy, 115
self-engineering, 314
self-governing teams, 809
self-management skills, 148, 153–154, 608
self-organizing teams, 504
self-paced learning, 336, 364
self-protection, fixed mindset for, 124–125
self-sourcing content, 233
self-study, 252
self-talk, 154
senior leaders, 582, 694–695. *See also* executives
sensitivity training, 23
sensory register, 54
sentence length, in videos, 266
serendipity, 808
set-up beats, of story, 276, 277
Seven Transformative Story Beats, 275–280
70-20-10 framework, 499–500
shared conversation, 393–394
shared values, 304

shotgun mics, 264
shots, camera, 261–262
SHRM-CP certification, 100
SHRM-SCP certification, 100
side hustles, 571–572
siloed strategic workforce planning, 550
Simmel, Marianne, 272–273
Simmons, Michael, 567
simple personalization, 229–230
simulations, 375, 378, 655
single data point risk, 584
single source of truth (SSoT) approach, 622
sit-stand activity, 42, 45
Six Bs framework, 553–554
Skelia, 817
skills and skilling
    business need for, 70–71
    complexity of skills, 9, 10
    for developmental managers, 540–541
    digital learning mindset about, 516, 517
    in Kirkpatrick model, 289
    learning team skills, 72
SkillsFuture program, 821
skill stacking, 111
Skinner, B.F., 18
slide design, presentation, 388, 448–449
slide notes, 447–448
small companies, 837
SmartBuilder, 378
social awareness skills, 148, 154–155
social component of adult learning, 37–38, 45–46
social engagement, 246, 388
social learning, 27–29, 113, 231, 232, 767
social media, 269
social presence, in virtual training, 390–392
Society for Human Resource Management (SHRM), 110, 778
sociotechnical-systems theory, 22–23

software training, e-learning for, 378
solo consultant practice, 603–614
solutions, aligning, 192
"so what," of communication, 470
spacing effect, 57, 246, 328, 485–486
speaker, role of, 46
specific learners, 40, 162–163
speed, learning, 518, 764
SPHR certification, 100
sponsorship, 583–584, 634, 653
spot learning plans, 112
stakeholders, 67–68, 73, 294–295, 304, 634, 638, 639
Startup phase, for solo practice, 612–613
storyboards and storyboarding, 261, 381–382
story-minded training programs, 271–283, 323, 394–395
strategic alignment
    and impact, 716–720
    in learning cultures, 759
    in organizational design, 802, 805–806
    in partnerships, 793–794
    of people analytics, 850
    in systems-oriented framework, 190–192
    of TD and organization, 663, 693
strategic imperative, for change, 827–828
strategic integration of digital ecosystem, 527–528
strategic objectives, 234, 235, 424–425
strategic performance objective (SPO), 234, 235
strategic planning
    embedding DEI in retreats for, 494
    of TD efforts, 425–428
    by TD professionals, 406–407
    workforce, 511, 547–559
strategy (generally)
    developing, to maximize transfer, 357–359
    executing, in learning culture, 761

    people analytics to enhance, 848, 849
    purpose of, 848
strategy blueprint, 206–207
strengths-based training, 111, 657–658
subject matter experts (SMEs), 432, 439–453, 530, 730–731
subscription-based e-learning authoring tools, 366
Successive Approximation Model (SAM), 180–183
suites of authoring tools, 376
summaries, 476, 694–695
supply and demand assessment, 553
support, 291, 526, 538, 681–683, 732–733, 736
support materials, 639–640
Surround, in LCD model, 229
surveys, 484, 723, 785
Sustainability phase, for solo practice, 612–613
sustainable change, 659–660
sustainable diversity, equity, and inclusion (DEI) efforts, 773–787
sustainable organizations, DEI at, 480–482
sustainable practices, defined, 775
Sustain Over Time stage, of learning journey, 205
synergistic delivery style, 392
systematic training, 17–19
Systems Approach Model, 176–178
systems-oriented framework for assessing needs and opportunities, 187–196

T

taking a stand, with executives, 473, 475
talent continuum mindset, 59
Talent Development Body of Knowledge (TD BoK), xiv, xvii, 96
Talent Development Capability Model (Capability Model), xiv, xvii, 83–93, 109, 664–666

talent development cohorts, 543
talent development field
    contributing to, 102
    evolution of, xiv, 13–31
    future trends in, 313–317, 741–746
    relevance of, 101
Talent Development Framework, 664–666, 672
Talent Development function
    agility of, 745–746
    DEI within, 483–484
    as department of one, 725–737
    learning science on impact of, 58–60
    ownership of culture by, 745
    strategic alignment of, 693
talent development initiatives
    demonstrating results of, 720–723
    initiating, 423–437
    integrating DEI in, 482–483
    reactive alignment for, 719–720
talent development leaders, global mindset for, 414
talent development (TD) professionals. *See also specific topics*
    essential skills for, 411–421
    growth vs. development for, 98
    learning science on, 60–61
    mindsets of, 79–82
Talent Development Reporting principles (TDRp), 26–27
talent development structure, 663–672
talent gaps, strategies to close, 553–554
talent management, 27–28, 88
talent optimization, 803–804
talent strategy, in Capability Model, 88
Talent Wheel, 784
talking head-style videos, 260
Target, 776–777
target audience, video, 259

target performance, delivery based on, 241–242
task, defined, 633
task analysis, 189–190
task-based trust, 620
Tata Consultancy Services (TCS), 818–819
teams, 617–629
    Capability Model for use by, 91–92
    DEI in training for, 492
    dysfunctional, 626–629
    effective, 619–626
    for initiating TD effort, 430–432
    modern, 618–619
teamwork, 512
technical detail, in presentations, 473
technical integration of digital ecosystem, 527–528
technology
    applying, in Capability Model, 87
    for blended learning, 335
    in business environment, 66–67
    and future of talent development, 314
    generational differences in use of, 830
    in learning cultures, 766
    learning technology ecosystem, 515–531
    for onboarding, 707–709
    and partnerships with executives, 796
    for personalized support, 253
    for strategic workforce planning, 555
    in successful learning strategies, 73
technology providers, 525–526
TechSmith Camtasia, 378, 380
TechSmith SnagIt, 378, 380
TED Talks, 543
testing, of technology ecosystem, 528
themed presentations, 215–217
thought leadership, 102
360-degree multirater feedback, 654, 657–659
toe touch review, 41

tone, of video script, 266
tools, considering (story beat), 275, 276, 278
TopGear platform, 751
top 10 list (activity), 45
Torres, Patricia, 101, 103
total cost of ownership, 526
touchpoints, 538, 808
Track, in LCD model, 229
tracking tools, e-learning, 383
trade schools, 16
trainer role, 46, 61, 443–444, 455–466
training. *See also specific types*
    modeling leadership in, 646–649
    pull learning vs., 332
    in TD department of one, 735
    work-based learning vs., 500
Training Arcade, 379
training development, defined, 24
training directors, 19
transactional roles, 551
transfer, of learning, 250, 351–361, 506–507
transferable skills, 568–571
transition strategies phase of consulting, 597
translation capabilities, authoring tool, 372
trend analysis, 111
triple bottom line, 775
tripod, 263
trust, 593, 596, 620–621, 744
Turning Learning Into Action (TLA) model, 357–358

U

Uhl, Trish, 359
UL, 758–759
Ulrich, Dave, 801
understandable web content, 343
understanding step, in learning, 54–56
unexpected materials, 214
universal accessibility, 138–139
University of Michigan–Ann Arbor, 320–325
updated materials, 250
update infrastructure, 232–233
Upgrade, in LCD model, 229
upskilling, 29–30, 70–71, 112, 511, 556–557, 760–761, 818–820
up-to-date content, 231–233
US Access Board, 343–344
user-driven learning, 767
user experience, 202–203, 322
utilitarianism, 133

V

validity, data, 193
Value, Flow, Quality (VFQ) program, 502, 506
value, user experience and, 202
value chain, 67
value creation, 295–296, 564–565
value definition, 506
value delivery, 506
value proposition, 595, 607
values modeling, 420
Vandesande, Olivia, 817
Vermueulen, André, 821
vertical development, 125–126
vestibule training, 17
video(s), 258–266, 374, 380, 543, 840–841
virtual instructor-led training (vILT), 244, 247, 268
virtual presence, 390–392
virtual reality (VR), 398, 838–840
VirtualStory workshop, 282
virtual teams, 618–619
virtual training, 214–215, 364, 385–398, 451
virtual worlds, 841–842
vision, 517
visual access concerns, learners with, 347
visualization, 506
vocational education and training (VET), 16

voice-overs, in videos, 266
volunteering, 563, 568
Vyond, 380, 381

W

wall chart list, 45
Walmart, 792–796, 820
warning stories, 280–281
Watson, Russell Wayne, 173–176
Web Content Accessibility Guidelines (WCAG), 344
webinars, 268, 330
Welch, Jack, 651, 652
We Learning, 667, 670
well-being, 763–764
What's in It for Me (WII-FM), 37, 818
whiteboards, online, 394
wide shot, 261
Wingron, Sharon, 412–413
wipe transitions, 265
Wipro, 751

word choice, in scripts, 266
work assignments, 542
work-based learning, 497–507
work environment, 241, 246
workforce assessment, 552–553
workforce development, 558
workforce readiness, 30
working memory, 54
workshops, 244
wrap-up strategies, 464–466
written communication, for executives, 472

X

xAPI standard, 371

Y

You Learning, 667, 669
You-Me-We Learning model, 666–672

Z

Zoom, 268, 625

About the Editor

Elaine Biech, CPTD fellow, believes excellence isn't optional. Her passion is helping others achieve their passion. She specializes in maximizing individual, team, and organizational effectiveness using her expertise in OD, training, and consulting. She custom designs every project to address each client's unique needs. She conducts strategic planning and implements organization-wide systems including process improvement, change management, leadership development, onboarding, and mentoring programs. She has developed hundreds of training courses and apps. As the founder and president of ebb associates inc, Elaine helps organizations implement large-scale change and is particularly adept at turning dysfunctional teams into productive teams.

As a management and executive consultant, trainer, and designer, Elaine's clients include the US Navy, China Sinopec, China Telecom, PricewaterhouseCoopers, Banco de Credito Peru, Lockheed Martin, Outback Steakhouse, FAA, Land O'Lakes, McDonald's, Lands' End, Johnson Wax, Federal Reserve Bank, Department of Homeland Security, American Family Insurance, Marathon Oil, Hershey Chocolate, NASA, Newport News Shipbuilding, Kohler Company, American Red Cross, Association of Independent CPAs, The College of William and Mary, and hundreds of other public and private sector organizations. She designed the first process improvement programs for The Newport News Shipbuilding Company and McDonald's as well as Hershey Chocolate's first creativity and innovation program; she also presented one of the first ever virtual training sessions in 1986 for NASA.

Elaine's been called a titan of the training industry. She's written 86 books with 14 publishers, including the *Washington Post* number 1 bestseller, *The Art & Science of Training*. She recently served as the principal author of ATD's Talent Development Body of Knowledge. Her books have won national awards and have been translated into 13 languages. She was the consulting editor for the prestigious *Pfeiffer Training and Consulting Annuals* for 16 years. Elaine has also been featured in dozens of publications including *The Wall Street Journal, Harvard Management Update, Washington Post, Investor's Business Daily,* and *Fortune*. Elaine has presented more than 400 times for national and international conferences, including keynote presentations to 7,000 trainers in China. She has presented 35 consecutive years at ATD's International Conference & EXPO.

Elaine has been active in ATD since 1982, serving on the National ASTD Board of Directors and as the Board's secretary from 1991 to 1994. She initiated and chaired Consultant's Day for seven years and was ATD's International Conference Design Chair in 2000. Elaine also designed ATD's first training certificate program and has since written five other certificate programs for the association.

A talent development thought leader and ATD's inaugural CPTD Fellow designee, Elaine is the recipient of more than a dozen national awards, including ATD's 1992 Torch Award, 2004 Volunteer-Staff Partnership Award, 2006 Gordon M. Bliss Memorial Award, and the 2020 Distinguished Contribution to Talent Development Award. She is also the recipient of the 2001 ISA Spirit Award, 2012 ISA Outstanding Contributor Award, and 2022 ISA Thought Leader Award, and Wisconsin's Women's Mentor Award. Elaine sponsors several scholarship funds and currently serves on the board of directors for ISA and CCL.

The Associa
ing by setti
organizatio
ment, servi
was founde
of global bu
designers, d
professional
developmen

Today,
professional
ment profes
- The
- Educ
- Certi
- Mem
- Indu
- Rese
- Book

Learn more

About the Association for Talent Development

The Association for Talent Development (ATD) champions the importance of learning and training by setting standards for the talent development profession. ATD is the largest, most trusted organization for the professional development of practitioners in training and talent development, serving a worldwide community with members in more than 100 countries. Since ATD was founded in 1943, the talent development field has expanded significantly to meet the needs of global businesses and emerging industries. Classroom trainers and facilitators, instructional designers, data analysts, coaches, and performance improvement consultants are among the professionals ATD supports with resources, membership, tools, courses, and credentials. Talent development professionals rely on ATD to establish benchmarks and capabilities for best practice.

Today, change is constant for organizations around the world. ATD's mission is to empower professionals to develop talent in the workplace. The resources we provide help talent development professionals increase their impact and effectiveness include:
- The Talent Development Capability Model
- Education courses
- Certifications and credentials
- Membership
- Industry-leading events held around the world
- Research
- Books and magazines

Learn more at td.org.